The Contested Quill

The Contested Quill

Literature by Women in Germany, 1770–1800

Ruth P. Dawson

Newark: University of Delaware Press
London: Associated University Presses

© 2002 Rosemont Publishing & Printing Corp.

All rights reserved. Authorization to photocopy items for internal or personal use, or the internal or personal use of specific clients, is granted by the copyright owner, provided that a base fee of $10.00, plus eight cents per page, per copy is paid directly to the Copyright Clearance Center, 222 Rosewood Drive, Danvers, Massachusetts 01923. [0-87413-762-4/02 $10.00 + 8¢ pp, pc.] Other than as indicated in the foregoing, this book may not be reproduced, in whole or in part, in any form (except as permitted by Sections 107 and 108 of the U.S. Copyright Law, and except for brief quotes appearing in reviews in the public press).

Associated University Presses
440 Forsgate Drive
Cranbury, NJ 08512

Associated University Presses
16 Barter Street
London WC1A 2AH, England

Associated University Presses
P.O. Box 338, Port Credit
Mississauga, Ontario
Canada L5G 4L8

The paper used in this publication meets the requirements of the American National Standard for Permanence of Paper for Printed Library Materials Z39.48-1984.

Quotations from *The History of Lady Sophie Sternheim: Extracted by a Woman Friend of the Same from Original Documents and Other Reliable Sources* by Sophie von LaRoche, translated by Christa Baguss Britt are reprinted by permission of the State University of New York Press © 1991, State University of New York. All rights reserved.

Library of Congress Cataloging-in-Publication Data

Dawson, Ruth P., 1943–
    The contested quill : literature by women in Germany, 1770–1800 / Ruth P. Dawson.
      p. cm.
    Includes bibliographical references and index.
    ISBN 0-87413-762-4 (alk. paper)
    1. German literature—18th century—History and criticism.   2. German literature—Women authors—History and criticism.   3. Women authors, German—Biography.   I. Title.
PT289.D38   2002
830.9′9287′09033—dc21   2001027758

PRINTED IN THE UNITED STATES OF AMERICA

To my beloved Steve and Robin

Contents

Acknowledgments   9

1. Introduction   13

2. Between the Spinning Wheel and the Book: Friderika Baldinger (1739–86)   37
   "Essay about the Education of my Intellect": Depicting Women's Basic Education for Cultural Participation   41
   Beyond Literacy to Scholarliness   51
   Marriage as Women Experienced It   61
   Concluding an Androcentric Woman's Self-narrative   71
   Writing and Desire   74
   The Enlightenment Woman's Failed Transition into Publishing   80

3. The Enabling Effect of Difference: Sophie La Roche (1730–1807)   92
   Feeling Woman, Educated Man: The Uses of *Empfindsamkeit*   99
   Representing Women's Experience of Unhappy Marriage in La Roche's First Novel   103
   The Tale of the Beautiful Band and Another Marriage Resister   110
   Menacing Mothers, Dangerous Men   116
   The Monthly *Pomona* and Its Audiences   122
   Women and the Possibilities of Literary Groups   131
   After *Pomona*: Writing for Women, Inventorying the Self for Men   141

4. Longing for Respectability: Philippine Engelhard née Gatterer (1756–1831)   155
   The Rules of Gender in the *Empfindsamkeit* of Sympathy   161
   The Call to Poetry   168
   Complex Relations with Male Mentors and Female Literary Confidantes   175
   Philippine Gatterer and Gottfried August Bürger   184

Poetic Versions of the Self within the Rules 191
Reception: Formal, Informal, and Nominal 202
Productivity after Marriage 213

5. Confronting the Lords of Creation: Marianne Ehrmann (1755–95) 221

Women's *Sturm und Drang*, or the *Empfindsamkeit* of Alienation? 228
"If . . . I would become the first female rebel" 236
Disastrous Marriage and Innovative Aftermath: *Amalie* As a Novel Thematizing Divorce and the Theater 245
Mapping Misogyny: Ehrmann's Contemporary, Emilie von Berlepsch 258
A Journalist's Experiments with the Macabre and the Mundane 263
Protofeminist Overtures: Ehrmann, Berlepsch, and Others 274

6. Examining Passion: Sophie Albrecht (1757–1840) 286

Poetry of Passion 290
An Uncommon Life 295
Theresgen, Drama of a Woman's Love and Suicide 302
Women as Playwrights and Issues of Objective Alienation 313
Negotiating Subjectivity in Poetry About Femininity, Freedom, and Death 319
Women, Genre, and Issues of Change 328
Unraveling Marriage and the Reinterpretation of a Fairy Tale 334
From Legends to Cookbooks 341

7. Conclusion: The Contesting Discourses of the Needle and the Quill 346

Notes 353
List of abbreviations used in the notes 353
Select Bibliography 383
Index 403

Acknowledgments

IN THE BEGINNING WAS THE GRANT; AFTER IT CAME DAYS AND WEEKS IN archives and libraries, spread out over years and years. Before the grant came the nub of an idea, but without the grant, the nub would have become nothing. Yet now it is a book. And so it is that I am intensely grateful to the German Academic Exchange Service (DAAD) for the funding that got me started and to the almost innumerable librarians, archivists, and scholars, who helped me along the way. My search for the German women writers of the late eighteenth century began with stays at two glorious research libraries, the Archiv für deutsche Literatur, in Marbach, and the Herzog August Bibliothek, in Wolfenbüttel, where I located a wealth of material and began my encounters with the five women whose writings and life stories make up this book. Finding the women's published work in those pre-internet days required numerous quests and a lot of serendipity. In addition to thanking the DAAD for their generous support right at the start, I wish to thank the many librarians and archivists who assisted on later trips when I searched for two-century old books and journals at the university libraries in Basel, Bonn, Göttingen, Hamburg, and Münster, at the Staatsbibliothek Preußischer Kulturbesitz in West Berlin, Pfälzische Landesbibliothek in Speyer, the Koniglige Bibliothek in Copenhagen, and the Oesterreichische Nationalbibliothek in Vienna. I was also fortunate to receive outstanding help on the other side of the rigid political divide slashing through the middle of Europe. In the German Democratic Republic I benefitted from the collections of the Forschungsbibliothek in Gotha, the Anna Amalie Bibliothek in Weimar, and, in East Berlin, I was able to use both the Staatsbibliothek and the library of the Humboldt University. At home, the Interlibrary Loan staff of Hamilton Library at the University of Hawaii at Manoa skillfully located the unending list of secondary literature that I needed, and the University itself granted me a sabbatical at a critical time.

Soon after starting my project I discovered that catalogs of manuscripts, such as Frels's MLA-sponsored 1934 volume, listed many letters written by eighteenth-century women writers to each other.

At the time, practically none of these documents had been published, and yet the continued existence of the letters themselves was tantalizing. I added archival work to my plan. I wanted to use these resources to construe the material (including ideological) conditions under which the women lived and, when possible, to surmise their connections with each other. When I was fortunate enough to locate a letter in an archive, I faced the task of transcribing it from the handwriting systems then used in Germany; only a few of the variously ornate or jagged letters have anything in common with the script styles of the rest of Western Europe. Again, archivists frequently came to my rescue as I worked to decipher letters in the manuscript collections of the university libraries of Göttingen, Hamburg (in the Theater Collection), Munich, and Münster, and also at the Deutsches Literaturarchiv in Marbach, the Freies deutsches Hochstift in Frankfurt am Main, at the Wieland-Archiv in Biberach, the Staatsbibliothek Preussischer Kulturbesitz in (then) West Berlin, at the Städtisches Museum in Göttingen (letters now in the possesion of the Stadtarchiv there), and especially at the Goethe- und Schiller-Archiv, Weimar, which contains a trove of La Roche correspondence with women, as well as the Jagiellonian Library in Cracow, Poland. I am thankful to all these institutions for permission to use their wonderful resources and for the professional assistance of their staffs.

For their helpful readings of my manuscript in its late stages, I thank Cornelia Moore and Lucy Frost. I am grateful to Maren Klotz for her timely assistance with the mechanics of my last revision. And finally, without the endless support, good nature, patience, and encouragement of my husband and my daughter, who has grown up along with this book manuscript, I would never have finished.

For permission to use illustrations, I am grateful to the following institutions. For Sophie Albrecht, and for Sophie La Roche to the Stiftung Weimarer Klassik. For Friderika Baldinger to the Goethe- und Schiller-Archiv of the Stiftung Weimarer Klassik. For the title page of Ehrmann's *Amalia,* to the Royal Library of Copenhagen. For the painting of Gatterer to the Deutsche Fotothek at the Sächsische Landesbibliothek, Staats-und Universitätsbibliothek Dresden.

The Contested Quill

1
Introduction

A SOCIETY HIGHLY STRUCTURED BY GENDER RELATES EVERY SIGNIFIcant aspect of itself—daily activities, the personalities of its people, the spaces in its farms and towns, its cultural processes and products, even its tools—to the concepts of masculinity and femininity. In eighteenth-century Germany, for example, the needle and the quill were tools with very different meanings depending on the gender of the person holding them. With every woman of the time expected to be proficient with the needle, this simple and ancient utensil was a sign of woman, peasant and aristocrat, illiterate and cosmopolitan alike. It was also a sign of women's labor, immobilizing, often domestic, and either unpaid or underpaid. In a man's hand, however, a needle suggested a paying profession, albeit in some eyes a tainted one. To Rousseau, the needle was so strong a signifier for woman that in *Emil*, his vastly influential codification of eighteenth-century gender roles, he proclaimed: "The needle and the sword cannot be wielded by the same hands.... If I were sovereign, I would permit sewing and the needle trades only to women and to cripples reduced to occupations like theirs."[1] Although many women, including a sizable number in the emerging educated middle class, which Goodman and Waldstein call the "incipient bourgeoisie,"[2] earned all or part of their living through stitchery, women using needles were women. Men using needles were tailors.

The quill functioned quite differently as an eighteenth-century sign. It was a mark first of class—for it excluded the peasantry—and second of gender, again with different meanings for men than for women. In the hands of literate men, which, at least on a rudimentary level, included most men in towns and cities, the pen was associated with what was recognized as their work or their cultural participation. Men used pens to keep shop accounts, to conduct correspondence, to write or copy documents, to compose poems, and for many other purposes. But women too, at least those of either the aristocracy or the educated middle class, were expected to conduct correspondence and, if necessary, to keep household accounts, although these activities were typically categorized as duty or pleasure, not work. Other uses of the quill by women were suspect, as a woman attempting to write novels and stories noted: "For as soon as anyone appears, out comes my needlework, which is as dear to me as my papers and books: especially since I have noticed that men of high birth and intellect show me more respect for the domestic industry of my needle than for the occupation of my quill; the only papers they accept seeing in my hands are the housekeeping accounts."[3] The woman narrating this text, an anxious reader of men's responses, claims here to receive the message that a literary pen in her hand is not approved, and, she asserts, the veto by men of high rank governs her behavior in the presence of "anyone." More than that, she herself transmits the proscription explicitly to other women—by writing it.

Her task is simplified by the fact that dominant Western gender notions then and now allocate human beings into only one of two categories, men or women. Much feminist criticism today is inclined to stress the constructed quality of the biological, social, psychological and other markers that delimit the two groups, a process that oversimplifies differences within categories, ignores overlaps, and composes the two groups in many respects as bipolar opposites.[4] Yet, even if there is no natural foundation for sex or gender, the notions of "women" and "men" as they are defined in a particular time and place nonetheless have a historical reality and long-lasting aftereffects, well worth our scrutiny despite our skepticism. I can admit gender attributions as historical constructs and then go on to examine how assignment to the category "women" affected the opportunities and shaped the experiences of individuals and groups. Just as one can study "witches" without believing in them in the way that seventeenth-century people believed, one can study "women" of, for example, the eighteenth century, without accepting that period's (or any other's) definition of the category as an adequate description of some underlying reality. Indeed, the disruption of gender produced by race and class makes it hard to think that most societies applied their gender notions as sweepingly as they claimed, since statements purportedly about "women" in general are so often not meant to include women of all classes and all races.[5] In eighteenth-century Germany, especially in its preserved texts, the two classes vying in writing for cultural dominance, the aristocracy and the new group of educated bourgeoisie, were most of all interested in applying their preferred sex/gender framework to themselves. They omitted in particular the rural peasants, who nonetheless formed the numerical majorities in the scores of large and small German-speaking duchies, archbishoprics, kingdoms, and other principalities, if not in the free imperial cities, all of which collectively made up the fragmented "Germany" of the time. Within the aristocracy and educated middle class, the polarization of gender made it predictable that once men were expected and accepted as writers, women would not be. Femininity, the construction of how being labeled "female" should be socially and culturally expressed, made almost no allowance for a woman desiring to write for publication, and even less for her to bring her works to press. Yet, write and publish women did.

Between 1770 and 1800 the numbers of women writing and the quantity of texts they produced far surpassed any previous period in German literary history. The purpose of this book is to examine the texts, especially those written for publication, by members of the first sizable contingent of women writers in eighteenth-century Germany, to analyze the strategies that enabled the women to write, and to suggest the meanings that their texts and strategies had for other women at the time. I argue that once these writers began to write, they produced texts using and interweaving almost all available genres and that, taking the Enlightenment's proclamations about shared human potential seriously, they sought in their writing to attain cultural agency typically expressed as a sense of self. The version of feminine subjectivity represented in their writing might in various places and on various levels in a text meet or approach or challenge middle-class culture's dominant prescription for being a woman, prescriptions that in the last third of the eighteenth century were themselves evolving. I argue that the texts by women resisted the abdication of identity that men philosophers and writers were beginning to advocate for women. The difficulty of this resistance is a theme in many of the self-histories women produced in an array of different genres. Yet, the self-assertiveness of women writers in eighteenth-century Germany is readable, for instance, in the way they openly signaled their gender when publishing their texts, even though women philosophers and writers did not necessarily adopt for themselves or for other women the notions of autonomous identity then current among and for men. Whether by name (such as "Marianne Ehrmann") or more cautious designation (such as "Verfasserin" "authoress," its suffix marking gender), readers of the writings of late eighteenth-century German women were and are almost always notified when the gender of the author varied from the default, "male." I am interested in the kinds of texts thus flagged as feminine, as the products of women, and in the array of representations of female literary productivity available in the late eighteenth century. What did the texts by these women signal to their readers about women's literary place? I attempt to explain and interpret the texts in part by examining the conditions of their production, that is the woman writer and the culture and ideology that constituted her as a woman and, to varying degrees, tolerated her as a writer, and in part by examining the messages about women that eighteenth-century readers may have gleaned from reading this material. But I am concerned with the understanding made available to readers in the twenty-first century as well. Agreeing with Laura Finke that feminist literary scholars struggle "to expose the political violence that inheres in the institution of literary studies under the guise of neutral and objective scholarship,"[6] I am exploring five writers who have been variously marginalized, neglected, or never even registered by most literary criticism until the 1980s at the earliest; I accompany these individual portraits with a reconsideration of women's place in the literary movements of the eighteenth century.

At the very time when the notion of an autonomous, freewilled self was accompanying the rising middle class in the last third of the eighteenth century, exhortations were beginning to appear for women of that class to be selfless and to accept their meager individual subjectivity as inherent in "female" nature. Karin Hausen connects this deprivation of a self with the redefinition of women's work as nonwork, acts of love that require a "male" audience, preferably in the form of a husband, for validation. This was a change, Hausen asserts, from the time when women's labor, recognized as economically vital, gave them status equal or almost equal to men. Hausen describes the dominant ("male") narrative of both selfhood and women. Other possibilities for women to establish identities and thus to constitute their own adult selves loom larger when texts by more women writers are folded into the account of the period. Furthermore, even in the time, and in the often agricultural setting, when women's work had been recognized as work, they had suffered from subordination and thus had learned to act both submissively and subversively.

It is the combination of submission and subversion that requires special note. Sophie La Roche, the author of the passage about bringing out her needlework whenever she had an audience, asserted that the most prestigious members of society, "men of high birth and intellect," enforced the prohibition against women writing. In a fairy-tale reversal, the kings and fathers in La Roche's account perversely urge their daughter to occupy herself with needles, and presumably spindles, so that she will remain in a long cultural sleep. The point of the needle in a period of emerging leisure is to prevent time or place for the quill. One cannot use both simultaneously. Sophie La Roche, as the best-known and most highly-regarded German woman writer of her day, makes an apt princess for the story. If the important people in eighteenth-century society recognize so respected—and cautious—a writer as Sophie La Roche more for her needlework than her writing, the ban on the quill would seem to be all the more effective for other women. It appears impossible for a culturally active woman to have a relationship as a writer to the culturally powerful, hence, "male" members of her society; they would only recognize her as a "woman," holding the signifying needle. But that is not the end of the story. For while La Roche in this passage overtly tells her readers that she puts away her writing when anyone comes, implicitly she also says that when she is alone she writes, and not just to keep household accounts. She treats her acquiescence to powerful disapproval as a show to appease men, but in this case with minimal effect, since "male" disapproval does not deter her from writing, as both the words and the existence of the text testify. This tactic has consequences for La Roche and her texts, but the consequences are not an immediate and definitive abdication of the self or of writing.

Contesting for the quill was becoming more important as a gender issue in the late eighteenth century in Germany because now large proportions of women—within a few narrow but powerful segments of society—had been educated in how to use this specialized instrument. Education was as important as work for the educated middle class's sense of self; Karin Hausen points out that the new middle class in eighteenth-century Germany is distinguished from its counterpart in England by being less engaged with industry and commerce and marked, instead, by its learning. For German women of this class, education was more available than before but with a gender-based cap imposed on how much of any particular subject they could learn. For an individual woman of the time aspiring to become a writer, that limit was the initial barrier both to literary activity in general and to genre choice in particular, since some genres required a scholarly immersion closed to women. For educated middle-class men, on the other hand, seeking expression for their growing economic strength and frustrated in their search for political power, cultural participation had other implications. An activity such as writing served both to demonstrate that in the arts these men were as important as the aristocracy and to broadcast their conviction that in terms of ethical behavior the educated middle class was superior.

As the campaign of middle-class men for power and authority progressed, the cultural participation of middle-class women was solicited too. In moral weeklies and new journals published just for them, women had been encouraged since the second third of the century to begin extensive reading, replacing the old intensive reading and rereading of the Bible, the hymnal, and a few collections of sermons or devotional readings. After all, to expand and thrive, middle-class writers needed as many readers and buyers as they could get; for economic purposes, the readers' gender mattered little. Furthermore, as the paid work performed by many men of the educated middle class was being physically separated from their thus increasingly private homes, women had new functions to fulfill, requiring that they be more educated than before. Women married to the men of the educated middle class (the class assignment of such women derived from the class of the men to whom they were attached) managed the household, kept its accounts, supervised its servants, and, as a new task growing out of the relocation and greater regulation of men's workplaces, women as wives were expected to help their husbands recuperate from the stresses of working outside the home. To accomplish this, women of the educated middle class were supposed to be culturally literate partners for their husbands. They were also more frequently responsible for overseeing the education of their children; this task, educating both sons and daughters, men had previously reserved mainly for themselves. Despite the new responsibilities of women and because more domestic goods and services were available through purchase, middle-class women also had new time in which to learn and to pursue other activities, such as in the arts. Along the way, there were proclamations of alarm about women reading to excess, especially novels,[7] but the very proclamations kept the idea of such reading in constant circulation.

Yet, if women's improved learning led them to consider serious study or to desire to participate in literary life by writing as well as reading, they diverged both from class discourse and from prevailing economic interests; men were determined to continue their monopoly on jobs for which eighteenth-century women—if adequately educated—could have been well suited, an idea rarely articulated at the time. Polarized gender notions, however, were an effective way for men to quell women's potential aspirations. Since scholarship, the elite level of education, was masculine and hence not feminine, gender made it virtually impossible for women to get the standard tools expected of ("male") writers (as well as bureaucrats, lawyers, and pastors and all the other positions of educated middle-class men) of that time and place. Attaining cultural and intellectual legitimacy without advanced educational credentials, I argue, was one of the crucial steps for women in becoming writers, choosing genres, and constructing feminine subjectivities in texts.

My project is to apply feminist criticism to an assortment of texts written by late eighteenth-century German women and to propose ideas, based on these texts and on a limited array of other resources, about how educated women of that time and place represented the world and the place of women in it, how they explained their writing strategies, and how they depicted the way their world both supported and impeded them in their literary activity. The main thesis threading through this book is that an unprecedented cluster of eighteenth-century German women, caught between their own wishes to become writers and society's confining versions of femininity, validated themselves through their emotions and through the incorporation of feeling into their texts, a choice that had important consequences for their writing and for its later reception, indeed suppression. I am assuming that even though the texts are written in language and thus in a medium that—no matter how creative the user—restricts, distorts, and takes over what can be said, still the texts in some way mediate the ideas, responses, and stories of their individual authors. I am looking at the literature by women as the writings of individuals conspicuous to their readers, themselves, and us, for the gender into which they had been firmly enmeshed and to which they themselves draw attention. Katherine Goodman has pointed out that "it makes a great deal of difference who is speaking. The discourses of authority, of patriarchy, of morality can be spoken very differently from various vantage points."[8] And yet, sometimes I have asked myself what would happen to my analysis if documents appeared proving one of the writers I was studying was a man. But what would that mean? What evidence would prove it? A doctor's report on the writer's genitals? A letter from her mother saying . . . what? All I can claim is that publicly and privately, as far as the record shows, the writers I am studying identified themselves as "women," and were accepted as fitting that category. The vantage points discernible in their writings therefore were taken to represent vantage points of "women" (to some extent even when the author chose a male narrator) and as such influenced late eighteenth-century notions of the kind of people "women" were and the kinds of writing "women" did. But this is not the same as saying that the author's gender had any particular effect on what or how she wrote. As Rita Felski observed in discussing twentieth-century literature:

> It is clear that a range of textual positions is available to both sexes, and that it is often impossible to construct a straightforward determining relationship between the gender of the writing subject and the distinctive formal and thematic features of a literary work. For this reason, a feminist approach to women's writing needs to proceed from a recognition of the heterogeneity of texts produced by women writers in different periods and cultures which cannot be reduced to exemplifications of a single underlying essence.[9]

In Germany between 1770 and 1790, the multiply-mediated relationship between gender and genre is particularly interesting because it was a time when an occasional woman of the right class might be allowed to write if she agreed to do so "as a woman." But who determines what that means and on what basis? As theoretical studies have repeatedly shown, doing anything "as a woman" is far more complex than at first appears.[10]

I find it useful to understand these women writers as confronting the demands of femininity in the form of life scripts that were acceptable for them to play. Starting from the small spaces within existing scripts that could tolerate the acts of learning and writing, some women attempted to produce new scripts. But producing change of this kind is fraught with difficulty. Bronwyn Davies explains:

> The polarised social structure, created through a multitude of different discursive practices, is something individuals can attempt to change through a refusal of certain discursive practices or elements of those practices, and by practising new and different forms of discourse. At the same time it is important to recognize that individuals are constrained by existing structures and practices. These are not simply an external constraint (or potentiation), they provide the conceptual framework, the psychic patterns, the emotions through which individuals position themselves as male or female and through which they privately experience themselves in relation to the social world. As well, they provide the vehicle through which others will recognise that positioning as legitimate, as meaningful, as providing the right to claim personhood. The development and practice of new forms of discourse, then, is not a simple matter of choice, but involves grappling with both subjective and social/structural constraints.[11]

In the face of the eighteenth-century German versions of these multiple constraints, women, including women writers, could not create alternative practices as complete and comprehensive as the already available ones still endorsed by dominant patriarchal discourses.

But when, after all, does a woman count as a writer? From one point of view, any woman writing anything can qualify as a writer, a definition that for late eighteenth-century Germany would include virtually all women in the educated middle class and aristocracy, since letter writing was such an important practice at the time. This is the perspective of Eva Walter in a book that concentrates on the nonliterary documentation of eleven women whom Walter categorizes as writers; at least two of the eleven can only be included under the most generous interpretation.[12] For the purposes of my study, such sweeping inclusiveness obscures more than it enlightens. My definition of a writer is someone who spends or spent a lot of time writing during at least one period of her life. If a woman's writing was extremely limited and of neither primary nor secondary importance to her life for any extended time, her situation is very different from that of a woman whose commitment to writing was prolonged and who used the commitment to produce more than the most occasional small text. What any woman wrote need not be ignored, but the mere fact that she for some brief moment composed a few poems or published several letters does not qualify her to be a writer. Although drawing the line exactly between writers and, in this sense, nonwriters is impossible, the general distinction is important nonetheless if one is trying to understand the women writers who made an impact on their contemporaries. This is so even though the barely documented but often prolific letter-writing of many women of the time can make it especially difficult to know the writers who existed.

Indeed, for eighteenth-century women, the category "writer" requires further refinement. I distinguish between two groups, private writers and public writers. Public writers are those who published their works commercially; private writers are those who produced a considerable body of written work but refused to publish—often despite specific offers.[13] The distinction locates the writers in a context that was already problematical for women and that was highly contested in the eighteenth century. This was precisely the time when the publicness of princely and royal courts was beginning to be challenged by a new publicness emerging out of the world of literature, literary exchange, and literary discussion, and promoted especially by the educated middle class and lower nobility (who were in turn often employees of the court). Paradoxically, the new publicness could arise precisely because it located itself within the realm that the court defined as private, not connected to the state or its ruler. "With the rise of a literary market and a bourgeois reading public from the late seventeenth century onward, the private society of market exchange formed itself into a network of communication, generated its own 'universal' moral standards through the communicative process, and eventually applied those standards critically to the state and its policies."[14] Feminist scholarship from the start has drawn attention to the relegation of women to the intimate realm of the house and family and the corresponding specification of privileged activity as men's, including that as head of the family, a model that comes under attack when it is hastily universalized.[15] The gendered division of spheres was familiar in Europe already in the eighteenth century, in Rousseau, for example. Thus, Gatens argues: "By privatizing familial concerns and making them the special province of women, Rousseau leaves men free to move between the private world—where 'natural' relations between the sexes and between fathers and children are conducted—and the public world of culture, citizenship and politico-ethical relations with other men."[16] But such a conceptualization omits the imbrication in the eighteenth century of at least the cultural version of the public (less so the political) and the private realm. As Dena Goodman argues, in this century "a new form of publicity developed within—and precisely because it was within—the private sphere."[17] When a woman considered publication, as opposed to private circulation of her writing, she was considering granting herself a larger role in the new literary public. Not as large a role as men, to be sure, for publication did not have to mean personal public appearances. Still, public writing as it was conducted in the late eighteenth century had become partially reconcilable with a woman's shunning the world outside her usual circle. Furthermore, the line between public and private in Germany was not drawn in the same places in the eighteenth century as it is in the twenty-first century, and it wavered far more. Most of all, it was not necessarily a line between home and an office located elsewhere. While the middle-class home had private zones, many homes specifically of the educated middle class still contained public areas as well—evident, for example, when a professor's home included a lecture hall—and even the private areas could host the events or provide the writing table where the discussions were provoked through articles, letters, books, reviews, and many other forms of oral and written discourse. When women writers wrote at home they were often there with their husbands. Altogether, "public" is a more abstract, more ambiguous, and less physical concept in the eighteenth century than is often noted.

Change for women is often the unintended result of alterations that occur in another realm and introduce discrepancies and contradictions into the discourse of femininity. Thus, the shift of literary production away from the courts toward the bookstores, monthly journals, reviews, subscription lists, and other devices that constituted the eighteenth-century literary marketplace, profoundly changed the circumstances under which private writing could become public "literature." Once the new literary institutions enabled women's writings to be published commercially without the author appearing in person before an audience composed completely or mainly of adult men, public women writers did not specifically offend against the most literal meaning of "women's place." Still, the choice between being a public or a private writer continued to pose difficulties and to have special consequences for a woman.

The choice of genre is frequently one of those consequences. Private writers wrote mainly in forms that, in a woman's hand, were not considered literary, especially letters, diaries, and autobiographies.[18] Public writers, on the other hand, experimented both with nonliterary forms, such as cookbooks and housekeeping guides, and with all the literary forms popular in their day: verse tales, tragedies, love lyrics, novels, essays, travel books, and more; they were typically prolific letter writers as well. Public women writers often posited a relationship to the audience that fit into an acceptable "female" role (mother, aunt, sister, etc.). For genres (such as scholarly writing) that exceedingly few women read, the construction of audience and claimed relationship to the audience were more difficult. As long as almost no women read scholarly books, the tiny number of women sufficiently educated to compose such works could not use a female readership to explain their writing in the genre. For most forms, however, women were at least a noticeable part of the readership.

The author's relationship to her audience was also important in another way. The actual readers in the literary marketplace differed—though not completely—from those reached when a woman's letters were read aloud or circulated among friends, and then perhaps copied and passed on to their friends. Despite the possible extensiveness of private circulation, a woman who decided to publish relinquished more control over who her audience was. The work of public writers, in short, became available to a wider circle of potential readers, some of them also writers or potential writers.

On the other hand, private writers were not without influence, especially when their work was published posthumously, like Friderika Baldinger's personal history. Especially impressive among private writers of the time is Rahel von Varnhagen, whose letters had a greater influence on later readers than the writings of many of her more forward sisters who dared see their work in print. Aware of the pressures on women not to publish, feminist critics have given sympathetic and often extensive treatment to private writers such as Varnhagen.[19] For the literary life of their own time, however, the impact of private writers was usually limited. In this respect, publishing a body of work distinguishes the meaning and effect of a public writer's accomplishment from that of most private writers—unless they died early and their work was then promptly made public. The willingness and ability of more and more women to publish is one of the momentous developments in the late eighteenth century.

Once the floodgates opened, once German women discovered in the late eighteenth century that they could indeed become public writers, they were minimally limited by genre—aside from the matter of a claimed female audience. Since women until then had essentially not been writers, no genre was held in reserve for women writers, and I would argue, along with critics such as Susanne Kord and Rita Felski, that their gender did not predestine them for any particular genre.[20] Thus the eighteenth-century German women's literary energies were not channeled in any particular direction and they had more freedom then than later to try many different forms and subforms. Although to attempt one of the most prestigious literary genres, such as tragedy or epic poetry, represented a bold assault on high culture, German women tried these, too. In England, by the time Sophie La Roche began composing *Geschichte des Fräuleins von Sternheim* "The History of Lady Sophia Sternheim," novels were already predominantly the compositions of women, so much so that Eva Figes says this is the deepest point in the cultural divide between men and women there.[21] In Germany, however, during the entire eighteenth century, women were identified with the novel as readers but not as writers. If one looks at the century as a whole, women's writing is concentrated in plays—during the first two-thirds of the century most notably those by Luise Gottsched and Caroline Neuber—and poetry, not in novels. The early poets were, for instance, Unzer, Zäunemann, Karsch, Ziegler, Volckmann, and Fuchs (all represented in poetry anthologies edited by Cocalis and Brinker-Gabler).[22] Occasionally, the poet and playwright groups overlapped or almost overlapped, as in the case of Henrietta Elisabeth Ekkard (or Eckhard), who purportedly wanted to write plays but, lacking the time, composed poetry instead.[23] In the year 1770, women's concentration on plays and poetry is neatly shown in the just two literary books published by women, one volume containing both poetry and a play for reading by Hedwig Pernet, and the other containing a successful play for the stage by the actress Friederike Sophie Hensel (later Seyler). The forty-six novels published in 1770 were all by men.[24]

During the thirty years between 1770 and 1800, women's choice of genre changed decade by decade, as an examination of new titles published during those years shows. In 1771, the year *Sternheim* appeared, the list of new literary books by other women included another novel (by Maria Anna Sagar), one collection of poetry (by Henrietta Ekkard), and one play (a new version by Seyler of the play she had published the year before under a different title). Throughout the 1770s, the books that women published continued to be chiefly plays and poetry collections, joined by the occasional devotional or pedagogical work. With the exception of two novels by La Roche and two by Maria Anna Sagar,[25] all the other several hundred novels published in the 1770s were by men.

Not until 1780 did the mix of women's writing—produced by a new generation of women writers—change. Women born in the 1750s (including Philippine Engelhard-Gatterer, Marianne Ehrmann, and Sophie Albrecht) were taking over. Their fathers had imbibed the early Enlightenment message of improving the education of their daughters (though only to a point).[26] They themselves had been influenced by the *Empfindsamkeit* (the Sensibility movement as it developed in Germany) and *Sturm und Drang* "Storm and Stress," had probably read *Geschichte des Fräuleins von Sternheim* at least once, and had benefited from the bypass around education that La Roche devised for women in that novel. In the 1780s, with a score of these young women writing, poetry continued to thrive, with new volumes (often also containing other small genres such as idylls, short essays, or letters) every year. As the decade advanced, plays by women became less frequent and novels more. Early in the period, one author, Amalie Froriep, in her novel *Amalie von Nordheim* (1783), showed her specific indebtedness to La Roche by creating a character with many of La Roche's attributes and named Madame Laresche. It was in the next decade, the 1790s, that La Roche as novelist was finally joined by a large number of other women, a development that occurred as part of an overall increase in women's literary activity, in journalism, in poetry, and, on an unprecedented scale, in the writing of novels and again plays, all of this happening at a time when the upheavals of the French Revolution were raising possibilities in the German states, terrifying to many members of the middle class as well as the aristocracy, of political and cultural participation by all sectors of society, elite and nonelite.

Even before this prospect arose in its revolutionary form, a common response to women writers in the public discourse was to trivialize them, thereby making it harder for women to have enough paying readers to take an important next step: earning a living from their writing and becoming professional public writers. Furthermore, if to be a professional writer a woman had to openly profess literature as the occupation to which she dedicated her time and by which she sustained herself financially, then professional writing was essentially out of the reach of women. The fractured conglomeration of German political entities did not have the big city subcultures to accommodate women who avowed such a tremendous deviation from recognizably feminine positions. But if the fact of intensive writing and publishing and the achievement of thus earning one's living—even if these facts were kept secret—are the measures of professionalism, then women who presented themselves in quite other ways, including three, Sophie von La Roche, Marianne Ehrmann, and Sophie Albrecht, of the five I examine in this book, unmistakably qualify for at least part of their lives. Indeed, the story of women's professional writing addresses the alienated resistance of a small group of women to powerful rebukes from their society; despite their own resistance however, the women in many respects also reaffirmed society's interdiction, posing themselves as minor exceptions.

The choice of public women writers, whether professional or not, to publish anonymously made little difference to readers in the late eighteenth century who wanted to discriminate between men and women writers, because the women writers' practice was to flag their gender—by calling themselves "A Lady of Rank," or "A Fräulein from the Country," or identifying themselves as the "authoress" of another work.[27] This means that while their individual identity might at least temporarily by sacrificed to feminine propriety,[28] the pseudonymous or anonymous signature on their work still announced a crucial element of their identity as society constructed it, namely gender.[29] Even for their names, anonymity seems seldom to have offered total protection—and perhaps was not intended to. This is evident in the work of the remarkable Carl Wilhelm Otto August von Schindel (1776–1830), collector, writer, and editor of all the information he could find about all women writers alive between 1800 and 1825. Because many late eighteenth-century women writers were still living after 1800, they, too, are included in Schindel's invaluable biobibliography, *Die deutschen Schriftstellerinnen des 19. Jahrhunderts* "German Women Writers of the Nineteenth Century," which appeared in three volumes from 1823 to 1825. In fact, Schindel had been able to identify the authors of most of the works he had located, regardless of pseudonym or disguise. But even if a woman remained genuinely anonymous—for most of her life, Benedicte Naubert accomplished this—she was still participating in literary life more than if she refrained from publishing altogether. She had a chance, for example, to read reviews of what she had done or to note the absence of any critical response. She could know how her work sold. And she could respond to attacks and adjust her behavior, sometimes by publishing nothing more. Most of all, regardless of whether she signed her name to her works, the woman who signaled her gender even though she remained anonymous affected the image of writing women and drew attention to their existence (which is not to say that choosing to be pseudonymous or anonymous was insignificant in other respects). A woman who flagged herself as a woman was one whose words about women and as a woman countered, confirmed, or reinterpreted the far more widely disseminated words about women by eighteenth-century men.

Despite (and to some extent because of) their sense of separation from women of their class as a group, eighteenth-century women writers felt that if they had to present themselves as opposing conventional oppression of women, they would never succeed. Even the public and professional writers among them crafted identities as (writing) women, not as women writers. By presenting themselves as fitting—or ostensibly trying to fit—the prevailing ideology of gender in every way but one (writing), they negotiated adequate levels of social approval, or at least tolerance, for themselves. But by advocating dominant ideology they imposed on other women the same difficulties that they individually were struggling to escape; they rarely saw their needs and achievements as representing the potential of all or most women, or even of all women in their own socioeconomic class. As long as the women writers of the late eighteenth century considered themselves as exceptions and represented themselves that way, then their accomplishments could have only limited impact on the general understanding of women's needs and capabilities.

Despite the bans that gender should have imposed, German women in the late eighteenth century pressed their way into the palace of literary creation. German men perhaps perceived the same domain more as a busy and increasingly crowded, though male-only market town of literature. They, especially the men of the educated middle class or aristocracy, could stride with freedom and confidence through the site, perhaps avoiding an exclusive dwelling, being rebuilt in Greco-Roman style as the century ended, which some said was in the town's center and where only an elite few were welcome. Women, however, to whom literary creation was a closed off palace that most had so far seen only from outside the fence, found it important not only to pass the gates but to do so openly, and fully marked as women, not in masquerade. But to know how to comport themselves in this awe-inspiring setting, the newcomers watched carefully to see how more experienced (men) visitors went about things. Thus, although the arriving newcomers were marked as eighteenth-century women, their actions were inflected by both the category of behavior designated as feminine and the category designated as literary, a category constructed until then by and for men. The newcomers explored the prestigious rooms labeled drama and lyric poetry; they lingered in the chamber of the novel, and surveyed several important alcoves, such as those called journalism, travel writing, and essay. And although the palace was a large and rambling one, only partially updated into eighteenth-century style but still containing many rooms and apartments in older wings and in outbuildings, the women began to hear tell of each other. Sometimes they were able to pass notes back and forth and around, despite their dispersion and despite the difficulty of coming up with a pfennig for a messenger, who might, in fact, also be a woman, but one with very different cares and concerns because of her class. The intruders did not, by the way, find themselves directed off to a remote apartment for women's writing; indeed, that artificial ruin was not constructed until later. Still, the choices and activities of those early "female" interlopers were regulated in several interrelated ways, through what they could learn of the palace's ground plan and of how to open the secret panels in its desks and treasure boxes, and through the constant demand that they adhere to the rigid decorum prescribed for women of their class and religion. Operating within these sanctions, few considered the idea of rereading the palace as a market town to which both men and women would have access on equal terms. Instead, the women in the palace were willing to help bring in the occasional stranger, such as a barely-educated rural woman, for example, or to spread the word of other women writers elsewhere. They undertook modifications of the furnishings and even some of the rooms of the palace, but they did nothing to enable either Jewish women or the men or women wearing the homespun clothes and the wooden shoes suited for field work any closer than before to the palace's polished floors and silken upholstery. And the unfree women and men called "Moors" from distant lands to the south might pass trays, clean the furniture, be painted into the background of pictures, or even suckle the white women's babies but were not allowed in German or in one of the African languages they may have spoken to leave traces in their own written words, though they were occasionally noted in others'.

Of the five women whose failed and successful entrances to the palace in the last three decades of the eighteenth century are discussed here, one is a private writer and four are public. Using materialist feminist notions that stress "the materiality, which is to say in this instance the historicity, of culture,"[30] I try in this book to look carefully at their texts and contexts, including issues of social history, such as age at first marriage among women of the educated middle class or their frequency of divorce. As Valerie Wayne puts it, "materialist feminism . . . helps us understand how all persons, in ways that we are asked to attend to for their differences as well as their similarities, are constrained by ideologies and social practices."[31] Five writers seemed to me a large enough number to suggest both divergences and commonalities within the larger group of late eighteenth-century women writers. And by organizing the work around the five, the variety of genres in which individual late eighteenth-century women wrote becomes evident. I began in the 1980s by reading texts by many different women, looking for those that interested me—which at that time generally meant that either they approximately fit my still mostly male-ordered notions of what a well-constructed literary text was like, or they surprised me by their deviation from what I expected (dimly) of proper eighteenth-century womanhood, or they pleased me by seeming to represent some "advance" in women's opportunities.[32] As I gradually became aware of the profuse variety of genres in which women had written, from epic poems to travel essays, and from epigrams to tragedies, I decided I must include as much of that richness as possible. Still, a different selection of writers would have yielded a different account of the nature and value of the texts, and of their author's strategies for becoming and surviving as women writers.

The published texts by late eighteenth-century German women demonstrate four paths whereby women might enter the palace of literature, or appear at one of the palace's windows, or enter through a new gate or door. One was boldly to ignore society's constraining expectations and plunge ahead without explanation. Another was to avoid the use of one's own name, but rather to appear pseudonymously or anonymously. Third was to receive authorization from a literary man who might, for example, in a preface offer a metanarrative about how a woman could acceptably come to write and be published. And fourth was for a woman, often the writer herself, to produce the metanarrative, either separately, or embedded in the rest of the text. When explanations were offered by either a man or a woman, or sometimes even in the circumscribing pseudonym, several strategies could be deployed, such as fashioning the writer as a thoroughly respectable woman, with writing her only nonconformity, or claiming that her writing was not deliberate, or at least not intended for publication. These paths and strategies imply a commitment, large or small, to developing a community of literary women by writing "as a woman" rather than resorting to the other approach, the least common one at the time, of writing "as a man," accomplished either by genderless anonymity (with "man" as the default gender) or by invoking a male pseudonym. The five women whom I discuss in the chapters that follow use different combinations of paths and strategies in their texts, and not always successfully.

The autobiography of the private writer Friderika Baldinger tells the story of a woman who pushed against the prevailing practices that limited women's education, attempted to write her own self-justifying metanarrative, but failed to reconcile her position as a woman writer with her position as a patriarchal woman. The learning that gave her a reputation for scholarliness also trained her in androcentric thought and values, and to acquire that learning she had needed to undertake marriage to a man who crushed her will and who did not take it upon himself to sponsor her public appearance in writing. Ultimately, she was neither educated nor independent enough to write for men and was no longer able or willing to present herself as writing primarily for an audience of women, a situation that truncated her autobiography and prevented virtually all publication. The induction of a woman into the particular knowledge and practices called the Enlightenment coerced her into insurmountable dilemmas. Despite probably thousands of pages of writing, including two preserved letters to Sophie La Roche, Friderika Baldinger, the subject of the first chapter, is a private writer.

The next chapter is about Sophie La Roche, who, with her first novel, entered the struggle of the educated middle class for social and cultural recognition and tried to renegotiate the terms by which women could become writers. La Roche applied the attribution of emotion to women as a way out of the Enlightenment impasse regarding women and reason that silenced Baldinger. By the end of her career, La Roche had used all four community-building strategies to deal with her difficult status as a woman writer. In novels, tales, a monthly journal for women, travel accounts, and innovative autobiographical volumes, La Roche explored the world of women, occasionally envisioning empowering change and often promoting connections among literary women. She was aided at the start by Wieland's powerful endorsement, which later was reinforced both by her own self-justifications and by her adherence to respectability. Yet, she established, I will argue, a literary group that enabled other women to write and publish without such difficulties. To place La Roche into literary history requires, I believe, refining our notion of *Empfindsamkeit* "Sensibility," recognizing three sequenced but also overlapping phases, religious *Empfindsamkeit*, *Empfindsamkeit* of sympathy, and *Empfindsamkeit* of alienation. I illustrate religious *Empfindsamkeit* briefly with texts composed before 1770, and locate La Roche in the *Empfindsamkeit* of sympathy, along with the third writer, Philippine Engelhard nee Gatterer.

Engelhard-Gatterer rejected a male metanarrative of women's writing and insisted, instead, on writing her own account of herself as a poet, a project she took up repeatedly in her texts; she also aspired to respectability as a woman—while yet wanting to compose and publish poetry. Her work refines our understanding of how a woman used feelings to position herself in the literary world at different stages of her life, as she published her first collection while a single young adult, her second shortly after marriage, and her third after the death of her husband. Although her texts, analyzed in my third chapter, reproduce correct bourgeois womanhood within the terms of the form of *Empfindsamkeit* that stressed sympathy, Engelhard-Gatterer's poems also modify femininity to accommodate the woman writer. And in Philippine Engelhard-Gatterer's case, it is more possible than usual to glimpse a woman writer's informal as well as formal reception, especially from women readers, as well as to trace the kind of help she got from male mentors and a female literary confidante.

Marianne Ehrmann, construing women as living in conditions of oppression that she was determined to change or at least alleviate, produced a body of protofeminist work, including short stories, journals, and novels, that challenges the dominant discourse about women and is addressed in many cases explicitly to women. Nor was she alone, as the work of Emilie Berlepsch and several other writers shows. In addition to her protofeminism, Ehrmann, drawing on emotional appeals, themes, and language similar to those of the *Sturm und Drang*, stretched the boundaries of *Empfindsamkeit* to include a strand of alienation, signaled by her texts about the macabre and uncanny.

The final chapter concerns the poetry, prose, and plays of Sophie Albrecht, and especially the way she uses the emotional discourses of love and death to circumvent issues of reason and education. How, asked Jakob Grimm, a distinguished philologist and one of the famous Grimm brothers, could a woman write about a kiss?[33] Sophie Albrecht, reclaiming eroticism for women,[34] could and did. She and Ehrmann wrote little metanarrative about themselves as writers, leaping instead into cultural agency without elaborate explanation or excuse. Her work represents another version of the *Empfindsamkeit* of alienation, this one close to the emerging discourse of Romanticism, yet another movement with only a problematic space for women.

These five writers struggled with a series of contradictions, many of which resulted from their difficulty in conceiving and practicing comprehensive alternatives to the dominant discourse and the approved feminine life scripts within the educated middle class to which they belonged. Friderika Baldinger shows the smallness of the space for writing and publishing that the discursive practices of Enlightened femininity allowed her. Sophie La Roche much more successfully addressed this small space, devising a specific strategy of enablement, a special form of permission whereby a woman's emotions allowed her to write within the scripts of femininity; she also used this emotional permission to write critically about marriage. But while La Roche gave women a justification for writing, and while her style made writing (as well as reading) more accessible to women, she also accepted and propagated a discourse of polarized gender that imposed tremendous limitations on women's cultural activities. Philippine Engelhard-Gatterer, who insisted that her feelings flowed unmediated onto the page, ready for the properly feeling reader, nonetheless repeatedly showed how modesty curtailed women's access to speech, while yet presenting herself as modest. Marianne Ehrmann more aggressively asserted the need for society to better accommodate women and for women to be more thoughtful members of society. She oscillates between late-Enlightenment reasoned optimism and the claim of special insights derived from feelings of melancholy, anger, and depression. Finally, Sophie Albrecht, never particularly interested in either reason or education, glorified love but could find no way to embed it in positive social narratives, connecting it instead directly and indirectly with death, and particularly, suicide.

Jakob Grimm, who was reviewing Schindel's biobibliography of women writers when he questioned the permissible topics about which women could write, estimated with horror that the number of such scribbling women had doubled during the last three decades of the eighteenth century compared with the first seven, and vengefully added that if the works of eighteenth-century women writers had never been published, it would have made no difference to the history of German literature. As that history has been written until now, he was right.[35] The absence of texts by women from studies that claim to examine the literature of the time but include only writings by men is a serious and thought-provoking flaw in most literary history as it has been presented until the advent of the feminist critique and in many cases until today. According to the usual account, in the 1770s, the *Aufklärung*, the German version of Enlightenment, was commencing its vigorous late phase, in which faith in orderly rationalism in the world was leavened by receptivity to empirical and psychological experience, all with the goal of enhancing human happiness, as viewed by the relatively prosperous and educated (men) practitioners of this philosophical, political, cultural, and literary movement. Meanwhile, *Empfindsamkeit*, the German version of Sensibility, was reaching its bloom as a form of Enlightenment that stressed the moral insight possible through gentle subjective sensations, such as sympathy or sensitivity to beauty. But during the decade of the 1770s and later, when *Aufklärung* and *Empfindsamkeit*, these two closely related movements of the middle class, were at full strength, they received an angry challenge from their ungrateful sons, the founders of *Sturm und Drang*, who expressed intense political distaste for the status quo and searched instead for a utopia of passionate freedom. By the end of the century, new challenges had arisen. Goethe and Schiller had withdrawn into a highly refined semi-collaboration known in German literary history as *Klassik*, and subsumed in other accounts under Romanticism. Meanwhile, the somewhat different impulse and aesthetic of another group of writers identified in German literary history as Romanticism was also emerging. Together, the *Klassik* and *Romantik* became the first major movement in modern German literature whose influence pervaded all of Western Europe. Can this division into movements also include the writings of women that were (and are) not taken into account? Years ago, Joan Kelly-Gadol asked the now classic feminist question: Did women have a Renaissance? For my purpose in this book, the question could be reformulated: Could women have an Enlightenment? Could it go beyond the occasional essay or dialog? If German women did not and could not fully participate in the central discourses of the *Aufklärung*, as Friderika Baldinger's story will suggest, then that is a failure that literary and intellectual history should clearly register, although so far the subject has hardly been raised. As for *Empfindsamkeit*, what varieties of it did women develop over the years? And could women be members of the *Sturm und Drang*, or was that movement too thoroughly misogynist for such a revisioning today?

When women passed the gates into public writing, they were not welcomed, they were not made comfortable, they were not really encouraged by male literary critics—though sometimes by middle-class male nationalists. Although women were occasionally reviewed as if their gender made no difference, more often they were belittled as women or ignored. But it was not reviews and reviewers or male cultural popes and pope-aspirants who deeply influenced the decision to write or not for most for these women, who, after all, in most cases lived away from the most powerful cultural centers. Rather, it was the women's readiness to write, a condition promoted by the early phase of the *Aufklärung*, and their audience's readiness to respond, a condition promoted by the *Empfindsamkeit*. Especially when the women defined their desired audience, as Engelhard-Gatterer did, as people with feeling hearts, (read: predisposed to like her texts) the women were sufficiently well received to keep going. But few women were willing to compete with men. In some cases, to minimize the problem, the women chose an audience (such as the urban girls whom La Roche addressed), not a genre. In other cases, by openly acknowledging their gender to the audience, the writers expected and wanted a different reception than a man, again in an effort to avoid competition with men writers. Women did not want their audience or the critics to judge them by standards designed for educated men, and they did not want to compete in any way except as women, a point underscored by the rarity with which eighteenth-century women used male pseudonyms.[36]

The texts I discuss do not just fling into view literary history's inadequacies and blind spots, but also rattle the sets of values that literary critics and literary historians commonly use when we read and judge eighteenth-century Western writings. Thus, when I note that the texts I am examining are of a kind traditionally considered literary, I raise for many readers questions of the texts' aesthetic qualities, a topic gynocritical feminists, those of us who focus on writings by women, often find daunting, given the notions of aesthetics in which we have usually been schooled. The texts themselves often proclaim an explicit aesthetic program—the special invocation, for instance, of approval by kindred spirits—not necessarily an aesthetic system we find helpful today. Less blatantly, the selection of the texts in a book of this kind, introducing many long forgotten writings to modern readers, can be said to signify at least preliminary evaluative judgments, even if the selector does not identify what her criteria were, whether aesthetic or otherwise. In fact, my wish is to have it both ways. I attempt to work with the texts as pieces of language that can claim the status of linguistic art works, as literature—and simultaneously as social and historical documents. In the process of reading the texts "as literature," I as the critic and reader who notes their structured language, for example, or their shifts of voice, choice of meter, or evocation of character, confer on the texts the status of literature, fictive though that status may be. After all, Terry Eagleton has persuasively argued that there is no such thing as literature in itself.[37] Eagleton goes on to argue that it will not do to say alternatively "that literature is just what people whimsically choose to call literature. For there is nothing at all whimsical about such kinds of value-judgment: they have their roots in deeper structures of belief . . . [which] refer in the end not simply to private taste, but to the assumptions by which certain social groups exercise and maintain power over others."[38] Nonetheless, I plan to pretend for considerable stretches of the following book that by producing literary critical readings of the texts, I can make them become literature for many of my readers; I want to resist the powers that long excluded these women and their writings from what counts as literature. By producing the critical readings, I hope to make the texts be "literature" for many of my readers, in turn. At the same time, these are texts of interest to me for their (mostly indirect) representations of women's strategies for negotiating gender and writing, for their explorations of "women's experiences"—impure and mediated though these experiences are through hegemonic ideology—sometimes as experiments in which writing women modified existing forms or introduced little-used themes and topics, and always because these writings contain decipherable traces of the still inadequately understood and insufficiently studied conditions under which they were both produced and originally read.

As the women in this book threaded their ways among their desire to write, their gender-structured circumstances, including the expectations, demands, and concessions of readers, and the changing discursive practices of their time, they had to undertake a number of different kinds of tasks. They invented new subject positions and new discursive practices whereby they could think about and live women's lives. They experimented with genre and language in order to find ways to write and speak, for instance, about what it meant to be women. Given the interior and exterior contexts in which they worked, their intellectual positions, gendered practices, and literary experiments proved to be diverse, and often fragmentary, didactic, and egocentric. The choices of whether and how to validate their writings through their feelings turned out to be especially important for their writing and their reception, past and present. This book is concerned with the new scripts, both as lived experience and as written document, that German women writers composed in the late eighteenth century, and with the story of how these writers grappled with both the subjective and the social and structural constraints that confronted them.

2
Between the Spinning Wheel and the Book: Friderika Baldinger (1739–86)

FRIDERIKA BALDINGER'S TEXT ABOUT HER EDUCATION IS ONE OF THE recuperated documents of the "other" eighteenth century, the one inhabited by women. It is a controversial self-narrative whose seemingly imposed terms are renegotiated even in the opening paragraph: "I am supposed to write down the history of my intellect? As if I had so much intellect that it would be worthwhile to seek out its path. I am not writing like that but as a contribution about my education, to the extent that it had an impact on my whole character."[1] The resulting "contribution," as she calls it, entitled "Versuch über meine Verstandeserziehung" "Essay about the Education of My Intellect," is prefaced by two failed authorial efforts at justification, which are in turn preceded by an editor's introduction. Friderika Baldinger, in short, wrote an autobiographical sketch and decided to publish it, thought about the matter again, and chose to keep it in manuscript after all. She was a profoundly misogynist woman, a fact that led her to irresolvable problems about herself, to extraordinary limitations and omissions in her account of her life, and to failed strategies for justifying publication. Little wonder that when the publication finally appeared posthumously in 1791 with the new title, *Lebensbeschreibung von Friderika Baldinger von ihr selbst verfaßt* "Description of the Life of Friderika Baldinger Composed by Herself," it totaled a mere thirty-nine pages, of which sixteen were the foreword, a dedication, and two prefaces. Still, despite her failure to publish it, Baldinger's autobiography became one of the very few works of self-narrative by a middle-class German woman actually published in the eighteenth century, and as such, was part of her century's published literature by contemporary women.

In my terms, Friderika Baldinger was a writer, the quantity of whose writing in the form of letters was originally enormous (although only a minute fraction seems to have survived until today). By her count, she had written twelve to fourteen hundred letters to one correspondent, at least some of which she herself considered publishable, and to others she had written hundreds more.[2] Despite this productivity, her scanty record of publication, consisting of a few letters in a journal, categorizes her, again in my terms, as a private writer.[3] As such, Friderika Baldinger is an important subject for the examination of the differences between public and private writers, while the particulars of her intellectual and educational history make her invaluable as a model of women's strained relationship to the Enlightenment.

In broadening her topic to address the impact of her intellectual education on her character, Baldinger creates a self-narrative with space to discuss four problems confronting most intellectually ambitious eighteenth-century German women of the educated middle class and above: access to sufficiently advanced education, the material conditions associated with marriage, the prevailing androcentric discourse on femininity, and the operations of desire, the latter two hiding in plain sight in Baldinger's text. In other words, Baldinger modifies the notion of a history of her intellect to take into account the fact that this intellect belongs to a woman. "I wanted so badly to become learned," Baldinger writes, "and was exasperated that my sex excluded me from that. Well then, you'll at least have to become smart, I thought, and that's done with books—you'll have to be a good reader."[4] For women of the educated middle class and lower levels of the nobility, educational access, marriage, and femininity operated as control mechanisms that allowed passive cultural consumption but hindered, among other things, women's active participation in literary or scholarly productivity; desire tended to undermine such constraints. The first factor, education, meant at the time a set of tools, skills, and knowledges profoundly connected to reading, writing, and books. Aside from university levels, education of one's intellect, as Baldinger repeatedly designates it, was only partially organized into institutions, and was much less available to girls and women than to boys and men. It was clearly a form of discipline, but not yet permeated by the state. For men, obtaining increasing levels of education offered a means of social advancement; for women, the possibility of leveraging more education into social advancement occurred almost solely through the different marriage prospects that education might bring. The second factor, marriage, was an institution of both state and church. Then as now, marriage was the site for reproducing gender through the process of child rearing, in eighteenth-century Germany usually including at least the early phases of "education," and was characterized by a gendered division of labor, wealth, and power. Because of this, feminist scholars often distinguish the husband's marriage from the wife's. They also often understand marriage as the principal patriarchal institution for male control of female sexuality and reproduction, both topics that Baldinger also briefly raises. Baldinger's self-narrative also raises other important, little understood points about the marital history of women of the time: their age at marriage, for example, and the incidence of death in childbirth. Marriage helped Baldinger definitively overcome her ignorance and her physical isolation, but it simultaneously clamped androcentric notions of femininity firmly over her vision. The third factor, femininity, is the part of gender discourse that refers to a society's class-inflected expectations of women's bodies, behaviors, and characters. In addition to impeding women's education and redirecting them toward marriage, the dominant versions of femininity for women of the educated middle class in eighteenth-century Germany discouraged their active participation in the cultural life of their time, a situation which many women resented ("I was exasperated that my sex excluded me"), and sometimes resisted. The fourth factor, desire, provided the energy for the accomplishments of women (and men, of course) despite constraints. For the women in this study, expressing desire was often a convoluted process; desire might be displaced onto others and then repackaged as duty or obedience, or mentioned in a belittling way, or offset by an opposition between the desired ("I wanted so badly to become learned") and the undesired ("all physical love was disgusting to me," 21).

To look at the issues somewhat differently, eighteenth-century Germany had a society and culture in which gender and class were powerful social categories that influenced virtually every aspect of human relations, including what it meant to be human. Thus, the four problems of education, marriage, femininity, and desire that confronted women in the efforts to be producers as well as consumers of culture are all highly inflected by the master statuses of gender and class. "Gender," then, has dimensions both on the level of the individual subject and on the level of the specific society. On the level of society it is an encompassing system of ideas, pressures, expectations, and practices that permeate the social world in a form commonly called patriarchy. Comprehensive though patriarchy was in eighteenth-century Germany (as it is and was in various forms in most of the world then and now), it was also messy and inconsistent and for many individuals, especially women and girls, quite uncomfortable, and it was crosscut by other structures and discourses. This combination of messiness, inconsistency, discomfort, and crosscuttings, of course, is exactly what made Friderika Baldinger's self-narrative both possible and interesting as well as cramped and hard to publish.

When Baldinger's sketch of the education of her intellect and its impact on her character paradigmatically addresses the four interlocking factors of education, marriage, femininity, and desire it also suggests the effects of the four on her as a (woman) writer. As its original title promises, the body of the account focuses on the development of the author's intellect and reason, but it simultaneously tells the story of a woman's capture by misogynist discourse of inferior femininity. The author's multiple prefaces to her work show her several attempts to explain publishing that story, none of which, however, met Baldinger's own need to reconcile writing and publishing with the Enlightenment version of proper, educated, middle-class womanhood. After all, Baldinger's discussion of femininity includes her movement from early rejection of male superiority and privilege to eventual "mature" acceptance of this discourse. This was a perspective that could not help a woman find a place in the literary and intellectual life of her time, as the autobiography's extreme brevity, conflicted statements about sexuality, multiple defensive introductions, anxious praise of male friends, and final resignation indicate. The little volume thus appeared in print only after Baldinger's death at the age of forty-six. For a patriarchal woman, only the most circuitous arrangements could suffice to permit publication, even when she was being coaxed by the female contemporary best established in the German literary world, as Baldinger's responses to letters from Sophie La Roche show. In this chapter, the self-narrative will be scrutinized both as to what it includes and what it omits; it will be read as a sample account of eighteenth-century girlhood and young womanhood within patriarchy, an account that concentrates on education, marriage, femininity, and desire; in my analysis, I will be alert to the ways that the critical categories of gender and class intertwine with these four issues and others. In the last section, I will explore the metanarrative introductions and Baldinger's correspondence with La Roche as to their illumination of the dilemmas of writing and publishing for women, topics that lead, in turn, to a brief inquiry into the relationship of women to the Enlightenment.

"Essay about the Education of My Intellect": Depicting Women's Basic Education for Cultural Participation

Born on 9 September 1739, in the Thuringian village of Grossengottern and raised in the nearby small town of Langensalza, Friderika Baldinger nee Gutbier grew up under circumstances like those of most women of her class in the eighteenth century. She lived in a town, not a city, was closely supervised by her only slightly educated mother, and had limited access to learning. She was middle-class, a member of that group of people, town and city folk, who were politically disenfranchised in most of Germany but economically of long-standing significance. Because her father was a pastor (a fact she did not mention in her autobiography), and thus, held a position that required a greater degree of literacy and education than the craftsmen and guild workers of the traditional middle class, he and his family are assigned to the group within their socioeconomic category that was of greatly increasing importance as the eighteenth century advanced: the educated middle class. Friderika Baldinger's older brother, in accordance with this class membership, with his gender, and with his corresponding career expectations, was sent first to the famous boys' school at Schulpforta, and then to university. Friderika's education was also geared toward her class, gender, and correspondingly expected future: these factors narrowed her prospects to domestic life rather than a life of display at court, such as aristocratic women could expect, or of heavy physical toil that was the assignment of peasant women. Like both aristocratic and peasant women, the woman of the "educated" middle class required no formal learning. Beyond household skills, the main things society asked women of Baldinger's class and rank to know were basic reading and writing so that they could carry out their womanly duties in the family and, if Protestant, be confirmed in the church.

But Friderika Baldinger was not to be content with that. As women became readers, they did not always immediately realize that the universalizing language of Enlightenment tracts did not include them. The resulting double readings, one including women as eligible and even obliged to become educated and independent-minded, and the other reserving that vision of the enlightened person exclusively for men, opened contradictions that could sometimes produce opportunities, at least for individual women. Baldinger's autobiography tells a complex story, explaining how she deciphered the coded hierarchy of power around her and sought to improve her position within the system she found. The lessons she learned make up the subtext of the descriptions of her father, her mother, her relationship to the town, and her reading. They pertained to the few possible sources of respect and status in her society, and the interaction of these status markers with gender and class.

For men of privileged birth in the aristocracy or even educated middle class, two social institutions, the military and education, offered means of consolidating power and status. For men without privilege, one of these institutions, education, was sometimes available as a means of obtaining status and economic improvement; education, especially advanced education, hinted at class mobility in the eighteenth century. For women (unless they represented themselves as men), the military was unmistakably closed. Education, however, given its humanist rhetoric and the possibility of attaining it or a semblance of it outside any formal setting, was not so obviously precluded. Thus, Baldinger's narrative describes education as the key that gave even a member of the middle class the status approximating a member of royalty as she saw it. When she chose, as she explained in her opening words, to write her autobiography as an essay about the education of her intellect, she was addressing the central theme of her life, a theme that the autobiography shows brought her into innumerable conflicts with positioning herself as a woman at the same time that it located her sometimes pleasurably, always insecurely, in the highly esteemed discourse of Enlightenment.

Baldinger's account repeatedly connects her education and its basis, her intellect, with men, beginning with her father. The second paragraph of her account indicates, amidst questions about biological inheritance, the way in which the absence of Johann Christian Gutbier could turn into the presence of a value system: "My father died even before I knew him. If intelligence were hereditary, then, based on all the descriptions of this wise and intelligent man, I could have inherited mine from him. Perhaps he gave me the ability to perceive the intellect of others and to make use of it. But I for my part believe in no such inheritance" (15). Her father embodied intellect and intellect's ability and right to appropriate from others. His example could thus reinforce his daughter's choices as she later began to define herself in terms of her reason. As for the references to biological inheritance, by rejecting this idea, the adult Friderika Baldinger was both denying a role to her father—and thereby asserting her own independent talents—as well as casually, but clearly, staking a position in a scientific debate—and thereby boldly proclaiming herself interested in academic matters.

She was also distancing herself from her mother, whom she could have viewed as the other source of her intellect. But scholarly women in eighteenth-century Germany were constantly tempted to dissociate themselves from other women. In describing her mother in four short, significantly worded paragraphs, Baldinger has a difficult path to negotiate. On the one hand, she makes it perfectly clear that she accepts society's devaluation of women, properly mystified behind a screen of admiration; on the other hand, she must allow for the fact that she herself is a woman too:

> My mother was the most upright woman whom I have ever known. But in every sense a *woman*, who was distinguished in no other way.
>
> She raised me according to her views, pious and Christian. But I could summarize all her teachings in the following words: *Pious* and *chaste* is what you must be.
>
> To the impression that these very important lessons made on me I owed all my later happiness.
>
> Yet even without my suggestion one can well imagine that in terms of my intellect she could have no further influence on me. (her emphasis, 15).

These words are a cruel revelation of how little it meant to be "in every sense" a woman. The statements can be brief and unelaborated because they represent not just Friderika Baldinger's personal judgments, but society's dominant evaluation of women. Yet, their very brevity and the pauses introduced by the frequent paragraphing draw attention to the awfulness of the verdicts from the mouth of the daughter. The text operates paragraph by paragraph with a series of sharp contrasts. The first paragraph beginning with superlative praise about the mother as the "most upright" "rechtschaffenste" woman the narrator has ever known is followed immediately by a sentence fragment equating being a woman with being undistinguished in any way besides rectitude. Indeed, the sentence fragment puns on the key word "Verstand" "intellect, sense," which also appears in the opening sentence of the essay, "Die Geschichte meines Verstandes soll ich aufzeichnen?" "I am supposed to write down the history of my intellect?" as well as in the original title, "Versuch über meine Verstandeserziehung" "Essay about the Education of My Intellect." In the sentence fragment, "Verstand" is linked not to knowledge and distinction, but to femininity ("in allem Verstande *Frau*" "in every sense *woman*"), and featureless lack. The second paragraph similarly begins with a positive claim, which also is promptly restated in the negative. In this case, emphasis on the reductiveness of the mother's teaching only piety and a gendered version of Christianity, truncated in the restatement into chastity, reverses the tone. The third paragraph then switches back into the positive again, this time with a euphoric one-sentence proclamation of the daughter's indebtedness for her happiness to her mother. But here, too, the praise is immediately undermined by a matching one-sentence paragraph dismissing the relevance of her mother's teachings to the education of the daughter's intellect. Overall, the superlatives about the mother's uprightness and the daughter's debt for her later happiness cannot soften the negative judgments so baldly attached to each seemingly positive claim. The mother is associated with limitations; her lessons are restrictive; she has no impact on her daughter's intellect and learning, and these will soon be all that counts. By identifying her mother's deficiencies explicitly with her existence as a woman, Baldinger displays her own alienation from her gender. It is a strong current through all her preserved writings.

As the text goes on to explain, in the daughter's eyes her widowed mother had another important strike against her: she had lost her assets in one of the wars then afflicting the region. When the daughter noticed, with pain, that her family's low economic status caused people to look down on her, she retreated to her room. Again she separated herself as she had done implicitly (and perhaps mainly retrospectively) from her mother. In this isolated situation, and piqued by the desire to attain status, Friderika Baldinger discovered *Die Göttingischen Anzeigen von gelehrten Sachen* "Göttingen Announcements of Scholarly Matters," a publication of scholarly news. She drew from it a startling conclusion:

> The announcements of so many little details about scholars, their promotions, deaths, etc., had a special impact on me. I compared these items of news with the announcements in *Der hinkende Bothe* ("The Limping Messenger") about kings and kaisers and got my first sense of respect for scholarliness, because scholarly men received just as much honor as did the potentates of the earth (16).

Baldinger had started reading the long-running scholarly periodical from Göttingen because its paper and print were good, but after her unexpected discovery, she realized the opportunity for recognition and self-assertion that scholarliness offered to people not born to influence. Here was a conflict in the making. For along with discovering the status attributable to scholarly men, Baldinger mentioned the exclusion of women from learning: "I wanted so badly to become learned and was exasperated that my sex excluded me from that" (16). Not that the fact of exclusion constituted a discovery—gender-based exclusions were a known and accepted part of the dominant discourse of patriarchy from which Baldinger could imagine almost no deviation. What had been unknown to her before she read the journal from Göttingen was the meaning of the exclusion. Until she realized the privileged life that scholarliness offered middle-class men, her exclusion from scholarship on gender grounds had not been important.

Baldinger did not recognize the barring of women from scholarliness as directly challengeable. She sought instead for an evasion of the ban, continuing in her autobiography with the observation, "Well, then you will at least have to become smart, I thought, and one gets that way through books: you will have to read diligently." In short, she attempted to enlarge a small space in the existing gender and class discourse. She saw the politics of higher education for the disenfranchised middle class and decided to keep on educating herself to the extent that she could. The class element of her situation is important. Aristocratic women, secure in their placement near the top of the social structure, did not have the same need to attain status as ambitious middle-class women did, while peasant women rarely had access to social mobility of any kind. For a middle-class girl, at least the first steps toward an education were relatively easy. Getting an education became Friderika Baldinger's strategy for status, a point few women writers of her time acknowledged so frankly.

According to her narrative, Friderika Baldinger's early reading, beginning at about age three, had seemed miraculous to her devout mother, who (contrary to the negative verdicts initially passed on her) encouraged the precocious child by having her read aloud from the Bible. That was the usual reading primer for eighteenth-century girls, especially in Protestant regions of Germany, where believers' Bible reading was an important part of religious practice and was virtually required in order for both girls and boys to be confirmed in the church. In addition to her mother's encouragement, one of Baldinger's male relatives, a maternal uncle, gave the girl further inspiration toward literacy. This man, whom the adult Baldinger characterized in the autobiography as a rich but stingy Pietist from Halle, came to spend half a year with the little family in not too distant Langensalza. He insisted, she writes, that a large number of chapters from the Bible be read aloud at the daily family devotions and paid a penny for each chapter that his two nieces completed. Warmed by the uncle's approval and enticed by the pennies, Friderika read chapters until—long after her sister and the maids had dozed off—the frugal man told her to stop. Already this incident, in which the autobiographer again separates herself from others of her gender, declares Baldinger's insatiability for learning and men's complicity in both fueling and extinguishing her desire. More than that, intensively reading the Bible and the hymnal acquainted her with the one body of knowledge that women were likely to know well.

The autobiography of Charlotte von Einem (1756–1833), another woman from Protestant north Germany who described herself growing up in the eighteenth century, provides many useful comparisons to Baldinger's narrative of a girl's basic education. Einem's account, written in 1826 from the perspective of old age, also remained unpublished during its author's lifetime, finally appearing in print in 1923, when the sesquicentennial celebration of a small but influential circle of student (= male) poets, named the Göttinger Hainbund (the "alliance of the Göttingen grove"), drew renewed attention to the young woman who had been their friend. Like many eighteenth-century children, including Friderika Baldinger, Einem did not grow up in a family with her two biological parents. According to her narrative, Einem's parents had decided while she was still an infant that in the midst of the troubled times in which she was born, her grandparents would be better able to take care of her; the glorification of maternal care had not yet become strong enough to make such arrangements uncommon. When Einem was nine her mother died; she continued living with her grandmother until the grandmother died, too. By then about fifteen years old, she went to live with the father whom she presumably barely knew. Like many members of the landed aristocracy in eighteenth-century Germany, his properties did not produce enough income to support him,[5] and rather than enter the military or the government as most of his peers did, he had given up his aristocratic status in order to take a job otherwise unavailable to him, as a teacher at a school in Münden, not far from Göttingen— where the adult Friderika Baldinger by then resided. But although her father was a teacher, Charlotte von Einem, like Baldinger, never went to school. Nonetheless, she had many more kinds of learning experience than Baldinger, her older and less prosperous contemporary.

Einem's education at scattered locations enabled her to comment on the experience of girls of all classes. For aristocratic daughters, tutors were usually hired, but what they taught was often trivial, as Einem observed when her grandmother arranged for her to attend the lessons a French governess gave to two local girls from the landed nobility. Proper aristocratic girls learned little except manners, submissiveness to superiors, and piety, the adult Einem writes (38). At the bottom of the class structure, on the other hand, peasant and village girls went briefly to village schools, at least in most of the many principalities that offered and even required schooling for village and rural children. While they learned to read well enough to be accepted for confirmation by the church, girls from the peasant class nonetheless attained the lowest level of reading skill, in comparison both to boys and to other girls, and rarely learned how to write enough to compose sentences and paragraphs on their own.[6] Einem mentioned a school for peasant children in her village that she did not attend, although she shared in the same weekly confirmation classes conducted at the church by the local pastor.[7]

Middle-class girls, in imitation of the aristocracy, usually learned how to read and write in lessons given at home. Occasionally these lessons, too, were given by tutors. Charlotte von Einem also tasted this kind of instruction, sometimes spending several months at a time with a pastor's family where a tutor was employed (43). What middle-class girls rarely experienced was school. In Baldinger's autobiography, for example, no reference to school appears—except the name of the one her brother attended. Lacking access to this kind of institution, she and many other women who became writers in the eighteenth century obtained the chances to read and learn beyond the elementary level with the help or at least the crucial acquiescence of the better-educated men or boys in their own homes. Often the decisive assistant was a brother, and his aid may have begun in childhood.[8] Some daughters were allowed to participate routinely in the regular lessons that tutors gave to sons in the family.[9] In many cases the teacher was the child's father (not the mother until very late in the eighteenth century).[10] Friderika Baldinger's father was dead, her brother away, and her mother minimally educated. She lived in a household of women consisting of her mother, her older sister, and a female servant or two. Probably all of these women—depending on the background of the servants—were literate, but none knowledgeable enough to be a sufficient teacher. In the autobiography, Baldinger attributes her lack of instruction in part to her widowed mother's impoverishment, although, of course, Frau Gutbier continued to send her son not only to a famous boarding school but also to university. While such discrepancy in treatment of sons and daughters was so ordinary it required no comment, still, it is characteristic of the narrative's acceptance of the status quo that it received none.

A childless and often ailing paternal aunt of wit and much intellect, that is a woman marked in Baldinger's text by the keyword "Verstand," took delight in the company of her clever niece and encouraged her reading. At this point, separated from any comparisons with the opportunities of boys and men, Baldinger notes that when the aunt was growing up, women got practically no education; she thereby indirectly suggests that in the changing times she herself should have gotten better opportunities to learn. The narrative avoids allegations of unfair advantages enjoyed by boys but not the less controversial "me too" approach of hinting at unfair disadvantages imposed on girls. Such a disadvantaged aunt, like the virtuous but disadvantaged mother earlier in the account, is characterized in the autobiography by her lacks: no children, poor health, no education, despite her strengths of native intelligence and wit. Her helpfulness was thus limited to shared reading.

Especially in light of girls' and women's restricted access to education and often even to educated people, getting good reading materials became a major obstacle. Friderika Baldinger and her aunt together read everything they could put their hands on. It was very little, the old-fashioned and unliterary volumes belonging to the uncle, a doctor, a man whom the text twice denounces as lacking in taste.[11] His library included conversations with the dead, ghost stories, and the two journals that led Baldinger to see scholarship as a middle-class form of royalty. Two decades later, Charlotte von Einem, too, was intensely interested in the news of royalty, which she read about in *Der Hamburger Correspondent*. Even in her old age, Einem looked back on the paper affectionately, and remembered accounts of the coronation of George III, his wedding, and the births of his children.[12]

But Baldinger, for her purposes of becoming smart, needed a more intellectual kind of reading, a kind not found, she asserts, in the market town of Langensalza.[13] With her critique of Langensalza as merely a place of business, Baldinger disclaims economic ambition, which in Germany was not a striking marker of the educated middle class, while continuing to endorse educational ambition, which would resonate strongly with her readers. She continues: "I read . . . everything that was given to me and I was admired more than a little when I read the difficult names of the old kaisers without any trouble." Again, learning is a source of status for the girl of shaky class standing, given the absence of a father and the poverty of her mother. But she repeatedly depicts herself as impeded from taking better advantage of her skill by the absence of good reading material: "How many an evening did I sit by the sickbed of my dear aunt and read and would have gladly read something better if I had had it" (17).

Fortunate girls had reading materials of the several kinds valorized in their century. Charlotte von Einem's reading, for example, although it has the same biblical starting point as Baldinger's, also includes works culturally validated for girls and young women at the time. Thus, while Einem recalled being given her first Bible when she was about six, she also received a popular and entertaining secular book at the same time, a translated volume of a children's magazine by Jeanne-Marie Leprince de Beaumont[14]; it contained, among other things, what would become the classic version of the fairy tale about Beauty and the beast. Later, Einem received a hymnal and a catechism, and then, in 1766, when she was ten, the works of Christian Fürchtegott Gellert (1715–69).[15] In 1746, operating firmly in the rationalist tradition of the Enlightenment and drawing on foreign models such as Richardson, Gellert had published the first German novel that a respectable middle-class woman could read without pangs of conscience, *Leben der schwedischen Gräfin von G.* "Life of the Swedish Countess of G."[16] Most of the rest of his writing was considered equally acceptable to women: a manual for good letter writing, collections of fables and tales in verse, and religious poetry, as well. All this, along with his elegantly readable style, made him thoroughly welcome to women readers during the rest of the century, including many who became writers.[17] Einem does not mention the other writer of her time most approved for women, Friedrich Gottlieb Klopstock (1724–1803),[18] whose sublime poetry, participating in both *Aufklärung* and *Empfindsamkeit*, achieved the main functions that reading had for eighteenth-century women: entertainment, devotion, and education. Goethe suggested Klopstock's importance to women readers when the idealized pastoral young woman, Lotte, in his sensationally popular first novel *The Sorrows of Young Werther*, breathed Klopstock's name at a critical moment to show her emotional and cultural sensitivity. Despite the erudition of much of Klopstock's poetry, women were able to read and enjoy it because it drew on the detailed Biblical knowledge they possessed.[19]

As the dependence of Baldinger and her aunt on the uncle's library suggests, women's access to books meant relying on men, usually a male relative.[20] After Charlotte von Einem went to live with her father, she got books from him; he constantly received—

she writes—the newest publications from an excellent bookstore in Göttingen. Because of *his* literary interest, she was able to read *Werther*, for example, as soon as it appeared. And earlier, while she was still living with her grandmother, a young uncle who had just returned from the university gave her the foundation of her literary education by reading aloud to her whatever stories and plays he thought would be useful. She writes that he was very well supplied with reading material, especially new publications, which he got from a friend in Bremen as often as he wished. In this way Einem became acquainted with the operas of Weisse and the translations of both *Don Quixote* and the *Thousand and One Nights*.[21]

Ultimately, for Friderika Baldinger, access to books as well as to intellectual training and inspiration depended on the presence of a helpful man: her educated brother came home. Johann Christian Gutbier—she does not name him—had already influenced his sister by giving her a reason to practice her literary skill by writing letters to him.[22] As important as the occasion for this early writing was the advice that went with it. Baldinger's brother urged her to ignore the rules for letter writing and write as she saw fit, advice that freed her from meeting standards about which she had received no instruction. By the time she was an adult she had developed a refreshingly informal style, as we will see.

Although the encouragement the brother sent was useful, his homecoming was of even more help, for now at last his sister had access to a person with a trained mind, an interest in her, and a collection of books. As she writes,

> How I looked forward to the arrival of the brother who planned to bring daylight into my dark brain.—He came at last, and I would try in vain to describe how much we loved each other—one heart and one soul. To this eternally beloved brother I owe the beginning of all my knowledge—my whole happiness, and I would have been able to have more if my good mother had not believed [that books were bad for girls].[23]

The brother is described in the language of the Enlightenment as the bringer of light. Like the mother, but without the surrounding web of retractions, he is also described as the source of all her happiness. In addition to sharing his library, the brother offered to teach his sister skills that she could not learn by reading, such as how to speak French and how to play the piano. Yet, despite her desire and determination to learn and the opportunity the brother presented, the results were far from equal for brother and sister. As Friderika Baldinger had known from the start, gender roles in eighteenth-century Germany prohibited female scholarship.

Beyond Literacy to Scholarliness

Baldinger's decision to become "smart" instead of scholarly did not challenge conventional male prerogatives but was an at least theoretically realistic way to move beyond the mere basic literacy widespread among women of her class. For a time early in the eighteenth century, the prolific and formidable professor of literature and arbiter of language, Johann Christoph Gottsched, had argued against the most negative assessments of advanced learning for women. Gottsched thought the opportunity for intellectual accomplishment should be available to them, proclaiming in one of the moral weeklies he pioneered in Germany that women had the same intellectual capabilities as men. As part of the middle-class effort to gain authority through its cultural accomplishment, Gottsched recruited middle-class women into literary and scholarly activity, arranging recognition for women poets, for example. A select few women were granted prizes and even memberships in the influential Leipzig literary society that Gottsched headed. As further encouragement, Gottsched presented women with models to emulate, such as the brilliant and famous seventeenth-century scholar Anna Maria van Schurman (1607–78) and his own impressive literary wife, Luise Adelgunde Culmus Gottsched (1713–62).

Yet, with opposition to advanced learning for women growing in exact proportion to women's efforts to become scholarly, these apparent inroads quickly dissipated; scholarliness remained overwhelmingly difficult for women to attain. Sophie La Roche once explained what it entailed:

> No one is called scholarly unless he has mastered a major discipline, such as, for example, mathematics . . . , philosophy, law, world history, theology, natural science, medicine, literature; to do this, one must understand perfectly the learned languages—the Latin of the ancient Romans, and Greek—because the people from whom we have received the fundamentals of these invaluable fields of knowledge were Greeks and Romans.[24]

For her time and place she was right. Among the eighteenth-century German requirements for scholarliness, knowing Latin, the language of erudition, was the mandatory first step. It was a step routinely forbidden to women.[25]

There were exceptions. When Charlotte Amalia Henrici died giving birth to her tenth child in 1779, her husband, a professor in Altona, wrote a tribute to her describing her life and accomplishments. He reported that she spoke and wrote Latin to perfection. This meant that they could enjoy together their favorite authors, including Cicero, Livius, and Horace. She could recite Horace by memory from beginning to end, had persuaded a local composer to set the poet's most beautiful odes to music, and herself wrote Latin poems.[26] The scholarly achievement of Ernestine Reiske (1735–98) is even more impressive, for although she did not begin to learn Latin and Greek until she married a famous classicist and translator, she became a respected translator in her own right after her husband's death.

But these women are rare. Most did not approach the educational standards of educated middle-class men. Only a tiny handful of the already select ten percent or so of all women who had good reading ability and adequate writing skills in a modern language could admire Horace in his original language or read Homer in Greek. And during most of the century, denying women the chance to learn Latin and Greek effectively excluded them not only from enjoying classical literature, but also from reading a significant percentage of contemporary scholarship. Almost a fifth of the books published in Germany in the year 1765, when Friderika Baldinger was 21, were in a classical language.[27] Even when books about literature, for example, were in German, they might be so laden with classical references as to be unintelligible to most women readers.[28] Lack of advanced education was a tremendous inhibiting factor for women's entry into the world of writing. Women's own acute awareness of the deficiency of their education was one of the psychological hurdles for those who might have begun or did begin to write;[29] it would be up to Sophie La Roche to devise a way to overcome it. Only when women's literacy and learning began to rise could the aspirations of larger numbers of women to scholarliness became realistic. The response to this changing situation was twofold: a much higher level of female education was accepted as good, but the epithet "scholarly," which would have previously applied to this degree of learning, especially in a woman, was denied.[30] The category of scholar was thus vigorously maintained as masculine; given the logic of polarized gender notions, women were necessarily excluded.

The woman who aimed for scholarliness was seen as inappropriately defying her sex and encroaching on male prerogatives. In a time, from about the middle of the century on, when the middle class sought public credibility for itself, certain kinds of pedantic male scholars also were more frequently becoming the targets of jokes for being excessively engaged with issues of no social or cultural consequence, but the comments about women and education have little to do with that. Scholarly women in the second half of the century were rejected as mere consumers and displayers, not—with rare exceptions, such as Luise Adelgunde Gottsched had been in the decades before—as public writers.[31] Most of all, according to the common lampoons of them, they pursued scholarship at the expense of domestic duties, leading both men and women to denounce too much learning for women, although in a larger context many of these denunciations lose force. Sophie La Roche in her monthly *Pomona*, for example, wrote of "true manly scholarliness," which, "if everything is as it should be, is not a matter for our sex and cannot be one,"[32] but aside from the true manly version La Roche worked energetically to enlarge women's access to scholarship. Similarly, A. L. Schlözer, a Göttingen professor who carefully educated his brilliant daughter Dorothea, said years later that his purpose had been, "not to make a scholar out of her but rather through a somewhat better than usual literary education to enable her to marry according to her wishes." Remarkably, he used the masculine form of the word scholar and pretended to have given his daughter a literary education, when in fact she had also pursued such topics as mineralogy and mining. Also striking is his claim that the components of her education were determined by her marriage prospects.[33]

Judging by the frequency with which women later rejected the epithet "scholarly" for themselves, the campaign to limit their education appeared to be successful. There was much talk of the dreadful excesses of scholarly women and their neglect of household duties. The stereotype comes up clearly in an essay that purported to praise Dorothea Schlözer:

> When a scholarly woman is mentioned, one generally pictures someone who is neurotic; and if she goes beyond literature into the higher sciences, well, then one can definitely predict that her clothes will be neglected and that her coiffure will be outmoded, that she will understand the cooking of Apicius but not the simple composition of a modern omelet, that she will force her way into the circle of men for whom she is nothing more than a book, while the women whisper against her. . . .[34]

The young Dorothea, the author reassured readers, was nothing like this image: "Mademoiselle Schlözer sews, knits, understands normal middle-class homemaking, is healthy, likes to dance, loves conversations with her own sex, and one must have earned her trust before finding out about the scholar in her." One of the weapons used to cudgel women away from scholarly learning was the discourse of housework, with use of the needle, not the quill, being the first item on the list. Housework, with its marital connotations, is an indispensable element in maintaining the category of the good woman. Most of all, however, given the negative stereotype of the learned woman, fortunate girls hid indications of their exceptional education ("one must have earned her trust before finding out").

In the last third of the eighteenth century, the concealed education of an apparently merely domestic woman was endorsed over and over again when real women were described. A Frau Zitzmann in Leipzig, for example, was described as a woman who was praiseworthy precisely because what she had learned had no detectable impact on how she lived: "Scholarliness and the inclination to read and study have—and this is what I admire most about her—had no bad effect in any way on her as woman, as wife, mother, and housekeeper, but rather she fulfills all these duties so exactly and so well, that in her spheres of influence one can detect no trace of scholarliness about her" (48). This disembodied concept of education is combined with a transparent insistence that women stick with their marriage roles: "Everyone who knows her testifies that running the house and motherhood are the main and best loved business of her life." Not only did a woman have to perform her marital duties, she also had to love them. Nor could the author apparently reiterate his praise of concealment often enough: "She dedicates herself to knowledge only as recreation in her free time, simply out of inclination, not to dazzle anyone, not to be called a scholarly women and to strut with learning in society—oh, she is without any pretension just that which she is, in the most modest quietness and humility—a model of the Noble German Woman." Women's education, to be acceptable, had to be both secondary to her and invisible to others. In her old age, the peasant writer Sophie Ludwig (1764–1815) made this point colorfully:

> I am heartily glad that I am only lame in my foot and not in the upper story. But that is just between you and me, because you know very well that one dare not let much be heard from or out of the upper story because so many men . . . absolutely cannot stand to see lights on up there, and whenever someone tries something like that they shout at the top of their lungs, "Lights out! Lights out!"[35]

This ideal of the woman with invisible education recurs also in novels by women.[36] In the contest between the discourses of education for enlightenment and of preserving gender differences, this device made it possible to avoid a direct denial of learning to women, but nonetheless the concept of invisible learning deprived a learned woman of any externally detectable benefit from her achievement. Invisible learning was never recommended to men. While learned women had been extremely rare, they could be glorified because they were too uncommon to jeopardize the fundamental distribution of cultural power. Once comparatively learned women became more numerous, mechanisms of containment were devised to control them. Remarkably, these mechanisms did not however include "real-life" stories of women who embodied the negative stereotype of the female scholar.[37] There is no negative counterpart to the hagiography of Frau Zitzmann.

In this situation so precarious to middle-class girls and women seeking education, Friderika Baldinger was always vulnerable to whatever changes occurred at home. A crucial change when she was still a young woman was the departure of her admired brother. Fortunately, before he left, he had introduced his sister to another educated man in the town, the new pastor named Johann Wilhelm Kranichfeld, who became, Baldinger wrote, her spiritual father, without whose help she would never have become the wife of a scholar.[38] He had books—with her brother's departure she needed a new source. He enjoyed intellectual conversation and was quite willing to share with the eager young woman. "He often laughed," she writes, "when, in a cloud of tobacco smoke, I sat beside him and listened with joy to what he was discussing with the others, while the remaining female company got aggravated about the eternal book-jabber" (19). One of the first volumes Kranichfeld lent to her, and the only book whose title is named in the autobiography after the books of her avid aunt, was Luise Adelgunde Gottsched's translation into German of the *Spectator*. Baldinger noted her original reaction to this famed work of the English Enlightenment: "I regarded the book with amazement because I had never in my life read anything more beautiful." But in the meantime, her esteem for the six-decade-old collection had sunk drastically: "Last year I tried to read this book again and could not. That is how I am now, compared to then" (19). Baldinger interpreted her more recent reaction as a sign of intellectual improvement. Her pride in this critical attitude is bolstered no doubt by the confidence that her opinion of the book was shared by some of the widely respected men whom she knew in Göttingen. As a young woman, however, her confidence in the rightness of her judgments and the legitimacy of her learning was still fragile. She associates this insecurity with her brother's validating presence or disqualifying absence, writing that when he died around 1759, she plunged into a terrible depression and became convinced that having a refined intellect was no longer appropriate for herself; she rejected her earlier ambitions, decided to become "dumber," as she put it, and gave up reading. The crisis affected her profoundly: "For a long time I did not read a book, I even condemned reading, and my intellect lay fallow . . ." (19). The strategy of including this episode in the account of how she got her education is important. Baldinger represents herself as inherently gifted, but highly vulnerable to her environment; she must constantly negotiate between her desire for learning (depicted as a gift for learning) and a social world that makes few allowances for a girl or woman like her. Her vulnerability is not, she implies, mistaken; she shows herself as fully receptive to the values of her class and time, thus making her deviation into scholarliness less defiant.

Women must have often felt it would be better to stop seeking a controversial education. Yet, education, as Magdalene Heuser points out, had practical benefits for women. One was a chance to improve one's social status by marrying an intellectually ambitious man of higher or rising status; this could be the starting point for a new relation between women and men; another was women's improved ability to use their critical facilities to examine both their own individual situation and broader gender relations, as conducted, for example, through the institution of marriage.[39] To this list I add that education beyond the rudimentary was also the prerequisite for women to become writers, which was, among other things, a way to earn a living independently. In Baldinger's case, the death of her brother is represented as a turning point in her education. It caused her, she wrote, first to drop and then to reshape her desire for learning, perhaps—although she does not say so—with more attention to these practical issues. What she does say, instead, is that gradually her mentor Kranichfeld helped restore her, though she remained melancholy. Her brashness changed to quiet solemnity, which made her seem older than her twenty or so years. Since, as a result, intelligent people talked seriously with her now, she decided to work to deserve the respect that she was receiving and thus resumed her studies (21). In this way, Baldinger managed to reinterpret her own inclination toward scholarship (and her desire for the status and power that it signified) as the fulfillment of an obligation she had to other people. The request device, which had purportedly induced the writing of her self-narrative and structured its opening sentence, would become a characteristic maneuver for many women and one Baldinger used repeatedly.

But opposition to the scholarly woman was so widespread that the claim of studying in order to please others was often unavailable. Many women, especially older ones, opposed all but the most rudimentary steps toward female education. For women at the bottom of the middle class or belonging to the peasantry, the ceiling that a girl should stay beneath was especially low. Thus, village woman and poet Anna Louisa Karsch told how, in her childhood, her great-uncle taught her to read, using the Bible, and then, at her request, wanted to teach her also how to write. Her grandmother, however, vigorously opposed this wish, though the child and her great-uncle were eventually able to prevail. Still, the next opponent to Karsch's learning was again a woman, this time her mother, who came to the uncle's home when the child was ten years old to take her back to her own family, explaining: "I am afraid she will go crazy in the head if she continues day and night mulling over books. She knows how to read and write; that is everything that a girl has to know!"[40] Uneducated themselves, the women in authority in the home often objected to the changing patterns they observed in girls.

Even for the middle class, the limits on girls were often strict. Friederike Koch, a poet born in 1772, had the unusual opportunity of going to school, a school for middle-class girls, where her male teacher gave her Gellert's fables to read, and she began experimenting with writing verse. Her mother, a strict, orderly housewife, tolerated such behavior until her daughter's school days were over. Then, in place of books and the pen came the spinning wheel, cooking pots, and often even the spade in the fields. The daughter, unable to devise new practices within the comprehensive framework that enclosed her physically and mentally, submitted to the will of her mother and found consolation only on Sundays, when she was permitted to peruse her father's collection of books.[41] Except for these reprieves, domestic labor and field work were now declared more important for the young woman than reading or writing. Anna Louisa Karsch, on the other hand, although she was never able to negotiate reprieves from her mother or, soon after, from her husband, nonetheless found ways to pursue her learning by extensive reading and writing, mostly in secret from them.

Clearly, the roles of women and men in the education of girls differed significantly. According to Baldinger's self-narrative, once her mother's early admiration ended, the uneducated aunt was the only *woman* who encouraged the girl's intellectual inclinations, but her encouragement could only minimally advance what was recognized as learning. Friderika Baldinger's aunt's lack of both recent books and systematic education meant her inability to provide the up-to-date and orderly learning approved by men and given to boys of the educated middle class. And Baldinger's mother was no more sympathetic to her daughter's cultural aspirations than Koch's, though more than Karsch's; after all, Baldinger's mother had reduced all learning to the two principles of piety and chastity, which in her interpretation had nothing to do with further education for her daughter. According to the autobiography that Charlotte von Einem wrote in old age, her grandmother also stressed traditional values: industry, humility, modesty, the fear of God, and a general willingness to be of service.[42] Although the grandmother demonstrated considerable learning within the discourse of religion, citing verses from the Bible and lines from hymns to reinforce these lessons, she discouraged her granddaughter from exceeding the minimum of learning. Einem described her grandmother as a very religious woman whose hands touched only Bibles, hymnals, and collections of sermons. And these were the books she recommended to the child whenever she expressed a desire to read. (This woman's husband, Einem's grandfather, in contrast, had a whole library of books in Hebrew, Greek, Latin, German and French, 47.) Einem's uncle was reprimanded for giving the girl "Historienbücher" "story books," as the grandmother called the literature he brought into the house, literature from which the girl could learn nothing but bad tricks (46). Friderika Baldinger's mother, her "good mother," was even more averse to her daughter's learning and even more limited in her view of acceptable reading matter: "Reading books, except for the Bible and hymnal, was a deadly sin, a waste of time for girls."[43] Baldinger did not have to stress the point. For boys, extensive reading was important and worthwhile; only on girls was intensive reading and rereading imposed. Daughters wishing to participate in the increasingly secular culture of their time had difficulty overcoming the resistance of mothers intent on preserving their own culture of religion.

Girls and young women, negotiating between their desire to read secular literature, on the one hand, and the moralizing assertion that extensive reading was a waste of time, on the other, tried to combine reading with work. "Since I could read so well," Friderika Baldinger wrote, "I put my book on my left knee and did the spinning with my right hand. But now when the yarn got wound it would break; that happens, it would be said then, because she spares her left hand and is always reading" (18). The effort to read and perform domestic work simultaneously is typical of women in the eighteenth century. They tried to use their strict adherence to one set of practices to offset their deviance from another.

2: BETWEEN THE SPINNING WHEEL AND THE BOOK

It was a strategy derived from women's training to keep busy, training so compelling that one older woman, discovering her granddaughter momentarily idle, told the child that a girl with nothing to do should cut a hole in her apron with the scissors and spend her time sewing it back up again. The next time the child followed her advice to the letter.[44] Sophie La Roche's mother had a very different attitude toward learning, but exactly the same insistence on preventing her daughters from having any idle moments, training that La Roche defended when she wrote about her upbringing:

> I am certain that my mother's wise division between reading and work kept the entertainment value of books fresh to us, because the linen, clothes, dressy things, and the kitchen all had to be taken care of, and we had to read the Bible and some devotional literature every morning as a duty, while my mother and the others were working, and then after the noon meal and in the evenings we had hours for other reading and for practicing French and Italian. But when we had mastered the art of reading and knitting well at the same time, then we were allowed to do that too.—This division has become the basis for true comfort. Doing handwork that is useful or attractive—what noble, just self-satisfaction derives from that and how much it enhances the joys of leisure time![45]

This position readily accepts basic learning for girls, but also insists on a fundamental commitment both to housework, which is strongly intertwined with religion, and to merely decorative but traditional handwork, that monopolizes a woman's hands. As long as this kind of handwork was required of respectable women, they could not do the concentrated reading required for scholarship or use their hands to hold a quill for writing. Even more than housework, decorative handwork is never done.

Most often, it was from their mothers that women learned how to do "women's work." The education of the novelist Wilhelmine von Gersdorf (1768–1847) illustrates this in an elaborate and seemingly favorable way: "Her governess prepared her for the outside world, in which [the governess] had lived for a long time, her noble mother prepared her thoroughly and strictly for her female destiny, and her father, who loved the Socratic method, for all the more serious fields of study."[46] Rather than being a well-rounded education, as the writer implies, however, this training was laden with contradictions. For although her father taught her history, geography, and, remarkably, Latin, von Gersdorf's mother's stress on her duties as a woman led her into conflicts if she felt inclined to pursue her learning further. Of course, some women were more fortunate, receiving intellectual help and encouragement from their mothers, but this was rare.

The more usual pattern was what dominated Friderika Baldinger's horizons. When she described the contrasting reactions of her mother and her brother to her desire to learn, Baldinger felt that both sides were acting as they were supposed to, each practicing an appropriate form of discourse. It was a mother's role to socialize the daughter according to the strict code that applied to all women; because her own mother was thoroughly dedicated to this task, she was "good." It was a man's prerogative, on the other hand, to offer an eager young woman a share in the education that he had been privileged to enjoy and which—he could be sure—she would never be able to duplicate while she remained at home, no matter how much he might share with her. His privilege and its certification (attending the university) were safe. A reasonable and intelligent brother need not be overly concerned with an individual woman's private deviation from the reading restrictions that usually applied to her gender.

Baldinger seems to have accepted the contradictions between the two sides as resulting from their two different subject positions, one as woman (specifically as a good mother), the other as a man (specifically as a man of the educated middle class). When she herself became a mother, she in turn undertook the mother's repressive task of training her daughters to meet society's norms. This brought her into direct conflict with advocates of change. Yet, she offered no thoughts on the topic in her autobiography. Indeed, it is striking that after criticizing the way her mother raised her, she wrote nothing in her autobiography about how she was raising her own daughters. Her younger daughter, however, recorded some observations on the subject much later, including one particularly telling instance that deals with the ultimate eighteenth-century European sign and fact of the restrictions imposed on women, the corset.

As the girl was being dressed to visit a neighboring professor in Göttingen, she reminded her mother not to tie her corset too tightly, for Professor Kästner was convinced, like many educated men in the eighteenth century, that tight corsets were detrimental to female health. The man's was a voice of both reason and authority and had to be deferred to, but Friderika Baldinger was very well aware that he represented only a small faction among all men. A much larger faction, the one from which her daughter's future husband would probably have to be attracted, still demanded corseting, as the leading fashion journal of the period made clear: "The corset holds the body straight without effort, it protects the body in winter against colds, and without it the slender stature is not attained that is after all a decisive element of beauty in the judgment of men."[47] The reasoning combines a nod to female health considerations with unexamined acceptance of male demands. Baldinger as mother was the enforcer of male preferences, even when enforcement was contrary to reason, and when she prided herself on how enlightened she was. When she bound her daughter's ribs and waist, she showed again that for her, the discourse of enlightenment and abstract reason was secondary to the discourse of femininity (and marriage). Given the scanty alternatives to marriage as a way for a middle-class woman to survive socially and economically, her choice was indeed practical.

As Helga Madland points out, an analysis of the eighteenth-century debate about corseting "suggests that the corset is not simply a garment, but that the social practice of wearing it is a 'sign' representative of a condition." She goes on to explain, "The corset signifies both the condition of women as a sex, and their class status as ornamental luxuries." In its first aspect, "it signifies the female situation itself—imprisonment and enmeshment in the whalebone structure of patriarchal society's restrictions and demands." In its second, it "gives politically charged class significance to the corset wearer." This happens because "the threat of the elimination of the garment is subconsciously perceived . . . as a threat to the privileged classes," the upper middle class and the hereditary aristocracy. In Baldinger's case, the privileged class is the group of women attached to admired scholarly men. In order to join that middle-class aristocracy, Baldinger had herself long since internalized the restrictions and demands of patriarchal society, as her autobiography makes clear ("I wanted so badly to become learned and was exasperated that my sex excluded me from that"). This being the conceptual framework and emotional system through which she positioned herself as a woman and a person, she imposed it also on her daughter. Accepting a new and not yet widely used social practice was too much for a woman who had staked her life's meaning on the status quo. As Madland observes, "While the corset is designed to *shape* the female body, its elimination implies the *reshaping* of society, a political implication."[48]

Marriage as Women Experienced It

Baldinger was not prepared (as far as her daughter knew) to discuss openly the issue of corsets with the objecting Professor Kästner, although he was one of her closest friends. To the extent that she interpreted the disagreement as the usual difference between the conceptual framework and social practices of privileged scholarly men, who had a wide range of prerogatives, and those of women, who did not, Baldinger's resolution to the conflict was simple: she appeared to acquiesce. When the daughter visited this particular professor, she did not make the corset tight. Otherwise, she did. Either way, the corset on body—and mind—remained, for a harness of inflexible restrictions on women affected Friderika Baldinger's whole relationship to the life of the mind and to literary participation. Her own mother had taught her vividly about women's position, as she recalled: "How often my love of reading was made bitter to me, the books sometimes locked up, and I sent to the spinning wheel."[49]

The education of girls and young women in eighteenth-century Germany was tailored to please presumed future husbands, who, it was assumed, would want feminine wives with some educational background, but not as much, and certainly not more, than the husbands had themselves. Thus, the third main source of constraints on women, marriage, was intertwined with education and femininity. Baldinger's self-narrative shows this interaction of the three factors when, after the ambitious daughter defends her efforts to learn by saying that she is too young to take up more important employment, her mother tells the girl she will never be able to marry a professor anyway (18), which implicitly is the only justification for letting her learn what her brother could teach her. A girl's education must be capped to guarantee her potential husband's superiority; the results for the girl were "femininity" and the promise of marriage.

Women's thoughts about marriage and their choices of husbands were crucial for their lives. Faced with this realization, Baldinger's response to her mother's assertions is simple, according to her retrospective account: she does not want a husband. She writes that she has already begun to find a large part of the people in her town "unbearable," a word she uses again later in another important statement. Especially unbearable were men who were not scholarly (18). Her reasoning had to do with her own experience of discrimination as a woman: "I had gotten an idea into my head: men must simply all be smarter than women, because they had claimed control over us; I found only the smallest number however who had a right to that based on superiority of understanding. This turned me against a whole sex, which I, ignorant girl, judged on the basis of the narrow circle where I lived" (18). From her perspective as an adult woman fully imbued with patriarchal values, she apologized for her radical opinion as a girl, and dismissed it as the result of her narrow experience at the time. As she stressed in the rest of the autobiography, once she had met men who exceeded her in education and intelligence, she accepted the doctrine of male superiority. Nevertheless, these early thoughts and her decision to record them show that even a young woman in the provinces did not internalize submissiveness smoothly. Patriarchy was not so self-evident as to be internalized without resistance; instead, it required serious techniques of enforcement. In fact, much as she attempts to stress that her topic is the education of her intellect, Baldinger's self-narrative also tells her education to patriarchy and full induction into it. Caution about exploring this other education explains much of what Baldinger includes and omits from her text. And of course, there is also the matter of her implied audience. The first sentence indicates that the text was originally written for a male friend; indeed, it is dedicated on the first page of the body to "one of my friends," with the friend's male gender evident in the German word choice (15). Baldinger was not writing for women.

So it is with a playful, self-mocking tone that she discusses gender issues. Accounting for her education into patriarchy and into its most common embodiment for women, marriage, requires that Baldinger explain her initial resistance. In addition to her disdain for men, the young Baldinger writes of other reasons to oppose marriage, including "because all physical love was disgusting to me" (21). Perhaps Baldinger was able to state this position so candidly because, by doing so, she was writing within the traditional framework that polarized mind and body. Having declared herself interested in the life of the mind, she could dismiss the body. Indeed, doing so validated the completeness of her dedication to learning. It was, nevertheless, not a perfectly comfortable claim, for she tried to defuse it with a joking comparison: "I had all the talents for being a saint, I was pious, a vestal, I was gushy; the only thing I could not do was perform miracles, because for that, according to all the rules, I would first have to die so that stories could be told about me" (21). Like many women in other times and places, eighteenth-century German women resorted to self-deprecation to deflect criticism from themselves.

While physical love was disgusting to her, Baldinger also felt wary of marriage for another reason, as she explained in a biting comment: "I often had . . . opportunities to make my fortune and happiness by marrying, if you can call it making a fortune when, in exchange for food and drink, you sell your body for life to a man whom you do not love" (21). Men disputed about marriage, too, but it was primarily women who saw it from this perspective. When Baldinger, as a young woman, had begun to hunger for status and perceived scholarship as a means to it, she was overlooking or dismissing the one institution that ideology would have proclaimed available for her purpose. Why did she ignore marriage as a means of socioeconomic self-improvement? Not because sexuality disgusted her; if anything, the causal relation was probably reversed. Sex disgusted her because it signified marriage and, in several ways, a loss of control of her own body, perhaps further because marriage (which usually meant pregnancy) in turn signified the thwarting of a woman's independent ambitions (in other words, her capitulation to patriarchy). Marriage also required submission to something she already knew well and disliked: domestic work. But most of all, it entailed submission to something less familiar, but not attractive: men such as those of her town.

In fact, many men and women in the eighteenth century never married. Among women writers who remained single all their lives—to what extent by choice can no longer be determined—were Friederike Jerusalem (1759–1832), Karoline Kamienski (1755–1813), Henriette Pauli (1754–1837), Karoline Rudolphi (1754–1811), Wilhelmine Schlieben (1765–1852), and Katharina Stolberg-Stolberg (1751–1832). Several other women who are known because of their connection to famous literary men also never married, including Julie Bondeli (1731–78), Susanna von Klettenberg (1723–74), and Luise von Göchhausen (1752–1807). And it was not just literary women who stayed unmarried, or who did not remarry after losing a husband. A statistical study of the town of Durlach in the 1700s showed that at the beginning of the century, more than half the population over the age of fifteen was unmarried. Even allowing for the fact that a large contribution to this percentage would be made by sixteen, seventeen, and eighteen-year-olds who did not ordinarily expect to be married yet, this points to a sizable unmarried population. By the end of the century, the population of unmarried adults and young people in the town had risen to about 60 percent.[50] Avoiding marriage was a real possibility for Friderika Baldinger.

She quickly learned that being unmarried gave her a certain amount of independence, but also left her financially insecure. After her older sister married and moved away, Baldinger, who was in her early twenties, was left alone with her mother. Especially after her brother died she had to work to support the household—what kind of work this involved she does not write—and she and her mother were both often sick.[51] Nonetheless, this stressful period had a positive aspect, for she notes she had more time then than ever before to devote to her studies. And she knew that marriage was not a perfectly reliable financial arrangement either, as her mother's widowhood proved. When reporting her brother's death and her own extreme response to it, Baldinger comments that her mother mourned because she had lost in her only son the last guarantor of her subsistence in old age. (Baldinger reports nothing here or later about what eventually happened to her "good" mother, who was, after all, irrelevant to the intellectual education of importance in the text.)

Baldinger posits a warning given to her by her brother, and thus patriarchally validated, as justification for her reticence about marriage. He had, she wrote, told her: ". . . if you should ever marry, do not accept anyone but an educated and especially intelligent man, because if you once see through your husband, you will be the most unhappy creature whom I know" (18). Meta Klopstock had a similar insight about herself and expressed it in much the same way:

> How much I feel every hour that nobody but Klopstock could have been my husband. How I tremble sometimes when I think that there was even a *possibility* of getting a different husband. But my heart was always alert when it did not want the people who had so many *other* advantages—Heavens! what would I have done with a creature whom I could see through![52]

As long as women were supposed to be subordinate, and Meta Klopstock believed they were, just as Friderika Baldinger would later, it was important to find a husband who was not inferior. For patriarchal marriage to work from the point of view of the middle-class woman with a relatively good education or with continuing educational aspirations, she must seek out a man to whom she was, by the standards of her day, intellectually second. The actual operation of such a system created interstices for alternatives. Thus, doctrines like this had the effect of giving a young woman a good reason in her own mind for rejecting suitors.

Baldinger's fraternally certified marriage guideline left open the possibility that she might decide against marriage altogether, but gradually, she wrote, it became more credible to her that she would marry after all (evidently as she discovered how difficult it was to earn a living on her own), and it became correspondingly more urgent that she not make a mistake. "The good advice of my blessed brother was always in my mind along with my own consciousness that with the wrong marriage I would make the man unhappy as well as myself, if I could not have the proper respect for his intellect."[53] When the woman's respect for the man's mind was crucial, the woman was positioned as judge. Something else was at stake, too: the woman's future access to more learning. In Baldinger's case, access to knowledge would constitute part of her happiness. Given men's advantages in education and in cultural participation (book ownership, for example), Baldinger needed to accede to this patriarchal institution in order to pursue her own not inherently patriarchal goals of learning and extensive reading.

Baldinger's attitude of selectivity was not always welcome, as she went on to report: "My family, who could not understand me, made accusations against me about this, which I ignored, because I thought too honorably to build my own fortune on the misfortune of an otherwise good man who was just not right for me" (21). The potential punishment for a bad decision was unhappiness, probably on both sides. Friderika Baldinger plainly was not leaving the decision in anyone else's hands. Particularly in the absence of a father, she had a powerful veto, no matter what her family wanted. Thus, it was that she was still unmarried when she met the Prussian army doctor, Ernst Gottfried Baldinger. She describes him as scholarly, intelligent, and honest, in that order, and she promptly accepted his offer, even though he was by no means wealthy: "I would have considered myself fortunate even if I had had to starve in his company, and indeed our prospects then weren't much better than that" (22). This was not, Baldinger is indirectly stressing, a marriage of convenience—the rank of army field doctor was not prestigious.

In 1764 when the wedding took place, the bride was twenty-five. The median age of first marriage for educated, middle-class women like her was around twenty-two in the eighteenth century, with three out of five women getting married between the ages of twenty and twenty-five.[54] The pattern remained fairly constant during the century. Examples among women writers can be cited approximately decade by decade: Luise Adelgunde Gottsched was wed in 1735 at age twenty-two, Meta Klopstock in 1754 at twenty-six, Henriette Ekkard in 1769 at twenty-four, Karoline Herder in 1773 at twenty-three, Caroline Böhmer (later Schlegel and then Schelling) in 1784 at twenty-one, and Sophie Mereau (later Brentano) in 1793 at twenty-three. Despite famous exceptions, such as the rural Karsch, who had been married off at sixteen, marriages at fifteen and sixteen were uncommon except perhaps in the aristocracy.

The countess Solms-Wildenfels, for example, having married at fourteen, was widowed at nineteen.

Within the educated classes, however, a significant number of women married much later, in their early thirties. Among women writers, Charlotte Seidel was thirty when she married; Christiane Karoline Schlegel (née Lucius), thirty-five; Nantchen Goeckingk, thirty-two; and Sophie Schwarz, thirty-three. Luise Boie married in 1785 when she was thirty-eight, and Benedikte Naubert, born in 1756, did not marry until she was forty-one. Many eighteenth-century women married considerably later than scholars writing today generally suggest, and thus had more time in which to develop their sense of self or sense of dependency (or both) before entering marriage.[55]

One of the factors that may have contributed to Friderika Baldinger's lack of haste in marrying was her continuing distaste for sexuality. At the time she wrote her autobiography, when she had been married nineteen years, sexuality (at least in the heterosexual form to which she seems to address her comments) still disgusted her. She established her aversion in contorted syntax that perhaps reflects her hesitations about making this statement: "Since the higher powers of my soul always outweigh everything lower, I do not know whether, considering me as a woman, [my husband] has always found me according to his wishes" "Da meine oberen Seelenkräfte immer das Übergewicht für allen Niedern behalten haben; so weis ich nicht, ob er sich, als Frau betrachtet, bei mir allemal nach seinen Wünschen gestanden hat."[56] Baldinger went on to draw a connection between the repression of her sexuality and the cultivation of her education. She said that in reaction to her own aversion she tried to improve herself spiritually and intellectually, putting friendship in the place of what she called "animal love." As a result, she believed that there could be no nobler love than hers and her husband's because it was grounded in mutual respect.[57] This interpretation of love and rejection of sexuality puts Friderika Baldinger squarely within the main Christian tradition of her time. That she brought the subject up in the account of her education she explained by its role in favoring her intellectual development. Despite the jumbled language of the first statement, her remarks are again startlingly candid, the sort that makes Baldinger's autobiography instructive reading to twenty-first-century readers who may not expect middle-class women of the eighteenth century to discuss their experience of sexuality. Perhaps Baldinger had another reason to bring the subject up twice, and to emphasize that spiritual qualities, valorized as higher, displaced sexuality for her.

She was countering a suspicion that women who were perceived as excessively interested in learning might also be excessive in other respects; women who did not position themselves as modest and silent might not be chaste, either. Baldinger did not want her unusual appetite for reading to be seen as accompanied by unusual sexual appetite. Yet, the disinterest she claims in the autobiography written for publication did not prevent her from speculating briefly in a letter to her friend Kästner about the sexuality of Jesus.[58]

Baldinger connects her brother's advice to exercise great care in her choice of a husband with "my stubbornness, with my inclination to mock everything, and with my will to be free and independent from the whole world."[59] The proclamation of this desire, "my will," for freedom and autonomy, a desire exactly fitting the central notion of the Enlightened person, is not pursued elsewhere in the text except negatively in the assessment of her marriage; there she writes that her husband had "cultivated my intellect, and improved my will and my heart." The possibility of reading his "improvement" of her will as making her better fit prevailing gender norms is ominous for her as an individual and as an aspirant to membership in the Enlightenment. In fact, Magdalene Heuser, reading late correspondence after Baldinger had been devastated to discover her husband's long-term affair with a domestic servant, has located a letter to Kästner in which Baldinger alludes to her husband's power plays in teaching her "patience" and correcting what she calls her "excessively high notions of the happiness of independence and freedom."[60] At first, she claims that her husband had bound "chains of love around the foolish woman" (168), but then, continuing at first to refer to herself in third person, she writes more explicitly:

> She voluntarily . . . became obedient, cooperative. [This happened] because she found she was very happy when she pleased him and very unhappy when she displeased him . . . I missed too much when my misbehavior caused him to close his spirit to me and when his wit did not entertain me. I learned to overlook things, tolerate them, at the cost admittedly of my health and my stubbornness, which repeatedly tried to break through. In order to please him I learned to tolerate people. That is, to hide my self from them. (169)

The process of becoming "patient" was clearly painful, but Baldinger seems to have perceived it as the cost of preserving her marriage—and pursuing "love of knowledge."[61] Yet, if this training meant the end of her independent will and judgment, no amount of reading would qualify her, as we shall see, for full participation in the Enlightenment project.

Beyond such psychological considerations, the practical resources necessary for the continued intellectual development of married women of the educated middle class depended overwhelmingly on their husbands. In Baldinger's case, after the couple had spent the first four years of married life in Langensalza, where her husband worked as a doctor, he was called to become a member of the highest educational elite, a professor first in Jena, and then in 1773, at the much admired new university in Göttingen. There, he played a decisive role in finally establishing practical experience as an essential part of the training of medical doctors.[62] More important for his wife, he owned many books—a library of 15,000 volumes by the time he died[63]—and was an avid reader. In his wife's company he could discuss what he read, and in his company she could read extensively: "My love of learning grew the more I became acquainted with it. I believe I would have become a scholar if providence had not destined me for the cooking pot, and I still find that one can use the understanding of men in their books when doing women's work."[64] She asserted her talent but acquiesced in the script assigned to her—while also claiming that her learning from men's realm was useful to her in women's. She no longer challenges either realm. To the extent that Baldinger's autobiography is about "learning patriarchy," it is less surprising that she does not identify any of the subjects that interested her, nor that, after mentioning the *Spectator*, she names no other books that she read or admired. Similarly, even though at the time of writing she had lived in two important university towns, Jena and Göttingen, she says nothing about intellectual life there or about her participation in it. She tells virtually nothing about the famous people she knew, omitting, for example, any mention of the novelist and poet Wieland, whom she had met on a visit to Weimar, and omitting, as well, all information about her husband and his career. Taking education in its relation to scholarliness, Friderika Baldinger tells how she got her education but not what it taught her. By the 1770s and 1780s, Enlightenment discourse made no allowance for married women in any contributing role involving learning. The invisibility and irretrievability of all Baldinger's expertise and interests—assuming that she did indeed have some—means that ultimately she, too, despite writing a narrative of her education, was a scholar in secret. On the other hand, taking the education of her title as learning the discipline of patriarchy, the autobiography demonstrates a coherence and provides a kind of closure that it otherwise lacks. Thus, less than a third of Baldinger's work describes her life after marriage because she needed in that section only to demonstrate her acceptance of male values and patriarchally determined gender roles. A few pages sufficed.

As is typical for women's autobiography—and different from most men's of the time—Baldinger emphasizes the people who had had a strong influence on her more than her own accomplishments. In discussing her marriage, she writes that she owes all the development of her spiritual powers to her husband. In one respect it is an obvious overstatement, especially in the light of the whole story she tells. In fact, it is precisely the same sort of statement she made about her brother, and Kranichfeld. In terms of one of the multiple stories she was telling in her autobiography, the shifts in identity of the person to whom she owes all her happiness from her mother to brother, (spiritual) father, and husband, signal her acceptance of patriarchy. In terms of the other story, the one about her pursuit of scholarliness, these men were virtually the only possible source for the knowledge she craved. Indeed, while in one way Baldinger professed her deference to intellectual men, she also, in another way, and within the ideological constraints she had accepted, depicted herself as pursuing a course toward learning and reading that she had early decided on. She attempted to stake out a special place for herself as a woman of accomplishment within an ideology of misogyny.

Baldinger illustrated her continued devotion to learning by telling about one of the opportunities she seized for reading—childbed. She brought up the topic in one of the most extraordinary paragraphs of her autobiography: a description of childbirth that totally elides babies and family: "Six childbeds contributed not a little to the growth of my knowledge, for usually I started to read again as soon as I was out of the hands of the midwife. And the six weeks of recuperation afterwards, when I could read undisturbed, were usually a recovery for my soul, admittedly at the cost of my eyes, which were still too weak to read book printer's signs and letters" (22). Again she fled the body for the mind, and considered that it was her soul that needed to recover from pregnancy. In the history of her intellectual education there was no place or interest for the newborn babies or for the waiting older children.

Goodman, writing about the autobiographies of German women, points out that to the extent the women autobiographers of Baldinger's time followed male models of the genre, they had no place in which to discuss their children, as well as no reason to expect public interest.[65] Nonetheless, it is striking that the self-narrative of

Friderika Baldinger, who proclaimed her acquiescence in her assigned gender roles as mother and wife, provides no information about her children beyond mentioning the childbeds.[66] By omitting her children, Baldinger was again distancing herself from other women. Children were not going to be part of *her* education, and she did not use them as a justification for her learning. This is noteworthy because women's responsibility for giving children their early education was a reason for women's learning that was gradually coming into vogue by the time the autobiography was being written. Instead of claiming a role in the intellectual education of her children, Baldinger invoked another, equally gender-specific way of demonstrating the usefulness of her learning.

Because of her intellectual insights, she wrote, she was able to behave rationally during childbirth, resisting the temptation to say special prayers or exhibit special piety before delivery. This resistance, she believed, was an example of how an educated woman should conduct herself. From here she proceeded to discuss how education helped a woman practice her religion rationally. For women, she pointed out, marriage, religion, childbirth, and death were intimately connected. Thus, Baldinger brought up the topic of death—and the philosophical approach her learning enabled her to take to it—in connection with childbirth. Yet, the references to death are entirely self-centered, for Baldinger mentioned six childbeds, yet, other sources allude to only three children. How had she responded to the deaths of the other three? The autobiography ignores the children and their fates.

Financial considerations for themselves and other family members, household duties, physical stresses and dangers (especially from childbirth), responsibilities for children, and intellectual openings (and closures) were all associated with marriage for women of the educated middle class. Marriage was an institution expected to consume the time, energy, creativity and identity of wives (unlike husbands). Neither scholarship nor serious writing had a place in the usual script.

Concluding an Androcentric Woman's Self-narrative

The thought of dying in childbirth led Baldinger to chart a general assessment of her accomplishments. What she wrote is notable for its patriarchal messages. She stressed the favorable impact that excellent men friends had had on her. Two were especially important, Georg Christoph Lichtenberg (1742–99), the sharp-tongued and hunchbacked physics professor whose wit and close observation are evident in his brilliant aphorisms, and the much older Abraham Gotthelf Kästner (1719–1800), who had the distinction of being both a mathematics professor and a writer of poetry, specifically epigrams. Baldinger mentioned these two friends when she discussed herself: "If you look step by step from me to the heights where Kästner and Lichtenberg became my friends, I believe that even the dumbest person would gain from both with regard to understanding. Does it deserve admiration if I have become bearable through such good company?"[67] One of the strengths that she depicted herself as sharing with her father was the ability to sense other people's intelligence and to know how to use it. "In addition to these, I have gotten acquainted with several other worthy men, and each one has done a service for me without knowing it. My receptive soul is only too inclined to gather treasures, and often I may decorate myself with strangers' feathers without realizing it because they have accidentally gotten mixed up with mine. Can anyone who has so much wisdom and wit from Kästner in his desk remain completely simpleminded?" (24). This is her second reference to Kästner and a cautious one, since the passage does not indicate how Baldinger happened to possess a private hoard of the professor's wit and wisdom.

Kästner's wife had died within two years of his marriage, almost twenty years before he met Baldinger. He had very definite ideas about women, progressive in some respects (he supported women writers by buying their books, sometimes in multiple copies), but was fundamentally convinced that women must be kept secondary to men. The mathematics professor and his colleague's wife, even though living in the same town, were avid correspondents. In 1783, Lichtenberg commented on the relation: "Kästner is unbelievably after the woman. With any other pair of people the *Chronique scandaleuse* would unquestionably have all sorts of tales to tell."[68] To Friderika Baldinger, Kästner's attentions were flattering and a further step in her climb up the unsteady ladder of female success as wife to and friend of people like those covered in the scholarly news she had read in Langensalza years before. If she could combine this wonderful public role as honored friend of Kästner and Lichtenberg with intellectual flirtatiousness, so much the better, she may have thought.

Baldinger's autobiography ends with a ringing affirmation of patriarchy, using words in which modesty and pride are inseparable: "As a woman I have become bearable, how little I would be however as a man!"[69] The sentence sums up her accomplishment in a typically understated way, and declares, also, her final position on the problem of the relations of men and women that had so long vexed her. Striving to find a praiseworthy formulation, she is overmodest about herself and obsequious to men. The final sentence implies that if Baldinger, as the exceptionally bright, well-read, and rational woman that she depicts herself to be were only bearable, then most women must be unbearable. That she was now fully absorbed into this misogynist Enlightenment discourse is evident in the letters she received from a friend in Göttingen after she had moved to Kassel in 1783. Dorothea Wehrs Spangenberg, herself the author of religious poems, never hesitated when she wrote to Baldinger to pass sweeping negative judgments on the other women in Göttingen; presumably she knew well that Baldinger agreed.[70] And when Georg Forster brought his new wife, Therese Heyne, to visit, he gave a vivid description of Baldinger's reaction: "(She) behaved very nicely to Therese, rather like a ferocious animal that retracts its claws and, contrary to its habit, flatters those who stroke it softly. Therese, I must say, kept up the stroking assiduously."[71] Inevitably, Baldinger liked few women.

The outside evidence and the conspicuous absence in the autobiography of any women whom Baldinger seriously admired corroborate the misogyny of the autobiography's concluding comment. Baldinger had carefully avoided writing a book that could be used to claim any intellectual equality between men and women. Her view of herself was utterly dominated by how she thought rational men saw her. She evaluated herself by the educated, middle-class, male standards of the Enlightenment. When she described herself as bearable, she meant to people—especially men—who had absorbed Enlightenment notions of learning, rationality, and autonomy. Behind her misogyny lay also the circumstance that, when a woman obtained glory by associating with famous men, it was important that this glory not be too diluted by letting many other women share the privilege. Patriarchy could only tolerate (and use) a small number of exceptional women. In order to maintain the status of being special that she so much valued, such a woman had a stake in keeping other women out. This Friderika Baldinger did.

Friderika Baldinger's misogyny was part of the prevailing discourse of her time, but as her book itself shows, it was not uncontested. Theodor Gottlieb von Hippel, the civil servant and secret writer, makes the same point a few years later, asking near the end of his feminist book on the status of women, *Über die bürgerliche Verbesserung der Weiber*: "Does not the modesty of Friderika Baldinger imply a criticism of our own sex in reference to our tendency toward self-exaltation?"[72] Hippel recognized that Baldinger's statement revealed the superior position that powerful men had arrogated to themselves, and that impacted the material (including psychological) conditions of women, even of those who were the most spirited and intelligent. Women's psychological discomfort was one of the important factors affecting their struggle to become either private or public writers.

Writing and Desire

Baldinger, in her account, struggling not to jeopardize her conventional gender position, depicts herself as if she had not invaded male sanctuaries, although at the same time she assiduously separated herself, her tastes, and her activities from those of other women. She attempts to make herself unique so as not to open a path for more women behind her, presumably not even to her own unmentioned daughters. In the main text of the autobiography, omitting the prefaces, Baldinger employs the strategy of demonstratively endorsing the conventional version of educated middle-class womanhood. Although by the very act of writing a biography of herself, she enlarges herself in her readers' view, she also simultaneously diminishes herself by writing so short a work and by positioning herself firmly within patriarchal discourse. She omits all description of the cultural climate of her times, reports almost no specific incidents, and makes minimal effort to set the scene. Indeed, after her marriage, no places are specifically named. She also positions herself innocuously by writing in a nonacademic, colloquial style that was easy to understand and unpretentious.

The casualness of the writing does not disguise the difficulty Baldinger confronted in becoming first, a writer, and second, a writer who seriously considered publication. The desire that provided the energy for these accomplishments is discussed in three ways in the text: displaced onto others in such a way that it can be repackaged as duty or obedience, described as suppressed or negative, or mentioned in a trivializing way. The displacement/obedience technique is shown, for example, in the claim in Baldinger's original dedication letter that she was publishing the autobiography at her husband's request and that obedience to him, not "vanity on my part," motivates her deed.[73] Displacement and obedience are a gender-inflected tactic that permits the woman author, by submitting to the wishes of others more authoritative than herself, to represent herself as adhering to patriarchal femininity. The others, of course, are usually men, as when she says her brother wanted to bring light into her dark brain (17), but when Baldinger identifies sympathy and duty as her reasons for visiting the smart aunt with access to a small library (16), she displaces her desire onto an older woman relative.

The second method of describing desire, representing it in the negative, is evident when Baldinger writes that her "love of reading" was made bitter to her by her mother's condemnations (17). After her brother's death and her sister's marriage, she says vaguely that she had three years under Kranichfeld's supervision in which she was able to "live for her inclination" and "read as much as I wanted," quickly adding that "this joy was made bitter for me by worries about sustenance" and by the obligation to do work that neither her spirit nor her body could tolerate (21). Baldinger understands her body not as demanding but rejecting: it cannot tolerate certain kinds of work (presumably some version of spinning, sewing, lacemaking or other fancy work that impoverished middle-class women did in their homes on commission) and is repulsed by physical sexuality. Furthermore, this is a body that requires protection from stimulation; Baldinger mentions her hope of not being conscious when she dies so as to be spared the bodily pains, her body being "extremely sensitive" (24). As already seen, she offsets her desiring mind with this undesiring body.

As for trivialization of her desire to write or learn, this is evident when Baldinger describes her desire for scholarliness ("I wanted so badly to become learned") as a childish wish. Even though almost everything in the self-narrative is built around precisely this wish for learning and its accompanying promise of upward mobility, she says extremely little about the pleasures she herself derived or hoped to derive from this goal. Yet, in a different case she is not so reticent: when she describes getting acquainted with Kranichfeld, she writes, "My strong desire [*Begierde*] to please the man, eventually drew the man to me, and he became my friend" (19). In the context of seemingly intellectual passion, she can speak emphatically of desiring to please a man. And she gives additional detail, mentioning his almost daily visits and stating, "I preferred to be nowhere more than in his company, I sought it where I could, and received advantages which are for me the most important part of my life" (19).

The request that provides the transition from desire for knowledge to writing an autobiography is another version of the displacement and obedience technique. The initial appearance of authorial pride and confidence, suggested by her choice of title, "Essay about the Education of My Intellect," is immediately offset by the first sentence, presenting her writing as the fulfillment of someone else's request, thereby allowing Baldinger to displace responsibility for her writing from herself to another person, an unnamed male friend. She repeated the maneuver in an introductory cover letter to her husband, where she mentions being obligated to write the sketch because of a friend's request (15). The request, as a version of the displacement and obedience technique, was a common method of disclaiming intention. Meta Klopstock had used the request pretext when, after denying categorically for years that women were justified in writing, she began composing a series of letters from the dead. Since her husband, she noted defensively in correspondence with her sister, had asked her to write the pieces as a favor to him, she claimed to feel it was her duty to respond, but she wanted the unconventional deviation kept secret.[74]

The motif of the man's request is important because femininity operated to constrain women not only from "too much" learning but also from most kinds of writing. Autobiography was a genre that German women, especially from the middle class, had hardly tried in public before; Baldinger's account was not written so that she could privately register her progress in religious devotion or take stock of her weaknesses in Pietist fashion; rather, she was writing explicitly for someone else to read. Friderika Baldinger had a long interest in biography, and especially in a subgenre that thrived in the eighteenth century, the scholarly biography. For years, her husband published a journal of biographies of famous doctors and scientists. Some of the articles were written by their subjects; some of the others that were published without attribution may have been written by Friderika Baldinger working to assist her husband. Besides letters (a few of them published during her lifetime)[75] and the autobiography, only one other piece of her prose is now known, an unpublished sketch of several incidents from the early life of Therese Forster's father, Professor Heyne; perhaps because these were events he had told Baldinger himself, she wrote her account in his first person, taking on a male voice. Her other writings are evidently lost; four years after her death, Georg Forster mentions them in a letter to his wife: "What you wrote to me about the Baldinger woman and her essays has shaken me very much. There really is more misfortune possible than good people believe. . . ."[76] What could have happened to evoke this comment, and what writings are meant is a mystery since the texts either remained unpublished or appeared without acknowledgement of any authorship by Friderika Baldinger. As for the choice of scholarly biography as a form for Baldinger's own biography, Magdalene Heuser argues strongly that this was especially effective, since it "offered her the foil against which her desire and the impediments to it could best be displayed."[77] Heuser goes on to point out that although Baldinger claimed to have originally written her self-narrative only for private purposes, she chose an established form that fit well with the possibility of future publication (167).

In the second sentence of her narrative, Baldinger doubts that the course of her education is worth retracing. Such self-trivialization was most commonly expressed in women's claim that writing was nothing more than a leisurely pastime, done only when their real duties were concluded; this claim in turn addressed the main reason overtly stated against women's writing, the old requirement that they be constantly busy with housework or handwork. Once writing became another way of keeping a woman constantly busy, however, the claim that a woman wrote in her spare time could be considered praiseworthy. Schindel, composing his biobibliography of women writers, offered several examples. His praise of housework at the expense of serious writing was explicit, for example, in the description of Susanne Bohl (1738–1806). Schindel mentioned her essays,

> which have the greatest value from the fact that they were composed solely in moments of leisure and that this woman, along with complete care for sustaining and educating a numerous family and along with the most pressing household worries, still knew how to save time for the practice of her talents; often, even during the most onerous housework, her mind was creating a clever work of the muse that she only wrote down after the housekeeping was finished.[78]

Small wonder if only two of Bohl's poems have been preserved.

Schindel was writing in the early nineteenth century, but eighteenth-century commentators were similarly eager to reinforce the view that all women's intellectual activity was secondary to domestic engagement. Even when sheer economic hardship did not force a woman to work as hard as Susanne Bohl, she was still praised if she was extremely dedicated to domesticity, as the eighteenth-century biographer of Charlotte Seidel shows:

> To satisfy her fondness for poetry she permitted herself least of all to neglect or omit other occupations that had to seem more important to her in her situation; . . . she always regarded being occupied with reading and poetry as a pleasure, and she was convinced that one should not sacrifice duties to pleasure, no matter how permissible and innocent it

might appear. She tried therefore at every chance to instruct herself diligently and eagerly in all female occupations and indeed possessed outstanding skill in all of them; not only did she make her own finery, but she also made her dresses with her own hands, and was so little idle that even when she was reading or writing poetry she had the spinning wheel in front of her or the knitting in her hands.[79]

And it was not just Seidel's biographer who attributed this attitude to her. She herself felt it necessary to explain how she had time to write poems. In a letter in 1769 she notes, "at the spinning wheel, in the kitchen, or during other occupations my thoughts are still mine, and instead of turning them to endless little things, I can follow the desires of my heart without missing out on any of my duties" (361). Her discouragement with some of the aspects of a woman's life ("endless little things") shows through even when she is trying to be absolutely correct, asserting that thinking was not hindering her duties. Conflict permeates her words. To the extent that women indeed used only slivers of leisure time for writing, they had made a pernicious compromise in which unending domestic duties preempted everything else.

The doctrine of the primacy of women's domestic duties was deemed so crucial that critics took it into account in their judgments of women's writing. An anonymous reviewer comparing the poetry of Nantchen Goeckingk (1743–81) and Philippine Gatterer (later Engelhard) states unequivocally his preference for Gatterer because of her domesticity:

For this dear young woman considers German poetry as a secondary matter, as recreation after the day's duties; she never sings except when the desire to do so takes hold of her soul; she is training herself, by the way, entirely for the duties of home life, as her poems show on every page. Certainly, in this respect it is praiseworthy when a young woman composes a song or plays the piano with more then usual knowledge, paints, draws, etc.[80]

Writing poetry was becoming acceptable as a "female accomplishment" so long as it was kept in the proper bounds. This limitation was, however, a problem, as the reviewer comments:

The demands of home life almost always suffer when girls' heads are lowered from soft German sense down to a sensitive type of mood, and when they are too weak for determined, noble deeds. The latter we believe we must properly criticize in Nantchen's attitude in her otherwise lovely songs. She says:

> "Für einen Mann zu kochen und zu spinnen,
> Unwürdiger Beruf!"
>
> (684)
>
> [Cooking and spinning for a man, / Unworthy vocation!]

The reviewer acknowledges the poetic merit of Nantchen's writing, but condemns it, nonetheless, as containing sentiments that conflicted with the thoughts and practices of a proper woman (mystified as "soft" but also "determined").

Inevitably, the reviewer admonishes Nantchen for her harsh description of housework as an unworthy profession: "No, that is not right, dear young woman! It is your duty to take over the care of the house for your husband; through contrary behavior his household, his peace and even his fortune, no matter how large, will suffer!" (685). The androcentrism of the idea that housework should always have priority for women could hardly be more clearly suggested than by the repeated use of the word "his." The quality of the woman's writing and its importance to her are entirely omitted from consideration.

Occasionally, however, a conflict was acknowledged between this doctrine of writing only during leisure time and the other view, usually applied exclusively to men, that effective writing was serious business that should be pursued without distraction. When the discourse of art rather than the discourse of gender was applied to a woman writer, she was castigated for excessive timidity in pursuing her literary goals. This happens in Schindel's analysis of Karoline von Klencke, the daughter of Anna Louisa Karsch:

> Totally feminine, she could have become a model of virtue and could have been, if not happy, at least peaceful; yet one must admit that once she became a writer, she did not devote herself to the studies and the industriousness which art demands and spent whole days instead with very unimportant and really useless needlework. *Gleim* pointed this out to her very often and asked her just to write, but the ingrained habit of constantly being busy in some feminine way was victorious and she wrote only in her leisure hours. . . .[81]

Schindel here envisions the women writers' situation as a choice between being a personally admirable ideal ("a model of virtue") or being a writer. Klencke and many other women writers of her time faced a dilemma. Neither alternative was attractive, for one way the woman was feminine and domestic but intellectually and artistically inert, and the other way she was artistic and serious, but no longer legitimately positioned as feminine. Making the artistic choice yet harder for a woman to pursue was a lifetime of training to keep her hands busy with housework.

Sophie La Roche tried characteristically to find the good side of women's obsessive domestic behavior:

> Oh how dear our needle was to us and how happy I am that I need to keep myself occupied. It is an even greater distraction when one is unhappy than reading. If I had not known the value of diligence, then I would never have enjoyed the sweet feeling of treasuring the virtue of industry. I would not be able to say from the heart that if some higher authority forced me to choose between the quill and the needle, I would (although, I admit it, with pain) lay down my quill.[82]

Three quarters of a century later, in 1844, Fanny Lewald felt the same compulsion toward domestic industriousness—even after she had moved to Berlin alone to become a writer. Unlike La Roche and Klencke, however, the nineteenth-century Lewald realized that her continued conformity to female training was counterproductive: "Accustomed to dependence and obedience more than I myself knew, . . . I still regarded my literary activity as if it were something granted to me but revokable at any time, so that I considered myself obliged to do a quantity of handwork because that had been my task before."[83] These activities prevented women from focusing on serious writing. If, on the other hand, their writing was ostensibly not intended for publication, and was not in a form that was considered literary or scholarly, it drew much less fire, as Friderika Baldinger's case shows. She had had to defend her extensive reading, especially given her circumstances in a small town. But once this had been accomplished, she did not have to defend her private, nonliterary writing of letters. This is especially striking given her claim to have written a huge number of letters to just one of her several correspondents. She did not pretend to have composed these letters only in the dead of night after taking care of husband, children, and house; she simply stated that she had written them. If she wished to publish them, however, the story was again different.

The Enlightenment Woman's Failed Transition into Publishing

One of the remarkable aspects of Friderika Baldinger's autobiography as it was published is its layering of indicators that, for a woman, publishing was a highly controversial act for which the prevailing notions of femininity made almost no allowance. Even after Meta Klopstock had begun writing her letters from the dead, for example, a form that could not be justified the way ordinary correspondence could, as mere private communication, she still rejected the idea of women publishing. In fact, in her first letter to the English novelist Samuel Richardson, Klopstock took it upon herself to say she had heard one of his daughters was an accomplished writer, and she proceeded to warn her, as a woman, against publishing. Richardson quoted his daughter's response: "Thank her, dear Sir, in my Name, for her Opinion, so kindly given, in relation to our Sex's being ready to make an appearance in Print. I am doubly secured from such Presumption; by the Consciousness of my own want of Talents; and by being entirely in this Lady's way of Thinking in this Particular."[84]

Despite the discouragements and inhibitions women confronted when they considered both writing and publishing, there were also at least occasional enticements and aids. Although the discourses within which women were thinking, feeling, and acting were perceived as individually internally consistent, different discourses might significantly conflict one with another, so that an unacceptable notion in one might be acceptable in another. Furthermore, groups of women operating on the margin were striving to create new social practices and new discursive systems. For Friderika Baldinger, the greatest encouragement came from the most noted German woman writer of her day: Sophie La Roche. Proclaiming her conformity to prevailing gender standards whenever she could, La Roche simultaneously used middle-class ambition and financial need to justify new practices for women. The correspondence between Baldinger and La Roche offers one of the infrequent records of women discussing with each other their ideas about publication. Only Baldinger's side of the correspondence is preserved, but the references contained there permit inferences about La Roche's letters.

In 1783, at the suggestion of a friend, La Roche wrote to Baldinger asking for help in locating subscribers for the new journal she was publishing for women and, more importantly, requesting that Baldinger contribute some of her own writing. About subscribers in Kassel, where she was then living, Baldinger replied: "I would wish that I could get a lot of readers for your book, but our ladies here read *nothing*."[85] To distance herself once again from other women, Baldinger exaggerated their lack of interest in literature; Philippine Engelhard, in contrast, seeking support in the same town for her poetry book for children just a few years later, was able to find eighteen women willing to subscribe in their own names. As for La Roche's suggestion that Baldinger submit something for publication, it received an equally discouraging initial response. Baldinger refused on three grounds: first, because she did not meet *male* standards ("The surest proof of my intellect is for me that I myself know and feel how infinitely much I fail to deserve the praise of . . . men");[86] second, because she was afraid; and third, because she had already said no to others who invited her. She was worried about the ideological condemnation of forwardness in women and about her reputation. But as her reply to La Roche grew longer, it became clear that her feelings about publishing were much more ambivalent than this opening rejection of the idea suggested.

Characteristically for the suppressed nature of her interest in La Roche's invitation—and symptomatic of the importance of the margins in women's writing—Baldinger's more positive discussions of publishing occur in the postscripts, not in the main bodies of her letters. The constraints Baldinger was operating under meant that she could publish her work if it were anonymous (so that it would not affect her public reputation), and if the work she submitted could be letters, either those other people had written to her or—acceptable since they had not originally been intended for publication—those she had written to someone else. She began to explain this in the postscript of her first letter to La Roche:

> I can't really write for publication, but I have a friend who possesses easily 12 to 1400 letters I wrote, among which something here and there could probably be found that would be usable. The work of going through the collection again would admittedly be awful for me. But what wouldn't I do to make myself worthy of your applause.[87]

Baldinger labored to represent herself here as just a private letter writer and one of so little consequence that finding anything worth publishing among her writings would be a distasteful and onerous task. At the same time, she indirectly made the point that her letters were good enough for one of her correspondents to have maintained an enormous collection of them. By adding that she would probably consent to find some publishable ones because of her important correspondent's request, Baldinger denied any ambition or intention of her own. Even though La Roche's invitation had supplied her with an excuse for publishing, Baldinger still engaged in an elaborate maneuver of near refusal.

Her next letter again contains an illuminating postscript. In it, the cautious Baldinger cited her second condition, anonymity: "I ask you to forgive such a long letter and never to use my name—if I should sometime dare to get something printed under your supervision."[88] In effect, in both postscripts Baldinger was repeating a message of many women of her time: publishing was one thing, and taking responsibility for it was another. This distinction fed directly into the "institutionalized namelessness in literature of German-language women authors" of the eighteenth and nineteenth centuries, a protection racket that enabled them to avoid the accusation of being women writers at all.[89]

Letters, as the one genre in which women of the middle class and aristocracy were routinely encouraged to be adept, had the special advantage for women of being both private (and thus uncontroversial in gender terms) and yet, potentially public. Meta Klopstock once more offers an excellent example. After her marriage, as she thought about writing to her sisters, it seemed possible to her that her letters would someday be published because they were part of the documentation of her famous husband's life. The woman who was adamantly opposed to publication of women's writing made no objection to the prospect of some future member of the family editing her correspondence. On the contrary, she worked to make her writing better, as she explained to her sisters: "If the letters are too very natural, then the scoundrel will probably drop the thought of publishing after all."[90] And so, to ensure that her writing was indeed publishable, she made it lively. To do this well, her next sentence reports, she consulted the most famous woman letter writer in literature: "I have been reading Sevigni today. . . . The sweet lady! She probably wrote so beautifully just because she never had the ridiculous idea of publishing." Madame de Sévigné (1626–96) was constantly admired in eighteenth-century Germany, and women in particular found her an inspiration, usually invoking the private nature of her art to explain its attractiveness. The lack of intention to publish, which the dominant interpretation proclaimed for Sévigné, had the effect of reinforcing women's exclusion from recognized literary activity by connecting their art with privacy and unintentionality. In many fields of accomplishment, women were told that to be successful they must abjure intentionality. One way to fulfill that repressive dictum, as applied to writing and publishing, was to write and die. That, unfortunately, is how Meta Klopstock became a second Sévigné. In 1759, the year after her death in childbirth, her husband published a selection of her correspondence, not including the words about reading Sévigné.

Thus, Meta Klopstock, too, could be praised for the purportedly unintentional art of her wonderful private letters. For women an important aspect of letters was that, as long as they avoided any direct responsibility for publication, they could write copiously in this form and their work could potentially appear in print almost without censure.

In Baldinger's case, the epistolary form was congenial as well as socially acceptable. Her letters, unlike most women's writing in the eighteenth century, and to the limited extent that they have been preserved, frequently have a folksy, homespun manner. For instance, when La Roche asked her about advice for young women reading her monthly *Pomona*, Baldinger said girls with any understanding needed no advice; as for the others: "to someone without any [understanding], my advice would be like the prescription of a great doctor in the hand of a dumb peasant He uses it for fever when it was supposed to cure something like gout"[91] (many of Baldinger's sentences end without periods). The anecdote, part of her condescending stance toward La Roche's *Pomona* project, reiterates by analogy both Baldinger's identification of herself with male authority figures and, in comparing *Pomona*'s readers with the ignorant peasant, her low estimation of women's educability. At the same time, Baldinger's punctuation, and, in other places, her orthography show the limits of her own education. Nevertheless, humor, informality, and folk wisdom are the hallmarks of Friderika Baldinger's few surviving letters, quite unlike the educated and often stilted prose that most aristocratic and middle-class women cultivated. Baldinger's words are still fresh, especially in comparison to the copious sentimental phrases of Sophie La Roche.

In the end, La Roche published none of Baldinger's letters in *Pomona*. In the second letter, Baldinger offers a sample piece of correspondence, a letter of consolation addressed to Kranichfeld "when his son-in-law . . . died in Jena, who had only lived there a quarter of a year and now left behind the daughter with less than nothing, with three children, the oldest of them six years old, and an eighty-year-old mother."[92] In short, Baldinger's proposal of a contribution to *Pomona* is a letter to a man about two women, one old and one young, both in dire straits after the death of the male breadwinner. Why it did not appear in La Roche's journal is unclear. Perhaps Baldinger had (more) second thoughts, possibly because of the challenge that she sensed *Pomona* represented to the gender hierarchy on which she had staked her way of life. Inevitably, there was tension between Baldinger and a public woman writer such as La Roche. Thus, in her first reply, Baldinger had im-

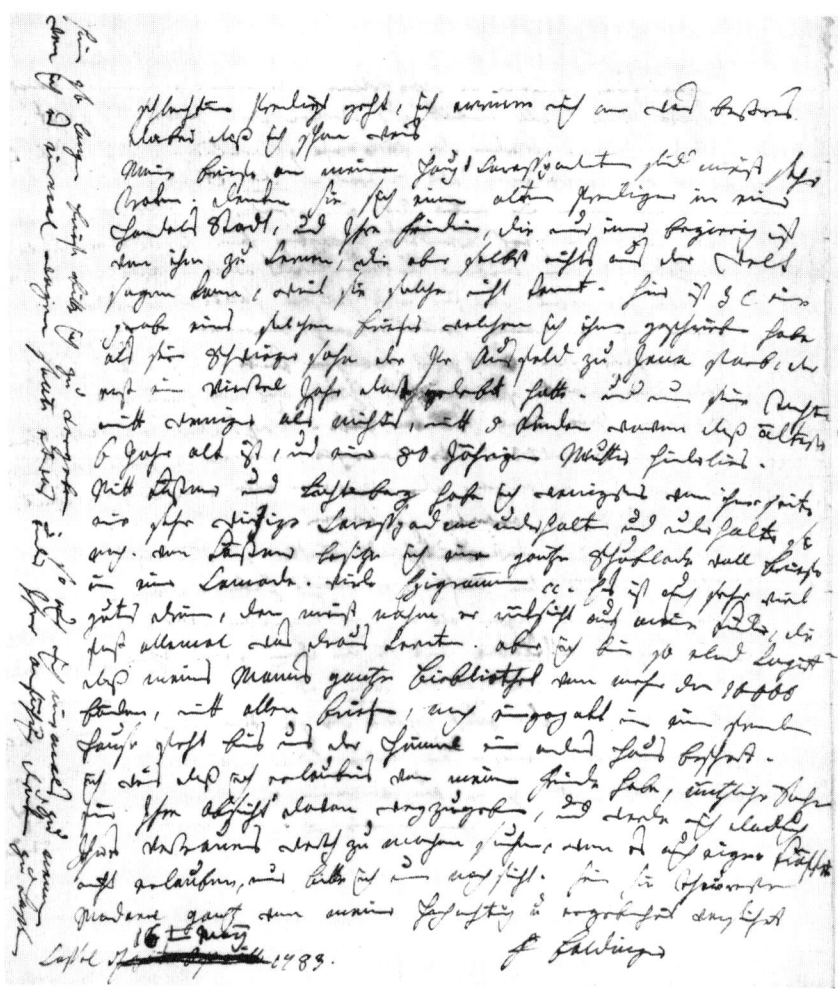

Page from manuscript letter from Friderika Baldinger to Sophie La Roche, dated 16. May 1783, with a marginal note asking La Roche not to identify her if she publishes something in *Pomona* (Goethe- und Schiller-Archiv manuscript, La Roche, I,4,16).

plicitly criticized La Roche by claiming to earn the approval of distinguished men—whose opinions unmistakably counted most—in that she was always aware of her own shortcomings, which meant fearing public appearances. Small wonder if La Roche, who also sought male approval at the same time that she made abundant public appearances in print, felt compelled to defend herself (as can be deduced from Baldinger's second letter).

As it happened, in the same days when she was corresponding with La Roche about publishing letters, Baldinger was also struggling with the question of publishing her autobiography. Justifying this move without jeopardizing her status within patriarchal discourse as an admirable woman was again difficult, even though by this time an increasing number of polite middle-class women were indeed sending their works to press. Yet, for her self-narrative, too, Baldinger constructed a series of elaborate excuses to clear an indirect path for herself. Her act of writing she had already attributed in the first sentence to the wishes of a friend. Publishing she discussed in two brief metanarrative prefaces that preceded the main text, one in the form of a dedicatory epistle,[93] the other a birthday letter,[94] both addressed to her husband. In the dedicatory letter, Baldinger describes publishing as a matter of obedience to her husband because, first, he had suggested the piece be printed as a memento for himself and their children—why publication was necessary for that purpose is unclear—and second, it was his birthday in particular that she had decided to celebrate by giving him a published copy as a present. And yet, she wavered. In the birthday letter (apparently written to accompany a manuscript copy of the text instead of the planned published copy), she claimed amidst lavish praise of her husband to have changed her mind about appearing in print because of her own insignificance and her husband's possible reservations about having such a work dedicated to him. Publishing one's autobiography implied a degree of self-assertion that women could seldom muster. They did not feel worthy of that sort of attention, and certainly not bold enough to let the neighbors and the general public know if they did feel worthy. The birthday letter offers her husband this "child" of her "spirit" (a metaphor particularly notable given the elision from the text of her biological children), to which he, through his wisdom, was so very much the "father" (11). She gave him permission to do with the work as he pleased; in effect, she asked him to publish it.

While Baldinger feared that no audience would be interested in her story, she claimed in one of her letters to La Roche that she cared little about obscurity: "My husband wanted to have this essay published, but I am too little known in the world for anyone to read it and I never want to be."[95] Fame, she claimed, was undesirable, although, since she was glad enough to be associated with famous men, this undesirability is again gender-linked. That is, fame was undesirable for women, not for men. But the question of audience for a male-identified woman such as Baldinger is more complex than the issue of fame. Given her lack of respect for women, she could not particularly desire women readers. On the other hand, given her low estimation of herself compared to men, she could not anticipate men's interest in her either, except perhaps as a curiosity. Since she did not want other women to emulate her, and could not openly expect men to admire her, Baldinger could identify no audience for her work, and on this ground, too, had to choose not to publish.

As a result of her decision, Baldinger's record of herself was still in manuscript form at her death in 1786 in Marburg, the university town to which the Baldinger family had moved in 1785. Her husband, who had published many volumes of short biographies and autobiographies of his male contemporaries, seemingly could find no means by which he himself could get his wife's brief account into print.[96] In about 1791, he wrote, instead, to her old correspondent La Roche and peremptorily requested that she take on the job. La Roche, who had never met either of the Baldingers in person, cleverly quotes his letter in the opening paragraph of her foreword: "I am giving [the essay] to you; you were her friend; my wife loved you; write a forward to it and have it printed."[97] If this is the form in which Enlightenment men made their "requests" to women, small wonder that patriarchal women felt compelled to obey.[98] Of course, as Heuser points out, this particular man had a complex problem to solve: trying to publish a text in which his deceased wife extravagantly praises him and expresses devotion to him, the husband who had been deceiving her for years; he had now brought his mistress into his home as "housekeeper," and would soon marry her.[99] It was much to his advantage if someone of La Roche's stature could be brought unwittingly to publish this "tribute to her," which is really a tribute to himself.[100] La Roche naively proclaims herself flattered by the opportunity.[101]

Now, finding a path to publication of the little-known woman autobiographer became Sophie La Roche's problem. She solved it with a combination of well-established techniques, first, using the authorization from a powerful man, Professor Baldinger, second, including the explanatory metanarratives that the author had already written, and, third, adding her own foreword in the form of a letter to a woman friend, rather than Baldinger's own twice-used choice of a wife's letter to her husband. La Roche thus wove another layer of apparently private writing, including, also, an excerpt from Baldinger's last letter to her, around Friderika Baldinger's narrative. Caroline von der Lühe (1754–post-1800), to whom the introductory letter is addressed, was herself a published poet.[102] Baldinger's book would interest her, La Roche said, because von der Lühe was always curious to find out how people had acquired their educations, and especially how they had overcome obstacles to reach their goals. La Roche's remarks drew no special attention to the gender of the author, or the particular aspects of a woman's autobiography. Instead, she presented Baldinger's account as encouraging young women to improve themselves through education, and she argued very conservatively that Baldinger's case showed obstacles to be beneficial to that process. With this claim, La Roche minimized the autobiography's potential for disrupting conventional gender roles.[103]

Women's autobiographies required especially vigorous justifications regardless of the author's fame. Elizabeth Winston points out that nineteenth-century professional women still felt uncertain: "Their need to assure readers of their womanliness results in apologies, disclaimers, and words of self-deprecation."[104] Among German-speaking women, the successful Caroline Pichler (1769–1843) is an example. Writing her autobiography four decades after Baldinger, she explained what she thought would be the value of her account to readers: "What she was and experienced as a girl, a daughter, a wife, as mother, can really only be significant for the closest circle of her friends and relatives; but how her intellect was trained, how she became the person who is known to the reading public could indeed have some interest for the world."[105] Her specifically womanly experiences, identified chiefly as personal relationships (daughter, wife, mother), did not offer any justification for autobiography, Pichler believed. What was left for her to include was much affected by her gender, of course, but was nonetheless ostensibly the same stuff from which most men's autobiographies were made. Under these circumstances, it is appropriate that in her ruminations Pichler distanced herself from her own story far enough to use the third person. Justifying an autobiography was an alienating experience. And the need for justification applied particularly to women.

Friderika Baldinger was always aware how different life would have been for her if she had been a man. Even on the next-to-last page of her account, she imagined that if she had not been female, she would have become a scholar. Instead, acceding to her society's prevailing misogynist denial of serious scholarliness to women, Baldinger discounted her own accomplishment: "As a woman I have become tolerable, how little I would be however as a man!"[106] Feminine modesty, so central to patriarchal gender concepts, required both this humble evaluation of herself and the avoidance of publicity, which meant the rejection of published writing. Seen in the context of her original goal of joining the alternative aristocracy of scholars, this brilliant final sentence—and it is both a grammatical statement and a culminating judgment of herself and her society—reiterates that it is still gender and not knowledge that stymies her efforts. She would be little as a man not because of men's superiority, but because of the patriarchal gender system. The resulting double standard, although it may appear to give her status, ultimately devalues her.

Yet, Baldinger came close to the line between a public and a private writer. Indeed, she allowed the editor of a journal for women to publish two letters by her and two from Kästner to her younger daughter.[107] In her correspondence with La Roche, she tried to work out a way to do something similar. Furthermore, in the case of her autobiography, Baldinger actually wrote for publication, one of the criteria for being a public writer. Yet, in the end, she did not publish her work; she deliberately stayed among the ranks of the private writers, those who wrote diligently but saw little or none of their work into print. Meta Klopstock belonged to their ranks also. She carefully wrote her private letters in the hopes that they would later be published. Then, when she attempted forms—a drama and letters to the dead—that would usually have been intended for publication, she insisted on keeping her writing secret.

The very fact that the writings of both Klopstock and Baldinger were soon published despite their personal choices makes the distinction between public and private writers more, not less, important. The posthumous publication of the refusal of these women to publish reinforced the social practice of private writing for women. Meta Klopstock, in particular, had this effect, for her published letters and other writings represented a much more substantial body of work than the brief autobiographical essay of Friderika Baldinger. Furthermore, Klopstock's husband was the most eminent literary figure in Germany when she died; her poignant death and her husband's edition of her work ensured more widespread public attention than Baldinger could attain. Meta Moller Klopstock became a model of the modest woman, one who might write, and write well, but not publish. The autobiography of the educated Friderika Baldinger did nothing to dispel this image. Even a much younger woman, such as Charlotte von Einem, who wrote her personal history a few decades after Baldinger, still followed their pattern.

The contradiction between writing and society's conventional scripts for women is clearly represented in Friderika Baldinger's autobiography, in the documents that preface it, and in her correspondence with La Roche. Just as significant is the presentation of the complex effect of the invariably patriarchal education of her day, which separated women from themselves and each other. Baldinger had written to La Roche that she would go to great lengths "to make myself worthy of your applause." If she had seriously valued La Roche's praise, it would have been an important development for her even though it was one that other women had already accomplished. But in the end, she did not want and value that praise enough to jeopardize the more satisfying and more widely acknowledged praise that powerful men (in Baldinger's case, this meant Enlightenment intellectual authority figures) gave to cooperative women. Part of the price, especially for educated women, of this androcentrism was alienation from what society construed as their femaleness, from their bodies, as is evident in Baldinger's attitude toward sexuality and toward the experience of childbirth. At the same time, Baldinger shows that women were emotionally coerced into giving up their will to be free and independent. Thus does the small corpus of Baldinger's writings reveal the inhibiting forces that discouraged even qualified and interested women from writing in what the *Aufklärung* considered literary or scholarly forms, and from publishing almost anything at all. To examine Friderika Baldinger's autobiography is to go a long way toward understanding not only the lives of the eighteenth-century German women of the educated middle class, but also the literature produced by many of those women and the usefulness of distinguishing between public and private writers. Friderika Baldinger's writings illustrate well the retarding factors with which women in the eighteenth century had to deal—and which she herself in many ways perpetuated.

Did eighteenth-century German women have an Enlightenment? Since women's opportunities both as children and as adults were so hemmed in by gender restrictions, the answer suggested by Friderika Baldinger's life history is no. But using the definition of Enlightenment—he used the term *Aufklärung*—proposed by Kant suggests the question should be revised. Kant wrote: "Enlightenment is man's emergence from his self-imposed nonage. Nonage is the inability to use one's own understanding without another's guidance. This nonage is self-imposed if its cause lies not in lack of understanding but in indecision and lack of courage to use one's own mind without another's guidance."[108]

Baldinger's inhibitions about publishing and low esteem for herself because she was a woman signal that after years of training in "patience," she no longer had the ability to use her own mind independently of (male) approval, as Kant indicates an enlightened person should do. Yet, the status of women, their exclusion from formal or informal advanced study, not to mention their intensive socialization to obedience, makes it hard to identify their intellectual position as self-imposed. A few paragraphs later, Kant proposed that if the public "is only given freedom, enlightenment is almost inevitable." But again, women were not given their freedom and were still struggling to envision the possibility of taking it. Under these circumstances the question becomes whether eighteenth-century German women *could* have an Enlightenment, and the answer again, by the standards of Kant and his contemporaries, is no. To a certain point, German women could be objects of the *Aufklärung*'s educational project, but the very education they received was not liberating to them, and the world in which they lived did not allow them to become independent subjects in the Enlightenment framework.[109] Women could be the targets of *Aufklärung*, its recipients, but not its autonomous, self-directing givers; they could participate in much of the Enlightenment's sociability, which was an important element of Enlightenment discourse, but they had no standing for converting their spoken thoughts into the printed word, which was especially privileged within the movement. Trouille's phrase, "enlightened domesticity," fits Baldinger and other women like her well since it alludes to them as wives, cooks, house managers, affirming listeners in the household, a realm lacking philosophical importance within the movement.[110] "Enlightened domesticity" is not about independence or autonomy but has, instead, to do with support functions; enlightened domesticity is knowledge applied—and actually a ghetto in which women are confined.

Goethe's last words, spoken in 1832, but still embedded in the central image of the Enlightenment, were supposed to have been "More light!" The undiminished and permissible desire contained in these words contrasts powerfully with the observation of Sophie Ludwig, that to women the message of the eighteenth century was "Lights out!"

3
The Enabling Effect of Difference: Sophie La Roche (1730–1807)

*G*ESCHICHTE DES FRÄULEINS VON STERNHEIM "THE HISTORY OF LADY Sophia Sternheim," the first publication of Sophie von La Roche, was an enormously successful book, attracting the approval of readers and critics. It can be read as addressing a painful eighteenth-century theme, the struggle of the educated middle class for recognition and prestige, which is to say cultural power, with Fräulein von Sternheim herself as the champion in the fight. The aim of the contest is not to disassemble the hierarchy of ranks, however, or to end absolutist rule, but rather to defend the admission of certain members of the educated middle class to the standing and privileges of the aristocracy, and to reshape the standards for that admission. And the opponent of this goal, as depicted in the novel, is the elitist aristocracy, especially that gathered at court.

In most of late eighteenth-century Germany, when people without rank served the court in some special way, they might gain enough attention and enough supporters to have nobility conferred upon them, and sometimes upon their descendants as well. For men of the educated middle class, this system worked relatively well, since the activities for which they were rewarded were usually achievements in the eyes of the educated middle class as well as the aristocracy. For women, however, admission, in the rare instances that it happened, was usually for sexual services, as mistress to a prince, for example, an activity incompatible with educated middle class approval.

Sternheim presents a woman's struggle between the two groups—on one side, the hereditary aristocracy attempts to seduce the heroine so that she will be on the same footing as other upstart women and can assert none of the educated middle class's usual self-righteousness, and on the other side, a coalition of the educated middle class and the landed aristocracy resists seduction and asserts virtue and knowledge as standards applicable to both men and women. The battle over rank is thus, in part, a gender struggle, a struggle to legislate the reigning meaning of womanhood, focusing either on pleasure or on virtue, the flirtatious courtesan or the well-behaved daughter. One of the novel's extraordinary moves is to let a woman, the title character, lead the virtue coalition. Even though La Roche accepts most of the usual terms of the argument as the educated middle class framed it, and thus does not challenge, for example, the rightness of a class society or the wrongness of female sexual experience outside of marriage, she changes the picture by relocating women's place in it.

Friderika Baldinger's publishing plan had been stymied in part because she was not well known enough to expect public interest in her story. Sophie La Roche, after the huge success of *Geschichte des Fräuleins von Sternheim*, had no such worry. This chapter will examine the book that brought her fame and some of the ways she later used her renown. In the course of her long literary career, La Roche argued for the improved cultural status of middle-class women, and devised an interpretation of women's gifts that offset the importance of learning for women's writing, even though the debate about women's learning, I will show, is one of her important themes not only in *Sternheim*, but also in various later texts, such as the moral tale, "Der schöne Bund" "The Beautiful Band," and the journal *Pomona*. Although she is known as a pedagogical writer, I will argue that she wanted to explore taboo subjects and to some extent accomplished that, addressing, especially in fiction, women's experience of unhappy marriage, difficult mothers, and dangerous men. When she undertook to edit *Pomona*, a monthly for women, she not only established a venue for her pedagogical agenda, but also initiated what I argue is a literary group for women. After the demise of the journal, she attempted to sustain the *Pomona* group while producing writing in genres rarely used by women until then, such as a modified travel journal and essay collection (*Briefe über Mannheim* "Letters about Mannheim") and an autobiographical fragment collection (*Mein Schreibetisch* "My Writing Desk"). While often deploying a selection of the ideas and goals of the Enlightenment, La Roche championed a version of the *Empfindsamkeit* that appealed especially to women.

The first volume of *Geschichte des Fräuleins von Sternheim* lays out the terms of the struggle over class and gender, showing how the protagonist's qualities represent the two partners in what I call the virtue coalition of the educated middle class and the lower-level landed aristocracy, the two groups in the novel that shared their opposition to the Frenchified excesses and frivolity of Germany's numerous large and small aristocratic and royal courts. In the opening section, occurring largely before her birth, the text seeks to validate Sternheim's genealogy as incarnating both sides of the coalition. Her father is university-educated and middle-class, with a record of military service so distinguished that he is rewarded for it with the military title of Colonel. Since the upper echelons of the army were reserved for the aristocracy, his new military title is accompanied by honorary aristocratic rank. He proceeds immediately to consolidate this status by buying an estate, hobnobbing with a baron, and then marrying advantageously. The social benefits of the marriage are negatively emphasized: the Colonel valiantly resists his love for the stepsister of his friend the Baron because he respects the difference in their status. It is the Baron who pushes for the union and learns from his stepsister that she, too, is in turmoil, having fallen in love with the Colonel on the basis of his letters to the Baron, and the Baron's accounts of the Colonel's virtue. Yet, just when disembodied love and virtue have been posed as motivating the marriage, the social consequences of such a union and the insufficiency of the Colonel's honorary nobility are reasserted. The Baron's sister, who thinks her own chances for a promising marriage may be damaged if her stepsister infringes on correct aristocratic behavior, asks whether she, too, will be tossed off to the next university friend of the Baron's who might appear. What counts to her are the privileges of birth. The sister argues in a dialogue with her brother that the issue is the admission of outsiders to the hereditary aristocracy. Although the marriage is allowed to proceed, the status of the Colonel as fundamentally middle-class is reestablished.

His new wife, as a member of the landed aristocracy, has impeccable moral qualities, exactly those endorsed by the educated middle class, and her virtues are reinforced, as in the middle class, by a palette of emotions that purportedly compensates for her limited education. The daughter of these two paragons, the middle-class man of achievement and the landed-aristocratic woman of virtue, is the heroine Sophie von Sternheim. Drawing the best from both parents, she is intelligent, practical, diligent in her projects, frugal, empathetic, and faithful in fulfilling her duties.[1] As has often been noted and as a minor antagonist in the text explains,[2] the Fräulein too embodies the self-proclaimed markers of the educated middle class[3]; indeed, for a considerable part of the novel, she explicitly assumes middle-class status. Yet, since she is also partly aristocratic, with access to aristocratic society, Fräulein von Sternheim can observe and report the weaknesses of the nobility from within as well as without. She is given this opportunity on a larger scale when her parents die and she leaves the countryside, where virtue prevails, for the iniquitous town, location of the princely court and home of a conniving aristocratic aunt, in fact, the Baron's rank-obsessed sister.

Among the tactics used by the educated middle class in its scramble up the cliffs of the social structure was the mobilization of virtue as attributed to the women of its group; the fitting antagonists to the chaste, virtuous, fundamentally middle-class heroine were sensualist aristocrats, sensuality and sexuality being tropes for the aristocracy at court. If the court can ensnare Sternheim sexually, the logic seems to be, then she will have become one of them. This part of the novel is a temptation story, with Fräulein von Sternheim being enticed with fine clothes and engrossment in her body, then with pastimes focusing on wealth and pleasure, and finally, with the possibility of special status and again body absorption—as the mistress of the prince. Although Sternheim participates in many court practices as her aunt directs her to do, and although she rarely voices her objections to people who think differently than she does, she does not share the court's pleasures and satisfactions. She remains fundamentally unmoved in her evaluation of the court, which she considers unnatural and immoral. But when the prince's seduction plot, along with her aunt's complicity in his desire, and the rumor that the people at court consider her hypocritical about her virtue, overwhelm her, she tries to extricate herself. At this point, she makes a mistake that generates the second half of the novel. She marries—at least she believes that she marries. And her new husband is an aristocratic man, Lord Derby, who had feigned interest in philanthropy and virtue to overcome her defenses against being sexually exploited. The shift in her pursuers from the prince to the courtier makes the point that it is not the prince as prince against whom the novel construes the middle-class battle to be directed, but rather, against the whole category of sensuous and hence reprehensible court aristocrats and their venal and unscrupulous behavior. Indeed, the prince and Derby as representatives of misguided court aristocrats are matched and balanced by two other young noblemen, Lords Seymour and Rich, representatives of the landed aristocracy that in the novel has the wealth, authority, and wisdom to enact the enlightened schemes that the educated middle class could only propose.

The second volume of the novel begins with the question of what

Sternheim's behavior will be like in the intimate company of a seducing nobleman, the same question that Gotthold Ephraim Lessing posed in his influential play *Emilia Galotti* (first performed in 1772, the year after *Sternheim* began to appear). In the presence of others and in her aunt's home, Sternheim had acted with strict virtue, even if the appearance was sometimes otherwise. Would she continue to resist sexuality in private? In the process of making the answer be a triumphant yes (without killing the heroine, as Lessing did), the novel defines Fräulein von Sternheim as asexual. The virtue that the protagonist invokes in her frequent homilies erases sexuality, and the knowledge that she usually pairs with virtue is not carnal. This resistance to sexuality, along with her unwitting revelation of her preference for Lord Seymour, is so exasperating to Lord Derby that he angrily reveals their wedding was a fake and then abandons her.

The stunned and revolted heroine, taking on the status of a middle-class widow, proceeds in the rest of the second volume to demonstrate what her definition of nobility as virtuous achievement can do to preserve class society. She shows that the educated middle class offers new techniques for keeping people of lesser rank in their place, by making them more content.[4] Sternheim works at this incessantly and gains great psychological satisfaction from it. She knows that her privilege depends on the labor of servants and peasants and does everything she can to make sure they keep working. At the same time, the particular variety of pacification program she chooses fits her definition of educated middle-class womanhood: La Roche's eponymous character, as a model of virtue and in a motherly role, engages in innumerable works of educational philanthropy. In her first charity case, for example, the young heroine instructs a hapless mother on exactly how to educate her sons and daughters and sends a basket of books so that the instruction can be carried out correctly. At all the distressing moments of her story, Sternheim finds solace in instructing girls—for the class to which they were born. She trains the nieces of an innkeeper to be glad that they can become ladies' maids instead of ladies, while insisting that a bourgeois woman, despite her crushing poverty, must have her daughters learn drawing, music, and modern languages. The ethic of blessings and gratitude that La Roche advocates precludes a closer investigation of what poor workers and peasants earn, and thwarts the other danger that commercial success, in itself, might become a ticket to high social status, a situation posed as a problem in some of the English literature that La Roche devoured. The novel does not object to wealth—after all, one of the heroes is named Lord Rich—but wealth is not the proposed basis for social mobility.

The novel comes to its close after one final test of Sternheim's steadfastness in virtue. Derby, whose violation of her trust (the false marriage) had sent her into middle-class exile, abducts her again, consigning her this time to extreme working-class poverty. Again, Sternheim proves resilient, gathering strength once more from helping a poor miner's family learn how to survive better—without leaving their social station—while devising ways of making her own return to aristocratic privilege and security. This she must accomplish almost entirely on her own, the hero of the story, Lord Seymour, being passive, inept, and always absent or mistaken in a crisis. At the end of the novel, however, Sternheim's marriage to him is presented as securing for her the economic, social, and cultural privileges that she sought and that, in the prevailing terms of the book, she and the classes she represents deserve. The degenerate Derby is killed off, but only after he has capitulated to Sternheim's version of what counts: he dies repenting his abuse of her.

The book concludes with a myth of idyllic unification of the educated middle-class (Sternheim's status in the second half of the book), with the landed aristocracy (Seymour). It attempts to reach complete closure, the end of history. Sternheim has attained high aristocratic standing through her heart and mind, not her body, although her brilliant performance of the principle duty of an aristocratic wife is a bodily one, producing two male heirs. She reincarnates herself in male progeny, literally one for each of the two good brothers who wooed her, since Sternheim gives Lord Rich one of the boys to raise. In effect, both men can thus be the fathers of Sternheim's children, and the novel ends with the thinly disguised image of polyandry as a reward for Sternheim's excellent conduct. It is a remarkable conclusion to a novel in which the author had also successfully avoided raising the question of whether Sternheim's virginity had remained intact after the wedding that she had incorrectly believed authentic. La Roche arranged a situation, marriage, in which Sternheim would ordinarily receive a sexual initiation. Within the discourse of the *Empfindsamkeit* that La Roche deployed, which stressed (good, mild) feelings at the cost of (bad, vigorous) passions, sexuality is repressed; "My virtuous tenderness constitutes my husband's happiness,"[5] Sternheim writes in her final letter (though not the last letter of the book).

Her life in the idyll is not merely domestic, however. Bringing middle-class notions to her exalted position, she can get her plans acted upon promptly, and with all the desired results; not only is there no unrest among the servants and peasants, but, in a move that shows the dependency of this idyll on the existence of harsh exploitation elsewhere, the poor are grateful to the rich, sending their "thanksgiving and good wishes" with every step of their master. In terms of its glorification of a heroine who acts with a remarkable degree of confident independence, the book ends with a tactical obfuscation, turning the final pages of the narration over to a male voice, Lord Rich, thereby reconfirming to readers that such a heroine can win male approval of the most important kind, that coming from a high-ranking, educated aristocrat. But it is also remarkable that the authority figure is not the protagonist's new husband, Lord Seymour. His satisfaction is cited, but by placing the narration in the voice of Lord Rich, Seymour is again prevented from attaining undue importance. The husband, in this construction, is indeed nothing without his wife's approval.

The novel, then, can be read as advocating the admission of the educated middle class into the upper tier of a class society, and justifying that admission on the basis of qualities characteristic of this class and the stabilizing effect of those qualities on society overall; the argument is also based upon a critique of certain aristocratic behaviors that are categorized as correctable abuses. But although the aspiring group frequently called itself educated or scholarly—and is called so today—and although Sternheim is constantly involved in projects of education, especially for girls, women of the educated middle class had no opportunity to meet the educational standards typical of the men, as Friderika Baldinger's life story has already shown. Thus, the fictional Sternheim did not enjoy the university training that had been the birthright of her father, himself the son of a professor (who is also, inexplicably, wealthy). Still, the novel does not allow the educated middle class to be defined and validated by men. The text recruits women into the contest not just as useful auxiliaries, but as central players. This centrality must be justified, however, and the way women's qualifications are explicated was particularly important and controversial. Part of the result of the justification that Sophie von La Roche devised for her first heroine was of enormous importance for another admission struggle that marked the late eighteenth century, the effort of women to be admitted to literary production. *Geschichte des Fräuleins von Sternheim* created for women of the educated middle class a usable stepping stone to cultural activity across the treacherous path of extensive education that otherwise had forced women either to dress themselves emotionally and intellectually as men or to feign unchanged ignorance as women; in the first case they risked paralysis (as Baldinger showed) or derision; in the second, as women whose learning was invisible, they were (allegedly) admired, but just as likely to be immobilized as the others.

Feeling Woman, Educated Man: The Uses of *Empfindsamkeit*

In the midst of her uncongenial stay in the vicinity of the court, Sternheim has a brief outing to the country, a place emblematic of right thinking. There she meets a shaman of the educated German middle class—a man, of fatherly age, educated, a writer, a German,[6] in short, an unimpeachable authority figure within the terms of the book. What he tells Fräulein von Sternheim enlarges the field of her potential intellectual activity and transforms her qualifications: "With tender delicacy he reproached me for my timidity and reserve in judging the works of the mind; and he ascribed to me a right perception ["eine richtige Empfindung" "proper feelings"], which, he said, justified speaking my thoughts as freely as others do."[7] Sternheim's feelings authorize her to express her thoughts just as much as men's formal educational credentials could authorize them. This is a major revision of the prevailing gender discourse.

Precisely at the moment, the second half of the eighteenth century, when the learning of educated middle-class women had improved, the claim of their unfitness for scholarly activity (and cultural productivity) had received a new justification, most influentially codified in Rousseau's *Emil*. His explanation, a concept of sexual characteristics to replace the old gendered division of labor, had been couched in terms women, too, might find palatable, for they were now readers themselves. Emil's ideal mate—that the relationship would be heterosexual went without saying—was described as a woman with "a feeling heart," along with a constant awareness of public opinion: "Sentiment without opinion will not give [women] that delicacy of soul which adorns good morals with worldly honor; and opinion without sentiment will only make them false and dishonest women who put appearance in the place of virtue."[8] The concern with public opinion is a persistent theme among eighteenth-century women writers, as Friderika Baldinger's debilitation has already shown. The valorization of sentiment had very different implications, some of them occurring at the cost of women's learning. Rousseau described Emil's Sophie as having "taste without study, talents without art, judgment without knowledge. . . . O what lovable ignorance!" (401). At an earlier point, in a passage addressed to men Rousseau had explained why a woman who fitted this description could be ideal: "You constantly say, 'Women have this or that failing which we do not have.' Your pride deceives you. They would be failings for us; they are their good qualities. Everything would go less well if they did not have these qualities" (363). Viewed from the perspective of many twenty-first-century American feminists, Rousseau's model woman, excluded as she is from serious learning and consigned to rely on her intuition and emotions (and any teachings her husband chooses to give her), appears to be a thoroughly discouraging development in the representation of women and in the implied prescriptions for their development and education. Indeed, eighteenth-century German men almost gleefully set about defining the exact list of bans that Rousseau's ideas implied.[9] Among certain eighteenth-century German women with literary inclinations, however, the result of Rousseau's argument was dramatic and unexpected: They dropped the needle for the quill.

For late eighteenth-century women, especially those aspiring to be writers, inadequate education had been the byword. The inadequacy came in different forms depending on the woman's class, with women outside the middle class and aristocracy usually lacking enough education to write sentences, much less compose paragraphs, while more privileged women, in contrast, now possessed the minimal language skills (or more) for becoming writers, yet still felt unqualified for full cultural participation. The middle-class women's sense of inadequacy took two forms. For those especially well versed in the dominant intellectual tradition, like Friderika Baldinger, the invidious androcentrism of all extensive education and the polarized scripting of femininity so crippled their self-esteem, and so limited their positioning as feminine, that writing was especially difficult and publishing might be impossible. For others, like Sophie La Roche, although androcentrism in their learning and in all available discourses necessarily drenched them, too, the problems were the lack of systematic learning and the absence of any recognized credential, formal or not, such as men routinely achieved before joining in overt cultural production. La Roche, for example, more than most other daughters or wives of the male intelligentsia of her time, had received a good childhood education, studying religion, history, natural science and mathematics,[10] as well as gaining fluency in both French and Italian.[11] She had gotten no instruction in geography or German, and none in literature, which boys and men studied under the titles of Latin and Greek, but, as Verena Ehrich-Haefeli points out, as a young woman she had one excellent and relatively sustained period for reading while she was engaged to the absent Wieland, and as a young wife she had an unusually good opportunity to be in an intellectually stimulating setting while living at the palace of Count Stadion. Still, there were key ways in which her learning and reading there were necessarily superficial and fragmented, weaknesses she later failed to overcome.[12] La Roche herself mourned her lack of systematic education, especially as taught at Latin schools and universities, which an elite group of boys from—in some cases—all socialeconomic classes attended from the age of sixteen or so, and which, in effect, offered eighteenth-century Germany's standard credentials for literary production.

With positive readings of Rousseau, however, the license of the feeling woman could be applied to enable women to write and publish without educational credentials. Within *Sternheim*, this occurs on two levels. First, the text purports to result from the writings most of all of three women: Sternheim, a prolific and indeed compulsive writer of letters (as well as of one poem, a love song);[13] her confidante, whose letters do not appear but are presumed; and Rosine, the fictional editor, who is posited as having collected the letters and composed the connecting material. Rosine, the fictional editor, is especially interesting because she, too, is of anomalous class: her father is a pastor, she was educated with Sternheim, one of her married sisters is Sternheim's confidante, and yet, she herself, remaining unmarried, has taken on the position as Sternheim's maid. The fictional editor, in short, is a self-supporting single woman. Letter writing did not require the special dispensation that the feeling woman offered; nor did the purported copying and editing by Rosine—since it is presented as a private act carried out at the request of yet another friend, another instance of the request defense that Baldinger uses. But within the novel in another sense is also the unnamed woman author of the text, as she is invoked in the signed introduction by La Roche's well-known and rather self-important editor, the writer Christoph Martin Wieland. Wieland's metanarrative about his woman "friend" [*Freundin*], as he calls the author, contains his justification for her audacity, his assurance to readers that his friend had written during her leisure time and without intentions, either to write a book or, once it was unintentionally written, to publish it. In other words, the three paths to publishing a woman's writing that can most reduce her responsibility for the act—through an anonymity that veils the individual but signals her gender, through the reputable man's metanarrative, and the woman's own metanarrative (appearing in

Wieland's quotes from La Roche's letters)—are invoked here. Yet, the feeling-woman notion within the novel changes La Roche's writing from an affront that desperately needs explanation into an affirmation of her most womanly qualities.

For some women, the feeling-woman rationale was unusable; for Friderika Baldinger, writing a dozen years after *Geschichte des Fräuleins von Sternheim*, the endorsement of emotion was of no help, since her purpose was to depict herself not as a woman of feeling, but as a woman of learning. Ehrich-Haefeli criticizes La Roche, even while she sympathizes with her, for so thoroughly proclaiming the importance of women's feelings and, in effect, amputating her own head.[14] Even women for whom emotionality was welcome found it difficult to hold to the feeling-woman rationale consistently. After all, resistance to the amplified version of women's emotions had begun instantly, in Wieland's introduction. Much as he praises the character of Sternheim and admires her principles, he considers the book flawed as a work of literature as he tells his "friend": "Your Sternheim, amiable though she is, has—when considered as a work of the mind, a literary composition, or even merely as German writing—certain faults that will not remain hidden from the hecklers."[15] He goes on shortly after to itemize some of the novel's weaknesses, especially the lack of a plan made in accordance with the rules of art, the absence of everything that might be called the skills of an author, and the sloppiness of the style—all implicitly connected to the author's lack of education. Much as many readers and reviewers disagreed with Wieland's introduction, it reasserted the incompatibility of women's literary aspirations, no matter how presented, with the dominant discourse of art as the province of the highly educated, always men. Sophie La Roche engaged in a lifelong struggle to locate herself and other women both as writers and as acceptably, recognizably feminine in the framework of the educated middle class.

Nonetheless, emotional qualification, along with her parentage, secured Sophie von Sternheim as a representative of the virtue coalition within the class politics of La Roche's first novel, and the outcome of the novel verifies her effectiveness. She is admitted into the ranks of the high aristocracy. Outside the novel, when women were able to assert their emotional qualification in the face of considerable resistance, the feeling-woman model enlarged the scripts of middle-class femininity and minimized the issue of women's learning. Because it entailed no unfeasible prerequisites and contained far fewer contradictions to current notions of femininity, it increased the number of women eligible to become public writers and located them within the *Empfindsamkeit*, with its emphasis on feelings, rather than the *Aufklärung*, with its emphasis on thought. The model of the feeling woman influenced what and how many women wrote, but did not resolve their ambivalent wavering between the desire for serious learning and notions of domesticated, emotional womanhood. Although women got improved access to the pen by truncating their educational aspirations, many, including La Roche, tried in their writings to advance the education and expand the realm of experience of other women.

La Roche also wrote that she wanted in her writing to articulate taboo thoughts. While the constrictions of femininity and the operations of the dominant discourse made this difficult, there are slippages and resistances in even the most comprehensive system. La Roche developed moments of marginality and techniques of juxtaposition to address some of these areas, such as the suffering of women in bad marriages (the assumption that there were good marriages was not challenged), the attractions of remaining single, and the desire of many women for an education exceeding the basic; she also problematized both mothers and men. Not separating herself from other women, La Roche constantly gestured to herself as a woman, as defined—partly through her own writings—by and for the educated middle class. Although she had no immediate disciples, she became the center of the most important women's literary network in eighteenth-century Germany. All this requires further elucidation.

Representing Women's Experience of Unhappy Marriage in La Roche's First Novel

Neither reading literature nor writing it has ever been a mere pastime. In eighteenth-century Germany, these two activities were entangled in many different and changing discourses, especially as the population became more literate and as small technological and economic improvements gave women (and men) of the educated middle class and lower nobility more time for cultural activities. One of the discourses in which literature was enmeshed—and which, therefore, also entangled women readers and writers—was sexuality. Examining the period's fascination with infanticide as a coded interest in the sexuality of unmarried women, Isabell Hull argues convincingly that over the century, absolutist faith in judicial regulation of sexual behavior was replaced by a more liberal concept (based on cameralist thinking) that the state does not have effective tools for this area of control. Cameralist thinkers turned their hopes more toward social control through education, which, for girls and women, who hardly attended schools and were excluded from universities, mostly meant reading. Reading, in turn, especially the reading of novels, was associated with sexuality.[16] Women writers then, because they were always expected to include women (and sometimes girls) in their audiences, were taking on functions of the state, having to do with sexual behavior. Furthermore, another cameralist position that had gained wide acceptance, especially because of the relative prosperity of the period, was the new idea that a state's wealth increased as its population grew; rather than disallowing marriage if the couple could not prove in advance its ability to be economically self-sustaining, the new attitude encouraged marriage[17] and ultimately made marriage more firmly patriarchal.[18] So women writers were coming on the scene not only when literature had a larger audience, but also when the dominant discourse expressed both fear of writing/reading as an incitement to sexual activity and hope for it as a mode of social and self-control, a tool for persuading readers to channel their sexuality into a socially approved form, marriage. The clash in views between absolutist and cameralist views, in this case of sexuality, which would be further complicated in the 1790s by more extreme notions of freedom provoked by the French Revolution, gave writers room for many variations in their representations of marriage and sexuality. Sophie La Roche used some of that space not just to reinforce women's submissiveness to patriarchal marriage but to question it.

A central event in *Sternheim*, forming the end of Part I and the beginning of Part II, is the protagonist's hasty courtship and presumed marriage with Lord Derby. Before the first six weeks of the marriage were over, Sternheim had realized that it might be impossible to please her husband while remaining true to herself.[19] On Derby's side, the letters about his feelings and motivations leading up to the wedding and during the six weeks afterwards are especially important. He rejoiced cynically over his successful ruse in capturing Sternheim, but he also suggested that her virtue and goodness were beginning to influence him in a more sensitive and moral direction. If all had gone well, he wrote, he might really have married her (174–75). His possible conversion to goodness was disrupted not simply by his own incorrigibility, but by his recognition that his wife, which Sternheim considered herself to be, cherished another man. "Yes, she was even careless enough," Derby writes, "to answer my amorous request to name the attributes that she would most admire in me by painting a picture of none other but Seymour" (169). Thus, the unhappy prospect for Sternheim's married life resulted not exclusively from the badness of the husband, but also from the wrong choice made by the wife and by her continued affection for the other man. The novel ultimately arranges a situation in which the woman does not and should not abandon her own wishes in order to placate her family, her husband, or any other representative of patriarchal society.[20] Through the device of the false wedding, Sternheim and Derby are released from what would otherwise have meant, again within the terms of eighteenth-century middle-class discourse, a thoroughly unpleasant married life, or years of self-abasement by the woman, perhaps ending in her death (a life course that Friderika Baldinger's marriage, especially as illuminated by her letters, brutally describes). Their marriage is instead dissolved: once Sternheim learns that the wedding had been conducted by a fake pastor and that she is therefore free to end the relationship, she does.

This is presented as a traumatic event for Sternheim. In terms of the novel's class politics, however, her extrication from the sexually obsessed court aristocrat is a victory for the educated middle class; when Sternheim takes stock of herself after her initial horror and bewilderment, she confirms herself as still meeting middle-class standards: "My heart is innocent and pure, the powers of my intellect are undiminished, the faculties of my soul and my good inclinations remain in full measure, and I still have the capacity to do good."[21] As to the weeks during which she believed she was married, she makes almost no analysis and draws no conclusions, although in her disguise as a widow she gives herself the status of a previously married woman.

A later passage in the novel stages a discussion of unhappy marriage that ends by allowing women the right to decide to remain single. Sternheim, to be sure, is positioned in the discussion to take the ideologically dominant stance of defending marriage, but the minor character who produces the critique is Sternheim's alter ego, taking stands similar to those Sternheim herself had proposed in a curiously parallel conversation she had held with the prince in the first half of the novel (147–48). Frau von C., a young widow (such as Sternheim purports to be), refuses to remarry, even though she has four seemingly attractive offers. When the heroine talks with her about this decision, the widow states simply that she wants to enjoy the freedom now that she has had to purchase with so much bitterness earlier.[22] Sternheim responds with a mixed message: "It is not wrong of you to love your freedom and enjoy it in every possible manner; but would not its best use be to make someone happy of your own free will?"[23] Sternheim proclaims herself attracted by the idea of female self-sacrifice—an assertion not supported by her actions: she had not become the prince's mistress to make her aunt happy; she had not altered her behavior to make her presumed husband happy, and later, she does not marry the utterly worthy Lord Rich to make him happy. Sternheim's alter ego in the discussion is not lured by martyrdom, arguing, instead, that the result of a new marriage could well be unhappiness on both sides. One's own happiness, in this thoroughly secular book, is an important standard for determining the success or failure of a choice. The alter ego explains: "You did not know that beneficence directed my first choice, but I have learned too well that one can make others happy without being so oneself. I don't have the heart to venture once more onto the uncertain ground where the flowers of pleasure soon fade under the blight of care" (196). Relying on metaphor, the widow alludes frequently to the misery of the married state as concealed—a hidden chain (189), "the mass of thorns under these roses" (189). These figures are summarized in the name that Sternheim chose for herself after her own experience of marriage: she calls herself Madame Suffering (rendered in Britt's English translation as Mrs. Leidens), thereby both announcing and concealing her sorrows in her proper name. Disguised by the device of the false wedding, the disastrousness of Sternheim's first marriage is similarly proclaimed and concealed right in the middle of the book.

Sternheim produces another argument that subordinates the woman's interests to those of others. She says Frau von C. should marry for the sake of her daughter and her father; both of them have unspoken stakes in keeping the woman enmeshed in patriarchal forms, the daughter because it affects her own marriage prospects and the father because his prestige and authority are connected to the propriety of his daughter's marital behavior. The widow, however, does not let these considerations overrule her own feelings and wishes, either. Again she answers that for her own sake, she would not undertake such a commitment and continues: "You embarrass me deeply . . . but my sad experiences make me rebel against the idea of *any* union. I wish worthier wives for these men than I would be, even if I were as they imagine me; but my neck is so bruised from my first yoke that even the lightest silk tie would oppress it" (190). Monika Nenon suggests that the episode entails both the assertion of women's right to lead a life independent of men and criticism of male behavior for turning marriage into a yoke.²⁴ Yet, if even a silk ribbon is oppressive, the problem is the constrictions that marriage itself places on women. The very fact that the men whom the widow rejects are not rogues or tyrants also aims the criticism more bluntly at marriage. Sternheim's acceptance of the widow's decision against marriage, grudging and patronizing though it is, gives moral validation to a young woman of the educated middle class or lower aristocracy living on her own. The novel allows for the possibility that an experience similar to Sternheim's could legitimately lead a woman to reject marriage.

The many writings of Sophie La Roche, beginning with *Sternheim*, and continuing for over three decades, are nonetheless often read as diligently preparing girls to meet the conventional late eighteenth-century notion of middle-class womanhood, with its predetermined roles as submissive wife, self-sacrificing mother, and well-disciplined manager of the home. Bernd Heidenreich, for example, acknowledges the economic security that Sternheim achieves through her marriage to Lord Seymour, but sees the union primarily as a reward for her virtue, especially because, in his interpretation, the only place in which a proper woman can experience love is in marriage. He categorizes the book as a "middle-class family novel" ["bürgerlicher Familienroman"].²⁵ Nenon, in response, points out that for considerable stretches, the novel shows no family life at all, but instead depicts an independent and unmarried young woman on her own; Nenon describes the autonomy of the subject, Sternheim in particular, as a principle theme of the novel, one in tension, as she sees it, with the propaganda for female subordination as wife-mother-housekeeper.²⁶ Silvia Bovenschen, on the other hand, describes the same novel as stressing the notion of passive, receptive femininity posed by (male-ordered versions of) *Empfindsamkeit*, and as minimizing women's claims to scholarliness, since learning was associated with qualities of active sensibility, intelligence, and aesthetic capacity that were irreconcilable with such femininity.²⁷ Sally Winkle, categorizing *Geschichte des Fräuleins von Sternheim* as a transitional novel in a transitional time, responds to Bovenschen by arguing that the qualities of Sternheim associated with *Empfindsamkeit* are "conducive to the activity and participation of women in the public sphere."²⁸ Winkle writes that "La Roche's positive portrayal of numerous independent, single or widowed women in her first novel stands in juxtaposition to the emphasis placed on marriage and sentimental love evident elsewhere in the narrative" (66). My argument is that juxtaposing contrasting values and ideas is a principle technique of La

Roche throughout her writings, along with locating daring discourse in marginal figures.

Over the years, Sophie La Roche made a number of comments about the unsayable, referring at one point to "ideas that I did not want to say aloud."[29] She sensed the possibility of other notions about women and men, notions excluded by the very framework in which her emotional, intellectual, and cultural world was situated. Sometimes she could even name them, although it was unacceptable, she wrote, to do so "at home,"[30] (one of the small signals that her husband had reservations about the practices she was living and writing). She wanted writing, especially writing in which she was not obviously bound by the familiar constraints of "real" life, to give her a locus for deviant ideas. Most of what she wrote was easily sayable to be sure; she was a skilled mouthpiece for the dominant discourse. Originally, she had thought that the novel would permit her to write as she wanted, but the narrative strategies available to her in the genre were inadequate. In a letter penned immediately after *Sternheim* was published, where La Roche reported she had hoped to use the novel's characters to express thoughts that she did not dare to espouse directly, she noted that to a large extent she had failed, unable even through the mouthpiece of fictional characters to say everything that she thought, felt, and saw (155). La Roche asserted a disparity between what she thought she would do in her writing and what she actually did, and she connected the issue with genre. The novel did not assist her as she had hoped. The recognition of self-censorship loomed most clearly to her—and so she blamed herself for being cautious. Overcoming the web of inhibitions would become more difficult later. Like Fanny Burney in England writing *Evelina*, Sophie La Roche had been able to compose her first novel in obscurity and publish it anonymously. But once her anonymity was punctured, her freedom vanished: she had a reputation to protect. Then, as Eva Figes observes of Burney, La Roche's novels "became more sentimental and more self-consciously didactic." Also like Burney, she "struggled to avoid anything contentiously 'political.' "[31] Figes calculates that for Burney, and also Maria Edgeworth, the result of this "enormous, even if insidious" moral and social pressure was that "their first book remained their best one" (23). But since La Roche also connected the threshold of the sayable with genre, she searched to see if another genre might be more satisfactory, trying moral tales, a journal called *Pomona*, travel books, and eventually innovative books about herself and her personal world. Still, not being an iconoclastic thinker, La Roche wanted to say the unsayable, not necessarily to argue for enacting it.

Also, even with the feeling-woman model, the gaps in La Roche's education still undermined her confidence. In *Pomona,* the monthly periodical for girls that La Roche produced in 1783 and 1784, one of the letters that she addressed to a hypothetical model girl named Lina was again explicit on this point:

> Your brother knows me enough to be certain that I never like to judge anything, partly because I feel that I lack a quantity of fundamental knowledge, and partly also because in my character and in my taste I am aware of something strange that very often causes me to look at matters from a different side and thus also gives me different ideas from what other people have.[32]

As long as men had the right to ordain how women should think, women had to worry about the deviancy, the "something strange," they might fall into if left on their own. La Roche both does and does not want to write her deviancy. Not comfortable with what she did write, she was nonetheless fearful of what she might write.

She also knew that "something strange" in the form of resistance and refusal was often brought about when people were given rigid instructions about their behavior: "Prescriptions and assertions about this and that signal domination, and it is so appealing to resist domination, to avoid doing what is wanted, and to evade the circle where it prevails." She proposed another way of inculcating right conduct, through stories, since, "A storyteller on the other hand seems to want only to entertain and to pass the time pleasantly; that is why people like him and are glad to take from his hand the flower of a beautiful insight or a fruit of useful ideas" (207). La Roche's fondness for representing discussion in her writings produced possibilities for invoking resistance (without having to bear full responsibility for it) through one character's strong assertion of a conventional truth and another's opposition. The sporadic resistance against prescription could help locate the invisible barriers to alternative discourses.

La Roche's writings repeatedly show inconsistencies, fragmentary experiments with other possibilities, and contradictions. It is precisely these breaks, as postmodern criticism often argues, that can be particularly interesting. Winkle, for example, characterizes La Roche's conversation with the wise man as an anomalous insertion of the retrograde ideology of sexual characteristics into an otherwise progressive text (71–73). Yet, it is here, I argue, in La

Roche's embellishment on the doctrine of sexual characteristics, that the text makes a crucial move empowering women, equating the value of feeling in women with thinking in men. Nenon describes the discussion between Sternheim and the widowed Frau von C. as appearing in the text unexpectedly. Yet, this unexpected intrusion makes the valuable contribution of allowing the consequences of an unhappy marriage, such as Sternheim and Derby had had, to be analyzed from the perspective of a former wife, a perspective hard to articulate in a patriarchal society. In addition to material that breaks into the narrative, marginal figures such as the widow often pose marginal ideas that help change the options available to women. These techniques and their effects are evident in La Roche's introduction of controversy into several standard topics, including education, mothers, and men, and they in turn flavor her relationships with other women.

The Tale of the Beautiful Band and Another Marriage Resister

In her narrative writing, La Roche continued to depict women who did not fit the usual prescriptions for proper behavior; she had begun with Frau von C. in *Sternheim* and proceeded with certain characters such as Madame Guden in *Rosaliens Briefe*. In the tale "Der schöne Bund" "The Beautiful Band" (1789), the unusual figure is a studious young woman, one of the band of four friends named in the title. The story that La Roche creates for this girl participates in determining the late eighteenth-century meaning and evaluation of such a young woman whose ambitions differed from the prescribed norms. To characterize the four girls, all educated at a small boarding school, which is vaguely described—without mentioning anything taught there except the expansion of the girls' hearts—the text begins by stressing the admirable qualities they share: they are all good, eager to learn, capable of friendship, calm, obedient, properly industrious, and neat. The differentiation among them is schematic: "Elise always distinguished herself by being the most precise; just as Auguste liked to undertake the most difficult and most artistic work, Julie preferred occupying herself with books, and Mina with music and singing."[33] The basic format of the story is typical of La Roche, character testing: "Soon . . . the four friends came into different situations, in which their attitudes and principles were tested in several ways" (205). It at first appears that the testing will involve marriage, the event that was almost relentlessly constructed for women in eighteenth-century literature by men, but for two of the girls in La Roche's story this is not so. Julie perceives her desire for book learning as probably excluding marriage. Auguste wants, instead of marrying, to find fulfillment through her three female friendships. By describing these two as neither beautiful nor rich, La Roche used the iconography of eighteenth-century women's literature to confirm that marriage might in fact not be a suitable arrangement for them. Only Elise and Mina hope for noble-minded husbands with whom they can have satisfying lives.

Julie's case, the first in the story, is a positive representation of a

Sophie La Roche at a desk. Engraver, C. Schule. Source: La Roche, *Mein Schreibetisch*, 1799.

scholarly young woman in the late eighteenth century. Julie desires for herself plenty of reading material, chances to learn languages, and a place to live in a community of scholars who would help her to perfect her learning (186). Not infringing directly on male prerogatives, the girl does not seek to attend the university, for example, or to become an independent scholar herself. On the other hand, the story makes no effort to apologize for Julie's intellectual aspirations and initially offers no ostensibly womanly justification for her deeds. It emphasizes, instead, what a young woman goes through to pursue learning. Among the factors are her parents:

> Julie's father, a respected legal scholar and a man who was rather proud of his learning, was delighted about his daughter's desire for knowledge because he regarded it as part of the contribution of his own intellect, and he dedicated every hour of his leisure to her, gave her books, and even read with her. The mother on the other hand, a woman of little intellect but with an inclination toward stinginess, regarded the continued development of the understanding of her daughter and the attention she got with displeasure, and the neglect of necessary household tasks served as a pretext for her complaints about wasting time and buying books. . . . (205–6)

La Roche represents the parents' attitudes as determined by the extent to which the girl resembles each of them, and thus, by their own gender-based relationships to scholarliness; it is not the designation of Julie as female that affects their behavior as much as it is their own gender. The father, seeing Julie as an admirable reproduction of himself, is proud of her and assists her in pursuing the scholarship that, by implication, he as a man has readily received; the mother, disinterested in book learning, and presumably not well acquainted with it because of her categorization as a woman, feels that her intellectual daughter has no relation to her and is taking up her husband's attention (and perhaps also affection). She tries to force Julie back into the traditional script to which she herself conforms.

In La Roche's fictions, the mother often has as an ally a young woman who is intent on marriage and who pursues this project by fulfilling conventional expectations. To her, the heroine is a dangerous rival and, because of her unconventionality (shown in La Roche's writing most often by an interest in learning), a worrisomely unfamiliar one. In "Der schöne Bund" the mother's ally is her spoiled younger daughter, Babette, who claims, for example, that she cannot sleep because of Julie's reading light. Julie consults with her friend Auguste, the young woman devoted to friendship.

Auguste suggests that Julie try waking up to read in the early hours of the morning. But Babette, trying to prevent Julie from reading altogether, complains about this solution, too, so that Julie promises to give it up. Again Auguste has a suggestion, showing Julie how she can write at night in the dark, using the fold of paper to guide her hand. Subtly, reading has turned into writing. But again, the sister foils this attempt by screaming when the rustling of paper awakens her. Both parents are roused and Julie confesses to her father what she has done. The incident, offering more proof of Julie's "irresistible desire for knowledge" and also displaying the harsh reaction of the girl's mother, who threatens Julie with blows, stirs the father so much that "he comforted Julie kindly and scolded Babette" (209).

This, however, is not a solution; in fact, now Julie's mother forbids her to see her friend Auguste, and allows only occasional letters between the two young women. Julie becomes a prisoner to her mother and to the submissiveness required of girls. Auguste recommends precisely this behavior: "Endure, my dear! Show them that learning improves our hearts and our minds. Whoever exerts all his energy toward the fulfillment of his duties, still always has time left over for the enjoyment of noble pleasures" (209). Auguste tries to reconcile the usual didactic incantations about duties with a degendered version of the discourse of learning. It is the implacable Babette who finally drives matters to an irreversible point, and Julie begs her father on her knees to separate her from her sister. This produces the necessary happy end, for Julie is sent off to live with a brother, "where she enjoyed the double happiness of learning a thousand useful things by being with her brother and his friends and receiving help in reading everything that cultivates women's intellect." It was the exact fulfillment of her wishes.

Julie's desire to follow her "irresistible" urge is accepted in the end. She continues her studies even though it means leaving her family, or rather, leaving the company of her anti-intellectual mother and controlling sister, for that of her understanding and scholarly brother. Again, the conventional relation of learning to gender is the unspoken framework, with the brother's devotion to learning never at issue. The penalty, however, that La Roche imposes on Julie for her independence, and for partially breaking society's gender-linked expectations about "true manly scholarliness" is that she has to perform compensatory service. She does so in the only way that is both bookish and available to women, by teaching children. The task is described in metaphor: ". . . she took over conducting her niece, leading her with equal doses of cleverness and love along the path of virtue to the temple of female merit" (211). In certain respects, this outcome, which positions Julie like the aunt of Lina, was simply another form of motherhood being foisted off on a mildly deviant woman to bring her back into the fold.[34] And yet, teaching fits the scholarly life that Julie desired.

Of the two women in "Der schöne Bund" who are interested in finding husbands, only one has the romantic experience usually depicted in eighteenth-century fiction about financially secure women. Elise's family asks her to marry a man she does not like, and she acquiesces. In the conventional sense, Mina is the only fortunate one: after being cured of her unacceptable fondness for making sarcastic remarks, she marries happily and wholeheartedly. Julie and Auguste, on the other hand, never marry, and yet, escape without blame on that account. Most important, by devising a studious life for Julie, La Roche proposes an alternative to marriage, making that institution less compulsory than is usually acknowledged. As Rachel Brownstein notes in her discussion of the lessons girls learn from reading fiction, "the marriage plot most novels depend on is about finding validation of one's uniqueness and importance by being singled out among all other women by a man. The man's love is proof of the girl's value and payment for it."[35] Part of "Der schöne Bund" repudiated this message. This is a distinctive and important accomplishment.

Yet, at the same time Julie's rejection of marriage was in part an acceptance of an important mechanism of social control, a mechanism that defined female scholarship as irreconcilable with family and home. Wieland, for example, had argued in an essay about the famous seventeenth-century scholarly woman, Anna Maria van Schurman, that all unusual women should remain virgins—a stipulation he did not apply to men. If a woman were going to be unusual, she should not marry and have a family, he contended, and conversely, if she wanted to marry and have a family, she should not be extraordinary.[36] Although Sophie La Roche worked to allow women as much opportunity for learning as the equation of men with intellect and women with emotion would permit, she usually also repeated the familiar argument that housework was women's primary duty: "Make sure, my dear, that your first knowledge is always of your duties."[37] And when La Roche wrote her own brief account of Anna Maria van Schurman, she praised the scholarly women's statement that women's right to intellectual activity disappeared whenever child care, or housework, or other "necessary work" required their time and energy:

3: THE ENABLING EFFECT OF DIFFERENCE 115

> For what help would it be to the weak child, the sick husband, and the housekeeping, if the woman spoke every language but did not know how to take care of her child, raise her son or daughter, care for and comfort her husband, and direct the business of the home? Knowledge in the head can always be acquired from books in order to be dazzling, but active, useful goodness of the soul, helpfulness, advice, joy, instruction in a thousand affairs of living are found only in the heart that knows and loves its duties.[38]

This is the perspective that could exclude almost all women from making learning a major part of their lives. La Roche does not connect such pronouncements with her own early efforts at child bearing and child raising while writing. She gave birth eight times (between 1756 and 1768), with five of the children surviving infancy. When the last was born, she was thirty-eight. She had already secretly started to compose *Sternheim*. The both/and possibility of learning and family is dimly left open even in pronouncements about duties—since the multilingual woman could also know how to care for her children, comfort her husband, and manage the home, if, as these duties imply, she had the help available to the educated middle class, and if the children were not too numerous and the husband not too emotionally needy. But such a woman, who combines learning with marriage and family, is visible in the texts only when La Roche writes about herself, or, in some cases, when others write about her. After an afternoon visiting the famous woman, a young visitor, Johann Heinrich Landolt, testified:

> she seems to be a true model of the excellent woman. She is not ashamed, as many who want to appear learned are, to be a woman—she considers it an honor and pleasure to be a housewife and mother of five children, whom she loves tenderly and by whom she is loved the same way in return. With the female virtues she combines strength and solidity of intellect, and love of knowledge. Her thoughts she always expresses in the most appropriate and best words, without however anxiously searching for them.[39]

Although he mentions nothing about La Roche's writing, which must surely have been the reason he had stopped to visit her, he stressed her identity as housewife, mother, and learned, articulate woman. Julie in "The Beautiful Band," in contrast, had to flee the first two of these roles in order to pursue the third.

La Roche had derived opportunities for cultural agency from the idea of the sensitive woman, she had produced arguments that allowed herself and other women to extend their learning (despite marriage and children), but her discontent with the exclusion of women from serious eighteenth-century scholarship endured.[40] In her *Briefe über Mannheim*, La Roche alludes several times to women learning Latin, in one place writing, "The writings of the ancients fill my soul with respect and sadness; the spirit of the Greeks and Romans gave immortality to the works of its sons and used them as the foundation of science—and for millennia to follow as the model of every great and beautiful thought—why is their language not as familiar to me as it is to my friends Mariane F——s and St——n and my Jenny S——s and Madame N——n?"[41] The hope that, despite everything, women would one day be admitted to scholarship persisted in La Roche's writings.

Menacing Mothers, Dangerous Men

"Der schöne Bund" is distinguished both by the persistence with which an approved heroine pursued her desire to read and by the depiction in some detail of an unreasonable, selfish, and jealous mother. More than once in her novels and stories La Roche presented such women, often, as in "The Beautiful Band," showing them fearing and rejecting women's learning. This text and many others, including the autobiography of Friderika Baldinger, have no room for another perspective of this tension between mothers and daughters. And yet, the effort to identify such a perspective helps in constructing a hypothesis about an aspect of women's participation in what was recognized in the eighteenth century as literary life: Women who sought scholarly learning and the culture that went with it were rejecting the artistic culture that women themselves had devised under conditions of considerable separation from men. Little recorded and hard to characterize though that culture is to us, it is possible to use the asides about women's activities, to recast the negatives in descriptions of traditional women, and to draw on the theories about the cultural consequences of a society highly polarized by gender to propose some of its possible characteristics. Women's traditional culture was probably pious, daily, repetitive, produced and often used in the home, not usually requiring a grand design (certainly smaller in scale than the palace-building, mural-painting, encyclopedia-writing culture of elite eighteenth-century men), often performative (singing, playing keyboard instruments) and group-oriented. It was also probably less inclined to value individual accomplishment than group satisfaction, with the group including children, at least at those levels of society where women did some or all of the mothering of their babies and children; this culture was not scholarly and not recognized as literary (fairy tales transmitted orally, for example, were not validated as literature) and it was always subordinate and secondary to "real" culture, which was male. It was a culture that women had developed for themselves outside formal education, outside printing presses, subscription lists, and the other male cultural machinery. Women did not need a man's permission to enter women's culture (such as Fräulein von Sternheim needed and got from the German poet in the form of the feeling-woman notion in order to enter men's culture). But women's culture was devalued, which is one of the reasons so little of it is preserved today. Of course, men neither wanted nor sought admission to women's culture. Yet, the women who participated in women's culture also struggled to get recognition and approval from men—and, at least in the usual depiction, were competing with other women for husbands. In fact, the view of marriage as success for women, and as partly based on their skill in women's culture (stitchery, cooking, music, for example), is the only way in which women and their culture are legitimated in men's literary culture (it should be gratuitous to point out that in "real" life, women's culture probably proved its worth and functionality in many other ways, in child rearing, for instance, and in supporting the transition of middle class women to becoming operational managers of the home in early capitalism).[42]

From the perspective of women devoted to this culture, scholarly learning lured women to abandon their own already devalued culture and join men's, instead. Scholarly learning thus separated women oriented toward women's culture from those oriented toward men's culture—in many cases a separation of mothers from daughters and of sisters from sisters, since it was apparently very difficult for women to demonstrate allegiance to both cultures at once (although La Roche at some points tried to accomplish this, too). In short, the feeling-woman notion as a way of giving women access to male culture contributed to the estrangement among women, a situation often demonstrated by the lack of a positive place for mothers not oriented toward male culture in the writings of the daughters. The daughters' desire for "knowledge," conflicted though it was, meant rejection of the mothers' lives and disparagement of their kind of cultural activity. Thus, in her autobiography Friderika Baldinger dismissed her mother with patronizing phrases, and left her sister almost completely out while writing considerably about her older brother (as an instrument for her learning). Sophie La Roche's mother and sisters (and brothers—all younger) are similarly faintly praised or omitted from her numerous self-histories;[43] the other women in her family seem to have remained within the culture of women (and the boys were too much younger to matter).

The situation of mothers is impacted in another way, too, by their daughters' attraction to male-ordered thought: the depiction of female characters, such as Julie and Fräulein von Sternheim, is rooted in androcentric Enlightenment notions of personhood that emphasize the autonomy of the heroine. In many instances, the heroine's father, and especially her mother, are killed off in order to produce the independence and autonomy this notion requires. "The mothers of fictional heroines are usually bad and living or good and dead."[44] Motherlessness is much more important for female than for male protagonists. Werther has no father, but Goethe could grant him a shadowy mother without any difficulty. (Neither Werther nor Sternheim has siblings.) For female heroines, the pattern is reversed: the female parent must die first in order for the girl's sense of self to develop. Fräulein von Sternheim's mother died very early, her father many years later (though still early in the first part of the book). The dead mother became an adored saint, while the live daughter was justified in doing all kinds of unusual things that a "good mother," in person, could not have permitted, but that gave the girl an independent identity.

And yet, La Roche herself frequently took on the role of aging mother, almost grandmother, to her readers. To men, the role positioned her in a way that was sexually neutral and thus simplified the interaction.[45] To women, the role drew attention to La Roche's age. Figuring herself as a paper mother (the counterpart to the "paper daughter" she wrote of creating in the figure of Sternheim), she called herself Mama to a series of almost grown girls and young married women to whom she addressed letters and works, such as the correspondence in *Pomona*. The age status she thus attained operates to free her from some of the constraints of femininity; Rousseau, for example, writing in *Emil* about the differing consequences of their sex for men and women, had made a glancing possibility of exceptions for older women: "The male is male only at certain moments. The female is female her whole life or at least during her whole youth."[46] La Roche had been over forty when *Geschichte des Fräuleins von Sternheim* was published, and in her early fifties when writing *Pomona*. She was old enough to command respect and a degree of authority, yet, as a mere paper mother, she did not jeopardize her readers' and correspondents' autonomy;

similarly, as herself a literary woman, she provoked minimal conflict with younger readers aspiring to enter literary life.

But the power and authority of women, regardless of their age or maternity, in the world that La Roche inscribes, is always limited by the greater power and authority of men. It is a situation she shows men routinely abusing. Indeed, La Roche's writings contain many passages criticizing men. Sometimes her tone is humorous and understated: "The division between Apollo, the god of the sciences, and Minerva, the goddess of wisdom, was very pleasing to me, and I found it often accurate; for (speaking very softly) wisdom is not always present among the sons of Apollo."[47] Sometimes the tone is blunt and resentful: "Men always consider themselves to be masters of all creation" (1784:171). Sometimes it is wary, as in an answer to a *Pomona* reader's question: "What is politics and does it also serve us women? I hope my valued friend has not let herself be misled by any volatile male head into posing questions to me that are like a kind of trap in which my mind could be very wickedly ensnared if I were to express myself incautiously" (1784:203). Indeed, her admonitions to Lina about contentment with class begin to take on a different ring in the context of her comments about men. Practicing the renunciation required to keep the class structure unchanged seems like a rehearsal for an even more irksome, because more immediate, submission—submission to men (of the woman's class or higher).

La Roche explicitly defends women's submission to men in several places, but she often does so in a dialog form that enables her to say her partner, always a younger woman, is not satisfied with her incantation of the dominant discourse. A note of helplessness creeps in here. It is vivid in the issue of *Pomona* where La Roche announces she is acquiescing to the advice of several men to drop from the journal the excerpts from "The Seasons" that she had been periodically using (1783:31–84, 474–99, 770–84). She defends her choice of the poem, but capitulates to the male advice nonetheless. In writing to her readers about this situation, her confidence and sovereignty have vanished. La Roche had assumed an authoritative voice originally because, as she said at the immediate outset of the first issue of *Pomona*, she could speak "as a woman"; she uses the phrase "ich als Frau" (1783:1). Now she tries to frame her action as a matter of being pleasing—to men: "For since it is ordered by Nature and the law that we are supposed to please men, it is good when we know what they like most. This attention seems however to prove our dependence and could arouse an unpleasant thought in some of my readers" (1783:831). On the next page she produces such a reader, a younger self, saying, "Yes, Mama La Roche, if it were only a matter of the wishes [of men], then it would be acceptable, but soon this turns into a matter of orders and demands for a certain obedience. How should one regard that? especially when they are often unjust and wrong" (1783:832). La Roche can only claim that it takes more strength to submit in such a situation—and then acknowledge that the younger woman was "not quite satisfied" with this explanation. She does not refute the young woman's characterization of men as wrongly and unjustly demanding obedience.

In fact, from the beginning La Roche had created unjust and violent male characters who practice their brutality, or threaten to practice it, on women. One such man says: "If I could have robbed her of her charming figure and all her talents, I would have done it at that moment. It would have been easier for me to see her miserable, ugly—yes even dead, than to be a witness to her moral destruction."[48] These are the words in *Geschichte des Fräulein von Sternheim* of the hero Seymour, rabid in his self-righteousness. His sense of moral superiority (unaccompanied by courage) led the masked Seymour to tell Sternheim at a ball that her jewelry and vile costume, financed by the prince, were the price of her virtue, and that all present despised her for her fall (153); these were the charges that precipitated her flight into marriage with Derby, the only person offering help. Although Derby is the designated villain in the novel, La Roche names Seymour's cruelty and has Derby point it out to him.

> [Derby] laughed at me and maintained that with all his reputation for wickedness, he caused less damage than I through my virtuous zeal. He says his wickedness carries a kind of warning with it that puts people on their guard, whereas the severity of my principles leads me to judge apparent and inevitable human faults with such cruelty that the wicked become more obstinate and good people are driven to desperation. How could *Derby* utter this truth? I feel—yes, I feel that he was right, that I was cruel, that it was I—wretch that I am—who have made the best of women miserable! (163)

Both men are sadistic in their dealings with women. As Kathy Ferguson notes, "Sadism organizes a narrative of investigation in which the choice between kindness and cruelty is secondary to the prior claim to an unqualified right to define."[49] Derby attempts to define Sternheim as sensual, while Seymour defines her as contemptible—once she has appeared to deviate from his notion of virtue. And to make sure that his right to define is unqualified, Seymour appears in a mask and disappears without allowing his victim a chance to speak.

The "narrative of investigation" that Ferguson associates with sadism appears at several points in La Roche's accounts of men's relations with women. The original premise of Seymour's behavior toward Sternheim, for example, was based on the instructions of his uncle, who knew that Sternheim's aristocratic aunt (the one who had opposed allowing the colonel to marry into her family) and uncle had brought the young woman to court so that she would become the prince's mistress. Seymour's uncle forbade him to warn the unwitting young woman, and said he would not countenance the marriage of his nephew to a woman of doubtful reputation; Seymour should simply watch (and judge) how events unfolded. Seymour quickly agrees: "I imagined the struggle of virtue as a delightful drama."[50] He assumes a voyeuristic stance, with the woman's sufferings presented as a performance staged for his pleasure and for the purposes of his sadistic investigation. In another place he writes of "the beloved image of suffering virtue" (193). La Roche's next novel, *Rosaliens Briefe*, contains a similar situation, perhaps even crueler. Rosalie's husband decides to test the character of his young wife by pretending to be in love with another woman. The result for Rosalia is pain and suffering,[51] and yet, the husband, Cleberg, is set forth as a model man. Men of all kinds—not just the villains—are dangerous to women.

Some of the men in La Roche's writings are simply selfish and cruel (and misogynist) without any particular note of sadism. In one of the moral tales, for example, the hero's father is such a man: "His father was a handsome but also very hard man, who loved display, sucked on the marrow of his underlings, and was raw and harsh to his amiable wife because she gave him too many children and was too kind with the people. He was actually happy when, shortly after giving birth to twins, she died, and the two children followed her, for the poor creatures were girls as well."[52] Although other male figures that she creates show no cruelty, it is striking that those who do include the ostensibly good men as well as the bad ones.

The indicators of cruelty and sadism in the male characters and the caustic, wary, or seemingly jocular comments about men by the narrator (often in the guise of quotations)[53] occur amidst a glut of obeisances to men, such as a patriarchal accolade to Sophie von Sternheim's father that opens the novel, or, in the letters to Lina, the letter writer's displays of servile deference to Lina's brother.

Nonetheless, despite the importance of men, good and bad, in the world of La Roche's writing, she is strikingly interested in women and in their support for each other.

THE MONTHLY *POMONA* AND ITS AUDIENCES

Ulrike Prokop, Barbara Duden and other feminist scholars studying the late eighteenth century have argued that it was a time of narrowing opportunities for women of the educated middle class. Duden sees a culture depriving women of the sense of self that was the key to self-worth, and instead, orienting them toward their husbands.[54] Prokop, emphasizing the exclusion of middle-class women from recognized cultural production, sees them herded into hopelessness and self-destruction, with marriage as their only option for social viability, symbolized by the notion of the "great pair" as the only source for womanly fulfillment. The pair was rigorously conceptualized as heterosexual; indeed, a key element of Prokop's argument is the separation of women from each other and their inability to derive productive emotional satisfaction (as opposed to the emotional sedation that could come from their roles as passive consumers of culture) from other women, or from their own work.[55] Prokop's examples come chiefly from among women who were close to the men who dominated eighteenth-century Germany's cultural landscape, especially Goethe. Duden's analysis of how women were discouraged from developing a sense of self concentrates on the popularized philosophy that reached so widely through the middle-class population. In her conclusion, Duden acknowledges that her argument is painted in broad strokes even as she recapitulates her key hypothesis: "With the apparent liberation of woman from the 'raw' conditions of the 'old society' the new form of her oppression was relocated into the woman herself. Nevertheless this new form of repression was never complete and certainly never unresisted; but whoever wanted to oppose it had to fight with the difficulty of needing to rebel against her 'own' cultural femininity."[56] Even more, the relative decline of real women's status into decorative domestics is reinforced by the appearance of the feminine as an ideal, for instance in the literature of Weimar Classicism. In this context, an important part of the accomplishment of Sophie La Roche is the encouragement she gave women to formulate their own agendas and to act together, rather than lapsing into idealized passivity. Indeed, it is precisely during this period that unprecedented numbers of women entered into active literary life, an indication that not all women were absorbed into selflessness.

Beyond her public starting point as a renowned novelist, La Roche's support for alternatives for women came in six ways, in the depiction of satisfying relationships among women (such relationships form the context for the beautiful band and the writing situation of the heroine in *Fräulein von Sternheim*), in her promotion of education for women at the same time that she offered women a way to circumvent unmeetable educational prerequisites for writing, in the representations she wrote of herself as a successful model of a culturally productive woman, in the incorporation of different women's voices into her writings, in her experiments with genre and style, and, finally, in her own direct efforts to encourage women to write, particularly by initiating a literary group for women. While La Roche was not able to devise a line of argument objecting to women's cultural idealization, the image she created of herself was a potent form of resistance, as was her increased inclination toward fragmentation and toward the relatively literal use of language.[57] The public construction of La Roche as a woman enjoying her literary ties and talents and using them in cultural production contrasts strongly with that of her contemporary Catharina Elisabeth Goethe, who also represented herself as enjoying her literary ties, but stressed having acquired them through reproduction, thereby leaving cultural productivity an intact male preserve and defining her own position strictly in relation to a man, the mother-son relationship also being a version of the great pair.[58]

In the early 1780s, when La Roche decided to be the third woman in Germany to publish a monthly journal for other women, she had a vehicle for working on all four areas of her program for women, beginning with education. Education, of course, was a vital topic for women in the upper strata of the middle class and indirectly for those in the aristocracy, too. La Roche's writings are filled with reports of educational schemes and proposals for how to teach and learn, always with class and gender together as the determinants of curriculum. And class in these texts is beyond the individual's control. After *Geschichte des Fräuleins von Sternheim*, La Roche was less inclined to depict members of the middle class being elevated into the aristocracy or marrying up; having attained praise and financial support from the aristocracy, she emphasized contentment with one's existing station in life. This, in fact, is one of the primary messages of the letters to Lina that are a frequent part of *Pomona*. The point is made already in the first sentence of the first letter: "I want, my dear, to keep the promise that I made to you when we were talking at your brother's about happiness and pleasure, and I claimed that Providence had assigned a certain amount of each to all classes and to every period of human life."[59] Later, several of the Lina letters structured around the rooms of a house continue to stress being satisfied with whatever class one is in. Since Lina is a member of an educated middle-class family with no wealth, she receives the gender and class-related advice to restrict her aspirations for learning. At one point, for instance, a letter draws Lina's attention to a book called *Schauplatz der Natur* "The Theater of Nature" and says this one volume contains "everything that a reasonable girl of your class can wish and should wish to know" (1783:288). Similarly, in a brief essay called "Knowledge of Scholarly Disciplines" explaining some of the logic of the Lina letters, La Roche writes, "Here I must repeat to the dear readers of *Pomona* that I do not want to have my Lina be scholarly."[60] Further consideration of such statements capping girls' educational ambitions makes an important point about the way La Roche uses context to modify her conventional messages.

The juxtaposition of unreconciled opinions and ideas and the inconsistency of La Roche's prescriptions for individual others with her reports about herself are her two most important techniques for diluting her frequent restatements of conventional propriety. Thus, although it is possible to identify in the Lina letters a series of statements arguing that girls' education should be limited, the seriousness of such statements, or rather the indications of their applicability to other girls of the educational middle class, is considerably curbed when the Lina letters are considered in their original setting in *Pomona*. The modifications appear in the fact that the stands taken in the letters are juxtaposed with conflicting images and advice elsewhere in the same publication, in the form of the narrator's presentation of herself and of other women whom she admires, and because the intended audience of the Lina letters is restricted. In the first issue of *Pomona*, La Roche wrote briefly about her expected readers:

> I hope that my readers will allow me here to say frankly how I imagine them. Many of them already know everything that they will find in *Pomona*, and more. They will go through my articles with reasonable curiosity about how a German woman, who until now wrote only novels, will go about talking in separate pages about all the things that have occupied the greatest men for so many centuries. . . .
>
> Other readers, *whose home and circumstances are not so favorable that they can enrich their minds as they wish*, will find it not displeasing

that Pomona thinks she is speaking with all of them about what their lovable companion Lina wants to hear.[61]

According to this, the letters to Lina are not at all the centerpiece[62] of *Pomona*, and do not represent general advice presumed to be valid for all young women in the journal's audience. Instead, they are an effort to respond to the limitations imposed on a less fortunate subset of readers, those who are not allowed to learn as they wish or cannot afford a life that is intellectually rich.

Pomona was the first widely read educational and literary journal published by and for women, and the letters to Lina there are embedded in a context that from the start displays a generous educational vision, providing useful information, introducing educational schemes, and proposing intellectual skillbuilding techniques, all quite different from many of the prescriptions for Lina. The first *Pomona* issue, for example, included an explanation of what inspired La Roche to publish a periodical, and two letters to Lina, followed by a short passage called "Knowledge of Scholarly Disciplines for the Beautiful Sex," an essay entitled "Poetry, Mythology, and the History of Didactic Poetry," a long elaborately annotated excerpt from "The Seasons," and finally, a lengthy moral tale, "The Melancholy Youth." The Lina materials are indeed only a small part of this menu. Later issues contain essays about the national literatures of England, France, and Germany, emphasizing literary women in those countries, articles offering information about classical mythology, useful not only for reading poetry but for composing it, too, more moral tales, and contributions about social institutions, such as law.[63]

Nor does La Roche want to underestimate her audience, as is evident in her identification of the group of already well-informed readers, or her comment, in the essay about poetry, that mythology will "not be unfamiliar" to her audience (1783:26). The annotations to Thomson's poem particularly indicate La Roche's broad educational agenda and corresponding assumption that her readership is intellectually curious and receptive. For example, she glosses the names of dozens of famous Greeks and Romans whom Thomson mentions, and suggests further readings; she recommends looking at the stars, briefly explains the rotation of the earth on its axis and suggests an experiment using a ball that will enable readers to visualize this motion; she discusses the northern lights and the discovery of ice skating, all in the name of commentary to the poem (1783:35–75). ("The Seasons," written in 1726–30, had been influential in Germany in the first half of the century, although it was no longer so when La Roche elucidated it in *Pomona*.)

Such material changes the impact of the Lina letters and of other disclaimers of scholarly aspirations. In her other writings, too, La Roche mixed her message. Thus, in one of the pedagogical sections of *Fräulein von Sternheim*, for example, Sternheim is asked about whether a group of girls of the educated middle class should be taught to be scholarly [*gelehrt*]. "May God preserve you from that intention, for even in the leisure class there is hardly one among a thousand women for whom learning would be suitable," she replies.[64] Direct questions about scholarliness almost always provoke denials in La Roche's text; and yet, she depicts Sternheim as an avid reader of books—mentioning Shakespeare, Thomson, Addison, and Pope as the character's reading material soon after arriving in England (203)—and as seizing all opportunities to learn from scholarly people, such as Lord Rich when he holds a lecture about a seeding machine. In *Pomona*, La Roche had seemed to reject scholarliness in the very introduction. In a passage presenting a conversation about starting the journal, a young woman asks La Roche to undertake the project and promises: "Then I will study very hard in order to attain some scholarliness too," and La Roche replies, "Scholarliness, my dear, you will not find in it, first because I have none myself and then also because it often gives an uneven pace to the goodness of one's heart and to what is called one's good humor."[65] When the girl responds that there are many scholarly women today, La Roche retorts: "They are exceptions of nature and chance" (1783:14). At that point, the conversation is interrupted by the arrival of two men. The defense of scholarliness for women is put in the lips of a young woman, one of the generation after La Roche; its rejection is assigned to an older, authoritative one, La Roche herself, who is aided in her argument by the silencing power of the representatives of patriarchy. The men need not join in the discussion since their presence speaks for them. As disavowals, women's statements disclaiming scholarship mean that women should not be measured by standards that they had no chance to meet. As reassurances, they mean that women are not intruding on male territory.

Yet, when the word "scholarly" is not at stake, La Roche often urges better education for women. In the *Pomona* issue about France, for example, while the impressive achievements of French women are being represented, the question is raised why France had such a large number of intelligent and perceptive women

(1783:136) compared to Germany. La Roche's answer, in the form of an example, is education; she asks:

> When giving us the letters of Madame Sévigné, which we all like so much to read, why doesn't someone say to us: "This woman would never have written these excellent letters if she had not enriched and trained her intellect beforehand with serious and beautiful writings: she knew ancient and modern history, read the sermons of great preachers of her day, Bourdalone and Flechier, the moral works of Pascal, Nicole and Arnaud; the best poets of Italy and France were hers, as well as the particular history of her country: that is how she could judge the events of her time and the works of more recent writers so well. . . ." (1783:137)

For women to participate in the production of culture, they needed significant education. Such passages form the contradictory context in which La Roche's various rejections of extensive learning for women appear. The disparity between the stress on contentment within limitations on the one hand, and the cultural exuberance and devotion to education of much of the rest of the journal on the other is left unresolved.

In *Pomona*, the inconsistency is even more striking when it occurs in the author-editor's representations of herself. After the first two issues, the journal began to contain letters and references to letters to and from La Roche and her readers. The letters raise many issues of concern to eighteenth-century middle-class women—child rearing, learning, relations with men; they also contain requests that La Roche write more about herself. These requests, like the one Baldinger had used to justify writing an autobiographical sketch, give La Roche the opportunity to become subject and object of her writing simultaneously. The third issue of *Pomona* opens with an essay called "Answer to Questions about my Room," in which La Roche describes the view from her window and what she associates with it, the pictures on her walls, the way she spends her day. She has, according to this account, an art-filled room of her own, with a desk in it that is very important for her identity ("the place that is my own," as she calls it, which is "ein grün Tischelgen" "a little green table," 1783:248), and she keeps a regular time of day for writing despite the presence of children (she mentions two young sons) and despite responsibilities in the management of the household. Two issues later, she answers another question about herself, having found out that the question about her room had been intended as an indirect query about her books. She does, indeed, sit in the midst of a lot of books, she writes, naming natural history, travel descriptions, the works of Raynal, Rousseau, and Littleton, and a volume of church history (1783:420); but since she suspects that the question is really about her learning and not her library, she goes on to give an "excerpt of the history of my head" (1783:420). This subject becomes an affirmation of girls' desire to learn. Having, like Baldinger, heard from childhood about the value of learning and the honor one could attain through it, her "natural desire for advancement" became a "noble ambition" to use knowledge as a means to distinction. With such phrases La Roche explicitly and repeatedly naturalizes girls' desire for knowledge. At the same time, she portrays education as belonging to boys: "But circumstances hindered the fulfillment of my wish *to be educated as a boy in order to become properly scholarly*" (her emphasis). She continues: "Thus the main point of my pride was lost, but the desire to know and the taste for knowledge remained in my soul" (1783:421). Sophie La Roche gave variants of this account a number of times during her career. She often represented herself as frustrated in her desire to get the best education available to men in her day: "I would gladly have combined all branches of knowledge in myself. Since that could not be, however, I turned my desire for learning the way the circumstances permitted and tried to acquire for myself at least its silhouette."[66]

Like Friderika Baldinger writing of her girlhood exclusion from scholarliness, Sophie La Roche specified a moment in her early adolescence when she found out that male-ordered learning would be denied to her and when she decided to redirect her energies. Addressing a man who had been her friend for a long time, she writes:

> You must have seen something in me that I too sense, namely that I have a heart in place of a brain. When I was thirteen, the great Bruckner wanted to take over my education and the training of my mind. I implored my father on my knees for his agreement, but he refused, and my emotional [*empfindungsvolle*] mother enriched only my heart, into which all the activity of my mind has shifted. As of now, circumstances have kept only it in practice.[67]

As already evident with Baldinger, Karsch, and von Einem, and in fictional representations, the problematic relationship of eighteenth-century girls with their mothers is closely tied to the mothers' attitude toward their daughters' education. Men play more varied roles, some, like Bruckner, offering help, and others, like the father, prohibiting further studies.

In the history of her head, La Roche concludes with the effort to depict her exclusion from systematic learning as ultimately for the best, since perhaps she would not have made any important discoveries anyway, and she might also have begun looking down on other people, so that she would not have been as happy as she proclaims herself now.[68] These images derive from the association of scholarship with ambition for social distinction and, although the passage does not acknowledge it, have no more application to women than to men. A few pages later, she indicates her continued desire nonetheless for more learning, saying that, after observing how educated men such as her father knew about many things besides their particular specialties, she decided she "could also be a good mother and housewife and know and learn a lot of other things in addition" (1783:428). Here La Roche was beginning to formulate the both/and position about women's work in the home and their yearning for cultural participation that became, as we shall see in a later chapter, a hallmark of protofeminist efforts, such as those of Mary Wollstonecraft in England and Marianne Ehrmann in Germany.

Earlier, in *Sternheim*, La Roche had proposed drawing on the discourse of virtue to give women more space in the discourse of education, writing: "It was true, he said, that women had indeed equal claim with men to all virtues and to all such knowledge which fosters their exercise, enlightens the mind, or improves our feelings and moral conduct."[69] As long as learning had a bearing on a woman's ability to exercise virtue, she could invoke virtue to justify acquiring that knowledge. This argument too Mary Wollstonecraft would try to propound in England two decades later, when she reasoned that if the virtue to be striven for by men and women were the same, then they must be allowed to learn similar things and to share a wide variety of experiences in order to attain the highest level of excellence. La Roche routinely and repeatedly pairs the notion of virtue with knowledge [*Tugend und Kenntnisse*]. Not stopping at virtue, however, she also includes in her justification of learning for women two other aspects of knowledge commonly identified in the Enlightenment, illuminating the spirit and imparting sensitivity and morality.

In *Pomona*, a few issues after the history of her head, La Roche answers another set of questions that had, at least purportedly, arrived from readers. Again she gives this autobiographical material prominence by making it the first item in the issue, thereby drawing further attention to herself and continuing to flag the issue of learning for women. This time the questions are "whether I am really not scholarly, or just avoid the appearance of it," and "how I gathered my knowledge." The answer to the first question depends on the definition of scholarship: "If by scholarly one means that a person knows more than it is necessary to know, well, then I am almost scholarly—but oh how far away from the shining, glorious goal of true manly scholarliness. . . ."[70] The goal of "true *manly* scholarliness" was unattainable, the rest of her answer makes clear, because she had not learned Latin.[71] Even though popular expectation might be less stringent, especially when describing women, La Roche separates her self-taught, unsystematic learning from the kind that required knowledge of classical languages. In other places she used "scholarly" [*gelehrt*] quite differently, talking about scholarly families, for example, to identify the educated middle class, but this designation too derived from the learning of men, not women. In short, the self-representations of Sophie La Roche suggest complex messages to readers in the context of her other writings. The way, for instance, she represents herself in autobiographical passages of *Pomona* (and elsewhere) usually contradicts her prescriptions for the less fortunate Lina. Readers inferred that the author, who stressed her categorization as female, could not be as educationally limited as many of her female characters if she were to write effectively. Yet, since the texts seek authority because they are written by a woman, and implicitly by a woman with the moral authority to educate other women, then the author's kind of woman must be good, too.

Many women, indeed, read La Roche as encouraging learning and supporting the training of women's minds. An anonymous reader of *Pomona* thanked her for her efforts "to make us better and more reasonable,"[72] and Judith Gessner, wife of the bookseller and idyll writer Solomon Gessner, wrote to La Roche after reading the magazine's first issue that La Roche had demonstrated "true reason" there. She went on to criticize the usual writing for women: "I believe also that we would have more reasonable women if we were not always talked down to so much. The usual writer makes things as simple as possible for our comprehension and generally treats us like large children. If our intellect were given stronger nourishment, then head and heart would have to benefit. . . ."[73] Women recognized the disempowering strategies of men, even though it was difficult to counter them.

Given the limited opportunities for learning usually available to women, and despite her statements eschewing scholarliness, the writings of Sophie La Roche vigorously promote women's education; after the Lina letters that appeared in *Pomona* were extracted and published as a separate volume, she composed second and third volumes that are compendia of knowledge about the physical[74] and moral world,[75] among the rare such attempts by a woman in the eighteenth century. But she was still intimidated by the label "scholarly woman," and generally formulated the purpose of women's education as related either to men or children. Thus, it was the first *Lina* volume, the one with the less intellectual agenda, that was published in four editions in La Roche's lifetime. The compendia volumes found no imitators, with one possible exception, the women's encyclopedia for which Isabella von Wallenrodt collected subscribers but which was not published, La Roche noted in 1799, because of the chaotic times.[76] As for imitators of the first volume, a small number of other women, including Luise von Krockow (1749–1803; later Brauneck), Elisabeth Eleonore Bernhardi (1768–1849), and Wendula Hedwig Möller (1741–1804) composed conduct books for girls. The asymmetry of authorship in this genre is typical: none of the books written to guide the behavior and education of young men were by women, but most of the ones for young women were by men.[77]

Women and the Possibilities of Literary Groups

From the beginning of La Roche's publishing career, women of the privileged socioeconomic ranks had responded to the authorship of Sophie La Roche with great interest. Whether she was an important figure to minimally educated women of the traditional middle class, which comprised the crafts and trades, and to women domestic servants, in short to the late eighteenth century's increasingly literate women below the educated middle class, is hard to trace; she mentioned a few occasions when such a woman, for instance, an innkeepers's wife, recognized her. Within the better educated levels of society, La Roche was unmistakably famous. Aristocratic women, who traveled rather often, especially within Germany, came to see her. Prominent among La Roche's visitors in Koblenz, where she lived at the time of *Sternheim*'s publication, was Duchess Anna Amalia of Sachsen-Weimar (1739–1807), the woman who brought Wieland to work in Weimar in 1772 and would soon persuade Goethe to follow. The duchess was accompanied by her talented, letter-writing lady-in-waiting Luise Göchhausen (1752–1807). Princess Amalia von Gallitzin (1748–1806), an independent-minded intellectual woman of the day, also came. Later, when La Roche and her husband had moved to Speier, others appeared, including Charlotte von Kalb (1761–1843), a friend and helper first to Schiller and later also to Jean Paul and Hölderlin, and Charlotte von Lengefeld, Schiller's future wife. Other aristocratic women who did not meet La Roche in person subscribed to her various publications and, at her request, to those of other women writers and left records of their attention to her. Pauline, Princess of tiny Lippe-Detmold, herself an occasional contributor to magazines, avidly read La Roche's writings.[78] Among the men even of the highest ranks she was known, too, so that when the King of Prussia met Elisa von der Recke at a reception, they discussed the writings of Sophie La Roche.[79]

La Roche's endeavor to give women recognized sites for self-assertion through writing and publishing is most evident in *Pomona*. With the publication of *Pomona*, I think her role in relationship to women's literary life in eighteenth-century Germany underwent a qualitative change. She shifted from having an unorganized audience of readers for her books to leading an unacknowledged but historically describable literary group, homosocial (composed almost entirely of women), nameless (as women themselves often are), with members who are partly self-identified and partly not (since I claim for its members all women who read *Pomona* regardless of how they saw their relationship to the journal). It was a literary group with an acknowledged leader even though she pretended to be doing other things (educating girls to be good wives and mothers) and with disparate subgroups meeting in gardens and drawing rooms rather than masonic lodges or university quarters. Jürgen Habermas, identifying the multiple forms of literary participation that were preliminary to the development of a bourgeois public sphere, acknowledged the widespread exclusion of women from most of the public-building activities and their confinement, instead, chiefly to the intimate world of the family house.[80] My proposal is to construe *Pomona* as one organizing point that enabled women to shift between the intimate and the literary, or, continuing the spatial metaphor, to establish literary zones within intimate territory and intimate zones in literary territory, with literary here understood as having to do with the written word, not restricted to traditional forms of creative literature.[81] The notion of a literary group cuts through the usual categorizations of literary history in a different way, not relying on thematic or stylistic similarity in the manner of literary movements, nor identifying close-knit coteries such as the Göttinger Hain, nor expecting the geographical proximity presupposed when the literary culture of a city or town is examined. It is more open than the friendship model of interaction that Ruth-Ellen B. Joeres urges us to recognize as a locus of self-chosen, homosocial, reasoning relationships among women of the eighteenth and nineteenth centuries and less geographically limited than the literary salon.[82] The importance of the literary group notion that I wish to develop is that it enables us to name forms of concrete literary participation and association that are otherwise too diffuse for our attention and which involve non-hegemonic and neglected participants, especially those who can only minimally be read as preparing for participation in the bourgeois public sphere. Isabel Hull emphasizes that what I am calling the public-building activities of the Enlightenment were confined to men: "The producers of Enlightened discourse were men, and no other sociological observation is as important for our purposes as that one."[83] Joeres, looking at developments around 1800, also clearly sees the exclusion of women from the most visible public scenes of cultural activity, but she emphasizes the importance of exploring possible alternative spheres "different from either the public or private spheres as they have generally been defined."[84] It is such an alternative that I seek to describe with the term "literary group."

To substantiate my declaration of a *Pomona* group, I borrow from the terminology and analysis of the social psychologist J. E. McGrath.[85] I propose understanding the readers of *Pomona* not as the kind of unorganized aggregate that is the usual reading audience, but rather as a loosely-organized but geographically dispersed literary group. An "audience" can be described as a minimally interactive collection of individuals responding to a shared set of stimuli and aware of the existence of other members but "not necessarily in physical proximity or direct communication" with each other.[86] A literary group is a more interactive, more coordinated, and longer-lasting aggregation of people still responding to a shared set of stimuli (such a response being basic in the perspective of social psychology for the existence of any kind of group), but also addressing interdependent literary goals. Coordination means that a literary group's internal relationships occur in patterns, flexible and changing though these may be, and interactivity means that the group has at least a small degree of reciprocal communication, such as can be built around a special periodical. While a literary group, of course, can have a location—a literary salon is thus a special kind of literary group that exists in a specific locale—as long as the members have some means of communication the group does not require mutual acquaintance of its members—the *Pomona* group is specifically not based on friendship even though the story La Roche writes in the first issue about the journal's founding grounds it in her friendship with a younger woman. Nor does a literary group require members' physical proximity, a point crucial for the ability of this notion to include women's literary involvement at a time when they were relatively immobile. The group members' interdependent literary goals may concern reading, writing, or disseminating texts; for economic, political, social, cultural, or more specifically literary reasons they may also have ideological goals. Also, a literary group need not have a name, self-chosen or otherwise, at the time of its functioning; it need not bill itself as literary or even as a group.[87] Rather, the reasons for cloaking a group's goals, or for mixing those goals in with other matters, should be sought in the relation of the goals to the prevailing social and cultural system; for women, a hegemonic system privileging men and limiting women's cultural participation is often decisive. Yet, as Joeres mentions in her discussion of friendship as a form of counter-public, groups can also involve "the presence and production of power," including "the power of creativity, of creating a sphere for one's self and for others who resemble that self,"[88] thereby producing psychological effects on identity formation. My proposed conception of a literary group is very broad and embracing, intended not at all to exclude men's forms of literary association, but rather, to be capable of including women's.

Obviously, the journal *Pomona* as it was organized, presented, read, and responded to, and as a literary and ideological manifesto for readers is the crux of my argument that there was such a thing as a literary group around Sophie La Roche in the early 1780s, and to a lesser extent thereafter. By publishing *Pomona*, La Roche automatically created an audience, since the magazine itself provided a common set of stimuli for its readers, who in turn were aware that there were other readers, no matter where they might be. And this audience, even more than the ones created when La Roche published a book that appeared in installments of volumes over time, could expect to exist simultaneously for an extended period, with monthly seasons of shared higher awareness among its members. But La Roche from the start structured her journal as a polyvocal place for exchanging ideas not just for women but also by women, and thus, from the start of her work on *Pomona*, she set up the conditions for the emergence of a literary group. She worked to give her readers at least the minimum skills to undertake to write, commented on issues—including literary issues—familiar to them, published contributions virtually exclusively by women, stressed the accomplishments of women, discussed her own experience as a writer, and invited her readers' comments and questions. *Po-*

mona gave potentially all its readers incentive, latitude, and a place to improve their learning and to practice writing.

The first issue of the journal well demonstrates the opportunity for reader participation. In it, La Roche describes the idea of the journal as something proposed to her by a young woman friend (and then validated by worthy men), she includes a letter from an idealized, empowered reader, "Caroline," and she asks all her readers to tell her their wishes for future issues. In short, La Roche represents the project as initiated by a young woman friend—age is again a frequent reference point—who was simultaneously a potential reader, as supported by a woman friend who immediately became an informal, but lively and appealing contributor, and as open to the influence of all women readers ("was meine Leserinnen . . . wünschen" "what my women readers wish").[89] Once the first issue appeared, readers indeed responded with letters, ideas, and references to discussions they had with other *Pomona* readers, and their contributions began to be included in the contents of the issues along with La Roche's own compositions. With these many interactions, *Pomona* was a site and stimulus for multidirectional communications. The journal, from its inception, was a vehicle for what Hull calls "the organized cycle of publication, reading, discussion, and publication again."[90]

The *Pomona* group members' interdependent (but not necessarily identical) goals were an important reason for the readers' responsiveness. Among their ideological aims were the improvement of women's education and the demonstration of women's cultural capabilities. Some of the men who offered La Roche advice about her journal, not recognizing or not wanting to encourage the ideological lessons about women's creativity and strength that La Roche was incessantly drawing from the cross-cultural references in *Pomona*, urged her to stress the national dimension of her work and not to be so interested in other countries.[91] La Roche and her literary group, however, were more devoted to gender solidarity than to incipient nationalism.

Among a literary group's interdependent goals are, of course, literary ones concerning the writing, dissemination/acquisition, and reading of texts. La Roche, as leader of the *Pomona* group, had literary goals both for herself and for her readers. She wanted to establish a venue in which she could try writing new genres and could guarantee a number of readers for her writings. But she also wanted to stimulate more women to write. The journal's subscribers presumably sought first to gain more reading materials for themselves, and in some cases, also, to recruit more readers (in effect, more group members) with whom to share and discuss the materials. But most impressive is that in many traceable instances, readers also sought to take on public dimensions of the identity "writer": they submitted texts in the form of letters and other genres for La Roche's response and for possible publication. In short, the *Pomona* group enabled La Roche to expand her position in the literary sphere and to get responses from readers. It enabled readers to conduct forays out of the intimate sphere and into the literary and then to receive responses from an editor and potentially from other readers as well.

The recasting of readers as writers happened quite deliberately and began even before the first issue of *Pomona* appeared. La Roche elicited the names of possible women contributors from friends, writing to them, cajoling, canvassing for contributions "for *Pomona*'s basket."[92] Not everyone responded favorably. Friderika Baldinger stalled, criticizing La Roche's project. Luise Mejer declined, but Friederike Jerusalem (1759–1836) accepted, sending poetry.[93] Among the other women who used the opportunity to contribute were Marie Katharine von Grävemeier (1756–1849),[94] and Juliana Giovane (also called von Mudersbach, 1757–1805), as well as two writers who will be discussed in later chapters, Philippine Engelhard-Gatterer and Sophie Albrecht. One of the anonymous contributors was probably Friederike von Rothberg, lady-in-waiting to the princess of Nassau-Usingen (1753–?).[95] Some contributors requested and got anonymity, and some La Roche herself could not identify; in her travel book about Holland and England, she told about two young women who sent an article that reached her too late for publication, but whom she could not thank since she knew neither their names nor their residence. La Roche used her magazine to encourage women to write and to give them a place for their work to be published, with or without their signatures.

Numerous sources, both passages in *Pomona* and letters there and elsewhere, mention these solicitations. Since the references are often from third persons, it is evident that invitations to write for *Pomona* were not a confidential matter between La Roche and her contacts, but that these solicitations were themselves the subject of small subgroup interactions. Thus, in 1782, some months before publication began, Friderika Baldinger knew that La Roche had asked Philippine Engelhard for contributions,[96] and Luise Mejer knew that Molly von Grävemejer had received an invitation to send in work.[97] Indeed, recruited contributors became recruiters themselves, as seems to have been the case with Friederike Jerusalem, who was evidently first approached by Jenny von Voigts nee

Möser.[98] When Jerusalem also received a direct invitation from La Roche, she wrote back in a tone as if speaking for many women: "What could be more precious to us than to have some part in your enterprise! And which of us would not have gladly long since tried to acquire this possible good fortune for ourselves if we did not fear to seem forward. . . ?"[99] The sense of group membership is unmistakable.

And membership in the group of contributors was distinctively open since La Roche in *Pomona* elicited submissions from young women to whom the idea of writing had perhaps not previously occurred. Her use of the already widely practiced letter form reinforced the message of women's literary capability. The emotional style of writing that La Roche often used also functioned as a writing aid to some women. (Her equal facility with sarcasm and worldliness, best known in the letters from Derby, is seldom noted either by contemporaries or by scholarship since.) When Charlotte von Einem, for example, wrote of her in 1779—"How infinitely much blessing a creature like her can spread through her teaching and example!"[100]—she perceived La Roche as a model and described her in the novelist's own sentimental diction. Luise Mejer noticed the influence of La Roche's diction, too, when she read a travel description by a woman magazine writer: "If I am not mistaken, Grävemeyr is imitating La Roche. Not in the description of the objects—there La Roche paints more strongly and with brighter colors—but in the comments and the depictions of character."[101]

In the issue for January 1783, the first, and repeatedly thereafter, La Roche explicitly invited her readers to send in their responses to particular questions. Readers took up the offers. Thus, promptly on 29 January 1783, "Vigilande," in an amusingly written letter about the reception of *Pomona* in her small town, cites La Roche's specific request that readers tell her what they want in the journal. She explains satirically the self-interested suggestions of various townsfolk, such as the doctor who wants La Roche to include a health manual for women and girls (otherwise he will not subscribe) or the aunt who wants La Roche to write about bonnets, since, as Vigilande quite accurately points out, La Roche had mentioned metaphorically that women like to wear bonnets that men praise. A small number of unpublished letters locatable in archives also show that readers used La Roche's explicit requests in *Pomona* as starting points for their contributions. A reader named Christiane von Hagen (who was also becoming a published writer at the time of *Pomona*[102]) writes to La Roche, for example, in response to a passage, again in the first issue, asking readers to write down and send in their thoughts on whether *Pomona* inclines them toward the good.[103]

The treatment unsolicited letters received in *Pomona* was another crucial aspect of encouragement to readers who were considering writing. Some issues of the journal contain letters from readers along with La Roche's responses, and others contain answers from La Roche that strongly suggest the content of the original letters. While her answers were uniformly kind, they could also be disapproving. To "Auguste along the Rhine" La Roche wrote her surmise that, "You must have a charming figure and much cheerfulness,"[104] adding, "That you have sympathy for the poor and that you shed a tear for suffering humanity is very valuable and shows a heart with fine feeling," but then La Roche asks Auguste never again in writing or orally "to touch on the disgusting image which you describe with the story of handkissing" (1783:815). Isolated replies such as this tantalize readers with unexplained and ambiguous allusions. The letter to Auguste continues, "The doctor who spoke with you about your hand's little flaw did not deserve that Auguste would step over the bounds of such lovable modesty [*der so liebenswürdigen Sittsamkeit*] and give so much cause for asking questions and making comments about the hidden flaws of her person. I am especially sorry that you speak of your moral sense and yet cannot resist the seductive fashion" (1783:815). La Roche advises Auguste not to let anyone except her future husband kiss her hand—others can kiss her rings—and not to let mockery become a habit (1783:815–16).

Once she had established the pattern of kind though not inevitably approving responses, more readers wrote to La Roche unsolicited. Helene Gatterer, sister of Philippine Engelhard-Gatterer, testified that she got the courage to write a letter to La Roche because of the famous author's courtesy to other readers.[105] Implied or explicit in many of the readers' letters is the sharing of *Pomona* by reading or discussing it with others. Helene Gatterer writes, "If I want to present my young women friends—among them many who are good—with a true pleasure, then I read to them from your Pomona. Then they sit around me with their work, and, touched by your beautiful moral tales, they often as a group express the wish with me to be able to thank you warmly for the happy hours which have come to us thereby."[106]

The *Pomona* group's literary goals are closely related to its organization. All but the most loosely aggregated groups, literary or not, have patterned relationships internally, often including one or more leaders. For the *Pomona* group, as a literary group structured initially around a periodical, several roles, arranged in concentric circles, can be identified, with writer/editor/leader in the center and reader/writers gathered around her, with those who lived in Speyer closest in. Noncontributing readers form the outer ring, further divided into primary readers (subscribers) and secondary readers (non-subscribers who borrowed the journal or listened when it was read aloud). The distinctions are based on degrees and directionality of communication, with the writer/editor sending monthly communication to the whole group, in a centralized communication pattern, and every reader at least potentially receiving, although some secondary readers would have had only intermittent access. A portion of readers then responded back to the center, and of these some, whose words or requests were cited in *Pomona*, also came into communication with the whole group. In this way, all readers could feel themselves as potential writers and thus as active contributors to the literary and ideological goals of the group. In fact, aside from the central fixed role of La Roche, other members of the group could move, partly at their own choice, from one role to another; La Roche, however, retained the power of deciding which contributions from readers were published. On the outskirts of the group were subgroups with their own informal leaders, geographically-based clusters of primary and secondary readers who gathered to read and discuss together, such as the circle of friends that Helene Gatterer describes or the conversational afternoon and evening visits with other readers that Vigilande alludes to.[107]

Each of these categories of social identity—that is identity within the group, as opposed to personal identity—especially writer/editor and reader/writer, was difficult to reconcile with hegemonic categories for women (daughter, mother, wife, etc.). To offset this problem, the group's representation of its structure was cast in kinship terms, with the readers identified in the very title of the periodical as daughters and the writer/editor frequently giving herself a title such as aunt or mother. As aunt, her role in the letters to Lina, La Roche made her claim to leadership in the group obliquely, same-gender, earlier-generation than the "daughters," with less authority, however, and less responsibility than a mother.

As with many kinds of groups, membership in the *Pomona* group, as I am defining it, is based both on ascription, being labeled as "women," and choice, which, in this case, means deciding to read and perhaps also to respond to *Pomona*. A list published at the end of 1783 names 709 subscribers, including individuals, bookstores, reading clubs, and libraries, located from Copenhagen to Zurich and from London to Saint Petersburg. Total circulation could have been distinctly higher, first, because the list does not indicate numbers of orders per subscriber, and, second, because as a note at the head of the list mentions, many women subscribers asked to remain anonymous.[108] Many of the named subscribers are men. Indeed, men served as a common "other" in *Pomona*, some helping to solicit subscribers and contributors, and some identified as influencing decisions by the leader, but almost none addressed within the periodical as part of the audience and, aside from the English poet Thomson, few getting their work published there. Although men, mostly as fathers or husbands, might also read the issues, the texts' strong gender politics clearly positioned them as outsiders and they evidently responded that way, too. Thus, Boie wrote to La Roche that he read *Pomona* with pleasure "although this time you are not really writing for me."[109] To a considerable extent then, I read the men's names on the journal's list of subscribers as proxies for the unnamed women who I am considering members of the *Pomona* group. In short, since the journal that is the central vehicle of this literary group is explicitly addressed to women and girls, I see the *Pomona* group as a literary group of women. This makes the group, after the convent scriptoria of the Middle Ages, one of the early literary groups by and for women that, given the current state of archival studies, can be clearly recognized and explored.

To the extent that the *Pomona* group depended not just on the communications facilitated by the journal, but also found its existence in two and three-way correspondences as well as local conversations about the group and its goals, I argue that the group began approximately in October 1782, while publication of the journal was being planned, and continued even after publication ceased at the end of 1784. Women's sense of indebtedness to La Roche for many of her writings, not exclusively *Pomona*, endured over time, as did their responsiveness in the form of writing. Caroline Ludecus (1757–1827), who was fourteen when *Sternheim* appeared and twenty-six when *Pomona* began, acknowledged La Roche's influence many years later when she was forty-three and published her first novel, dedicating it to Sophie La Roche. As late as 1820, Luise Brachmann was signing some of her poems in magazines with the pseudonym of Sternheim.[110] In 1805, Sophie Mereau Brentano (1770–1806), dedicated one of her books, *Bunte Reihe kleiner Schriften* "Colorful Series of Little Writings," to La Roche, who was also the grandmother of the Mereau Brentano's second husband, Clemens Brentano. Of course rather than registering an enduring *Pomona* group these tributes may simply be the expected indicators that a writer of La Roche's stature had an impact on women after her. After all, the names of many of the members of the *Pomona* group are unlisted or hidden behind their fathers' names on the subscription lists (such as Mereau), or behind pseudonyms in the pages of the journal (such as Vigilande), or partial names there too (such as Caroline); several identifiable *Pomona* correspondents who published elsewhere (such as Helene Gatterer and Christiane von Hagen) remain obscure in history and in literary studies as these so far exist. Such factors make it extremely difficult to trace the longer-term impact of the journal and the group around it. Yet, specific evidence for the partial continuation of the *Pomona* group is to be found in La Roche's book of Mannheim letters (1791), which explicitly address again the women readers of *Pomona* and continue to model the exchange and discussion of ideas both in conversation and in letters. A later work, *Mein Schreibetisch* "My Writing Desk," (1799), while still addressing one of the *Pomona* group's thematic questions of how and where La Roche had created a physical and intellectual space for herself as a woman writer, shows how differently the answer is structured when the interlocutor is a man.

AFTER *POMONA*: WRITING FOR WOMEN, INVENTORYING THE SELF FOR MEN

I am contending that in addition to the impact of her renown as a novelist, Sophie La Roche supported women's entry into cultural productivity in six ways, first, by depicting satisfying relationships among women, which promised a sympathetic audience of readers and thereby allowed for writing about otherwise occluded topics; second, by arguing for more education for women—even while La Roche asserted that women's emotions could substitute for their lesser education; third, by offering readers a model of a woman, herself, who succeeded in being both recognizably feminine and an abundantly productive writer; fourth, by incorporating women's deeds and especially their texts into her own writings and thereby validating them; fifth, by elaborating a style that was relatively easy to imitate and by suggesting through her own experiments that many genres and genre variations might be appropriate for women, thus opening the floodgates so that women in the late eighteenth century wrote in virtually every genre of the time; and sixth, by directly encouraging women to write and publish. In *Pomona*, La Roche had worked on all six strategies. Her later writings, including travel books, but especially two works called *Briefe über Mannheim* "Letters about Mannheim" (1791) and *Mein Schreibetisch* "My Writing Desk" (1799), continue the efforts in other ways.

In the last half year of *Pomona*, La Roche had begun considering the project of travel writing. She explained to readers that the September issue was late because of a trip she had taken to Switzerland.[111] In the October issue, under the rubric of a letter to Lina, her first published effort at nonfictional travel writing appeared, an excerpt from her Swiss journal (1784:824–51). And that same month, she included a long summary of a book by a Mr. Houel about traveling in Sicily (1784:963–1005) as well as a short essay by Caroline endorsing travel (1784:1005–10). In 1785, after *Pomona* had ceased publication, La Roche made a journey to France and the next year one to Holland and England. Beginning the year after that, she published three travel books in two years: *Tagebuch einer Reise durch die Schweitz* "Diary of a Trip through Switzerland" (1787), *Journal einer Reise durch Frankreich* "Journal of a Trip through France" (1787), and *Tagebuch einer Reise nach Holland und England* "Diary of a Trip to Holland and England" (1788), followed five years later by *Erinnerungen aus meiner dritten Schweizerreise* "Memories from My Third Swiss Trip" (1793). Sophie La Roche was one of the early German women writers to compose in this form. Given its popularity among men, travel literature is the part of her ouevre least likely to have reached a readership chiefly of women, although none of her writings were read only by women (or women and girls), as the many male comments about her various works indicate. Still, La Roche's travel journals are all represented as addressed to her daughters. Indeed, despite her own declared great love of travel, and despite her frequent demonstrations and professions of concern for women, the chances for travel that she furnishes her own sons and daughters differ distinctly as described in the books, a discrepancy she struggles to ignore. Thus, accompanying her youngest son on his trip to boarding school is the pretext for setting out on her trip to Switzerland (while her now married daughters stay at their respective homes). From England, she rejoices to her daughters that she has met a woman who will buy up a hundred extra copies of *Pomona* and thereby enable La Roche to pay for the travel not of one of her daughters but of one of her sons, including a visit to Paris.[112] In this instance, *Pomona* was sold to women to benefit men.

Nonetheless, the travel books assiduously draw attention to women, especially women writers, to the life experiences of women, and to their educational opportunities, all themes La

Roche had stressed in *Pomona*.[113] The narrator also seeks out material about women and includes a sprinkling of caustic comments about men.[114] Worley notes that La Roche did her traveling "as a woman writing for women, and, in some ways, traveling on behalf of women."[115] But the books also contain comments on the history and character of the places visited, landscape descriptions, accounts of accommodations and road conditions, notes on galleries and museums. Occasionally, in keeping with the interest in natural history that she presented several times in *Pomona*, La Roche comments on geology and mineralogy. Although the travel books thus continue *Pomona* themes, another work, *Briefe über Mannheim* "Letters about Mannheim" (1791), continues not only these themes from *Pomona* but also, like *Pomona*, contains a chapter and other scattered passages of autobiographical writing, and furthermore sustains at least part of the *Pomona* group. The letters support five of La Roche's six goals for her women readers: female friendships, better education (and a circumvention of it), validation of varied female voices, positive self-depictions, and style and genre choices accessible to women, omitting, however, encouragement directly to her readers to write and publish. *Mein Schreibetisch* "My Writing Desk" (1799), written eight years later when La Roche was sixty-nine years old, again offers a self-depiction and encompasses writings by other women, but this time addressed to a very different audience and thus, with very different results. Both of these works are also experiments with form.

The Mannheim letters are a hybrid, part travel journal and part essay collection. Like the travel journals, the letters address the details of a particular place, in this case, the Mannheim theater and the lives of actors, the natural history collection of the prince-elector, the library, notable people, and a school for girls. Like both *Pomona* and La Roche's travel books, the letters contain information about other literary women and ideas about women's participation in culture. Most important, like sections of *Pomona*, the letters are mostly structured as conversations, some carried on in person and some in writing, and the conversations are overwhelmingly among women—not just to them and not primarily with men. Using the terminology of Carla Kaplan, *Briefe über Mannheim*, like *Pomona*, uses both the "politics of voice," in which women articulate their own more or less explicitly political agendas, and an "erotics of talk," in which the speaker, desiring "intimacy and recognition" seeks the ideal listener.[116] My argument is that La Roche does not expect to find dialogic intimacy, which Kaplan claims is fundamental to identity, in heterosexual relationships, but rather in friendships with other women, and that she seeks to model it in the Mannheim letters. Furthermore, the model she invokes always draws on the memory of the *Pomona* group.

The opening entry of the book is a letter headed "Pomona to Caroline" and beginning, "It is difficult, my dear, to pick up again nicely the long broken thread of your old Pomona's exchange of letters, since all the women with whom I corresponded lost connection or became tired because of the silence that began in 1785," the year after *Pomona* ceased publication.[117] In the letters, La Roche hopes to reestablish the interactive female audience of *Pomona*. To produce a similar effect without the situation of the monthly journal, La Roche, as the letter heading shows, resumed using the persona she had produced for herself in *Pomona* and asserted she was writing in response once more to the periodic requests and comments of Caroline, who had functioned as a conversation partner, informal editorial consultant, and occasional contributor to *Pomona*. The first chapter of the Mannheim letters contains a letter from Caroline, whose ability to influence the shape of the book is repeatedly stressed.[118] The third letter, for example, begins: "I interrupt the course of my story to answer part of your last letter."[119] Indeed, the very existence of the book is attributed to Caroline and her insistence that La Roche fulfill a promise, allegedly made as publication of *Pomona* was winding down, to write about Mannheim.

Caroline lends herself to readings as a self-confident, frank, and articulate woman, an enlivening, slightly irreverent alter ego to the *Pomona* La Roche. In the Mannheim letters, Caroline has a companion, Annette, in the role of conferring, advising, and questioning. She is figured as frequently coming to visit La Roche, serving as a partner in dialog in a number of letters (often signaled by a peculiar systems of indents, for example in the twentieth letter—275–85). Less opinionated than Caroline, Annette acts as a receptive listener whose questions seek elaboration rather than posing challenges. But Caroline is not always bold, either. By quoting Caroline's assertion that she does not talk to her husband in the same language that she uses to La Roche, the point is made that this woman, too, is anchored in a patriarchal world; to get along with powerful men, the most common suggestion in the writings of La Roche is tactical deference and concealment, and Caroline apparently uses this system, too.

The sections of the Mannheim letters in which Caroline (by means of letters) or the young friend appear often concern topics unrelated to Mannheim but of interest to women. One example occurs when Caroline asks that La Roche compose "a kind of dictionary of concepts" and Annette proposes a sample word for it, "mood" "*Laune*," which La Roche, deploying gender analysis, identifies as a privilege of powerful men (278–82). More important, in the year that Sophie La Roche published Baldinger's conflicted autobiography, with its representation of repeated failure to justify publication, the situation of communication among women in the Mannheim letters provides another ready locus for self-biography: Caroline is depicted as insisting that La Roche again compose a brief account of her life as a writer until that point (199–212).

The extensive incorporation of quotations and contributions from Caroline into the Mannheim letters resembles the work of a woman whose correspondence La Roche describes: "It is certain that she always makes excerpts from everything that she reads and that she likes all too well to place contradictory ideas one beside the other" (291). This system of writing is especially evident in La Roche's works that do not claim to be fiction, travel books, and memoirs, and is marked by its unreconciled combination of conflicting ideas, some in the form—or guise—of quotations, occasionally very extensive. It is a technique that allows disharmony to stand, that does not insist on an overall clarifying system. One chapter of the Mannheim letters begins: "My work table—and the knitting bag of my friend; this heading leads . . . far from the scenes of the archbishop's residence" (258). Both the technique of juxtaposition and the renunciation of a general philosophical integration of its parts make this kind of writing intellectually and aesthetically remote from the high culture being proffered out of Weimar under the name of "Classicism" (*Klassik*), with its confidence about what was essential, its determination to slough off the unessential, and its avowed refinement of the ideal into the symbol of the feminine. Worley speaks of the "additive, associative style" of the travel journals. She suggests that to understand the different roles La Roche assumes in the books it is useful to give up the assumption of "a harmonious unified self possessing a consistent world view." She continues:

> La Roche's different "selves" as expressed in her travel journals—the didactic mother advocating a feminine model of harmonizing self-sacrifice, the sentimental heroine, the woman hungry for knowledge and travel, the champion of women's achievements—obviously exist concurrently. The journeys may have given La Roche the freedom to activate these "selves," most likely originating in different periods of her life. The travel journals, not bound by concepts of unified plot and char-

acterization, enabled her to place herself in a variety of situations and roles, allowing her multifaceted subjectivity to surface.[120]

While Worley's idea that the "selves" identified here were grounded in La Roche's biography is not necessary—most of these subject positions were ready-made in available discourses of the time—her depiction of the concurrent existence of multiple voices in the journals and the rousing of precisely this diversity by the travel situation itself help locate the ways La Roche's travel books differ from the more harmonious, integrated travel writings of her male contemporaries. La Roche could then extend this associative style to her other writings, such as *Briefe über Mannheim* and, far more blatantly, *Mein Schreibetisch*.

In some ways, juxtaposition is a continuation and expansion of the multiple perspectives La Roche achieved in her epistolary novels, beginning with *Sternheim*. There, she used several letter writers with different values and different purposes, each addressing a symbolically situated correspondent (moral Sternheim, for example, writing to the daughter of the German country parson who had also been her teacher, virtuous Seymour writing to the serious and high-minded Doctor T. in England, and iniquitous Derby writing to a licentious friend in Paris) to produce different accounts of the same events. With each writer's version valid in its own way and each also incomplete, the main characters depend on the others for an effective conclusion to the story. Thus, Fräulein von Sternheim, unwilling or unable to acknowledge her wish to marry Seymour, talks of remaining single. Meanwhile Derby, who had long since recognized her suppressed love for Seymour, reveals it to the hero and thereby facilitates the conventional happy end. When this technique of multiple perspectives is used in genres that make more direct truth claims, such as the hybrid *Briefe über Mannheim*, it suggests the legitimacy of the various women's ideas and concerns, and thereby admits differences among them along with interdependence. This parries Classicism's glorification of the unified "feminine" by dislocating it onto women of differing ages, styles, and views. But it also suggests the difficulties of achieving the conversational intimacy of the "erotics of talk"; as La Roche notes at the beginning of the chapter after she has written her latest account of herself as a writer: "Caroline, how different are our fates and our attitudes! You have lost almost nothing, I *everything*. You are so many years younger than I—can therefore also still expect much with time—I nothing—nothing more. You prove to me what J. J. Rousseau once said: the poor must always give from what little they have—so that the rich have surplus. . . ."[121] Depending, as Kaplan points out, on whether the speaker/writer desires an interlocutor with whom she identifies or not, these differences between La Roche and Caroline hinder or help the conversation. In fact, La Roche does not seem to desire a conversational setting of personal intimacy but instead, one of philosophical trust, modeling discussions among women that are equivalent to the (presumed) discussions and debates among men on general topics of ethics, science, and, very abstractly, politics. La Roche desires conversational partners who will take her seriously and respect her intellectually. In the Mannheim letters, she searches for these partners among young matrons, adult women who nonetheless look up to her as famous, experienced, and informed.

Later writings continuing La Roche's self-depiction counter the Classicism in other ways and also structure a different relationship with her conversational partners. *Mein Schreibetisch* "My Writing Desk," for example, is the first of La Roche's books to be overtly about herself, with "desk" standing in transparently for "life as a writer" and "my" boldly heading the title.[122] La Roche in this book faces the same problem that Friderika Baldinger confronted when she tried to find a way to produce an autobiography for publication. How could a woman of the educated middle class write about herself as an intellectual or a writer? The topos of the male requester, which Baldinger had also used, has important consequences. As Loster-Schneider points out, when the requester is a man, the woman respondent is nudged into adopting a male perspective and male interests in examining her own life.[123] Given a male interlocutor, only her intellectual life is likely to be treated as of any import, and yet, that topic is, within eighteenth-century thought, extremely difficult for a woman to address, since she should be neither scholarly nor culturally productive on any significant scale. La Roche represents herself as writing *Mein Schreibetisch*, to fulfill a promise to a particular young man. In citing his role as instigator/reader/interlocutor, and alluding both to his friendship with her deceased son and to his respected position in society, she depicts him as a son-substitute, as well as a busy and important man whose opinion counted in the world and whose request must be met. Nonetheless, to write a book about herself as a woman of cultural achievement and as an active participant in literary life required other ways to explain and validate her text.

She returns to the model of self-inventory used for her first novel and, within that novel, for Sternheim's letters. Thus Wieland, in his introduction to *Fräulein von Sternheim*, mentions La Roche's transmission of the manuscript to him as a checkup on her ideological correctness, quoting—or claiming to quote—her: " 'I send it to you,' you [La Roche] wrote me, 'so that you can give me your opinion of my sensibility, of the point of view from which I have become accustomed to judge the affairs of human life, of the considerations that customarily arise in my soul when it is vividly moved, and so that you may rebuke me where you find me in error.' "[124] Sternheim, likewise, writes so that her correspondent, Emilia, and Emilia's father, Sternheim's moral tutor, can evaluate the condition of her soul. In *Mein Schreibetisch*, La Roche says she will reveal her desk to her reader so that he can decide how well she has survived the blows of recent years, "whether my mind and character went forward or backward."[125] She has promised to "give a completely honest description of this table and of the wall around it without . . . changing, omitting, or adding anything, because the one could be detrimental and the other advantageous to me" (1:3). Despite this appeal to male authority and male judgment, structuring the book as a strict and complete inventory reduces the extent to which La Roche articulates herself through the perspective of her interlocutor—although it leaves the reader in that subject position.

Fundamentally, however, the book gets its meaning by being about the famous Sophie La Roche. She describes the objects on and around her desk because, she asserts, they offer "a very exact blueprint of my head and my inclinations" (1:6). Although La Roche has authority because of her cultural achievement and connections, which she frequently mentions, in writing to a man she needs a man's approval, and thus refers to her authorizing male reader both on the title page and throughout the book. It is a complicated situation. As Loster-Schneider points out, the narrator of *Mein Schreibetisch* carefully maintains the fiction of a speech situation (narrator and her listener) into which all the many excerpts and citations are embedded, and in this and other ways, La Roche's situation as a writer (rather than speaker) is omitted from the text and from the perception of the narrator's (male!) interlocutor (1:307). On the other hand, the erasure is glaringly obvious and the many invocations of the male interlocutor provide a context for this omission. Thus, we have again both a representation of the male-ordered ban on women writing and a woman's quite evident noncompliance with the ban, indicated by the text itself.

In *Mein Schreibetisch*, La Roche assembles the parts and leaves it to the reader to produce the whole—rather as she had let the reader synthesize the parts of her epistolary novels, too. In eschewing making large-scale sense of things, La Roche again retreats into the relatively literal without giving up the notion that she herself is valid and valuable. The book is organized around memorabilia La Roche had collected over the years, lists of book titles, inventories of pictures, poems copied long ago, and writing implements (such as the ruler, "with which I knock on my door if I want someone from my family while I am writing" 1:167). They are accompanied by commentary and remarks, moral anecdotes, words of praise for friends and acquaintances, sentimental memories. The narrator repeatedly indicates the disjointedness and triviality of her material as problems, but the need to avoid taking too authoritative a stance in her text (unlike the stance in her family implied by the summoning ruler) and the promise of complete exposure lead her to this form. By confining her attention to her desk and her study, she can compartmentalize the intellectual aspects of her life and thus avoid Baldinger's problem of how much to tell about other possible components of an autobiography, such as girlhood, courtships, childbearing and rearing, changing domestic duties in the quite varied settings in which she lived, her relationship with her husband over time, illness and health, dealing with criticism, the responses of her family and friends to her increasing fame, and so forth. Within the confines of her study she can, quite unlike Baldinger writing earlier, reprise Rousseau's famous autobiographical pact to withhold nothing.[126]

Similarly, in positing herself as a female subject, within the interrelated terms that she has set for herself as an author and that the eighteenth-century reading classes allowed for women, La Roche has no place or language in her book for her aging female body nor, unlike Baldinger, for her sexuality. La Roche shifts her physicality onto the desk and its contents, this "old servant in a gray cloak, who for many years has empathized with his master, has patiently born all the work and difficulty, and has quietly and loyally kept every secret."[127] As the desk and the things on it are described, sometimes in lavish detail, layer under layer, the effect is to unveil the female self presumed to underlie it all. La Roche's gendered self is disconnected from the body, which is replaced by the desk, but, given the lack of legitimacy for women in cultural life, La Roche is necessarily insecure about so much self-exposure. She also often mentions the difficulty of this kind of writing, something to which she had not frequently referred before: "But now I have come to the catalog of the packet wrapped in pale yellow paper. How shall I write it? How will you read it?" (1:20).

La Roche in *Mein Schreibetisch* uses situations and ideas she had previously addressed to girls and women and addresses them here to men—as indicated by the requester—and certainly also to women. In this setting, she represents herself as a champion of women, although always with reservations. For example, after entering several quotes from an old galley sheet she had found and ironed back into presentable condition (1:78), she writes that her reader was perhaps saying she saved the page because of the praise its late medieval author gave to women (although only one of the excerpts she had included touched on that subject). "I answer: no! The spirit of the man pleases me in general, but certainly also because, *out of the cage of his narrow time*, he . . . observed everything with an acute mind, judged with sympathy, and, even though a monk, was just to my sex" (her emphasis, 1:85). She does not recant her advocacy, but tries to embed it in an agenda that is signaled as broader. In other places she follows praise of women with the citation of a misogynist crack. She mentions, for instance, a prizewinning essay about Madame de Sévigné by Mme. Brisson, and comments:

> I love everything that originates from the quill of a person of my sex, and have always especially loved the letters of Madame de Sévigné as a model *of narrative letters full of feeling and grace*, and [I] was therefore very happy to receive this indication of respect for the accomplishments of a woman, since several of the submitted laudatory essays were authored by men, and yet the work of a woman won the prize. (her emphasis, 1:103–4)

Now comes the misogynist moment: "Some people had the meanness to say that this happened because of the rarity of the case of a women being so just about the accomplishment of another woman." La Roche had no theory by which to evaluate such material, using instead her own repetition of the put-downs of women to show her open mindedness.

Still, she remains distinctly woman-centered, with tributes to several outstanding women. Wanting to identify a female literary tradition—having the "desire" [*Begierde*] to know everything that came from a feminine pen—La Roche treated as valuable for women the awareness that there were, and had been, other women writers in other places and other times, and she regularly insisted on including her findings on such women in her writings. One is Susanne von Klettenberg, whose poem "An die Spindel" "To the Spindle" La Roche published for the first time in *Mein Schreibetisch* (1:329–31). Another occurs in the second volume of the book where La Roche takes it upon herself to publish substantial parts of the correspondence she had received from Julie Bondeli (1731–78), whose intellectual and cultural significance La Roche tries to articulate (2:146–366). The excerpts from Bondeli's letters, in French,[128] show the literary topics the two women discussed, including the ideas of Rousseau, the poetry of Anna Louisa Karsch, and the reactions of Bondeli and her friends to *Sternheim*.[129] In editing and publishing this lengthy correspondence, La Roche boldly publicizes the life, thought, and writings of a woman. It constitutes by far the largest section of the book and the portion positioned at the climax of the text, the last item connected with the desk itself before other objects nearby and on the walls of the study are described. As Loster-Schneider points out, Julie Bondeli in these letters becomes the woman muse to a woman writer whose texts—for this section of the book—are not a taboo subject.[130]

I have argued that women were excluded from the *Aufklärung*; yet, La Roche's choice of a biographical form that stresses her intellectual life shows her vividly at work in Enlightenment activities, indoors, reading voraciously and desiring to read even more; the book does not show her cultivating intimate friendships (the one with Julie Bondeli that she features existed entirely on paper and never face to face), not walking along the Rhine or in her garden (although these were activities she mentions elsewhere), not surrounded by her children or grandchildren, or, retrospectively, in the company of her husband. Although much of *Mein Schreibetisch* uses the language of *Empfindsamkeit*, that does not conceal its Enlightenment aims. But because women could only present themselves as objects of the Enlightenment and not as subjects, La Roche represents herself through a desk. *Fräulein von Sternheim* is the story of a woman whose enlightening books are forcibly taken away from her; *Mein Schreibetisch* is about a woman who has acquired books later in life, though not always the books that she wanted, and who has written, but who nonetheless knows she, too, is excluded from the movement to which she obviously aspires.

Bettina von Arnim nee Brentano, one of La Roche's granddaughters, wondered once what the inside of her grandmother's head looked like since she was always stringing together the most unusual topics.[131] In her own way, Arnim-Brentano carried on this tradition. Christa Wolf, writing about *Die Günderode*, stresses exactly its nontraditional form:

> What is especially striking about the letter book is most easily overlooked since it is not formulated in words: the statement, which lies in the structure of the book, namely its refusal to submit to the aesthetic

canon. Bettina senses that the structures of the aesthetic that she knows must somehow be connected with the hierarchical structures of society. It is an insoluble paradox that literature depends on orderings which it however must continually breach in order to be literature.[132]

Arnim-Brentano's grandmother had breached these orderings, too. La Roche's late works, these verbal scrapbooks of juxtapositions and associations, do not aim to fulfill the various aesthetic imperatives that came and went during her long writing career.[133] They counter the disparagement of women's everyday world by bringing what was usually considered trivial to the center of attention, even though the inventory, organized as it is by the structuring locus of the desk in a small study, necessarily omits many typically feminine aspects of her and other women's lives. Goethe, offended by La Roche's writings, said of her: "She is one of those whose nature it is to level everything; she elevates that which is common and drags down that which is excellent."[134] In elevating the common into writing, La Roche was insisting on the specificity and practicality of herself and other women of her class, and was negotiating a way to write about herself still largely within dominant eighteenth-century ideological terms. When, as in *Mein Schreibetisch*, her interlocutor is a man, the result is especially unsystematic, an indication again, as Friderika Baldinger had also discovered, of the impossibility within the system-building male discourse of the *Aufklärung*, for a woman to speak coherently. But La Roche did not let such problems silence her. In 1806, the last of her self-depictions and her final publication, *Melusinens Sommer-Abende* "Melusina's Summer Evenings," appeared, like her first, with a preface by her old friend Wieland, but this time addressed to a woman reader. Sophie La Roche worked hard almost to her death on 18 February 1807. Her writings show a woman taking herself seriously as both literary subject and object.

Over her long literary career, La Roche's actions and influence occurred in a context of conflicting discourses. Operating within the thought of her time, La Roche accepted the notion of male/female duality and corresponding ranking. As with the presentation of class in *Fräulein von Sternheim*, she argues not against male supremacy (in the privileged classes) but for female adequacy (again, in the privileged middle and upper classes). She points at male abuses, but unlike the convenient localization of aristocratic abuse at the court, sees abusive behavior by men afflicting wives or future wives in many settings. In the last letter to Lina in *Pomona*, when the young woman is about to marry, the narrator quotes Lina's brother as writing: "Before marriage, the happiness of the man seems to depend on the girl, but after the wedding her happiness is certainly forever in his power. We do not want to deceive our Lina with an ideal of happiness. She should know, that the most perfect man is nevertheless an imperfect human being."[135] Even in their endorsements of patriarchal structure, La Roche's texts suggest its weakness, its need for constant shoring up, and its dangers to women. Her writing, in its mixture of resistance to patriarchy, and insistence that women play along, draws attention to rickety corners of the system, and to the constructedness of femininity, since women needed extensive coaching in order to fill their scripts.

The dominant discourse of femininity had essentially no room in it for a woman writing and publishing. Yet, the effectiveness of eighteenth-century German literary women and of women's literary groups, including those still to be identified, is suggested by the number of their daughters and granddaughters who also became writers. Aside from Sophie La Roche and her granddaughter Bettina Arnim-Brentano, the most famous case is Karsch, whose daughter Karoline von Klencke (1754–1802) wrote and published plays and poems and compiled a major edition of her mother's work, introduced by a biographical essay;[136] Klencke's daughter in turn, Helmina von Chézy (1783–1856), wrote poetry, travel books, and essays, and composed the second biography of her notable grandmother. La Roche's own unhappy daughters were not part of this pattern. If they showed any creative literary inclinations, there is no record of their receiving parental encouragement; perhaps La Roche did not have the psychological and other resources to assist her daughters while continuing her own work—which was itself none too highly encouraged at home. One of Philippine Engelhard-Gatterer's daughters, on the other hand, Caroline Engelhard (1781–1855), was a prolific writer in the nineteenth century. Even a daughter of the publicly reticent Friderika Baldinger, Amalie Gehren (1769–1819), published occasional poetry and edited a collection of the letters that Kästner had sent to her, and Gehren also had a daughter, a namesake Amalie von Gehren (1799–?), who, likewise, wrote and published.[137]

The notion of the feeling woman that La Roche articulated in *Fräulein von Sternheim* and elsewhere gave many eighteenth-century German women tickets into the forecourt of the literary palace that they parleyed into door passes to literary productivity. La Roche used her opportunity as a visible woman enacting a new combination of discursive practices to abet other women writers. If she could form a literary group and persuade many of its members to join her in literary practices, she gained their validation of her acts; this behavior contrasts with Friderika Baldinger's strategy of preserving her own singularity. Sophie La Roche enlarged the discursive space for women writers by showing them helpful and fulfilling relationships of women with women, by helping to educate her women readers and finding a way to make their limited education sufficient, by answering their questions about herself, by elaborating an accessible style compatible with the dominant androcentric discourse of femininity—I will locate her style in the *Empfindsamkeit* of sympathy—and by mediating culturally productive connections among women through a literary group (unnamed though it was), which also published their work. La Roche opened the floodgates to literary productivity (even though her contemporaries did not immediately rush to the genre choice that had made her famous, the novel). With her emphasis on the relatively literal and the everyday, her complex placement as an intellectually active woman writing for other such women—sometimes under the imposing guise of writing for a man—La Roche abstained from the language and thought of her most esteemed male colleagues. Younger women, such as the poet Philippine Engelhard-Gatterer, more thoroughly explored some of the possibilities La Roche had opened.

4
Longing for Respectability: Philippine Engelhard née Gatterer (1756–1831)

A LETTER TO A FRIEND BY A YOUNG WOMAN READER IN THE HOME TOWN of Philippine Gatterer contains a passage discussing the reception of the poet. It begins: "Of course—thanks to the goddess of Fame— you surely know our Göttingen muse, Mlle Gatterer, and her poems." By the eighteenth century, fame for a member of the middle class depended most of all on the written word, such as that of the personal letter and various published forms such as reviews, announcements, annual collections, and book copies. At the time of this letter, in 1780, Philippine Gatterer, still in her early twenties, was the author of several poems that had appeared in influential annual poetry anthologies, as well as of a poetry book of her own. But fame for a woman was an overarching signal of her transgressiveness, a major aspect of the irreconcilability of proper womanhood with writing. In the effort not to appear too presumptuous and not to infringe too harshly on the requisite female modesty, many public women writers denied serious ambition and thereby accepted self-trivialization. A respectable woman was unknown to "the goddess of Fame."

The letter from Göttingen veers from a possible discussion of the writing of a young woman to the normative question of femininity and fame, so Gatterer's poems are mentioned only in the opening sentence of the letter passage and then dropped. While it is clear that the letter writer knew the poet, her comments were written from the position of an uninvolved spectator, one who, however, agrees with the prevailing condemnation of her errant compatriot. The first explicit judgment is cast in terms that seem unrelated to Gatterer's gender: "How true the saying is that no prophet is known in his own country and how very right Miss G. is when she says that people here have no idea how to value her." Judith Grant, conceptualizing gender as a system of crime and punishment, argues:

Like any power structure, gender has rules, and breaking these rules amounts to what we can call "gender crime." These gender crimes represent, in a sense, tears in the otherwise seamless and natural quality of the structure of gender. Gender crimes exact a sort of punishment. In fact the punishments are what clue us in to their status as crimes in the first place. Gender crimes and their punishments can tell us a lot about the nature of gender itself.[1]

In this framework, I see the letter writer as signaling to her friend, another young woman, that Philippine Gatterer has committed a gender crime, which is being punished by social ostracism, a point the letter writer reinforces: "Here no one talks about her, no one admires her, despite her lively understanding, and her fiery wit—on the contrary the latter has exposed her to various unpleasantnesses." Given the social nature of gender, qualities such as wit and understanding are evaluated in terms of their reception by others, taking Gatterer's gender into account.

While it was permissible for a young woman to have wit and understanding, both of which the letter-writer herself assiduously displayed in this private letter to another young woman, the rules of gender stipulated a public marker for women, modesty, that would substantially diminish the non-private impact or even visibility of their intelligence or cleverness. The letter writer emphasizes modesty for Gatterer in terms of its effect on others: "If [she] only had more modesty, she would be much more appealing." Criticizing a woman for breaching modesty was an effort to maintain gender boundaries and to keep women's literary activity as ineffective as possible, for it is precisely transgressions against the rules for women, transgressions expressed as courage and the ability to talk and think freely, that are required for the kind of poetry that has been most admired in the West in modern times. Again the letter writer elaborates: "Her heart is certainly good, her intellect beyond reproach, but for a young lady she has too much courage, she thinks and talks too freely, and has in general too little soft female character to be pleasing from that standpoint."[2] The letter writer's judgment is based on an assessment of Engelhard-Gatterer's femininity, in particular, the unseemly freedom of her thought and language summed up in her insufficient modesty.

The eighteenth century has taken on significance in the late twentieth century as the originative period of the bourgeois public sphere, a notion of a locus and process of ideas and of rational thought to which all men who passed a certain threshold of education and training in reasoning in words could be admitted, a rehearsal room for democratic government. Beginning with Habermas's *The Structural Transformation of the Public Sphere*, scholars have often acknowledged, though less often explored, the limited access of women to much of this development. Regardless of their education or their skill in argumentation and debate, women had little chance to join in the new public discourse. Yet, if activities such as book buying and reading, subscription collecting and extended discourse on literary matters suggest the emergence of a public, then women in late eighteenth-century Germany were also establishing a public. For women, print was becoming a medium for emotional and intellectual exchange that could connect them across both geographical and some social distances. Although the vaunted democratization practiced in the bourgeois public sphere failed women, instead buttressing the separation and segregation of people by gender, still women contributed to its emergence by participating in the literary sphere that led up to it.

In her argument that gender can be understood as a system of crime and punishment, Grant cites Durkheim, who "described crime as a violation and punishment as the expression of collective sentiments against it. In fact, the function of punishment is to sustain social cohesion by sustaining a common consciousness. . . . Durkheim contended [that] all crimes have in common the fact that they provoke a punishment."[3] Grant goes on to explain:

> even though gender's power is hegemonic and exercised through ritualized practices in daily life, the power of gender is also always contingent and contested. The fact that it is an ideological structure that mediates humans' interactions with each other and the world means that its power can at times face crises. . . . Just as crime is a kind of crisis for state power so can certain transgressive behaviors represent a kind of crisis for gender if the "crimes" are revalued through feminist (or other critical) interpretations as heroic, rebellious or otherwise transformative acts.[4]

The formulation of a bourgeois public sphere that overtly proclaimed itself open to all who could meet its standards of reasoning and discourse led some women to define themselves not as women, whose responsibilities and capabilities lay elsewhere, but as rational beings, and thus, to join the public discussion. At the same time, the bourgeois public sphere also provided a framework for interpreting the gender-defying efforts of these women as heroic. These efforts and activities, however, seriously jeopardized the existing gender system and provoked frequent punishments. Thus, by this analysis, too, as well as according to the case studies of Baldinger, La Roche, and others, for women of the educated middle class in late eighteenth-century Germany, there were constant lures and penalties to negotiate. Readers, such as the one who discussed Gatterer in her letter, played a key role in meting out the rewards and punishments.

Yet, readers' situations, too, varied by gender in several ways. Anthony J. La Vopa explains the Enlightenment's perception of the man reader's experience (La Vopa's pronouns imply the reader's gender) as that of the solitary individual who attained "moral autonomy" by being "insulated from the social or political effect of the author's presence."[5] The implication of this expected situation for men (available to women only if they assumed at least some masculine roles or were willing to have masculinity attributed to them) was important: "When print connected a producer (i.e., the author) to a consumer, it empowered the latter by lifting him out of specific contexts and their power relationships; the consumer read with the potentially universal receptivity of the 'human being' (*Mensch*), despite the constraints of his particular station as *Bürger*" (11). La Vopa's comment on the independence of the critic also applies to other kinds of writers as long as they were men: "There was a sense in which market exchange, because it was impersonal, ought to insulate the critic [or other man writer] from his readers' prejudices" (8). If the writer were a woman, however, this model had less effect. Now the consumer read with awareness and attitude addressed quite specifically at the producer, and typically invoking virtue or modesty, salient attributes used to control the texts as well as bodies of all women of this time and class. If a woman poet were properly modest, she would curb her speech, never expose herself to the charge of being courageous, and perhaps not publish, as the Göttingen letter writer implies.

Engelhard-Gatterer's not completely successful circumvention of the impasse between fame (in the form of public writing) and femininity was to stage modesty in much of her writing, and to address its aspect of severely restricting the circumstances under which women could speak. In one short poem, for example, a young woman dreamed that charming Damon had told her he loved her. Modesty, of course, had prevented her from showing any indication of her feelings while she was awake, but now in the dream, since he had revealed his love, it was possible for her to confess, with proper embarrassment, that she loved him, too. While the poem presents a woman remaining within conventional restrictions, in a small way its final lines disturb the naturalness claimed for this gender rule (as for most of the others) by declaring it painful. The young woman in the poem suffers from a secret pain that gnawed her during waking hours but was wonderfully relieved in her dream when she had the chance to speak. The poem reiterates women's need for relief from modesty in the speaker's request that sleep bring her this dream again: "Guter Schlaf, o willst du mich beglücken, / Schenke öfter solche Träume mir" "Good sleep, oh if you want to make me happy / grant me such dreams more often."[6] Yet, her brief reprieve did not overtly disturb society's still dominant rule of female confinement and silence: the speaker suggested no extension of freedom to her waking life, no rousing herself to deal with the world around her. Similarly, the setting of the poem as an idyll allows Engelhard-Gatterer to minimize the appearance that her poem could have any practical message to her readers. Still, in its status as the work of a writer who proclaimed herself a woman on the title page of the collection, the poem unsettles the expectation of feminine silence and reserve.

Another poem using dream as a liberating device also sketches an overt message of female modesty being covertly undermined. In this case, a woman talked aloud, although asleep, and confessed her love by convenient chance in the presence of the loved man. He then himself had the courage to admit his love, too. The dream thus came true in the poem, aptly and significantly titled "Der Lohn der Bescheidenheit" "Modesty's reward" (159–62). Indeed, because modest behavior entailed so many obvious drawbacks, its rewards had to be energetically portrayed. But first a rule as restrictive as modesty had to be circumvented in such a way that punishment could be avoided. By putting the heroine to sleep in a garden (the only place even in an idyll where a man might properly be near a healthy, sleeping, unmarried woman), the woman was deprived of intention, and a circumstance was thereby created in which a woman could actually initiate a love declaration. Engelhard-Gatterer simultaneously made the heroine helpless and vulnerable and empowered her to speak.

As Engelhard-Gatterer would have known, not the moral autonomy that La Vopa identified for men but rather moralizing unanimity was promoted (though not attained) for women as readers and as writers, and the woman writer could expect little, if any, insulation from readers' prejudices. The woman reader was expected to read not as a sovereign "human" being but "as a woman," which is to say within the male-ordered moral, intellectual, and behavioral bounds of eighteenth-century educated middle-class femininity.

The woman writer, of course, was first and foremost not expected at all. But eighteenth-century poetry, for example, with its emphasis on the individual poetic voice, offered women an opening for presenting hitherto little tried versions of the womanly self, even though the opportunity was circumscribed by the conventions of genre and the available discourses of gender. In fact, the very possibility of deviation meant that women's poetry and women poets were vigilantly watched as they negotiated the varying sets of notions and activities associated with femininity. Women, whether as critics, novelists, poets, or mere letter writers, could not expect the literary marketplace to insulate them from social pressure in the way that it insulated men.

Since incursions of women's writing, rather than men's, into the masculine preserve of the public, published word, were a possible gender crime, indications that the writer was a woman endowed readers with a sense of entitlement to judge both the writer and her texts in terms of femininity and to accept, reject, or demand revisions in either area. Readers—including women readers—often took themselves to be more qualified than the author herself for making judgments about her femininity. Women's rigorous patrolling frequently occurred in the social form designated as gossip, a form preserved mostly in letters. Some women, however, had the role of literary confidante to a woman writer, a position that gave the writer a chance to discuss her writing and gave the confidante a degree of influence over the writer as well as a possible mediating role between the writer and others. A literary confidante was, in short, a mentor without the literary skill, experience, or clout that the term suggests when applied to eighteenth-century men. Men, on the other hand, did much of their patrolling in the far more privileged modes of mentoring, editing, and reviewing. But in the changing cultural world of the late eighteenth century, neither all men nor all women were consistently or vigorously engaged in the tasks of maintaining the gender status quo; many opposed it in various ways, some of which had an impact on women writers, who were themselves inevitably at least partial resisters to the gender rules limiting the behavior and opportunities of people designated as women. Reader responses to women writers were part of the contest over redefining (or not) what was acceptably feminine.

This chapter examines how the relations of Philippine Gatterer (later Engelhard) with her readers and with the dominant rules of gender and genre in late eighteenth-century Germany affect her texts and how, to the lesser extent permitted by the evidence, her texts affected her readers. Letters of several different kinds, reviews, and subscription lists, together offer many clues as to the responses of men and women readers to Engelhard-Gatterer's poetry and to her position as a woman writer. The influence of two particularly powerful kinds of reader is also evident in the documentation still available on Gatterer, the influence of (male) mentors and a (female) literary confidante. Together with the poetry itself and its context in a particular strand of the movement of *Empfindsamkeit*, the documentation permits an examination of the poet's responses to them and her efforts to select and control some of her readers, while protecting herself from others, always with her gender and sometimes with theirs very prominent in the interaction. Of the five main strategies that women developed to explain themselves as writers—having a male sponsor, writing one's own explanatory metanarrative, fashioning oneself as, aside from writing, irreproachably respectable, using a pseudonym, or boldly proceeding as though there were nothing to excuse—Gatterer very briefly used a pseudonym but then positioned herself as both respectable woman and competent writer by concentrating on producing metanarratives of herself as woman writer and by endorsing in her writing the conventional femininity of the educated middle class. The responses were not always what she wished.

The Rules of Gender in the *Empfindsamkeit* of Sympathy

Despite its ostensible obeisance to gender rules, one of the important strengths of Engelhard-Gatterer's poetry is that it deals with contradictions between the discourse of femininity, marked most frequently by modesty, virtue, and silence, and the emergent discourse of feeling and speech. The literature of *Empfindsamkeit* is situated at exactly this junction of discourses, and Philippine Engelhard-Gatterer, like Sophie La Roche, had absorbed much of its usefulness for women. *Empfindsamkeit* developed as writers and thinkers began modifying the Enlightenment's focus on reason and logic by attempting to balance head with heart. For educated men the *Empfindsamkeit* meant enriching reason with sympathy; in recent efforts to reassess this literary movement, one scholar, Jochen Schulte-Sasse, has formulated the term "empfindsame Hochaufklärung" "sentimental High Enlightenment" in an attempt to connect the *Empfindsamkeit* directly with the widely recognized (and currently widely debated) achievements of the High Enlightenment.[7] Silvia Bovenschen, however, argues that *Empfindsamkeit* images of the feminine were not an empowering assignment of new competency for women through their emotions, but only an enlargement of competencies for men (adding emotion to reason for them) and a reduction of competencies for women (to an emotionalism that essentially condemned women to domesticity); she illustrates with analyses of Herder, Schiller, Kant, and especially Rousseau.[8] Some women, however, resisted the disempowerment propagated by their male contemporaries and found validation of themselves as writers and thinkers (as opposed to scholars) through the new movement. I identify the women in the earliest strand of *Empfindsamkeit* as concentrating on religious feelings, religious themes, and depictions of the soul. This strand, very evident in the work of Meta Moller-Klopstock (1728–58) and Charlotte Lange-Seidel (1743–78) overlaps with Pietism, especially in the pattern of self-examination and in the frequent assertions of religious faithfulness. The second strand of *Empfindsamkeit* among women, the one to which Philippine Gatterer chiefly adhered (although religious *Empfindsamkeit* is also apparent in many of her poems) entailed feelings and intuition as valid sources of action and cultural participation, which in turn meant women's qualification to join publicly in literary life as writers, as we have seen in the argument of Sophie La Roche, the best known woman writer of the *Empfindsamkeit*. This second strand I call the *Empfindsamkeit* of sympathy because, opposing both the ethos of (usually aristocratic) hedonism and the logic of abstract rationalism, it stresses instead the notion of "Mitleid" "sympathy" between and among morally sensitive souls.[9] Together, Engelhard-Gatterer and Sophie La Roche, appealing to sensitive, sympathetic readers, used the instability and multiplicity of standards in the period of competing discourses so that they could claim to be respectable while also writing, even about previously taboo subjects.

A compact poem in eight folk song stanzas (with alternating lines of tetrameter and trimeter, all iambic), set in the brief time between the speaker's wedding and her wedding night, is an excellent example of Gatterer's solicitation of reader's sympathy even as she crossed the usual bounds of propriety to anticipate her first experience of sexual intercourse. "Nach der Trauung. Den 23. Nov. 1780" "After the Wedding" (quoted in its entirety over the next paragraphs) is one of the many poems Gatterer wrote in the mode of personal history. Along with substantial portions of conventional marriage ideology, the first three stanzas contain expressions of the bride's joy, and apt allusions to the wedding ceremony, at which a pastor friend officiated. In the opening lines, a confident woman speaker proclaims herself as possessor, not possessed, and follows with a firm statement of her own wishes:

> Es ist geschehen! Er ist mein!
>   Der Tod nur soll uns scheiden!
> Gern will ich immer um ihn seyn,
>   In Freuden und in Leiden.
>
> Im Tempelchen ward ich getraut
>   Wo ich oft Tröstung hörte;
> Wann mich—von Red' und Sang erbaut—
>   Kein eitler Städter störte.
>
> Oft wünschte meines Freundes Blick
>   Und Wort mir frohes Leben—
> Jetzt hat er selbst mir Lust und Glück
>   Im Gatten übergeben.

[It has happened! He is mine! / Only death will part us! / Gladly will I always be near him / in joy and in sorrow.
In the little temple I was married, / where I often heard consolation / when—edified by speech and song— / no vain city fool disturbed me.
Often my friend's glance / and word wished me a happy life— / Now he himself has given me to delight and happiness / in my husband.]

The speaker positions herself firmly in the category woman, presenting an internalized repetition of the marriage vows from the perspective of the dominant version of femininity ("only death," "in joy and in sorrow")—and also claiming to be on the approved, rural side of the eighteenth-century country/city dispute. But in the second stanza, dissonant tones quickly enter, first acoustically in the repeated *t*-sounds, many in consonant clusters, and then thematically in the strongly alliterative phrase ("eitler Städter störte") about city fools. Contrasting with the pastor friend's good will is their ill will, presumably because they are critical of the speaker's boldness in becoming a public literary figure and possibly, since she calls them vain, because they are jealous. Yet, by not specifying why some people criticize her, Gatterer avoids raising issues that might reduce her readers' sympathy for the depiction of herself as respectable and sensitive:

> Zwar hört ich Fluch für Weib und Mann—
>   Und bebt'—und schwamm in Zähren!
> Doch faßt' ich mich, denn Tugend kann
>   Auch hier uns Trost gewähren!

> [To be sure, I have heard curses for wife and man— / and have quivered— and swum in tears! / but I pulled myself together, for virtue can / give us comfort even here.]

The poem conveys the impact on her of the others' ill will through her specific reactions of trembling and tearing and through the truncated phrasing of the first two lines. Then the discourse of virtue, itself effectively a list of gender rules, is quickly deployed again to counter society's efforts. A display of how she continues to solve problems by positioning herself as a virtuous woman provides a transition from the immediate past events to the future:

> Drückt schwere Arbeit meinen Mann
> Mit Zentnerschwere nieder,
> So scherz ich mit ihm, lach ihn an—
> Und sieh—er lächelt wieder.

[If heavy work presses down on my husband / with the heaviness of a hundred weight / then I will jest with him, smile to him / and, look, he smiles again.]

This weak stanza of conventional marriage ideology, with its clumsy wording (two uses of "schwere" in two lines) and metrical awkwardness ("so scherz ich mit ihm, lach ihn an"), contains the argument that the speaker will voluntarily play the role of caring and attentive wife. This is in contrast to the usual notion of submissive obedience, as she explains in the next stanza:

> Mein Fluch war Unterwürfigkeit
> Zwar will er's nie begehren—
> Auch würde seine Billigkeit
> Mir nie dieß Loos erschweren.

[My curse was submissiveness / To be sure, he never intends to ask it—/ Also his sense of what is right / would never make my lot heavier.]

Now it is her load rather than his that is heavy and the husband rather than the wife who should be caring and attentive. The "lot" that has befallen the speaker is so commonplace as to require no explanation since it, like her next fear, is the same for many women; the word "us" in the next stanza signals the presumed shared experience of the speaker and a knowing subset of her readers:

> Und Schmerz, der uns zu Müttern macht,
> Den will ich gern ertragen.

> Wann erst das Kind am Busen lacht—
>   Vergißt man Angst und Plagen.
>
> Nur das Geheimnis dieser Nacht!—
>   Die Augen gehn mir über!—
> Das ist es was mich angstvoll macht—
>   Ach wär sie doch vorüber!![10]

[And pain, which makes us mothers / I will gladly bear. / Once the child is laughing at the breast / one forgets fear and worries. Only the secret of this night!— / My eyes fill with tears! / This is what makes me anxious—/ Oh, were it only over!]

It is neither the man's possible claim that she subordinate herself to him nor fear of childbirth that disturbs the speaker most, but rather, the impending experience of sexual intercourse, which she faces with fear and ignorance. She cannot feel herself free and capable in this situation of unequal knowledge. While feminine virtue made a respectable woman's ignorance mandatory and her fear inevitable, Gatterer found a way to make her discomfort speakable. The syntax and punctuation of the final stanza signal the climax of the poem, which ends abruptly and without resolution: there is no morning-after epilogue, no companion poem written on the next day. In that respect, the speaker does nothing to prevent other young women from confronting their wedding nights with the same ignorant trepidation. Yet, by positioning herself first as an admirable woman (getting married, claiming her allegiance to virtue), she can strike at the gender rule that requires women to be submissive to men and can bring up the subject of the female experience of sexuality. A few years later, in a collection of poetry that she composed for very young children, Engelhard-Gatterer wrote relatively explicitly about childbirth, calling attention to parallels between human and animal birth processes and especially to the pain experienced by the human mother; in her introduction she defends this approach to reproduction against expected criticism.[11] Despite her adherence to respectability, Gatterer's explorations of topics that for women of the educated middle class were rarely problematized or discussed make up much of the interest of her poetry today.

  Magdalene Philippine Gatterer was born in Altdorf near Nürnberg in 1756.[12] Three years later, when her father, Johann Christoph Gatterer (1727–99), was called to become a professor of history at the new university in Göttingen, the family moved to the territory ruled at a distance by King George of England. Philippine was the third of fifteen children. It is certain that, by the standards the eighteenth century applied to women, Philippine and her sisters had a reasonably good education. Their father benefited from whatever he expended on the girls' education by putting them to work for him. Whether it was copying manuscripts or tabulating historical statistics or tinting maps, the daughters were kept busy by such responsibilities. As for her mother, all that is known of Helene Schubert Gatterer (1728–1806) is that she was the daughter of a cooper (hence, probably minimally educated) and that she bore fifteen children. Given the nutritional and medical conditions under which she was living, this presumably occurred at considerable biological and psychological stress to her. Her role in the talented daughter's life, as Philippine Gatterer publicly described it, was the conventional one, imposing social expectations on her daughter; in particular, she worried about the chances for marriage of a young woman who wrote poetry.

But marry Philippine did, in 1780, at age twenty-four. Three years later, the young Madame Engelhard—the French loanword "Madame" was used in German for married middle-class women of the time—still thought of herself in terms of her important father. When she and her husband were asked to write autobiographical sketches for a book on scholars and writers in Hessia, her husband, Johann Philipp Engelhard, began his in a straightforward and ordinary way: "I was born on Jan. 21, 1753, in Kassel."[13] The sentence is about himself. As a man he saw himself as an independent subject. Quite different is the approach of his wife, who began: "Johann Christoph Gatterer, Councilor and Professor in Göttingen, is well enough known to the reading world. When he was still teaching in Nürnberg at the school there, I was born to him as his third child, in 1756, on October 21."[14] There could hardly be a more striking model of the different self-presentations of men and women. Engelhard-Gatterer described herself in terms of relationships, as her father's daughter, dependent on him, his reputation, his decisions. Although she was already a mother, she still thought of herself in terms of her rank order among her siblings. Furthermore, the gender rules of her time required of her a more circuitous route to self-assertion—through her father, through good works, through a language of self-effacement. Altogether, in a way that is characteristic of many women, she envisioned herself less as a subject than her husband did; she could say "I" only after she had established herself within a network of kin.

It is true that her father was a remarkable man, a prolific publisher of historical facts and statistics, producing numerous handbooks on historical reference and two journals that ran consecutively from 1767 to 1781. Literary women of eighteenth-century Germany came from the homes of scholars, unlike many of their male counterparts, who came from the homes of pastors.[15] (Friderika Baldinger, the daughter of a pastor whose scholarliness is unknown, was one of the few exceptions, although she was left fatherless very early.) The scholarly lineage of women writers results from the better chance at a minimally adequate education available to girls in such households. Scholarly households were themselves concentrated in university towns. Of these, none boasted a more broadly active intellectual life than Göttingen, and in no other place of comparable size between 1770 and 1790 was there such an extraordinary group of women. One was Caroline Michaelis (1763–1809), whose correspondence at age seventeen with her friend Luise Gotter had criticized Gatterer's too free thinking and talking; herself later freed from many of the rules of female propriety by early widowhood, Caroline Michaelis was arrested for sympathizing with the importation of the French Revolution to the left bank of the Rhine, as well as threatened with harsh social sanctions for becoming pregnant extramaritally. Her legacy of letters, which continued when she married the scholar and critic August Wilhelm von Schlegel and then divorced him to marry the philosopher Friedrich Schelling, rank her as one of the outstanding private writers of German Romanticism. Other notable Göttingen women of Gatterer's time included Friderika Baldinger, Baldinger's friend and correspondent Dorothea Wehrs (later Spangenberg, 1755–1808), Therese Heyne (later divorced Forster and married Huber, 1764–1829), Margareta Wedekind (later divorced Forkel and married Liebeskind, 1765–1853), and Dorothea Schlözer (later Rodde, 1770–1825). Not far away, in Münden, lived Charlotte von Einem (later von Emminghaus, 1756–1833), who in the nineteenth century would write her useful autobiography about growing up in the eighteenth century and who, as a young woman, was a friend of Philippine Gatterer. The women on this list who were not the daughters of scholars had married scholarly husbands. And through fathers, brothers, or husbands, all but Einem had practically daily indirect contact with Göttingen's new university. Although none of the women was permitted to attend, their lives were nonetheless enriched by the presence of this major academic institution, and one of them, Dorothea Schlözer, was granted a degree.

Even among the outstanding women of her town, the young Philippine Gatterer was known for her strong personality. Her new friend Charlotte von Einem sketched her in a letter shortly after they became acquainted:

Strength and majesty in her looks, in which her heroic soul is perfectly reflected. German and unshakably honest: one of the rare members of our sex who says much with few words. A young woman who has extraordinary talent for poetry. Sometime you should see what bold wit this girl has . . . A girl for whom I can never have too much respect. Every week I learn from her marvelous letters to treasure her great soul more.[16]

(As often is the case, the woman to woman correspondence of Einem and Gatterer mentioned here was apparently not preserved; their only surviving letters are to men.) Einem's words contain no traces of the punishments that would flag infringements of the gender rules; Einem sees her friend as heroically flaunting the rules, as her words a year later indicate: "That is a girl such as hardly exists in the world any more. So completely master over her feelings, so strong, so free from all weaknesses of our sex."[17] Words of praise for a rule-breaking woman entailed making her an exception to the stock versions of gender behavior accepted in the society and internalized by women themselves. Although, as her poems about modesty show, Gatterer was not exempt from the urge and need to fulfill the dominant gender rules, her friend interpreted Gatterer as a bold transgressor who meets the (hypothesized) more energetic standards for women in the distant past.

One of Gatterer's own public accounts of her negotiations between the two important positions of being a respectable (and therefore unexceptional) woman and transgressing the rules is contained in a verse autobiography, "Mein poetischer Lebenslauf" "My poetic career," which formed the introduction (six pages long) to her first book.[18] As a self-justification, the poem makes a valuable barometer of how a public writer constructed an identity that she believed would be acceptable to polite readers by positioning herself favorably in terms of the gender rules, yet excusing her writing.

The Call to Poetry

The first of several narratives composed by Engelhard-Gatterer about herself as a writer, "Mein poetischer Lebenslauf" is a repertory of strategies drawing on both dominant and emergent discourses. It starts, quite differently from her prose self-history, with herself as called to be a poet:

> In Kinderjahren schon fühlt' ich Beruf zum Dichten,
> Und hohe Gluht in meiner Brust;

> Kein Spiel, kein Puppentand konnt' ihn in mir vernichten,
>   Den Trieb zu edler, bessrer Lust!
> [Already in my childhood years I felt the call to write / and high ardor in my breast; / no game, no doll's trifle could destroy that in me, / the drive for a nobler, better joy!]

The claim that she had felt called to poetry since childhood is one of Gatterer's recurrent motifs. Much later she wrote, "How I arrived at poetry, I hardly know myself . . . the spark of genius was ignited by Mother Nature."[19] Among the explanations that public women writers advanced for their seeming deviation from gender norms, the new conception of the poet as inspired and summoned by an outside force freed the bold woman from individual responsibility for her rule-breaking activity (as the dream state did in the modesty poems) and countered the naturalness that society claims for its gender rules with the naturalness that poets could now claim for their verse. The exalted quality of having a special calling is unmistakable here, too. Gatterer both defended and glorified herself in these stanzas.

The call to poetry, if it could be added to the permissions granted to women of the educated middle class, would allow a considerable expansion of women's options. While the feeling-woman notion had dispensed a general validation for cultural participation, it gave an individual woman no specific permission to write. To explain this deviance from the usual rules and roles of an educated middle-class woman, a litany of other rationalizations and pretexts was usually invoked, such as the one that Wieland's introduction to *Fräulein von Sternheim* had helped to establish. Addressing the originally unnamed woman who wrote the novel, Wieland described her composition as an act of private entertainment: "a work of your imagination and your heart, which was written down only for your own diversion."[20] He went on by quoting a letter by the unnamed author in which she wrote:

> You know what prompted me to devote the few idle hours that remained to me after the discharge of essential duties to this recreation of the spirit. You know that I have always cherished the ideas I sought to realize in the character and actions of Miss von Sternheim and her parents; and with what does one occupy one's mind more gladly than with that which one holds dear? There were hours when this occupation was a kind of necessity for my soul. Thus, before I knew it, this little work came into being, though I began and carried it on without knowing whether I would be able to complete it, and though I feel its imperfections as keenly as you do. But it is intended only for you and

me—and if, as I hope, you approve of how this daughter of my mind thinks and acts, for our children. If through their acquaintance with her, they were strengthened in true, general, active goodness and honesty—how that would delight the heart of your friend!

The litany includes writing as a pastime after more important duties are performed, as therapy for unnamed problems ("you know what . . .", "necessity for my soul"),[21] as a form of self-reflection or as a self-inventory for the reader to judge, as involved with family ("Sternheim and her parents"), as an extension of motherhood both in the sense of the text as a child ("this daughter of my mind") and its purpose as educating children (an explanation Friderika Baldinger had also proposed in one of her failed attempts to explain the idea of publishing). All of these were congruent with educated middle-class notions of femininity in that women of this group were to keep themselves busy, find secular solutions to emotional matters, and engage themselves in the discourse of motherhood. Gatterer's invocation of genius was different. Lacking any special connection with femininity, it seemed to operate similarly for women and men. Nonetheless, since assertions about calling entailed the risk that Gatterer would sound immodest, she often accompanied them with depictions of herself as insignificant and with unpretentious domestic metaphors (such as picking feathers). In "Mein poetischer Lebenslauf," Gatterer uses a stanza form that incorporates the same duality of the grand and the homespun: the rhymed quatrains consist of alexandrines (iambic hexameters, usually with a caesura in the middle), which were the high literary line of drama and epic, alternating with iambic tetrameter, one of the common lines in folk songs and ballads.

Her first desire to write could be reconciled well with respectable femininity, as conceived by her class, since the thought of imitating nature poets did not lead to action:

> Kaum wuchs ich auf, und sah in mannigfachen Bildern,
>   Die immer wechselnde Natur,
> So seufzt' ich: Könnt' ich sie, wie meine Dichter schildern!
>   Doch noch blieb es beym Wunsche nur.
>
> [Hardly had I grown up and seen in multifarious images / always changing nature, / then I sighed: If I could only describe it like my poets / but still it was no more than a wish.]

Unexplained is how and when she as a young reader became engaged with poetry sufficiently to have identified a group of poets she could call hers. In another stanza, she writes that when she actually began to compose poetry, she still maintained social proprieties, singing her poems to piano music, an encouraged form of artistic exercise for a well brought up young woman. She labels the activity innocent and says her songs were secret. It might appear that if the exercise were innocent to her, there would have been no need to conceal it. While genius had been posed as excusing or at least explaining the action of the woman herself, secrecy deflected blame for the woman's writing from one of the other parties most likely to be thought culpable, the woman's parents (or later her husband). A few stanzas later, Gatterer mentions her fear that people would accuse her of seeking fame:

> Ich sing' auch wahrlich! nicht um die mir kleine Ehre,
>   Daß man mit Fingern auf mich weist,
> Und dann der Fremde spricht: In aller Welt!—das wäre
>   Denn also Euer schöner Geist?
>
> [I do not sing, truly, for the little honor / of having people point at me / and then the stranger says: What on earth—this / is the mind you admire?]

She tries to prove her modesty by anticipating the scoffing of observers. Since fame broke the rules for women, such demurring was, of course, common among women writers. Karsch, for example, insists that she does not write in order to become famous. She starts one of her poems: "Lady, do I write for fame, and for eternity? / No, for the pleasure of my friends!"[22] And Susanne Bandemer, a reliable voice of society's gender rules, writes decades later:

> Für Dichternachruhm hab' ich weniges Gefühl;
> Mir gab mein Genius ein kleines Seitenspiel,
> Hiermit versüss' ich mir des Lebens bittre Leiden;
> Und die Erinnerung an die entflohnen Freuden
> Ist für mein Herz Genuss. . . . [23]
>
> [For the poet's fame I have little sense; / to me my genius gave a small lyre / with which I sweeten life's bitter sufferings; / and the memory of long gone joys / is a pleasure for my soul.]

Proper women, in yet another move of self-trivialization, eschew any desire for fame.

Gatterer denied ambition for publicity and anticipated the punishment (strangers pointing fingers and making mildly derogatory comments) fame would and did bring (as shown in Caroline Michaelis's letter, written after the publication of Gatterer's first poetry collection, which was introduced by this poem); she attempts to vouch for her poetry in part by asserting her own conformity to educated middle-class expectations of young women. When the narrator brings her self-portrait into her present time (she was twenty-two), she again invokes modesty, deprecating her appearance and claiming no adornment except a smile:

> Jetzt ganz erwachsen—zwar mit wenig Reiz beglückte
>   Das Schicksal mich und mein Gesicht;
> Unschuld'ges Lächeln war's, das Wang und Lippen schmückte,
>   Und zu gefallen such' ich nicht.
> [Now all grown up—but fate adorned / me and my face with little charm; / Innocent smiling was what embellished my cheeks and lips / and I did not try to be pleasing.]

The lines describe a young woman's experience of herself as that experience was construable within the ideological possibilities of the time; in the process they reinscribe the dominant understandings of educated middle-class femininity. When a properly modest woman believes that her beauty is an important measure of her worth, she can never feel adequate; the self-critical element entailed in modesty will force her to discover defects in herself. Gatterer seeks relief from this in a way that is highly conditioned by her times. Her innocence, that slippery feminine virtue bitterly glossed by Mary Wollstonecraft as ignorance, which, like modesty, enforces passivity, is what partially makes up for her insufficient beauty. Gatterer's innocence is expressed in smiles, the traditional expression of the subordinate and the one seeking to please. In a variation of the unintentionality topos, Gatterer writes that her smiles are uncalculated; she dares not admit trying to please (even though another gender rule of the time stipulated that she must be pleasing). The contradiction is apparent. The woman avows that she is not attempting to please, but, as the continuation makes plain ("Doch fand ich, daß allein nicht Schönen nur gefallen, / Sah Männerherzen mir sich weihn" "Yet I found that it is not just beauties who please, / I saw men's hearts dedicated to me") she is aware that her "innocent smiles" are effective. Gatterer depicts herself as modest, and yet, she also asserts her attractiveness to the people whose approval—among educated middle class women—counted most, the approval of (educated middle-class) men.

When her self-depiction is analyzed for its participation in modes of social control, it is evident the poem suggests that every woman (of the educated middle class to whom Gatterer directed her attention), not just the beautiful ones, had a good chance in the existing system of wife allocation if she behaved as expected. Gatterer, participating in the circulation of this ideology, presented herself as an example. Despite her plain features, she begins to hear the notes of love around her. She responds, she goes on to assert, by joining in "with her lyre," and then quickly reassures readers, in metaphorical language that mixes painting and poisoning, about the propriety of everything she writes:

> Nur werd' in süsses Gift ich nie den Pinsel tauchen,
>   Nie frischen Reiz der Wollust leihn,
> Nie heimlich glühend Feu'r in junge Seelen hauchen;
>   Mein Lied sey, wie mein Leben, rein.
>
> [Only I will never dip my brush in sweet poison / never lend fresh charm to lust, / never secretly breathe glowing fire into young souls; / my songs shall, like my life, be pure.]

This disclaimer is yet another assertion of her innocent virtue, rather than a comment on her poetry. By writing only the primmest and lightest of love poetry, such as the compositions on modesty, Gatterer avoids the risk she describes of secretly poisoning her unsuspecting readers. The metanarrative poem is thus used to deflect charges that Gatterer anticipates from critics about her subject matter, motivation, deviations from traditional poetic standards, and effects on susceptible readers.

One of her subjects, for instance, was religion:

> Auch wag' ich Stammelnder den Herrn der Welt zu singen,
>   Und flöge gern erhabnen Flug.
> O könnt ich ihm dereinst der Andacht Psalmen bringen!
>   Doch ist ein Mädchen dem genug?— —
>
> [Also I, stammerer, dare to sing to the Lord of the world / and would like to fly the sublime flight. / Oh if I could some day bring him psalms of devotion! / But is a young woman up to that?—]

Religious poetry was not a conventionally female genre in Gatterer's time. Indeed, much religious poetry in the eighteenth century was distinctly tied to exactly the kind of scholarship unavailable to women. Klopstock, for example, admired by women readers as well as men, used for his religious odes forms derived from the Greek; this reinforced in women the sense that to write poetry they needed an education few could attain. One of Gatterer's younger contemporaries, for example, Friederike Koch (1772–1812), the one whose reading after leaving school was limited to Sundays, is depicted as experiencing the full impact of the scholarly disqualification. She had already written poems at school, inspired by Gellert, but now at home she discovered the influential eighteenth-century theoretician Sulzer. What she learned from him, her biographer reported, was discouraging: "For the demands that Sulzer in his theory made on a good poem took away all her courage to make new efforts because she doubted that she possessed the talent and education to meet these demands and to satisfy herself and the world."[24] She stopped writing. Not until years later, when she discovered that Sulzer's requirements were no longer universally accepted did she resume composing poetry. Women, as newcomers to the domain of poetry composition, and especially the serious realm of religious poetry, were seldom confident enough to disregard what they thought was prevailing practice, and in their isolation, they were often misinformed even about that. Gatterer was comparatively fortunate to know that she need not master Greek metrics to write poetry that was acceptable in the 1770s, although religious poetry in the exalted form she thought of remained largely beyond her reach.

Gatterer's statements in "Mein poetischer Lebenslauf" about herself and her poetry show her negotiating a relationship with her readers. The *Empfindsamkeit* of sympathy emphasizes a broad audience of readers without advanced education, whose hearts, in the rhetoric of the time, are directly touched by the moral emotions of the writer. Thus, the *Empfindsamkeit* deployed an aesthetic of affect and a comparatively egalitarian notion of literature that empowered new groups of inexperienced women readers—including domestic servants, for example, or middle-class girls in homes hostile to female education beyond the most basic skills. Gatterer addresses her relationship to her readers explicitly, saying she wants her poems to be honored and read aloud in chaste circles, where listening girls would blush because of their tender feelings and not out of shame. She expected readers of both sexes, but all of them should have pure and feeling hearts. Hers is an aesthetic of shared sentiments based on acceptance of eighteenth-century middle-class morality. Having worked so hard to establish her own purity and modesty, she dismissed two groups of critics, both the flirtatious ones, who were not as respectable as she, and the narrow-minded, who might find her too free.

Most women writers were disheartened by the possibility of being charged with excessive freedom. At exactly the time when freedom was being endorsed as fundamental to enlightened thought and enlightened political behavior, women were being taught to deny it to themselves. An older contemporary of Engelhard-Gatterer's, Charlotte Seidel, concerned that she might look too opinionated and too different from the norm (for women), was constantly scratching out words in her letters.[25] Gatterer, however, both because she draws on an emergent middle-class discourse that privileged freedom and feelings over the older categories of either flirtation or prudery, and because she knows she herself has carefully censored the poems in her volume, professes in her introductory poem to be unconcerned about appearing too free. To the extent that she succeeds in being inoffensive in terms of the dominant discourse of her time, Philippine Gatterer is usually uninteresting today, but because her standards of censorship were loosened by the new discourses and because of their possibilities for giving words to her lived experience, her poetry remains readable two centuries later.

Gatterer concludes her introductory poem by identifying the readers and judges whose response she seeks. First, she wants evaluation by experienced poets. And then she desires the approval of readers who belong to the aristocracy of virtue, the new idealized group valued not for their public rank but for their private qualities:

> Der Edlen Beyfall nur such' ich mir zu erwerben,
>   In denen Geist und Tugend wohnt;
> Und wär's der Lieder Loos mit mir zugleich zu sterben;
>   Bin ich durch ihn genug belohnt.[26]

[The applause of the noble ones I wish to earn / those in whom spirit and virtue live; / and if the fate of the songs is death along with me / I will still have been rewarded enough.]

Praise from the moral and intellectual elite is declared a more important achievement than enduring literary fame. Traditional aesthetic criteria are secondary. Literature of the *Empfindsamkeit* frequently characterizes readers and critics steeped in knowledge of literary forms and techniques as unreceptive to the literature of sympathy. This attitude complicated Gatterer's relationships with her would-be literary mentors.

Complex Relations with Male Mentors and Female Literary Confidantes

For beginning writers, an especially influential kind of reader is the man, or perhaps woman, of letters who offers advice and help with the stages and elements of literary productivity. Discussing the literary help given by eighteenth-century men writers to women writers in England, Jane Spencer describes how Richardson, Fielding and others "enjoyed themselves by offering gallant compliments to ladies of letters who remained flatteringly inferior."[27] Gottfried August Bürger, one of several men who played the role of mentor to Philippine Gatterer, wrote to her: "Learn prettily, little doll of my heart, to work on a few lines for whole days, on a stanza for whole months, and on a song that can be sung in one breath for whole years."[28] There is a contradiction in Bürger's message, one part delighting in Gatterer's attributed childishness, and the other encouraging her to cultivate a serious (and adult) approach to her literary activity. Gatterer never accepts the notion of obsessive polishing, perhaps because to do so she can not remain a little doll, and thus, might lose her place in the hearts of the people who count most in the literary world. Perhaps also because, for herself as a woman writer, and thus, as a poet of comparatively limited education, such fine-tuning is impossible. In the introductory poem she describes her earliest response as a reader of poetry:

> Las ich dann Dichter—Wie, dacht' ich, in lauter Reimen?
>   Und doch bemerkt man keinen Zwang.—
>   Und schon versucht' ich's selbst . . . . [29]

[Then when I read the poets—What? I thought, all in rhymes? / and yet one feels no strain. — And already I was trying it myself. . . .]

The impression of effortlessness helps Gatterer feel able to write. Writing without straining or training remains her choice, to the consternation of systematically educated men.

For women writing in the eighteenth century, male mentors were both an advantage and a hazard. The women constantly felt the danger of being dominated or of having their work interpreted as the work of the man. And yet, they had little choice, for there were few women in a position to offer other women the help of an important mentor—and in late eighteenth-century Germany the most famous of these few, Sophie La Roche, was not a poet. On the whole, even literary women lacked the prestige, the experience (with critics, publishers, and audiences), and in many cases, the basic education to be mentors to other women, although they fulfilled another less recognized role of literary confidante, a role in which one woman advocated for another with the purpose of furthering her literary career. The more comprehensive teaching, advising, encouraging tasks that constitute mentoring, however, were still necessarily in the hands of men. As she began her writing career, Philippine Engelhard-Gatterer had an important literary confidante, Charlotte von Einem, and three notable mentors: her father, Heinrich Christian Boie (1744–1806), and Bürger (1747–94).

Although Gatterer was fortunate to have a father who, though largely self-educated, knew much that could be helpful to her, he was not her first literary mentor. That was Boie, the leading critical mind of the Göttingen Hain group of poets, and editor of a literary almanac that in the early 1770s first made the Hain poets famous. Gatterer writes about Boie's role in her life in another metanarrative poem:

>   Ich sagte zu Aeltern und Schwestern und Brüdern
> Zu keinem ein Wörtchen von meinen Liedern,
> Bis BOIE einst hinters Geheimnis kam
> Und sich von einigen Abschrift nahm.
> Als drauf ich die Dinger im Almanach sah —
> Da stand ich halb lachend, halb weinend, euch da!
> Freund Boie gab auch den Gevattersmann ab,
> Der mir den Namen Rosalia gab.[30]

[I said to parents and sisters and brothers / not one little word about my poems; / til BOIE finally got wind of the secret; / and made several copies. / When after that I saw the things in the Almanac— / there I stood half laughing, half crying! /
Friend Boie also was the godfather / who gave me the name Rosalia.]

According to the description, Boie's mentoring was both limited and important: Gatterer's first publication was entirely his doing. The frequently invoked topos of a man's purportedly chance intervention in a woman's private writing, yet another variant of unintentionality, had also been used to explain La Roche's first novel, deployed by Wieland in the first sentences of his introduction where he asserts her unawareness of the publication until the printed volume is in her hands: "Do not be alarmed, my friend, to receive, instead of the manuscript of your 'Sternheim,' a printed copy, which reveals the whole treason that I have committed against you."[31] "Treason" suggests the enormity of this particular gender crime, the one that kept many women writers private, as Friderika Baldinger's case has illustrated. Gatterer too claimed Boie had not asked her advance consent—"Was war zu machen? Es war geschehn!" "What was to be done? It had already happened!" When Gatterer, La Roche, and their contemporaries appealed to unintentionality and chance, they justified behavior they thought praiseworthy even though it deviated from the gender rules for women. Unintentionality overtly rendered the behavior useless to others, for usefulness would derive from emulation, but if emulation were admitted, the deed would no longer be unintentional. Along with it came the suggestion that only a woman who had not (visibly) studied and striven for an accomplishment, such as writing, could perform that accomplishment well. For women, the praiseworthy was supposed to be natural rather than learnable.

In the same vein of conventional feminine modesty, Gatterer uses the passage of verse autobiography that prefaces a long verse tale to remind her readers that her first publication was under a pseudonym. She then vaguely places the responsibility for the ineffectiveness of the false name on rumor, before hastily moving on to mention the most important consequence of the spreading news, the need to divulge the truth to her parents, especially her father. She performed the task in a birthday poem for him. While he might have been alarmed if women had attempted any large scale revision of their situation, the astonished Johann Christoph Gatterer was not disturbed by one daughter's departure from silence and public invisibility. He gave her a reprimand, but softly, she says, not scornfully (118–19).

The attitude of the men close to aspiring women writers was an important but little discussed matter. La Roche, in one account of writing *Fräulein von Sternheim,* includes a reference to the issue. She records her anxious thought: "What will your good husband say? and what about Count St——n, his great friend and the head of the house—what will they say if they were to see me writing so much or if they were to find such a piece of paper?"[32] Georg La Roche and Count Stadion were the two most powerful men in her life when she started writing. Although, as her wording indicates, her relationship to Stadion was through her husband, who was the count's employee and perhaps also his illegitimate son, she too was a member of the courtier's daily social circle, living, when she began *Sternheim,* at his Warthausen castle with the rest of his family and attempting along the way to raise her small children there. (Sophie La Roche's experience of intimate connections with the aristocracy was quite different from that of Philippine Gatterer and the other more exclusively middle-class late eighteenth-century women writers in Germany.) Yet, important as these men were in her life—they appear as judges and police in her words here—she does not depict herself seeking their permission in advance, and she does not say whether her worries materialized. Using her technique of juxtaposition, La Roche simply switches from the men and their possible wishes to her own goals: "But I wanted to raise a paper girl now, because I did not have my own any longer" (202). She hints at a conflict between men and her writing, but, returning to her interest in girls—and her own role as mother rather than wife—she leaves the problem unreconciled in her account, although she and other women writers must have addressed it in their "real" lives.

Confronted with his daughter's transgression, Gatterer's father becomes a supportive reader of her writing. Recognizing her deficiencies according to the dominant literary culture, he offers to teach her the fundamentals of metrics, as she explained in the second verse autobiography:

> Zu der Zeit wollt' er mir gütig erklären
> Was Dacktilus und Spondeen wären,
> Und alles das—. Doch ich muß bekennen,
> Kaum weiß ich noch die Namen zu nennen.
> O was so schwer ist, begreif ich nie!
> Ich liebe nur Praxis, nicht Theorie.
> So mach ich mir Hauben und Kleider und Hut—
> Nie lernt' ichs nach Regeln—doch stehn sie mir gut.[33]

[At this time he kindly offered to explain to me / what dactylic and spondaic mean / and all that—. But I must admit, / I hardly still know the names. / Oh anything so difficult I'll never understand. / I only love practical things, not theory. / That's how I make bonnets and clothes and hats— / I never learned the rules—but they look good on me.]

The lessons, being incompatible with the rest of her education, for which she chooses a specifically feminine and domestic metonymy, are useless. Gatterer herself realizes she did not know "the rules" of poetry but also decides that she does not want to learn them. She considers them crutches, and perhaps she also senses that the elite literary practice her father would teach her would not assist her in speaking of her own main concerns, concerns not addressed by scholarly or literary theory. Drawing on *Empfindsamkeit*'s stress on sympathy between writer and readers and on women's emotional sensibilities, women poets as well as novelists could offset their lack of education.

Professor Gatterer did not find a way to teach his daughter about metrics. And yet, his supportive attitude was basic to her accomplishment, as she explains in another poem, which contains some of her best stanzas. Written in 1778, when her father was acutely ill, "Den 15. October" "The 15th of October" describes their relationship. As in "Mein poetischer Lebenslauf," the lines alternate between two contrasting lengths, in this case pentameter and dimeter, at least for the first six lines of each octave. The effect is a meditative slowing of the poem's rhythm with each line of dimeter. The couplets of iambic pentameter that then conclude each stanza again produce a contrast and sense of almost unexpected closure, especially since these lines are tightly stitched into the whole by means of an *ababcdcd* rhyme scheme:

> Wie gütig nahm an meinen kleinen Freuden
>   Mein Vater Theil;
> Und war ich blass—besorgt er innr'e Leiden—
>   In welcher Eil'
> Dacht er dann drauf mich wieder zu erfreuen
>   Durch Freundlichkeit!
> Hieß mich in Fluren gehn, mich zu zerstreuen,
>   Und gab mir oft auch selber das Geleit.
>
> Kam ich, die Stille suchend, auf sein Zimmer,
>   Voll Phantasey—
> Im Busen mein Papier—in Händen immer
>   Die Strickerey,
> Und sas und strickt' aus allen Leibeskräften,
>   Schrieb dann ein Wort;
> So sah ich oft den Blick auf mich ihn heften,
>   Und wurde roth—dann sagt' er: Schreib doch fort.
>
> Und hatt' ich glücklich ein Gedicht vollendet,
>   So kam's heran.
> Er las—ich stand und forschte, unverwendet,
>   Sein Urtheil dann.——
> So, dacht' ich, würd er mich noch lange führen,
>   Mein Muster seyn.
> Da kam der Tod, ihn langsam zu entführen,
>   Doch jezt strahlt wider froher Hoffnung Schein!
>   (89–91)

[How kindly my father joined in with my small joys / and if I was pale—if he worried about unspoken sufferings—in what a rush / would he think of cheering me up again / through his friendliness! / He would tell me to take a walk in the fields, to distract me / and often came along himself. If I came, seeking quiet, to his room, / filled with imagination— / my paper in my bosom—knitting always in my hands, / and sat and knitted for all I was worth, / then wrote down a word; / that is when I would often see his eyes on me / and would blush—then he would say: Do keep writing.

And when I had successfully finished a poem, / it got handed over. / He read—I stood and scrutinized, resolutely, / his judgment then.— / Like this, I thought, he will continue to guide me for a long time, / be my model. / Then came Death, to take him slowly away, / Yet now shines happy hope again.]

Altogether the relationship between mentoring father and writing daughter is deftly drawn, another illuminating representation of the writing experience of a young woman in the eighteenth century. While the speaker went to her father's study to write because of the quiet that she could find there and because the man's study was probably the only reliably quiet room in the house, as well as the only one reserved for intellectual work, with books and a writing table, she was also seeking the protection of her father, who supported her writing while her mother condemned it. After all, she especially mentioned going there when her father was also using the room. He was, as she explicitly noted, her model for how writing was done, even though she would never be able to write under the conditions available to him. Her later descriptions once she married, of writing at the kitchen table, make the contrast unmistakable. Even in her father's space she claims to have combined writing with knitting, something certainly her father neither did nor found it necessary to claim when he was writing. Precisely when she was most explicitly breaking gender rules by actually doing literary work in a distinctly patriarchal place reserved for a man's study and a man's writing, the young woman attempted to assert her simultaneous fidelity to women's work. While writing, she tried to use both the quill and the knitting version of the needle.

The only adult offspring whom fathers could mentor as poets in the late eighteenth century were daughters. Male poets, striving for the intellectual autonomy advocated by the Enlightenment, were unlikely to have close artistic relations to their fathers. As for mothers, given women's lack of literary authority and usually of literary training, the relation of a poet, daughter or son, to a mother was not a problem of intellectual or artistic independence,[34] although for some, such as Philippine Gatterer, the mother's negative judgments could pose personal and familial difficulties. Although her father's offer to explain the technicalities of her craft was unacceptable to Gatterer, she was willing to hear his judgment after she had composed a text. The woman writer let herself be strongly influenced by a male reader. From this perspective, regardless of Professor Gatterer's intentions, he was also his daughter's censor, framing the discourse in which she wrote. She composed literally under his gaze, submitted completed poems to his scrutiny, and read every reaction on his face. As Eva Figes has put it, "any woman living at home, without independent resources, is bound to be influenced by those in authority, and the authority of someone who is loved and respected is the most insidious."[35] This is not usually the way to explore ideas and techniques that deviate from the dominant, or to experiment with writing about aspects of women's lived experience that did not support notions of the prevailing system as natural and right. In this respect, the apparent divergence of views of Gatterer's parents about the issue of her writing may not have been so great after all. The mother was an openly disapproving reader, according to Gatterer. The father seemed supportive, but by virtue of his membership in the dominant group, was a reader likely, at least occasionally, to overpower any inclination of his daughter to give critical voice to the distinctive experience and concerns of the subordinate group. It becomes understandable then, that one of her best poems (the one concerning his illness) was written when he was unavailable as a reader and several others (the marriage poems) appear when her sense of congruence with the dominant group—as she considered the changes her impending marriage was likely to force on her—was at its lowest. On the other hand, her mother was the married woman role model with whom she lived in closest proximity, particularly important because Gatterer knew no other women poets. The idea of being the only one made her see herself as both important and freakish.[36]

Despite the role-constraints imposed on women and the infrequency, or in many places, the total absence of women with the literary education, the publishing experience, and the willingness to mentor other women, responsive women readers nonetheless played important encouraging and guiding roles for women writers. In Gatterer's case, the woman most involved with her writing, to the extent that a record of literary confidantes for Gatterer exists, was Charlotte von Einem. Her critical assessment was based in the belief that technical mistakes were endemic in women's writing, as she wrote to a male friend: "For it seems to me I have observed that we women seldom, almost never, can write poems that are completely free of errors with regard to meter and style." Calling Gatterer by her pseudonym, Einem hastened to add, "Rosalia is to be sure in this last matter far superior to most, but still it affects her sometimes."[37] Einem expected that Gatterer lacked the technical skills important for poetry ratified as excellent in the eighteenth century—and since then, as well. Although she had expressed no previous reservations about her friend's poetry, now, when what had been mere private writing was on the brink of becoming public text, she was concerned that it would not measure up. She was not confident of the *Empfindsamkeit* compromise that Sophie La Roche had pioneered for women of feeling. Einem's anxiety marks her absorption of one of the new tools for excluding women from the public sphere. Following Habermas again, and work by Kramnick based on him, the emergence of a literary public, which was the proving ground for a political sphere separate from the state, "endowed taste with new importance as the vehicle of sociable affiliation . . . [so that] the broadly social project of abstracting 'polite' language resulted in a rather strident fetishization of grammatical correctness and metrical regularity."[38] While Engelhard-Gatterer herself claimed to be addressing a public that she construed on emotional, not literary, terms, the widespread assertion of women's grammatical and metrical incapacity showed an underlying recognition that any literary productivity by them could jeopardize men's domination of literary life. (And by the time when in Germany, too, as in England earlier, in the process Kramnick outlines, "the emphasis on decorous ease gave way to a revaluing of difficult obscurity,"[39] new tactics of excluding women had again been devised.) Demands for grammatical and metrical correctness, hard to meet without advanced education, were a new but quite imperfect tool for excluding women. Again, the feeling woman and her feeling readers could circumvent this barrier.

Not skilled enough in language or literature to help Gatterer directly, Einem, as literary confidante, had suggested male protection for her, hoping an editor would take the poems into his own hands and also compose an introduction, as she wrote to the male friend:

> My Rosalie's poems will come to light at Whitsuntide with her own and not, as was planned until now, with an introduction by Bürger or Kästner. No one admires R., even from this side, more than I do, but still I would wish that some discerning and honest poet had polished them here and there—though not à la Boie of course.[40]

The reference to Boie suggests that his editing had been too drastic. But Charlotte von Einem thought that either of two other writers might be better: the fifty-eight-year-old Kästner (1719–1800), Friderika Baldinger's rationalist friend, or the thirty-year-old Bürger (1747–94), famous author of folk song-like ballads such as "Lenore," and teller, in German, of the Munchausen tales. Gatterer's acquaintance with Bürger was the accomplishment again of Boie, who had arranged for them to meet and had urged Bürger to correspond with the young woman in Göttingen. Since Einem was convinced there was such a thing as correctness, she was not disturbed by the drastically different poetic styles the two men (and their two generations) represented. If any form of male sponsorship and male aesthetic endorsement was preferable to a woman's exposure alone, both the intellectual logician and the reviver of popular forms seemed equally appropriate candidates.

Philippine Gatterer and Gottfried August Bürger

Literary mentors acted variously as first readers, editors, and sources of information and advice about the book trade. Gottfried August Bürger seemed well positioned to perform at least some of these tasks for the young Philippine Gatterer, a fact that delighted Charlotte von Einem, as she told her friend Sprickmann:

> You should see how he wrote to her recently, like a friend and a father: "Dear child, I fear you have been too hasty with several things and will regret it later! I wish I had been able to lend my two eyes to yours, Oh having an honorable critical friend, who has honest intentions and is plain spoken, is a precious thing!" I would like to kiss Bürger because he means it so honorably with the girl and I love him now so heartily![41]

(Einem's citation is corroborated by comparison with Bürger's original letter, published in his correspondence with Gatterer.)[42] The characterization of Bürger's attitude as fatherly is perceptive and ominous, since Philippine Gatterer has already resisted one father's efforts to influence her writing; a poet-to-poet mentoring relationship was far more promising than father-to-poet.

If she does not want Bürger in the role of father, Gatterer is not enthusiastic at the prospect of Bürger as editor either, as Einem unhappily adds: "Yes but then she says no one is supposed to be able to say: Bürger helped her, polished her writing and such pitiable trifles. Otherwise the girl is so clever but here—I plan to send you the little work as soon as it is available." Philippine Gatterer is adamant about her own creation. She wants to get and deserve full credit, a point that for her outweighs Einem's worries and Bürger's warning that instead of credit, she may receive criticism.

A woman writer's attitude toward an editing reader was strongly affected by the isolation in which she had begun writing, even if, like Gatterer, she lived in the midst of a major intellectual community. In her first letter to Bürger, in September 1777, Gatterer describes her situation: "If I had been in the circle of the poets perhaps it would have been good for me—So many were here, and

I didn't even know what they looked like." In a later letter to Bürger, she mentions her isolation again: "How much I would like your silhouette, you are the only one among the poets with whom I am personally acquainted. . . . And now I know you—may our friendship be eternal, like your fame!" (66–67). Writing is a solitary act, but for women in the eighteenth century, this was reinforced by the cultural, educational, and literary exclusions imposed on them. Isolation had many consequences. For Gatterer in particular, it means important areas of ignorance, an attitude that was often both defensive and suspicious, and then the appearance of arrogance, the self-protection of the autodidact. Most of all, in keeping with her assertion of feeling called to poetry, she tries to be thoroughly independent by asserting the absolute integrity of her poetry as her own accomplishment. She refused to let any individual man have a substantial influence on the subjects, diction, meter, or structure of her compositions.

In England, Ann Yearsley (1752–1806), one of the infrequent working-class poets of the eighteenth century, illustrates both the trap that Gatterer was trying to avoid and a solution similar to the one Gatterer chose. Yearsley's first collection appeared with a preface written by her patron, the established writer Hannah More. Linda Zionkowski comments:

> By sentimentalizing Yearsley as a struggling Shakespeare or as Gray's unlettered muse, and by assuring subscribers of the poet's docility as one of the deserving poor, More tries to evoke readers' sympathy and deflect their criticism. But the character that she constructs in the preface also undermines whatever subjectivity that Yearsley's poems might express.[43]

Within two years, however, Yearsley decides to oppose this treatment of herself. She "not only rejects these attempts to label and contain her subjectivity; she also rejects the ruling-class culture that allows this containment to occur" (103). Furthermore, in one poem Yearsley "states that her alienation from this literary culture empowered rather than inhibited her writing" (104).

Gatterer too tries to turn her isolation into an advantage, to avoid a problem that peculiarly afflicted women writers. In her first letter to Bürger, after telling him that she had been unable to meet any of the poets of the Göttinger Hain when they were in her city, she had continued:

> Yet on the other hand it is also good, because otherwise the world could believe that those people had honed me so long that a little something

> had become of me. Most people know that (as far as poetry is concerned) I grew up like a wild tree without any tending; and yet I hear here and there that a professor, or even students are said to help me. Yes, I wanted to teach them! You yourself admitted that you had heard that my admirers made the poems for me. . . . Even when people of the earnest good sort were favorable to me, first, they rarely got to see anything; and second I would have strongly rejected their corrections.[44]

Her pride as a writer and, specifically, as a woman writer was at stake. And now that she had come this far by herself, she wants the credit for it and does not want to have anyone treat her as a puppet—or a daughter.

That Gatterer finds the discrediting rumors exasperating is understandable. Even Charlotte von Einem admits how much the rumors about Nante Goeckingk, one of the well-regarded women poets of the day, affects her reading of Nante's work.

> To be sure, Nante is free from mistakes as far as I know, but what did Amaranth do? And then, it's too bad—and sometimes I threw the book aside when I thought of it—everyone says the songs are not original, just sung by Amaranth in her name, the similarity proves it. Oh that anyone deceives the world like that, and yet, who disproves this talk?[45]

Einem sees the loss to the woman caused by the rumor of help from her husband, L. F. G. Goeckingk ("Amaranth"). While the woman reader, distressed to have the authenticity and independence of a woman writer undermined, throws the book aside, Gatterer, as woman writer, declares her sensitivity to such charges, writing: "Tell me, dear Bürger, what it means that I sometimes can't keep myself above such tittle-tattle. I usually can about other topics."[46] One answer to her question is that such rumors challenge her sole claim to public importance, being a poet. Men, presumed to be competent, did not have their very authorship routinely doubted.

Publicly, Gatterer denies being concerned about issues of authorship and influence. In the poem introducing her first collection, she anticipates claims that she had help from others, quickly challenging such doubters to identify who her helper had been. But the consequences of this independence are great. If she accepts offers of help, she lends a shred of support to rumors that her work is not her own; if she does not accept the offers, she does not learn the elements of poetics that might assist her to improve her writing according to the elite culture. Hard though it is, she plans to make an exception for Bürger, and the way she tells him this reveals the posture she has defensively developed: "You shall have permission to say: This and that I don't like." Even this limited grant was given only because she had judged him worthy, telling him he was one of few people whom she took seriously, "because you understand the difficult art of writing according to the taste of the majority" (36). Her judgment has nothing to do with Bürger's catastrophic economic problems or the low-level civil service job he held—and hated. In her eyes, Bürger, as a university-educated man who had published a recognized body of poetry, resides high on Parnassus, which she, in her literal and figurative long skirts, is impeded from climbing without help. She feels a kinship with Bürger because he successfully writes for the general reader. So on one condition she gives him permission to critique her work, the condition of mutuality: Bürger must also send her some of his work in progress.

Bürger's response is cheerful and amusing—and shows his confidence that he can teach her a great deal.

> I feel a powerful drive in myself to do a critic's job on your children with all my might. Leaving it at "This and that I don't like" is really not enough, when I get started. For don't you know that a well-loved child is kept under the rod?—Philippine's genius is the child that I have begun to love. Either it should turn into something good—or nothing at all. . . . I am glad that you take me seriously, I will make an effort to really be so. Then afterwards the child, when it has grown big and strong, can play games on gramp's nose. And the old gramps, while he is sitting in his grandfather chair weak and sated with life, will have his last joy and happiness in that. (40)

On one level, the offer looks both generous and persuasive. Bürger has not missed the signs Gatterer's letter contains about her difficult situation, although he attributes her touchiness to her character, not to the problem of gender-biased reading that meant that the more competent a woman was as a writer, the less likely she was to get credit for her work.

He tries to explain that accepting criticism is not a bad thing:

> But listen, my little daughter, you seem to me, if I may say so, to be a proud thing if you just plain don't want to owe your education to any mortal. Of course at the end of one's career it is a marvelous sublime thought that one has become what one is entirely by oneself. But how many mortals since Adam can make this claim? And is it really any shame to the grownup hero that a nurse trained him in his childhood? So my Philippine should also not be ashamed to pay attention to this or that hint by a friend—who takes her seriously and is serious himself.

> And how much better it is when such things happen secretly and in private rather than later in public with beardless boy critics. (40–41)

Bürger envisions Gatterer's situation in developmental terms, with himself in the role of educating father and his correspondent (or earlier her genius) as receptive child; to his credit he thinks of the child as outgrowing the parent, not remaining in a state of perpetual childhood, a common eighteenth-century perception of women. He thinks Gatterer should prefer to be tutored privately by a father-figure rather than publicly by arrogant young men who, though younger than she, would be better educated and in fact fully qualified to criticize.

In her answer (1 October 1777), Gatterer discusses the matter in terms of pride, first denying then admitting that she does feel a bit proud of writing so many poems secretly, and thus entirely by herself (47–51); indeed, secret writing, in addition to exonerating people around the woman writer from responsibility for her behavior, also asserts the independence of her writing. Secrecy is one of the pervasive themes when women of the time describe their writing.

Try as she might, Gatterer can find no way to consult with Bürger and still both appear and feel independent. (Bürger, for his part, seems not to have accepted her request to critique his work.) Also because she uses poetry as a form of self-assertion (not necessarily self-expression), Gatterer is unlikely to appreciate either the corrections or the advice of her would-be mentor. Although she sent him poems to critique, Bürger never gave her as much help as he had planned. To Boie, for example, he wrote that he had a whole collection of her poetry in his desk, and that he scolded her very much, no matter how badly it hurt what he called her "considerable vanity" (19). Nonetheless, Bürger's letters to Gatterer, as they have been published, contain no responses to her individual poems. Fundamentally, Gatterer, like Yearsley, wanted "her exclusive control over her writing,"[47] and was careful not to jeopardize it.

Soon after Gatterer decided to publish her first collection of work without consulting Bürger on the matter, he took an action that reinforced her resistance to him, publishing without her approval an edited version of one of her poems. Gatterer's response combines acquiescence with resistance and protest:

> I send you . . . my sincere thanks for the changes to the poem in the almanac. I recognize that this choice of verse is fierier than mine was.

> It would be very nice to collect the judgments, the comments of knowledgeable people on my unpublished poems; but before I write them out twice, or leave them in strange hands for a long time—and run the risk of losing them in the mail, it is better that they and I live and die without fame.[48]

Her poems are not long, but she claims to dislike making copies of them, something Bürger said he could not understand, perhaps because he was not being asked to do copy work for his father, as Gatterer may have been, and also because when he consulted a friend, it did not jeopardize his claim to authorship.

Although he was unable to understand the several threats his criticism posed for her, Bürger knew of Gatterer's sensitivity. He writes her the answer he gave when he was asked whether he edited her poetry as rigorously as everyone else's:

> I answered: *Why not? Anyone who goes along gets caught. Even if it were the empress herself.* He replied: *Ay, you'll get a fine reception with that. Because she said: If Bürger has the nerve to change anything in her poems then this or that fellow take him. Then she would . . . yes and then . . . and then she . . . and would . . . etc.*
>
> That of course should have given me a scare so that I would not dare to lay my murdering hand on the others without your advance knowledge. But as I said! I had no time to talk about that with you. And because of the sins that I had already committed, I also didn't, to tell you the pure truth, completely dare. (His elisions and emphasis, 81)

Here, Bürger blames Gatterer for his failure to consult her about his editing. Yet, he continues to write of all the things he can do for her poetry:

> Believe me, I still can't get over my discomfort that I wasn't able, before the publication of your poems, to talk with you about this and that, for which you would certainly have thanked me eventually. But it was, is and remains impossible to deal with all that adequately in letters. An oral conference of two hours gets more done than ten letters, each as long as a printed sheet. Nevertheless I have still thrived on your wonderful talents . . . Girl! Girl! What would become of you if you had a lover who understood just exactly [the technicalities of poetry]! (79)

Bürger blithely reminds Gatterer that many educated men can teach her the basics that she had never had the opportunity to learn, for, of course, many men were given this training as part of their education, while women were not. Even such ostensibly well-meaning asides tend to belittle Gatterer, just as the many intimate names for her position her as childish while Bürger is authoritative and mature.

Bürger most often makes general statements of praise or warning to Gatterer. In a letter of 17 July 1780, he writes that of the poems she has sent him for his annual volume, none is worthy of being published under her name. Again he gives her advice:

> You, my charming maid, should make a nice try at learning how to hold your course. Because after many lines that are so beautiful that even the best poet could not wish them better for himself, it drops off so fatally that one would like to give you a whack. Especially you should learn, my esteemed Maid Blackbird, to limit the chattiness in your verses. (107)

He proceeds to give her a painful parody of her versifying, saying that just stringing rhymes together is not art, and that if it were, he could make poems in enormous quantities.[49] These statements must have been deeply wounding to Gatterer, who had a high esteem for rhyme. And Bürger goes on to point out that sheer productivity is not important either:

> Wenns damit ausgemacht nur ist,
> So will ich ihr zu jeder Frist,
> Ohn im geringsten zu erblöden
> In Versen ein langes und breites reden,
> Und jährlich marschiert ein dicker Band
> Voll Verse durch das ganze Land.
> (108)
>
> [If that were all there is to it / then I can by any date / without in the least being a fool / talk at great length in verse / and every year a thick volume full of verses / marches through the whole country.]

A lampoon of the cliches that inevitably accompany such easy verse making followed, and then came the sentence calling Gatterer the little doll of his heart and urging her to revise (but giving no clues how). By 1784, the correspondence had lapsed. Despite her own reasons to be wary and unreceptive, and his failures actually to give usable advice, this had been a literary relationship of considerable potential congeniality. Although Engelhard-Gatterer later met additional literary figures, such as Goeckingk, Sprickmann, Nicolai, and others, she had no other mentor after Bürger.

Having, she believed, rejected what could be taught to her, Gatterer relied on "genius," "instincts," "feelings," and the indulgence of her readers. Many other eighteenth-century women show a similar dilemma of striving to write in the style of the time without having the requisite training. Gatterer's British contemporary, Mary Wollstonecraft, wrote her convoluted English sentences without the assistance of the analysis that came to her male literary models from their knowledge of Latin. Unpreparedness belonged to the ethic of unintentionality, and was a continuation of La Roche's enabling effect of difference. Women's literary accomplishment was valued when it presented itself as feminine, even without revisions and without striving for formal correctness. Of course, in most cases, the women themselves could not privilege formal perfection, since they did not have the training to recognize it, much less produce it. Especially in light of the vision of the feeling woman, the image and self-image of a woman bent over her desk revising and rewriting had no place. Claims of spontaneity and of sincere feelings replaced those tedious chores. The movements of *Sturm und Drang* and *Empfindsamkeit* lent support to this view, but in contrast to *Sturm und Drang,* the feminine aesthetic of the late eighteenth century avoided posing any unnecessary challenges to the dominant discourse, the act of challenging being irreconcilable with conventional femininity. The less aggressive *Empfindsamkeit* was more compatible to those women who were trying to remain respectably feminine within the prevailing gender rules; not all women were so interested, as Marianne Ehrmann and Sophie Albrecht will demonstrate.

Poetic Versions of the Self within the Rules

Poetry as it was evolving in the eighteenth century was a framework in which poets inscribed the psychic patterns and the emotions by which they positioned themselves in the world, and through which they subjectively made sense of themselves and their circumstances. As poetry became both more secular and more engaged in creating and elaborating the realm of the personal, it gave women opportunities to present a variety of subject positions and claim them as both female and feminine. In 1778, just two years after her pseudonymous first poem was published, the twenty-two-year-old Philippine Gatterer brought out, under her own name, the collection of work, *Gedichte von Philippine Gatterer,* which Charlotte von Einem had both dreaded and longed for.

This volume and its companion four years later indicate the kind of poetry a relatively privileged late eighteenth-century woman was willing and able to publish under her own name, and thus can be

Painting by Johann Heinrich Tischbein of Philippine Engelhard-Gatterer after publication of her first book.

read, in its organization, diction, choice of topics, and evocation of a speaker, as a representation a woman poet was willing to make of herself to her readers. Once Gatterer had established this version of her literary self in her first collection, she changed it only slightly in later work. To make the book unmistakably her own, she omitted the common male intermediary—in the form of preface or endorsement—between her text and her readers, substituting, instead, her autobiography as a poet (in which she justifies herself by stressing her own conventional femininity). The later volumes also are structured as self-representations, signaled particularly by the arrangement of the poems by date of composition, hence in the order of events and experiences that moved the poet to write. The second volume also contains a poem of literary autobiography, this one including the authorizing reference to Boie; since this poem is in the middle of the book, however, it functions less obviously as a device for justifying publication and more as part of the poet's self-image. All three collections contain many more references in other poems to her position as woman writer.

The first collection thus establishes important patterns: the use of both metanarrative and correct femininity, genre range, poetic style and content. Gatterer moves from the opening self-description to a sequence of poems representing a variety of styles and moods, thereby displaying the poet's versatility in writing verse tales, odes, epistolary poems, prose idylls, songs (often with musical notes included), and a number of playful poems in Rococo style. The pieces frequently rely on the language and themes of the best established male poets of Gatterer's youth: Klopstock, Gellert, Hagedorn, Wieland, and Gleim. Not schooled in the unrhymed Greek poetry that inspired several of these models, Gatterer works instead mostly in the indigenous tradition of rhyme and meter; only a handful of the more than forty poems in the first collection are unrhymed. In many cases she uses one of two basic rhyme schemes, *aabb,* or *abab,* often dividing the poems into four-line stanzas. The meter, too, shows a predominant favorite: iambs. In short, Gatterer repeatedly employs one of the most common German stanza forms. Over the years, this pattern gradually changes, her second collection exhibiting a slightly greater formal variety, and the third, slightly more again. What is distinctive about Gatterer's work, beginning with the first collection, is the way in which the poet, acting within and between the discourses of her time, constructs versions of herself and of her own personal history in the poetry.

Far more often than might be expected from a poet whose gender rendered self-assertion problematic and whose published prose was often circumspect, an emphatic "I" appears in Gatterer's poems. First-person pronouns crop up repeatedly in the first lines of the poems. "Schwing meine Seele dich auf!" "Swing upward, my soul," "Ich irrte lauschend" "I wandered listening," "Ich dich trösten?" "I thee comfort?," "Schließe gütig meine Augenlider" "Close my eyelids kindly" and so on. Virtually the only pieces containing no first-person forms are the prose idylls, which, by tradition, are third-person narratives. Otherwise, Gatterer's willingness to say "I" in her poetry reveals itself even in poems that are ostensibly about quite different topics. The introductory "Mein poetischer Lebenslauf," in which Gatterer boldly uses her own self-representation to establish a first relationship with her readers, is followed by the moralizing "Der Soldat" "The Soldier," "Hymne," which is one of the two unrhymed odes, a poem of condolence, the first installment of a long verse tale that is continued intermittently through the volume, a patriotic song, the short poem about circumventing modesty, and an idyll.

A closer look at two more of the poems in the first collection, besides the modesty poems and the metanarrative already discussed, again shows the woman poet positioning herself within the gender possibilities of her day. "Der Soldat" portrays an encounter with a pious veteran soldier who, crippled, is forced to beg for a living. Although the poem strikes an occasional patriotic note, its central message concerns altruism. The first-person narrator, a middle-class young woman who seems to be yet another poetic version of Gatterer, would like to help the soldier, but has nothing to give. She thinks of the blessings and gratitude that come from caring for the poor. The sentiments, all respectably laudable and Christian, and familiar from Sophie La Roche, show the narrator focusing primarily on herself and not actually on the needy soldier, suggesting that self-satisfaction motivates the speaker's advocacy of alms-giving.

As is usual with such moralizing tales, contrast is one of its basic techniques. After the speaker has passed the begging soldier, the next person who happens by is a rich man who can well afford to make a contribution.

> Doch musst' ich hören—
> Es sprach der Thor
> Ihm harte Lehren
> Des Fleisses vor!
>
> Gab dann am Ende,
> Mit finsterm Blick,
> In seine Hände
> Ein—Kupferstück![50]

[Yet I was forced to hear / that the fool preached / to him hard lessons / about industriousness! /

Then in the end / with a dark look / put into his hands / one—copper penny.]

Despite the opportunity for social criticism that she creates ("Der drückt die Armen—/ Und ist so reich?" "He oppresses the poor—/ and is so rich?"), and which occurs in other poetry of her time, the narrator piously concludes that if this was the way the rich behave, then she will attain happiness by not being rich after all. The narrator's discourse of feelings and her politically conservative message of contentment eclipse the soldier's needs, blotting out him, his survival, and his happiness from the last nine stanzas of a poem named for him. The brief thought of social criticism elicits no thought about the role of gender in matters of money and class, even though that is suggested by the figures in the poem: poor man, rich man, woman without money of her own. Iambic dimeter in four-line stanzas can sustain the poem's initial ballad-like character, but does not lend itself to ethical and moral reflection.

"An die Muse" "To the Muse," less jarringly self-referential, demonstrates Gatterer's use of an entirely different poetic tone, the sublime, and again suggests the difficulties women experienced in gaining the skills often used at the time by poets who were men. This poem is unrhymed and Klopstockian, containing all the usual elements of this kind of poetry, beginning with its topic, melancholy. The first-person poetic voice says that only her muse saves her from melancholy, a fashionable ailment at the time, when nothing else avails: "Dann kamst du mit lächelndem Blick, und hauchtest begeisterndes Feuer, / In mein schon für alles erstorbenes Herz" "Then you came with smiling glance and breathed inspiring fire / into my heart that had been dead to everything" (47). The style of schooled sublimity deployed here is uncommon in Gatterer's writing. The word order, syntax, metaphors, and especially the reliance on meter rather than rhyme all distinguish this poem from the others and show that Gatterer's poetry does not always depend on rhyme to override metric irregularities. Like Hölty, one of the poets of the Göttinger Hain, Gatterer could write effective quatrains of alternating alexandrines and tetrameter (in this case with anapaests, not iambs), whether rhymed, as in her verse autobiography and in a poem such as "Elegie eines Schäfers" by Hölty, or unrhymed, as in her poem to the muse and Hölty's "Die Beschäftigungen der Menschen."[51]

If the unrhymed form was, nonetheless, a stretch, so were the mythological allusions that were almost obligatory in poems about melancholy. Becoming acquainted with mythology presented a problem to women writers untutored in the classics. Friederike Koch, for example, the young poet who was intimidated by her reading of Sulzer, rejoiced to find a volume of mythology in her father's collection of books, which were otherwise mostly technical. She read the mythology eagerly because only with its help could she understand the poems and other literature that she loved.[52] Gatterer found a similar solution, a well-known handbook of mythology by Christian Tobias Damm. With its help she could decipher the references in poems she read and check what allusions to use in poems she wrote. Near the conclusion of "An die Muse," for example, Gatterer uses the Fates to create a fiction of herself, possibly threatened by an early death:

> Verlängern die Parzen auch nur, mit ihren
> oft drohenden Händen,
> Den Faden des Lebens, der kaum erst entstand,
> So tret' ich, voll Schüchternheit, einst zur hohen
> Versammlung der Dichter,
> Und weihe den fühlenden Schwestern mein Lied.[53]

[If only the Fates will extend with their oft threatening hands / the thread of life that has hardly begun / then sometime I will step, full of shyness, into the high gathering of the poets, / and will dedicate to feeling sisters my song.]

With the nine elegant stanzas of this poem, she assembles the trappings of grandeur, but in a reduced form that can presumably be reconciled with the conventions of being female. Thus, she enters the gathering of poets "full of shyness" and dedicates her songs not to everyone with a feeling heart (her usual formulation), but only to her feeling sisters, to other women, a significant reduction in eighteenth-century discourse. The modest self-stylization involved here contrasts amusingly with the saucy confidence she expresses elsewhere and the challenges she flings out, especially to critical female readers. Still, this is a vision of herself that Gatterer likes and quotes in her letters.[54] Two stanzas later, she again imagines what will happen after she dies; she hopes her grave will be visited by lovers who have read her poems.

After all this deference and fragility, "An die Muse" ends on a heroic note: the poet is willing to continue writing even if her hopes are not fulfilled.

> Doch kennt auch die Nachwelt mich nicht, und lohnen auch
> jetzige Schönen [sic],
> Durch sanfte Erröthung und Thränen mich nicht;

> So bleib' ich dir dennoch getreu, und weih' in erhohlenden
>   Stunden,
> Dem Schöpfer—der Lieb'—und der Freundschaft, Gesang![55]
> [But even if the world to come does not know me, and if the beauties of today do not reward me / with their soft blushes and their tears / still I will remain true to you and dedicate in hours of recreation / to creator—to love—and to friendship, my song.]

Disclaiming any interest in fame was standard, as has been seen; the declared relegation of writing to one's leisure time was mandatory; and writing poems about religion, love, and friendship was equally conventional for the period—though not distinctively reserved for female writers, and not actually a good description of Gatterer. Most of all, in this final stanza, even though modified by the reference to leisure time, she proclaims her continuing dedication to poetry.

More often than she writes about friendship, Philippine Gatterer, as a public woman writer claiming respectability and trying to avoid punishment for gender transgressions, composes poems that inculcate conventional behavior and values, especially the prevailing gender rules as they apply to other young women. In "An Teutschlands Mädchen" "To Germany's Girls" (32–34), for example, she invokes the common androcentric premise that, to prepare themselves for life, young women should be guided by the desires of men, their potential mates. And men, Gatterer claims in the same vein, are interested in intelligence and understanding as well as a pretty face. To train women's minds, Gatterer contends, women should choose to learn such things as contribute to happiness—and only such things: "Nur solches Wissen, das beglückt" "only such knowledge as makes happy." Her position is the dominant one that women should not be completely uneducated, but also should not aim to be scholarly. Of course, they should not learn the classical languages:

> Sich mit der Grundtext-Sprache quälen;
>   Unübersetzt Homern verstehn—
>   Das ziemt sich nicht für Weiberseelen!
>   Latein—steht eben auch nicht schön.
>
> [Torturing oneself with the language of the basic texts; / understanding Homer without a translation— / this is not appropriate for womanly souls! / Latin—just doesn't look good.]

Unsure of the purpose of this renunciation, she multiplies the reasons for it: torturous, inappropriate, unattractive. Other areas associated with serious scholarship are also gender-specifically inappropriate:

> In tiefgelehrten Schriften lesen
> Die man für ernste Männer schrieb—
> Mein Trieb ist's mindstens nie gewesen;
> Weil ich in meiner Sphäre blieb.

[Reading in deep scholarly books / that were written for serious men—/ this at least has never been my desire / because I stayed in my sphere.]

Like Sophie La Roche, Gatterer correctly sees that scholarly books are written for male audiences. And, setting herself up as a model—that is, mindful of her own reputation—she declares women do not read such books. Aside from modern languages, history is the one academic subject about which the history professor's daughter suggests women should learn a little, and this, only to avoid conversational gaffes.

As for an inclination to the arts, under which Gatterer includes music, dancing, stitchery, and also poetry writing, this can be pursued within the confines of domestic responsibilities and thus, not very far, according to her ruling:

> Doch laßt dergleichen Euch nicht gnügen,
> Das nur als Nebensache schmückt;
> Könnt Ihr in Häuslichkeit Euch schmiegen,
> Dann ist einst Euer Mann beglückt.

[But don't let yourselves be satisfied with that sort of thing / which is only attractive as a secondary matter; / if you can mold yourselves to domesticity / then someday it will make your husband happy.]

Gatterer often positions women in androcentric terms—especially in policy statements such as this. The image of preparing oneself for someone else's future appreciation apparently offset the loss inherent in foregoing one's own present wishes, while the possibility of remaining unmarried is ignored since women are supposed to tailor themselves to please men whether they actually married or not. The claim that the future appreciation will be for the woman's domestic skills means that men want women to keep house—and to stay out of prestigious or influential realms of activity. Newly professionalized, exclusively male fields such as law were already so completely closed to women that it was not as necessary to work hard to keep intruders out of them as it was in the case of the arts.

To be certain that the message is clear, Gatterer repeats that gaiety and appearance are not enough, and concludes with the standard assurance that a limited amount of learning is a woman's best provision for the future, when age diminishes her physical charms, which then need to be replaced by mental ones, again for the happiness of the man.

> Sie wird bey wenig Reitz gefallen—
> Ist selbst im Alter noch geschmückt.
> Und froh wird der durch's Leben wallen,
> Den sie durch ihre Hand beglückt.
>
> (32–34)

[She will be pleasing even with little physical charm—/ is still attractive even when she is older. / And happily will he proceed through life / whom she has made fortunate with her hand.]

In a period that conceived the pursuit of happiness as an ostensibly human right, the definition of women's satisfaction as only derived and secondary among women writers is especially notable. Among men writers, the emphasis is slightly different. They asserted that domesticity was a direct source of happiness to women. When one of Philippine Gatterer's reviewers compared her ideological submissiveness to Nante Goeckingk's bold rejection of a servant role, he admonished his female readers: "Strive above all for domestic learning; in this way you will be happy."[56] This claim contrasts with that of women writers, who knew too well that domestic duties in themselves provided little satisfaction; they thus shifted the source of fulfillment elsewhere. But the slight difference in emphasis does not detract from the fact that both woman writer and male reviewer were reinforcing the androcentric assumption that the welfare of the dominant group was the chief source of happiness to the subordinate members of society.

Something else was involved, too. Gottsched's efforts for female education early in the century had been part of the general movement to make the middle class morally superior to the aristocracy; thus, women's educational improvement was a political tactic aimed at the class structure and was not necessarily a policy that the middle class was committed to in itself. Indeed, once the middle class had convinced itself that it held the moral high ground (a job of persuasion to which both Rousseau and Lessing contributed), another role was found for women, that of the inherently moral being. To prove that this characteristic was innate in middle-class women, and had not been destroyed as in aristocratic women, it was important that the individual girl had not acquired her goodness through formal education. In short, she must be innocent/

ignorant (though not illiterate). Such, for example, was Emilia Galotti, one of the famous heroines whom Lessing was creating during his engagement to Eva König, who bore little resemblance to Emilia. There is no female character in Lessing's works who echoes the practical, intelligent, mature Eva König. Perhaps, in fact, the problem of morality was even more complicated. The middle class wanted to justify its desire for political power by means of its moral superiority, but the men, not wishing to be too confined by moral standards, assigned this responsibility primarily to women. Emilia Galotti, after all, shows what often happened to the morally superior character in literature: she died. Innocence/ignorance is always shown as precious, but dangerous to the person possessing it. Philippine Gatterer does not recognize these connections.

Women writers valued writing, in part, for the opportunity for individual self-assertion that the mere fact of writing, and especially of publishing, meant, even when it was in the service of a fundamentally repressive discourse. Thus, when expression of feeling gained value in itself, the author, convinced she was writing from the perspective of her unique subjectivity, was almost inevitably blind to the conventionality of what she wrote, although as she got closer to lived experience, this acquiescence to the dominant discourse could lessen. Philippine Gatterer repeatedly demonstrates this pattern, especially in her poems about how writing intersects with marriage.

In one of the poems that Bürger praised, "Der künftige Gemahl" "The future husband," Gatterer presents a fiction of herself in which she wonders whether her future husband is someone she already knew or someone she has yet to meet. Trusting completely that God will bring him along when the time is right, she expresses no doubts or fears about marriage or about not finding a man. In simple four-line stanzas of alternating iambic pentameters and iambic dimeters (unlike the more complex eight-line stanzas using the same lines in the poem on her father's illness), Gatterer concentrates here on the role of obedience she will adopt as a married woman, a role the subsequent poem on her wedding day addresses more critically. Here, however, complete submissiveness and self-sacrifice are the message, including the cessation of poetry writing, depicted, yet again, as a leisure time activity:

> Du arme Leyer, wirst im Staube hängen,
>   Jetzt Zeitvertreib:
> Denn mancherley Geschäfte [sic] wird sich drängen
>   Zum jungen Weib.

> Doch löscht dein Angedenken, gute Leyer,
>   Nie ganz sich aus;
> Ich rühre dich bey jeder frohen Feyer
>   In meinem Haus.
>
> Oft stimm' ich auch die hellen Saiten wieder
>   Für Freundes-Ohr;
> Und singe meinen Kindern kleine Lieder
>   Von Tugend vor.[57]

[You poor lyre will hang in the dust / now my pastime; / for many tasks will be pressing / the young wife.
But your memory, good lyre, will never be / completely extinguished; / I will touch you at every happy celebration / in my house.
Often too I will tune the light strings again / for the ear of a friend; / and sing little songs to my children / about virtue.]

The activities she describes here are all correct and proper for a woman—and correspond to some extent with what actually happened to Engelhard-Gatterer's writing.

But in a poem written not long before her wedding took place, and included in her second volume, she begins to think differently about the glories of duty and the confines of a wife's lot:

> Ich darf doch tun, warum mich viele baten,
>   Darf sammeln meiner Leyer Lohn?
> Dreist wag' ich das, was Herrn und Grafen thaten,
>   Und folge aus dem Modeton.[58]

[I may nonetheless do what many asked of me, / may collect the reward of my lyre? / Rashly I dare to do, what gentlemen and counts have done / and follow out of fashion.]

This is a female version of defiance. Not really confident, the speaker couches her dissent in the form of a question and in terms of permissions obtained from authority. Yet, plainly she is presenting a wish to do something not expected of the usual good wife. As part of her ongoing literary account of her life, the poet also alludes to her engagement: "Ich bin versetzt in diese neue Sphäre, / Vor der mir mehr als halb gegraut" "I have been transferred into this new sphere / before which I feel more than halfway horror." Resentment and resistance seep through her second volume of poetry. In another account of her engagement, the fine poem "Das Jawort" "Accepting," she begins with remarks about her right hand, the one she has given to her fiancé (and the one in which she holds her quill). As she continues, she no longer presents herself as planning automatically to stop writing poetry and she indicates many reservations about the idea of marriage, especially about giving up the comparative independence of her single status. Of course, she ends on a correct note of rejoicing, but only after having already conveyed a picture full of ambivalence (205–6). In such poems, especially in the year before her marriage as she anticipates how the practice of conventional ideology will affect her, Gatterer begins to modify her usually orthodox claims.

Reception: Formal, Informal, and Nominal

A public writer could be staggered or inspired by readers' responses to her work. Part of the reception usually occurred formally, in published reviews in the journals of the prevailing elite. These, virtually without exception, were written by men; Charlotte Hezel's reviews in her pioneering *Wochenblatt* of 1779 are almost the only ones by a woman until the very end of the century. But just as important, though potentially very different, was the informal reception by the reading public, a group or collection of groups usually also versed in the literary culture circulated by the book trade and ratified (or rejected, as in the case of many novels) by reviewers. The informal responses of readers of the author's time, women and men, to the extent that they are preserved today, are found in letters and occasionally biographies or autobiographies composed in the eighteenth century or soon after. Taking "reception" to mean who read a work and what they made of it, another kind of eighteenth-century document, the subscription list, gives a third, different record of reception. Unlike formal and informal expository reception records, subscription lists tell more about who and how many the readers were, though not what they thought of the reading. But if, as I claim, readers played a key role in doling out the punishments that signal the presence of a gender crime or in revaluing transgressive behaviors as acceptable, then attention to the reception of Philippine Engelhard-Gatterer's poetry can inform us about her status as a woman/writer and about the struggles of other women writers as well.

Eighteenth-century reviewers wrote from within dominant literary conventions that had developed in complete separation from women's writing and from any theoretical or aesthetic account of that writing. The hesitation of many reviewers to apply their usual standards to women's writing was not, however, usually based on any doubts about the universal applicability of their literary standards, but rather derived from the discourse of polarized gender, which could mean that whatever applied to men either should not apply to women or would not apply in the same way. The intervention of gender and the application of the feminine aesthetic of the eighteenth century leads to a double standard, although at times the double standard could almost become the start of rethinking the qualities of women's writing.

Of course, book reviews also functioned as publicity for a work, and in this respect Gatterer was fortunate to have her first work reviewed in two of the most influential periodicals of the time,[59] the *Göttinger Anzeigen von Gelehrten Sachen*, published in her hometown, and the *Allgemeine deutsche Bibliothek*, published in Berlin by the vigorous exponent of German Enlightenment, Friedrich Nicolai. For her first collection, Nicolai's reviewer in Berlin began immediately with a gendered analysis embedded in a list of implicitly masculine qualities that the poems properly lack and implicitly feminine ones that they correctly embody: "The character of these poems is not so much sublime enthusiasm, fiery feeling and inventive fantasy as rather a pleasant, persuasive liveliness, unforced openheartedness and goodhearted sauciness, combined with much wit and soft feeling." The genderedness of the terms to late eighteenth-century readers is corroborated by their use in Caroline Michaelis's private letter about Engelhard-Gatterer. Three qualities, fieriness, softness, and goodheartedness, occur in both descriptions, and seem to have the same allocation there as to femininity, masculinity, or both, with Michaelis reporting that the poet's "fiery wit" had exposed her to social punishment, which indicates this quality is not acceptable for a woman of the educated middle class, even though she was properly good-hearted, a comment that helps us to recognize good-heartedness as acceptable in women. As for softness, Michaelis explicitly identifies this as a female characteristic. As Susanne Kord has pointed out, reviewers often confounded the work with the writer when reviewing women's texts.[60] The coincidence of terms between the informal analysis of Caroline Michaelis writing about the poet and the anonymous reviewer discussing the poetry suggests this may have occurred here as well.

Not surprisingly, the reviewer's next observations also touched on the particular situation of the poet as a woman writer:

> The ease with which the poet rhymes is uncommon. The short two-footed lines flow as if they had been made to the beat of the spinning wheel. I ask that this comparison not be taken badly. For that utensil has my great admiration, and Mdm G. seems to think very favorably of the lesser female duties. After all, she herself says:
> Ich sitz und spinne

> Den Flachs so fein
> Dabey ersinne
> Ich Reimelein.

[I sit and spin / the flax so fine / and while I'm at it / think of little rhymes.][61]

In short, the reviewer certifies Gatterer as meeting the standards of the late eighteenth-century feminine aesthetic: spontaneous, domestic and hence, correctly feminine, not challenging. Apologizing for associating poetic meter with a routine and exclusively female piece of equipment, the spinning wheel, the reviewer seeks to excuse himself by proclaiming his admiration for spinning and by invoking Gatterer's own assertion that she composed poetry while spinning. Calling spinning one of the "lesser female duties" (with "lesser" ambiguously applying to either "female" or "duties"), while making it clear that the spinning wheel is a tool he admires but does not use, the reviewer maintains, with this statement, the dominant polarizing notions of gender. The cited lines, considered in their original context, show the poet using them to position herself as a woman, by not writing poetry at the expense of domestic work. As part of the same posturing, it was the flax that was fine, while her poems were merely little, as indicated by the diminutive ending ("Reimelein"), which could also refer to the brevity of lines of iambic dimeter. But after the four quoted lines, the poem does not continue in this vein, shifting, instead, to the search for an appropriate subject, which the speaker seeks tentatively in the public sphere of kings and emperors, even though she returns at the end to the idea of writing about smaller, more intimate topics.[62] The reviewer, ignoring the long middle section of the poem that deviates from his prescription, tries to position Gatterer as feminine without letting the subordinate status of women or their work or their domestic place become an issue.

At the same time, just as Charlotte von Einem feared, the critic reproved the technical correctness—in the eyes of the elite critics—of the poetry and, like Bürger, chided her too-ready knack for rhyming. An educated reviewer did not want to allow a possible feminine aesthetic of spontaneity to impinge seriously on the dominant standards.

> But sometimes, the very ease of her rhyming lures her into prosaic lines; and with the speed of her quill she is not attentive enough to incorrect language or clumsy constructions. Considering her large outpouring of ideas and her ability with language, she could have easily avoided these small errors. To be sure, it is hardly more important than

when a lady puts a bow on crooked; it is just that both are so noticeable and would have been easy to avoid.[63]

In this last remark, the reviewer's gender-based condescension is palpable, since the gravity of a crooked bow was trivial compared to the lasting effect of the printed word, and the comparison of fancy bow to poetry would not have been used had the poet been a man. On the other hand, the comparison dramatically shows how the correct knot was construed as corroborating the social order, and the reviewer's words reminded women of their duty to pay attention to their appearance. He then mentioned certain poems individually. One, a Klopstockian unrhymed ode about the death of a baby brother, evinced "much strength and sublimity." The verse tales suffered more criticism "because of their inappropriate and much too uninteresting content." Other poems displayed "a fine wit," "much cheerfulness," and "a distinctively droll nature." Again, the tendency to examine the personality of the poet is apparent, a point made explicit in another review: "When flattery, friendship, or a misunderstood sense of proper behavior do not prevent honesty, then it is done through mixing up the total impression of her person with the impression of her poems."[64] As Susanne Kord points out in her discussion of the gender-inflected reviews and reception, "being recognized as female represented a substantial professional risk for the women writers."[65]

One of the literary functions that reviews could theoretically have, especially for isolated women writers, was to give them ideas for improving their writing. The Berlin reviewer of her first volume took this task seriously, urging Gatterer to revise more carefully, and, using the opportunity for reinforcing gendered writing qualities, endorsing her "soft feeling," while suggesting that she reconsider one of the genres she had tried:

> The idylls are composed in rather poetic prose and seem to have too little that is distinctive about them. In my view, if the poetess wants to essay this form of literature further, then she should bring in more of her pleasant, cheerful mood, which is so happily combined in her case with soft feeling, and should then write the shepherd poems in verse. This last request cannot be difficult for her.[66]

The Berlin review was thorough and contained specific suggestions that the poet could consider applying; it probably brought Engelhard-Gatterer readers. It was firmly embedded in a reading and judgment of the poetry as the product of a woman.

In some reviews, the interference of gender discourse excused reviewers from giving women the kind of expert evaluations of their work that the women could have learned from if they were to fit their work to the prevailing standards. The hesitation to criticize was explicit when Engelhard-Gatterer's second collection was examined a little over four years after the first. The reviewer in *Allgemeine deutsche Bibliothek* began: "The good reception of the first collection that the writer, then still as Mlle Gatterer, published in 1778, has probably encouraged her to bring out a second. A lady, especially as a poetess, is always at a disadvantage, because she so very rarely hears the pure truth about the worth of her creations."[67] In other words, the reviewer claims, women's books are not as good as their reviews. Germaine Greer, discussing eighteenth-century attitudes of art academies toward women artists, notes that they "alternately encouraged young and virtually untutored female talent beyond its deserts, and ignored and obstructed women who sought recognition as serious artists,"[68] and Susanne Kord points to the relative willingness of reviewers—and scholars—to accept a first book from a woman as good but increasing resistance thereafter. In the case of this seemingly reluctant reviewer, the impact of gender difference between reviewer and reviewed introduces the factor of courtesy: "Also a reviewer, even if he is not a friend or a social acquaintance and is isolated from all relationships that can slant his judgments, must still know how to live, and so we do not want to review this collection further."[69] The reviewer himself did not adhere strictly to his stated position, proceeding, instead, to give a brief description of the collection and to praise specific poems by name. Still, the ethos he described of accepting and indeed encouraging female mediocrity—as measured by the standards of the cultural elite—left women writers without the opportunity to benefit from a thoughtful reader's reactions. Thus, in several ways the reviewer essentially tells readers not to believe positive reviews of women's work. The notion of insulation of author, critic, and reader from each other supposedly promoted in the eighteenth century by the literary marketplace does not operate when the writer is not a man.

There were important voices in the eighteenth century arguing the other way, claiming gender, among other factors, should be of no concern to the reviewer or reader. Moses Mendelssohn (1729–86), the influential Jewish philosopher and critic, had argued that Anna Louisa Karsch had been ill served by uncritically enthusiastic responses to her poetry. Since she herself had not read widely, he pointed out, and thus, could make few comparisons, she lacked a good standard for evaluating her work and so had to rely very much on her friends for help. But they failed her. As long as the poems were simply passed from hand to hand in manuscript form, consideration for the poet's gender and circumstances helped to gloss over small defects and to polish good lines. But, Mendelssohn wrote, when the reader picked up a published book, all details about the author were forgotten—whether a king, a woman, or a Jew—and the writer was simply judged as a writer.[70] In this last point, Mendelssohn reflected the universalizing rationalist thinking of the eighteenth century, which supposedly could override the discourse of gender.

Gatterer's own expectations as to how critics would treat her were entirely gender-based. Before publication she had written to Bürger:

> How Masters Fipp and Fapp and Firlefanz will jump around with me, poor girl. When this one thinks the laurel wreath doesn't look as good on my high hairstyle as on his wig, and that one tries to push me roughly down from the small height which I have climbed with enough difficulty in my hoopskirt and high heels, or a third treacherously steps on the train of my skirt because he is afraid to come before me openly to insult me: oh, still there are certainly a few good souls who will offer me their arm to climb up to Helikon, or will warn me gently when I have stumbled, and give me friendly hints of how I can avoid this or that difficulty.[71]

Perhaps because she was writing to Bürger, a member in her eyes—though not in everyone's—of the literary establishment, she referred here only to male critics, whose pronouncements would count officially, and not to females, whose judgments would be spread over coffee cups or in private letters. Her language shows that she interpreted any vigorous disagreement or criticism from male critics as jealousy. (Quite possibly, she had the same interpretation of female critics.) Honest well-wishers would be soft, tactful, and courteous, giving her hints rather than instructions. In short, they would play a gallantly masculine role to her expressly feminine one.

She usually got exactly this treatment in published reviews, as has already been seen, but when her third collection of poetry, *Neujahrsgeschenk für liebe Kinder* "New Year's Gift for dear Children," was published in 1787, the reviewer in the *Allgemeine deutsche Bibliothek* followed the usual praise with a list of reservations:

> [A] more stringent critique would have several additional things to say. Here it might find a little poem too empty, there some of the morals not

natural or apt enough, here some ideas too worn or alien or dragged out or not clear enough, there it might wish more correctness, elegance, or harmony, which is all the more necessary in poems of this kind because so little poesy can prevail in them in other respects.

After this imposing tally of criticisms, the reviewer concludes with the inevitable reference to the poet's gender, because it neutralizes all normal critical standards: "But ladies on Parnassus, just as ladies in the world, can demand and expect gallantry."[72] More than Mendelssohn wished, women writers were judged by separate standards, whether their work was in printed form or not, and the formal reception of the work, conducted by reviewers, tended to encourage women to be conventional and conservative, showing "soft" rather than "fiery" feelings.

The informal reception of late eighteenth-century women writers, especially by women readers, contained its own doubts about the acceptability of another woman's writing. Thus, Caroline Michaelis had noted that Gatterer "thinks and talks too freely and has in general too little soft female character" (*see* 155–56 above). Nor is this the only instance of such a harsh assessment of Engelhard-Gatterer by a woman reader, as another personal letter also by a woman and, significantly, to a woman, shows. This letter was from Dorothea Wehrs Spangenberg (1755–1808) to Friderika Baldinger, who had meanwhile moved away from Göttingen to Kassel, where Madame Engelhard was by then living, too. Spangenberg, herself a poet, had published under the pseudonym Aephilia in the *Göttingen Musenalmanach*. Spangenberg expresses outrage at the poet's insufficiently submissive tone, which was not only offensive but unnatural: "I simply do not know how a young woman, to whom Nature gave modesty [Sittsamkeit] as her most beautiful ornament, can excuse that insolent tone, which makes her despicable even to those people whom it seems to please and who recite thousands of flattering things to [her] about it." The letter writer, one year older than the woman she was discussing, was sure that even the people who praised Engelhard-Gatterer also scorned her. Now Spangenberg commented explicitly about the new volume, Engelhard-Gatterer's second collection:

> Ph[ilippine']s new poems are again proof of how much she tramples on the duties of chastity [Schamhaftigkeit]. I have read them—and been put out of temper. Some are excellent, but for a wife and mother, and not interesting for a young public. In the case of one, called "[After] The Wedding," I was glad that my name was not on the subscription list— and a young woman could write that! My husband was amazed when

he read it and said: No man would write of such things with so little tact.[73]

The poem that Spangenberg singled out for shocked and male-ordered mention, the one in which Engelhard-Gatterer wrote of a bride's anxiety about what would happen on her wedding night (cited 162–65 above), suggests that the glimmers of women's lived experience in the poetry, especially concerning sexuality, constituted speech and thought that were too free. No man would write with so little tact about these matters? More to the point from a twenty-first-century view, eighteenth-century men had never attempted to put these important anxieties of the women of their time into literary form at all. The poems that Spangenberg approved were those that best matched the standards of modesty and virtue. Spangenberg, citing her husband as judge and attempting to delimit the acceptable audience for Engelhard-Gatterer's poetry, is not an example of a "consumer" who has been lifted "out of specific contexts and their power relationships" and reads now as a human being. Furthermore, it can be assumed that some of this disapproval was communicated to the poet; indeed, the supposedly common refusal to speak of her that Michaelis mentioned was part of this punishing communication.

In her letter, however, Spangenberg also mentions another group of readers who were responding quite differently to Engelhard-Gatterer's poetry, and whose behavior indicates the contingent character of the then hegemonic version of gender. "Madame E.," Spangenberg wrote to Baldinger, "has unfortunately found more imitators than is good for G[öttingen]."[74] Redefining transgressive behavior as worthy of imitation could jeopardize the structure of gender, as practiced in this case in Göttingen, and, for the writer, could perhaps offset or neutralize the social punishments she was otherwise receiving.

Letters by women that are also to women, such as the ones from Spangenberg to Baldinger and from Michaelis to Gotter, commenting on another woman's writing are especially useful because they reveal the nonautonomous standards and ways of judging of women readers reading books by women writers, and their statements are not filtered for acceptability to the poet. First, second, and even third-hand reports to the poet herself about readers' views are more likely to offer positive evaluations, especially when the author is controversial—as women writers automatically were in the eighteenth century. The reports to the writer help explain how she was able to resist the punishments others, perhaps the majority, imposed on her, and sometimes preserve remarks from people whose views are otherwise left unregistered. An instance occurs in a letter Bürger's first wife wrote to Gatterer about a note she had received from her brother. Among the guests at a dinner the brother had attended was a pastor named Spor, described as a scholarly man. Spor and the brother spoke at length about Philippine Gatterer, for the pastor had just read her first collection—not the one with the marriage poems in it—and was so charmed that the two men drank a toast to the poet's health. When Spor found out that Bürger's brother-in-law knew the young Gatterer, he asked him to inform her that one of God's minor rural servants had been heartily gladdened by her poetic genius.[75]

Many women writers in the eighteenth century got information about how their work was received from yet another source in addition to formal and informal reviews: subscription lists. These lists, part of a mechanism of presales that helped finance publication and that thus are analogous to journal subscribing, of course indicated subscribers' expectations, and not their specific responses to the book. Nonetheless, these lists, printed at the front or back of the book and naming the people who prepaid for copies of a forthcoming publication, show the minimum geographical and often numerical distribution of a work and, given the eighteenth century's penchant for titles, something of the social profile of the work's readers. The subscription list in Engelhard-Gatterer's third book, *Neujahrsgeschenk für liebe Kinder* "New Year's Gift for dear Children," shows that it sold better than either of her two earlier collections—at least in their original editions, and hence, not counting a major pirated Viennese edition. With approximately 600 copies sold by subscription,[76] *Neujahrsgeschenk* was one of the most successful subscription efforts by any German woman writer in the eighteenth century.

Of the subscribers, 60 percent came from well-known cities and towns, ranging in size from cosmopolitan Hamburg, with about 100,000 inhabitants and seventeen subscribers, to tiny Marburg, whose university faculty had totaled seventeen members in the 1760s,[77] but whose general population came up with eighteen subscribers for Engelhard-Gatterer's book in 1787. The other 40 percent of the people who ordered came from a variety of obscure villages and towns, including some that were insignificant capitals of several of Germany's thumbnail principalities. Finding subscribers in these places depended on energetic friends and supporters. The towns with the longest lists of names include Bielefeld, Bückeburg, Eisenach, and Münden, but also the nearby city of Hannover, as well as a distant southern princely residence called Öhringen.

Many of the subscribers came through university contacts, it appears, because university towns are well represented, including Giessen, Erfurt, Erlangen, Jena, Marburg, and Göttingen of course, as well as Rinteln, a university town on the Weser River northeast of Göttingen. The eleven subscribers there included four professors, the mayor, and the wife of an army major. For Göttingen, which is second only to Kassel in number of subscribers, many prominent professors' names are listed—Blumenbach, Claproth, Gatterer, Gmelin, Kästner, Meiners, Pütter, Schlözer—and many of the lesser lights, too. In addition to the famous scholars, all of them inevitably men, various literary women subscribed to Madame Engelhard's new book: Lotte Kestner, the prototype for the heroine of Goethe's *Werther,* the private poets Dorothea Spangenberg (this time she dared) and Julie von Bechtolsheim, the public poet and actress Sophie Albrecht, the journalist Karoline Kamienska, and others.

But the most striking part of the list for Engelhard-Gatterer's children's book, and the aspect that distinguishes it from most other subscription lists for literary works in the eighteenth century, is the number of craftsmen and tradesmen who entered their names. In Kassel alone, where Engelhard-Gatterer could solicit subscribers in person, 120 people obliged, including a citrus fruit dealer, the court chimney sweep, a goldsmith, an apothecary, several baker masters, butchers, the court wallpaper hanger, tavern keepers, a copper engraver, two belt makers, the keeper of the pheasants, many tutors and seminary students, court officials of all ranks right up to the minister of state, church pastors and officials, military officers and men, merchants, accountants, carpenters, and brewers of beer. If the children or parents could read, Madame Engelhard evidently encouraged them to buy, no matter what their class in society, from the countess of Hessia (who purchased six copies) to the forester in Gladenbach and a scribe in Herzberg.

Engelhard-Gatterer had also been effective in canvassing for her earlier volume, the second collection of poems. For that one she had found just under 400 subscribers, among them Lichtenberg, one of her father's colleagues in Göttingen; Pfeffel, a blind poet in Colmar who contributed to many magazines for women and advised La Roche about *Pomona;* and Herr von Zedlitz, the Prussian minister of state in Berlin. A bookstore in distant Liegnitz, Silesia, ordered twelve copies, and the rector in far northeastern Riga ordered twenty. Engelhard-Gatterer found buyers in tiny Betzigerode and Diepholz, Ermschwerd and Hoym, as well as in the far-flung cities of Nürnberg, Basel, Lisbon, and Triest. Soliciting enrollment was an arduous process: only 4 percent of her subscribers ordered more than one copy. Most of Engelhard-Gatterer's subscribers to the two volumes, *Gedichte von Philippine Engelhard* (1782) and *Neujahrsgeschenk* (1787), the two of her books that have subscription lists, were men. Women may have hesitated to put themselves forward even on subscription lists (or their husbands or fathers may have prevented such behavior), but, as with *Pomona*, women may nonetheless have been the main motivators behind the purchase and the main readers of the books.

Gatterer herself seems to have been satisfied with her readers. In a poetic epistle about the reaction to her first volume she wrote:

> Ja, manche Frau gewann mich lieb,
> Seit ich die kleinen Lieder schrieb.
> Und mancher Mann, sehr hochgelehrt!
> Hält jetzt mich eines Wörtchens werth.
> Frech hüpft kein Stutzer zu mir hin,
> Weil ich kein Püppchen für ihn bin;
> Doch mancher Jüngling ist mir gut,
> Voll Witz, voll Geist und Edelmuth.
>
> Mich liest sogar der Handwerksmann,
> Und gafft mich, freundlich lächelnd, an.—[78]

[Yes, many a woman took a liking to me / since I wrote the little songs / and many a man, highly learned, / now considers me worth a word. / No dandy hops freshly over to me / for I'm no little doll / but many a young man, / witty, intelligent, and nobleminded, / likes me well. / Even the craftsman reads me and gawks at me, with a friendly smile.—]

In rhymed couplets of iambic tetrameter, repeatedly anchored by the word "mancher" "many a," Gatterer discusses reader responses by gender (first women, then men), and, for the men, by subcategories of occupation and age.

One indication of her impact occurred long afterward. In 1790, thirteen years after her first, prenuptial, volume of poetry appeared, Postmistress Wirth in Hof sent her copy of Gatterer's first collection to the novelist Jean Paul, who responded with an ingratiating, flirtatious note: "I can hardly wait for Wednesday and you. I would not be able to think of any better prelude than your letter and the Gatt[erer]."[79] Despite often negative formal and informal reviews at the time, Philippine Engelhard-Gatterer attained good distribution and was remembered by her readers, who kept the

4: LONGING FOR RESPECTABILITY

work in circulation even during a period when the poet was distracted from the composition and publication of any substantial body of new work.

PRODUCTIVITY AFTER MARRIAGE

Philippine Gatterer had married and become Philippine Engelhard on 23 November 1780, when she was twenty-four and her husband twenty-seven; in his autobiographical essay, the young husband considered his wife to be one testimony that he himself was interested in the arts. Their first child, Karoline, was born fourteen months after the wedding. The new mother would spend the next twenty-five years of her life bearing and raising small children. Nonetheless, for the first nine years after her marriage, Engelhard-Gatterer still got her work published often, both in magazines and as broadsheets. She was not satisfied. In 1787, she wrote in a birthday poem for her father: "[Du] weißt, daß ich durch meine engen Gleise / Mehr tätig als begeistert bin" "You know that because of my narrow path I / am more active than inspired." The next year she was writing to Kästner in Göttingen, "For my poetry this is an unfruitful period now. . . . So little time is left for literature if one is a good mother."[80] Another two years after that she protested:

> Rollt von der alten Dichterader
> Kein Tröpfchen mehr durch Herz und Sinn?
> Dann künd' ich laut dem Eh'stand Hader:
> Er mordete die Dichterin.[81]

[From the old poetic vein flows there / no drop more through heart and mind? / Then I loudly announce my feud with marriage: / it has murdered the poetess.]

The slight displacements of accent to the initial syllable of the iambic feet opening the first two lines of the stanza produce an effect of barely controlled anger and give even more emphasis to the powerful word "mordete" in the fourth line when it receives the otherwise expected iambic stress pattern. One decade of marriage had extinguished the woman poet, in Gatterer's view.

In 1794, she wrote to Lichtenberg that she was disappointed to see her fame disappearing.[82] Indeed, for the nine years from 1790 through 1798, her publications ceased. Instead of sending out poetry, she nursed her children through a terrible round of smallpox; she did the sewing and spinning; she gardened; she did laundry; she cooked (usually with the assistance of a servant, but not with such a staff that she could keep her own hands either dry or free). Finally, on 15 June 1800, her last, tenth, child was born. Engelhard-Gatterer was forty-four. At first she had yet another infant to care for, but three years later, she reported to Nicolai that she was seriously getting back to writing. Parenthetically, she said that she was feeling stronger now that she had had three years without a pregnancy.[83] There is no hint here, by the way, of any disappointment or loss of self-esteem associated with the conclusion of childbearing.

With the end of pregnancies and fewer infants and small children left to care for, her poetic work reveals another way in which marriage, besides inclining her towards children's literature, influenced her writing. Because she had a large brood and because her husband was only a government functionary and not a rich man, Engelhard-Gatterer often found that she seriously needed money. She hoped to contribute to the family income through her poetry. Sophie La Roche similarly mentioned money as a reason for writing in private letters written in the years after her husband's withdrawal from public life—having been dismissed from his position at the court in Koblenz at the age of sixty, he did not enter other employment. La Roche too linked this with the maternal rationale by saying she was earning money for her sons.[84] Yet, as the analysis of Marianne Ehrmann's work will show, women so often invoked financial need to explain their writing that this claim must have been a widely acceptable justification for their deviance—as well as an indication of their vulnerable economic position.

Gatterer, as a poet, could earn money in other ways besides selling books, by receiving honoraria from magazines, or by writing occasional poems for wealthy and famous people who were potential patrons. Karsch, for example, had earned her living entirely from one book, from magazine honoraria, and from payments by wealthy patrons. To Engelhard-Gatterer, writing poems for magazines and patrons was appealing because it did not require the sustained effort involved in a book, and yet, it supplemented her income. With all her other responsibilities, contributing to magazines and writing for patrons entailed an effort of composing and selling that she could muster. In short, magazines and patrons were especially attractive for a woman whose time, energy, and attention were frequently deflected from writing.

When her children were small, Engelhard-Gatterer concentrated on these accessible targets. The topics she wrote about were usually state events, such as a visit by the Prussian king to Hessia, or the assumption of the throne by a new Hessian landgrave; later, during the Napoleonic Wars, the occasions also included military events, as seen in the 1814 poem "Über den Einzug in Paris und Napoleons Flucht und Entthronung" "The Entry into Paris and Napoleon's Flight and Dethronement." Sales in that instance were perhaps further promoted by the charitable purpose of the publication: "For the welfare of the unfortunate city of Vach." Karsch, too, had written war poems commemorating various battles and sold them by the sheet. Indeed, many women wrote war poetry, especially during the Napoleonic years.

Contributing to magazines was more reliable, however, than selling occasional poems by the sheet. In the early 1780s, Engelhard-Gatterer had written for two important women's magazines, *Pomona* and *Magazin für Frauenzimmer*.[85] Two decades later these had both ceased publication, but she wrote for another venerable pair that had continued from those earlier times, the *Göttinger Musenalmanach*[86] and the *Teutscher Merkur*. She also contributed to some of the newer journals of the period, like *Genius der Zeit*[87] and *Eunomia*,[88] as well as Cotta's influential *Morgenblatt*, where in 1818, a poem received a friendly, if condescending, introduction by her old friend from Göttingen, Therese Heyne Forster Huber.[89] Some of Engelhard-Gatterer's work in magazines appears, like her first poems in the almanacs a quarter of a century earlier, under a pseudonym, a signal in the new century that the tide had once more turned against the boldness of public women writers.

Convenience, accessibility, a changing literary scene, and her own separation from the cultural world in a university town induced Engelhard-Gatterer to publish in different forms and in new journals, magazines, and newspapers after her marriage. While an average of 787 books were published in Göttingen every decade between 1765 and 1805, the corresponding figure for Kassel was a paltry forty-nine.[90] The literary enterprise was simply not as developed in Engelhard-Gatterer's new home, and to continue writing in this new milieu meant adjusting on the local level to an audience less inclined to read. The resort to children's literature and occasional poetry was a well-chosen response to this situation.

Marriage had another effect on Engelhard-Gatterer, too. As a wife and mother she was somewhat more careful of her reputation than she had been before as a professor's daughter. Only in a few poems, especially those addressed to her father, did she express pain at the restraining effect of marriage on her writing. As long as her husband was alive these poems remained unpublished. Johann Philipp Engelhard died in January 1818. Three years later, when she was sixty-five, Philippine Engelhard-Gatterer's fourth and last collection of poetry appeared. On the title page she still identified herself with her maiden name, as well as her married one. The publisher was George Eichhorn in Nürnberg, her nephew.

Much had happened in the literary world since her first collection of poetry had appeared forty-three years before. Most of Goethe's and all of Schiller's works had been written, the entire literary careers of Hölderlin, Kleist, and of the Romantic poet Novalis had come and gone. Two other Romantics, Brentano and Arnim, had published their powerful anthology of folk songs and poetry, and the Grimm Brothers, whom Engelhard-Gatterer knew, had sent their fairy tale collection into the world. But Engelhard-Gatterer's writing remained unaffected by these developments. She still favored the same verse forms, the same rhyme words, the same attitudes, the same eighteenth-century moral lessons. In the third decade of the nineteenth century, when her old models Bürger, Boie, Hölty, and Claudius were all long dead, she was still writing the way she had during their heyday almost half a century earlier. Why this failure to develop?

The answer is complex, but fraught with importance for women writers. Engelhard-Gatterer's limited education was one aspect of it, making it more difficult for her taste in reading and her skill in writing to keep pace with the changing literary world around her. Her lack of literary contacts after leaving Göttingen also contributed, and unlike Schiller or Brentano or Wieland, she could not move herself—along with her husband and children—when an opportunity presented itself elsewhere. Then there was the fact that the very conventionality that made her popular also made her conservative. This important factor could afflict writers of either sex, but for women, conventionality was a trait that was especially encouraged and rewarded, as the reception of her work showed.

After her husband's death, Engelhard-Gatterer had thirteen more years to live, surviving until 1831, when she died at age seventy-five. She never ceased thinking of herself as a poet; her last work, a translation from French, appeared in 1830. It was fifty-four years since Boie and Voss had published her first youthful rhymes. Now she introduced the work of Pierre-Jean de Béranger (1780–1857), a French writer of poetry and popular songs. Engelhard-Gatterer claimed to have been prodded into the effort by a critic who wrote that Béranger was too difficult. She still could not resist a challenge, and she still wanted to do work that she herself would earn credit for, even when it involved translating. She explained in the foreword:

But just as the mother must first put in order the hair and clothing and wash the hands and face of a beautiful talented boy, whom fine guests would like to meet at the moment when the boy's high spirits have sent him roving around in puddles and thornbushes; and as she takes away from him the dirty toys and the crossbow with the mischievous arrows—and then brings him into the room; and he enchants everyone with his intellect and wit and gentle good nature (but a little bit of roguishness must still be there, or he wouldn't be himself): this is the way I, the old poetess, had to proceed with M. de Béranger. And thus decency and discretion permit his introduction to the polite German reader.[91]

To the very end, Engelhard-Gatterer let respectability and her assumptions about audience reaction dictate what could be presented to readers. In translating Béranger, she imposes the repression on another writer that she had always imposed on herself.

It is appropriate that at the end of her career Engelhard-Gatterer published a book that allowed her to speak in the (improved) voice of a male poet. In the last quarter of the eighteenth century, when she was starting to write, a common articulation by women of female exclusion from male privilege was in the wish to be male: the literature of complaint.

"Mädchenklage" "Young Woman's Complaint" by Philippine Engelhard-Gatterer expresses this wish and illustrates the complex problems women faced in the Age of Enlightenment as they attempted to gain knowledge of the world and of themselves but not to deny the womanhood whose evolving definition they were just beginning to explore and contest. The speaker in the poem stresses the frustrating limitations imposed on women's liberty. Men, in the view of the poem, have innumerable opportunities in all kinds of occupations and regardless of their age or status, while women, at least "respectable" women—and here Engelhard-Gatterer's class affiliation is unmistakable—are confined to the house.

> Oft hab ich mit Thränen
> Und innigen Sehnen,
>   Verwünschet mein Geschlecht!
> Es fesselt fast immer
> Mich Arme ins Zimmer—
>   Wie frey gehn die Männer, selbst Knabe und Knecht.
>
> Wie um sich zu schauen
> Ist Mädchen und Frauen

> Vom Schicksal vergällt.
> Als Diener, als Lehrer,
> Als Held, als Bekehrer,
>   Als Kaufmann, durchreisen die Männer die Welt.

[How often have I / with tears and a sigh / cursed this my sex! / To the house it confines me / alone and unhappy— / How free are the men, both lackeys and boys.

How fate makes it bitter / for women and girls / to glance past the hearth. / As servants, as teachers, / as heroes, as preachers, / as merchants, so travel the men through the world.]

Even as she complains about limitations on women, the poet demonstrates at least a degree of creative freedom with the innovative form of her poem. At first, she seems to be using the same cramped two-footed lines with alternating accented and unaccented endings she had employed in poems about spinning and meeting the crippled soldier. But those dimeters were clearly iambic, while here the poet creates an almost indeterminate line form following the pattern: Ăls Díeněr ăls Léhrěr. Are these incomplete anapests? overfilled iambs? something else? And while she establishes a very regular rhyme scheme (*aabccb*), the poet ends each stanza with a distinctive line, one twice as long as the others, a line suggesting her yearning for expansion, for more social, psychological, and artistic space. Indeed, seven of nine stanzas use this line to express an explicit wish or a hypothesis about having greater freedom.

The poem lists some of the adventures that men could undertake, exploring, visiting famous people (both kings and scholars, a pairing reminiscent of Baldinger), sailing the seas, climbing mountains, all quintessential activities during the eighteenth-century age of (European) exploration, culminating in the three voyages (1768–80) of Captain Cook; the poem hints, too, at the first stages of religious colonialism as well as expansionist capitalism ("als Bekehrer, als Kaufmann") and then states the narrator's wish to join these projects, too—by being a man:

> Ich traure fast immer
> Im einsamen Zimmer
>   O wär ich ein freyer und fröhlicher Mann!
>
> Wenn strahlende Seen
> In Heiden nur stehen:
>   Was spiegeln sie wohl?
> O könnt es mir glücken

Die Welt zu erblicken,
　　　　So säng ich oft hoher Begeisterung voll!
[I'm most always sad / in my lonely room. / Were I only free and happy, a man!
When shining ponds / lie still in the heath, / what do they mirror? / If I had the luck / to go through the world / then would I sing in ecstasy high!]

The speaker proposes a way to accomplish her goal, by cross-dressing:

> Zwar könnt ich entfliehen
> Und Länder durchziehen
> 　　Im männlichen Kleid;
> Doch Weisheit und Feuer
> Erkauft ich zu theuer,
> 　　Denn weh mir!—die Sittsamkeit hätt ich entweiht!
>
> Wie Stürme die Wellen,
> So thürmen, so schwellen
> 　　Oft Leiden mein Herz.
> Verlösche, mein Leben!
> Dann dort werd ich schweben
> 　　Auf Flügeln des Windes—und Traum wird mein Schmerz![92]

[Of course, I could flee / and wander afar / attired as a man, / but for wisdom and fire / the price is too steep / for—woe!—all of virtue I'd have to disgrace.
As storms toss the waves, / so sorrows swell / my pounding heart. / Burn out, my life! / For then I will hover / on wings of the wind—and pain becomes dream!]

When the speaker wants to go to isolated places and look in the ponds on the heath, she seems to have no idea what she will find, but she believes that if she could have this other assortment of experiences it would enable her to be a more elevated, rapturous poet. The reader is left to recognize that if the female speaker could leave her self-pitying lament and indeed undertake the travels and adventures she describes, then when she arrived at the ponds she would be able to see in them, in part, what they reflect—herself. As it was, the only means whereby she could undertake that journey to enlightenment/Enlightenment would have been in male guise; women's participation in the intellectual independence that was the proclaimed goal of the movement was precluded by the dominant discourse of gender and sexuality, as the texts of Friderika Baldinger and Sophie La Roche have already shown. Nonetheless, within Engelhard-Gatterer's poem, one could argue that to the extent that she refrained from exploring the larger world because leaving home would infringe on society's gender-specific notions of virtue, the speaker allowed herself to be confined. But in another respect male dress would have defeated her purpose; her experiences would not have been hers as a woman, just as—if she were cross-dressed—the pond's mirror would not have shown a self of her gender, so strongly marked is gender by appearance. The poetry of Engelhard-Gatterer repeatedly, even if obliquely, articulates the dilemmas of German women and their writing in the late eighteenth century. How could they be both women and writers in their time?

Philippine Engelhard-Gatterer and Sophie La Roche were similar writers in two important senses: Both were willing to disclose and explore the world of women. Yet, they were also both reluctant to follow through on problems except by suggesting acquiescence and coping strategies. La Roche hinted at emotional constraints when she allowed the possibility of unhappy marriage to appear fleetingly in some of her writing. Engelhard-Gatterer occasionally expressed her exasperation at the repressive effect of gender on women. Like Friderika Baldinger, neither of them explored the social structure behind these points of discontent. To perceive some of the broader patterns of misogyny underlying the individual experiences of eighteenth-century German women and recast them in literary form required a bold writer, Marianne Ehrmann, with a very different, unconventional background that carried her beyond the boundaries of even a good education.

5
Confronting the Lords of Creation: Marianne Ehrmann (1755–95)

Despite the enforcement of gender as a system of crime and punishment, some writings of eighteenth-century German women produced a discourse about women and femininity that can be called protofeminist. Hard though the contours of this category are to determine, I am using "protofeminism" to refer to texts that, selectively read, both describe women as an oppressed group and work to give women more control over their lives as individuals and as members of society at any of its levels and in any of its groupings, social, economic, or cultural. That the category protofeminism requires its illustrative tests to be selectively read is problematic. Of course, all readings are selective and partial, but the eighteenth-century German texts that most clearly or most cleverly subvert dominant notions of gender are always inconsistent and retract, drop, or forget on one page the arguments made on another. Works of such vacillation and such incomplete vision can only be called protofeminist if they are written at a time when a comparatively developed level of feminist thought or practice was unavailable, often because earlier feminist or protofeminist initiatives had been fought back and forgotten; when serious vacillation and retractions characterize works written while feminist discourse is in circulation, such works are at best unfeminist and at worst antifeminist. For texts produced in eighteenth-century Germany, the term protofeminist signals the internal inconsistencies, gaps, and incompleteness of their feminist vision but also acknowledges their potential future use—either in the years immediately after the works appeared or perhaps even today—as stimuli to the ever-developing, ever-changing body of feminist thought.

In this discussion, I will focus on the protofeminist strand in a wide range of Ehrmann's writings, as well as in an essay by her contemporary, Emilie von Berlepsch, and in several other late eighteenth-century German texts. I will attend also to parallels between

Ehrmann and her notable English counterpart Mary Wollstonecraft and to Berlepsch's remarks on Wollstonecraft, the only extended comments on her by an eighteenth-century German woman. I think that Ehrmann's alternative discourse about women, even though it mixed submission with subversion, and her new subject position for women, urging them to become thinkers, opposed the trends and pressures of the dominant discourse that Karin Hausen describes for the period.[1] Looking at Ehrmann's play, one of her novels, and her monthly journals for women, I argue that their narrative and thematic strategies put them into a strained counterpoint to the recognized literary movements of her time, especially *Sturm und Drang* "Storm and Stress," and I propose a new category for the hyperemotional, disaffected texts by women such as Ehrmann. "Geschichte eines Schnupftuchs" "History of a Handkerchief," (published in a posthumous 1795 collection of stories, *Erzählungen*) is an example of Ehrmann's literary and protofeminist boundary crossing. Indeed, for German women writers, protofeminist thought often emerged not in analytical writing but in literary texts, for example in genres that encourage imaginative or intellectual distance from the status quo. A parody of the picaresque pseudo-memoir, an autobiography of a nonhuman subject, for example, is a vehicle for just such an imaginative distancing.

The "Geschichte eines Schnuptuchs" establishes its parodic subgenre from the start by asking questions about typical autobiographical topics, birth and early childhood, and, after neatly modifying the questions to apply to the origins of a handkerchief, leaving them unanswered: "Where the home town of a handkerchief is, where I came into the world, who took care of me, tended me, took me to be bleached until I came back as white as snow, ready to wander the wide world in decency? Probably nobody will give any heed to such matters."[2] The narrator's dismissal of birth and childhood topics alludes to one of Friderika Baldinger's problems with publishing her autobiography, lack of an audience, and then sidesteps the problem by omitting what will not attract readers.

The language of the story is naturalistic and ordinary, not the language of high poetry or of the *Empfindsamkeit* of sympathy, but that proper to the ironic mode:

> as far as I know, my first master, who according to his trade was a linen seller, sold me to a fat, red-nosed storekeeper in a small imperial city. Then this man carried me along with my comrades to a dark stinking hole that presumably was supposed to represent a merchant's storeroom, even though it looked more like a dog kennel. (28–29)

The form of the story, which Christopher Flint dubs the "object narrative," entails a subject position for the narrator that permits society to be sketched from the underside, and the device of the apparently genderless narrator frees the woman author from middle-class feminine linguistic constraints.[3]

As the tale unfolds, the insignificant handkerchief changes hands with adventurous speed. Its first buyer, for instance, a sentimental lady, receives a visit from the "friend of her soul," a "co-crier of superfluous tears,"[4] who accidentally carries the handkerchief home, where his bad-tempered housekeeper discovers it, "noticed the stranger's name on it, and, since in this house it was the custom that everything was common property, instantaneously took it for herself" (34). Using irony and humor to describe casual immorality is notable in the story and characteristic of it as a parody of the *Empfindsamkeit* of sympathy, which rarely employed comic effects and regularly spelled out the value readers should attach to an object or activity. The moralizing intent of the parody is unmistakable, but its form invited readers to draw conclusions for themselves.

As a parody, too, the story critiques overly sensitive characters, such as the lady who is too delicate to understand correctly anything her straightforward German husband says and the young dandy who wants to use the handkerchief-narrator to hang himself when his hairdo goes awry. Accompanying such assessments is something very unusual in eighteenth-century German literature by women: sexual innuendo and episodes involving unsublimated and unloving sexual activity. Handkerchiefs were, of course, a standard piece of equipment in flirtations of the time, but what is described in the story considerably exceeds conventional flirtation scenes. The young dandy, for example, visits a bordello. Describing such a place created difficulties in a woman writer's relation to her audience, since a minimally respectable woman writer of the educated middle class, one whose writings other women of the same class could admit reading, was defined as much by the knowledge she should lack and the practices she should omit as by the knowledge she had or the acts she performed. In the handkerchief story, the tone of social criticism permits a solution to this problem; the narrator comments:

> I won't detain myself for long with a description of the house or its arrangement. There are after all enough men, with or without wigs, to whom these houses are not unfamiliar—even though by the light of day in polite society they complain about such places that they nevertheless sneak off to by dark of night, wrapped in their cloaks. (37)

An attack on male hypocrisy, including men of the middle class, those wealthy enough to afford wigs, substitutes for a description of the forbidden scene. The attack also preempts moral criticism of the author's awareness of brothels by casting doubt on the morality of her possible critics; at the same time, the passage seems to suggest that the handkerchief narrator expects its readers to include men.

The substitution of attack for description does not detract from the effectively presented climax of the incident. The helpless handkerchief is frightened to realize that the harlot is stealthily picking the pocket of the dandy now asleep on her breast:

> I became scared to death. The purse lay under me.—Not far from my side the watch struck its last, sad, muffled stroke and . . . it was gone. Now it was my turn! The skillful little fingers of the whore, already morally dulled from stealing, knew how to snitch me and the purse so softly that my lust-drunk master had not the slightest inkling of what had happened. (38, Ehrmann's ellipsis)

A noise is created, someone tells the young man to flee, claiming the police are coming, and so he is induced to leave the brothel so quickly that he does not check his belongings, and thus, discovers his losses too late to have any chance of relocating his possessions. This part of the story of course does not fit well with the necessarily narrow narrative perspective of the handkerchief, but it is reported so economically and the point of view of the handkerchief is returned to so quickly and smoothly that the deviation does not distract from the general consistency of the narration.

Despite such episodes, the experiences of the narrator, surprising though some of them are, match what by misfortune might befall an urban or small-town woman in bad circumstances. In fact, the handkerchief narrator is feminized in several respects. It is a narrator who, with certain striking additions, sees much the same world as urban and small-town women, from servants to mistresses, saw. Narrators with an approximately similar range of experiences are frequently found in texts by women writers of the time. Sometimes the narrators are young women who were orphaned and, thus, less protected than was customary; Sophie La Roche's Fräulein von Sternheim and several protagonists in Ehrmann's novels and short stories are typical examples. Sometimes the narrators are men, such as those of two novels with scenes from the French Revolution, La Roche's *Schönes Bild der Resignation* "Beautiful Image of Resignation" and Sophie Mereau's *Blüthenalter der Empfindung* "Blossom Time of Feeling." But the men narrators may not be convincing as representatives of their gender. In fact, they usually have many attributes of conventional women characters, being sensitive, tender, and ready to make sacrifices. What distinguishes them from women is their masculine freedom to move and to meet people unchaperoned. The handkerchief, a liberated narrator in the same vein, is charming and clever, domestic and personal, but, unlike the narrators in the novels of the Revolution, does not invoke political or historical events or direct intellectual or artistic development. This is especially important in the story given the (pseudo)autobiographical genre. Thus, the handkerchief is present almost exclusively for private occasions and sees almost nothing of the public world.

The handkerchief is feminized in other ways, too. In its beginning self-description, the two attributes the handkerchief claims are a tender nature and humility, both feminizing characteristics that match the demands that women give up a sense of individual self (29). Both hint at the fact that no matter how alert and attentive the handkerchief may be to its world, it is invariably a passive, even helpless, and thus feminized, observer. Flint, reviewing eighteenth-century English object narratives, notes fittingly that "despite their narrative capacity," the speaking objects "are not adequate subjects themselves."[5] The handkerchief, in its aspect as a piece of property belonging for good or ill to an owner, also represents an important element of women's status. In short, the handkerchief, to whom no gender is assigned in the story, is like an urban woman from the educated middle class or the liminal populace of new readers below it, though not from the culturally almost invisible lowest levels of society. The range of scenes within the urban setting and the assortment of socially and economically situated persons encountered thus resembles the world and the role that might be familiar to the daughter or niece of the fat, red-nosed linen seller in a small imperial city, a daughter or niece working, perhaps, as a domestic servant, or in a shop. The parodistic pseudo-memoir of a "handkerchief" in this respect allows women of the lowest literate levels to read a slightly protofeminist version of their own history and world.

The handkerchief's unpredictable wanderings are basic to the story's success in telling about both a woman's life story and women's world. The handkerchief does not get into its various predicaments because of decisions it has made, but "innocently," without intention on its part, although not without neglect or malice on someone else's side. After the earlier episode with the thieving prostitute, the handkerchief is in the possession of the mean and stingy madam of the brothel, who frequently takes walks to look for "fresh wares" for her business; on one such occasion she accidentally drops the handkerchief. The narrator's predicament is dramatically presented and credible both in terms of the story and in its explicit analogy to the (sexual) vulnerability of a respectable woman, especially a young one, whether from the new middle class of the educated professions or the old middle class of the guilds, who, through misfortune, loses the protection of her family:

> There I lay on the hard earth, like a thoughtless, inexperienced girl, exposed to whatever villain came along first, who might spare me or might trample on me. In this helpless condition my future fate was a true riddle to me. I looked here, I looked there, and saw not a soul who could rescue me.[6]

The sexual innuendo of the description (lying on the hard earth, inexperienced, exposed and helpless) all belong to the picaresque, and appear frequently in Ehrmann's writings, although very infrequently in the works of other late eighteenth-century German women. The autobiography narrates the intertwining of sexuality and economics in the downward mobility of a middle-class young woman whose falling status is caused not by seduction (the usual device for such dysphoric narratives,[7] an example being Friederike Helene Unger's *Julchen Grünthal*), but by the foreclosure of alternatives to her as a woman without the protection of money or family.

Thus, in later episodes the handkerchief is picked up by a drunk actor who is trying to learn his lines, lifted from him by an actress who—like most women in her profession, the handkerchief comments—did not have enough handkerchiefs and underwear, and then given to a girlfriend who has a nosebleed. This young woman, who pretends to be virginal in mind and body, receives a visit from the man who is courting her: "Soon there was kissing, then fondling, then nibbling on each other's mouths, then Werther-izing, Siegwart-izing; even I, poor handkerchief embellished with blood, now came into view."[8] The story's parodistic critique of the *Empfindsamkeit* of sympathy is evident in its reduction of the emotional charge of popular sentimental novels to flirtatious hypocrisies. As the story continues, the lover, seeing the blood spots from the girl's nosebleed, falls on his knees begging for the handkerchief as an eternal remembrance of his friend—and shortly afterwards arranges a meeting with another woman.

Another scene, also stressing sexual innuendo, takes place in a convent, where a young nun hangs handkerchiefs over a screen in the church to signal her secret lover, the convent administrator, that they can meet. This time, the handkerchief ironically attributes a number of amusingly favorable and generous motives to the schemers: "But hardly had the trusty administrator seen me on the treasonous spot when he ripped me down and poked me in his pocket, out of fear that the nun in the delirium of her joy might forget me altogether" (45). The administrator's acquisitiveness is transformed into thoughtful concern for the nun, whose sexual excitement is written as all-purpose joy. Likewise, the handkerchief's description of the two lovers meeting also turns the entire event into an acceptable, even high-minded encounter:

> The visit took place. The two little people had a marvelous conversation with each other. They chatted about better convent arrangements, disputed bills, about vain worldly pleasures, etc. If I were a gossipy woman, I could probably tell here and there about a repeated sweet little kiss. But who will think something bad right away? (45)

It is a teasing style, hinting at acts and then retracting the hints.

Ehrmann describes a world of hypocrisy, where people of all ranks and in all walks of life reveal themselves to the private observations of the narrator as much less honorable than they pretend to be. Flint argues that object narratives, which in English literature reached their zenith between 1770 and 1800, frequently "uncover a disorganized and venal world" and that in complex ways such stories represent the difficult relationship of authors to their commodified printed texts.[9] Only near the end of Ehrmann's story, when the handkerchief, now old and tattered, is given to a beggar, does a person appear who is honest. Not a hypocrite himself, the beggar is the victim of hypocrisy and of moral insensibility. Having lost his money through an unfortunate lawsuit, the beggar often receives nothing but the words "God help you" from the self-righteous and prosperous people who pass him by. In desperation, he sells the kerchief to the rag man, who takes it to the paper mill. This is the equivalent of a traumatic transition to old age, but also makes links to manuscripts, authors, and the highly competitive book trade: " 'O you Gods!'—I thought often under the heavy iron hammer that was crushing me—'o you Gods, do not separate my best parts from each other, and reunite them again in a sheet of pretty white paper, so that even in the hands of a conscientious author I can yet do something good!' "[10] The wish is partly fulfilled, for the handkerchief still has enough power of thought, sight, and hearing to observe the miserable room of the poor writer who purchases it. When the proposals the author writes on the sheet of rag paper are rejected by a publisher, the paper is torn to shreds and thrown to the wind, a more honorable end, the handkerchief reports, than being eaten by worms or used to wrap cheese. And so concludes the "Geschichte eines Schnupftuchs" "History of a Handkerchief."

The picaresque entails a series of misadventures without coherent purpose, a reversal of the quest. While the events chronicled in the handkerchief's pseudo-memoir are entirely beyond the control of the protagonist-narrator, and therefore, disconnected from any purpose or goal on the protagonist-narrator's part, still the narration of the events, within the terms of the story, is entirely governed by the pseudo-memoirist. The handkerchief, then, this crypto-woman, is not entirely passive and dependent on rescue after all. She shapes her account in language and thereby affects the meaning of her experiences. By going against the grain, writing parodistically and whimsically, the protagonist-narrator projects herself in ways that allow new possibilities for being and acting in the world and thus—potentially—are protofeminist. Thus, while the narrator condemns immodesty and illicit sexual activity and to that extent supports conventional morality, which is a fundamental tool in the social control of women, she treats sexuality as pleasurable and exciting for women; she does not accept the prevailing double standard for women and men, and she does not engage in prescribing a morality that women (but not men) should follow. Marianne Ehrmann in this story and others wrote episodes quite different from what other German women of her time usually wrote—or even openly read. From the peculiar subject position of the handkerchief, Ehrmann could suggest some of the limitations of conventional femininity, which she also touches on in other work, thereby continuing to produce protofeminist criticism.

Women's *Sturm und Drang*, or the *Empfindsamkeit* of Alienation?

For an eighteenth-century woman of moderate or high literacy to dissent strongly from the usual manners and mores of her class and to frame her dissent as connected with her situation as a woman, she needed to be familiar with the operation of her society and yet, marginal to it—this was, in some respects, the situation of most women in the aristocracy and educated middle class—but, more distinctively, a dissenting woman had a diminished stake in the status quo (she might be tainted as déclassé); she also needed access to texts and traditions that in recombination or with radical rereading would elicit new ideas and make the new ideas expressible. Among texts of the eighteenth-century public women writers in Germany, Marianne Ehrmann's include the boldest explicit protofeminist criticism of the situation of women, especially in the educated middle class and lower aristocracy, and the most vigorous protofeminist discussions of key issues facing such women. Writing about late twentieth-century conditions for the emergence of feminist consciousness, Sandra Lee Bartky says that it occurs "only when there exists a genuine possibility for the partial or total liberation of women"; she goes on to argue that "the feminist apprehends certain features of social reality as intolerable, as to be rejected in behalf of a transforming project for the future," and she claims that often, as part of this project, "features of social reality are first apprehended *as* contradictory, as in conflict with one another, or as disturbingly out of phase with one another...."[11] Drawing on intellectual space already created by other women (signaled, in Ehrmann's case, by her use of Sternheim as her stage name) and then seeing it enlarged as the tumult of the French Revolution raised entirely new possibilities for change in late eighteenth-century Europe, especially for change that could be grounded in the Revolution's notions about the implementation of basic individual rights and about their extension to previously excluded groups, a small number of German women who were simultaneously social insiders and outsiders began tentatively applying human rights principles to their analysis of women and, thereby, perceiving contradictions. Women writers a decade or less earlier, such as Sophie La Roche and Philippine Engelhard, had inserted into their overall reiteration of conventional ideology some comments that partially disrupted their usual endorsement of conventional femininity; these often appeared in connection with self-descriptions. Ehrmann's texts, on the other hand, show her situating herself from the start in a new nexus of discourses, first as a woman philosopher, then as a woman philosopher writing novels and stories drawing on the picaresque to posit deviations from conventional femininity and to identify the intolerable aspects of social reality, and finally, as a journalist identifying the fads and foibles of bourgeois society, especially as seen from her view as a woman. Writing in the decade in which the French Revolution erupted, Ehrmann perhaps sensed a "genuine possibility" for change that Bartky stipulates for feminist thought. Using the role of woman philosopher, though embedding it in the dominant androcentric discourse, Ehrmann articulated protofeminist positions.

In certain respects, Marianne Ehrmann resembles her famous English contemporary Mary Wollstonecraft. Both of them journalists as well as novelists, they were middle-class by birth, yet marginal to their class in the way they lived. Wollstonecraft was born in 1759, four years after Ehrmann, had as her first publication a rather conservative tract about women, *Thoughts on Educating Daughters*, in 1787 (Ehrmann's similar first publication appeared in 1784), and published her first novel in 1788, one year after Ehrmann. Both women were basically self-educated and economically independent from an early age. Wollstonecraft died in 1797, two years after her German counterpart. Ehrmann was one of the early women in Germany to write professionally. Perhaps more than Wollstonecraft, she also was willing to experiment with literary forms, although so far, Ehrmann's writing and life have received only a small fraction of the attention that Wollstonecraft has quite rightly gained.[12]

In the little more than ten years of her literary career, Marianne Ehrmann wrote much that was conventional, but as she grappled with emerging new notions about women, she also tried techniques and forms that women writers seldom used, and she engaged in a kind of writing that brought her close to the *Sturm und Drang*, a literary movement routinely understood to have been exclusively male (although rarely explicitly described that way). Two scholars writing at the beginning of the twentieth century about women's participation in eighteenth-century literary production, Christine Touaillon and Edith Krull, both suggested Ehrmann's affinity to the *Sturm und Drang*.[13] It is a tempting placement that forces the consideration of whether women (could have) devised and deployed a version of this movement and, if so, to what effect. A preliminary answer can be found by briefly examining to what extent the literary production of Marianne Ehrmann and some of her women contemporaries match with the standard descriptions of the *Sturm und Drang*.

Since *Sturm und Drang* is understood as a movement running simultaneously with the larger and longer period of the Enlightenment, the dates of the movement help to locate works to be included in it. Andreas Huyssen in an often cited overview of the *Sturm und Drang* agrees with much other past scholarship in selecting the years as 1770 to '85/'86, from the encounter of Herder with Goethe in Strassburg to the end of Schiller's Mannheim period and the departure of Goethe for Italy.[14] Among potentially appropriate texts by women that these dates might include are Christiane Karoline Schlegel's play *Düval und Charmille* (1778), Sophie Eleonore Kortzfleisch's *Lausus und Lydia* (1776), Sophie Albrecht's *Theresgen* and the first installment of her "Fragmente aus dem Tagebuch einer Unglücklichen" "Fragments from the Diary of an Unhappy Woman" (1785). Marianne Ehrmann's play, *Leichtsinn und gutes Herz, oder die Folgen der Erziehung* "Frivolity and a Good Heart, Or the Results of Education" would squeak in (1786), and, under another title, the first eighteen letters of her epistolary novel *Amalie*, just one of the works by Ehrmann that Touaillon, Krull, and more recently Madland have connected with *Sturm und Drang*[15]; the complete *Amalie* and Ehrmann's first monthly journal were published in 1788 and 1790–92. The argument could well be made, however, that if literary history is to take women's writing into account, it will have to redraw its time lines, in this case recognizing that Schiller was not the only member of a second phase of *Sturm und Drang*. A later closing date would also allow consideration of Eleonore Thon's *Adelheit von Rastenberg* (1788), another play with many *Sturm und Drang* resemblances.

Of course, literary qualities of genre, ethos, diction, and theme are as important as date of publication for categorizing a work or writer in literary history. Thus, the fact that Kortzfleisch, Schlegel, Albrecht, Ehrmann, and Thon all wrote dramas is significant for their possible placement within the *Sturm und Drang*, since this was a movement known overwhelmingly for its plays. The debt of several of the women writers' plays to Lessing's two bourgeois tragedies [*buergerliche Trauerspiele*], *Miss Sara Sampson* and *Emilia Galotti*, also fits, since these plays were greatly admired and in many ways rewritten by the *Sturm und Drang*'s eager playwrights. Ehrmann's version of this *Sturm und Drang* reception of Lessing, *Leichtsinn und gutes Herz*, repeats the *Emilia Galotti* situation of effectively middle-class daughter (despite the nominally peasant father, as we shall see) abducted from her stout-hearted and adoring father by a lustful nobleman, who in turn is goaded on by a venal, misogynist retainer. Sophie Albrecht's *Theresgen* reverses this plot, having the rural stepdaughter fall hopelessly in love with the unattainable and unwitting local count and vigorously reject the respectable man of her own status who wants to marry her. Whereas Lessing's heroine asks her father to kill her to make her immune to the prince's seduction, Theresgen kills herself in final refusal of social and moral convention and to preserve her own choice. Schlegel's *Düval und Charmille*, on the other hand, reiterates the constellation from *Miss Sara Sampson* of an aristocratic man torn between two women (although neither of them replicates the unprincipled Marwood of Lessing's tragedy). *Lausus und Lydia* and *Adelheit* do not draw on the themes and figures of bourgeois tragedy, but instead use another tradition also beloved by the *Sturm und Drang* dramatists, with settings in supposedly more heroic past eras. All of the plays show what Albrecht's most obviously demonstrates, a rejection of abstract moral norms when these conflict with the free development of the individual, a stand that is highly characteristic of the *Sturm und Drang* and its valorization of the creative person, the "genius." Especially in the canonical dramas of the movement, this genius is prominently represented in two figures, the *Grosser Kerl* (the great chap—a heroic, amoral, macho, male figure) and the *Machtweib* (the woman of power—an amoral, powerful, often seductive, always vilified, female figure). *Sturm und Drang* protagonists in their vigorous pursuit of a life unregulated by conventional society often end either in narcissism and self-glorification, or in depression and alienation. Again, several of the central characters in the women's texts fit this description. Düval, convinced that society has foreclosed all options for his love, murders his beloved and himself—but Schlegel (unlike her *Sturm und Drang* male contemporaries) does not seek audience sympathy for her often brutal and always selfish male protagonist. Theresgen, equally sure that society is about to crush her, drowns herself. *Ninas Briefe*, a novel by Ehrmann, also matches the style and issues of *Sturm und Drang*, especially its critique of an excessively rational *Aufklärung* that dismisses the importance of strong feelings;[16] the title character, a woman artist (writer), is unable to endure either the regulations imposed by aristocratic snobbery or the ignorant moral self-righteousness of the petite bourgeoisie, and withdraws in despair to the countryside.[17] These protagonists and others are and remain outsiders.

Sturm und Drang literature is considered to have had "the historically important function of promoting the identity formation of the German bourgeoisie across the borders of [Germany's] small principalities."[18] Given the embryonic state of early capitalism in late eighteenth-century Germany, this literary identity formation, as already seen in the constellation of class opponents and allies that La Roche posed in *Fräulein von Sternheim*, was often enacted not just as opposition to the aristocracy at the numerous princely courts, but often in alliance with portions of the aristocracy that were anti-court. Generally, such anti-court groups were the diminishing land-owning aristocracy living on country estates and the lowest levels of aristocracy so reduced in their circumstances that they had given up the privileges (and prohibitions) of their rank in order to earn their own livings by work. As in *Fräulein von Sternheim*, literary representations of such bourgeoisified aristocrats could act as supraterritorial representatives of middle-class values, complete with separate value systems for men and women. Düval's ill-used aristocratic wife, for example, demonstrates the patience, marital fidelity (despite numerous infidelities by her husband), sympathy, and motherliness (shown on stage in her love for her twelve-year-old son) required of middle-class women, while her husband embodies the desire for independence and freedom that the *Sturm und Drang* sought for men. Düval's final rage is conditioned in part by his lack of options as a nobleman without an estate, completely in the power of a court that is deaf to his hopes, feelings, and wishes. Personal autonomy is a typical *Sturm und Drang* formulation of the identity issue for both the middle class as a group and for the great individual whom the movement glorified. It also meant that in the very act of creating a greater identity for the (male) middle class, the *Sturm und Drang* sharply critiqued the group's existing narrow and trivial concerns, while leaving women's constrained lives unaffected.

Hartmut Dedert has noted that the themes of the *Sturm und Drang* plays also occur in the movement's short prose texts, identifying such characteristics as the use of autobiographical material to depict the pettiness of everyday life clashing with the individual's desire for self-realization. Thus, when fulfillment is accomplished through love, the joys and sorrows of that emotion can engulf and disempower the protagonist. Indeed, the search for fulfillment often culminates in melancholy, depression, and, as in the plays, even suicide.[19] Dedert, too, although he omits any materialist analysis, notes the preference for the life and values of the country, not of the overly civilized, calculating city or the immoral court. He also identifies characteristic *Sturm und Drang* language approximating speech, including colloquialisms and overtones of dialect, as well as richly metaphorical and hyperbolic diction. Much of this, of course, fits the story of the handkerchief with its autobiographical claims, its characters drawn from everyday life in such a way as to reveal the misery of petit bourgeois existence (inglorious shopkeepers, dandified youth, unscrupulous servants, sanctimonious town fathers, thieving prostitutes, and predatory madams), and the mixture of colloquial and literary style. While this short story lacks the hyperemotional protagonist of much *Sturm und Drang* prose, figures such as Nina in Ehrmann's other works well fit that bill.

Yet, despite the many ways in which texts by women can be read as meshing with *Sturm und Drang* agendas and style, it is striking that the figure of the *Machtweib* is missing from most of the prose and theater of the women writers. While the play texts by women in several cases include conniving, villainous women, only Bertha von Wildenau, in the late play *Adelheit von Rastenberg*, matches the scale of this standard *Sturm und Drang* figure. Huyssen notes of the *Machtweib*:

> Despite reservations and exceptions it is fundamentally true that that for which the great individual man is praised is turned into a grimacing caricature in the case of the great individual woman. It is easy to recognize that here the male misogyny of the patriarchal middle-class social order is expressing itself and, unable to include the greatness and individuality of a woman in its utopia, imposes double sanctions as a matter of principle on female efforts to escape. It is not only that these women fail as the men do, but that the sympathy of the audience is withdrawn from them. This becomes even more evident when the positive female characters of contemporary drama are considered who are always distinguished by domesticity, submissiveness, and suppression of sensuality. . . .[20]

To make matters worse, the passively suffering heroine often becomes the target of attack by the raving villainess, and then the *Machtweib* in turn is punished, frequently with death, by the male-dominated society—a penalty carried out in the less important netherworld of a subplot. Huyssen summarizes: "The bourgeois emancipation of men does not correspond in drama with a demand for the bourgeois emancipation of women."[21]

Indeed, the conspicuous misogyny of the *Sturm und Drang*, marked especially by the *Machtweib* and by the movement's fondness for bourgeois tragedies that systematically engage in the removal of women,[22] is one of two reasons not to pursue the characterization of texts by Ehrmann, Schlegel, Kortzfleisch, Albrecht, Thon, or other women as belonging to that movement. Why would feminist literary scholarship argue for women to be counted as members of such a misogynist literary program? To be sure, the women writers resist (with partial success) the extreme disregard for women of their male contemporaries, not only generally omitting *Machtweiber* from their casts of characters, but also showing serious and valuable female friendships (such as Lehngen's for Theresgen and even the strained efforts at solidarity between Düval's wife and his latest lover, Charmille), not glorifying domesticity (a female protagonist such as Lottchen in *Leichtsinn* is more notable for being a reader than for her housewifery), and allowing for passionate outspokenness and bold deeds (such as Ehrmann's Lottchen pulling the trigger on the count who has seduced her). If their works are added to the understanding of the *Sturm und Drang* repertoire it could draw attention to the usually unremarked misogyny of the male material, but—and this amplifies my first reason not to advocate the addition of women writers to the *Sturm und Drang*—such an addition would also offer a counter to that misogyny and thus, seem to redeem the movement from its offensive posture of despising and denigrating women.

The second reason not to claim a *Sturm und Drang* designation for potential women candidates is timing. In order to include the full scope of literature by women that closely resembles *Sturm und Drang* values and styles, the dates of the movement would have to be extended by almost a decade, until the end of Marianne Ehrmann's life. This means adding two thirds of the current length of the *Sturm und Drang* to its term, changing it from the period 1770–86 to the period 1770–95. And considering that the three high points of the movement, as identified by Huyssen are the years 1773–74, when Goethe's *Götz von Berlichingen* and *Werther* were published, the drama year 1776, with its plays by Leisewitz, Lenz, Wagner, Müller, and Klinger, and finally 1781–84, the early years of Schiller's play writing,[23] this revision would cast much of the work of the women as lagging long after the currently recognized main events, and hence as epigonal.

Considered from a historiographic perspective, literary historians have not been receptive to a revamping of the *Sturm und Drang* to include women.[24] Those working on the movement have evidently not sought to locate dissenting or deviating perspectives that might moderate the androcentrism of the movement as it is usually understood. Even the most recent "general" (not feminist) literary historians, including some (such as Dedert) who address genres and authors marginal to the movement, have neither taken up the long-standing assessments made by Krull and Touaillon nor the more recent repeated proposals by Helga Stipa Madland that connect Marianne Ehrmann with *Sturm und Drang*,[25] nor evidently sought out other women authors for late inclusion. This is important since the works proposed by Krull, Touaillon, and Madland are protofeminist texts that repeatedly address patriarchy and its impositions on women. This protofeminist element is exactly what tips the balance for me. Thus, rather than stretch our understanding of *Sturm und Drang* to include women, that literary moment should be left as it is: a male-ordered, misogynist, exclusionist movement that proposed to emancipate men while (and to some extent by) reinforcing women's subordination.

To accommodate the many impassioned texts by Marianne Ehrmann and her compatriots, to recognize their distinctiveness, the tradition within which they work, and their timing, I recommend we refine our notions of the *Empfindsamkeit*, especially as women writers participated in it, by identifying a third strand of the *Empfindsamkeit* after the religious and sympathetic strands. This third strand is based not on active sympathy but on the irritable sensitivity of loneliness, difference, thwarted desires, and secularized alienation. I propose to call this third strand the *Empfindsamkeit* of alienation. The name suggests estrangement from the lopsided rationality and masculinist bias of the *Aufklärung*, from the optimistic first two versions of *Empfindsamkeit*, and in tension with the *Sturm und Drang*, the male movement with which the third female strand of *Empfindsamkeit* overlaps in many respects. Presumably the women who wrote the texts of this strand were well aware of the much-debated *Sturm und Drang* literature of their time and were writing partly in response both to those works and to the same socioeconomic, literary, and intellectual conditions that inflected the *Sturm und Drang* texts. For Marianne Ehrmann, perhaps reading the impassioned literature of the *Sturm und Drang* functioned as a weaker print version of the radical community of intellectuals in which Mary Wollstonecraft developed her ideas about gender.

"IF . . . I WOULD BECOME THE FIRST FEMALE REBEL"

The history of Marianne Ehrmann's life is only now being written. Like the origins of the handkerchief, her birth—aside from its date in 1755—and childhood are obscure—few documents remain about any part of her life outside of her literary activity. She was baptized in Rapperswil on Lake Zurich, one of ten (or perhaps eleven) children in her family.[26] Most of the children died young, however, only two of them surviving her mother, Maria Sebastian Brentano nee Corti (1732–70), who died when Marianne was fifteen. Five years later, her father, Franz Xaver Brentano (1727–75), a prosperous man of business who fell into bad times, also died.

Marianne Brentano was able to get advice and limited assistance from an uncle, the priest Dominikus von Brentano. At about age twenty-two she married an unidentified man who soon abandoned her, threatening her thereby with the long-term danger of joining the growing underclass of day laborers, small jobbers, and other workers, both male and female, who performed tasks considered not sufficiently respectable to be in guilds. (The countryside also had an underclass of peasants who had lost all or most of their land or had inherited unworkably small divided portions, and who thus had become agricultural day laborers, or the equivalent of share-croppers, or both.) Once her abandonment had evidently concluded with a divorce,[27] she seems to have begun to earn her own living, first in a socially suitable job that, however, no woman of the educated middle class undertook unnecessarily: as a governess.[28] Her apparent second employment, as an actress, was far more questionable at the time. With a nod to Sophie La Roche's heroine and in an obvious bid to combine a déclassé social role with a claim to middle-class respectability, she took Sternheim as her stage name. Later, when she began to write, Ehrmann often—and usually sarcastically—described the hard life of most actresses, stressing their ignorant, inferior performances, as when the autobiographical handkerchief, in a departure from the private sphere she/it otherwise inhabited, is taken on stage by a young prima donna:

> O how I loved the applause, which we two with our shameless impudence got from the blind public more often than we could actually demand it! In this situation I performed no small service for my prima donna. Often when she was supposed to cry and had no tears in readiness, she held me in front of her ice-cold statue's face and the public thought it was real feeling. If she had to say a line that she did not understand, then she would swing me around quite ridiculously. If she wanted to imitate nature in important details or did not know how to help herself in powerful places, then she would drop me....
>
> In short, in these enlightened times, when the true art of acting is actually practiced exactly as seldom as it is encouraged or properly judged, we two carried off no small triumph.—[29]

Ehrmann commented frequently on the need to give actors proper training; she also joined in the characterization of actors as morally and socially suspect. After her own career in acting, which exposed her to a kind of life that few women of the educated middle class ever glimpsed, and probably also gave her some opportunities to travel beyond Germany, she began her career as a writer and married Theophil Friedrich Ehrmann, a travel writer seven years her junior. They lived in Strassburg, a small city on the left bank of the

Rhine, close to France and connected to the more economically developed cities of Switzerland, thus again in a place in which early capitalist class formations were evolving somewhat in advance of the rest of Germany; like Frankfurt, Strassburg had also been one of the predominantly southwest German locations of *Sturm und Drang* activity.

Marianne Ehrmann's first independent publications appeared in 1784, one called *Müssige Stunden eines Frauenzimmers* "Leisure Hours of a Gentlewoman"—this was the publication containing the first letters of what would later become the novel *Amalie*[30]—and the other *Philosophie eines Weibes* "A Woman's Philosophy," a booklet of only seventy-two pages, but successful enough to justify translation into French and a second German edition the next year.[31] It is an undistinguished retelling of Rousseau that bears almost no trace of the ideas that would later make Ehrmann interesting. In 1786, she published her play, *Leichtsinn und gutes Herz, oder die Folgen der Erziehung* "Frivolity and a Good Heart, Or the Results of Education," in which she explores issues of class, using as her virtuous heroine a girl of mixed-class background. The girl's father is a prosperous and educated peasant who had traveled before returning to country life. Her mother, who does not appear on stage, is a woman from the city and implicitly from the urban middle class. Lottchen has been educated in the city, by a woman "who inflamed her sensitive spirit [*ihren empfindsamen Geist*] toward reading and foolish fantasies [*Schwärmerei*]."[32] When Lottchen tries to shoot the young count who has seduced her, she briefly takes on some of the heedless anger of the *Machtweib*, thus, as Karin Wurst points out, combining qualities that most eighteenth-century drama rigorously divided between its passive, good female characters and its powerful wicked ones.[33] Because the gun is not loaded, Lottchen remains innocent of crime, though not completely ineffective: she scares the count into taking the steps necessary for their marriage, which provides the play's happy end, as conventionally defined.

In 1788 Ehrmann published a collection called *Kleine Fragmente für Denkerinnen* "Small Fragments for Thinking Women" along with three novels: *Amalie, eine wahre Geschichte in Briefen* "Amalie, a True Story in Letters," *Graf Bilding, eine Geschichte aus dem mittlern Zeitalter, dialogisirt* "Count Bilding, a Story of the Middle Ages, in Dialogue,"[34] and *Ninas Briefe an ihren Geliebten* "Nina's Letters to Her Beloved." This level of productivity was aided by the fact that at least one of the novels had been started four years earlier: the beginning of *Amalie* had been published in *Müssige Stun-*

Amalie.

Eine wahre Geschichte in Briefen.

Von der Verfasserin der Philosophie eines Weibs.

Erster Band.

1788.

Title page of the novel *Amalie* by Marianne Ehrmann.

den. At least two of the novels, *Amalie* and *Ninas Briefe* were published in handsome format but listed neither publisher nor place. After this rush of publishing activity, there is a pause of one year before Ehrmann began editing and writing the two periodicals for women, first *Amaliens Erholungsstunden* "Amalie's Recreational Hours," then *Die Einsiedlerinn aus den Alpen* "The Hermit Woman from the Alps," that continued until a few months before her death.

Then, in February 1795, as she was closing down the second journal, she announced a plan to publish a whole series of her works, old and new, with a novel called *Antonie von Warnstein* listed as the second and third volumes of the collection.[35] The novel appeared posthumously (1796–98), under the guidance of Ehrmann's husband, who evidently tried to extract what publications he could from the work his wife had left behind; he produced three volumes of *Amaliens Feierstunden. Auswahl der hinterlassenen Schriften von M. Ehrmann* "Amalie's Rest Hours. Selection of the Posthumous Writings of M. Ehrmann" in 1796–98 and in 1802, published her correspondence with Gottfried August Bürger, Engelhard-Gatterer's mentor years earlier. The name Amalie appears repeatedly in Ehrmann's book titles; it is the original name of *Antonie von Warnstein*, too. This provocative book, with its examination of an unhappy marriage and its description of the life of an actress, is nothing more than a new edition of *Amalie, eine wahre Geschichte* with the names of the main characters changed. How and why it happened that the novel received this late (and long unrecognized)[36] reincarnation is unclear. Regardless of title, the two volumes of *Amalie, eine wahre Geschichte*, or *Antonie von Warnstein*, are Ehrmann's most comprehensive depiction of the emergent protofeminist discourse about issues that talented, energetic, educated, and hence, comparatively privileged women could face in the late eighteenth century if they suffered financial distress and had no family help. Ehrmann looks particularly at marriage and work, specifically the work of a professional actress. The literary composition of new feminine subjectivities and of impassioned alienation accompanies and reinforces the novel's protofeminist discourse.

Amalie, eine wahre Geschichte consists of the correspondence of two young women with each other, Amalie and Fanny (or in the later version Antonie and Betty). From the beginning, the correspondents have a sense of belonging to an intelligent, moral, and emotional elite. In their view, most people, especially most women, are neither so sensitive nor so principled as themselves. Fanny and

Amalie consider each other thinkers and call each other philosophers, and in so doing, they offer a new form of feminine subjectivity indeed from the pen of an eighteenth-century German woman writer. In keeping with the *Sturm und Drang* critique of an overly rationalistic *Aufklärung*, the thinkers are also emotionally volatile, but here, in keeping with the innovations of the *Empfindsamkeit* of alienation, the combination of strong reason with powerful emotion occurs in positively depicted women.

Ehrmann's protofeminist interest in women's situation is established early in the novel, especially in a vivid and acrid description of the different rules and judgments imposed on women from those set for men. The heroine, the young Amalie, exclaims: "Often I have thought to myself how much I would like to be a stout-hearted boy! This is a wish that I am constantly chasing around in my head and whose basis I can hardly figure out. If I ask myself often why, then my answer keeps coming back to the restriction of our sex."[37] The common motif, which both Baldinger and La Roche had also used and which Engelhard-Gatterer had described so clearly in "Mädchenklage" "Young Woman's Complaint," the wish to be a boy or to have some of the privileges of a boy and thus, to escape the social and cultural confines of femininity, continued long past Ehrmann's novel. One of Ottilie von Pogwisch's friends, for example, wrote to her in 1813, three years before Pogwisch's engagement to Goethe's son:

> Why aren't we men, Otilie? You would be happy and I certainly would be too! For that is precisely my misfortune, that for my tasks I don't need my head, and so I cannot control the thoughts that are constantly chasing each other there. If I were a man, I would use my thoughts in effective dealings; I would take action and be happy! How different it is with us in this respect![38]

Many women of the eighteenth and nineteenth centuries comment on the feeling of having energies, thoughts, and emotions with no culturally acceptable outlet, and they frequently associated this sensation, though rarely so clearly as here, with the restrictions they faced as women. Pogwisch-Goethe's friend's thoughts are expressed in a typical situation: when young women are speaking or writing to each other. The result is typical, too: complaints about the privileges that society gave to males, but no deeds, and no further discussion of the matter.

Ehrmann's heroine is somewhat different. She considers the matter in more detail, focusing on the things women are either excluded from or punished for:

> Can there be anything more unnoticed in the world than a woman, and is there anything more miserable than she if she is too much noticed? Aren't we a real sacrifice to a certain prejudice and isn't this prejudice necessary for our education in order to scare back our vanity and to bring an offering to men's craving for dominance? That is really very dear! What is counted against us as a vice is what embellishes their freedom, and even if it may not bring them honor, still no one punishes them or snorts at them because of it, least of all they themselves among each other.[39]

The fictive letter writer here depicts women as victims (and as victimizing each other in the process) and characterizes men as totally overweening; her allusion to women's vanity is readable on one level as a reiteration of a long-standing charge against women and on another as a sarcastic reference to women's self-respect, a quality men were beginning to find dangerous. Furthermore, Ehrmann names and stresses again the cruel double standard that ridicules and punishes women for things that men are praised for. Her words also mesh well with the twentieth-century conception of gender as a system of crime and punishment, as discussed in connection with Philippine Engelhard-Gatterer.

Amalie mentions how the sexual double standard applies to sexual behavior and refers to a key male misperception of women: "They lure us into false steps, we listen to them, and if things then go wrong, the whole burden falls on us alone. They call us weak, and yet we are in certain cases much stronger than they. Altogether I find them in many things extremely unjust. . . ." (1:16). Amalie's rejection of women as weak is particularly unexpected since weakness is repeatedly invoked in the descriptions both Amalie and Fanny give of women, including themselves. Here, however, when directly confronting weakness as attributed to women by men, Amalie rejects it.

The conclusion Amalie draws from her recital of injustices leads her toward a rebellion against men's arrogation of power and privilege to themselves, an idea from which she then quickly retreats:

> if there were not so many empty, brainless puppets among us, I would become the first female rebel, stirring everyone up to healthy reason. That we are so dully educated and that so few of us distinguish ourselves and know how to control ourselves, this may be the reason for such a strict set of laws; and men are in the right there. For dumb women are often virtuous out of necessity and smart ones avoid licentiousness out of vanity. (1:16–17)

Suddenly, Amalie shares men's low regard for women. Previously, she seemed to consider that women's inferiority was at least partly men's creation, but now she ignores the implications of that position, which would suggest that women cannot fulfill their capacity to become equal until they escape the oppression she described men imposing on them. Now she uses women's inferiority to justify male superiority. She ends, then, by justifying the status quo.

Despite the typically protofeminist collapse of her tentatively feminist analysis, her ideas require an answer. The reply is ambivalent, too. Fanny, accusing Amalie of being an extremist and of ignoring men's side of the story, points to the dangers to which men with their greater freedom are exposed. Then, taking a position that makes the whole discussion moot, she questions the possibility of change: "It is after all the custom now that we have to act on the world stage as different creatures [from men]. Can it well be otherwise?" (1:18). And she claims that women who are oppressed are not the worthy ones, but rather are unworthy and deserving of being controlled or even abused. She continues with a virulent attack on these women, using a dehumanizing language that bears all the marks of misogyny: "An uneducated woman is the worst creature on earth, a thing that wanders around burdening humanity, a creature full of obstinacy and pride, a creation that martyrs everything around her almost to death. When a woman is bad, then she is so to a degree that a man can seldom reach" (1:18). It is women like these who make the policy of oppression correct, Fanny argues, in agreement with Amalie, and in confirmation of the dominant discourse after all. But note the initial marker of these horrendous women: uneducated.

The new positions and interpretations of social reality in the novel exist intermixed with the dominant discourse of the time, which Ehrmann herself had reproduced effectively in her slender essay on a woman's philosophy. In it she had written such platitudes as "Only the innocence and virtue of a young woman can bring happiness" and "The education of girls is different from that of boys because they are the same neither in character nor in temperament nor should they be the same" and "The greatest value of the virtuous and righteous woman is to remain hidden; her fame consists in the high regard of her husband, and her pleasure is the happiness of the family."[40] But even here there are also discordant claims, such as the statement that "a woman without a system against love—against men . . . is a miserable thing" or the warning to men not to "write up all of your weakness on our bill" (8, 10). A twentieth-century feminist critic has observed, "The growth of the novel, with its structural demand for conflict, undoubtedly helped to throw the adversary relationship between men and women into sharper focus."[41] Amalie's retreat from the protofeminist notion of leading women out of ignorance and bondage suggests the uncertainty and confusion associated with an emerging discourse and the difficulty of taking unequivocal stands, moving beyond the vacillations of protofeminism, when the dominant discourse is still overwhelmingly, pervasively in place.

Still, many sections of the novel explore the cracks and inconsistencies in women's opportunities for living full lives in the late eighteenth century. The starting point for these explorations is the female protagonist's situation of increasing independence, which, for a bourgeoisified young woman of the lower aristocracy in late eighteenth-century Germany, required killing off her parents and putting her in a diminished financial situation. Thus, in the first letter, Amalie announces with dismay and grief the death of her mother and mentions that her too good-natured father has allowed himself to be so viciously exploited by his brother that they are now besieged by creditors. Soon after, the trustee in charge of the inheritance that Amalie and her younger sister are to receive from their mother also begins to behave suspiciously and refuses to give Amalie an accounting of her inheritance. When the uncle and his unbearable brood of children, of whom most are daughters whom Amalie detests, come to live with them, Amalie and her father argue vehemently. As much as she wants to be a good housekeeper (substitute wife) for her father, Amalie is glad when the need to pressure the trustee about her inheritance gives her a chance to go on an extended trip, initially accompanied by the obnoxious uncle, but mostly on her own, staying with friends and relatives. Her taste for adventure whetted ("I would so like to see the world and get to know different people"),[42] she is next allowed to board with a family from whom she can learn how to make items of fashion, an activity that strangely produces no commentary from her or Fanny and yields no skills that she uses later. Soon, her father, too, is dead (1:83), but Ehrmann does not grant her protagonist complete independence, transferring her, instead, to the care of a kind uncle, a Catholic priest. As a priest, who cannot bring Amalie to live in his home, this transitional male authority figure functions as an idealized father—kind, generous, trusting, respectable, and mostly absent—whose main task is to endorse Amalie's plans while minimally interfering with her freedom.

Disastrous Marriage and Innovative Aftermath: *Amalie* As a Novel Thematizing Divorce and the Theater

The conventional goal for the heroine of an eighteenth-century German novel is marriage, a social institution, Karin Hausen argues, that in the last third of the century was changing rapidly from a practice overtly organized around the division of labor to a practice claiming to be founded in love and in the complementarity of sex/gender characteristics that assigned rationality to men and emotion to women. Ehrmann's *Amalie* challenges both parts of that discourse, representing the dangers of a seeming love marriage and the perils facing women not skilled at rationality.

Amalie, longing for love, is infatuated with various men beginning with the novel's seventh letter, but all had rather quickly proved unworthy. She had also repeatedly been importuned for sexual favors by strangers and acquaintances. Her response to such harassment is typically connected to her sense of superiority to other women. The report of one instance, for example, opens: "My woman cousin, the fool, is jealous of me" (1:33). The novel, at this point, seems to try valiantly not to side with women. When the uncle locates a post for Amalie as head of the house of another priest (1:104), she again finds herself warding off unwanted attention. The quality that enables her to resist these approaches despite her status as a human [*Mensch*], which means in Ehrmann's terms as a sexually excitable being, is the capacity for reason that helps her hold to her principles. Since most women are not so educated, they are not so capable of resistance. This is the novel's message again and again. Marianne Ehrmann's thinking woman then is a change from the feeling woman of Sophie La Roche for whom sexuality was not posited as a powerful issue. While La Roche's feeling woman was also relatively educated (and indeed La Roche herself would have welcomed scholarliness for her), Ehrmann rejected scholarliness, welcomed feelings (which she considered both useful and inevitable), but repeatedly and explicitly stresses "thinking," although without giving an educational recipe for it. Ehrmann discusses education infrequently and does not propose a particular curriculum that will yield rational women. Very importantly, she stresses the social and personal benefits of "thinking" for men as well as women. Rarely do the two thinking correspondents in the novel encounter others of their ilk, however.

Amalie certainly does not find thinking women at the convent where she goes to escape the lecherous priest. The location gives both Amalie and Fanny opportunities to blast the stupidity, narrow-mindedness, and insensitivity of nuns (1:135–45). Whereas the priest-uncle is clearly fallible, as incidents beginning with placing Amalie in the employ of the lecherous priest show, he is always respected and never ridiculed. The nuns, on the other hand, are always ridiculed and rarely respected. If they are transitional surrogate mothers, analogous to the priest-uncle's role as transitional father, then no wonder Amalie's mother died at the very moment the novel as a discussion between two *thinking* women started. Mothers and their replacements are treated as foolish, uneducated, and unreasonable. As depicted, the nuns provide a home to which one would go only in the most extreme need, and they impose restrictive rules on Amalie that are irreconcilable with emotional or intellectual growth and that are, of course, intended to forestall sexual behavior. Amalie views the cloistered repression of the nuns' sexuality as ultimately futile: "As a martyr of cruelty, many a good young woman wilts there with the teaming drives of nature in her bosom!—All of Nature reminds her in the gloomy convent garden of freedom, of love; with sadness she sees the smallest insects mating, and horribly heavily then the thought of impossibility weighs on her unhappy heart" (1:136). Since the text argues that sexual desire cannot simply be repressed as it will return undiminished, it is not surprising that the sexually repressed, unmarried nuns make a decision that drives Amalie into a hasty marriage: they refuse to let her answer a desperate call for help from her sister. Frantic to take action (why Fanny does not act for her is not mentioned), Amalie hastily agrees to marry a man who promises aid. The sister dies before he can reach her (why Amalie herself does not go is also unclear). And the marriage is a disaster, as well.

Key situations in the book are preceded by theoretical statements and by predictions (invariably correct), usually by Fanny. Thus, marriage is discussed in terms of its dangers and difficulties. As in most novels of the time, few words are spent on arranged marriages;[43] the emphasis, instead, is on the usual topics associated with love marriages, especially the problem of choosing a mate well, the probability that affection and love will dwindle with time, the harm that disenamoured husbands can inflict on their wives, mistreating them, plunging their children into misery, and even leaving home altogether. Such a breach of marital responsibility, Fanny is made to write, is fiendish and inhuman.[44] This time it is Amalie, who, taken aback by her friend's grim views, reasserts the dominant acceptance of male privilege by accusing Fanny of becoming an enemy of men (1:74). The two correspondents continually monitor each other's attitudes toward men and women. Disliking women, which is part of the dominant discourse, is clearly more acceptable than disliking or simply criticizing men, which is treated as an indicator of dangerous notions and practices. However, when Fanny writes about the patience and tolerance that marriage partners have to develop for each other, she adds an important clause: "Contributions toward this must however be made by the man as well as the woman; otherwise one only works to strengthen the other in evil" (1:71). This is a significantly different condition attached to the usual ideal of the totally patient and forgiving wife on whom alone the burden of adaptation falls. The notion of equality, in the limited form of equal responsibility, is fundamental to Fanny's analysis of marriage.

Despite Amalie's disappointments with other men, and despite Fanny's warnings about the dangers of being misled, the young heroine, who is posited as smart, highly principled, and, of course, a thinker, voluntarily marries a man with a seriously defective character. Since the possibility that a good and intelligent woman can make a bad mistake in her choice of a partner was not supposed to be part of the story of goodness (in which virtue is rewarded, not punished), this misadventure, as in *Fräulein von Sternheim*, is shown to result from a series of unfortunate events (the convent situation, the sister's plea for help, the uncle's absence at the critical moment). But *Amalie*, like many of Ehrmann's texts, also has a pessimistic strain (evident in the autobiography of the handkerchief as well and characteristic of the *Empfindsamkeit* of alienation) in which it is precisely the good people to whom bad things happen and bad people who prosper. So the heroine discovers that her new husband is a compulsive gambler. Through the marriage, he gains control of her money and squanders it, as Amalie discovers by having him watched (1:273). At first, she tries the same strategy as the heroine of Karoline von Wobeser's later immensely popular *Elisa oder das Weib wie es seyn soll* "Elisa or a Wife as She Should Be" (1795): tranquil and constant forgiveness. This is the proposal of the dominant discourse, initially advocated in the letters of Fanny. The husband in Ehrmann's novel initially responds well to his wife's patience, but then reverts to his addiction. Amalie persists with patient passivity. When she is about to seek help from strangers, she refrains out of consideration for her own and her husband's good names. And although the agony of her predicament nearly strangles her, she claims never to have directly expressed disapproval to her husband even in a single syllable (1:170). In one especially awful incident, the husband comes home in a fury, drags the pregnant Amalie around the room by her hair, and causes her to miscarry (1:174–75). Fanny had indicated earlier that husbands sometimes resorted to physical abuse, but she had assumed this happened only among the ignorant, not in the educated middle class or among the gentry (1:46). Even though Amalie plays the virtuous martyr, willing to suffer anything, and thus, seemingly following Ehrmann's own earlier advice in *Philosophie eines Weibes*, in the novel her efforts meet with failure. Having discovered that class does not protect her, Amalie leaves home.

The two friends conduct a long and vigorous argument about what to do next. Fanny approves Amalie's flight: "You have done well, my friend, to depart. Duty is only holy when our self-preservation does not suffer as a result" (1:177). Relying on the discourse of human rights and happiness, she asks: "Who could advise you to sleep beside a barbarian who is ready at any moment to become your murderer? Who could be so insensitive as to leave a beloved female creature any longer under the tyranny of a crazy man?" What this rhetoric does not make explicit is the practical choice available. (Nor does it list among the husband's transgressions Amalie's miscarriage, an event that is dropped.)

Fanny had introduced her passage with comments about Amalie's femininity that lead to entirely different conclusions: "And this monster had the effrontery to drag you around by your hair, poor patient one? And you, angel of gentleness [*Sanftmuth*], let yourself be so devilishly treated without complaining, without making the slightest sound!—Oh this steadfastness is incomprehensible, is the greatest strength of soul that ever lived in a woman!—Let the woman appear, some woman somewhere, who could wrestle with you over the prize of such virtue!—Maly!—Maly!" (1:176). This language mystifies weakness as strength, a tactic Rousseau had also used and that Ehrmann had urged in her *Philosophie eines Weibes*: "The first and greatest quality of a woman is gentleness."[45] By praising Amalie, affectionately called Maly in this passage, for her feminine gentleness, Fanny makes it unfeminine for Amalie to summon the strength to leave or to fight back in other ways, although at a critical moment, at the end of her letter, she suggests that precisely that could happen—Amalie might become so provoked she would literally fight back, with disastrous consequences: "Who knows whether frenzy might not have misled you into a bloody decision!—I know the degree of your passions and your melancholy."[46] In a typical Ehrmann move, offsetting her harshest criticism of men with criticism of women, it seems as though Amalie might murder her husband (or herself), although the woman had so far been inclined only toward pathological passivity, not aggression.

In her response, Amalie ignores the possibility of assaulting her husband, but pursues the issue of virtue: "Your love for me made you forget that small virtue demands small sacrifice, and great virtue demands great sacrifice." Now she begins to dismiss the importance of the man's assaults on her and even to excuse them: "What would it have mattered anyway if he crippled this miserable body of mine with his shoves, since sooner or later it will turn to dust?—His mistreatment was in fact just haste and sickness of spirit. If I could be so fortunate as to discover even a trace of improvement in him, then a thousand such abuses would be nothing to my patience!" (1:178–9). She quickly goes even further, castigating herself for having abandoned him: "Why did I leave an unhappy husband, who was overwhelmed by his passion for gaming, just to save this mug of a youthful face, to spare these unsound bones?—Ha!—I am a condemned woman!—an undutiful woman!—a worthless woman!—How could I lower myself like that to the common run of women?" (1:179). She summarizes all her self-accusations by saying she had sunk to the level of ordinary women. Amalie goes back to her husband.

Changing course again, Fanny soon invokes the stand she had taken at the beginning of the novel, rejecting carrying a virtue so far that it may result in self-destruction: "Your steadfastness is a sin that you are committing at the cost of your life and your health." She then demands: "Why haven't you been listening to my warnings long since?—Why did you not follow my advice?—Why did you open your heart to him again for that unscrupulous man to shred?" (1:206). This is the correspondence between two women friends who are approximately equals in authority, although Fanny has the role of stable adviser. It is not the situation of La Roche's Lina letters, in which an experienced and highly respected older woman addressed advice to a compliant and obedient younger one. Fanny can tell Amalie what to do, but Amalie need not follow the advice.

And then Fanny again briefly introduces the discourse of femininity that sanctions or at least explains Amalie's behavior (and that deauthorizes her own female voice, as later events make clearer): "You are a woman in the full sense of the word, a weak woman; otherwise you would not offer your neck yourself to your murderer." The continuation indicates that Fanny does not approve of this form of complete womanhood: "Your unpardonable goodheartedness is contagious, you befuddled your uncle with it and are taking him with you into ruin!" (1:206). Within the terms of this novel it is, on the one hand, good for a woman to be a woman, which is to say weak; on the other hand, women can also be defined as persons with responsibilities and rights that do not vary by gender. The mediator between the two is provided, the text argues, by thinking.

As a thinker, Fanny recommends divorce, which raises an issue seldom addressed in eighteenth-century German novels: confessional difference. Amalie is Catholic and Fanny Protestant, an important factor, since divorce was virtually impossible within the Catholic church. So Fanny suggests Amalie undertake an informal separation: "And given too that the ears of the ecclesiastical judges among you Catholics would be deaf to such misery, still your own should not be deaf toward a life for whose foreshortening you will someday have to answer to your creator!" She follows with another strong denunciation of the "villain . . . who in a frenzy of depravity wallows in filth" and asks rhetorically, "Or are an addiction to gambling, bloodthirstiness, and fraud not sufficient reasons for an eternal separation?" The criticism of Catholic ecclesiastical courts and of their attitude toward divorce is extensive. Fanny says religion is profaned when the impossibility of divorce drives couples into despair and causes them to lead lives of secret dishonor (1:208). In concluding, she invokes the eighteenth-century authorities, humanity, reason and nature, rephrasing the problem as it affects everyone for whom divorce is inaccessible: "O human race, human race! When will your laws begin to be an honor to sweet reason and to beautiful nature?" (1:209).

The answering letter, not directly addressing the ideas that Fanny raises, is situated first in Amalie's worsening psychological predicament: "Yes indeed, everything in my situation looks hopeless to me!—Not deaf to your begging, not deaf to reason, but incapable of any action, I drag my fate from thought to thought and can find none that calms me." As she explains the matter further, she again positions herself as a model of gentle passivity: "Am I not tired of the abuses by my husband?—O my dearest!—My weak body has been tired of them for a long time already, but my heart is not." Amalie frames her position explicitly within the terms of femininity: "You are right, amiable thinker, I am a weak, weak woman, who obligingly hastens to her death! By god, woman is, just as all the observers of human nature say, either an angel or a devil." The recourse to femininity makes action impossible; it poses the alternatives of being either weak, incapable, immobilized and an angel, or strong, capable, active, and a devil. Given these choices,

Amalie must reject her friend's advice: "And now for the last time, my friend, leave off your demand; I cannot, I will not leave him!" (1:210). Nonetheless, she sketches what might happen if she sued for divorce: "Should I be brazen enough to put forward his weaknesses in front of others and let even greater [weaknesses] be ascribed to me by his gall? Only common women can stand in a courtroom and insult their husbands and themselves in public!" The need to separate herself from other women again cuts off choices from her. She concludes with the trump card of religion, "And if it turned out to my advantage, this divorce, what would it avail me given my religion?" (1:211)

Fanny doggedly responds again: "You are too good. . . . When this goodness nourishes vice, it becomes unforgivable. My words for moving you to a decision that sooner or later you will have to make are almost exhausted" (1:213). She inserts Amalie's psychological state into her argument: "You would really not be leaving a husband; you would be leaving a torturer, who torments you all the worse because he knows your discouragement . . ." (1:214). Again, Fanny acknowledges the problems with the courts, but argues that Amalie can leave her husband on her own. Her letter concludes with a positive vision of the kind of love that is based on virtue:

> It is undeniably true, my Amalie, that only virtuous love grounded in principles makes the human being into a true human being. O, what feelings one has about this! In the arms of love is enough blessedness to suppress every other passion with ease! But as long as people do not love and do not learn to think by loving, just so long will many-headed vice still be at home everywhere. Goodbye for today, dear Maly! Your Fanny—(1:216)

In this paragraph, Fanny invokes two themes of the book: love (and sexuality—"arms of love") as essential to full humanity, and love allied with thinking as the best promise for human goodness. With this vision and an affectionate farewell, the first volume ends.

Sophie La Roche, like Fanny Burney in *Evelina*, had used the epistolary novel as a "literary device to obtain contrasting voices."[47] In most respects, Ehrmann did not. Amalie is narrator of almost all of the events of the novel and respondent to Fanny's comments; Fanny is the commentator on the events and the predictor of what they mean, which turns out to be a rudimentary technique of foreshadowing. In the marriage and divorce discussion, Amalie's and Fanny's analyses are most differentiated; on other topics, the two substantially agree. And both share the subjectivity that Ehrmann privileged for women: both are thinkers who enact their thinking through discussion. Yet, it is very significant that they cannot reach agreement about the topic of divorce, and founding the disagreement in harshly criticized religious institutions does not resolve the conflict. After all, Amalie herself thinks that if priests experienced marriage, they would have different ideas about divorce.[48] The inconclusiveness of this discussion, then, can be understood as another indication of the alienation threading through Ehrmann's texts, an alienation stemming in part from a world full of contradictions, many of them unhappy: "Unhappiness always has the upper hand among humankind, and anyone who hopes for something better is clinging to a soap bubble which can disappear with every breath" (1:85). But unhappiness and depression in Ehrmann's texts has its own validity: "To a healthy person, one who is not depressed, the secret worm, gnawing inside, is as strange as to a depressed person are the joys that volley back from his dulled, sick nerves" (1:94). These are ideas she will develop further in later writings.

The second volume opens with further episodes of outrageous behavior by Amalie's husband, including one that requires Amalie to take on the role of rescuing hero: dressed as a man of the middle-class, she rides to extricate her husband from danger. But the husband makes another violent assault on her, which at last precipitates the right authority to produce an informal separation without jeopardizing her womanly submissiveness. That authority resides in men, men of rank, and men from her family. Although the battered Amalie, bleeding from mouth and nose, begs her uncle to forgive her husband, the uncle is determined to report the batterer to the prince. When a baron walks into the room and recommends the less public and less drastic option of separation, the problem is resolved. Amalie decides to go to a convent again as a boarder. Fanny greets the news with joy, calling it Amalie's "salvation and release" (2:26); Fanny's arguments for divorce, or separation, in the case of the Catholic Amalie, are accepted in a protofeminist way—when they are placed in the mouths of men.

Throughout the marriage and divorce discussions, as if to offset the implications contained there about men, opportunities are produced to lambaste various groups of women, aristocratic ladies, merchants' wives, nuns. Now when the separation of the marriage partners has finally occurred, the convent once more provides an opportunity to assail the nuns, this time an order devoted to educating girls, a project carried out very unsuccessfully, according to Amalie. Ehrmann's invective against women is another way in which her work resembles some of Mary Wollstonecraft's; Claudia Johnson comments that "her censoriousness of women as well as her commitment to ostensibly masculinist, enlightenment values have disappointed those who expect feminism to produce, as she does not, a positive culture of the feminine and of female solidarity."[49] While Johnson goes on to argue that Wollstonecraft's stance is a part of her commitment to a republican agenda as well as a feminist one, Ehrmann's mixed positions seem to indicate an effort to maintain male support. Thus, much as Amalie professes the importance of her epistolary conversations with Fanny, Amalie's actions are generally incited by men. When she grows depressed during her separation, her uncle, at the suggestion of a kind doctor, sends her on a trip to Italy to recover. Wise men help her leave the company of foolish women. The action of the novel, in keeping with Amalie's philosophy, assiduously distinguishes her from the other women.

The letters from Italy pick up again on picaresque events in the first volume, but also contain, in abundance, the kind of general observation about Italians and comparisons with Germans that are typical of travel writing of the time. About Italian men, for example, one comment in a whole letter full of judgments is this: "The basic trait of their character remains goodnaturedness until it is put to the test by a passion, and then it turns into fiery vengefulness."[50] What is interesting about passages such as this is Amalie's ready appropriation of a subject position as judge and evaluator; she assumes the respected Enlightenment role of observer without qualms about her legitimacy. Yet, at the same time, she attends to the much less high-minded sexual escapades happening around her. There are crowded coach rides, venal innkeepers, aristocratic parties, and, at the insistence of her male cousin, a visit in men's clothes to a brothel. In short, an array of incidents quite different from the usual German sentimental novel and far exceeding the usual experience of German women readers of the educated middle class or its near neighbor, the lower aristocracy. The story of the handkerchief rewrites this same material.

The next stage of Amalie's story also parallels the handkerchief's autobiography: forced, or enabled by the sudden death of Amalie's husband and the depleted finances of her priest/uncle, she becomes an actress in order to make her own living. Money was only part of the choice, however. Amalie could also have earned a living as a governess, but even the mere process of seeking such a job proved humiliating to her (2:114). Acting, the main subject of almost half the letters of the second volume (especially letters 115 through 152, out of 163 letters in the novel), was a different matter. Near the beginning of the book, after seeing her first play, *Romeo and Julie* (perhaps meaning the much produced play by Weisse in which Sophie Albrecht often performed), Amalie had written: "I have never in all my life found a form of entertainment that could become more of a passion to me than this" (1:70). Amalie becomes an actress after first having been an avid spectator and then organizing performances for and by the schoolgirls being educated in the second convent. By the time she begins her stage career, she knows the theater relatively well and continues to find it exciting. After many difficult experiences, she still explains to Fanny the attraction of her profession: "My feelings are fiery, they have learned to soar, they don't willingly tolerate restriction, they need occupation, they must have an object.—Previously, love was my main occupation, but since I have tasted its bitternesses, now [my occupation] has become my propensity for the theater" (2:153). Work as an actress, then, is an outlet for her energies and emotions—but it is also morally dangerous.

The morality of actors, so often discussed in the novel, can be understood as a stand-in for questions about the role of rationality in human behavior. Karin Hausen argues that the polarization of the sexes, which, beginning in the last third of the eighteenth century, attributed rationality to men and emotionality to women, sprang up among the educated bourgeoisie in part because that was a class in which education had "almost certainly brought about considerable real though socially engendered character differences between the men and women . . . with respect to rationality."[51] Ehrmann's *Amalie* can be read as confirming that women "had evidently preserved modes of behavior which diverged from those of the formally educated men as irrational, emotional, spontaneous, uncontrolled, etc.,"[52] but even though Ehrmann is especially vitriolic in her accounts of irrational behavior among women, she finds these modes among men, as well. The theater is a particularly interesting site for her critique since this is a rare public workplace in the eighteenth century in which numbers of originally middle-class men and women worked side by side. (In private workplaces, men and women worked side by side when family members, for example, were engaged together in a trade or craft in a workshop not separate from their home.) While, as Hausen argues, many men of the educated middle class were working in settings separate from their homes in "increasingly specialized fields of productive, distributive and administrative activity" that required "disciplined, rational and impersonal behavior," a professionalized notion of the theater required disciplined, rational, impersonal behavior (as well as creativity and emotionality) from both the women and the men who would make up a troupe. Ehrmann's text, then, in its demand that both women and men should become thinkers, and that both would practice rationality publicly, as well as privately, offered a different solution to the instability of roles that the separation of "home" and "work" was producing in late eighteenth-century Germany. Instead of following the dominant discourse in reinforcing the separation of the two places by naturalizing polarized sets of characteristics for men and women, Ehrmann argued that women as well as men should practice rationality to the benefit of both home and work. She depicted "home" as a site of possible abuse for women and "work" as a site of escape. Even though particular theater troupes can also be abusive, *Amalie* shows actresses able to leave them and find new employment quickly.

With respect to rationality, then, Ehrmann does not accept different standards of gendered behavior for public and private settings, and she thinks that higher levels of rationality are evident in higher standards of morality. While in the first volume of the novel Amalie was becoming more adept at seeing the weaknesses of theatrical performances, she was distressed to realize that the actors who spoke fine words and performed good acts on stage were not moral and good behind the scenes. Fanny explained this bluntly by asserting that most people who became actors were unhappy misfits who used art as a cover.[53] When in the second volume Amalie becomes an actress, she argues that the chance to observe the behavior of her colleagues will give her ample material for thought. What follows are colorful and credible references to ignorant oafish directors, their incompetent wives, and their spiteful mistresses, the occasional leader with good sense and good taste but little money, the skilled and unskilled colleagues (some facing painful declines in their fame), the intrigues among them, the claques, and cabals. Brief travel description is part of these letters, too, with references to Hungary and its bleak landscape. The heroine performs in many different roles, including as the mistress in Schiller's *Kabale und Liebe* (a late *Sturm und Drang* play that had first been produced in 1784), and, despite her inexperience, she enjoys mostly successes from the start. Yet, of course, there are many disappointments and difficulties, including fans and directors seeking sexual favors. Whenever possible, Amalie blames the artistic, economic and sexual foibles of the many directors for whom she works on their ignorant (and thus immoral) wives or mistresses (or both).

Ehrmann sees vivid public consequences of poorly educated, unself-disciplined women.

Until the longer travel and theater episodes, most of the letters in the novel are about two pages in length, usually with two letters from Amalie for each one from Fanny. Ehrmann takes care to keep the epistolary form evident, with varied openings and closings, and also with occasional tidbits about Fanny's personal life. One letter, written in the dialogue form that Ehrmann handles especially well, describes Amalie's first interview for a position with a theater troupe. Along with making the classic sexist evaluation of her body and appearance, the director asks her whether she can read, explaining in response to her expression of wonderment that many actors cannot; by the end of the piece, Amalie has forced the director to acknowledge that he is illiterate, too. This lively letter opens with one of the incongruities that mark the book at several points. Fanny has just written about her horror that Amalie must take up so disreputable a profession; Amalie responds that her heart is bleeding, too, and then, in the same sentence, begins with obvious relish to report on her comical discussion with the director.

The lack of transition matches the sometimes discordant intertextuality of the book, combining the comic picaresque with the sentimental.[54] *Amalie* draws on sentimental novels such as *Clarissa* for the correspondence relationship but also has elements of adventure novels, such as *Tom Jones*, for its numerous raunchy scenes. *Amalie, eine wahre Geschichte* is especially indebted to *Geschichte des Fräuleins von Sternheim*, borrowing its spunky heroine and its structure of multiple courtships followed by a traumatic misguided marriage at the midpoint of the book; the end of this unfortunate marriage leaves the protagonist unencumbered by familial direction and earning her own living, a situation that enables each to travel to distant countries (England and Scotland in the case of Sternheim, and Italy and Hungary in the case of Amalie) and ends with a second marriage, this one flagged as good. Both books are organized by the notion of the heroine writing letters to a female confidante; but while *Sternheim* also includes letters from the protagonist's rival suitors, *Amalie*, in contrast, contains the confidante's answers to the protagonist's outpourings. The continuing dialog situation of the two writers in *Amalie* and their consistent self-presentations as lively, thinking, but also fallible, women minimize the disruption to the aesthetic and psychological texture of the novel caused by the conventionally incompatible intertextualities of the book.

To end her book, Ehrmann moves to give her thinking protagonist the usual reward: a fitting husband, quite unlike the first fiendish one. At the same time as Ehrmann's publication of the first letters that became *Amalie*, Isabelle de Charrière published *Lettres de Mistriss Henley publiée par son amie* (1784), in which the heroine also faces a disastrous marriage; Mistress Henley, however, tells her husband about her distress, then, refusing to take any further action, finally enacts "the silence, the living death," which is the "unwritten sequel" to the eighteenth-century novel of courtship.[55] Ehrmann, in contrast, depicting a husband so violent that real death could have been the result of staying with him, offers a serious debate about divorce in her novel; and if divorce can be considered as the death of a marriage, Ehrmann gives her protagonist a symbolic divorce via the convenient death of the dreadful husband. Yet, Ehrmann's critique of marriage is less stringent than Charrière's because, in the end, she holds out the promise of a happy marriage, which the French author had profoundly questioned, and because Ehrmann, like Sophie La Roche, offers her heroine a second chance after her first mistake. Just as *Amalie* is not a tract that argues singlemindedly for divorce, it also does not feature only unhappy aspects of marriage.

After Amalie rejects a nobleman's invitation to be his companion, the right husband, a thinker of course, is finally found and proves to be a friend of Fanny's equally honorable new husband. Amalie's acting career does not prevent marriage (although Wilhelm's parents object to it); once she can marry someone who is able to support her, however, necessity no longer justifies her career. Yet, whether she leaves the stage or not is unclear. Was it simply self-evident? In any case, Amalie assumes the woman's traditional submissive position: "All my wishes are now fulfilled! My good heart has found an even better one! my soul can pour itself into its mirror image; my spirit finds nourishment through Wilhelm's reason; my little weaknesses are now under the care of a kind, loving husband. . . ."[56] And so forth. At this point, the novel must, and does, end.

Prior to this positive version of the "unwritten sequel," *Amalie* shows how a strong eighteenth-century woman character attempts, in a male-defined world, to find out some of what it might mean to live life independent of family control. The two letter writers in the novel are both women, and no individual man figures prominently for more than a limited time, although men as a group are a constant censorious presence. Such a pattern of emphasis is not rare among late eighteenth-century novels and tales by women. Yet, despite the extensive dialogue between Fanny and Amalie about women's problems, there is no analysis of women's legal, economic and social status in marriage.

Embedded as they are in the dominant discourse of the time, the two correspondents often take androcentric positions and make harshly misogynist statements. This situation of the emergent discourse reproducing part of the dominant discourse under challenge is typical of eighteenth-century texts that I am labeling protofeminist. Hausen describes the late eighteenth century in Germany as a period in which the legitimacy of "the traditional subjection of the woman to her husband and her limitation to the domestic sphere" was in doubt; while the dominant group developed the notion of polarized sex characteristics to reimpose controls, another discourse demanded "female emancipation from conjugal or paternal authority and integration on equal terms with men into bourgeois society."[57] Identifying Theodor Gottlieb von Hippel's *Über die bürgerliche Verbesserung der Weiber* (1792) as her German example, Hausen claims this emancipatory option appeared "in the wake of the French Revolution."[58] I am arguing that three prominent exponents of emancipation were Hippel, Ehrmann, and Emilie von Berlepsch, and that their first tentative versions of the emancipatory option, written before the Revolution (evident in Hippel's case in the gradually reversing argumentation of his book about marriage), focused on the wife's experience of marriage and its implications. In Ehrmann's *Amalie, eine wahre Geschichte*, protofeminist discourse occurs in the correspondence of two thinking women confronting injustices of several kinds (botched inheritances, greedy and lecherous relatives, a gambling and violent husband) and leads to a shocked sense of the incoherence of the world, a sense I am labeling the *Empfindsamkeit* of alienation. In the early books of Emilie von Berlepsch (1755–1830), a protofeminist analysis of marriage, but one less prone to alienation, is practiced that is later far more widely disseminated through a two-part essay in a prominent journal. In it, Berlepsch transforms Ehrmann's narrative of Amalie's marital exploitation into a more theorized critique of women's situation in marriage and thus, complements the writings of Marianne Ehrmann.

MAPPING MISOGYNY: EHRMANN'S CONTEMPORARY, EMILIE VON BERLEPSCH

Berlepsch's most dramatic statements representing the new discourse on women's experience of marriage are incongruously located within an essay entitled "Ueber einige zum Glück der Ehe nothwendige Eigenschaften und Grundsätze" "Some Characteristics and Principles Necessary for Happiness in Marriage." The essay appeared in Christoph Martin Wieland's famous journal *Der teutsche Merkur* in 1791, after the French Revolution had begun but before it had become notably bloody, thus, in the period when some German intellectuals were willing to engage with its propositions. Whether the essay was written during that period is uncertain, however; Wieland's introductory note claims it had been composed ten years before publication.[59] The aristocratic Emilie von Berlepsch, born in 1755 to a countess and the vice chancellor of Altenburg and Sachsen-Gotha as Emilie von Oppeln, had married Friedrich Ludwig von Berlepsch, the president of the high court in Hannover, when she was sixteen and he twenty-two. She had several children, including an especially beloved daughter who died very young, before her unhappy marriage ended in divorce at about the end of 1787;[60] Emilie von Berlepsch was thirty-two. Her first publication, a series of travel letters, had appeared in 1785, her first book, a collection of essays and poems, in 1787, the same year as the divorce (and the year before Ehrmann's *Amalie*), and her essay on happiness in marriage four years later.

While Marianne Ehrmann in *Amalie* articulates reservations about the disrespect for women at the same time that she also invokes it, Berlepsch went further. She produces in her essay an extensive critique of society's low esteem for women and gave that low esteem its unacceptable name: misogyny.[61] She argues that misogyny contaminates the husbands' minds and made it impossible for women to derive satisfaction from their traditional roles as wives. While Ehrmann writes about a disastrous marriage in *Amalie*, Berlepsch in her essay writes about routine marriages as experienced by everyday women of the class who read Wieland's journal, the educated middle class and lower aristocracy. Taking the position that for a woman to survive the tribulations of marriage, the usual characteristics of submissiveness and orderliness were utterly insufficient, Berlepsch saw herself as "fighting against the prejudice that wants to grant women neither a will of their own nor the courage to express it." She disapproves of the version of femininity that idealizes "a languishing eye or a lisping voice or slinking bearing," and argues that a woman with sharply drawn facial features and "a bold swift tongue" could still have the best heart. She sarcastically notes the objections of the dominant version of femininity when "a certain firmness in making judgments let one feel that the woman who possesses this might possibly be able to—say no" (69). Berlepsch's essay, composed in the form of a letter of advice to her soon to be married younger sister, denounces the weak and helpless image of women that her society cultivates; she defends strong women who neither looked nor acted the prescribed feminine role.

But Emilie von Berlepsch also did not have a comprehensive analysis with which to counter the dominant discourse. Like Ehrmann in *Amalie*, Berlepsch mixes passages advocating the release of women from compliant, childlike behavior with passages of routine androcentrism:

> How sad is the fate of the man whose home a raving, quarrelsome, impertinent spouse makes into hell, who dares not try to express his opinion if it deviates from hers because he always runs the danger of . . . being made to lose his temper and getting into such tumults of feeling as are equally detrimental to the health of the body and the soul. (70–71)

Here, the outspoken woman is blamed when the man loses his temper. The inconsistency of Berlepsch's perspective again demonstrates how difficult it was for a writer to separate herself from the powerful and pervasive claim that men should be in control in a marriage and to put into words new ways in which women could experience themselves in relation to the world, a new feminine subjectivity.

Both the Ehrmann and Berlepsch texts accept the stated ideals of the dominant discourse. Thus, the essay, like the *Amalie* novel, accepts the conventional view of the husband as proper head of the family; it gives advice to men about how to exert control and still get along well with their wives. The Berlepsch essay, however, published three years after *Amalie*, insists on women's dignity. One of the passages addressed to husbands gives a clear statement of the new practices Berlepsch attempts to promote:

> Instead of destroying her self-confidence with imperious coldness and unjust contempt, or—as always happens then in the case of strong souls—rousing her to rebellion against him, it would be easy for him through gentle care and consideration to make precisely this self-consciousness into the indestructible basis of an attachment that is perhaps the first and strongest need of the female heart. (76–77)

The dominant version of women as delicate and dependent by nature does not here preclude reading some of women's destructive behaviors as reactions to the common peremptory behavior of husbands. In this protofeminist version of the dominant discourse, men should temper their behavior to fit the nature of women and to preserve women's sense of self.

Eighteenth-century women, such as Emilie von Berlepsch, could adopt in their thought two positions that for substantial periods of late twentieth-century feminist discourse have been considered irreconcilable alternatives. Eighteenth-century writers often envision women as suffering from negative social conditioning, part of it provoked by profound male misogyny, and simultaneously consider women as tied by nature to certain specific social roles and characteristics. Renate Möhrmann, in her study of German women writers in the early nineteenth century, has commented on the dilemma that this position entails: "If male insufficiency of feeling and female capacity for love, i.e., the characteristic qualities of the sexes, are seen not as socially conditioned but as biological constants, then all ideas about improving the situation of women are condemned to failure from the start. Chromosome structures simply cannot be changed through campaigns of enlightenment."[62] But it is not so clear what eighteenth and early nineteenth-century writers meant by "nature"—certainly not chromosome structure. And, that problem aside, the disposition attributed to women can only be adequately evaluated in comparison to that attributed to men, and vice versa. Emilie von Berlepsch, for instance, apparently thinks that while women are by nature dependent on strong emotional attachments, men are not condemned by nature to be tyrannical. Both parties can and should change their methods—although men retain supremacy.

Arguing, however, that a woman cannot rely upon attaining the ideal relationship of respected dependency, Berlepsch attempts to displace the central problem from the nature of women or men onto the culture of misogyny. Men are so misogynist that they could drive "good" wives to become "bad." Misogyny, Berlepsch points out, affects both men and women. Men's writings about women, she says, teem with "biting attacks, exaggerated assertions, half-true, over-generalized accusations, . . . chilling censure and even more humiliating praise."[63] Women, she argues, suffer not only from criticism, but also from approval when it is of the wrong kind. Berlepsch proceeds to explain more directly what sort of women result from this misogynist world, where all women are judged by the behavior of a few who are bad—and even the defects of those few are not difficult to explain:

> If an error-ridden education, bad example, and the deafening whirl of the world of society mislead some women into dissolution and foolish-

ness, should therefore the larger number of those who lead a useful, innocent life also be condemned and be robbed of their well-earned claims to public respect and domestic trust? Is female virtue an absurdity because there are still many women who are weak and a few who are wicked, because some make themselves ridiculous by their oversensitive affectation or carry on some monkey business with their so-called pretension to wit and culture—to which, carefully examined, men themselves probably gave the first impetus?—Can it therefore be decisively claimed that women lack feeling, lack genius, that nature overall has denied them all strength and warmth of soul, all sense of what is great and beautiful, yes, even the necessary power of the brain, as an otherwise intelligent writer asserts? (83)

The text argues for giving all women another chance against the harsh judgments that have so long been circulated against them. Furthermore, it is men's low opinion of women that makes it impossible for women to be their naturally mild, tender, pure selves (a characterization of women that does not fit with her defense of the strong-willed, straightforward woman earlier). When a woman is subjected long enough to male disapproval and belittlement, "The soul is demeaned, courage weakened, energies crippled, and every fiery striving for greatness and perfection stifled" (88). Misogyny distorts women and diminishes the opportunity they have to demonstrate their abilities. Especially since male observers are also subject to misogynist discourse, misapprehensions about women and their abilities are inevitable. This observation is used to neutralize the most powerful eighteenth-century opponent of protofeminism, Rousseau. His writings, too, which are cited admiringly in other Berlepsch texts, suffer from contamination by the prevailing misogyny, she here argues, and men who came after him constantly appeal to his authority. "Those cutting moralists, who, no matter how vigorously and proudly they strut around, still like to barricade themselves behind a great name" (85), they quote everything Rousseau wrote in criticism of women but never cite his words of praise.

Because the best men, as well as their pretentious followers, are tainted with misogyny, the essay contends, the danger to women is great and urgent, and a proposal for change acutely needed. The text acknowledges that the proposed response does not attack "the evil itself," but hopes it offers women "a means of self-preservation." The notion of preserving (or perhaps more accurately, developing) women's sense of self is emphasized throughout these passages of the essay. Solutions that do not take women's self into account are not effective; meekness [*Sanftmut*], which Rousseau particularly recommended to women (and which *Amalie* too continued to endorse), "will preserve peace and decency outwardly," the essay contends, "but it will not be able to deter the inner grudge, the enervating loss of courage, and the soul's gradual decline into discord." The opposite approach, "vehement resistance," is even more destructive. The proposal for a "shield that can guard the soul and protect its delicate sensitivities against harm" is *"self-reliance"* (her emphasis, 89). Women, the argument goes, must learn to be independent. In the face of the grim situation of women in marriage, a protofeminist proposal inconsistent with the earlier depiction of female "nature" and the earlier acceptance of traditional marital roles emerges.

The pages that follow fend off various objections. Yes, it will be very difficult for women, especially young women, to learn independence, since their entire education inculcated submissiveness. Yes, the proposal conflicts with the view that women's obligation is to be pleasing to men, but such notions are inappropriate for an enlightened world: "But we, whom a better fate and brighter recognition of reason protects, we who share and enjoy the inviolate rights of humanity—at least in many respects—with men: why should we not also keep our inner, spiritual existence independent and individually our own?" (91). The text here alludes very cautiously to the possibility that women, too, might share in inalienable "human" rights. It briefly proposes the notion of independent personhood as extending to women in ways that would change women's relationships, and then, in a characteristic protofeminist move, the text veers back into traditional advice and comments about marriage.

Despite the comparatively thorough argumentation about misogyny and the need for self-reliance in this essay, Berlepsch, too, cannot sustain a liberatory argument through an entire text. Meanwhile, her contemporary, Marianne Ehrmann, although not advancing theoretical arguments about women's situation, found another vehicle through which to offer reformist appeals to women, and in which she could develop her literary skills.

A Journalist's Experiments with the Macabre and the Mundane

Marianne Ehrmann became a journalist. This work began when her new husband started two journals. One, *Der Beobachter* "The Observer," was for the general reader and had a subtitle appropriate to what would become Marianne Ehrmann's usual work: "a weekly magazine with political-moral-satirical contents" (1788–90). The other, *Frauenzimmer-Zeitung* "Gentlewoman's Newspaper," started a year earlier, used its subtitle to promise safely uncontroversial reading: "a historical-moral entertainment journal for the fair sex." It appeared in 1787 and 1788 in the south German town of Isny, not far from the border of Austria. Involvement with these two periodicals was a crucial development for Marianne Ehrmann, for journalism was to become her final area of outstanding accomplishment.[64]

Shortly after the couple moved to Stuttgart in 1788, the year that saw her three novels published, Ehrmann started planning and preparing her own new periodical. Without the advantages of fame that Sophie La Roche enjoyed when she started *Pomona* five years earlier, Ehrmann worked particularly hard to make her new monthly magazine a success.[65] While she published *Amaliens Erholungsstunden* "Amalie's Recreational Hours" herself at first, it was quickly taken on by Cotta, in Tübingen, the publisher who was soon to become an important force in the dissemination of classical German literature. Although working with Cotta undoubtedly had advantages, it also led to so many disagreements and misunderstandings that late in 1792, Ehrmann was replaced as editor and her journal rechristened *Flora*.[66] Unwilling to accept this blow, Ehrmann promptly founded another journal, *Die Einsiedlerinn aus den Alpen* "The Hermit Woman from the Alps," published this time by the respected firm of Orell, Gessner, Füssli und Comp. in Zürich. But the dogged editor's health had been failing for the past five years. *Einsiedlerinn*'s 1794 issues, the last, did not appear until mid-1795. Then, on 14 August 1795, three months before her fortieth birthday, Marianne Ehrmann died.

The contents of *Amaliens Erholungsstunden* are energetic and diverse: admonitory stories, articles, poems by diverse contributors, essays, and anecdotes offering an array of information, entertainment, and instruction. In a move typical of the eighteenth century, Ehrmann wraps her editorial persona in layers of claims to both fiction (since she has already used "Amalie" as the name of the title character in her first novel) and truth (her novel, likewise, claims to be "a true story" and is later asserted by T. F. Ehrmann to be autobiographical).

As tools of persuasion in her journal she is more likely to use fear or ridicule, tools deriving from a feeling of alienation in a disorderly world, than coaxing or the promise of happiness, the tools of empathy and order. And when she combines her harsh and defiant words about women with frequent prods and subtle jeers at men, she tends again to move toward an emergent protofeminist discourse in which women have rights and abilities not subsumed by marriage. She includes comments about careers for women, again not dwelling on governessing, but on writing, a new and risky possibility, as well as acting, the morally stigmatized choice she explored in *Amalie*. She continues prodding women to cultivate not the serenity and acquiescence that La Roche prefers, but rationality and often autonomy. Ehrmann consistently privileges blunt language and associates it with being German, not part of the high aristocracy and not Frenchified. She did not identify a separate diction for women. The editor of the journal presents herself as an outspoken woman who shows other women their foibles and, instead of concentrating on tedious virtues, constantly reveals the shocking consequences of error and folly.

Nor did she insist that one group of people, women, should preserve a happy demeanor or emphasize the possible good side of every issue. Quite the contrary. Ehrmann's texts are likely to identify unhappy, uncomfortable moments and feelings, and often, to leave them unresolved. The very form of the journal allows for constant disjunctions between one item and the next; since these disjunctions often accompany highly emotional texts, here, too, the label *Empfindsamkeit* of alienation can be applied. One of the pieces in *Amaliens Erholungsstunden*, "Die schlaflose Nacht, oder Glossen über Welt, Menschen, und Tod!" "The Sleepless Night, or Glosses on the World, Human Beings, and Death!"[67] is a characteristic hybrid form; it might be called a meditative, almost plotless story, or an essay with a first person narrator, or more adequately (and vaguely) a sketch. It describes the dark and morbid vision of life that evidently helps Ehrmann separate herself emotionally from a defense of the status quo and thus, assists her in developing a critical perspective on women's status in society. The piece begins with stormy weather and a series of analogies with people in extreme situations: "What a terrible, dreadful, sleepless night this is again! The winds howl like the despairing evildoer whose piece of villainy did not succeed. The rain trickles onto the stones as quickly as the tears of the unfortunate in the unharkened midnight hour. The thunder claps as horribly loud as the storm in the soul of the inconsolable!" (1792, 1:144). Along with the bombastic heaping of analogies are the setting, mood, and ideas of the *Empfindsamkeit* of alienation, which in turn suggests themes and modes of the Romantic period to come. The tumult heightens the narrator's perceptions, and she is able to transcend time:

> This stormy, raving weather, this solemn darkness, this deathly silence alternating with the storm of infuriated nature, tune my roused feelings to a higher level of comprehension for past, present, and future! Perhaps some people will misjudge my present mood, which is unintelligible to them. I willingly admit it. How would it be possible for people with less irritable nerves to understand the feeling of one who is, perhaps to his own misfortune, more delicately modulated? They are healthy in body and soul, they skip with fluttering carelessness over the black behavior of people without feeling it deeply enough. (1792, 1:144–5)

There is plenty of emphasis here on feelings, but a kind of feeling quite different from the optimistic *Empfindsamkeit* of sympathy that Philippine Engelhard and Sophie La Roche demonstrated. Ehrmann values darkness ("dieses feierliche Dunkel" "this solemn darkness") and despair and writes stories suggesting it is preferable to be sensitive but unhappy rather than wholesome but unaware. The slighting of happiness in favor of "higher comprehension" contrasts starkly with the happiness doctrines of many women writers of the late eighteenth century and with the combination of *Aufklärung* and *Empfindsamkeit* these writers represent.

In the piece about the sleepless night, even more than in similar earlier passages in *Amalie*, ordinary healthy people seem superficial and uninteresting, their lives of physical contentment base: "They are not misunderstood, because they do not want to be understood. They fear no slander, because they have enough effrontery to defend themselves with counterattacks. . . . Their lot is as dull as their feeling. They are happy in their narrow circle of influence—if one can call such a sensual spiritless life happy" (1792, 1:145). Ehrmann privileges the life of the mind and the imagination at the expense of appreciating both corporeality and life itself.

The sketch presents a bleak view of human behavior and human nature in this night vision that healthy people, it argues, do not share:

> They do not know that there are faithless friends who brush one off at the exact moment when one needs them the most. They do not know that self-interest makes people sly, wicked, hardhearted, because they believe it has to be this way, and they give tit for tat. They do not notice that usually brother tries to take advantage of brother, friend of friend, and beggar of his benefactor. (1792, 1:145–6)

No one is exempt from viciousness, but, Ehrmann hints, it does not have to be this way. What the essay uses here, and then develops further, is the topos of the world upside down. It is elaborated in a series of images and variations. "Jeering scoundrels, hardhearted stony souls, thankless creatures, spoiled boys and girls, unite their efforts in order to persecute, worry, drive out, oppress, and rob the better people, whom they envy" (1792, 1:147). The descriptions are hallucinations that only the narrator and other ultrasensitive people can see, grim visions of an unforgiving world, a world without justice:

> Here one of the happiest of marriages is torn apart by scandal mongers; there to the jubilation of hell a disharmonious one is made. Here a family is undeservedly hungry; there someone else is gorging himself full on what was stolen from them. Here an honest man dries the bloody tears from his pale cheek; there a good-for-nothing is sweating voluptuous sweat beads of wantonness. Here a poor widow cries for lack of bread; there a harlot at the cost of a nobler woman devours huge sums in riotous living! (1792, 1:147)

It is a chaotic scene crowded with images, some of them perhaps suggested by the social criticism propagated in the French Revolution; the text speaks of sympathy for the downtrodden, again different from La Roche's confidence that each social class was properly occupying its god-given place. To the narrator, such a view is a screen behind which churns immorality.

But death, as the sketch's title promises, is also an important motif here. Death represents a release: "O dear state in and after death; how much I, with all the delicate feeling ones, long for you!" (1792, 1:152). Eighteenth-century women were frequently expressing a desire for early death; their writing on the topic continues even when men let the tradition lapse. Meta Moller mentions the idea several times in her letters to Klopstock, commenting once, for example, in 1751, that an early death is her "constant wish."[68] Charlotte Seidel, writing in the mid-1770s, also appropriates the topos of longing for death in many lines such as these: "O eilt zu träge Tage! / Bringt mich ins Thal des Todes, / Des Todes?—Nein der Freude!" "Oh hasten, too languid days! / Bring me into the valley of death, / Of Death?—No, of joy!"[69] Because Seidel frames her desire in terms of Christian otherworldliness, often using Biblical language to emphasize the connection, I consider her a representative of the religious *Empfindsamkeit*. By the end of the eighteenth century, Marianne Ehrmann's use of the death wish is secularized, omitting Christian language and imagery, and thus, more alienated.

As the vision in Ehrmann's short and moody essay concludes, the weather also clears, and the narrator becomes aware of a hearse beneath her window. She is drawn to it and her body takes over involuntarily: "Already my hand braces itself firmly on the four cold irons that serve the coffin as a more comfortable resting place. Already the smell of death, which was drawn into the black cloths, wafts toward me, and I do not shudder. Already I hear the man dressed in black with the ice face and his equally unfeeling horses clanking along, and I am not horrified."[70] She incorporates all the senses in her vivid descriptions, with the whole essay written in high pitched rhetoric. At the end, she falls back asleep, but the division between nightmare and waking has been dissolved throughout the piece. This is certainly not the usual stuff of women's periodicals at the time. It may derive its mood partly from the Gothic novels that were then becoming popular, particularly among women readers, constrained as women were in most respects from expressing either revulsion or desire. In Ehrmann's writing, sensitivity to the macabre, awareness of the loathsome, employment of altered physical and mental states as sources of inspiration are found several times and are not limited to a particular form of fiction. But what is effective in making this passage uncanny is that the speaker is attracted by what should ordinarily be repellent.

There are other bizarre visions in *Amaliens Erholungsstunden*. At the beginning of the journal's second year, Ehrmann explains that two issues appeared late because severe illness had interrupted her work.[71] (Whether this illness in 1791 is connected with her terminal illness in 1795 is not known.) The next issue contains a description of the physical and psychic stages of being sick, "Empfindung in und nach einer schweren Krankheit" "Feelings in and after a Bad Illness" (1791, 1:128–34), and, a few pages later, there follows a grotesque tale, "Das Ei" "The Egg," a story of the sort she did especially well (1791, 1:139–47). The story describes two women taking a walk together in a familiar woods, but on a foggy day that keeps the usual fashionable set at home. In the midst of the darkening forest they unexpectedly discover a beautiful palace, to which the friends are drawn with as much expectation and curiosity as Eve to the apple. The doors open of their own accord, and servants signal the two women to enter. They pass silently through a series of magnificent rooms bustling with male and female servants. Almost blinded by the gold, silver, and mirrors, the friends, clinging to the arms of the serving maids, finally arrive in the most splendid room of all where sits an elaborately dressed and coifed woman, the owner of the palace. They watch as she sighs fashionably, coughs fashionably, even cleans her nose according to fashion. And then they notice that the silken cushion on which she is sitting resembles a nest. "What a discovery! we thought, when she suddenly jumps up, threw herself with a sigh onto the sofa, and we saw in the nest a large egg" (1791, 1:142). At this point, Ehrmann moves into the terrain of the grotesque in which, among other possible combinations, the human is adjoined abruptly to the animal: a woman broods an egg. The horrible egg hatches, producing a being that is also grotesque, a double creature both male and female joined at the back and fully dressed in a constantly shifting array of the latest fashions, with which both parts, the male and female, are equally obsessed, but which are rigorously differentiated by gender. When the narrator's friend's revulsion at this vain self-absorption becomes noticeable, the two women are attacked. Suddenly, the first person narrator realizes she has been dreaming. In the poetry of Philippine Engelhard-Gatterer, dreams were used therapeutically to enable women to express desires excluded from their conscious lives, but otherwise appropriate and wholesome. Ehrmann grants dreams a power of disruption far different from Engelhard's. Thus, despite the story's allegorical elements as an attack on fashion, "The Egg" is a very effective recreation of a nightmare experience, somewhat like Romantic fairy tales that would be written six to ten years later. In stories such as this, Marianne Ehrmann seems refreshingly unworried about the dangers of stimulating the fantasy of her female readers, which most moralists warned against;[72] indeed, she herself condemns readings that might rouse too much fantasy and unfulfillable hopes for one class of readers: servant girls.[73]

Nevertheless, as Helga Madland notes, she also uses nightmarishly "horrifying example[s] as a didactic tool,"[74] writing, for instance, in one of her numerous admonitory tales about fallen women and unwed mothers: "Here—hoo, hoo, I shudder!—here a ghost glides softly forth from the corner!—it is the murdered husband, who stretches out his hand to his children and casts a vengeful, fire-spitting glance on the coffin, as if even today he wanted to summon the adulteress to the court of judgment!"[75] The texts exult in the chaotic and creative. They assert the superiority of irritable nerves over wholesomeness, and endorse the insights to be gained from sickness and dreams. Even a period so alien to the Enlightenment as the Middle Ages is promoted at one point by the publication of poems by the Minnesänger in side-by-side Middle-High, and modern German versions.

Yet, along with strange and disturbing stories and sketches, and inserted medieval and pre-Enlightenment texts, are other contributions by Ehrmann that are perfectly consonant with Enlightenment goals and style. They stress reason, combat superstition, and take place in the plain light of day. Illustrating the abrupt mixture of discourses, the disturbing sketch of the sleepless night is followed immediately by an excellent dialogue that meets all the criteria of the Age of Reason. "Eine Szene aus der wirklichen Welt" "A scene from real life," which constructs, as its title suggests, a version of everyday life in the educated middle class, concerns an effort to reform two ignorant women, one a spoiled and selfish adolescent and the other her weak mother.[76] Using a favorite Enlightenment target, this piece, too, like "The Egg," ridicules extravagant addiction to fashion, applied here to the question of hairstyle. In good dramatic form, the dialogue relies on the speakers to reveal the situation. It begins:

> Mother. (*To her daughter sitting at the dressing table*) Lorchen, do see to it that you drink your coffee for once; it's getting cold.
> Lorchen. I don't care, my hairdo is more important.
> M. You bad child, you! Am I supposed to have breakfast alone again?
> L. As you like, just keep my coffee warm for me.
> M. Aye, you surely don't expect me to take it into the kitchen?
> L. Then leave it till the maid comes. I simply can't get up now and that's that!
> M. (*To herself*) What am I supposed to do? The more reasonable one always has to give in first. (*Carries the coffee away.*)
> L. (*To herself*) Aye, Madame Mama can very well take care of things like that.
> M. (*Comes back*) What were you saying as I went out?
> L. That you are a very good mother.
> M. If you would just really grasp this truth for once, then . . .
> L. (*Interrupting*) For heaven's sake, Mother, not another sermon already! (*Angrily rips out the half-finished hairdo.*) Now look how you have mixed me all up again with your eternal moralizing! That's how a cuckoo probably gets its hair done. It is so awful that my obstinate father wants to save the few guilders that it costs for a hairdresser for me! In all eternity I can never get my hair style right if you are always preaching in my ears. I think I'm going crazy because of this dumb hairdo if it doesn't work right today either. (*Throws all the hairdressing equipment on the floor*) Take the stuff; I'm sure to get a bilious fever from sheer irritation!
>
> (1792, 1:155–7)

The mother has already given in once on the coffee warming; now she will give in again. Striking here is the daughter's vigorous reaction against her mother's moralizing, another item unthinkable in most earlier stories for women, such as those of Sophie La Roche. But La Roche concentrates on model girls, while Ehrmann's characters are often negative, in this case including both mother and daughter.

As the piece continues, the mother, faced with emotional blackmail from her daughter and thinking her husband is absent, sends the maid for the hairdresser. The girl's father enters, instead, and announces he will be the hairdresser as soon as Lorchen takes down her hair. "Down with this dreadful bird's nest!" he orders (1792, 1:161). As usual, Ehrmann's language is vigorous. When the wife protests, the husband reproves her bluntly and appropriates all authority to himself: "Woman, don't get mixed up with my affairs; what I do has to suit you and her. Without delay, girl, sit yourself down; I am going to give you a hairdo that will satisfy you. (*In a firm tone*) Well, are you going to act quickly or not?" Whereupon he cuts his daughter's hair. Speaking to his wife, he gives an explanation for this deed that would have been officially persuasive to adherents of the Enlightenment: "I want to lead you and your spoiled daughter on the path of sound reason! Her hair looks good this way, she saves powder, pomade, hairdresser fees, and is finished with the whole business in three minutes" (1792, 1:162). Yet, the father's arrogance in preempting his daughter's choice does not go unchallenged in what follows.

Indeed, one of the elements that distinguishes this sketch from others of the time is that the scene does not end here: the mother and daughter do not bow gratefully to male reason, and they do not express contrition. Instead, the daughter is dismissed and the argument continues, the husband telling his wife she must cease allowing her daughter to take advantage of her. Ehrmann uses the man as a mouthpiece for what would have been considered enlightened ideas, but she does not grant him or his ideas a definitive victory. Far from it. The sketch concludes with the following pungent exchange:

> F[ather]. . . . now you know my opinion and that's that!—
> M. As you wish, gruesome despot! (*Leaves crying*)
> F. Where the devil did my wife pick up that language! She is usually not so well read?—Ever since the French threw off their yoke, it's no good anymore being prince or husband; the good ones get this bitter name thrown at them just as much as the bad!—
> (1792, 1:164–5)

So the dialogue ends not with a smooth resolution of conflict, but with dissatisfaction on all sides. Although neither mother nor daughter is reaching a solution on her own, the father speaks and acts in an arrogant, highhanded manner that prompts a sudden aperçu from the mother: a parallel between her powerful and domineering husband and an insufferable tyrant. She briefly connects oppression on the level of the family with oppression on the level of the state and—given Ehrmann's other invocations of male/female disputes—between women and men. These are not routine scenes in the eighteenth century, and the unresolved emotional outcome is unexpected. Furthermore, it is the mother's emotional state, crying, not a calm and dispassionate analysis of the situation, which has led to her insight. Strong feelings and often pessimistic alienation are depicted as a productive combination in Ehrmann's versions of both *Empfindsamkeit* and *Aufklärung*.

In some cases, the alienation is represented by means of the linguistic daring that distinguishes Ehrmann's writing. Like her British contemporary, Maria Edgeworth, who wrote a short novel with a first person narrator who is a servant speaking a broad regional dialect,[77] Ehrmann wrote dramatic pieces in dialect and one in imitation of the broken German of a foreigner. "Der Marmottenjunge" "The Marmot Boy,"[78] depicts a street performer, evidently Italian, spinning a tale that is interspersed with snatches of song. He tries to persuade a watching woman to toss down food and money for himself and his animal, saying the two of them are as feeble as a fly in winter. Again, Ehrmann discovers a topic not usually dealt with in literature at the time, and she breathes life into her hungry beggar boy by having him mix Italian words into his uninflected German.[79]

Both *Amaliens Erholungsstunden* and *Die Einsiedlerinn aus den Alpen* evince intense interest in the world of women, especially their contemporary world. Along with "true stories," for example, of wetnurses who by their negligence cause the death of children entrusted to their care, there are items resembling news accounts of distinguished individual women. In *Amaliens Erholungsstunden*, for example, under the title "Noch ein edles Weib," is a brief report on one of the women active in the French Revolution, commending her for presenting to the national assembly in Paris a work she had written about the best means of perfecting female education.[80] *Die Einsiedlerinn aus den Alpen* includes writings by other respected women writers, such as the then increasingly admired Friederike Brun, who wrote, appropriately for the Swiss-born Ehrmann, about Switzerland, Mme de Stael (1766–1817), represented by her story "Zulma," and the black American slave poet Phillis Wheatley (1753–84).[81] A poem by Wheatley is presented in English along with a translation into German and a short biographical introduction. Ehrmann extends her interest in gender across the boundaries of race, although without acknowledging the racial issues raised by the presence, for example, of black African women in late eighteenth-century Germany.

One of the features sometimes appearing in other magazines for women, including *Pomona*, but not employed in Ehrmann's journal, is a section of letters from readers requesting personal advice. In fact, Ehrmann avoids the directly personal most of the time. She wrote little that was explicitly about herself, although this changes slightly in *Die Einsiedlerinn*, where she publishes letters written on a journey from Stuttgart to Zürich and a moving account of the baby boy she adopted. Besides her own work, contributions, especially to *Amaliens Erholungsstunden*, came from her husband. T. F. Ehrmann wrote about geography, anthropology, women's education, and current events. Otherwise, the prominent male contributors were chiefly poets, including Herder, Schiller, and, more frequently, the blind poet Gottlieb Konrad Pfeffel (1736–1809), who contributed verse fables to many magazines for women. It is especially impressive that in *Einsiedlerinn*, Marianne Ehrmann publishes several poems by the young, unknown Friedrich Hölderlin (1770–1843). Neither of the Ehrmanns wrote poetry. Many issues of *Amaliens Erholungsstunden* carry book announcements and reviews, including a publisher's announcement for Sophie La Roche's edition of Friderika Baldinger's autobiography, and a favorable review of an anonymous novel, *Alf von Dülmen*.[82] Many years later, it was revealed that the author of this and a large collection of other novels, mostly historical romances, was a well-educated woman from Leipzig, Benedikte Naubert.

Altogether, Marianne Ehrmann's journalism was an enormous achievement. Edith Krull characterizes it well:

> She must . . . have possessed astonishing capacity for work, for the largest part of the approximately hundred-page-long issues always was from her pen, and these are works of the greatest variety: observations, aphorisms, novels, travel reports, anecdotes, character descriptions, all of them naturally one-sided and challenging in respect to the publicity intentions of the author but also captivating because of her incredible temperament.[83]

Furthermore, partly because of her judicious use of outside contributors, Ehrmann was able to sustain her journals longer than most other women editors of her time.

Protofeminist Overtures: Ehrmann, Berlepsch, and Others

Much of Ehrmann's criticism of ignorant behavior and ridiculous fashions and taste was directed against her own sex, but in her periodicals, the criticism is almost always an introduction to a passage on improving women. The protofeminism that Ehrmann espoused in *Amaliens Erholungsstunden* entailed naming and deploring female oppression and believing women were better than their reputation indicated. As Karen Offen has written:

> feminism raises issues that concern personal autonomy or freedom—with constant reference to basic issues of societal organization, which center, in Western societies, on the long-standing debate over the family and its relationship to the state, and on the historically inequitable distribution of political, social, and economic power between the sexes that underlies this debate.[84]

Eighteenth-century protofeminism rarely explicitly argued that men and women, equal as persons, should have equal rights—Emilie von Berlepsch had only tentatively suggested women's access to human rights. The eighteenth-century protofeminism to which Marianne Ehrmann adhered, similar to that of other German journal contributors of the early 1790s, objected to oppression but not to subordination.

Despite the limitations of her ideas, it is important to acknowledge the audacity of Ehrmann's writing: she was willing to assert publicly what other women wrote privately. Dorothea Schlözer, for example, had commented in 1785 to a friend: "Women are not in the world just to amuse men. Women are human beings like men: each should make the other happy. . . . Now, does a woman make a man happy just by being his cook, seamstress, and spinner? Well then I would rather rent myself out as cook, seamstress, and spinner, and that way I could escape from that devil, if a devil is what [my employer/husband] turned out to be."[85] And Rahel Levin (later von Varnhagen) earned praise for her feminist insights by writing in private letters in 1793 about such topics as the impossibility that women could find fulfillment vicariously through their husbands.[86] But by then, Ehrmann had already boldly raised her concerns about women's status in print.

From the beginning of her independent journalism, Marianne Ehrmann saw women of the educated middle class and aristocracy as rendered helpless and infantile by their conditioning and lack of education—she spoke for example of "das ewig gegängelte Geschlecht" "the sex that is eternally on leading strings"[87]—but she did not theorize about the general symptoms of women's condition. Instead, she described particular types of objectionable women: the coquette, the pious woman, the woman of leisure—all noted, for example, in the handkerchief's story. She did not dwell long on the reasons why women had not escaped from the condition of oppression, though she suspected that, to a considerable extent, men were content with women's deplorable situation. Sometimes she suggested that men found female inferiority convenient because it made cajoling sexual favors easier: "Oh yes! You men are the most responsible for this. You have to first stop praising *lead* and *iron* to women's faces as if they were *gold* so that by this lie you can wheedle sensual advantages. That is the crux of the matter!"[88] Other times, she thought that having a boring and ignorant wife made it easier for men to justify spending their time away from home: "They are satisfied if they can yawn over the dull conversation of their wives, in order to be able with more right to run out of the house in search of pastimes" (1791, 2:240). Ehrmann recognized the interest men had in preventing women from improving themselves since they derived advantages even from women's faults. At another point, in an extended exchange of letters between herself and an anonymous male critic of her journal, Ehrmann wrote tartly: "Speaking frankly, everything that comes from you lords of creation is suspicious to me!" (1791, 2:266). Ehrmann was looking seriously for other forms of discourse besides those that women received from the powerful and privileged male "lords of creation." The estrangement from conventional gender relations that this sarcasm indicates is another mark placing Ehrmann in the *Empfindsamkeit* of alienation.

When her male critics declared themselves unwilling to accept responsibility for female inferiority, Ehrmann firmly asserted that they were accountable for it nonetheless: "Also you ask me . . . since when men had taken over the duty of educating us? Naturally since the moment, when they took it upon themselves to care for the entire moral wellbeing of the state, whose members we are also. . . ."[89] Ehrmann gave some of the blame to older women, too, especially for preventing the younger ones from escaping the traditional degradation. Mothers come in for particularly sharp criticism for not wanting their daughters to know more than they did. Yet, Ehrmann thought that women wanted to improve themselves and that they were capable of doing so: "I now know my sex better; they do not lack the good intention to become all that they could and should be but only the opportunity."⁹⁰ By implication, Ehrmann attributes to women ability as well as desire to change.

The purpose of Ehrmann's monthly journal, and much of the rest of her writing as well, was to help and encourage women in a program of self-improvement. The goals of this program are clear: "We want despite the prejudice to brighten up our heads, to clean our souls of sludge and to learn to fulfill our duties through good books and reasonable society!"⁹¹ The reform projects that Ehrmann stressed most throughout both her journals were the two Enlightenment tasks of teaching women to use their reason and giving them an education. These, she asserted, were the best ways to improve her readers' characters, help them perform their duties, and enhance society. And the means that she advocated was for women to take over their own education: ". . . I think I am not mistaken when I assert that it would be good if women's education were also left to women."⁹² The tentative formulation shows that she expected resistance in this matter, and she did not in fact repeat the claim that women should be in charge as emphatically as some of her other ideas, but it was still an underlying message, one that she shared with Sophie La Roche. Like *Pomona*, Ehrmann's journals, too, are in their own way a case in point of a woman instructing other women. Of the readers who considered Ehrmann's main goal to be educating and improving women, one wrote a letter to her praising her intent but predicting her failure on the grounds that women as a group would never be able to meet her expectations. Ehrmann's responses to this and two succeeding letters from the same correspondent (1792, 1:57–66, 117–38) contain much of her strongest protofeminist argumentation. Yet, one letter is followed immediately by a long essay (by another contributor) disqualifying women from public service, and the others occur along side Ehrmann's own multipart treatise extolling housework and the fulfillment of traditional duties.

At other points, however, Ehrmann herself supported women's interest in public affairs, a controversial move since it challenged the public/private dichotomy that was a major patriarchal technology for controlling women. In her brief description of the French Revolutionary woman, Madame Morat, Ehrmann had noted: "It is a joy to see in our times that women also try to offer their intellectual powers to the general good" (1790, 2:73). Later, she was incensed to hear that women in Strassburg had been intimidated for trying to start a patriotic society:

> How can this oppressed sex bring forth good mothers before they can be good citizens? . . . Is this tyrannized sex supposed to remain eternally

excluded from the enjoyment of freedom and be respected by the male sex only when they, the women, want to beg love from the men? Or does it perhaps flatter male pride to be able to command the feelings of helpless slaves???[93]

Ehrmann could pen fierce invective when she chose. Like Mary Wollstonecraft, she uses motherhood, which was increasingly valorized in the dominant late eighteenth-century discourse on middle-class women, as a justification for political claims.

Her zealous words about women were different from what had preceded her. She articulated the humiliating inferiority to which women were consigned, something that Friderika Baldinger accepted as natural, and Sophie La Roche and Philippine Engelhard-Gatterer protested but hardly explored. When Ehrmann saw women's low status and objected strenuously, proposing better education as the remedy, her thinking was different from that of Gottsched at the beginning of the century; alert as she was to women's practical needs, Ehrmann did not advocate so abstract an education as he did, and to justify her proposals, she used the demands made of women by the dominant discourse, claiming that the learning she advocated would help a woman to perform her duties and improve her mind and character. Similarly, she made no general arguments for admitting women to new careers, aiming, instead, to find ways for women to survive in the status quo.

Perhaps it was Ehrmann's limited education (both formal and informal) combined with the immediacy of the needs she was addressing, that inclined her away from a theoretical analysis of the discrimination that she observed; Emilie von Berlepsch, somewhat like Mary Wollstonecraft, had benefited from her friendship with a well-trained and highly practiced male theoretician, Herder, when she wrote her protofeminist analysis of marriage and misogyny. Ehrmann, on the other hand, focusing on the practical, tended to accept at face value other arguments that claimed to be practical, too, such as one that the poor reputation of women writers was derived from cases when such women had sacrificed all their other responsibilities to their literary whim: "Various women turned writing into their main occupation and forgot thereby their far more necessary domestic business. That is how there arose . . . that general prejudice, which still affects the few women who, under favorable circumstances, try to combine the one activity with the other."[94] The dominant discourse again speaks through her, making her receptive to the criticism of women writers, so that she allowed the rare cases—and rare they must have been, given what is known about eighteenth-century women writers—to determine the rule and to justify a negative public opinion of her women colleagues.

Defensiveness is understandable given Ehrmann's isolation and the newness and uncertain status of the emergent discourse, as well as the edginess of a dominant discourse still formulating, as Hausen argues, its responses to changing circumstances. Since Ehrmann seems not to have known the writing of Theodor Gottlieb von Hippel, she had no male standard bearer to assist her.[95] Yet, very soon after she began writing her critiques in *Amaliens Erholungsstunden*, other protofeminist voices arose, too, some of them in the most unexpected places, in *Flora*, for example, the magazine that Cotta had founded when *Amaliens Erholungsstunden* had been dropped. The new editors had pledged not to publish anything that could offend the sensitive guardians of young women's virtue and morality, and had stuck to their promise with such an inoffensive collection of stories, poems, and anecdotes that even Schiller, who was far from progressive in his ideas about women,[96] complained they were underestimating women: "You seem to me . . . to have the opinion that writings which are going to succeed in the female world must simply be mere play, a slander I would not like to be guilty of," he wrote.[97] Nonetheless, in *Flora*, too, there was an occasional glimpse of the new thinking about women that Marianne Ehrmann represented. One instance occurred in 1793, in an essay about the strength and bravery of the beautiful sex. After using history to show that women are courageous, the author, who in anglophile style called herself Sophie Strongness, commented: "If we had made the laws, women would be on the thrones, women would fight at the head of armies, women would pass judgments, women would play every male role, and verily! things would go, if not better, then at least no worse on this little speck of earth. . . ."[98] The very way in which this is written shows men's exclusive hold on powerful positions in the government, the army, and the judiciary as contingent, not as a decree of God or a law of nature. By making patriarchy conditional on who holds the legislative power and by suggesting that women could exercise that power, too, the narrator denaturalizes patriarchy and challenges its unspeakability. The narrator further asserts that, given women's abilities, male readers should be silent in the future and not blame women for a weakness that men themselves had cleverly condemned them to acquire. The letter writer, who purported to be in Paris, signed off with an appropriately androgynous phrase, calling herself a "strong and courageous brother in female form."

Even more surprising, because more extensively argued, is a letter that appeared in *Flora* in 1794. One of the earlier issues that year had contained a satire against educated women, "Last Testament of the Husband of an Educated Woman," which condemned all scholarly women, but especially those who wrote. Letters by unhappy reader-husbands were a common misogynist genre.[99] The disgruntled speaker in *Flora* proposed sending women back to the spinning wheel away from the ink bottle, something the author hoped to accomplish in part by giving more respect to women's handwork: "Why do we value a pair of cuffs less than an ode, a shirt less than an idyll? Without this injustice we would perhaps be able to admire in Karsch an excellent netmaker and in Sophie Albrecht the best spindle virtuoso."[100] And he promised from this reform a great improvement in the households of men with educated wives: "If the *culture* of your women has produced *barbarian* conditions in your household, then from now on instead of lyrical confusion simple prosaic order will prevail there. In the future the right to blacken a female hand will be granted at most to the meat pot instead of the inkwell."[101] Women (meaning only, of course, those of the educated middle class and above) could and should have no role in what the speaker defined as culture.

A vehement reply, purporting to be from the wife, defending herself against these accusations and against misogyny in general, appeared soon after the "Last Testament." The respondent blamed her husband's outburst on his jealousy that she had become a more successful and better received writer than he. Quickly, she proceeded from that to assertions about women, not a defense of herself in particular, not the claim that she was an exception, but a mustering of arguments, drawn mostly from earlier writers, that women were equal to men. This, too, was a well established technique for the defense of women. The speaker cited the brilliant Anna Maria van Schurman and Sibylle Schwarz, and pointed out that Plato and others vouched for female talents. She also quoted male misogynists, like Jean Chapelain (1595–1674), who thought women had only half as much reason as men, Jean-Louis Guez de Balzac (1597?–1654), who claimed he preferred a woman with a beard to one with learning, and Euripides, who, she said, declared he would not let a woman cross his hearth if she knew more than she should. In response to them, she summoned the spirits of great women of the past, both historical and mythological, including Sappho, Agnodicea, and Hypatia, as well as more modern women, too:

> And all you uncounted women writers among the English, French, and Germans! Come up from the realm of shadows! Come up to torment

the insolent scoffer who condemns you to the spindle and needle! Appear to him in the form of the Furies; press and pinch the offender in poetic explosions of your revenge! Drive him into the corner with syllogisms until the sweat of fear drips from his brow![102]

It is a passionate evocation of her predecessors and contemporaries, with the quill contesting the needle.

This anonymous writer in the persona of a married woman author traced misogyny back to men's fear that if they did not keep women inferior, they would not be able to retain their positions of superiority. The writer looked at the campaign of intimidation that men used to keep women down. And she (if it was a she, which cannot be known definitely) also produced an impressive list showing that women in the past had, indeed, won respect and fame for their handwork.

Most of all, she had a high vision of what women were capable of in the future:

Yes, friends! we may claim for men and for ourselves what Father *Klopstock* claimed to the people who were overfond of foreign culture
    They have high Genius!
        We have Genius, like them!
        That makes us their equals!
    They penetrate science
        Into its deepest marrow!
        We??——
Ha, we *would* have done it long since, if we also attended your *secondary schools* and *universities*, you gentlemen with your *doctors* and *masters degrees*!—(her emphasis)[103]

The speaker's enthusiasm for women's ability and her sarcasm about men make this short essay one of the most interesting pieces in the many volumes of *Flora*.[104]

The chances are good that Marianne Ehrmann knew these issues of *Flora*, but that journal's sporadic support for positions she espoused came very late for her, so often embattled alone. In part, her isolation may explain the fact that, despite the urgency and firmness of her advocacy of improvements for women, there were distinct limitations to her demands for reforms. In the midst of her plea for women's right to patriotic feelings, she had acknowledged once again the traditional limits: "For once let the female sex be given the freedom to think, to act, and to delight in patriotic virtues, and give it a warning only if we forget the main female duties because of this or if we hastily unwind ourselves from all femininity and want to play male roles everywhere."[105] For all her denunciation of women's condition, Ehrmann still endorsed women's assignments to be good mothers, dutiful housekeepers, faithful wives, and charming companions. Her ability to practice and articulate a new form of discourse for women was constrained by the protofeminist framework in which she operated with its acceptance of limitations of the ways in which individuals could position themselves as women.

The resulting restrictions on learning and reading are familiar. Thus, although Ehrmann constantly advocated thinking, she denounced scholarliness for women.

> What would become of us women in the end if we wanted to occupy ourselves with complete scholarly knowledge, in order, contrary to our destiny, to get in the way of men? A woman who does not wish to deny her femininity should be merely a thinker and not an educated scholar. . . .[106]

Women as "thinkers" rather than "scholars" did not dispute women's place; they did not make the kinds of demands for serious scholarship that could threaten the male monopoly of learning. On a more broadly applicable level, since most girls and women would not have aspired to be scholars any more than most boys and men did, Ehrmann tried to limit what and when a woman might read:

> In general . . . a girl should only *read* when she has fulfilled all her other duties and read such things and so much as is appropriate to her class. She must know what kind of husband she will later be able to expect and adjust her education according to the situation in which he lives, in order later to attain that sweet harmony in her marriage that can make her and him happy.[107]

This is hardly a revolutionary guideline—Friderika Baldinger's mother had tried to employ it four decades earlier, in the 1750s—and one might question whether it was at all usable, since a woman might well miscalculate who her future husband would be. Furthermore, Ehrmann exempted three groups of women: ladies from the higher classes, governesses, and writers, which is to say, herself. Ehrmann wavered as to whether a talented woman was a special exception or a signal of female potential. Nor does she recognize the unpredictability—well shown in her own *Amalie*—of when a woman will need to be self-supporting, and thus, perhaps depend on her education. Ehrmann acknowledged that women undertaking certain forms of paid work, governessing and writing in particular, needed learning, but she continued to see such female employment as anomalous. It was Theodor Gottlieb von Hippel (1741–96) who saw women's options for work in a broader context.

Hippel's book, *Ueber die bürgerliche Verbesserung der Weiber* "On Improving the Status of Women," was unquestionably the most thorough protofeminist manifesto written at the time by a German.[108] Published in 1792, it contains not only a detailed attempt to explain the origin of female oppression, but a varied program for combating it. Part of what Hippel promoted was allowing women to choose their own occupations, not excluding them from any profession except perhaps the military. He justified his proposal in terms of giving women the same right to choose their own activities as men enjoyed; he did not discuss women's economic dependence or propose that this widespread and routine dependence was a major factor in the whole of women's subordination. But Hippel's arguments, too, framed in a playful and satirical manner, contain so many elements of the dominant discourse that nineteenth and twentieth-century interpreters long debated whether Hippel's intentions were parodic or programmatic; regardless of that question, his book was clearly readable as advocating new ideas about women.

The record thus shows a series of German writers in the late eighteenth century beginning to explore feminist ideas, but in texts always also pervaded by the dominant discourse: Emilie von Berlepsch (a divorced mother), Marianne Ehrmann (a childless wife living in economically marginal circumstances), and Theodore Gottlieb von Hippel (an unmarried man), and a number of journal contributors whose names and circumstances are unknown. The different material and social conditions of the three prominent protofeminists seem to have affected their writings—Hippel, protected both as a man and as an anonymous writer, was able to state many things that Ehrmann especially, as a woman writing under her own name, could do only with far greater difficulty, and Berlepsch and Ehrmann had both had experiences unacceptable in their social classes (divorce, self-support) that diminished their stakes in the status quo and increased their receptivity to possibilities generally not admitted in the literary, intellectual, and practical life of their time—but all three, probably independently of each other, were certainly influenced by ideas from the early years of the French Revolution.[109]

Events in France and writings about the events were also crucial in England in producing the conditions under which Mary Wollstonecraft composed the best known feminist document of the eighteenth century. The impact of *A Vindication of the Rights of Woman* on her German contemporaries is difficult to trace. Whether Hippel was aware of Wollstonecraft's classic feminist text is uncertain.[110] Since it appeared in English in 1792, and in German in 1793, Marianne Ehrmann might have seen it before she died in 1795, two years before Wollstonecraft, but it did not noticeably affect Ehrmann's writing. As for the aristocrat Emilie von Berlepsch, she read Wollstonecraft, and later described her response. Her detailed (though retrospective) account stresses the tumultuous and (to her) threatening context in which she read the English book:

> When in the first, most violent years of the Revolution the *Vindication of the Rights of Woman* fell into my hands, the title of the book, which made me expect a sequel and echo of the work of Paine, created a repugnant impression. But how I found myself deceived in my presumption! How my soul flew to the sister soul, which revealed itself to me in the thought and spirit, in the whole direction of the book! What power, what self-reliance! What a pure, definite, nowhere exaggerated concept of female dignity and destiny! What a deep insight into the sources of social ruin![111]

Wollstonecraft impressed Berlepsch because she embodied the prime characteristics Berlepsch had said in her essay of 1791 that women needed, independence and self-reliance. And Berlepsch recognized that Wollstonecraft, too, intended the improvements in women to help them better fulfill their traditional roles. In short, it was the very entanglement of Wollstonecraft's notions in the prevailing system of gender roles and characteristics that made her acceptable to a cautious German protofeminist such as Berlepsch.

Nevertheless, as was inevitable for a woman as thoroughly tied to the German intellectual establishment of her time as Berlepsch was, she hastened also to identify a list of Wollstonecraft's shortcomings:

> The deficiencies did not escape me. Something raw and desultory, I might even say boastful, which could not be pleasing to a pupil of Herder, Wieland and Garve, the harsh attacks on meritorious writers who consider their topic in a different light, and especially the overly strong, often tastelessly expressed, one-sided contempt for the impressions made by external beauty and grace, for the tender relationship which because of the strength of the one sex and the weakness of the other, according to the eternal laws of nature, must exist between the two.[112]

Rousseau's notions of masculine and feminine continue here unchecked. Berlepsch explained her reservations about Wollstonecraft in terms of her loyalty to a group of writers who prized refinement in literature and her unwillingness to accept Wollstonecraft's rejection of grace and beauty, even though Berlepsch herself had defended women who deviated from that ideal; Marianne Ehrmann, whose aesthetics had far more room for unpolished colloquial language and for jarring, ungraceful ideas, might well have reacted differently to Wollstonecraft's writings if she knew them. In Berlepsch's case, however, despite her criticism, it is her fundamental public approval of Mary Wollstonecraft that is especially important, particularly in contrast to what women at the time were writing in England, where "repudiation of Mary Wollstonecraft became . . . a way of establishing the respectability of the writer's views and forestalling or propitiating male criticism."[113]

Emilie von Berlepsch called *Vindication of the Rights of Woman* "an inexhaustible source of truth and ennoblement for us." And even the contradictory quality of the woman Berlepsch saw as instructive: "Blameless mediocrity can be a friendly sight for us; but the contemplation of a great, independent character, of the internal and external dangers that accompany such a character, and of the sufferings which that person cannot escape . . .—this is what makes our progress toward the goal of free refinement more beautiful, firmer, and more secure."[114] Berlepsch was able to use ideas of Romanticism about greatness to narrate the Englishwoman's stature. It is with praise of Mary Wollstonecraft that Emilie von Berlepsch concluded both the narrative of her intellectual encounter with Wollstonecraft and the travel book in which the narrative appears.

Feminist ideas tended to undo the conventional forms and arguments of Berlepsch's work, as they had Mary Wollstonecraft's, too. Thus, *Caledonia* (1802–4), about Berlepsch's journey through Scotland, does not conclude with words about the country she was visiting, and an earlier work containing encouragement to women to be interested in politics, *Bemerkung zur richtigen Beurtheilung der erzwungenen Schweitzer-Revolution und Mallet du Pans Geschichte derselben* "Remarks on the Correct Judgment of the Forced Swiss Revolution and Mallet du Pan's History of It" (1799), did not conclude with comments on Switzerland or on Mallet du Pan, but, like *Caledonia*, with a passage for and about women. The essay on happiness in marriage had, likewise, been disrupted by the analysis of misogyny; the commonplace thoughts that make up the essay's entire second part are invalidated if the reader takes seriously the author's protofeminist arguments of the first part. In the writing of Marianne Ehrmann, protofeminist thinking is often equally disruptive, as in the dialogue on the hairdo when the wife's naming her husband a tyrant prevents the usual closure. Yet, it is precisely the emergent notions about women's status and women's potential and the formal impact of these notions on various women's writing that lend special interest to much of the work of authors such as Marianne Ehrmann today.

Ehrmann's accomplishments are several: innovative use of small forms, especially dialogues, essays, and short stories; bold and sometimes risqué language; capable work as a journalist who founded and edited first one creative periodical, *Amaliens Erholungsstunden*, and then, slightly less successfully, another; open professionalism at a time when this was unacceptable for women; unconventional exploration in a novel of the life of an actress and the experience of an acutely unhappy marriage; and, finally, conscious efforts to better women's lot, especially through thinking. Although Ehrmann was vehement in her opposition to female degradation, her theoretical insight into women's oppression was narrower than that of her contemporaries Hippel and Mary Wollstonecraft, and in some respects, not as bold as Emilie von Berlepsch. But mixed in with the social criticism that confirmed the proclaimed values of the status quo, Ehrmann dared to write discordant thoughts and to do so in her own name. She should be considered one of Germany's most important eighteenth-century advocates of changed conditions for women and one of the key representatives of the *Empfindsamkeit* of alienation. In her alienation, she has a distinguished sister with a very different take on the eighteenth-century world, Sophie Albrecht.

6
Examining Passion: Sophie Albrecht (1757–1840)

THE DICHOTOMIZED POSITION OF WOMEN AS VIRGIN OR WHORE IN LITerature by men has been a commonplace of feminist literary analysis, along with the consequent limitations on real women's participation in literary discourse. Writing of German literature, for example, Susanne Zantop notes, "While men created heroines who were either models of incorruptible angelic purity or demonic, obsessed despots (*Machtweiber*), women were developing strategies of dissimulation, hiding behind 'rituals of modesty,' suggesting that they were indeed harmless and 'virtuous,' not prone to any such misdemeanor or overt sexuality."[1] But it was also possible, as Sophie Albrecht demonstrates, to develop a maneuver of claiming virtue and simultaneously proclaiming sexuality. To write and publish poetry that made this double move was as radical a deed as were the more overtly contentious protofeminist gestures of Marianne Ehrmann and Emilie Berlepsch. Friderika Baldinger and Sophie La Roche shunned writing about passionate love. Philippine Engelhard-Gatterer expressed her conventional and disembodied notions of love mostly in the guise of dreams. Marianne Ehrmann, who saw sexuality as part of the human condition, considered it perilous, especially when it took even a rational woman or man by surprise. She obsessively sprinkled issues of her journal with warnings to women (and men) of the dangers of lost chastity. Her heroine in *Amalie, eine wahre Geschichte in Briefen* stressed her future husband's excellent moral qualities and mentioned no romantic or sensual love for him. Sophie Albrecht reverses the narrative of disembodied love, writing, rather, of love as a corporeal and spiritual experience combined. To do so, she decontextualizes the lovers, omitting any overt socioeconomic references, and deinstitutionalizes their relationship, avoiding the usual culmination in marriage. Her oeuvre begins with three extraordinary volumes containing two plays, two lengthy sections of fragmentary prose, a few idylls, and many pages of poetry in which Albrecht explores the language of desire and of death. The volumes are later followed by a small body of Gothic and religious tales composed at the turn of the century. Her published writing concludes with a very late work in yet another genre, a cookbook with an introduction in which Sophie Albrecht adopts the rhetoric of protest.

Where does this oeuvre fit in the schemes of literary history and criticism? In the last chapter, I argued that both the literature designated as *Sturm und Drang* and the discussion of that literature in literary history and criticism is so thoroughly masculinist that it seems misguided to claim space under the banner of *Sturm und Drang* for writings by women—especially since some of the candidate writings are distinctly protofeminist. I proposed, instead, to locate this literature within the movement where women writers have been welcomed, or perhaps relegated, the *Empfindsamkeit*. But since writers such as Marianne Ehrmann and Sophie Albrecht are strikingly different in style and tone from other women of the *Empfindsamkeit*, I also proposed a third strand of this movement, adding the *Empfindsamkeit* of alienation to the religious and sympathetic strands. Alienation, however, is itself an unfashionable concept in recent years, relying as it generally does on essentialist notions of the human that have allowed it to conflate descriptive accounts of human relations with normative ones. Can it be salvaged for the description of eighteenth-century German women's writing, and if so, what does such a reformulated alienation mean? Richard Schacht in *The Future of Alienation* offers suggestions for a nonessentialist notion of alienation, proposing to begin with two broad varieties, subjective alienations and objective alienations, each with its own multiple versions. Schacht sees all alienations as forms of discord, with subjective alienations being kinds of psychological dissatisfactions and objective alienations being social-structural dysfunctions. To avoid essentialism and the predetermined value judgments that have generally accompanied conceptions of alienation, Schacht notes, on the one hand, that discord is itself not necessarily bad, and on the other, that even when it is decided that the discord should be resolved, it is still unclear which party should change or, indeed, whether both should.[2]

Schacht's two basic forms of alienation are useful in elaborating two aspects of the situation of women writers. First, there are the writers, such as Marianne Ehrmann and Sophie Albrecht, who write about their subjective feelings of isolation and disaffection, thus fitting the description of subjective alienation. Second, there are also writers such as Baldinger, La Roche, and Engelhard-

Gatterer, who only intermittently claim feelings of dissatisfaction with society but whose actions, it can be shown, were socially dysfunctional in terms of eighteenth-century prescriptions for femininity (although the same actions were not dysfunctional in other eighteenth-century terms, such as, for example, those of middle-class German patriotism). In this chapter, the representations of subjective alienations by Sophie Albrecht will be pursued, with additional references to Marianne Ehrmann.

At first glance, Sophie Albrecht would appear to be an odd choice to represent subjective alienation since she writes lyrical love poetry describing satisfying union, not separation or distance. For considerable stretches, her writing contains only the faintest traces of alienated subjectivity. Yet, her notion of love, because it does not reconcile itself with marriage, is intertwined with a sense of social estrangement; also, because it can be disrupted by an unwilling or changeable lover, her commitment to love always carries with it the possibility of personal estrangement from the lover as well. A few of Albrecht's love poems contain no glancing references to either of these dangers, but many of the poems and most of her other kinds of texts dwell on the extreme subjective alienation of the loving protagonist, either from her society, from her lover, or both. And the solution the texts propose to the resulting psychological isolation is a radical one—death, especially suicide.

Because the ability to feel, in Albrecht's texts, usually meaning to feel passionate love, is so closely linked with vulnerability to alienation, I consider that the *Empfindsamkeit* of alienation is a useful name for Sophie Albrecht's writings, different though her version of subjective alienation is in many ways from the *Empfindsamkeit* I read in the works of Marianne Ehrmann. Ehrmann's texts, in my construction, stress a pained awareness of injustice and hypocrisy that is apparent to a sensitive few but does not bother the sturdy and self-satisfied majority. Ehrmann's texts repeatedly address psychological vulnerability to injustice; Albrecht's address psychological vulnerability to lack of love. Both problems lead to subjective alienation, psychological dissatisfaction, in the texts—occurring, however, against a background of possibility, the possibility of a just and open-minded society in Ehrmann's case, and the possibility, sometimes vividly described, of rich and satisfying—and socially decontextualized—love in the texts of Sophie Albrecht. At the same time, Albrecht's oeuvre contains a smaller set of writings that seem to address the social and political context, which is consistently described as repressive. Like some of Ehrmann's sociopolitical texts, Albrecht's poems and plays of this kind usually envision death as the solution to the narrator's subjective experience of social estrangement. Death is thus Albrecht's second obvious theme after love, and love she represents in many ways, often with triumphant, if carefully engineered, optimism.

"An *. 1781" "To *. 1781" imparts a woman's passion for her lover. Employing direct address to the lover in a manner that suggests physical intimacy and immediacy, the poetic speaker describes the touch of his lips, the warmth of his cheek, and the match of their two bodies.

> Wenn dein Kuß auf meinen Lippen schwebet
> Und mir glühend jede Nerve bebet,
> Deine Wange heiß an meiner Wange lieget,
> Und dein Busen sich an meinen schmieget
>
> Hah! wer sagt das ganz, was ich empfinde
> Und vielleicht ist dieses tiefe Sünde,
> Rufet dann die bange Seele oft mit Schaudern,
> Und doch bleibt mit wollustvollem Zaudern
>
> Noch der Mund auf deinen Lippen glühen,
> Heisser wird die Wange, statt zu fliehen
> Drück ich trunken dich an meinen Busen fester,
> Ach was hält mich stärker—weißt du's, Bester?[3]

[When your kiss hovers on my lips, / and each of my nerves trembles, / when your cheek lies hot on my cheek, / and your breast clings to mine, / Ha! who can say then exactly what I feel, / and maybe this is a deep sin, / my fearful soul calls often with a shudder, / and yet with passionate lingering

My mouth stays glowing at your lips, / hotter grows my cheek, instead of fleeing / I press you drunkenly more firmly to my breast, / Oh what holds me more strongly—Do you know, my best one?]

The speaker registers her physical sensations in the arms of her lover (whose gender is not indicated until the last syllable of the poem, where a masculine referent is signaled in the German text by the ending -er). The resort to the indescribability topos in the second stanza is a cry of defiance that the speaker's erotic feelings do not fit the descriptions and judgments of others. Briefly, the thought of others makes her think also of the possible charge that her love is sinful, an idea that comes, she says, from her timid and fearful soul. The notion of sin indicates the relationship's lack of social sanction; whether because of marital status or considerations of rank or something else is unclear. In any case, the idea of "sin" does not deflect the lyric speaker. Confronted with it, she becomes more passionate and determined; the physical loci of sensuality of the first stanza—lips, cheeks, and bosom—are all repeated and reinforced in the third stanza: "my lips" echoed by "your lips," the hot cheek being hotter, and the embrace firmer. In the last line, the lyric speaker playfully consults about the matter, neither with her apprehensive soul, nor with the arbiters of sin, but with her lover himself. Love, she decides, holds her faster than fear, and she can think of nothing that would surpass love's power over her. Implicitly, she rejects marriage as an institution for binding people together. She does this not only through the logic of her question ("Ach was hält mich stärker?"), but even more effectively by totally omitting marriage from consideration. By focussing on the romantic dyad and emphasizing sensual experience, Albrecht minimizes the socioeconomic context so that any impact on the lovers' standard of living or class placement or institutional acceptability is neither a motive nor a by-product of the relationship. She releases herself from the new discourse linking love directly to marriage, a discourse that Karin Hausen sees as unsettling the old explanations of women's subordination (based on her function in the household). When passionate love was treated as a preliminary event to marriage, as happened increasingly in literature in the 1790s,[4] and when the functional explanation for the division of labor and allocation of power to men was replaced by new notions of sexual characteristics (women as passive and emotional, men as active and rational), control over women remained in the hands of men (often mediated through the church or the state). Sophie Albrecht's omission of marriage gave women control of their own affections and bodies—to the extent that this was medically possible in the late eighteenth century. So situating her work, Albrecht could write poetry from the perspective of a passionate woman speaker—previously almost unthinkable in the eighteenth century.

Poetry of Passion

What makes Sophie Albrecht's poetry effective and fascinating today is her exploration of the possibilities a woman could derive from the then still controversial discourse of romantic love, with emphasis on both the spiritual and the erotic union of the lovers. This notion of profound and unaccountable sensual and emotional passion had occurred frequently in German literature in the *Sturm und Drang* and afterward, but in its corporeality, it had not been welcome to the *Aufklärung* or in the first two strands of *Empfind-*

samkeit, religious and sympathetic, and had, until Sophie Albrecht, found no outstanding woman exponent.

Most of the behavior Sophie Albrecht describes in her love poetry exceeds what was socially acceptable for a respectable middle-class woman, since it did not conform to the requirements of virtue and innocence. The poet realizes this; she mentions, for example, what happens to virtue and innocence in a struggle with passion. By using love, however, as a transforming lens, a poem like "Liebe" "Love" can begin with the words "sweet torture," but by that, not mean agonizing over moral or philosophical problems:

> Süße Qual in meinem Herzen,
> Die sein holder Name giebt,
> Ruft mit tausendfachen Schmerzen:
> Nie als jetzt hab' ich geliebt!

[Sweet torture in my heart, / which his beloved name produces, / calls with thousandfold pains: / never until now have I loved!]

The poem opens with the declaration that the lyric voice's present feelings are her first true experience of love, although, by implication, not her only experience of it. Albrecht's decontextualized love poetry places great emphasis on the present, omitting both the legacy of the past and the consequences for the future.

As the poem goes on, she names some of the symptoms of her condition, asking whether they signify lust or virtue. In fact, stanzas two and three consist entirely of questions, an appropriate device to express the speaker's wonderment and turmoil:

> Dieses Klopfen, dieses Sehnen,
> Ha!, wem gilt der Flammenstreit?
> Sind der Tugend diese Thränen?
> Sind der Wollust sie geweiht?
>
> Sehnsucht, wie sie keine kannte,
> Seit die Lieb' ein Weib gekannt,
> Knüpfst du himmlisch unsre Bande?
> Wirst du Unschuld noch genannt?

[This pounding, this longing, / Ha, for whom is this flaming battle? / Are these tears dedicated to virtue / or to passion?
Longing, as no one has known it, / since woman has known love, / are you tying our bands in heaven? / are you still called innocence?]

The speaker, explicitly positioning her questions in the context of women's experience of love, appears to leave the questions open;

any marriage ("unsre Bande" "our bands") resulting from the relationship is spiritual and the result of emotion, not formal, nor regularized through the church or the state.

With the self-accusations of immorality or impropriety unanswered, in the fourth stanza, the speaker bluntly admits that her feelings are bold and that her heart is wild.

> Tausend kühne Wünsche beben,
> Zum vermessnen Herzen hin—
> Wollt' ich ihnen Namen geben
> Würde Schaam die Stirne glühn

[A thousand bold wishes tremble, / to my emboldened heart— / If I wanted to give them names / shame would glow my brow.]

She acknowledges that the labels conventionally assigned to her wishes would make her ashamed. With this stanza, the tone of the poem changes. Her way of dealing with shame is to avoid the offensive naming. As the last stanza makes clear, this avoidance can happen because all the ideas that are supposed to restrict and intimidate her are transformed under the influence of her passionate love.

> Selbst der Tugend ernste Büste—
> Einst mein schönstes Heiligtum—
> Wandelt, seit sein Mund mich küßte
> Sich zur Liebesgöttin um.[5]

[Even the earnest bust of Virtue— / once my loveliest sacred object— / changes, since his mouth kissed mine / into the goddess of love.]

The erotic confession does not force the speaker into the position assigned her by the ideology of virtue. Despite the strong language she uses to describe herself ("Wollust" "passion," "vermessne[s] Herz[]" "emboldened heart," "Schaam" "shame"), she does not have the pariah sensation, which would indicate deep emotional estrangement from society. She resolves her questions and alleviates her strong language by depicting virtue and love as intermingled. By omitting the institutional and socioeconomic aspects, she also avoids having her texts about relationships channeled into a few well-known narratives of love-and-marriage or misapprehension-and-fateful-seduction. Instead, with a light touch of rococo flirtatiousness, she shows the bust of virtue turning into the goddess of love. In this radical vision, with its truncated context, the two deities, both represented in the poem as feminine, are equally valid—and alienation in the form of thwarted desire is eluded.

Understanding Sophie Albrecht's expressions of sensuality and sexuality in the context of her time, gender, and class is difficult. Judging by such evidence as the private correspondence of Meta Moller, it seems to have been permissible for a woman to register her sensuality midway through the eighteenth century. After she became engaged to Klopstock, Moller wrote to friends about the first days of their acquaintance. Most interesting is her description of the moment when she and Klopstock first touched. Although she begins her account by justifying the position of her hand, she ultimately strives most to recapture her sensual response:

> I, in order to better see the letter, because we could not read it completely aloud, had—really quite by accident—put my hand behind Kl's back. He pressed it very softly with his back. This pressing aroused in me a feeling that made me take notice but that was so sweet that I was not capable of pulling my arm back (which I would certainly have done right away with any other man).[6]

She mentions her heightened awareness of physical sensation, her sweet feelings, and her lack of desire to end the experience. Nor is this an isolated comment or an isolated instance of Moller's awareness of sensual experience. At another moment early in their acquaintance, Moller noticed Klopstock looking down the front of her dress and sighing. Although she asserts that she would have ordinarily reacted by despising the man and feeling angry, this time she was not cross. Instead, she was interested and surprised: she had imagined the poet Klopstock as exclusively spiritual. Now, however, she tells her friends in the letter, she knew quite differently: "Now I know well that he has an equally sweet body."[7] Moller apparently does not hesitate to comment on the "sweet body" of the man who wrote the most exalted religious epic in German literature. Not only did Moller include this kind of physical detail in her account of her first meetings with Klopstock, but she also wrote to third parties. Her comments suggest a less inhibited standard of behavior than came later, though it is also significant that Moller did not continue with such attention to sensual experience in her letters after the wedding.

Private letters written by other similarly situated women two decades later show dramatic changes. For one group of letter writers, probably the vast majority, female explorations of sensuality were completely repressed. Thus, Eva König and Gottfried Ephraim Lessing exchanged letters for the seven years of their courtship and engagement, from 1770 through 1776, without ever exceeding impersonal formulaic expressions of physical affection. Another group, writing under the influence of the *Empfindsamkeit* and the cult of friendship, penned passionate expressions of love that were purely rhetorical. Schiller, writing to a friend whom he addressed formally (as *Sie*) rather than intimately (as *du*), still called him "my dearest." The candid but proper Luise Mejer wrote to Heinrich Christian Boie about embracing him and giving him her heart, but turned down his proposal of marriage (years later she accepted after all). That ambiguity would arise from such expressions of passion was unavoidable: the village woman Anna Louisa Karsch, transplanted into both courtly and middle-class urban literary circles, misread the code of her citified contemporaries and so, mistaking Johann Wilhelm Ludwig Gleim's sentimental words of affection to her, thought a mutual love affair was underway. Similarly, the young Lotte von Einem fell seriously in love with Anton Matthias Sprickmann, partly as a result of the emotional charge inherent in the cult of friendship. Nor were the gestures of friendship expected to be exclusively linguistic. Tears and embraces were notoriously abundant in friendships both between and among men and women. Luise Mejer wrote that at one encounter Jenny von Voigts held her so close and so long she thought she would suffocate.[8] Nonetheless, a distinction between sexual love and the kind of passion or flirtation permitted in the cult of friendship was usually carefully maintained.

Some of Sophie Albrecht's poems seem to be in this vein, too, charming flirtations. One example, "An den Mond. Nachts 3 Uhr. 1778" "To the Moon. 3 o'clock at night. 1778," is a poem of a favorite type in the eighteenth century. The small mid-century group of writers known as Anacreontic poets cultivated moon poems, Goethe wrote poems to the moon, and Sophie Albrecht herself wrote several of different kinds:

> Blick diesen Kuß dem fernen Freunde zu,
> Du kennst ihn ja, er liebt so herzlich dich,
> Und schläft er schon, so wink ihm sanftre Ruh,
> Vielleicht küßt er im süßen Traume mich.[9]

[Look this kiss to my distant friend, / you know him well, he loves you so much, / and if he sleeps already, then wave him softer rest, / perhaps in a sweet dream he is kissing me.]

In keeping with Anacreontic practice, the four-line poem uses the language and gestures of love, but is undisturbed by any hint of passion, except perhaps the unusual degree of longing implied by the time in the title: three o'clock at night. Within the poem, the feeling between the two people is so veiled and deflected that it is the distant friend who loves—the moon. The poem is conventional but nicely done, with its juxtaposition of rhyme words "dich" "you" and "mich" "me" neatly matching the exchange of kisses, and the deferral of love syntactically echoed in the last line when the pronoun object of the kissing ("mich" "me") is postponed until the last word of the poem. Despite the conventionality of the words employed, including "süß" "sweet," "sanft" "soft," and "herzlich" "heartily," the poem contains one usage that is distinctive, though not unprecedented: "zublicken" "look" as a transitive verb.

An Uncommon Life

The eighteenth-century woman who dared to mix passionate love poetry in with her flirtatious verses crossed other discursive boundaries, too. Sophie Albrecht had been born 17 November 1757, in Erfurt, a small city in Thuringia in central Germany, not far from Langensalza where Friderika Baldinger had grown up not many years earlier. Erfurt was a Catholic enclave in an otherwise Protestant region; in some of her few religious poems, Albrecht wrote as a Catholic. Albrecht's mother, Johanne Maria Rebekka Christine nee von Teuzel, came from Saxony, and her father, Johann Paul Baumer, was a professor of medicine at the university in Erfurt, an undistinguished institution at the time. From the few descriptions of her youth (none by her and all by nineteenth-century men) emerges the picture of a girl who was rebellious, stubborn, and unafraid. These characteristics were not encouraged in her sex, as one of her biographers made clear; he wrote with distaste that there was something manly and firm in her character, although he quickly and approvingly added that she could also be sentimental.[10]

When the professor's daughter was ten years old, a young medical student from the north German town of Stade, the fifteen-year-old Johann Friedrich Ernst Albrecht, came to board in the professor's house. Four years later J. P. Baumer died, and the year after that, in 1772, Sophie Baumer married the newly graduated Dr. Albrecht. He was twenty, she fifteen, young to be a bride in the educated middle class. Perhaps Sophie's widowed mother arranged or encouraged the marriage in order to make sure that at least this daughter was taken care of in the way considered desirable for women.

Within a few years, the young couple began to get involved in the two enterprises that gave them both historical significance: writing and theater. The beginning looked inauspicious. In 1775, J. F. E. Albrecht published his first book, a pamphlet really, about reproduction in bees. In later years, he would be much bolder in his scientific, medical or pseudo-medical endeavors, writing numerous books about human sexuality that were reprinted right to the end of the nineteenth century. Meanwhile, the Albrechts' first effort at imaginative literature appeared in 1778, when the doctor published a five-act tragedy, "Der unnatürliche Vater" "The unnatural Father" and his wife wrote "An den Mond" "To the Moon" and several other poems.

When her husband edited an anthology of poetry, *Ehstländische Blumenlese für das Jahr 1779* "Estonian Anthology for the Year 1779," she contributed several poems, her first publications. The young couple at the time was far away from Erfurt, in Reval, on the Gulf of Finland. The next year, another volume of the annual anthology appeared with more of Sophie Albrecht's work. The great distance to Reval, where Dr. Albrecht was serving as the personal physician to a Count Manteuffel, may have itself been important to Sophie Albrecht for freeing her from the entanglements, obligations, and social expectations she faced in her home town, where her family had presumably been respectable citizens. Furthermore, traveling gave her a host of new experiences and new acquaintances. It was in Reval, or on the way there, in 1776, that Sophie Albrecht first saw a play performance that met contemporary critical standards of literary and artistic quality.[11] In 1781, however, the couple was back in Erfurt, where Sophie's mother was ill and going blind.

Having begun to publish individual poems in Reval, Sophie Albrecht had her first book appear in Erfurt in 1781. The love poems in this collection already show Sophie Albrecht's willingness to confront society. She had found what Ann Rosalind Jones, writing about the Renaissance woman poet Pernette Du Guillet, called "an experimental vision of sexually and verbally active femininity,"[12] which allowed her to transgress against the norms of her time without engaging in any introductory apology. Confident of her rereading of virtue and innocence, she spent only minimal energy defending them or seeking any external confirmation of her stance. Indeed, she proceeded to write, contrary to all the usual eighteenth-century injunctions to women, as though she were not being observed but were instead herself recorder and, together with her lover, valid interpreter of her own behavior. Conventional standards sometimes briefly confused the speaker in the poems, but a claim of innocence remained undamaged so that even in an unofficial moonlit "marriage" described in one poem, the couple's kisses are called chaste.

Nevertheless, one of the characteristics of Albrecht's love poems is that they often refer to the outside forces that would forbid, prevent, or object to the love affairs described, and it is in the responses to these obstacles that one aspect of Albrecht's subjective alienation can be identified. The impediments, as Albrecht represents them, were primarily social and religious, not economic and yet, indirectly related to class. The inhibitions society imposed were felt especially by middle-class women, as members of the class attempting to exalt itself above the aristocracy by its higher moral standards. Furthermore, middle-class women were inculcated with the prohibitions against unsanctioned love affairs much more thoroughly than men of the same class, for women were made chiefly responsible for the preservation of sexual virtue. A woman's virtue was considered above all to be sexual, unlike a man's. As a result, women of the educated middle class constantly remembered the prohibitions against even the slightest and most innocent erotic pleasure outside of marriage. Injunctions against pleasure, then, were an important part of the female experience of love. But the result was not invariably a sense of alienation due to thwarted desire. On the contrary, in some cases Albrecht's poetry suggests that once a woman learned to deal with the conventions, she might find herself to be bolder than a man.

One solution to social disapproval was to admit that she did not meet society's rigid standards, but still to insist that she was behaving morally. "Als er mir zur Verschwiegenheit rieth. Im Mai 1781" "When he advised secrecy to me. May 1781" is an example. The situation, as revealed in the title, again suggests an illicit relationship, and yet, as in the poem about "sweet torture," this one, too, conveys no sense of moral taint.

> Immer laß die Welt es wissen,
> Daß dich meine Seele liebt,
> Und mein Mund dein glühend Küssen
> Glühender sie wieder giebt.
>
> Daß mein Busen stärker strebet,
> Wenn mein Auge dich erblickt,
> Deine Seele wonnig bebet,
> Wenn mein Auge dich entzückt.

> Daß ich dir im Arme liege,
> Wenn nur unsere Liebe wacht,
> Mich an deinem Busen schmiege
> In der stillen Laube Nacht.
>
> Lieber! laß die Welt es wissen,—
> Sei die Laube noch so dicht:
> War bei unsern heißen Küssen
> Gottes keuscher Engel nicht?
>
> Sprach nicht unsre Seele Frieden
> Und umschwebt uns Ahnung nicht:
> Daß wir lieben wie dort oben
> Einst für Gottes Angesicht?—[13]

[Always let the world know, / that my soul loves you, / and my mouth your glowing kiss / more glowingly returns.
That my breast more strongly strives, / when my eye sees you, / your soul blissfully trembles, / when my eye enchants you.
That I lie in your arms, / when only our love is on watch, / press myself to your breast / in the quiet arbor's night.
Beloved! let the world know,— / No matter how thick the arbor: / was not God's chaste angel present/ as we were hotly kissing?
Did not our spirit speak of Peace / and did not the premonition hover around us / that we love here as we will above / sometime in the presence of God?]

Far from being circumspect or prudish, the speaker spends three stanzas describing the lovers' passion, simultaneously mixing this with claims of spiritual morality. She does not explicitly reject conventional moral standards. Instead, she transvalues the lovers' behavior as moral. It might be inferred that this claim to morality is connected to the reciprocity that characterizes the relationship; reciprocity is mapped onto the poem in its remarkable pattern of pronouns. The first two stanzas densely alternate first and second person pronouns, with five pairs of them in those eight lines, and no pronoun unanswered by a counterpart, shifting, then, in the last two stanzas to the joint statement represented by "we" and "us," a pronoun that occurs four times there, with the transition from "me" and "you" to "our" occurring in the third, and middle stanza, which contains both patterns. The lyric speaker weaves into this fabric of reciprocity no objections to the idea of chastity; she appeals, instead, to a notion of chastity as sanctifying the relationships she describes. God's chaste angel attends the lovers, for love is itself holy. The speaker invokes religion without addressing religion's institutionalization of love into marriage.

Sophie Albrecht's linguistic surefootedness helps her leap some of the chasms that the discourse of middle-class femininity usually kept uncrossable. More than most women of her time, Albrecht wrote poetry that is free of the blemishes in diction that can be detected against the normative complexion of eighteenth-century standard German (which was itself far less standardized than in subsequent periods). Her intricate grammatical control is shown, for instance, in a short untitled poem in which the speaker defends herself against a surprising charge. In complete disregard to middle-class ideological condemnation of a woman conducting any variety of passionate affair, she claims to be defending herself against women who say she is too restrained, charging that her devotion to virtue is merely a prudish self-deception. The speaker declares that the chaste kisses she exchanges with her lover are, in fact, as passionate and thrilling as the other women's hours of passion. By the time Albrecht wrote this poem, readers, aware of her acting career, might interpret the accusing women as actresses and thus beyond the pale, but Albrecht does not marginalize them that way herself.

> O, nennt es nicht getäuscht, ihr Schwestern! Tugend—
> Daß ich und er mit heißem Blick der Jugend
>   Nicht weiter gehn, als bis zum Feuerkuß;
> Ihr habt in allen euren Wolluststunden
> Nicht das, was wir in einem Kuß, empfunden,
>   Uns war er jeder Wollust Vollgenuß.[14]

[O, do not call it faked, you sisters! virtue— / that he and I with the hot gaze of youth / do not go further than a firekiss; / you in all your passionhours have / not felt what we feel in one kiss, / To us it was the full enjoyment of every passion.]

The poet rearranges word order into its pithiest form. The first line creates and then relieves suspense as it first defers naming what she is accused of faking and then, in the most important position in the line, reveals it: "Tugend" "virtue." Alliteration with "getäuscht" "faked" reinforces the word's significance. And yet, the poem turns conventional morality of the time upside down: Albrecht is accused of sacrificing her sensual satisfaction to a *false* sense of virtue. Her rejoinder is not the defense of virtue (and of her virtue in particular) that the opening lines suggest. Rather, she asserts that her firekisses, an apt word creation, are just as sexually fulfilling as other women's hours of voluptuous passion.

The intricacies in the poem's syntax complicate the poem's rhythm (without deviating from the iambic pentameters of which the poem consists), but Albrecht was equally adept at simple syntax and common versification, as in the poem discussed above disputing the lovers' need for secrecy. Folk song stanzas were an important part of her repertory, as they had been for Philippine Engelhard-Gatterer. In one of several poems called "Lied" "Song," for example, love is again perceived as, in part, an enjoyable kind of pain:

> Ach, wie ist mir so warm—so warm!
> Wie's mir zum Herzen dringt.
> Wenn, Holder! mich dein lieber Arm
> So liebevoll umschlingt.
>
> Und wenn mich küßt dein heißer Mund,
> Wie schaudert mirs durchs Herz;
> Es fühlt sich wohl, es fühlt sich wund,
> Und liebt auch seinen Schmerz.[15]

[Ah, how warm I feel—how warm! / How I feel a pressing toward my heart / when, beloved! your loving arm / lovingly encircles me.
And when your hot mouth kisses me / how it shudders through my heart; / it feels good, it feels bad, / and loves even the pain.]

The poem begins with the expression of surprise—and dismay—at the woman's reaction to her lover's clasp. In the first stanza, he embraces her and the sensation reaches all the way to her heart. In the second, he kisses her and in her heart there is a shudder. The first stanza refers to warmth, the second escalates this—as everything in the poem is escalated—to heat. And her reaction, the key point, is unexpected to her and paradoxical: her heart feels good and hurts simultaneously, and yet, loves even its pain. The man as a person disappears: only his arm and his mouth are evoked. In a way that is short, intense, and specific, the poem concerns the reaction of the implicitly female lyric speaker. Well before Romanticism had endorsed both passionate love and folk songs, Albrecht was not only using the common stanza form of these songs, but also capturing their apparent simplicity and directness. The language of "Lied" is simple and made even more so by repetition. There are no literary allusions of the type that appeared frequently in the poetry that influenced women in the late eighteenth century, and only one poetic word, "holder" "beloved."

Albrecht wrote about love over and over again, though not always about moments of passion; some of the poems are about other phases, including disagreements, anger, disappointment, and loss.

6: EXAMINING PASSION

In one with a title that she often used, "An *" "To *," she condenses a moment of frustration almost into an aphorism:

> Wenn ich für dich auf Lieder denke,
> Dir Träume, Ruh und alles schenke,
> Was Glück für mich auf Erden ist—
> Sinnst du auf Briefe mich zu qüalen,
> Weißt Blick' und Worte so zu wählen,
> Daß Gram mein liebend Herz zerfrißt.
>
> (160)

[While I am thinking of songs for you, / giving you dreams, quiet, and everything / which is happiness for me on earth— / You are pondering letters to torment me, / knowing how to choose glance and words in such a way, / that misery devours my loving heart.]

Again, she expertly employs parallels and contrasts, juxtaposing the different activities and effects of the loving woman and the critical man: her songs, dreams, rest, and happiness for him, against his letters, glances, words, and pain for her. A simple poem again, in fact a poem about writing poems, this one is composed in a single, carefully crafted sentence.

The focus on a woman's account of love makes these poems a woman-authored counterpart to much of the immeasurably more famous men's poetry of the time. Goethe, for instance, wrote about a man's impatience to see his beloved in "Es schlug mein Herz. Geschwind, zu Pferde!" "My heart was beating. Quick, on my horse!" In one of the less characteristic of Sophie Albrecht's poems, in which the narrative aspect outweighs the lyric, she wrote about a woman's impatience to see her beloved, but Albrecht's woman, in contrast to Goethe's man galloping to a tryst, must remain immobilized at home. The poem, "Als ich ihn erwartete. Im May 1779." "While I was awaiting him. May 1779." describes very economically the slow passage of a night as the speaker waits for the return of the man she loves.[16] Although the poem is addressed to the absent man, it is really about how solitary and abandoned the woman feels, and how hurt that he has left her alone when he promised to be with her by midnight. The dramatic moment is concentrated in the final stanza when the clock strikes one, she hears a noise, wonders if it is merely a dream, and then banishes all her worries when she realizes that he is at the garden gate. Her confinement contrasts with his freedom. Nonetheless, Sophie Albrecht, in her poetry, somewhat like her much older contemporary in France, Marie-Jeanne Riccoboni, "undermines the traditional gendering of the active/passive hierarchy, though without relinquishing her identification with feminine qualities of délicatesse."[17] Albrecht continued this subversive work in other genres as well, for instance, in her one full-scale play, *Theresgen*.

THERESGEN, DRAMA OF A WOMAN'S LOVE AND SUICIDE

When Sophie Albrecht published her first collection of work, it contained, in addition to poems, two plays. The plays testify to eighteenth-century women's extraordinary work as dramatists.[18] Writing plays generally required a different kind of public act than writing and even publishing novels or poetry. For, while the latter could be composed with relatively less infraction against the discourse of femininity, it was much more difficult to write plays without at least the appearance not only of infraction but of deliberate and desired transgression. Furthermore, the author of a play potentially went public not only through writing and publication, but also, if she was fortunate, performance. Some women avoided or minimized this incursion into the masculine public realm by writing plays intended for reading, not for staging, an example being *Selina, Komischer Trauerspiel in Verse* "Selina, Comic Tragedy in Verse" (1770, by the Austrian noblewoman Hedwig Louise von Pernet [1742–1801]). Others minimized their claim on the public realm by writing plays for private domestic performance, such as those in which children served as both actors and audience; for instance, *Der Besuch* "The Visit" (1759) by Katharine Helena Dörrien (1717–95) taught children, especially girls, correct manners when they paid calls on each other. And some tried to avoid the problem of public forwardness by working anonymously—although women novelists around this time hid their identities almost twice as often as their sister playwrights.[19]

Most of the plays by women, however, were composed for staging in a regular theater, and as such, women playwrights encountered three more levels of patriarchal gatekeeping than did other women writers. A playwright who authored a series of much performed original plays and became the earliest well-known woman writer of the century, Luise Adelgunde Gottsched (1713–62), is a good example. A woman playwright's actual composition, like most other women writers', was typically done virtually under the eyes of her father or husband, as also occurred, for example, in Gottsched's case. After that, the woman's script was scrutinized by one of the three new gatekeepers, a director, usually (though not always) a man, whose approval was necessary for performance. Second came the sometimes highly innovative performance and textual modification carried out by male actors, a situation Gottsched in one instance largely circumvented by making the three main characters women.[20] Third came published reviews of the play as performed, which is to say reviews by men; again, the case of Gottsched and her harsh treatment at the hands of Lessing is instructive (129). If the play was also published, the routine gatekeeping conducted by publisher, bookseller and the rest resumed. In short, the plays by eighteenth-century German women that have been preserved until today are not a promising site to seek ringing protests against patriarchy—although attentive reading can cue indications that here, too, women were groping for ways and means of establishing their authority as women and as women authors.[21]

Sophie Albrecht's two dramatic efforts, especially the longer one, suggest women's search for authority over their own lives and the difficulty women faced in being heard. The shorter first play, *Lauschen ist auch gut* "Listening is also good," presents in two acts a marriage proposal seen mainly from the perspective of a child. It opens as an eight-year-old boy, picking flowers for a little girl with whom he is infatuated, ruminates on the erratic behavior of his relative from the city. The relative, in turn, comes to the garden, where her monologue is overheard by both the boy and her aristocratic lover, who promptly proposes marriage, thus resolving the young woman's uncertainties. The play's awkward dependence on a series of purportedly private monologues is Albrecht's version of Engelhard-Gatterer's dream device or La Roche's many instances of secret watching. Deliberate spying usually involves men spying on women to check their virtue when they are off guard. Accidental spying, on the other hand, is a form of otherwise unavailable conversation. Participating in a discourse that posited emotions as directly speakable, women writers had to work hard to construct circumstances in which a plausible license to speak her feelings in the presence of the key listener could be extended to a woman without jeopardizing the character's positioning as respectably silent. Albrecht's sequence of monologues is an undramatic solution to the problem.

Her other play, the ambitious five-act *Theresgen* "Little Therese," more successfully produces dramatic tension as it explores the destructive consequences of a young woman's lack of influence on a crucial decision affecting her life. Formally, the play, drawing on strategies of the *Sturm und Drang*, mixed genres, most obviously including elements of *Singspiel* and bourgeois tragedy.[22] The *Singspiel* form, most familiar today in Mozart's *The Magic Flute*, intersperses songs within spoken dialogue. Albrecht's *Singspiel* operates in another tradition, too, one then current in France, the rosière play, which brought to the stage a village festival, in which a girl, selected as queen of virtue, was crowned for the day in the presence of the local aristocracy. The title heroine's name, Therese, is typical of the rosière play, as is the inclusion of two couples and the plot that depends on "misunderstandings and mistaken identities."[23] In Albrecht's version, Theresgen, after spending some years in the city, has returned to the country and to a stepfather who wishes only to marry her off to a young man named Franz. Theresgen, however, has fallen in love with the local count, whom she has met once by chance. The usual narrative of the sleeping encounter between boy and girl, familiar, for example, from Engelhard-Gatterer's poetry, aligns male with active and female with passive. Albrecht's heroine, reversing that pattern, is awake and the count asleep in the grass by a pond when first they meet. And it is Theresgen who also rescues the count a few moments later, when he rolls over, falls into the water, and is pulled to safety by the young woman. Prokop points out that for a woman to maintain her claim of uncalculating innocence, love must strike quickly.[24] This is especially important for Theresgen, since the attraction of a peasant woman to a count could so readily look like a shrewd choice of love object.[25] In this case, however, when the count awakens, unlike conventional love-at-first-sight stories, he does not promptly fall in love with his beholder/rescuer; indeed, he soon has a bride of his own class. It is to welcome her that Theresgen is selected by the village for a ceremony resembling the French rosière; like some of the French plays, Albrecht's includes a certain amount of social criticism in the allusions to the unthinkability of Theresgen's secret passion for the count. Class issues, however, are only one source of the protagonist's experience of profound alienation.

But before the audience knows any of these things, the play, in its rosière mode, appears to be something completely different, a dramatized rural idyll about nice young peasants in love. In the opening scene, the peasant bride of the first couple, Lehngen, impelled by the force of love to rise at dawn and sing of her emotions, meets Andres, the beloved peasant groom who has chosen her despite pressure from his father to marry another country woman more prosperous than Lehngen, even though Lehngen is already wealthy in comparison with Andres. This rejection of economic motivation—so that Lehngen will never have to worry that Andres married her for her money—ratifies the pair as truly in love and, therefore, properly rewarded financially (with wealth contributed by Lehngen and hard work by the energized Andres). Such a plot gets to have it both ways: the couple does not marry for money but benefits materially nonetheless. This first couple is soon joined by Lehngen's brother Franz, who asks their assistance in his so far unsuccessful wooing of Lehngen's friend Theresgen. In fact, with Theresgen's widowed stepfather demanding that Theresgen accept the offer, everyone supports Franz's suit, including Andres, Lehngen, and also, Franz reports, his employer, the count. The story of Franz's desire, the stepfather's demand, and Theresgen's refusal are the central elements in the action of the play, which Karin Wurst aptly and bluntly describes as depicting the psychological rape of a woman.[26] Theresgen is to be coerced into a marriage that is unmistakably against her will. Just before the wedding takes place, in the final moment of the play, the desperate Theresgen drowns herself in the pond from which she had rescued the count.

The tumultuous passions and dire struggle of the protagonist to combine personal integrity with a place in the world, the flavor of class conflict, and the protagonist's melancholy all are reminiscent again of the *Sturm und Drang*. It could be argued that Albrecht's drama is a woman's counterpart to *Werther*, Goethe's novel of a young man whose strong feelings permit no compromises in his personal life or his career. After the woman he loves marries a conventional man chosen for her by her mother, Werther shoots himself. *Theresgen* likewise involves a love triangle of two men and a woman, and the woman's marriage choice has been made for her by a parent. But Albrecht's play offers one of the rare instances when it is the woman whose subjectivity determines the outcome of events. Theresgen does not love Franz, a man of similar socioeconomic status to hers. Her strong feelings prevent her from accepting what convention—and her (step)father—dictate, and the result is disastrous, although the man whom her stepfather has accepted on her behalf is neither unattractive nor uncaring. Yet, while Franz claims he loves Theresgen, his sister points out that his insistence on marrying her immediately, even though she begs not to be rushed, hardly seems to match the feelings he declares. Theresgen, acting on her faith in romantic love (which validated her feelings) and her own immoderate subjectivity, withdraws from the arranged marriage in the most extreme way that the discourse of femininity allowed her to conceive of, by killing herself. When Werther goes to Lotte to borrow the pistols for his death, he manages to make the woman he loves complicitous in his destruction. Prokop argues that the men of the *Sturm und Drang* were haunted by a great fear: that men would become the victims of women.[27] In

Leichtsinn und Gutes Herz, Marianne Ehrmann toyed with that fear when she had her desperate female protagonist pull the trigger on her seducer, but in that very instant she discovers that she lacks the ammunition to destroy the man; she and her count subsequently marry. Albrecht's play, on the other hand, shows men's fear of being women's victims as utterly ridiculous, the reverse of the truth.

The play depicts a woman taking the premise of the love marriage very seriously, more seriously than society actually permitted. Much work has been done in recent years on the appearance of this form of marriage, inquiring why it became possible and began to spread in the eighteenth century. One argument is that love marriages were a functional accompaniment to the separation of work from home in the middle class. The educated, middle-class man's work could take place in an increasingly hostile and competitive environment, partly because he had a place of repair to which he could daily return, the emotionally healing private home. The function of the home, then, was structured around the psychological, emotional, and physical recreation of the paid worker in the public world, while the labor of the unpaid woman was increasingly disallowed as work and relabeled "love." This unpaid support labor thereby disappeared from the cost equations of capitalism. But the woman was induced to perform it in the name of love and to manage the household in her husband's interest (not necessarily the same as her own). By giving her play a rural setting, Albrecht reduces the visibility of this economic apparatus since the competitive industrializing work world did not (yet) operate there. Never mind that love marriage, which was seeping through the German middle class in the late eighteenth century, was rare to unknown in the peasantry—and uncommon in the aristocracy as well. Furthermore, Wurst argues that while the economic function of love marriages may have been the pattern in England, in Germany these conditions were not sufficiently widespread anywhere in the middle class in the late eighteenth century to explain the dissemination of this form of relationship; she argues that love marriages were an ideological import that occurred before the socioeconomic conditions arrived that justified the change.[28] In Albrecht's play, an idealized peasantry is the site for this middle-class issue.

Even so, class relations affect the action. It is all well and good, the opening scene between Lehngen and Andres points out, when love occurs between members of approximately equal socioeconomic status; it is quite different, the rest of the play suggests, when the two are not members of the same class. Drawing on ideas of the *Empfindsamkeit* about an "aristocracy of the heart" that Sophie La Roche had also invoked in the *Sternheim* plot, Theresgen asserts her equality with the count on the basis of her virtue; however, she can only envision a locus for this equality in death, in the "fields [of death], where equality reigns, where only love is wealth and virtue is high rank."[29] In life, she makes no effort to practice the equality of love and virtue; she sees her case as completely hopeless as soon as she learns the identity of the young man she has saved. In 1786, five years after *Theresgen* appeared in Albrecht's first volume of work, Ehrmann's *Leichtsinn* shows an uncannily similar situation, with a city-educated, rural heroine who is the daughter of a prosperous peasant father and dead mother and involved with a possible aristocratic suitor; the result of the relationship between the peasant and the aristocrat in Ehrmann's play, however, is marriage. If a cross-class marriage is not actually unthinkable, then perhaps Albrecht is using the rhetoric of class to produce a situation of impasse that can in turn raise other issues, especially of gender. Two of these gender issues are the limitations on women's right to speak and the limitations on women's right to choose their own marriage partner. For the matter of choice, Andres, a man situated comparably to Theresgen (though admittedly with a class-appropriate love object), successfully rejects his father's spouse selection; Theresgen, however, fails to prevent her stepfather's imposition of his selection on her. Women had less choice in marriage partners than men, a fact that suggests that marriage still functioned as the exchange of women among men. Gendered limitations on speech are a similar matter. First, Theresgen is, and does, what in this kind of eighteenth-century literature is conventionally needed in order to have her wishes recognized, even without her articulated speech: she is beautiful and accomplished, so that the count should recognize her merit without speech from her. But he fails at this recognition. Second, she talks to herself, so that she can be overheard by the beloved, a device that works perfectly to catalyze a marriage in Albrecht's other play. In *Theresgen*, however, the beloved does not hear, and the friend who does hear misunderstands. Third, although Theresgen can speak about her love when she is alone, when she knows she has an auditor she needs an enabling mechanism, which turns out to be a burst of crazy raving. Sufficiently pushed by Lehngen's loving questions, Theresgen makes a ranting speech in which she shifts her terms of address between the count's bride (who does not appear on stage) and Lehngen, and refers to herself allegorized as "love" and "poor love":

> Theresgen: Horrible! Terrible! Oh how I hate you, you fortunate countess! Love pines in vain for a glance from him; through all its suffering poor love can purchase not a glimpse. Then she comes, because she is rich, because she is beautiful, and tears him away. Is she really so beautiful, Lehngen? Do tears of love gleam in her eyes too? Or is it only her jewels that glitter?[30]

When Lehngen is still confused by this babble, in which the countess appears, in Theresgen's eyes, with the personal advantages (wealth, rank, and beauty) and calculating personality (signalled by glittering eyes) of a *Machtweib*, Theresgen says directly and reasonably that she loves the count. But even here, to explain how this could be, Theresgen needs a special form, this time a song, in which she describes seeing and saving the sleeping man. Nonetheless, especially since her auditor is a young woman, not a man of authority, this speaking, too, is useless in solving her problem of being forced into an unwanted marriage.

On one occasion, however, in the second act, Theresgen speaks directly with the count about love and marriage. Because she keeps her passion a secret from him, and because it is a passion he does not return, the discussion occurs, most painfully for Theresgen, when the count is speaking on Franz's behalf.

> The Count: You know that poor Franz loves you; I am requesting of you your love for him.
> Theresgen: Heavenly god! How can you demand this of me?
> (*sings:*)
> > Fordren Sie mein Blut und Leben,
> > Ach, wie gern will ichs geben,
> > Liebe nur für Franzen nicht,
> > Alles, was hier mein auf Erden,
> > Alles, was noch mein kann werden,
> > Aber Liebe hab ich nicht.
>
> [You may claim my blood and life, / Oh, how gladly I will give them, / Not however love for Franz; / All that is mine on earth, / All that could yet be mine, / But not love for Franz.]
>
> No, gracious sir, I do not want to [deceive] you and Franz; never can I, never will I love Franz.
> The Count: Your friends have assured me that your heart is free. Franz loves you, his happiness will depend on you in the future; you say, you cannot love him?
> Theresgen: No, never, never will I be able to love him. . . .
> The Count: Be at peace, dear girl. You have done your duty by telling him that you cannot love him. But what if he does not demand

love from you. What if he only wants your hand? You can surely allow him the hope that he will one day win your love.

Theresgen: No, my lips will not say Yes, when my soul says No. I will never love Franz.

Heinrich: But you are going to take him, or else not stay an hour longer in my hut!³¹

The count's manner is kindly and "enlightened," but, relying on incorrect information and drawing mistaken conclusions, he allies himself with the stepfather, whom he considers "ein ausgelernter Schelm" "a thorough jerk,"³² and against Theresgen, whom he believes himself to be helping. The *Aufklärung* fails women (and men) again. Thus, despite the difference in their tone and the seeming respect the count mentions for Theresgen's feelings, he and the stepfather, Heinrich, are two versions of the same voice, both pushing the young woman to marriage, ignoring and overruling the firmness and decisiveness of her repeated and unmistakable "no."³³

Indeed, the peasant characters, aside from Theresgen herself, repeatedly frame the issue as one of daughterly obedience to the patriarchal will. Albrecht has devised a situation in which a daughter vigorously and vehemently resists her (step)father's authority. Theresgen expresses no more guilt about refusing the orders of her father than about rejecting the languishing Franz. (Franz, it could be argued, is in a situation like Theresgen's: he loves someone passionately who is unreachable. But Franz does not get our sympathy because he already has all social forces on his side and he shows none of Theresgen's self-restraint in controlling her passion). On one level, then, the play is about Theresgen's insubordination, her refusal of patriarchy. When she refuses to obey direct orders from her father and an indirect order (in the enlightened style of a request) from the head of state, the count, she is staging a serious rebellion as a woman opposing paternal and paternalistic authority. The family is supposed to accustom its members to obedience,³⁴ but Theresgen, despite brief lapses, maintains her resistance. Her friends remind her several times that her "father" wants her to make this marriage. Her father reports to her in turn that the count wants her to make the marriage. Since everyone expects her acceptance ultimately to be coerced, her final choice is to move beyond coercibility, to die.

Theresgen's insubordination suggests that the play does not have to be understood as a love story. After all, the selection of Albert as the name for the count points for eighteenth-century readers to

Werther's dull and uninspiring rival of the same name, hardly an object of romantic love. Thus, the play is also readable as the story of a woman's passion for anything not conventionally available to women—perhaps a literary career, or learning, or poetry. The passionate woman first tries to conceal her desire behind something else (grief for a deceased benefactress in Theresgen's case). When she is tricked into revealing her unacceptable yearning, society reacts with horror and intensifies its pressure on her to get married, with love an irrelevant consideration now; the woman must be stitched back into her conventional social place. In the end, Heinrich's big threat against Theresgen, that he will tell the count she loves him, makes sense only in its aspect as a blackmail technique, which, unlikely as it seems, succeeds in controlling the woman's behavior. Every time he mentions it, she suddenly and languishingly cooperates. The point of this is that the stepfather has found a pressure point that attacks the daughter's wishes and sense of who she is. If she does not cooperate, he will violate her determination not to expose her feelings to the count. Whether or why this determination is important is less significant in the play than the woman's avid adherence to it and the stepfather's willingness to use it against her. In these terms, then, the play is about what happens when a gifted and beautiful young woman makes up her mind for something her community rejects, how patriarchal society then labors to rediscipline the woman through marriage.

It is striking that Albrecht does not raise choices beyond death or marriage for Theresgen, and in this respect makes her strictly a victim, although as Roebling points out, she makes an active choice to die and does so quite deliberately, by jumping.[35] In the last act, as the procession of villagers is on its way to accompany Theresgen to the palace, where her wedding is to happen in the presence of the count, the protagonist desperately considers what to do, saying, "And so, only a few more moments, and then [Franz's] forever. No, never. No, and if it means my damnation! Sooner would I—Ach, you poor lonely woman—What can you choose? Abandoned one!"[36] Having stopped midway into formulating any idea for rescuing herself, Theresgen offers no viable choices for women. As a relatively educated young woman who had already been to the city, it would seem possible that she could have sought alternatives there. But the city was not part of the diction of virtue that Sophie Albrecht is using for Theresgen, who aside from her aberrant desire, is supposed to be thoroughly proper. In fact, *Theresgen* uses topography very deliberately to underscore the situation of the protagonist: she is always out of doors, and, indeed, outside the garden enclosure as well, closer rather to the forest, thus suggesting more closeness to nature than to any form of domesticity.[37] As for religious orientation, unlike Marianne Ehrmann's *Amalie*, where ecclesiastical rules limited the protagonist's choices, propriety in *Theresgen* is dissociated from religion. Aside from stock phrases ("and if it means my damnation"), Theresgen ignores religious notions, especially about suicide as a sin. Although she is shown to be death-oriented, lingering in the cemetery that is the setting of her first appearance in the play, Theresgen does not want to die, and, unlike Werther, she neither plans her death nor deliberately implicates others in it. At the same time, it is noteworthy that Theresgen is not empathetic; she does not feel guilty or sorry about discomfiting or embarrassing her very disagreeable and misogynist stepfather or about disappointing Franz. At one point in her despair, she even badly misreads Lehngen's feelings and accuses her of spying.[38]

Both women in the play are equally stymied in the effort to envision alternatives for Theresgen's survival. When Theresgen begs her friend for help in the final act, Lehngen, who has already tried in vain to dissuade the men from going ahead immediately with the wedding, responds helplessly: "How should I—how could I save you?" The possibility of joint action by the two women is thus also suppressed in the text. In her last speech, Theresgen asks herself again, "Where can I flee?" She raises the notion of divine intervention, which she has already decided is hopeless, but repeats here, as a stage on the path toward her sudden decision to commit suicide, indicated when she abruptly shifts her address from God to the pond: "God, hide me in your earth, veil me in your clouds. Can't you in your seat of heavenly joy hear the scream of my misery! (torches approach from a distance) Torches! They are here— Who will save me? Who will help me? Franz! My father! You conceal me from their rage—" (187). The stage directions conclude: "She jumps into the pond just as the people arrive at the garden gate, and the curtain falls." *Theresgen* is excellent in its depiction of a determined woman who adamantly refuses society's dictates, but it crafts no options for surviving refusal and none for changing social pressures on women.

This absence of options correlates to the play's affiliation with the *Empfindsamkeit* of alienation. While that affiliation aided Marianne Ehrmann in her dissociation from key bourgeois limitations of women and in *Amalie* helped her address practical issues of divorce and employment, in Sophie Albrecht's texts, these issues are displaced by more personal issues of a woman's psychological survival in a hostile patriarchal world. Theresgen's profound sense that her strongest desire is proscribed in her society for utterly inadequate reasons separates her from the social norms and prevents her from pursuing a possibility that Albrecht argued was central to human experience: represented in the play as love. So Theresgen's feelings of love lead to her sense of alienation. This is Sophie Albrecht's main version of the *Empfindsamkeit* of alienation. It occurs when conventional femininity imposed by patriarchy (in the form of "the world" or a father figure) prevents the protagonist or lyric speaker or narrator from satisfying her own sexual or sometimes cultural desires, or when the love object (always heterosexual in her texts) withdraws or refuses. Many of the love poems show devices for avoiding the subject's sense of alienation from the world, through evasion or by transforming society's standards. But when those strategies fail, the resolution that Sophie Albrecht repeatedly offers in her texts is death, especially suicide.

After *Theresgen,* Sophie Albrecht wrote, or at least published, no more plays. Abandoning playwriting allowed her to stop repeating old plots in which desire and love appear to "participate in the process of social mobility."[39] By confining herself for several years to lyric poetry and prose fragments, she could evade the prominent socioeconomic issues associated with love—or rather with marriage—and concentrate on the emotional and sensual experiences that a woman might have of her lover and herself. Genre choice was profoundly important to the forcefulness of Albrecht's concept of love.

Fifteen years after *Theresgen,* Elise Müller (1782–?), wrote a play about another young woman facing similar pressure to marry a man she does not love. But in Müller's *Die Kostgängerinnen im Nonnenkloster* "The Boarders in the Convent" (1797), the defiant woman has two advantages compared to Theresgen. First, whereas Theresgen hopes not to marry at all if she cannot marry the count, Müller's protagonist specifies a willing and socially appropriate alternate to the husband chosen by her mother. Second, the parent whom she opposes is not her father or stepfather, not a man, who can get support from the established power system, but a woman, the protagonist's mother. The setting of the play in a convent in which the nuns are shown to be tyrannical and hypocritical (similar to their representation in Ehrmann's *Amalie*), signifies the abuses that occur when women are in authority. The protagonist succeeds in getting her own way, submitting herself to a particular man, despite her female antagonists. Less daring than Sophie Albrecht's work in its depiction of women's oppression, but more dramatically conceived, this play uses an independent-minded heroine to reconfirm the rightness of patriarchal power. Albrecht's play, on the other hand, raises doubts about patriarchy, since male pressure leads Theresgen to her death.[40]

WOMEN AS PLAYWRIGHTS AND ISSUES OF OBJECTIVE ALIENATION

Plays have the distinction of being the one literary form in the eighteenth-century German-speaking world at which both aristocratic and educated middle-class women, as well as a significant group of déclassé women, those who worked as professional actresses and director-managers, tried their quills.[41] The déclassé group, of course, had the theatrical experience needed to construct a stageable play. The middle-class women show the importance of such experience, too, since most of them, in addition to having better opportunities to educate themselves about literature in general, had somehow established a connection with the theater as well, at least temporarily. Thus, Marianne Ehrmann published her one play after her stint as an actress, and Elise Bürger (1769–1833), the scandalous young woman who had been Gottfried August Bürger's third wife before he divorced her, became an actress and later a playwright, too.[42] For aristocratic women, in contrast, theater experience was not likely to be accompanied by such trauma. Performing in amateur productions was a regular form of entertainment among the nobility; amateur performances in the educated middle-class also existed, but were less likely to take place in actual theaters or to have full theatrical trappings. Aristocratic women often had connections at courts where they could see plays in rehearsal, and where their own works could be performed by resident companies, sometimes with a mix of amateur and professional players. This degree of access makes it less surprising that writing scripts and libretti was an acceptable deed for a number of aristocratic women. In fact, writing for the theater was probably their most frequent form of literary activity in eighteenth-century Germany. The former German princess, Catherine the Great of Russia (1729–96), for example, was the author of a series of plays (including comedies in the style of Moliere, as well as dramas she considered to be in the style of Shakespeare, Russian proverb plays, and operas, too)[43]; the favorite sister of Friedrich II of Prussia, Wilhelmine, Margrave of Bayreuth (1709–58), wrote librettos and performed operas; Maria Antonia Walpurgis (1724–80), princess of Saxony, wrote and performed in her own operas (which she composed in French and then had translated into Italian), including a notably suspenseful and well-constructed one about the Amazons (*Talestri, regina delle Amazoni,* 1760); at the end of the century, Charlotte von Stein (1742–1827) composed a five-act tragedy about Dido (1794), and Elisa von der Recke (1754–1833) wrote a moralistic play about family life in the aristocracy (composed 1794, published 1827).[44]

German women in the eighteenth century wrote plays in every current form: historical drama, farce, high tragedy, bourgeois tragedy, dramatizations of Bible stories, tragedies with classical Greek settings, pastoral masques, dramas of virtue pursued, and of adolescent rebellion. They tend to have two kinds of themes and, correspondingly, two kinds of settings. The group to which the plays by Marianne Ehrmann, Elise Müller, and Sophie Albrecht belong focuses on domestic issues, especially marriage and love, and usually has indoor, pastoral, or garden settings. The other group, dramas with political themes, takes place in locations and situations far from the domestic world; sometimes pseudo-historical, sometimes mythological, and sometimes contemporary, they are not set in Germany. The women characters in these plays are usually strong in their own right, more forceful, better able to lay plans, and more outspoken than the women characters in the domestic type. In both kinds, suicide, committed or contemplated, is a common motif.

Of the women who wrote these plays, few, after Luise Gottsched and her contemporary, Caroline Neuber, were able to sustain their composing over both a sizable number of plays and a stretch of more than five years. Yet, the fact that approximately forty-five German women were public writers of plays in the eighteenth century is impressive; and women were also private playwrights to an extent that is hard to measure, although nine, mostly aristocratic women, can be named in this category.[45] Women were drawn to playwriting, but the support and encouragement necessary for extended growth and development did not appear until the next century when popular dramatists like Johanna Franul von Weissenthurn (1773–1847) would compose many plays and see them frequently performed. Meanwhile, in the eighteenth century, many women followed Sophie Albrecht's pattern of publishing only one play or two.

Unlike most of the other small number of middle-class playwrights of her time, when Albrecht wrote her dramatic works, she lacked theater experience completely. Not until the year after the plays were published (1781), did she go on stage in an amateur theater performance of Weisse's *Romeo und Julia.* She was a success.

Sophie Albrecht as actress. Engraver, Christian Gottlieb Geyser. Original Source: *Gotha-scher Theater-Kalender* 1786.

This was also the year, 1782, in which her mother died. The next year, 1783, she became a professional actress, making her debut with the respected Grossmann troupe in Frankfurt and then in Mainz. The fact that Albrecht composed no plays after going on stage reinforces the suspicion roused by the lack of sustained playwriting among other women that a nonaristocratic woman playwright faced high hurdles.

This must have been so despite the advantages of mobility and networking that a theatrical career offered a woman, especially if she was one of the uncommon actresses from the aristocracy or educated middle-class. For example, among the small number of aristocratic women who earned their living on the stage was Henriette von Montenglaut (nee v. Cronstain, 1767–1838), a woman who became part of Sophie Albrecht's circle of friends, especially late in her life. An actress had a contingent of women coworkers who gave her relationships quite different from what other women had. The actress also had an audience, and women of the audience, too, sometimes entered into a personal relationship with an actress, an indication of her social mobility—especially in unusual cases such as that of Sophie Albrecht, who at the time of her professional debut was married to a middle-class man. This social mobility helps to explain Elisa von der Recke's relationship with Sophie Albrecht in 1784, after Albrecht had been an actress for over two years. Elisabeth Charlotte Konstantia von der Recke (née von Medem), who combined the high moral sensibilities of the educated middle class with the impractical lack of skills of the aristocracy to which she belonged, would not have cultivated a relationship with a woman of whom she disapproved morally, but she cultivated her connection with Albrecht.[46] She also enrolled as a subscriber to Sophie Albrecht's second volume of poetry, listing herself as "Frau Kammerherr Charlotte von Recke" "Mrs. Gentleman-of-the-bedchamber Charlotte von Recke." In fact, this subscriber was a poet herself, with two of her own collections of poems already in print by the time she ordered Albrecht's second book. Her relationship with Sophie Albrecht seems to have been brief and never close, but it helped put both women into a network of literary women and it signals that Albrecht's status as an actress did not prevent her from associating with other very different women.

Although her playwriting career was short, Sophie Albrecht's acting career was considerably longer. In 1784, her second year on stage, she met the man who was to be her most famous literary friend: Friedrich Schiller (1759–1805).[47] At the time, he was the young author of one of the plays in which she had the lead. On 13

April 1784, she had performed Luise Miller in the premiere of his *Kabale und Liebe* in Frankfurt. In May, Schiller wrote about the actress to a mutual friend. His account is the most detailed extant description of Sophie Albrecht by an eighteenth-century contemporary:

> I have gotten acquainted with an excellent woman in Frankfurt—she is your friend—Madame Albrecht. Right away in the first hours we linked together firmly and intimately; our souls understood each other. I am happy and feel proud that she loves me, and that my acquaintance can perhaps make her happy. A heart, completely made for sympathy, exalted above the spirit of triviality of the usual circles, full of noble *pure* feeling for truth and virtue, and admirable even where one otherwise does not find her sex so. I promise myself heavenly days in her close company. She is also an emotional poet.[48]

This is the discourse of the cult of friendship, and, in this context, when Schiller described Albrecht as an emotional poet, he was not necessarily dismissing her. The brevity of his comment on her poetry, as compared to the elaborateness of his words about her heart, however, signal the relative weight he gave to the two aspects of his new friend. Schiller, unlike Elisa von der Recke, did not subscribe when Sophie Albrecht's next volume of poetry was published.

But *Empfindsamkeit* and the cult of friendship alone do not frame his words. Of the competing discourses of art or gender through which Schiller could have construed Sophie Albrecht, he chose to stress gender, as is discernible when his plans for her are contrasted with his plans for himself. In the continuation of the letter, he wanted his correspondent, also a man, to help him persuade Albrecht to leave the stage so that *she* could adhere to sentimental norms:

> Only, my friend, write to her to defeat her favorite idea and to leave the theater. She has very good qualifications to be an actress, it is true, but she won't develop them with a troupe like this; she will not make real progress in this career except at the risk of her heart, her beautiful and special heart—and even if she did that, write her, the greatest theatrical fame, the name of a Clairon and Yates, would be paid for too dearly with her heart. For my sake, my dearest, write her that with all emphasis, with all manly seriousness. I have already done it and our united pleas may perhaps save a beautiful soul for humanity, even if we steal from it a great actress.[49]

Schiller assumed that he knew better than Albrecht what was good for her. Although he criticized her chances of becoming an excellent actress as long as she stayed with the Grossmann troupe, that was not the reason why he thought she should leave the theater altogether. Since he himself had resisted extreme pressure in order to pursue his interest in the theater, his campaign to induce Sophie Albrecht to withdraw indicates that he measured her behavior, the importance of her "heart," and the value of her potential achievement (even though he admitted she could become a great actress) by a different standard than the one he applied to himself. It was more important for a woman to have a beautiful heart than for a man to, even if this meant sacrificing one's ambitions as an artist. The seemingly ungendered norms of the *Empfindsamkeit* were actually more strictly applied to women. Furthermore, it was authoritative male admonitions that he hoped would enable him to "defeat" her wishes, much as the authoritative men in *Theresgen* collude to overpower the woman's wishes about marriage. The men who were most important to women in their artistic careers and *potentially* most influential in enabling them to make artistic progress were quite as capable of being anti-mentors as mentors.

It is possible to make some tentative generalizations about women, genre, and audience in eighteenth-century Germany. Women poets, embarking onto alien and alienating territory long recognized as literary and hence, traditionally male, expected to write for an audience of men as well as women. Women novelists, vending a kind of text that lacked an acknowledged literary pedigree in the eighteenth century, and that appealed to masses of ill-educated readers, many of them also women, might well write for an audience mainly of their own gender. Women playwrights, seeing theater as a practical genre no more inaccessible than others and as one that draws on powers of imitation rather than innovation, using themes comfortable to women, such as family, love, and marriage,[50] did not necessarily appear more presumptuous to the readers of their texts than women who wrote in other genres; if their plays were performed, the woman playwright could, from the perspective of the audience, disappear behind the vivid and self-contained presence of a staging (even though, as I have argued above, that staging can also be read, from the perspective of the playwright, as another series of censoring layers). Subscription lists offer limited clues about the accuracy of such projections. In Sophie Albrecht's case, only a quarter of the listed subscribers for her poetry collections were women, but a large number of the men on the list may have entered their names on behalf of their wives or daughters. (It was unlikely to happen the other way around.) Perhaps the fact that 40 percent of the women who ordered were single is explained by their lack of a man's name behind which to hide.[51] The influence of gender on Albrecht's publishing history is noticeable in other ways, too. For example, unlike her husband's books, her first two were published "commissioned by Albrecht" rather than through a regular bookstore publisher, the more common pattern.

Negotiating Subjectivity in Poetry About Femininity, Freedom, and Death

Alienation did not necessarily prevent women from starting or continuing their literary work. Sophie Albrecht's second volume of work, no longer deploying drama, appeared in 1785, relying entirely on poems and prose sketches. It contains more love poetry, some of it excellent, and a few more poems addressed to friends—including Elise Bethmann, who was also a friend of Sophie La Roche; a Herr Tiedeböhl, an old friend from Reval; Schiller (about his drama *Die Räuber* "The Robbers"); and Karoline von Dachröden—and in the last portion of the volume, where the plays had been in the previous book, is an experimental "diary," another representation of disappointed love. Again, there is an undercurrent of subjective alienation running intermittently through the book.

Objective alienation, functional estrangement from the culture and institutions of one's world, is occasionally evident as well. Of the poems to persons, the one addressed to Karoline von Dachröden (1766–1829), future wife of the scholar, philosopher, diplomat, and educational reformer Wilhelm von Humboldt, reproduces the alienated situation of talented and ambitious women and girls who are prevented by conventional femininity from pursuing their aspirations for adventure and for learning:

> Oft wenn ich von Helden hörte,
> Die der laute Nachruhm ehrte,
>   Seufzt' ich tief in meinem Sinn:
>   Ach! daß ich kein Jüngling bin!—
>
> Rief, wenn ich von Weisheit hörte,
> Die man hier nur Männern lehrte,
>   Und mir doch so reizend schien:
>   Weh! daß ich ein Mädchen bin!—

[Often when I heard about heroes / whom fame loudly honored / I sighed deeply in my mind: / Oh, that I am not a boy!— Called, when I of wisdom heard, / which is here taught only men / and seemed to me so alluring: / Woe, that I am not a boy!—]

The poem continues for two more stanzas to stress the female voice's previous dissatisfaction with society's conventions that prevent women from enacting their intellectual or heroic impulses. (It is possible that the later biographers, treating the poem as an autobiographical statement, derived their characterization of Albrecht's youthful personality from these lines.) Stating in stanza four her possession of "manly courage" and reiterating her desire for learning, the speaker again emphasizes that these qualities have brought her into painful conflict with traditional female roles. Rather than being a call to action to change the roles, however, the first four stanzas contain the familiar expression, like Amalie's did in Ehrmann's novel, of a woman's alienation from her female body, since it is this body that (ostensibly) excludes her from male prerogatives. Acquaintance with Dachröden ends Albrecht's alienated discontent:

> Doch seitdem ich dich erblikte
> Die mich selbst als Weib entzükte
>   Gleich an Geist und Körper schön—
>   Ach, seitdem ich dich gesehn;
>
> Küß ich meine engen Bande,
> Rufe, froh mit meinem Stande:
>   Holde, schönste Zauberin!
>   Wohl, daß ich kein Jüngling bin.[52]

[But since I saw you / who enchanted me even as a woman / equally beautiful in soul and in body— / Oh, since I saw you
I kiss my tight bindings, / call out, happy with my station: / Lovely, most beautiful, enchantress! / How good that I am not a boy.]

A woman's or girl's desire to be a man or a boy, or rather to have the same cultural and psychological privileges as the males in their society, disappears upon seeing a woman who is beautiful in spirit and body, and who is thus simultaneously intellectual and female. The sight reconciles the speaker in Albrecht's poem with her lot. The noisy acclaim given to heroic men, according to the first stanza, and the knowledge kept secret from women, according to the second, no longer provoke the speaker, and, under the influence of the enchanting model woman, the poetic voice proclaims her complete satisfaction—satisfaction allegedly with women's role, though perhaps more deeply with the kind of intimacy her gender permits her to enjoy with her attractive friend. The speaker shifts from envying the privileges and status of men in patriarchy to endorsing the characteristics attributed to women, all because of her responsiveness to a physically and intellectually beautiful woman.

A study of the epistolary novel claims "the depiction of women speaking their amorous desire to be, among literary situations, particularly striking as a site of conflict between established representations of the female gender and transgressive visions of women rebelling against the roles provided them by the discourse of their times." Sophie Albrecht's love poetry fits this description as well, and the poem to Dachröden shows the peculiar corollary that "literary heroines who plead their loves often appeal to established perceptions of women's virtues and prerogatives, thus becoming complicit with patriarchal representations of Woman that are oppressive to women."[53] Sophie Albrecht could simultaneously lead a bold life and, when confronted with the dominant ideology of her day about women's roles, claim to accept conventional values. What she accepted as innocence and virtue would have been unrecognizable to anyone less creative, but to the extent that she proclaimed adherence to these conventional values she could and can be read as perpetuating the "tight bindings" [*meine engen Bande*] of femininity, while to the extent that her transformed meanings of virtue, innocence, and femininity are evident, she could and can be read as subversive.

Indeed, her very model of femininity, Karoline von Dachröden, appeared very different in the eyes of a less imaginative beholder. Sophie Becker (later Schwarz, 1754–89), Elisa von der Recke's friend and traveling companion on a 1784 journey through Germany, for example, had definite reservations about the young Dachröden. Becker noted in her diary: "This is a very good, well-mannered girl, although too early authorship seems to be harmful to her. O, it is really a dangerous thing, when our sex plays with the quill too much."[54] Thus, Sophie Becker, herself also a composer of verses, described a writing woman as merely playing with the quill, an image without positive, creative connotations in this context. Becker's words seem especially harsh because Dachröden's writing was very limited. Her only known publications are two short translations that appeared (after her marriage) in literary journals.[55] In short, she was at most a private writer. That Karoline von Dachröden could provoke criticism for being too devoted to writing emphasizes again how difficult it was for a woman who did any writing to achieve social acceptance. The whole construct of writing in one's leisure hours and writing as a feminine accomplishment was wobbly. For if in Dachröden's case the woman was a paragon of femininity with writing as her only blemish, the dominant discourse of gender required that the blemish nonetheless be harshly judged, even by another woman writer. Both Becker and Dachröden positioned themselves as women in the conventional way that some of Albrecht's poems overtly endorsed, but, I think, covertly undermined.

And Albrecht's poetry did not repeat all the paragraphs of the doctrine of femininity. Two topics that were part of the work and world of almost every other woman writer of the time are notably absent in hers: marriage and motherhood. One of the surprising gaps in knowledge about Albrecht is whether she had children. Only one source, written in the middle of the nineteenth century, makes any comment on this, asserting that as of 1784 (in the midst of her acting career) she had a daughter and a son.[56] Quite unlike other women writers of the time, Albrecht made no reference at all in her publications to children or to any experience of motherhood. In fact, the only explicit personal reference to family—aside from some of the love poems, which may be to her husband—concerns her father's grave, another indication of the important role of fathers in the development of eighteenth-century women writers. (On the other hand, Albrecht did write several poems about her favorite cats, such as one in her third collection entitled "An den Mond" "To the Moon," which asks the moon to watch over the grave of Mörgen, identified with an asterisk as her favorite cat.)[57] And she continued to make forays in other directions, such as composing patriotic poetry.

In general, the patriotic poems in the second volume, published four years before the French Revolution, are antiaristocratic and anti-French, sometimes also asserting an egalitarianism of feeling regardless of personal wealth. "An Thüringen" "To Thuringia" for example, is a stirring anti-French hymn that begins by extolling traditional strong roles for German men, but ends with two stanzas about the brave behavior the poet, too, would like to exhibit as a true German woman:

> Weg fremder Sinn!—in meiner kleinen Hütte
> Sei meiner Väter alte Biedersitte,
>   Und Freiheit sehe sich wie einst geehrt.
> Mein Lohn sei:—unter deinen grauen Eichen
> Der Tage Ziel als deutsches Weib erreichen,
>   Das kühn des Todes eh'rne Schritte hört.
>
> Dann, Mutterland, dann rufe du mir Einen
> Der nicht mit Kränzen, nicht mit schwachem Weinen
>   Und Modetand die kalte Tochter ehrt,

> Nein, stärker wälz er, nach der Väter Sitte,
> Den schweren Stein auf meines Hügels Mitte
> Und nenne mich des Vaterlandes werth.[58]

[Away foreign thought!—in my little hut / may there be the plain old customs of my fathers / and may freedom see itself honored as in the past. / My reward will be:—under your gray oaks / to reach the goal of a German woman's days / bravely listening to death's inexorable footsteps.

Then, motherland, then call someone to me / who will honor the cold daughter / not with wreaths, not with black tears and fashionable trivialities, / no, may he more stoutly, according to the fathers' custom, / move the heavy stone onto the middle of my hut / and call me worthy of the fatherland.]

If foreign ideas can be eliminated, the speaker suggests, then solid traditional virtues will return and freedom will once again be honored—although what this freedom means is unclear. The interplay between fatherland and motherland in the first and last lines of the final stanza nicely mirrors the complementary roles of men and women that Albrecht envisions, although it is evident in the context of her other poems that she thinks of her Germanic heritage primarily in terms of fathers.

When Albrecht wove a grave scene into her patriotic poem about Thuringia, she was evoking her other major theme besides love: death. Albrecht represents death as a relief from the entanglements of life, and, unlike her usual practice in other kinds of writings, she frequently writes about death without making even a glancing reference to the gender of the poetic speaker:

> Nur dem freywilligen Sklaven
> Ist diese Erde
> Gefängnis—
> Sie selbst reicht uns
> Die Schlüssel zur Freiheit;
> Und jeder Augenblick
> Ist bereit
> Uns ihre Pforten zu öfnen
>
> (124)

[Only to the voluntary slave / is this earth / a prison— / She herself hands us / the keys to freedom; / and every moment / she is ready / to open her gates to us]

A political element, suggested in this short untitled poem by the reference to being a willing slave, is almost always mixed into these aphoristic, thanatopsic poems; but death, or more specifically, suicide, offers only a blurry solution to the *political* issues of unfreedom. It could be argued that here and in other kinds of Albrecht texts about suicide, death is not in any usual sense political. *Theresgen,* for example, resorted to death as an escape from her impending marriage when all appeals for help had failed. In my view, however, Albrecht has more than one notion of what may lead to suicide, with escape from a love catastrophe as the most common catalyst, but defiance of repression as a different, political motive. Thus, the play, which is about the protagonist's resolute faithfulness to her own agenda, never poses Theresgen's dilemma as an issue of freedom; similarly, the unhappy and suicidal narrator of the journal fragments at the end of the second volume, and continuing in the third, writes of death in terms of escape from love's misery, but rarely as claiming freedom. In the short poem, however, "freedom" means death as an escape from unspecified repressive conditions on earth, and is, in this general sense, political. When Albrecht links freedom with death, she is also addressing alienation, this time as a sense of powerlessness in the face of an enslaving world, suggested by the notion of earth as a prison, albeit one in which some people remain voluntarily.

Another of Albrecht's exalted, pithy death poems, again untitled, unrhymed, and in irregular meter, explicitly raises the idea of freedom from imprisonment:

> Freyheit!
> Dein Harfenton wird nicht gehört
> Unter dem Geklirr der Felsen hienieden!
> Deine Palme
> Weht nicht in Thälern des Welkens!
> Dein Name ist nur die große Ahndung der Zukunft—
> Gegeben zur Stärke
> Dem Gefangenen des Lebens.
>
> (89)

[Freedom! / your harpsound is not heard / amidst the ringing of the rocks here below! / your palm / does not wave in the valleys of wilting! / Your name is only the great premonition of the future— / given to strengthen / the prisoner of life.]

Freedom in this poem, too, is ambiguous; it can be read as religious or political, or as an expression of world-weariness and melancholy. The tone is prophetic and the metaphors biblical, but the emphatic first line suggests the political and philosophical. This is unusual from the pen of an eighteenth-century woman because of women's long exclusion from both philosophy and politics, but Albrecht does little to moderate her intrusion. Unlike Ehrmann in her first tract, Albrecht does not, for example, adopt an overtly feminine perspective on her topic. She instead asserts her right to speak about freedom and about death.

Alienation and death also infuse her successful long poem, "An die Ruhe" "To Peace," but this time, in connection with the desire for inner peace and with little enticement to a political reading. Written relatively early, in February 1781, the poem shows the poetic speaker, drenched in melancholy, searching for the calm and serenity that she lost as a child. In the opening lines, peace is addressed as "Schwester des Todes und der Nacht! / Bewohnerin der Gräber und des Himmels!" "Sister of death and of night! / Inhabitant of graves and of the heavens!" The speaker goes on to say that she had lost her peace before she even knew that peace could leave, and then tells the ways she has looked for it since, first by traveling and then by seeking diversion. She describes her search for peace at the bedside of a dying man, who called in vain for peace until the moment of death:

> Die Gluth der Angst erlosch;
> In sanftes Lächeln schwamm der starre Blick—
> Und du erschienst in deiner Schöne
> Auf der blassen Gestalt,
> In deines Bruders Umarmung.

[The glow of fear was extinguished; / the fixed eyes swam in a soft smile / and you appeared in your beauty / on the pale figure / in the embrace of your brother.]

Albrecht had a good command of unrhymed poetry, better than Engelhard-Gatterer. She did not resort too strongly to the sublime, retaining, instead, a grasp of the specific. The poem is ceremonial, almost stiff, and full of gesture, with peace entwined in the arms of her brother death, an image beautiful and enticing in its austerity.

Since she has been unable to find peace in the valley of life, the speaker concludes that she must search for her at the home of death.

> Ich strekte meine Arme nach dir aus;
> Rief dich mit Thränen;
> Aber du hülltest dich tiefer
> In dem Schleier der Verwesung,
> Trostlos stand ich da
> Und rufe noch immer vergebens:

> Wer sagt mir,
> In welches Gewand verhüllt,
> Dein Genius wandelt im Thale des Lebens?
> Aber ich will mich aufmachen
> Und dich in der Behausung deines Bruders finden.⁵⁹

[I stretched my arms out after you / called you with tears; / but you wrapped yourself more profoundly / in the veil of decay, / inconsolably I stood there / and am still calling in vain.

Who can say to me / clad in what garment / your genius wanders in the valley of life? / But I wish to be on my way / and to find you in the home of your brother.]

Albrecht artfully repeats at the end of the poem the image she had introduced at the beginning—peace and death as mysterious brother and sister. (Sister images are surprisingly uncommon in German women's literature in the eighteenth century. Jane Austen produced sisters abundantly in England, but German women writers preferred heroines who had no significant siblings, male or female. Even the sister in Ehrmann's *Amalie* remained unnamed in the text until her death.) The language here, too, is biblical, and the poem, psalm-like in its construction, but conventional religious feeling is missing. Neither God nor salvation plays any part.

In her first volume, Albrecht had included several poems about dying for love, usually through suicide. In one, "Am Ufer eines Flusses, in dem einige Unglückliche ihr Leben geendet. Im Juli 1781" "On the Bank of a River, in which some Unfortunates ended their Lives. July 1781," a Gothic mood is set, with the woman narrator describing her strange attraction to the fatal river, saying, for example, "Ach, wer sagt mir: wessen ist die Stimme, / Die mich nachlockt deiner Schauderkrümme?" "Oh, who can tell me: whose is the voice / that lures me into your shudder-bend?" (98). Terry Castle writes of the spectralization of everyday life in the eighteenth century, precisely when the attempt was underway to root out ghosts and supernatural mysteries in the name of Enlightenment and rationalism.⁶⁰ Sophie Albrecht, until late in her writing career, evoked ghosts and apparitions mainly of the kind in this poem: as expressions of internal mental imagery rather than inexplicable external apparitions. Thus, when in Albrecht's play, Theresgen addresses the absent countess, no one believes she is seeing a specter—especially since the countess is very much alive. In Albrecht's first three volumes, in fact, spectralization is always incomplete, not containing traditional ghosts. In some instances, Albrecht sets up all the elements associated with the appearance of ghosts—night, tumultuous weather, a lonely, distressed, and frightened narrator, reminders of death—but leaves out the ghosts; in other instances, she includes apparitions, but they are clearly personifications of abstractions (such as peace, death, or freedom), which the speakers welcome without fear. Often written as apostrophes, the apparition texts, including poems and the fragmentary diary, derive their spectral character from their morbid associations with death and decay, but not through an evocation of the uncanny or terrifying. Sophie Albrecht's partial spectralizations thus are not philosophical commentaries in line with the Enlightenment, but versions of her notion of the crucial importance of love in a woman's life. As Castle explains with regard to Albrecht's contemporary, Ann Radcliffe, "to be haunted . . . is to display one's powers of sympathetic imagination."[61] In the poem alluding to the voice from the riverside, the sensitive speaker wonders whether the river may offer a solution for her as it did for the lovelorn suicide, and whether the blue flood can give her peace. This spectralization is also related to Albrecht's sense of alienation as a woman. Lacking a systematic critique of patriarchy, perhaps because she was able to appropriate patriarchal discourse so adroitly when she wished, and because her genre choice and her focus on the romantic dyad enabled her to avoid social questions and reduce social pressure, but painfully aware on occasion of the lack of place in patriarchy even for a heterosexually loving woman, Albrecht turns to the theme of death, and specifically of suicide, as a relief from a variety of often unspecified problems, both political and personal. But the attention to death frequently fits with her acceptance of patriarchal definitions of women's nature when she reiterates the notion that if a woman could not love, she would not wish to live, a notion that Albrecht explores repeatedly.

In the same thematic vein, the sketch series at the end of the second poetry collection, "Fragmente aus dem Tagebuch einer Unglücklichen" "Fragments from the Diary of an Unhappy Woman," (SA85 201–316), contains a shifting mix of prose and poetry without coming to (patriarchal) closure, thus anticipating the particular version of genre-melt favored only a few years later by the Romantics; the continuation in Albrecht's third volume contains longer entries and switches to straight prose.[62] The vaguely dated fragments in the diary describe a woman's despair and prolonged depression upon having discovered that the man, known only as "he," to whom she was committed, is betraying her. Melodramatic and indefinite, without names, places, or clear relationships, the diary is interesting for its genre-mixing, open-ended form, and as an attempt to understand the conflicting forces that made suicide seem right at one moment and wrong the next. In the diary, Albrecht has located a genre without the strong conventional plot pressure of plays. As in her poetry, the socioeconomic elements of love can be minimized to allow full attention to the narrator's subjective experiences of alienation, including humiliation at being rejected by her lover,[63] an (unexplained) estrangement from her former friends,[64] a sense of being isolated in the lonely crowd of the city (224), the draining of all positive affect from places and things that had previously been valuable to her (244), a sense of severance between body and soul (230), and repeated variations on the themes of despair and the desire to die, including the feeling that an apparition of death is near and the inclination toward suicide. An entry dated May 23, for example, begins with a nature description before shifting to thoughts of death:

> More loudly rushes the river through the quiet of the night. The winds' whisper in the reeds becomes brisker—the beetle heads homeward—the nightingale ends her song.
> Cloaked in midnight darkness, sleep sinks onto weary nature, offering me also his chalice of ecstasy [*Taumelkelch*].
> Sympathetically he wipes the tears of rejected love from the wounded eye, and beckons. I follow—I come—you dear comforter of the comfortless. I come. O! ever since I have loved you, friend of the melancholy, gatekeeper of peace, . . . ever since I have longed for you, cold escort, over the path of eternity!—Death!—since then I sleep gladly. (235–36).

The paragraphs are short and sketchy, and the nature descriptions serve as introductions to explications of subjective states. As in the poetry, Albrecht insists in the fragments on the female subjectivity of the narrator; the fact that the narrative voice is female is a notable accomplishment at a time when poems and narratives about the desire for both love and death were increasingly monopolized by men. Albrecht would retain her insistence on portraying a woman's subjectivity in all her writing to the end.

Women, Genre, and Issues of Change

Since women at the beginning of the period under study here were not supposed to become writers at all, there was no genre toward which society directed them. In the first six decades of the century, their published efforts had been primarily in poetry and drama, but this had not resulted in the identification of any genre or even subgenre as characteristically feminine. And although the new increment of women's literary activity in the late eighteenth century had as its first widely noted entry a novel, La Roche's *Sternheim*, this did not instantly become the favorite genre of women writers. Once La Roche and her contemporaries had discovered a way to use the ideal of the feeling woman to validate their literary activity, when they could thus start writing in large numbers, late eighteenth-century German women suddenly—and, as it turned out, briefly—wrote in almost any genre. The limits on them were mainly associated with audience; women avoided genres with a readership that would be exclusively male. Otherwise, as long as nothing had been categorized as peculiarly theirs, they could try anything. Some women composed novels, essays, travel books, poetry, and more. Some undertook to work in the most public of literary forums, the theater and journalism. Silvia Bovenschen, convinced that the novel was the preferred eighteenth-century German woman's genre—a situation I believe only obtained after the mid-1780s—argued that the novel's domestic subject matter and emphasis on subjective feelings made it an especially accessible form to women.[65] But other genres in *Empfindsamkeit* stressed subjectivity and used domestic settings, for example, plays, verse tales, and epistolary poems. Some of these shorter genres could be published in journals, a vehicle that, by allowing anonymous contributions and by offering a testing ground even when a woman had so far created only a small body of work, played a key role in getting women started toward public writing. Bovenschen also claims the novel could incorporate the pedagogical elements that were, she argues, a recognized part of women's responsibilities (213). Again, much of that effort could also go into other forms: conduct books, plays for children, or poems for children, for example. Not the questionable aesthetic status of the novel but its female and mixed readership, along with the possibility, as Bovenschen argues, of drawing on epistolary skills approved for women, explains the gradual inclination of many eighteenth-century women writers to this form (211–12). On the other hand, the comparative lack of social resistance to women writing in this form may be connected with the novel's relatively low status in German literature; nonetheless, neither the novel itself nor any of its subgenres was conceded to women writers as their own until the nineteenth century.

Bovenschen also contends that the "open form" of the novel encouraged women to try it (216). More recent feminist literary historians examining other national literatures have theorized a resistance among women writers to closure regardless of genre.

Writing of two novels by Mme de Graffigny and Mme de Charrière, Elizabeth MacArthur notes, "The fact that these inconclusive plots are accompanied by feminist commentary on society suggests that the failure to close might represent a protest against the 'closures' generally imposed on women."[66] The writings of late eighteenth-century German women offer numerous examples, from Sophie La Roche's late autobiographical pastiches and Marianne Ehrmann's dialogues, to Sophie Albrecht's diary of a woman pondering suicide. In most cases, the absence of closure is also linked to the use of fragments and to the mixing of genres, such as poetry and prose, all practices that suggest the spirit of Romanticism.

Although for many women writers, literary growth and development could be particularly difficult to accomplish, for Sophie Albrecht, the years brought both continuity and change. The second volume of Albrecht's work had appeared in 1785. Meanwhile, she was increasingly recognized as a distinguished actress. In 1786, the year after her second book appeared, she joined the prestigious Bondini troupe at the Dresden court theater. One observer described her talent and performance: "She learns easily and correctly, so that she never makes mistakes and usually has memorized the whole play. She casts hardly a glance toward the audience, is completely at home on the stage, understands its poets perfectly, declaims correctly and beautifully; she is best at soft, tender roles. Also the category of fury is not inappropriate to her. . . ."[67]

The season in Dresden alternated with summer months in Leipzig. Albrecht was again very close to Schiller, who was living with friends first in Leipzig (or in Gohlis, a summer resort town outside the city), and then in Dresden. Schiller's one preserved letter to Sophie Albrecht, dated 17 April 1787, makes the friendliness of the relationship clear; the playwright addresses the actress affectionately as "my dear" and "my dear doctor's wife" [*meine liebe Doctorin*]. But she was also a theater colleague on whom he could rely to represent his interests. He requested her to take care of the manuscript of *Don Carlos* for him, and asked explicitly when the troupe in Leipzig planned its first production of the new play, Schiller's first in the blank verse that became the hallmark of his classical style. He also playfully asked about Albrecht's love affairs, signifying the topic with the small figure of a heart. Decades later, at the end of her life, Sophie Albrecht evidently told a friend that Schiller had finished writing *Don Carlos*, in her house.[68] Five months after his letter to her, in September 1787, at the Leipzig premier of *Don Carlos*, Sophie Albrecht played the second female role, Princess Eboli.

In 1791 and 1792, Johann Friedrich Ernst Albrecht would publish a four-volume work called *Die Familie Eboli*. While there are many suggestions of collaborations and interactions in the lives and careers of Sophie Albrecht and her husband, there are also many indications of unconventional aspects to their relationship.[69] In 1788, Sophie Albrecht's career took a turn away from the major playhouses of the country to a much smaller court theater at Schwerin, where she played the roles of naive girls—and was evidently the favorite of a Count Bassewitz; if his first name was Ferdinand, then some of her love poetry dated 1788 could be addressed to him. By now, Sophie Albrecht had been married for sixteen years, and was thirty-one years old. A friend with whom she talked at the end of her life, a man very much of the moralizing nineteenth-century bourgeoisie, said that Albrecht had regretted her early marriage almost as soon as it happened, and indicated in elaborate circumlocutions, including calling her a "female Faust," that she had carried on a series of affairs.[70] Yet, for decades, the two Albrechts shared their main artistic interests. Most nineteenth-century biographical sketches omit any reference to possible adulterous activities by either partner and, instead, primly cast the relationship in terms of wifely submissiveness, specifically asserting, for example, that Sophie Albrecht accepted her first professional stage engagement only with her husband's approval.[71] However that may have been, it is clear that when she joined the Grossmann troupe J. F. E. Albrecht accompanied her. Schiller, for instance, commented about meeting him in 1784: "The doctor is also a dear valuable friend of mine."[72] In the years since this early acquaintance, Dr. Albrecht's literary production had grown considerably. In connection with Sophie's stay in Schwerin, it is perhaps significant that between 1778 and Dr. Albrecht's death in 1814, the only two consecutive years with no publications from him were 1787 and 1788, when his wife was apparently with Count Bassewitz. But starting in 1789, Dr. Albrecht averaged three works per year for seven years, beginning the series with publishers in the geographically disparate locations of Leipzig, Berlin, and Vienna. In 1790, his publishers were in the two main cities of Saxony: Leipzig and Dresden. Sophie Albrecht was probably back in Saxony by then, too, although no one mentions that exactly.

In 1791 came the peak of her career as a poet, with the publication of her collected works, including the previous two volumes and a new third one. Albrecht was the only eighteenth-century German woman to have her collected works published in her lifetime. Three years earlier, the journalist A. F. Geißler, Jr., had listed Sophie Albrecht among the best women writers of the time. Geißler was not a disinterested commentator, for he went on to say that since the first two books of her poetry were no longer available, he was about to announce a new edition, which would include a new third volume and revisions of the earlier work. He claimed that Albrecht had left the publication entirely to him.[73] The talk about revisions was a standard ploy to convince anyone who already had a copy to buy another, but such a tactic would not have been very necessary in Albrecht's case, since few copies of her first volumes had gone into circulation. Despite Geißler's authoritative tone, however, he was not in charge of the publication of her collected works when they appeared in 1791. Volumes one and two were reprinted, unrevised, including the original subscription lists, and a new third volume was added. This edition, published by the highly regarded Carl Christian Richter of Dresden, is the source of most surviving copies of Sophie Albrecht's poetry.[74]

The best poems in the third volume are again about love, and Albrecht once more found new aspects of it to examine. Like the second, the third volume contains poetry and the diary fragments, omitting the prose idylls and plays that had been included in the first volume. The third volume is more careful (two years after the outbreak of the French Revolution, but before the Terror) about quasi-political odes or aphorisms. Love was a safe topic from the perspective of the state. The poems beginning "When your kiss hovers on my lips," "Sweet torture in my heart," "O do not call it faked," "While I am thinking of songs for you," and "Ah, how warm I feel—how warm" all appeared in this volume, along with many more. A poem about disappointment, for example, brilliantly reverses the usual love poetry addressed to the moon. "An den Mond, den 9ten März" "To the Moon, March 9th" unmasks the moon's deceitfulness. The speaker sees the moon as a hypocrite and herself as a fool for having been taken in. Indirectly, as she builds her case against the moon, she also describes the passionate affair that is now over. She notes the qualities of purity, passion, and sympathy that she had attributed to the hypocritical moon, and the effect on the lovers:

> Wir freuten uns des hohen Himmels Zeugen,
>   Der nur für uns so freundlich niedersah,
> Und küßten keuscher in der Strahlentrauung,
>   Und glaubten uns dem Himmel selber nah.

[We were happy to have the high heavenly witness / who looked down in such a friendly way only for us / and we kissed more chastely in the moonbeam-wedding / and believed ourselves to be closer to heaven itself.]

Again Albrecht presents an instance of love as virtuous and chaste though irregular, as her word invention "*Strahlentrauung*" "Moonbeam-wedding" suggests. Again she uses conventional labels to endorse an affair that the labels are conventionally intended to condemn.

The description of happiness sets up the decisive change to her present pain and sadness, not because of wounded virtue but because the lover is gone. She seeks solace from the moon and discovers how untouched the moon is: "Ha! Falscher! Kalt und ruhig blickst du nieder, / Kein Wölkchen trübt die freche Stirne Dir" "Ha! False one! Cold and quiet, you look down, / not one cloudlet darkens your presumptuous brow." The moon represents the audacity, falseness, and unfeelingness of the formerly beloved man. Subjective alienation, Schacht points out, is perspectival, which is to say that a situation or its context can look entirely different to various observers and to the same observer at various times. The subjective alienation described by Marianne Ehrmann centers around the perception of injustice available to one group of observers, a hypersensitive few, but not to others, the healthy but insensitive majority. The subjective alienation described by Sophie Albrecht centers around attunement to desire and its satisfaction, as perceived by an individual speaker whose attitudes and feelings change depending on the circumstances. When the speaker's desires, which are usually sexual, but in some instances cultural or political, are thwarted, whether through social intervention, as in *Theresgen,* through some change in the beloved, or through undefined repression, alienation results, as described, for example, in the moon-chastising poem.

Once the lover has left her, the speaker sees the whole situation differently, with the moon as a cold planet where, as on earth, the tears of the virtuous flow along with the blood of the innocent ("ich seh dich wie du bist./ Ein kalter Erdball, wo, wie hier auf Erden,/ Der Tugend Thräne, Blut der Unschuld fließt." "I see you as you are. / A cold planet, where, as here on earth, / the tears of virtue and blood of innocence flow"). With these references to virtue and innocence, she is touching again two major motifs for women, here seen as bitterly painful. The process of subjective alienation reverses the interpretation of everything she had imagined before:

> Was meine Phantasie einst Lächeln nannte,
> Sind kahle Berge, wo der Müde sinkt.
> Dort rauchen Scheiterhaufen, schrecken Rabensteine,
> Wo man dem Fanatismus Opfer bringt.[75]

[What my fantasy once called a smile / are barren mountains, where the tired sink down. / There the stake smokes and ravens' rocks strike terror, / where sacrifices are brought to fanaticism.]

Now she is just as fanciful in the direction of alienation as she had been toward sympathy before. From here until the end, three stanzas, the poem looses momentum. Nevertheless, the main device of the poem, the reversal of traditional poems addressed to the moon, is apt and effective. Sophie Albrecht had continued to grow as a poet over the ten years since her first volume appeared. The changes that came next brought her to new places and to new genres.

Unraveling Marriage and the Reinterpretation of a Fairy Tale

Not long after the successful publication of her collected works, Sophie Albrecht's acting career began to decline. After appearances in Prague and Mannheim, she went to Hamburg to be a guest performer at the "Theater am Gänsemarkt" "Theater at the Goose Market" but received no regular appointment there. Still, the move north was momentous,[76] for it led Albrecht briefly to a new kind of theatrical career. In 1796, she and her husband, who was by now a popular writer for the stage, took over the direction of the national theater in Altona. Sophie commemorated the event with her "Antrittsrede bei Eröffnung des Nationaltheaters in Altona am 1. Sept. 1796" "Opening Speech at the Premiere of the National Theater in Altona on Sept. 1, 1796." That same year, the Albrechts also found time to publish a book of stories called *Trümmer der Vergangenheit* "Ruins of the Past."

The next year, when she was forty-one, Sophie Albrecht and her husband quit the national theater and were evidently divorced.[77] A striking number of eighteenth-century women writers got divorces, including Sophie Friederike Seyler, Juliane von Mudersbach, Auguste von Goldstein, Elisa von der Recke, Johanne Friederike Lohmann, Elisabeth von Stägemann, Juliane von Krüdener, Johanne Elisabeth Gregorius, Margarete Liebeskind, Emilie von Berlepsch, and presumably, Marianne Ehrmann.[78] The actress Karoline Dorothea Ackermann Unzer, who had quit the stage at twenty-six to marry a professor, was divorced from him eight years later. Susanne Bandemer, Henriette Hendel Schütz, and Albrecht's friend Henriette von Montenglaut were all divorced twice. Anna Louisa Karsch's divorce in 1748, the first in Silesia,[79] was followed by the divorces of her daughter, Caroline Klencke (1780), and granddaughter, Helmina von Chezy (in 1801). Early in the 1790s, the marriages of Elise Bürger (1792), Charlotte Diede (1794), and Karoline von Wolzogen (1794) all ended in divorce. So, even before the famous women of the Romantics who had their marriages legally dissolved—Dorothea Schlegel (1798), Sophie Mereau (1801), Caroline Schelling (1803), and Sophie Bernhardi (1807)—Sophie Albrecht would not have been alone among women writers in going through a divorce.[80]

As already suggested by Marianne Ehrmann's treatment of the matter in *Amalie*, divorce was a topic of increasingly open and vigorous debate. An anonymous essay in Wieland's *Teutscher Merkur* in 1793, published amidst the social turmoil of the French Revolution, claimed to describe the ease of divorce in Protestant Germany, especially in Prussia:

> here marriage is considered simply to be a contract, which can, according to the pleasure of the participants, be terminated or renewed. Because love moved them to submit to this ceremony, so there can be no further healthy results to be expected if the cause of it has ceased; the intention of marriage is just as much destroyed as would happen through the death of one or the other members of it, and both should be considered as widowed and have complete freedom to enter new commitments again. In the whole Protestant part of Germany divorces are granted without much difficulty if one of the parties can be accused of adultery or of debauchery disadvantageous to the property conditions of the other party.[81]

The year after this greatly overstated description appeared, the idea of divorce was approved for the first time in literature for girls.[82]

While Sophie Albrecht's life was changing, so was, very abruptly, her writing. The poet, who had written confidently and brilliantly of love, decided not to convert her experience of divorce into literature. In fact, after 1792, she published no more poetry, turning, instead, to short novels and stories of ghosts and the supernatural. In 1797, in Altona, she published a Gothic horror tale, *Das höfliche Gespenst* "The Polite Ghost." Another edition of the same story appeared at the same time under another title, *Legenden* "Legends," also with the publisher Bechtold in Altona. In 1799, she published another spooky story, *Graumännchen, oder die Burg Rabenbühl, eine Geistergeschichte altdeutschen Ursprungs* "Little Gray Man, or Castle Rabenbühl; A Ghost Story of Old German Origin." It got enough attention to be reviewed by the *Allgemeine Deutsche Bibliothek* and in a literary newspaper published in Erlangen.[83] As the new century began, Sophie Albrecht published another collection of legends. Five years later, in a move reminiscent of the republication of Marianne Ehrmann's *Amalie* as *Antonie von Warnstein*, Albrecht republished her story of the polite ghost under the new (third) title, *Ida von Duba*. Because it thus appeared in three editions, under three titles, this short novel was evidently an important one to Albrecht.

Albrecht constructed in *Ida von Duba* a world in which men are displaced to the margin; she argued that the image of the past was distorted by war and battle accounts featuring men but leaving out women. *Ida von Duba*, then, was to be the story of what happened after the battle, what the widow did after the hero was dead. Albrecht laid claim here to the untold stories of women and to their relationships to each other, and she hints at the distortions introduced when only men and male values are taken seriously. The tale is set along the Moldau after the Thirty Years War. A young woman, Katherine, fiancée of an officer who has died in battle, retreats from Prague to her country home on the Moldau to grieve, seeking especially the melancholy consolation of long walks at night by moonlight. An elderly aunt, a nun who had also lost a lover and then entered a convent, joins Katherine for a while and enjoys walking with her, but always insists anxiously on returning to the house before dark. When Katherine tries to reassure her that there are no dangers, the aunt responds with questions. Has Katherine seen no one on her walks? Has she never been approached? With a widow yearning to see her dead lover, a nun disappointed in love, moonlit walks, and an atmosphere of rising anxiety, the scene is set for the ghost's entry into the story.

Katherine, her curiosity aroused by her aunt's questions, begins to take more note of an old chapel along her usual way. It contains the graves of the von Duba family. The contrasting stones and inscriptions for a mother and her daughter lead Katherine to make inquiries, but to no avail. Not long after, on the eve of Easter, Katherine decides to spend the night watching beside the memorial she has erected for her husband. The tale shows Katherine and her aunt enacting constant and never fulfillable desire for their dead men.

For brief moments, female friendship appears to offer an alternative to this unending desire. While the young widow is keeping her vigil, she sees a beautiful woman in white, with many maidens attending her and one old woman who bears all the signs of being present against her will. Although Katherine and the beautiful woman become acquainted, the woman in white reveals almost nothing about herself. One evening, however, while the two women and, some distance away, their maids are walking together, Oda, Katherine's maid, beguiles the other into mentioning an identifying name for her mistress. Although she is too far off to hear their conversation, Ida instantly knows her maid's mistake and makes a face of such extreme and unexpected anger that Katherine cannot ignore it. She decides to find out more about her nocturnal friend, whom she does not recognize as a ghost. After many efforts that lead nowhere, she speaks with a priest who is able to direct her to a monastery containing an ancient manuscript, "The Polite Ghost"—one of the three titles Albrecht used for the book—about Ida von Duba—another of the titles.

At this point, the text shifts from describing the ghost's persuasively realistic visits to recounting the apparition's human past and explaining why she now haunts Katherine. Ida von Duba, a beautiful woman, was wonderful in every respect except for her extreme haughtiness and utter lack of feelings. When the day came for Ida to marry, she ordered her old nurse to come carry her train, but the nurse, shocked by Ida's peremptory manner, became too ill to comply. Then Ida had a bold and arrogant inspiration. She persuaded her proud and wealthy father to order her mother, who had been declared insane at Ida's earlier connivance, to perform this lowly service. The bridegroom was on his way, and the bride, her father, and her maids were just leaving the mansion when a horrible storm erupted, with terrific winds lashing the banners of the groom's party and sweeping the wedding wreath from Ida's head, even though it was weighted down with jewels. Lightening struck, and Ida was dead. Her arrogance, which she shared with her father, but which was less acceptable in her, became excessive when she made the older woman become her servant as she was about to take a husband. As befit a novel that claimed to be recovering the stories of women, Ida was not allowed to establish a relationship with another man while she behaved in such ways to women. The extremity of the daughter's depravity and of the father's (incestuously) misguided admiration for her is signaled by the next section of the novel, the section that most thoroughly draws on Gothic conventions of horror.[84] Ida's corpse is laid out in wedding finery. Mourners, paid to keep watch, flee as rumors spread that Ida is alive. Poor people who look at the corpse bemoan the burial of expensive jewels that could mean so much to them. When her body sits up in the casket, the burial is rushed to completion. The coffin is opened once more to dampen wild rumors, but the sight of Ida's decay is so horrible it has the opposite effect.

And there is further punishment awaiting her. The monk who recorded these events in the ancient manuscript that Katherine reads also reported how he became Ida's scribe. The passage shows how carefully Albrecht worked to establish a wild and mysterious mood for the events of her novel:

> Storm arose dreadfully, trilled the flags, shook the high trees, struck their anxiously murmuring branches against the windows of my cell, and curled the rustling greenery around the graves at the foot of our walls. I had often heard storm—it had already run through my locks, as now through the trees and dry leaves; then too I was alone on my cot; but the thousandfold terrors I felt only in this terrible night! Suddenly the doors of my cell flew creakily open; a light like sulfur danced around every object of my chamber; only my little altar stood dark—then there was a stirring like anxious groaning coming up to me, then the storm whirled more powerfully—then the sulfur flame flickered higher, and *Ida*, dreadfully enclosed in the blue light, stood in gruesome form before my fixed eyes; woe! woe! she called with a tone that I hope will be spared all fleshly ears—it shook the marrow in my bones: "I have been judged! restless wandering until I find a woman, more evil and proud than I. Write down, old man! my story, write according to the purest truth! I must tell you to do this; it is the first hour of my humiliation!"[85]

Nature appears at its most independent and unpredictable here, as suggested even by omission of an article before the first references to the storm. The world is in menacing motion. The weird weather fits the uncanny events, reported—to give them credibility—by a solid, reliable eyewitness, a monk. The closest Sophie Albrecht comes to the image of woman as victim of seduction is in this tale in which a woman is condemned to seduce another woman to evil—and fails. In Albrecht's love poems, a man might jilt or disappoint a woman, but the initial relationship was not produced by a male seduction plot, and the female seduction plot in *Ida von Duba* miscarries, too. After reading the disturbing manuscript, Katherine decides to leave her solitary life and go first to Prague and then to Saxony, where she dies a few years later. But Ida presumably "lives" on and, in this sense, the novel avoids closure.

This is a Gothic tale using many of the conventions popular then in both England and Germany. It is not, however, the story of an innocent girl trapped in a dreary castle by a wicked man. Nor, in the process of being scary, does it pretend to explain rationally every seemingly supernatural incident.[86] Instead, the short novel is a revision of the Snow White fairy tale with a proud and rich father, mother, and daughter living in a castle until, in their competition for this prized locus awarded to a few women privileged within patriarchy, one of the women gets the other expelled. In Albrecht's retelling, the woman who retains power in the castle is not the (step)mother but the daughter. To enlarge her dowry, the daughter plots against her brothers as well, telling her father they meant to murder him, and preventing any careful examination of the charges by begging for clemency for the offenders—exile for the brothers, and imprisonment in the castle for her intelligent mother. The daughter, who deliberately overthrows her mother's place in her father's affections and in the home is the wicked one, not the mother, the only one able to decipher Ida's intrigues. It is the daughter who then arranges a final humiliation of her mother, carrying her bridal train. Furthermore, the arrival of her prince charming, selected solely for his wealth and status—through him Ida will become a princess—is the start not of a happy life, but of a restless death for the bride.

In her last encounter with the monk, Ida tells him his manuscript should be shown to all wicked daughters who forget that they owe their deepest respect to their mothers. The forty-eight-year-old Albrecht seems interested in chastening younger women. To the extent that a moral is present—and it is only flimsily attached to the tale—it demands respect for older women (and distrusts younger ones), and it condemns marriages of convenience. *Ida von Duba*, with its undertones of incest (the daughter replacing the mother), is not about love in the way that Albrecht's poetry had been; because of that, it can be about marriage. None of the marriages represented in the tale are successful as a site for an ongoing fulfilling relationship between a man and a woman. Reversing the pattern of much of her poetry, which addressed love but not marriage, the Gothic tale was a genre in which Sophie Albrecht could write about marriage, while omitting love.

Different as Albrecht's *Ida von Duba* is from Ehrmann's *Amalie*, both are, emphatically, books about women. Sophie Albrecht justified this wild new kind of novel in her preface, where she identified her readers as people who did not feel comfortable with their present lives: "For souls drawn back into the past by some relationship in their earthly career that cannot completely fit the role that has been allotted to them here, this was written."[87] This is not the same kind of interest in the present and in promoting change that characterized Marianne Ehrmann. Yet, without addressing immediate social issues, Sophie Albrecht expressed dissatisfaction with the status quo. As Karin Wurst notes, "One could speculate that, in general, interest in the Gothic was a reaction against the obsessive focus on the domestic sphere and its value system. The Gothic seemed to emerge in the heyday of the domestic sentimental novel."[88]

Albrecht anticipated that critics would not appreciate the book, but reminded them that many other people, equally valid as individuals, were more concerned with their feelings than with logic, which she connects with maleness in the person of a literary critic:

> When the literary critic, when the more enlightened free thinker calls this excessive enthusiasm, let him consider that among the millions who weave around him are millions of equally free creatures, who have an independent ego as much as he, and whose opinion, whose inner feelings he has the right neither to judge nor to control. Those who feel with me will not find [the book excessive, but] will discover the spirit, which lies in these pages, and will find there nourishment for feelings, which—even if others do not recognize them—have precisely the greatest value for a person to whom they are a need.[89]

To Albrecht, the claim that the feelings to which her book appeals are not common increases their value. Albrecht suggests here an aesthetic code somewhat like Ehrmann's in her night vision. And it is a code that women might be especially likely to identify with. Not trained as critics, not educated as central members of the Enlightenment, women readers had different tastes than the critics advocated.

Terry Castle argues that "the eighteenth century in a sense 'invented the uncanny': that the very psychic and cultural transformations that led to the subsequent glorification of the period as an age of reason or enlightenment—the aggressively rationalist imperatives of the epoch—also produced, like a kind of toxic side effect, a new human experience of strangeness, anxiety, bafflement, and intellectual impasse."[90] For women, the Enlightenment was often also an experience of exclusion and alienation in itself, as Baldinger's autobiography showed. Sophie Albrecht reworks that alienation as a demand for expressions of the irrational. The pages of the copy of *Ida von Duba* preserved now in the university library in Göttingen are dark from the fingers of the many readers who borrowed it from the lending library to which it previously belonged. The only surprise is that Sophie Albrecht did not write more tales in this mode. When in 1808, she published a volume called *Romantische Dichtung aus der älteren christlichen Kirche* "Romantic Literature from the early Christian Church," she used an impersonal narrator who, in a tone of simple piety, recounts legends about miracles associated with various sites of the early church. The atmospherics of the Gothic are missing.

In the ten years since her apparent divorce, Sophie Albrecht had earned her living partly by writing, but she had not stopped using her other talents. In 1801, a work appeared that was connected with another source of her income. It was *Der Kummer verschmähter Liebe; als Declamationsstück mit musikalischer Begleitung des Claviers oder Fortepianos bearbeitet* "The Pain of rejected Love; for Declamation with musical Accompaniment on the Piano or Fortepiano." In 1798, Albrecht had left the failed theater in Altona to stay briefly in Hamburg with Schröder, the erstwhile mentor of Elisa von der Recke. Then she became an itinerant actress, traveling back to the northeastern region she had visited as a young wife, venturing as far as the border of Russia. Eventually, she left acting for her old sideline, declamation. Dressed in a black gown with a white veil, she made appearances in the cities and on the populated islands of the Baltic coast before turning south again toward home, toward Thuringia and environs. In Weimar, where she visited the grave of her former friend Schiller, the aging Duke Carl August rewarded her performance with a gift of two ducats.[91]

Meanwhile, Dr. Albrecht seems to have resumed his medical practice, while maintaining occasional contact with the theater. After a possible bout as a Jacobin, he undertook the intense publication of medical books, all printed in Hamburg. Fourteen titles appeared in four years, many of them about sexuality or about sex-related problems. In the nineteenth century, they were by far his most durable works, with numerous editions. In 1814, he died during a typhus epidemic at age sixty-two. Sophie, who was fifty-seven, had more than a quarter of a century yet to live. She returned north to Hamburg and Altona.

From Legends to Cookbooks

For many women, advancing age meant toiling anew to find a means for survival. Sophie Albrecht's last two decades were characteristically female in their increasing poverty and loneliness, as the fragmentary available information shows. Among the few documentary sources in which Sophie Albrecht wrote about herself is a letter composed in 1816 to an old friend, a man who had subscribed to her second volume back in 1785, Dr. Schütte in Bremen; of everything that she once had, she told Schütte, nothing remained but memories. Yet, she condensed those memories into two sentences and then, not withdrawing into the past, went on to congratulate the Bremen theater for hiring one of Hamburg's actresses.[92]

The aging actress was not completely isolated; she continued to use her theatrical prerogative to have unusual friends, such as Doctor Salomon Ludwig (Levi) Steinheim,[93] a doctor for poor members of the Jewish community in Altona. A short note he sent her in 1817 shows that he enjoyed her intelligent company. It may have been around this time, also, that someone arranged free admission for her to the theater; she was very grateful, though not excessively humble.[94] Then for a decade, from 1819 to 1828, while Sophie Albrecht was in her sixties, documentation is missing. In 1828, she made a contribution to a newspaper.

A letter written four years later by Henriette von Montenglaut shows that life was becoming more difficult for Albrecht, now seventy-five. Montenglaut had tried to arrange a pension for her by asking various theater people to contribute. The total amount, from a theater in Braunschweig, was three talers per month, which Montenglaut hoped would be augmented by support from Hannover and Dresden, too. Along with this news, she sent Albrecht a package containing a skirt made from an old coat, a pair of shoes that were too small for her but would be too large for Sophie, a homemade shawl, and a scarf that could be bartered. And she thought about coming to live with her old friend because inflation in Braunschweig was making it too expensive.[95] Six years later, Henriette von Montenglaut died in Prague. Sophie Albrecht lived on.

Very late, she devised another canny way to support herself with writing: she published a cookbook. It appeared in Erfurt, with the imprint of Hilsenberg, a publisher her husband had used long before. Hilsenberg published the book under two titles, presumably for two markets, one the *Erfurter Cookbook for the Middle-Class Kitchen* and the other the *Thuringian Cookbook for the Middle-Class Kitchen*.[96] The prologue shows that Albrecht was still an outspoken, lively woman, capable of the unexpected, here in the form of comments about men that are more reminiscent of Marianne Ehrmann's writing than her own previous work. She writes:

> Men are selfish creatures. We are pleasing to them in the array of the ballroom, where they woo us; we become wives. Now they stop liking

finery; now, using expressions of wisdom they demand that the young woman carry out the duties of the housewife in deep seriousness. And the philosophy *of the stomach* especially asserts itself among husbands. "What are you cooking today, dear child?" is the question at breakfast, because men are all lid lifters, even though they don't want to admit it; and if the wife wants to see a nice friendly face, then she must apply all her attention to the noble kitchen.[97]

This sarcastic tone introduces a collection of clearly written, well-organized recipes that sound sensible, simple, and tasty. Evidently the book was a success; it continued to be reprinted until at least 1865.

But it did not make the author wealthy. The last preserved letter from Sophie Albrecht is dated 22 April 1839, and is addressed to an unnamed woman friend who had sent a letter and some money. Albrecht was grateful to have been remembered and thankful for the money. She explained that her income was arranged chiefly by a man named Friedrich Clemens Gerke, who, following in the path of Henriette von Montenglaut, had collected money for her from a variety of sources and now paid it out to her weekly. In addition, a friend named Schütze, in Braunschweig, sent her a ducat every month. Other people, however, no longer sent anything. She concluded with a reference to her long-standing fondness for drinking tea sweetened with sugar, a luxury she did not want to give up in her last years.[98]

On 16 November 1840, one day short of her eighty-second birthday, Sophie Albrecht died in a Hamburg hospital for the poor. There was no money to pay for a headstone until Gerke published a small anthology of her poetry to raise funds. Not wishing to be too closely associated with this bold woman—it was he who called her a female Faust—Gerke published the anthology as Friedrich Clemens, without his surname. The subscribers came mostly from the theater world. The book they received contained much of Albrecht's inferior sentimental poetry, but a reasonable sample of her good work as well.

One of the poems chosen, "An den Todesvogel" "To the Bird of Death," bears a surprising resemblance to Edgar Allen Poe's later poem "The Raven." The speaker contrasts the usual fearfulness and awfulness of the raven with her favorable feelings toward it as a harbinger of the death she longs for. Not only is the choice of the raven to American readers a reminder of Poe, but so is the use of a refrain, otherwise not typical of Albrecht. The speaker's longing for death is repeated in each of the three stanzas, including the last:

> Siehe mich voll Sehnsucht lauschen,
> Auf dein dumpfes Sterbeschwirren!
> Ha!—ich höre Flügel-Rauschen
> Seh' dich kreisend um mich irren.—
> > Komm, o Friedensrabe!
> > Rufe mich zum Grabe![99]
>
> [See me listening, full of longing / to your muffled death whir! / Ha! I hear wings rustling / see you stray circling around me.— Come, o raven of peace! / Call me to the grave!]

The poem, originally published in 1785, aims for a feeling of the macabre and mysterious but is too short and too uninvolved to be quite successful. Still, the theme, the use of a refrain, and the word constructions, such as *Sterbeschwirren*, indicate yet again the creativity Albrecht evinced in her poetry.

Sophie Albrecht's writing, especially her poetry, probably fits more closely with the late eighteenth-century mainstream concept of literature than that of any other German woman writer of her time. Measured by the dominant elite standards of her day, her diction was excellent, her choice of topics was exemplary (also innovative and daring for a woman), and she respected composition as a craft, probably indicated not just by her correctness, but also by the many revisions detectable between her first books of poetry and the much later Clemens anthology, although there is no documentation about the exact source of those emendations. Unlike other women poets of her time, who, in the manner of Philippine Engelhard-Gatterer, deliberately relied on sentiments shared with readers to offset what were considered technical irregularities, Albrecht offered her poems with few or no prefatory instructions to her readers. She chose a more aesthetic and less didactic mode of writing than many of her female contemporaries, including La Roche, Engelhard-Gatterer, and Ehrmann. Of all the women writers of late eighteenth-century Germany, Sophie Albrecht is one of the rare ones for whom education was a topic of no special interest. She did not discuss it in her preserved letters, nor dwell on it in her novels, nor linger over it in her poetry.

Closer comparison with Philippine Engelhard-Gatterer makes Albrecht's distinctive accomplishment as a poet clearer. Not absorbed, like Engelhard, in her own biography, Albrecht could write more effectively than Engelhard on traditional poetic topics, such as death. While placing less overt emphasis than Engelhard on herself as an exceptional woman, she could still, of course, write from within the position of being a woman, as her best love poems show.

Because Engelhard was concerned with her public reception, she tried hard to please her readers with her propriety—even though she valiantly denied that pleasing concerned her. Albrecht, on the other hand, was more willing to write in ways that deviated from what society sanctioned for proper women, as represented by how rarely she made public statements of self-defense; Albrecht seems to have published no autobiographical sketches and few words in prose addressed directly to her audiences.

Sophie Albrecht used the notion of the validity of her feelings, a notion on which Sophie von La Roche had also drawn, for a radical new purpose: to redefine passion as virtuous. This strategy was powerful enough to release Albrecht from conventional morality, but not from the pressures of plot, which connected love with marriage (or the intention to marry) and marriage with upward mobility options for women. Only when she chose genres that evaded marriage narratives could she explore her new discourse of love as the interweaving of both sensual and emotional passions. In lyric poetry and in fragmentary diary form, she produced representations of love quite distinctive for her time, love between two partners relating to each other as near equals, love that empowered and emboldened the woman—perhaps even more than the man. Far more than Friedrich Schlegel in his androcentric novel of love, *Lucinde*, Albrecht shows love as mutually enriching in body and spirit, and, even when love stumbles, Albrecht shows it inspiring the loving woman, not the man, to literature. A woman's subjectivity and creativity are validated in Albrecht's writings, even though this subjectivity may get the woman into difficulty and lead her to suicide or its brink. Indeed, Sophie Albrecht infused a woman's subjectivity even into the most utilitarian of texts: the cookbook.

7

Conclusion: The Contesting Discourses of the Needle and the Quill

OPERATING WITHIN THE SLIPPERY UNIVERSALISM OF THE ENLIGHTENment, Friderika Baldinger had been unable to establish standing for herself as a legitimate writing subject. Truncating her text, reinterpreting "female" experience in educational terms, and paying obeisance to better educated and ostensibly brighter men had not sufficed. Her contemporaries who were less intent on the Enlightenment rubric were far more successful in smuggling themselves onto the podium of literature by using the more flexible, less prestigious banner of *Empfindsamkeit*. Within its terms, they could write in lyric, epic, and dramatic genres, as well as in mixed forms. They composed verse tales and love lyrics, epistolary novels and ghost stories, tragic *Singspiele* and comedies. They also wrote autobiographical texts, but not necessarily in the overt terms that Baldinger had attempted, trying verse and pastiche instead. Their works typically assert an explicitly female self and often a discontented one. After an early phase, mostly before 1770, when this self was represented in a religious context, came two secular strands, an *Empfindsamkeit* of sympathy, which stressed shared emotional responses and an *Empfindsamkeit* of alienation, which emphasized the social and psychological isolation of those who are most sensitive and artistic.

Indeed, alienation, especially the kind Schacht dubs "objective alienation," abounded among eighteenth-century women of the educated middle class.[1] It is located in contexts that are "social-structural, or, more fully and explicitly, socio-politico-economico-cultural" (29), and can be identified by examining "what the individuals and groups in question actually *do* in relation to the nature of some existing social *structure,* regardless of how they may perceive and feel about both what they do and this structure" (30). Thus, objective alienation can occur even though the alienated group does not feel itself estranged. Of course, it is also possible for subjective and objective forms of alienation to coincide, with the subjective alienation helping to draw our attention to the objective. Women writers in eighteenth-century Germany varied as to their own perception of estrangement or belonging, but there are many indications that on an objective level, in terms of discordant social relations, they were alienated from the dominant regulations and discourse of their culture. Male anti-mentoring behavior toward aspiring women writers is one example of a pattern of men providing disincentives to women so that they would not pursue full participation in the creation, critique, and use of culture, in this case literary culture, otherwise highly regarded in the period. Friderika Baldinger's autobiography exhibits how hard it was for a woman on her own to get an education, to justify writing, and then to excuse herself for publishing within the terms of the Enlightenment. Sophie La Roche's prescriptive writings and autobiographical sketches reiterate women's almost total exclusion from the scholarliness that male writers could enjoy. Philippine Engelhard-Gatterer's poems reveal the stress a woman felt between respectability and writing, and documents about her demonstrated the peculiar reception accorded to women writers, although for men respectability—though not necessarily wealth—could well accompany a literary career. Marianne Ehrmann's clash with Cotta illustrates the struggle women had to retain control even of their own work. The discouragements that artists, male and female, confronted were often vast and oppressive, but women artists had these challenges and more. In short, many women resisted the social steering to which they were subjected, and they contested, usually not wholly, but in significant part, their exclusion from functions that were clearly meaningful and often fulfilling to the men who performed them. Visiting a library in Mannheim, Sophie La Roche wrote, "I thought with envy of the good fortune of the men, who from their youth are destined and trained for a regular job and the enjoyment of this wealth [of their intellectual talents]: there I was with the feeling of a person who knows the qualities and the thousand uses of gold and silver, has read their natural history, sees the treasure of the fleet from Peru gathered, without being able to call even a sliver of all the gold and silver bars his own."[2] Yet, she was not able to convert this envy into a program for change. This statement combines both the subjective dissatisfaction elicited by gender-based discrimination and the objective alienation evident in the systematic discrepancies between women's options and men's.[3]

The gender-differentiated public reception of women writers is a clear instance of this socio-politico-economico-cultural stress, since it exercised tactics likely to lower women's self-esteem, brake their drive for accomplishment, and induce feelings of estrangement from their society. The *Almanach der Belletristen für's Jahr 1782* provides an example, even though it appeared, at first glance, to endorse the idea of women writing: "Germany also has women who write *belles lettres,* as France, England, etc., have always had and still have. To be sure their names are not so commonly known as Babet, Ninon Lenclos, Mistress Brook etc., but they can still become so!"[4] The achievements being singled out, however, are little more than variations on the usual feminine accomplishments, presented in a patriotic context: "It is praiseworthy, when ladies can do something more than write an unorthographic love letter, make and accept visits, trill a little song, etc. [It is better] when they learn a little of the sciences with the heart and head, when they try to get beyond the mediocre and be an honor to their Fatherland!" (5–6). The authors, with Rousseau, assessed women as lacking the talents that were necessary for significant literary achievement: "Even if, according to Rousseau, they lack all the qualities which distinguish us men in this regard, 'that heavenly fire which heats and inflames the soul, that encompassing devouring genius, that burning loquacity that sublime verve which communicates its enchantingness to our innermost hearts,'—still any lady who tries to become more than her sisters must be worthy to us." This is the negative, crippling interpretation of Rousseau's thoughts on women, which most men (and many women) read in his writing. Permitting women to try to achieve something valued in society does not obscure the presupposition that whatever they accomplished was bound to be inferior. In fact, Sophie Albrecht was his proof.

> So it is with *Madam Albrecht!* her poems, which she has had published now and then in anthologies, are, if one looks at them with critical eyes, mediocre; expression, tone are commonplace—but what of it! The noble, sensitive heart of the woman protrudes visibly everywhere, her will should become deed to us, and our wish is that Germany gets plenty of these good industrious women. (6)

In the case of a woman, it was almost enough to have a noble, feeling heart. Even though her poetry might be mediocre, the proof that Germany had women poets, too, was a patriotic good. Pronouncements such as this reinforced the subjective alienation of women from cultural production, and help us observe objective alienation in action: elements of the dominant masculine discourse trivializing women's participation in literary life. Indeed, uncontrollability and impersonality are two of the basic aspects of alienation. "There is an absence of control . . . and . . . a significant sort of separation here, between what one is as a person and what one does as an agent," Schacht notes, and he continues, "The crucial point is the fact that the character and occurrence of the actions involved in the kind of economic activity in question are explicable without any references to the personal identities of those who perform them."⁵ For women writers as women, their use of the quill was still contested.

What happened next was no improvement. At the very moment that the first version of Sophie Albrecht's *Ida von Duba* was being published (1797), the movement now known as Romanticism was about to begin. Its opening is typically marked in German literary history by such events at the end of the 1790s as the publication of Friedrich Schlegel's programmatic novel *Lucinde* and the joint Schlegel-Tieck translations of Shakespeare. This is when, although more women wrote more books in this decade than ever before, the proportion of them who were young decreased ominously. By now, the French Revolution had brought to Germans new ideas, a new sense of daring, and a new conservatism, including the notion that if bloody internal upheavals were to be avoided in Germany and if "natural" relations among people were to be preserved, then women, in particular, should not overstep the limits that philosophers detected for them.

It is possible to understand the French Revolution as one people's response to the bold promises made but not kept by the Enlightenment. These promises, condensed into the revolutionary phrase, liberty, equality, and fraternity, had not been—even in the most abstract of their possible meanings—extended across all socioeconomic classes of European (or American) society. Nor did the ideals apply equally to members of all races, as the behavior of Europeans overseas, the little documented treatment of isolated foreigners in Europe from other regions of the world—including black women and men living in eighteenth-century Germany—and the white American treatment of Black and Native Americans amply attested. Yet, perhaps it was women such as Friderika Baldinger, who were most aware, in complicated and convoluted ways, of their material (physical and ideological) exclusion from ideals that claimed to be universal but omitted whole categories of people—as the very term "fraternity" made clear. In Germany, women in culturally active layers of the aristocracy, and in much of the educated middle class, had read *The Spectator* and Rousseau. They knew the writings of Lessing and other major exponents of the *Auf-*

klärung, such as Moses Mendelssohn. And they recognized that when it came to practical applications of Enlightenment values, women had been left out. Romanticism and the philosophers on whom Romanticism relied, especially Fichte, offered an explanation for that omission in marriage, which is the "natural" condition of women. Fichte contended that a married woman "cannot rationally will to be free. Her relation to her husband being publicly known, she must, moreover, will to appear to all whom she knows as utterly subjected to, and utterly lost in, the man of her choice."[6]

Confronting this (wishful) thinking, La Roche's bargain of enablement had run its course and was not suited to the new terms of debate. Furthermore, male Romantics had commandeered the literarily productive aspects of emotions and intuition for themselves, even while continuing to insist that women were more emotional than rational. Lack of good education did not prepare women to confront the new challenges presented by these emotionally and intellectually intimidating Romantic men, or by the other advocates of the "character of the sexes" who essentialized gender differences. In fact, women's lack of advanced education reinforced the status quo, by preventing women from seeming as qualified as men to speak on any intellectual or cultural subject, even when the issues intimately concerned themselves and their being. The image of the feeling women was exposed as confining and one-sided; it had not changed the prevailing literary or intellectual standards, which still focused on men.

Indeed, the men of Romanticism used some of the very tools and techniques that women, relying on their less tutored skills, had developed since 1770: fragments, dreams, open-ended works, disorderly collations that disrupt the usual hierarchies. The very closeness that some women had attained to the Romantic aesthetic meant that, in a movement so deeply rooted in the polarized discourse of gender as Romanticism was, these women writers had to be first disregarded and then forgotten. Thus Romanticism, incorporating the ideal of the feeling woman into its philosophy, used this version of femininity for a very different purpose. Woman was not just to complement man functionally, but actually to complete him psychologically. An individual woman's ability to act independently and on her own terms, or even to contemplate autonomous action, was correspondingly reduced. In *Lucinde*, the scandalous title figure is a prop for the development of her lover, Julius, a writer.[7]

Faced with Romanticism's reactionary discourse, more writers than before hesitated to identify themselves as women, since high culture, invoking its doctrine of sexual characteristics, disqualified them from writing (first in certain genres, and then more broadly). The male pseudonym gained an attractiveness that would have baffled Engelhard, La Roche, Ehrmann, and Albrecht. Private writing became the locus of some of the best writing by women,[8] supplanting the public writing of the last third of the eighteenth century. Indeed, in the middle of the nineteenth century, other German woman writers were still struggling over the choices for women implied by the contesting discourses of the needle and the quill.

According to the canonical version of German literary history, during Romanticism certain women, for the first time as a group rather than as individuals, participate in literary life—mostly, however, as "muses," inspirations for the famous men. The feminist work of recuperating women writers challenges the adequacy of this understanding either of the muses, particularly Caroline Schlegel-Schelling and Dorothea Schlegel, or of other women writers of the time such as Karoline von Günderrode and Sophie Mereau. After noting that many twentieth-century feminist scholars have avoided confronting the relationship of women writers to standard literary periods, Susan Lanser examined possible feminist responses to Romanticism, and its relation to women writers, identifying "six positions—some mutually exclusive, others overlapping":

> first, that Romanticism is too intractably masculine, too invested in androcentric positions and tropes, ever to constitute a legitimate descriptor of women's writings of the period; second, that Romanticism is the creation of both women and men, and therefore that canonical revision can itself correct the apparent male-centeredness of the Romantic terrain; third, that many women practiced Romanticism somewhat differently from many men, so that a redefinition or expansion of Romanticism is necessary—but also sufficient—to accommodate women's work; fourth, that women and men Romantics thought and wrote so differently as to suggest two separate, gendered versions of the term; fifth, that far from being antithetical to women's interests, Romanticism enabled feminist goals; and sixth, that Romanticism is less a definable movement than an amalgam of the various tendencies that coexisted within a specific historical period.[9]

Whichever position or combination of these positions becomes dominant, it seems necessary to me, also, to reconsider the relationship of Romanticism (or its contemporaneous counterpart for women) to the *Empfindsamkeit* of alienation, and hence, to writers such as Sophie Albrecht and Marianne Ehrmann with their representations of independent women who resist the proprieties in love and even death. Under the changed conditions produced by the Revolution and soon by Napoleonic Europe, women who wanted to be active participants in the new movement had once again to set about the task of creating a space for themselves. Women writers had to find new terms in which to justify writing and (perhaps) publishing, new ways to acquire the experiences that enriched their imaginations, new subject positions, and new strategies to deal with gender in their work. They had to find new solutions to changed definitions of gender crime that once again pushed women into background roles as receptive audience or supportive muse. Resisting the changed definitions of femininity and of literary qualification was a task they could and did undertake. Yet, the newness of their strategies will quite possibly have a more familiar look when seen in the context of their older sisters, from La Roche to Albrecht. Even though women constituted only a tiny contingent compared to the fast-growing crowd of writing men,[10] significant enough numbers of them had become openly active participants in literary life—and with sufficiently distinctive voices that their agency in literary production has never, since the late eighteenth century, been completely reversed.

La Roche's heroine, Fräulein von Sternheim, was skilled in her use of the needle from the earliest stages of her life. While needlework is a classic element of women's undervalued traditional culture, it is also often posed as an alternative, indeed, as an obligatory detour, for women away from high cultural or intellectual achievement. But Sternheim deploys the needle with effects reaching beyond the expected: when she teaches an impoverished child in Scotland to sew, she is not merely reenacting a traditional motherly role, but deliberately attempting to give the child a skill that will improve her economic prospects. At the same time, she helps to lift herself out of depression, a process aided by her idea of transforming her needle into a quill. Thus, she decides that when her paper and ink run out, she can stitch her journal. The needle that signifies women's roles turns textile petticoats into another female text. But such a development is the product of extreme deprivation. Sewing words is a substitute for writing, not a program of reconciliation between needle and quill that could be sustained. The fundamental tension remained, and long continued to mark the texts of women writers.

Notes

LIST OF ABBREVIATIONS USED IN THE NOTES

Works cited in the notes are usually identified in shortened form. In general, when new editions are available for the most commonly cited eighteenth-century texts, the cited page references refer to them. The works most frequently cited in the notes are abbreviated as follows:

FB   Friderika Baldinger, *Lebensbeschreibung von Friderika Baldinger von ihr selbst verfaßt,* ed. Sophie von La Roche (Offenbach: Weiß und Brede, 1791. Reprinted in *"Ich wünschte so gar gelehrt zu werden." Drei Autobiographien von Frauen des 18. Jahrhunderts,* ed. Magdalene Heuser, et al. Göttingen: Wallstein Verlag, 1994).

ME-*A*   [Marianne Ehrmann,] *Amalie. Eine wahre Geschichte in Briefen*, 2 vols. (n.p. 1788).

ME-*AES*   Marianne Ehrmann, *Amaliens Erholungsstunden. Teutschlands Töchtern geweiht*, vol. 1, (Stuttgart: Im Verlag der Expedition des Beobachters, 1790; 2nd ed. Tübingen 1790. vol. 2–3, Tübingen: Cotta, 1791–92).

ME-*G*   Marianne Ehrmann, "Geschichte eine Schnupftuchs," in *Erzählungen* (Heidelberg: F. L. Pfähler, 1795), 28–50.

PEG-21   Philippine Engelhard, *Neue Gedichte von Philippine Engelhard geborne Gatterer* (Nürnberg: Georg Eichhorn, 1821).

PEG-78   Philippine Gatterer, *Gedichte von Philippine Gatterer* (Göttingen: Dieterich, 1778).

PEG-82   Philippine Engelhard, *Gedichte von Philippine Engelhard geb. Gatterer* (Göttingen: Dieterich, 1782).

SA81   Sophie Albrecht, *Gedichte und Schauspiele*, [vol. 1]. (Erfurt: Albrecht und Compagnie, 1781; also 2nd ed. Dresden: Richter, 1791).

SA85   Sophie Albrecht, *Gedichte und prosaische Aufsätze*, vol. 2. (Erfurt: Albrecht und Compagnie, 1785; also 2nd ed. Dresden und Leipzig: Richter, 1791).

SA91   Sophie Albrecht, *Gedichte und prosaische Aufsätze*, vol. 3. (Dresden: Richter, 1791).

SA-*ID*   Sophie Albrecht, *Ida von Duba, das Mädchen im Walde; eine romantische Geschichte aus den grauenvollen Tagen der Vorwelt* (Altona: Bechtold, [1805?]).

SA-*T*   Sophie Albrecht, *Theresgen* (from SA81 above), citations from reprint in Wurst, *Frauen und Drama im Achtzehnten Jahrhundert.*

Schi   Carl Wilhelm Otto August von Schindel, *Die deutschen Schriftstellerin-*

nen des neunzehnten Jahrhunderts, 3 vols. (Leipzig: Brockhaus, 1823–25).
SLR-*BM* Sophie La Roche, *Briefe über Mannheim* (Zürich: Orell, 1791).
SLR-*FS* Sophie La Roche, *Geschichte des Fräulein von Sternheim* (Leipzig: Weidmann und Reich, 1771). Unless otherwise noted, references to *Geschichte des Fräulein von Sternheim* and quotations from it rely on the English translation entitled *The History of Lady Sophia Sternheim* by Christa Baguss Britt (Albany: State University of New York, 1991).
SLR-*MS* Sophie La Roche, *Mein Schreibetisch*, 2 vols. (Leipzig: Gräff, 1799).
SLR-*P* Sophie La Roche, *Pomona für Teutschlands Töchter* (Speier 1783–84).
SLR-*SB* Sophie La Roche, "Der schöne Bund," in *Geschichte von Miß Lony, und Der schöne Bund* (Gotha: Ettinger, 1789).

Chapter 1: Introduction

1. Rousseau, *Emil or on Education*, 198.
2. Goodman and Waldstein, *In the Shadow of Olympus*, 5.
3. SLR-*P* 1: 248–49.
4. Of the many possible discussions of this major issue in feminist theory, Mohanty, Butler, and Fuss are especially prominent: Mohanty, "Under Western Eyes: Feminist Scholarship and Colonial Discourses," 51–80; Butler, *Gender Trouble*; and Fuss, *Essentially Speaking*. Much of the literature on this subject as of 1994 is reviewed in Young, "Gender as Seriality: Thinking about Women as a Social Collective"; a series of articles in the spring 1997 issue of *Signs* begins with an analysis of recent conceptualizations of gender: Hawkesworth, "Confounding Gender."
5. Spelman, *Inessential Woman*.
6. Finke, *Feminist Theory, Women's Writing*, 2.
7. Meise, *Unschuld und die Schrift*, 66–82.
8. Goodman, *Dis/closures: Women's Autobiography in Germany*, xi–xii.
9. Felski, *Beyond Feminist Aesthetics*, 49.
10. For example, Felman, in a brief assessment of Luce Irigaray, elaborates on some of the complications that arise from Irigaray's notions of women speaking, given Irigaray's claims that women are silenced; see Felman, "Women and Madness: The Critical Phallacy," 136–37. For the analysis of a particular case, that of a woman whose male mentor allowed her to write with the provision that she write as a woman, see Loster-Schneider, *Sophie La Roche*, 233–92.
11. Davies, *Frogs and Snails and Feminist Tales*, 13.
12. Walter, *Schrieb oft*.
13. The distinction between public and private writers, like the one between writers and nonwriters, is sometimes a matter of degree or of evidence, which for private writers is often in short supply. Some women who were prolific private writers had a handful of poems published or a couple of letters—Friderika Baldinger will be an example in the first chapter—and then decided not to take that step again. In my analysis, they remain private writers.
14. La Vopa, "Conceiving a Public," 99.
15. Ramazanoglu, *Feminism and the Contradictions of Oppression*, 62–64.
16. Gatens, *Feminism and Philosophy*, 95.
17. D. Goodman, "Public Sphere and Private Life," 14.
18. I am using the term "private writer" rather than "closet writer" precisely

so that I can include women who wrote only letters. "Closet writer" usually implies compositions in literary or scholarly forms that were kept unpublished. See for example Trouille, *Sexual Politics,* 297.

19. For example, Möhrmann, *Die andere Frau,* 31–33.

20. Schieth appears to argue that the novel was assigned to women in *Entwicklung des deutschen Frauenromans,* 220, 269. Felski argues against this position throughout *Beyond Feminist Aesthetics.* A recent vigorous rejection of the overhasty and often essentializing notion of gender-genre affinities appears in Susanne Kord, *Namen machen.*

21. Figes, *Sex and Subterfuge,* 11.

22. Cocalis, ed., *Defiant Muse*; Brinker-Gabler, ed., *Deutsche Dichterinnen.*

23. Schindel, *Die deutschen Schriftstellerinnen des neunzehnten Jahrhunderts,* 1:112.

24. Haferkorn, "Der freie Schriftsteller," 623.

25. This novel, *Karolinens Tagebuch ohne ausserordentliche Handlungen oder gerade so viel als gar keine* "Karoline's Diary without exceptional actions or just as many as none at all" (1774), has drawn favorable attention from Meise, *Unschuld und die Schrift,* 189–200.

26. Cocalis, " 'Vormund will Vormund sein,' " 41.

27. Sometimes the gender-flagging pseudonymous or anonymous signature appeared at the end of the foreword rather than on the title page. Such is the case with *Blüthenalter der Empfindung* "Blossom Time of Feeling," the first novel by Sophie Mereau, who signs the short foreword as Authoress ("Die Verfasserinn"). This modifies Sigrid Weigel's argument that in this book Mereau masks herself and specifically that as author she conceals her gender ("Der schielende Blick," 93).

28. Kord, *Namen machen,* 24–25.

29. Because her first publications appeared under her husband's name, Therese Huber is usually cited as an eighteenth-century woman who used a male pseudonym. I think that her case is slightly different, however, than when a woman chooses a pseudonym, for Therese Huber seems to have perceived herself, at least initially, as writing on her husband's behalf, enabling him to get more writing done by doing part of it for him.

30. Belsey, Afterword, 263.

31. Wayne, Introduction, 23.

32. I am grateful to the wonderfully helpful book *The Man Question* by my colleague Kathy Ferguson for the term "male-ordered."

33. Grimm, *Rezensionen,* 172.

34. I allude here to Laura Finke's assertion that "feminist theory has much work to do to articulate a feminist analysis of sexuality which reclaims eroticism for women as well as for men." While Sophie Albrecht's poetry offers no analysis of sexuality, it certainly attempts a literary reclamation of the erotic.

35. Grimm formulated the view clearly that writing, as a male preserve, was undesirable and even unnatural for women:

[I]f, by becoming a lawgiver, a judge, or a priest, a woman crosses beyond the limits of nature that are sacred to all peoples, why should literature seem to be any different than an office and business of men? All of history teaches that it is so. Public appearances and public speaking damage the woman's innate morals and dignity. True poetry does not put up with things, it does not require that which is less, rather that which is high and pure, it requires that the poet should sing freely from a breast free of inhibitions. . . . (*Kleinere Schriften,* 172)

Grimm did not consider the possibility that it was the conditions under which women lived which made the restrictions on their abilities look appropriate. He thought, instead, that they had a realm of their own, the house and private social gatherings, and he granted them talent as letter writers. But true literary authorship he reserved for men. Georg Gottfried Gervinus, the father of German literary history, was of similar opinion in the middle of the nineteenth century, although for a slightly different reason. He stressed that the range of experience necessary to become even a mediocre woman writer was incompatible with a woman's good reputation. Brinker-Gabler discusses his remarks in *Deutsche Dichterinnen,* 17–18.

36. Kord, *Namen machen,* 51–56.
37. Eagleton, *Literary Theory,* 1–16.
38. Ibid. 16.

Chapter 2: Between the Spinning Wheel and the Book

1. FB15.
2. Heuser gives the most complete information yet assembled on Baldinger's publications, and especially on the loci of unpublished letters to and from her. "Zwischen Kochtopf und Verstandeserziehung," 156–57.
3. Friderika Baldinger is listed in none of the standard comprehensive reference works for German literature. One American scholar, Timothy Sellner, after searching in vain for information about her, wrote: "Extensive research has failed to yield any evidence that Friederika Baldinger actually existed; most probably the book . . . Lebensbeschreibung von Friederika Baldinger . . . is a fictional work in the autobiographical mode, written by [the purported editor]" (translator's annotation to Hippel, *On Improving the Status of Women,* 217). She is granted neither a line nor a word in the recent nonfeminist studies of the eighteenth century.
4. FB 16.
5. Einem, "Jugendgeschichte," in Heuser, *Ich wünschte so gar,* 42.
6. Wartburg-Ambühl, *Alphabetisierung und Lektüre,* 93–99; Petschauer, "Improving Educational Opportunities for Girls," 56–57; and Petschauer, *Education of Women,* 141.
7. Einem, "Jugendgeschichte," 43.
8. Esther Gad (later Domeier, 1770–1830), growing up in Breslau, provides a good example; according to an early biographer, "the largest influence on her intellectual development came from her brother, whom she had loved dearly from earliest childhood and who taught her in the evenings the most useful parts of the things that he learned during the day . . ." (Sch 1:103). Even the daughter of a professor might have to depend on her brother to get an education. Thus, a biographical sketch of Therese Heyne (1764–1829), the daughter of a distinguished Göttingen professor, puts her neglected early education in a positive light: "She was not plagued with lessons. She learned how to read when she was three to four years old from her brother, who was two years older and was her playmate and ally from the cradle to the grave" (Sch 3:172).
9. Ernestine von Krosigk (1767–1843), living in Berlin, shared a tutor with her brother and learned from this teacher to love literature (Sch 1:272).
10. Fathers were rarely as attentive as the famous Professor Schlözer, who gave his daughter Dorothea (later Rodde, 1770–1825) such an excellent and thorough education that she received a degree from the University of Göttingen, with-

out, of course, being permitted to attend. Professor Schlözer also had other daughters and sons. Far more typical was the childhood education of Friederike Brun (1765–1835). Although she was the favorite of her father, who addressed her in English as "darling child," he completely neglected to give her regular instruction. "The young girl had actually learned very little, but she had read a lot that was good and heard even more"—her father's Copenhagen circle was a distinguished one—"and, aside from what she taught herself from the best German prose writers and poets, she had only gotten negative hints from her father when she made mistakes in language, euphony, or prosody in her prose essays and poetic outpourings." Her brother however, had been treated very differently, receiving regular lessons from their father. Friederike had benefited secondhand from what her brother had learned, "for she listened in whenever she could to the serious critical analyses which her father conducted on her brother's youthful poetic efforts" (Sch 1:169).

11. FB 16.
12. Einem, "Jugendgeschichte," 38.
13. FB 16.
14. "Jugendgeschichte," 30; Grenz, *Mädchenliteratur*, 36–41.
15. Einem, *Nachlaß*, 165.
16. Engelsing, *Der Bürger als Leser*, 308.
17. Charlotte Seidel (1743–78), niece of the poet and pastor Samuel Gotthold Lange, wrote a poetic tribute to Gellert on his death (*Hinterlassene Schriften*, 254–55). Maria Mnioch (1777–97), poet and daughter of a lowly customs official, spending her girlhood in a village outside Danzig, read Gellert in the 1780s ("Zerstreute Blätter," 286). At the other geographical pole of the German-speaking world, Caroline Pichler (1769–1843), dramatist and prose writer, whose father was a leading figure in Vienna's literary circles in the 1770s, read Gellert, too. Decades later, Pichler could still recite many of his rhymed fables and religious hymns (Sch 2:105). Even at the end of the eighteenth century, Gellert was the first poet whose works Johanne Schubert (1776–1864), a woman from a family of poor Silesian weavers, read and utterly admired (Sch 2:289). After women had read and reread Gellert from childhood, it is predictable that he also influenced what some of them later wrote as adults. One, Karoline Lucius (later Schlegel, 1739–1833), was fortunate to become his correspondent and to have her letters published with his (Sch 2:251), while others, like Sophie Kortzfleisch (1749–1823), imitated his verse (*Allgemeine Deutsche Biographie*).
18. Whether Friderika Baldinger in her girlhood isolation had read Gellert or Klopstock, she did not say. Her interests and style were closer to the prosaic, practical, and sometimes juicy Gellert than to the sublimity of Klopstock. Yet, because Klopstock was living in her town when the first cantos of his famous "Messias" appeared (in 1748, when she was nine), other people in Langensalza were certainly well aware of him. Given his connections to the place, it is striking that Baldinger did not mention him. In this instance, as in others, she was so intent on separating herself from her environment that she insisted on the total bleakness of her town. Baldinger had the instincts of a token woman.
19. Even the normally prosaic Sophie La Roche, who generally kept her ideas of religion neatly parceled for practical purposes (such as explaining to the lower classes why they should stay in their place), once described an experience of pantheism by citing Klopstock (*Tagebuch meiner Reise nach Holland und England*, 95). And Sophie Albrecht reinforced her theatrical successes, which will be discussed in chapter 5, by appearing as a dramatic reader of the second book of Klopstock's "Messias" (Eisenberg, *Großes Biographisches Lexikon*, 20).

20. Sophie La Roche's father gave her the key to his library and allowed her to read whatever she wished—as long as it was in her leisure time. Philippine Gatterer and her sisters also had a father with books that they were allowed to read (Gatterer to La Roche, 12 December 1784). In 1765, Goethe advised his fifteen-year-old sister to have her uncle borrow the *Spectator* for her from the library, since she could not borrow it for herself (Prokop, "Cornelia Goethe, 1750–77," 96), and in 1791, Georg Forster wrote to the librarian at the university in Göttingen, asking that Meta Forkel (later Liebeskind, 1765–1853), a married woman, be allowed to borrow books without harassment (Forster, *Werke*, 16:357–59). For permission to use the correspondence of Sophie La Roche with several other women, I am deeply endebted to the Goethe and Schiller Archives of the Stiftung Weimarer Klassik.

21. Einem, "Jugendgeschichte," 36.

22. Heuser has located biographical detail on Baldinger and her family, including her brother's name ("Zwischen Kochtopf und Verstandeserziehung," 154–56).

23. FB 17.

24. SLR-P 1 (1783): 924.

25. How much Sophie La Roche valued it can be seen in the report of a young traveler, Johann Heinrich Landolt, who talked with her in 1782. During his afternoon visit, the subject of classical languages arose. As they were inspecting a cameo depicting Phocion, La Roche said to Landolt, "You know Greek, don't you?—Be very grateful to your parents and teachers, because this language is the source of true scholarliness"—Albert Becker, *Schiller und die Pfalz*, 66.

26. [Hezel, ed.], *Wochenblatt für das schöne Geschlecht*, ed. Hans Henning, 251.

27. Kiesel and Münch, *Gesellschaft und Literatur im 18. Jahrhundert*, 196.

28. The women whose literary careers are of interest in this book, those doing their major writing between 1770 and 1800, got their educations primarily in the 1760s and 1770s. As the century drew to a close, Latin became less important and caused less frustration to young women to whom the language still remained largely inaccessible.

29. Even after the seventeenth century, when the most admired German literature was mainly by and for scholars, the overwhelming majority of male writers was still university educated and thus could, for example, read Latin and Greek. These qualifications were shared by men from a wide range of class backgrounds. Throughout the century, young men from the most modest or even impoverished homes—for example, the sons of tradesmen or of poorly paid municipal soldiers, or even village boys on occasion—were enabled to reach the university. Of course, many left without completing a degree, but they had still obtained a foundation incomparably better than that available to their sisters at home.

The point is well illustrated in the comparison between a famous brother, the brilliant embodiment of the best of the German literary Enlightenment, Gotthold Ephraim Lessing, and his obscure sister, Dorothea Salome. The well-honed language of the playwright's letters contrasts vividly with the miserable orthography and bad grammar of the sister's. Nor is the difference simply a matter of different intelligence, because the Lessing family had gone hungry and accumulated debts in order to give all the sons a solid education and good professional training. For the daughters, however, the Lessing family, like Friderika Baldinger's, could or would do nothing, so that Dorothea later, when she was an aging spinster with no way to earn a sufficient living for herself and her widowed mother, had to write to her brothers to beg for money in order for the two women to avoid starvation. Becker-Cantarino, "(Sozial)Geschichte der Frau in Deutschland," 246–47.

A generation later the disparity continued, as the case of Christian August Vulpius (1762–1827) and his sister (1765–1816) shows. Christiane Vulpius, Goethe's mistress and companion in Weimar for almost eighteen years and then finally also his wife, had received little or no schooling. She was certainly not illiterate, but practically all of Goethe's biographers describe her as uneducated. Goethe himself said in 1807, after he and Christiane had been together for almost two decades, that she had never read a line of his works. Her brother, on the other hand, had managed to attend the university and became a writer of sensational novels.

30. Meta Moller offers an example. In the 1750s, she reported in a letter to a friend that when Klopstock described her as his future bride to the king of Denmark, he pointed out that, despite her knowledge, she was not a scholarly woman: ". . . they talked about me at length. About my person, my heart, my intellect, about my taste and even about my bit of knowledge of languages and learning. Kl. said however that I was not at all what one would call a scholarly woman and the king was glad of that" (Klopstock, *Wunderliche Dinger*, 292–93). In this case, the label "scholarly woman" had more to do with how a woman behaved than with what she knew.

31. Meise, *Unschuld und die Schrift*, 85.
32. SLR-*P* 1:925.
33. Schlözer, *Dorothea*, 106.
34. [Müller,] *Schattenrisse edler teutscher Frauenzimmer*, 2:36.
35. Sch 1:365.
36. Meise cites a passage from *Maria*, by Margarete Liebeskind (1765–1853) which clearly shows through its language that when women endorsed the ideal of invisible superiority for talented women, they were doing so to please men (Meise, *Unschuld und die Schrift*, 84).

37. The Countess Luise Stolberg (1746–1824) is one example of the negative stereotype. The atmosphere of forced learning at her home in Tremsbüttel was so pervasive that Luise Mejer, who had been brought to the house as a combination of personal secretary and companion to the countess, said people were stuffed with reading material like a goose stuffed with noodles (Boie, *Ich war wohl klug*, 274). The countess herself kept meticulous records of her accomplishments and thus knew that in the year 1783 she had read seventy-five volumes of books, not including journals, and written 911 letters. To accomplish this, everything was rigidly scheduled, as Mejer reported.

> Breakfast is at ten o'clock. Then Stolberg reads us a chapter in the Bible and a hymn from Klopstock's songs. Everyone goes to his own room. I read from the "Spectator," the "Physiognomy" and a few other books which the countess has given me. She comes down to me while Lotte is translating and I read her "Pontius Pilatus" by Lavater for an hour. Then she has her Latin lesson; I do copying for her or read for myself until lunch. After the meal and coffee Fritz reads from "Lebensläufen," then Lotte comes down to me and I read Milton with her for an hour. Then we all go up and I read aloud to the count and countess out of Plutarch until it is teatime, at nine in the evening. After tea Stolberg reads a chapter in the Bible and a hymn from Klopstock; with that, good night. (274)

During the hour when Mejer was scheduled to be discussing Milton with the countess's niece, the countess would come to the door to spy. And, although this is not the point Mejer herself stresses, the countess, in her extreme dedication for scholarliness, neglected the matters that only a woman was expected to handle;

as a result, people sometimes went away from the dinner table still hungry. The coercive atmosphere and neglected household management at Tremsbüttel were not well known, however. Heinrich Christian Boie, the important editor of the Göttingen Hainbund poets, friend of Philippine Gatterer, and future husband of Luise Mejer, was a good friend of the Stolberg family. Yet, his fiancée's account completely surprised him. It is not likely then that Countess Stolberg was in anyone's mind when dire warnings about the evil effects of learning on women were issued.

38. FB 18–19.
39. Heuser, "Zwischen Kochtopf und Verstandeserziehung," 161–62.
40. Karsch, *O, mir entwischt nicht*, 168.
41. Sch 1:259–60.
42. Einem, "Jugendgeschichte," 35.
43. FB 17.
44. Möller, *Die kleinbürgerliche Familie im 18. Jahrhundert*, 15.
45. La Roche, "Mein Glüke, einer klagenden Freundinn gewidmet," 97.
46. Sch 1:153.
47. Quoted in Walter, *Schrieb oft*, 181.
48. Madland, "Three . . . Women's Journals," 178–79.
49. FB 17.
50. Möller, *Die kleinbürgerliche Familie im 18. Jahrhundert*, 171–72.
51. FB 21.
52. Klopstock, *Wunderliche Dinger*, 348.
53. FB 21.
54. This estimate is derived from an examination of the age at first marriage of 251 German women writers born between 1715 and 1779. Monter has shown that, in Switzerland, the age of marriage was even higher: "The median age at first marriage for Genevan-born women, about twenty in the 1580s, rose rapidly to about twenty-five a half-century later and continued to increase slowly until it reached twenty-eight by the 1760s." Monter, "Women in Calvinist Geneva (1550–1800)," 198. Rural women also married later than is generally thought. John Knodel, studying fertility in ten villages in Germany during the years 1750–1849, found that the average age of the women living there at first marriage ranged between 25.6 and 31.5. Knodel, "Natural Fertility in Pre-industrial Germany," 484.
55. Examples include Vogt, *Autobiographik bürgerlicher Frauen*, 34, and Prokop, "Cornelia Goethe, 1750–1777," 51–53.
56. FB 22. Heuser offers a fascinating biographical context for this comment. She points out that since approximately 1780 Baldinger's husband, Ernst Gottfried Baldinger, had been engaged in an affair with Lisette Charlotte Drebing, a servant woman "in various households" ("Zwischen Kochtopf und Verstandeserziehung," 170). Heuser asserts that Friderika Baldinger had definitive knowledge of this relationship as of fall 1784 (169) and goes on to explore the possibility that she already know about the fragility of her marriage "at the time of composing and dedicating the description of her life" (172). This seems to me to be persuasive only with regard to the preface that Baldinger wrote last, which was composed after the autobiography and after the initial preface (which is printed second). In short, knowledge of the affair and of the fact that many of her acquaintances knew about it before she did may have contributed to Friderika Baldinger's reluctance to publish.
57. FB 22.
58. Baldinger to Kästner, n.d. For permission to use this correspondence, I wish to express my sincere thanks to the manuscript department of the Niedersächsische Staats und Universitätsbibliothek in Göttingen.

59. FB 18.
60. Heuser, "Zwischen Kochtopf und Verstandeserziehung," 167–74, 168.
61. FB 22.
62. Günther Meinhardt, *Die Universität Göttingen*, 36.
63. "Baldinger," *Neue Deutsche Biographie*.
64. FB 22.
65. Goodman, *Dis/closures*, 29.
66. Four sons died during Friderika Baldinger's lifetime; two daughters survived her. The daughters are listed in the *Neue Deutsche Biographie* account of Ernst Gottfried Baldinger (with birth dates in Heuser, *Ich wünschte so gar*, 185) as Sophie Friederike Ernestine, born 1765 (married in 1790 to Georg Theodor Christoph Handel in Marburg), and Friederike Wilhelmine Amalie, born 1768 (married Bernhard von Gehren in Darmstadt), and the sons are listed in Heuser as Ernst Friedrich Baldinger (1767–84), Christian Ernst Wilhelm (1770–74), Johann Friedrich Karl (1772–73), and then his similarly short-lived replacement, Johann Friedrich Carl (1773–74). Heuser, *Ich wünschte so gar*, 185–86.
67. FB 24.
68. Georg Christoph Lichtenberg, *Schriften und Briefe*, 4:511.
69. FB 24.
70. Spangenberg to Baldinger. 3 May 1782, 26 May 1782, and undated.
71. Forster, *Werke*, 14:357.
72. Translation from Hippel, *On Improving the Status of Women*, 188.
73. FB 14.
74. Klopstock, *Wunderliche Dinger*, 410.
75. Heuser has done the important task of searching extensively for extant letters to and from Baldinger; see her essay "Zwischen Kochtopf und Verstandeserziehung," especially 156–57, and the notes to her edition of Baldinger, *Ich wünschte so gar*, 186–204.
76. Forster, *Werke*, 16:405.
77. Heuser, "Zwischen Kochtopf und Verstandeserziehung," 164.
78. Sch 1:48.
79. Seidel, *Hinterlassene Schriften*, 361.
80. Quoted in Wittmann, "Die frühen Buchhändlerzeitschriften," 684.
81. Sch 1:253.
82. La Roche, "Mein Glüke," 98.
83. Möhrmann, *Die andere Frau*, 127.
84. Klopstock, *Wunderliche Dinger*, 433.
85. Baldinger to La Roche, 31 January 1783.
86. Ibid.
87. Ibid.
88. Baldinger to La Roche, 16 May 1783.
89. Kord, *Namen machen*, 12–17.
90. Klopstock, *Wunderliche Dinger*, 366.
91. Baldinger to La Roche, 31 January 1783.
92. Baldinger to La Roche, 16 May 1783.
93. FB 14; the letter is undated but presumably before 16 May 1783.
94. FB 11–12, dated May 18, 1783.
95. Baldinger to La Roche, 16 May 1783.
96. Perhaps this is another point at which E. G. Baldinger's love affair affected the publication history of the autobiography, if he was somewhat reticent about publishing this text that contained so much praise of himself, given that he would

marry the servant woman Drebing in June of 1791 (Heuser, "Zwischen Kochtopf und Verstandeserziehung," 170). On the other hand, the fact that the author's husband had possession of the manuscript for so long, and that La Roche received it only from him, should also be taken into account when the omissions in the text are considered.

97. FB 9.

98. Friderika Baldinger's husband also claims in the passage La Roche quotes that the autobiography was written at his request. His wife, however, never identified the man for whom she had written it, always referring–in her subtitle ("To one of my male friends," FB 15), in the dedicatory letter to her husband (FB 14), in a letter to La Roche (cited Heuser, ed., 191), and in more detail in a letter to Kästner (Heuser, "Zwischen Kochtopf und Verstandeserziehung," 189)—to a male friend.

99. Heuser suspects that Friderika Baldinger may have known of her husband's continuing affair at the time she wrote both the self-narrative and the two prefaces, using them to try to woo him back to her ("Zwischen Kochtopf und Verstandeserziehung," 172–73). While I find it plausible that she sensed problems, or even harbored suspicions, neither the internal nor external evidence seems sufficient for the hypothesis that she had full knowledge of the matter, especially given how unmistakable her agony and her desperation are when she undisputably knows, as indicated in a letter of 1785 to Kästner (quoted in Heuser, "Zwischen Kochtopf und Verstandeserziehung," 170).

100. Ibid. 172.

101. FB 9.

102. Dawson, " 'Der Weihrauch, den uns die Männer streuen,' " 225.

103. Goodman, in contrast, argues that La Roche presented Baldinger's work "in an enlightened, even polemical, spirit" (*Dis/closures*, 6). In the single review of Baldinger's book that I have found, the conservative perspective on La Roche's tactic seems to prevail, for the reviewer, writing anonymously, argues that true education is hindered when the learner receives nothing but encouragement and faces no obstacles. The reviewer recommends the book especially for women readers and praises the writer's concentration on her education, adding that no one would have been interested if she had written about her whole life. He praises La Roche for publishing the work, criticizing only its brevity (Anon., "Kleine Schriften").

104. Winston, "The Autobiographer and her Readers," 94.

105. Sch 2:99.

106. FB 24.

107. Baldinger, "Ermahnungen einer Mutter," 827.

108. Kant, "What is Enlightenment?" 384.

109. Cocalis reaches a similar conclusion from a different starting point ("Vormund will Vormund sein," 43).

110. FB 22.

Chapter 3: The Enabling Effect of Difference

1. The extensive description of how Sternheim's parents manage the estates and what qualities they encourage in their daughter could be taken as a late version of the traditional *Hausväterliteratur*, discussed, for example, in Frühsorge, "Begründung der 'väterlichen Gesellschaft.' "

2. SLR-*FS* 105.
3. See for example Heidenreich, *Sophie von La Roche,* 53.
4. Hohendahl argues, somewhat differently, that La Roche, by polarizing good and evil in such a way that all evil is associated with the court and good with country living, leaves the class system untouched. Hohendahl, "Empfindsamkeit und gesellschaftliches Bewußtsein," 196–98. Heidenreich disagrees, calling it a revolutionary act to measure the aristocracy of birth by the standards of the aristocracy of virtue (*Sophie von La Roche,* 52).
5. My translation from the German edition: [La Roche], *Geschichte des Fräulein von Sternheim,* ed. Becker-Cantarino, 345; Britt's version is on p. 241.
6. The wise and knowledgeable German writer is contrasted in the same chapter with a "little French author" who, although more highly esteemed by the German aristocrats, is better at discussing furniture and clothing than books (SLR-*FS* 117).
7. SLR-*FS* 116. Wieland, La Roche's literary mentor at the time, and the prototype for Sternheim's adviser, reinforced the message that La Roche had already taken to heart. When she wrote in *Sternheim* that women's feelings were often better than men's ideas, Wieland added a heartily approving note (SLR-*FS* 81). Of course, La Roche was well aware of the contradictions between what Wieland wrote and what his actions showed, so she would have been cautious, for example, about his notion of accepting women as members of the body politic. Touaillon, *Deutscher Frauenroman,* 194. La Roche never seriously tried to explore such ideas herself.
8. Rousseau, *Emile or on Education,* 382.
9. Nenon, "Sophie von La Roche," 74.
10. In an account written almost fifty years after the events, and much cited by analysts of La Roche's life, she asserts that her girlhood fiancé, an Italian named Bianconi, had taught her mathematics and coached her singing. She writes that her father forced her to break off the engagement and to destroy all mementos of Bianconi, whereupon she decided to hide her knowledge of singing, piano, mathematics and Italian. The psychological and psychoanalytical import of this account needs further consideration, given La Roche's pride in her learning in every other situation, given the multiple traumas she was suffering at the time of her broken engagement (the barely mentioned death of her mother, Bianconi's invitation to elope, her father's eagerness to remarry), and given the newness of this event in an old-age text composed otherwise mostly of familiar material. For less skeptical responses, see Heidenrich, *Sophie von La Roche,* 2–3 and Nenon, *Autorschaft und Frauenbildung,* 28–31.
11. SLR-*P* 1783:927.
12. Ehrich-Haefeli, "Gestehungskosten tugendempfindsamer Freundschaft," 78–80, 82–85, 94–97, 116–23.
13. SLR-*FS* 221.
14. Ibid. 116–20.
15. SLR-*FS* 47.
16. Meise, *Unschuld und die Schrift,* 66–83; Isabel V. Hull, *Sexuality, State, and Civil Society,* 146.
17. Hull, *Sexuality, State and Civil Society,* 144–45.
18. Ibid. 184–90, 289–90.
19. SLR-*FS* 167–68.
20. Decades later, in discussing her first novel, La Roche wrote that she had, in the course of the story, deprived the heroine of everything: "Respect, good rep-

utation, the ability to do good, friends, the hope that she would be able to regain her *husband*'s affection" (my emphasis, qtd. in Maurer, "Das Gute und das Schöne," 122.

21. SLR-*FS* 178.

22. In 1788, when her husband died, La Roche referred to the event in a letter four days later as her "dearly purchased freedom"—La Roche, *Ich bin mehr Herz als Kopf*, 312—echoing the words of the widow Frau von C. whom she had created in *Sternheim* almost twenty years earlier.

23. SLR-*FS* 188.

24. Monika Nenon, *Autorschaft und Frauenbildung*, 95.

25. Heidenreich, *Sophie von La Roche*, 45.

26. Nenon, *Autorschaft und Frauenbildung*, 98–99).

27. Bovenschen, *Imaginierte Weiblichkeit*, 194–96.

28. Winkle, *Woman as Bourgeois Ideal*, 66.

29. Maurer, "Das Gute und das Schöne," 123.

30. La Roche, *Ich bin mehr Herz als Kopf*, 155.

31. Figes, *Sex and Subterfuge*, 39–40.

32. La Roche, *Briefe an Lina als Mädchen*, 63.

33. SLR-*SB* 184.

34. Meise, *Unschuld und die Schrift*, 90–95.

35. Brownstein, *Becoming a Heroine*, xv.

36. *Teutscher Merkur* 1777, 2:86–87.

37. La Roche, *Lina* 1: 191.

38. SLR-*P* 1: 746–47.

39. Becker, *Schiller und die Pfalz*, 66.

40. Her desire for "manly" scholarship in the form of Latin continued to the end of her life, according to the depiction by her granddaughter Bettina von Arnim nee Brentano (1785–1859). When La Roche was finally altogether free from male supervision—her husband was long dead and her male mentors were dead or far away, too—she tried to persuade Bettina to learn the language of Virgil and Horace. Bettina wrote that her grandmama took her by both hands and told her so urgently to learn Latin that she promised she would—and then fled to the garden where she prayed vehemently to be released from this hasty vow. This incident is described in one of Bettina von Arnim's partially novelized editions of letters, *Die Günderode*, 280.

41. SLR-*BM* 96–97.

42. Ulrike Prokop makes sporadic use of the notion of feminine culture throughout her analysis of the "great pair," e.g. *Illusion vom grossen Paar*, 1:188, 249; Alice Walker is the vivid proponent of this notion to American readers. Walker, *In Search of Our Mothers' Gardens*, 231–43.

43. An interesting exception is the article called "Alte Toleranzlehre einer Frau" in *Pomona*. Here, La Roche tells a story in which her mother decides to help a girl who had come to the door begging; she offers to send her to school and to have her learn handwork (again, the linking of the needle with the quill for women). " 'Yes,' she said, anxiously looking at my mother, 'but I am Catholic.' 'That doesn't matter—you shall go to the Catholic school,' was the immediate answer." (SLR-*P* 1784: 534–36).

44. Todd, *Women's Friendship in Literature*, 2.

45. Prokop, *Illusion vom grossen Paar*, 323

46. Rousseau, *Emil or on Education*, 361. It is a perspective that La Roche raises questions about, however, sometimes directly. In *Letters from Mannheim*,

for example, she quotes a young man: "True knowledge and feeling are outraged by the idea of a scholarly woman because she deviates from her calling and because through useless artifices with her understanding she looses the charms of modesty and gentleness, the only means by which she can please us and make us happy. . . . Only when her charms wilt is it permissible for the female spirit to dedicate herself to contemplation" (SLR-*BM* 298–99). These lines appear in the context of a letter that La Roche purports to be quoting, in which a sister writes her brother: "I am, my dear brother, at this moment again happy in my memories of you, for if you had waited until my cheeks wilted before you taught me to read, where would my head be? (SLR-*BM* 299).

47. SLR-*P* 1783:27.
48. SLR-*FS* 160.
49. Ferguson, *Man Question*, 151.
50. SLR-*FS* 95.
51. La Roche, *Rosaliens Briefe an ihre Freundinn*, 3:201–19.
52. SLR-*P* 1784:227.
53. One of the longest and harshest of the early instances is a satirical passage in the special issue of *Pomona* dedicated to France; it is a translation of a pamphlet by Mme. Beauharnais in which the issue of learning for women is discussed (SLR-*P* 1783: 164–83).
54. Duden, "Das schöne Eigentum," 125–40.
55. Prokop, *Illusion vom grossen Paar*.
56. Duden, "Das schöne Eigentum," 130–40.
57. Margaret Homans explains this notion and how it helps us understand women's complex relationship to writing and language in the first chapter of *Bearing the Word*, 1–39.
58. Prokop, *Illusion vom grossen Paar*, 1: 200–378, 400–404.
59. SLR-*P* 1783:16.
60. La Roche, *Lina*, 25.
61. SLR-*P* 1783:30; my emphasis.
62. I disagree with Nenon's assessment of the twenty-four letters to Lina as "certainly the most important contributions in the journal, and also those most treasured by the readers" (*Autorschaft und Frauenbildung*, 150–51). I see little evidence for either part of the assertion. Before publication, La Roche wrote to Lavater about *Pomona*, especially describing the letters to Lina and concluding, "All the men say it is the best thing I have written" (Maurer, "Das Gute und das Schöne," 246), but since she was writing to a man and reporting the reactions of the men around her, I do not find this statement a persuasive overall report of reader response. Heidenreich similarly argues for the centrality of the Lina letters, citing the passage to Lavater and another to Dalberg, again when *Pomona* was in its earliest stages (*La Roche*, 148, 367). By the time the journal was well underway, Lina was only one element in the mixture, and not one the readers overwhelmingly mentioned.
63. SLR-*P* 1784:141.
64. SLR-*FS* 198.
65. SLR-*P* 1783:13.
66. La Roche, *Lina* 1:75.
67. La Roche, *Ich bin mehr Herz als Kopf*, 155.
68. SLR-*P* 1783:425.
69. SLR-*FS* 116.
70. *SLR-P* 1783:925.

71. Nor was inadequate education in girlhood something that could readily be made up later. Catharina Elisabeth Goethe, for example, later mother of the famous poet, married a man who wanted to become her teacher; yet, although all of her life she complained about being unschooled, for years she rejected his efforts until he stopped. The problem, in the analysis of Ulrike Prokop, was that accepting instruction from her husband would have put her into yet another relationship of perpetual inferiority and dependence on him, since she would never be able to overcome his enormous head start, and, equally important, the kind of education he offered her had almost nothing to do with the education she sought (*Illusion vom grossen Paar*, 229–33). She read avidly and thoroughly on her own, but was nonetheless indeed uneducated by the standards of her son and his elite male friends, the men who determined, as much as anyone, what counted in the world of late eighteenth-century Germany.

72. Anon. to La Roche. [c. 1784].

73. Gessner to La Roche. 20 February 1783.

74. The presentation of material, however, is unreadably dry except where its scholarly standards are lamentable. Sheer ignorance lends interest today, for example, to this dramatic description of the tiger:

> Tigers, which can also retract their claws, the cruelest animal of prey with the most beautiful pelt, brown with black and white stripes, often grow to 14 feet in length; attacks everything, strangles it and only sucks out the blood, eats its young and rips up the mother that defends them, lives in Asia's forests and along rivers where other animals go to drink, plagues and persecutes elephants, squeezing their trunks until they suffocate or die of hunger. (La Roche, *Briefe an Lina als Mutter*, 2:181.)

75. The third volume contains thoughts on moral concepts, the history of the human soul, in accordance with the notions of d'Alembert. Besides the quotations from him, there are extensive excerpts from other writers too—Sophie von La Roche, *Briefe an Lina als Mutter*, 3:163–65.

76. SLR-*MS* 1:49.

77. Grenz, *Mädchenliteratur*.

78. Kiewning, *Fürstin Pauline zur Lippe,* 15–16.

79. von der Recke, *Tagebücher und Selbstzeugnisse,* 161.

80. Habermas, *Strukturwandel der Öffentlichkeit*.

81. Ruth-Ellen B. Joeres makes arguments similar to this in some ways but drawing on a later group of eighteenth-century women and reaching quite different conclusions about the relation of women to the roughly delineated public sphere (" 'Adjacent to Human Society' " 10).

82. Joeres, " 'Adjacent to Human Society,' " 39–57.

83. Hull, *Sexuality, State and Civil Society*, 207.

84. Joeres, "Adjacent to Human Society," 40.

85. McGrath's theory, dating from the 1960s, seems to me especially useful for diachronical application and because the abstract criteria he uses can readily include women and be modified for literary associations; his most comprehensive discussion of different kinds of groups, large and small, formal and informal, and thus, the one best adaptable to the literary sociology that I am attempting here, is in an overview essay written for the *Encyclopedia Britannica.*

86. McGrath's term is not audience but public. "Social Groups," *Encyclopedia Britannica*, 15th ed., 1979. Given the Habermasian meaning that I am using for that term, however, I consider it less confusing to substitute audience as a label for this level of aggregation.

87. Richard van Dülmen has written a useful book about various kinds of eighteenth-century German associations, but includes only those that identified themselves as organizations, which means omitting less formal groups, such as women may have had an interest in.
88. Joeres, " 'Adjacent to Human Society,' " 44, 51.
89. SLR-*P* 1783:[2].
90. Hull, *Sexuality, State and Civil Society*, 209. Of course, the cycle that Hull describes was not just an ideological or literary matter, but also an economic one. The readers whom La Roche sought for her journal were paying subscribers who would, she hoped, make *Pomona* a successful business venture for her, as *Der teutsche Merkur* was for her friend Wieland—and ultimately it was economic issues that led to the demise of the journal. Nicolay and Nicolai, *Die beiden Nicolai,* 188.
91. Hassencamp, "Aus dem Nachlaß der Sophie von La Roche,"493–94.
92. Boie, "11 Briefe von Heinrich Christian Boie und Luise Mejer," 88.
93. Boie, *Ich war wohl klug* 218; Jerusalem to La Roche. 14 ? 1784.
94. Grävemeier to La Roche. 23 August 1784.
95. Sch 2:228.
96. Baldinger to La Roche. 31 January 1783.
97. Boie, "11 Briefe von Heinrich Christian Boie und Luise Mejer," 88.
98. Jerusalem to La Roche. 14 ? 1784.
99. Ibid.
100. Jansen, *La Roche im Verkehr mit dem geistigen Münsterland*, 24.
101. Boie, *Ich war wohl klug,* 109.
102. Sch 1:160 and 3:114.
103. Hagen to La Roche. 27 November 1783.
104. SLR-*P* 1783:814.
105. Gatterer to La Roche. 12 December 1784.
106. Ibid.
107. SLR-*P* 1783:302.
108. Hutten, Verzeichniss der Abonnenten auf *Pomona*, [1].
109. Boie, "11 Briefe von Heinrich Christian Boie und Luise Mejer," 90.
110. Sch 3:51.
111. SLR-*P* 1784:859.
112. La Roche, *Tagebuch einer Reise durch Holland und England,* 611–12.
113. Watt, "Woman's Progress: Sophie La Roche's Travelogues," 51–58.
114. Worley, for example, quotes two in "Sophie von La Roche's *Reisejournale*," 97, 99.
115. Ibid. 100. Meetings with famous people are recorded, including the woman who had translated *Sternheim* into French, Mme La Fite; the English novelist Fanny Burney; the notorious mystic Cagliostro; the embattled governor general of British India Warren Hastings; the Methodist John Wesley (who, La Roche wrote, prayed so long before the first meal on their cross-channel sail that the rest of the passengers begged him to end so that they could eat). But the journals also include conversations with ordinary people and observations about where and how they lived. Although she occasionally speculated briefly on socioeconomic conditions and forms of government, political analysis and social comment are an insignificant part of La Roche's travel literature.
116. Kaplan, *Erotics of Talk*, 72.
117. SLR-*BM* 1.
118. Caroline deserves further investigation. Ulrike Weckel, in a book that has

reached me too late to fully utilize in my discussion, hypothesizes that Caroline is fictional. Weckel, *Zwischen Häuslichkeit und Öffentlichkeit,* 341. If Caroline was real, however, her role as a feisty collaborator of La Roche's, and as the author of several items in *Pomona* and elsewhere, should be acknowledged. If she was La Roche's invention, then La Roche's continued command of a a straightforward, zesty writing style deserves attention.

119. SLR-*BM* 25.
120. Worley, "Sophie von La Roche's *Reisejournale,*" 101.
121. SLR-*BM* 212; her emphasis.
122. Loster-Schneider has written an excellent analysis of this book. Although she initially acknowledges its title as an allusion to La Roche as writer—Loster-Schneider, *Sophie La Roche,* 293—she later asserts, based on La Roche's introduction, that the book is about her as "individual woman, mother, grandmother, but not as author" (295).
123. Ibid. 294.
124. SLR-*FS* 45.
125. SLR-*MS* 1:6.
126. Trouille, *Sexual Politics,* 302–5.
127. SLR-*MS* 1:9.
128. La Roche's friendship with Julie Bondeli is discussed in Becker-Cantarino, "Zur Theorie der literarischen Freundschaft," 47–52. In many parts of educated German society, French was the language of culture. La Roche made the decision to write her first novel in German rather than French only with Wieland's encouragement. It was not the language in which she had the most literary practice. In 1753, when at age twenty-three she married, Sophie La Roche had entered an aristocratic world in which not only correspondence but also daily conversation was conducted in French. Even earlier, with Wieland himself she had communicated in French, at least in writing, as they conducted a long and ultimately fruitless engagement. She persisted in writing to her elder daughter in French right up to Maxe's death. Fluency in French enabled aristocratic and educated middle-class women to participate somewhat in the world of their men. Sophie La Roche thus could assist her husband in the composition and copying of endless letters that were part of his work; Schiller on at least one occasion asked his sister-in-law, Caroline von Beulwitz (later Wolzogen, 1763–1847), not just to copy but to compose a French letter for him (Walter, *Schrieb oft,* 63). It opened to women an additional world of reading, which in turn enabled them to participate in literary life in another way, by becoming translators. Despite the advantages, knowledge of French was also in some respects a handicap for German women aspiring to be writers. Since aristocratic women in particular were lured more toward French than German, many women of their class were not routinely members of the reading public to whom German women writers addressed their works. This produced a different socioeconomic profile of the reading audience in Germany than in France or England. Detrimental to the German women who were inclined to become writers was that they had often gained proficiency in the foreign language by neglecting German. Sophie La Roche herself long had no confidence writing in her native tongue when she made her first adult efforts.
129. SLR-*MS* 2: 148–50, 285–309.
130. Loster-Schneider, *Sophie La Roche,* 309.
131. Arnim, *Die Günderode,* 259.
132. Wolf, " 'Nun ja! Das nächste Leben geht aber heute an,' " 574.
133. It seems to me that the first section of Loster-Schneider's book (48–88)

seriously overstates the duration of Wieland's aesthetic impact on Sophie La Roche, but if Loster-Schneider's detailed analysis of Wieland's ideas is read as a more general account of a widely available set of values and prescriptions that endured for a considerable stretch of the eighteenth century (summarized under the heading *Empfindsamkeit*), then the book helps to explain the intellectual context in which La Roche was writing and the repressive attitudes toward women that dogged her and her contemporaries.

134. Cited and translated by Britt, in La Roche, *History of Lady Sophia Sternheim*, 13.

135. SLR-*P* 1784: 1141–42.

136. Klencke and Karsch lived together most of the years from the birth of the daughter until the death of the mother, but the relationship was rarely really positive and, in fact, was often abusive, as is now becoming apparent in the most recent editions of their letters, addressed to Gleim (Pott, *Briefgespräche*, 42–43, 171). Ute Pott points out that aside from editing her mother's work, Klencke stopped writing when her mother died (*Briefgespräche*, 62).

137. Sch 1:148, 3:100–101.

Chapter 4: Longing for Respectability

1. My emphasis; Grant, *Fundamental Feminism*, 164.
2. Schlegel, *Caroline, Briefe aus der Frühromantik*, 1:31–32.
3. Grant, *Fundamental Feminism,* 163.
4. Ibid. 163–64.
5. La Vopa, "Herder's *Publikum*," 15.
6. PEG-78, 37.
7. Schulte-Sasse, "Poetik und Ästhetik Lessings und seiner Zeitgenossen," 318.
8. Bovenschen, *Weiblichkeit*, 150–256.
9. In an entry about the *Empfindsamkeit* that I wrote for *The Feminist Encyclopedia of German Literature*, I called this strand the *Empfindsamkeit* of empathy (Eigler and Kord, *Feminist Encyclopedia of German Literature,* 479). Further investigation of the terms has caused me to reconsider that choice. "Empathy" is a twentieth-century loan-translation into English of the German word *Einfühlung*, which is not at all the orientation toward *Mitleid* that I wish to express with the name of this strand.
10. PEG-82 219–220.
11. Brüggemann, *Handbuch zur Kinder- und Jugendliteratur von 1750 bis 1800*, 352.
12. Friedrichs, *Die deutschsprachigen Schriftstellerinnen*, 74.
13. *Grundlage zu einer Hessischen Gelehrten und Schriftsteller Geschichte*, ed. Strieder, 3:359.
14. Engelhard, "Engelhardin," 365.
15. Ruth Klüger proposes a different profile of women writers, seeing the backgrounds of the original and important ones as more profoundly separated from that of men. The value judgments entailed in originality and importance are crucial to her argument, which is thought-provoking, nonetheless. Klüger, "Zum Außenseitertum der deutschen Dichterinnen," 13–19.
16. Einem to Sprickmann, 13 September 1777. I am grateful to the Universitäts- und Landesbibliothek of Münster for permission to use and cite the correspondence between Einem and Sprickmann.

17. Einem to Sprickmann, 3 July 1778.
18. PEG-78 3–8.
19. Rotermund, *Das gelehrte Hannover*, cxxxxv.
20. SLR-*FS* 45.
21. Years later, in writing about the composition of *Fräulein von Sternheim*, La Roche elaborates on the therapy element, saying a friend suggested she write as way of dealing with her extremely unhappy feelings when her young daughters went away to school (SLR-*BM* 201).
22. Karsch, *O, mir entwischt nicht*, 34.
23. Bandemer, *Poetische und prosaische Versuche*, 26.
24. Sch 1:216.
25. Seidel, *Hinterlassene Schriften*, 263.
26. PEG-78 1–6.
27. Spencer, *Rise of the Woman Novelist*, 91.
28. Bürger and Gatterer, *Briefwechsel aus Göttingens empfindsamer Zeit*, 108.
29. PEG-78 1.
30. PEG-82 118.
31. SLR-*FS* 45.
32. SLR-BM, 202.
33. PEG-82 119.
34. The exception is the terrible, twisted, and evidently violent relationship between Karsch and her daughter; see, as mentioned in an earlier note, Pott, *Briefgespräche*, 42–43, 171, and Becker-Cantarino, Vorwort in *Gedichte. Nach der Dichterin Tode*, 12, 21–22. Also consider Prokop on Catharina Elisabeth Goethe's non-relationship to her daughter (*Illusion vom grossen Paar*, 1:318).
35. Figes, *Sex and Subterfuge*, 27.
36. PEG-82 117.
37. Einem to Sprickmann, 12 May 1778.
38. Krammnick, "Making of the English Canon," 1088.
39. Ibid. 1090.
40. Einem to Sprickmann, 12 May 1778.
41. Einem to Sprickmann, 25–26 July 1778.
42. Bürger and Gatterer, *Briefwechsel*, 72.
43. Zionkowski, "Strategies of Containment," 100.
44. Bürger and Gatterer, *Briefwechsel*, 35–36.
45. Einem to Sprickmann, 12 May 1778.
46. Bürger and Gatterer, *Briefwechsel*, 36.
47. Zionkowski, "Strategies of Containment," 103.
48. Bürger and Gatterer, *Briefwechsel*, 76–77.
49. This is a sample of Bürger's parody:

> Auf die Art ist, mit Gunst,
> Das Versemachen keine Kunst,
> Wenn man so ohne viel besinnen
> Die Verse lässt wie Wasser rinnen
> Dann mach' ich in einem Odenzug
> So viel daher, dass sie genug
> Vom Geborenwerden bis zum Begraben
> Soll Tag und Nacht zu lesen haben.
>
> (*Briefwechsel* 107)

[In this way, beg pardon, / versifying is not an art, / when one lets the verses run like water / without much thought / Then I can make in a single breath / enough of them that you will have enough / to read day and night / from birth to death.]

50. PEG-78 12.
51. Hölty, "Elegie eines Schäfers" and "Die Beschäftigungen der Menschen."
52. Sch 1:260.
53. PEG-78 49.
54. Bürger and Gatterer, *Briefwechsel*, 34–35.
55. PEG-78 50.
56. Quoted in Wittmann, "Buchhändlerzeitschriften," 684–85.
57. PEG-78 127–29.
58. "An Meine Freunde," PEG-82 217–18.
59. Reviews in the major reviewing organs were widely read. After the young author Georg Forster, who had just completed his account of circumnavigating the globe with Captain Cook, met Philippine Gatterer, he wrote to his father in London, saying the older man would surely be familiar with Gatterer's poetry from the review in the *Göttinger Gelehrten Anzeigen*. The poems were, Forster went on to comment, "very beautiful" (Forster, *Werke*, 13:168). Such fame had a general effect. Even two years after the first collection appeared, Caroline Michaelis expected that her friend in Erfurt, Luise Gotter, would know about Philippine Gatterer "thanks to the goddess of fame." Schlegel, *Caroline und Dorothea Schlegel in Briefen*, 31. Presumably, the gender of the poet was important in making her memorable.
60. Kord, *Namen machen*, 156–64.
61. *Allgemeine deutsche Bibliothek* 37 [1779]: 476–77.
62. PEG-78 132–36.
63. *Allgemeine deutsche Bibliothek* 37 [1779]: 477.
64. *Allgemeine deutsche Bibliothek* 54 [1783]: 156–57.
65. Kord, *Namen machen*, 158.
66. *Allgemeine deutsche Bibliothek* 37 [1779]: 476–78.
67. *Allgemeine deutsche Bibliothek* 54 [1783]: 157–58.
68. Greer, *The Obstacle Race*, 294.
69. *Allgemeine deutsche Bibliothek* 54 [1783]:158.
70. Karsch, *O, mir entwischt nicht,* 241–44.
71. Bürger and Gatterer, *Briefwechsel*, 64–65.
72. *Allgemeine deutsche Bibliothek* 80 [1788]: 2, 556.
73. Spangenberg to Baldinger, 26 May 1782. I wish to express my profound thanks to the Niedersächsische Staats- und Universitätsbibliothek in Göttingen for the use of the Baldinger and Spangenberg correspondence.
74. Given Spangenberg's record of pseudonymous publication, it is possible to consider her also as one of Engelhard-Gatterer's imitators. Her poems, which are described as full of feeling and often religious, included one that became a regular part of many funeral services of the time (Sch 2:332–34). Whether Spangenberg's authorship was widely known, especially whether Baldinger was aware of it, I have not been able to determine.
75. Bürger and Gatterer, *Briefwechsel*, 97.
76. The subscribers are listed alphabetically by place in the back of the little book. Although the only copy I have seen breaks off after St. Petersburg, it contains 435 names and accounts for at least 566 copies. Probably a little less than 10 percent of the names are missing, which means that the complete list would presumably show about 475 subscribers buying 600 copies or more.
77. Ingrao, *Hessian Mercenary State,* 76.
78. PEG-82 150–51
79. Jean Paul [Richter], *Briefe 1780–1793*, 3:295.

80. Engelhard to Kästner. 18 February 1788. I am deeply grateful to the Stadtarchiv in Göttingen for the opportunity to use and cite this correspondence.
81. PEG-21 64.
82. Lichtenberg. *Briefwechsel*, 321.
83. Engelhard to Nicolai. 19 December 1803.
84. In her later years, she was more willing to say it was for herself; by then she was aged, widowed, and suffering like many others from the economic side effects of the French Revolution (she had lost incomes from rents and fees that her husband had been awarded).
85. SLR-P 1783: 251–53; *Magazin für Frauenzimmer*, 1782: III, 755–56; IV, 857–58.
86. Itemized in Stummann-Bowert, "Philippine Engelhard," 41–42.
87. Rotermund, *Das gelehrte Hannover,* cxxxxv.
88. Ibid. cxxxxv.
89. *Morgenblatt* 1818, nr. 201.
90. Kiesel and Münch, *Gesellschaft*, 185.
91. Philippine Engelhard, trans. *Lieder,* by Beranger, 2.
92. PEG-82 157–59. The complete text of the poem and a rhymed translation are available in Blackwell and Zantop, ed. *Bitter Healing*, 194–99.

Chapter 5: Confronting the Lords of Creation

1. Hausen, "Family and Role-Division," 51–83.
2. ME-G 28.
3. Flint, "Speaking Objects," 212–26.
4. ME-G 32.
5. Flint, "Speaking Objects," 221.
6. ME-G 39.
7. Miller, ed. *Poetics of Gender*, xi.
8. ME-G 43.
9. Flint, "Speaking Objects," 215–16.
10. ME-G 49.
11. Bartky, "Toward a Phenomenology of Feminist Consciousness," 14–15.
12. Ehrmann's novel *Amalie* was reprinted in an edition of 500 copies in 1995 well edited by Maya Widmer and Doris Stump, who also edited the much less interesting *Kleine Fragmente für Denkerinnen*, under the title *Ein Weib ein Wort*. Ehrmann's play, *Leichtsinn und gutes Herz*, is included in a collection published by Karin Wurst in 1993. Most recently, Madland's biography, *Marianne Ehrmann*, contains extensive excerpts translated into English from a variety of Ehrmann texts.
13. Touaillon, *Frauenroman*, 228. Krull, *Wirken der Frau im frühen deutschen Zeitschriftenwesen*, 275.
14. Huyssen, *Drama des Sturm und Drang*, 1980.
15. Madland, "Introduction to the Works and Life," 177, 191.
16. Huyssen, *Drama des Sturm und Drang*, 48.
17. Roebling, writing about Sophie Albrecht's drama *Theresgen*, asserts that the *Sturm und Drang* notion of the artist as independent and self-guided genius is unimaginable in female form ("Sturm und Drang—weiblich," 63), but this is precisely what Nina represents.
18. Ibid. 53.

19. Dedert, *Erzählung im Sturm und Drang*, 8–9.
20. My translation; Huyssen, *Drama des Sturm und Drang*, 83.
21. Ibid. 84.
22. Hart, *Tragedy in Paradise*.
23. Huyssen, *Drama des Sturm und Drang*, 13–20.
24. Roebling, examining Albrecht's *Theresgen* for the pedagogical journal *Deutschunterricht*, argues for reading the play as "female *Sturm und Drang*" because, first, placing the play in relation to a known movement makes it more teachable, and, second, because, now that scholars such as Huyssen have enlarged our understanding of *Sturm und Drang*, we have an opportunity to further refine it—Roebling, "Sturm und Drang—weiblich," 64. I agree that it is useful both for our understanding of a work such as Ehrmann's "Story of a Handkerchief" or Albrecht's *Theresgen* and of a period such as *Sturm und Drang* to see works in their literary-historical context, although that does not necessarily mean designating a work (or a writer) as belonging to that movement. As for the rereading of *Sturm und Drang* in recent years, I still do not see serious reception there of women writers. It is the literary historiography of the also greatly revised *Empfindsamkeit* that seems to me much more receptive. Roebling also makes a third argument that teaching about women's contributions to culture is an important consideration; I strongly agree, but do not see this as connected with *Sturm und Drang* allocation.
25. Madland asserts that "Ehrmann's writing has an affinity to the Sturm und Drang" ("Introduction to the Life and Works," 171) and that her "aggressive Sturm und Drang mode is especially evident in *Leichtsinn und gutes Herz*" ("Introduction to the Life and Works," 177); she also elaborates on Ehrmann's infanticide fiction as fitting in with *Sturm und Drang* motifs ("Gender"). Touaillon, writing in 1919 about *Antonie von Warnstein* (not recognizing its identity with *Amalie*), considers that Ehrmann belongs to the *Empfindsamkeit* but notes that she has some of the marks of the *Sturm und Drang* as well as Enlightenment (*Frauenroman*, 228). Krull, on the other hand, focusing in 1939 on Ehrmann's journalism, argues that the only thing Ehrmann has in common with *Empfindsamkeit* is a few expressions but that her fiery style, often extreme demands, ethically motivated fight against the status quo, and choice of topics all align her with the *Sturm und Drang* (*Wirken*, 275–76).
26. Doris Stump has clarified long-disputed issues about Ehrmann's birth and childhood in her essay at the end of the new edition of *Amalie* ("Eine Frau 'von Verstand, Witz, Gefühl, Fantasie und Feuer,' " 481–98). In another recent scholarly work on Ehrmann, Madland's "Introduction to the Life and Works" gives full credence to the statements of Ehrmann's husband on biographical matters (172); Madland is only slightly less willing to accept his word in her new biography, *Marianne Ehrmann: Reason and Emotion in Her Life and Works*, even though it means ignoring a passage she cites in another credible biographical source in which Ehrmann's husband displays jealousy of her (159).
27. Widmer and Stump state simply that the marriage ended by divorce but offer no documentation in their annotated reprint edition of *Amalie* (490, 529). Madland thinks the matter is uncertain. T. F. Ehrmann wrote in his biography of his wife after her death (when he was publishing and republishing her work and thus may have had reason to represent her in conventional terms), that the first husband died (Madland, "Introduction to the Life and Works," 181).
28. This was the job Sophie La Roche urged her own daughter-in-law to take up after La Roche's son had abandoned her and her children—La Roche, *Ich bin*

mehr Herz, 366–67. Angelika Rosa's account of her life as a governess, included in her autobiography, helps makes it clear why this choice was unattractive —Heuser, *Ich wünschte,* 150–64.

29. ME-G 40–41.
30. Widmer, "Amalie—eine wahre Geschichte?" 500.
31. The best accounts of this small publication to date are in Wägenbauer's *Pathologie der Liebe* (36–41) and Madland, *Marianne Ehrmann* (25–44).
32. Ehrmann, *Leichtsinn und gutes Herz,* 189.
33. Wurst, *Frauen und Drama,* 85.
34. I have not read *Graf Bilding,* but see Madland, *Marianne Ehrmann,* 148–56.
35. Ehrmann, *Einsiedlerinn* 1794, 3:285–87.
36. Not only did Madland not know in 1989 that *Amalie* and *Antonie* were the same text when she wrote her "Introduction to the Works and Life" (173), but the entry on Ehrmann in the 1997 *Feminist Encyclopedia of German Literature,* edited by Eigler and Kord, also does not make the connection (109).
37. ME-*A* 1:16.
38. Goethe, *Goethes Schwiegertochter,* 14.
39. ME-*A* 1:16.
40. Ehrmann, *Philosophie eines Weibes,* 19, 35, 59.
41. Pomerleau, "Emergence of Women's Autobiography," 32.
42. ME-*A* 1:60.
43. An important exception is Wobeser's *Elise oder das Weib wie es seyn sollte* (1798), in which a good woman makes a bad marriage because her family wishes it, even though she is in love with someone else. Despite this contrast, neither Ehrmann nor Wobeser is interested so much in how a marriage is made as in how it works after the wedding.
44. ME-*A* 1:72.
45. Ehrmann, *Philosophie eines Weibes,* 59.
46. ME-*A* 1:178.
47. Figes, *Sex and Subterfuge,* 33.
48. ME-*A* 1:212.
49. Johnson, *Equivocal Beings,* 23.
50. ME-*A* 2:77.
51. Hausen, "Family and Role-Division," 69.
52. Ibid. 69–70.
53. ME-*A* 1:80.
54. Madland discusses *Amalie* as a mix of the earlier epistolary novel and the newer Bildungsroman (*Marianne* 118–19).
55. Lanser, "Courting Death: *Roman, romantisme,* and *Mistress Henley's* Narrative Practices," 52.
56. ME-*A* 2:245.
57. Hausen, "Family and Role-Division," 59.
58. Ibid.
59. *Teutscher Merkur* 1791, 2:63.
60. Berlepsch to Herder, 18 October (1787). For years, Emilie Berlepsch wrote to a close friend in Weimar, the critic and philosopher Johann Gottfried Herder (1744–1803), about her difficult marriage; perhaps his detailed awareness of her experience made him more sympathetic when Sophie Mereau later came to him for help in her own effort to obtain a divorce. Because Berlepsch avoided the word divorce in her letters to Herder—she depicts her husband as the one

seeking this change in their status—the legal events described in the correspondence are hard to trace exactly; other biographical sources about Berlepsch and her first husband omit the date of their divorce. Her first contribution to the *Teutscher Merkur*, in 1791, was a poem (1:113–7) addressed to Herder.

61. She uses the word adjectivally, writing about "the consequences of that misogynist tone" "die Folgen dieses misogynischen Tons." *Teutscher Merkur* 1791, 2:83.

62. Möhrmann, *Die andere Frau,* 110.

63. *Teutscher Merkur* 1791 2:82.

64. Schumann, " 'Lesende Frauenzimmer': Frauenzeitschriften," 156; Geiger and Weigel, eds. *Sind das noch Damen?* 13–28; Madland, *Marianne Ehrmann,* 158–63, 183–84.

65. One of the people whose help Ehrmann requested was Philippine Engelhard's old mentor, the impoverished and recently again widowed Gottfried August Bürger. Along with an announcement of *Amaliens Erholungsstunden,* Ehrmann sent him an excerpt from an issue of her husband's *Beobachter,* a poem by a young woman in Stuttgart expressing her love for the famous and popular poet Bürger. In the series of letters that followed, Marianne Ehrmann accidentally became the intermediary for Bürger's disastrous last marriage, to the bright and adventurous Elisa Hahn (*Briefe von Gottfried August Bürger*; see also Madland, *Marianne,* 44–50 and 114–15).

66. Madland, "Introduction to the Life and Works," 182–85, and Madland, *Marianne Ehrmann,* 215–25.

67. ME-*AES* 1792, 1: 144–55.

68. Klopstock, *Wunderliche Dinger,* 89.

69. Seidel, *Hinterlassene Schriften,* 94.

70. ME-*AES* 1792, 1:154.

71. ME-*AES* 1791, 1:96.

72. Grenz, *Mädchenliteratur,* 86.

73. ME-*AES* 1792, 3:131–32.

74. Madland, "Introduction to the Life and Works," 176.

75. Quoted in Krull, *Wirken der Frau,* 242.

76. ME-*AES* 1792, 1:155–65.

77. Figes, *Sex and Subterfuge,* 26.

78. Ehrmann, *Einsiedlerinn* 1793, 2:274–78.

79. The dialogue is almost untranslatable. Here is a sample of the marmot boy's language:

(Singt.)   "Ik bin si ein armi Marmottenbub,
             ak geb si mir dok was ihr Menschen!
(Spricht.) He *bella Signorina* da drob, mik nik vergas da drund! Kann si ein andermal von di Liebhab küß laß di And. Geb si mir nur su erst ein Stük Brod, das ik kan mein Unger still. Ik und meini Thier hab si eüd nok gar niks geß. Wir sin si so matt wie die Flieg im Wint, hab si dok *pieta* mit uns armi Kreatur. (277)

Again, Ehrmann seems to have been ahead of her time, closer to Büchner than to Nicolai.

80. ME-*AES,* 1790, 2:73.

81. Madland proposes that one of the satirical essays in the journal is by a Maria Dorothea Mezger (*Marianne* 238).

82. ME-*AES* 1790, 4:95.

83. Krull, *Wirken der Frau,* 251.

84. Offen, "Defining Feminism," 151.
85. Schlözer, *Dorothea von Schlözer*, 108–9.
86. Möhrmann, *Andere Frau*, 31–32.
87. Quoted in Krull, *Wirken der Frau*, 238
88. ME-*AES* 1791, 2:267.
89. Quoted in Krull, *Wirken der Frau*, 251.
90. ME-*AES* 1791, 2:240.
91. Geiger and Weigel, *Sind das noch Damen?* 23.
92. ME-*AES* 1790, 2:73.
93. Quoted in Krull, *Wirken der Frau*, 248–9.
94. ME-*AES* 1790, 2:126.
95. For her relation with other German protofeminists, see note 109 in this chapter. Madland argues Ehrmann's "chief allies are her wit, an unfailing faith in education, and her second husband" ("Introduction to the Life and Works" 179), but this depiction of T. F. Ehrmann is open to dispute. Thus, the passage from his introduction to one of his wife's novels that Madland reads as "uniquely supportive," I read as superfluous and condescending (181). And the way Ehrmann writes about his wife after her death is shaped, I suspect, by the interest he had in making her acceptable so that her writings were still marketable. Ehrmann was already an established writer when she married T. F. Ehrmann, and he may understandably have found it difficult to cope with this unconventional situation. Madland acknowledges that during an extended stay in the Ehrmann home a visitor was made distinctly uncomfortable by the way the husband and wife competed for his attention ("Introduction to the Life and Works" 190).
96. Bovenschen, *Imaginierte Weiblichkeit*, 220–224, 239–56.
97. *Flora* 1795, 1:101.
98. Ibid. 1793, 3:73.
99. Another example, from the *Berlinische Monatsschrift* of 1786, is extensively cited in Simon, "Schillers 'Berühmte Frau,' " 289–92.
100. *Flora*, 1794, 1:294.
101. Ibid. 1794, 1:297.
102. Ibid. 1794, 2:85.
103. Ibid. 1794, 2:87.
104. I have speculated elsewhere that the author might have been Marianne Ehrmann herself ("And This Shield" 173–74).
105. Quoted in Krull, *Wirken der Frau*, 248.
106. Ehrmann, *Einsiedlerinn* 1793, 1:146)
107. ME-*AES* 1792, 3:132.
108. It is extraordinary that a biographical sketch of Hippel in 1980 contains no reference to this important work (Stenzel, *Zeitalter der Aufklärung*, 89).
109. It is not known how much these three knew about each other's work. Marianne Ehrmann could, for example, have read the essay on marriage by Emilie von Berlepsch. Ehrmann knew something about the outspoken aristocrat, for *Einsiedlerinn aus den Alpen* contains a poem "An die Frau Präsidentin Emilie von Berlepsch" "To Frau President Emilie von Berlepsch" (her title derived from her husband's position; *Einsiedlerinn* 1794, 1: 117–18). Yet, because the essay in the *Teutscher Merkur* was signed merely E. v. B., even if Ehrmann read it, she might not have realized the concerns she and Berlepsch had in common as the strongest female public representatives of early feminist thought in Germany. Of course, there were differences, including differences of audience. Berlepsch's publications were in the hands of the formidable literary establishment of the time, which

means that although she usually ostensibly addressed her writing to women or to a particular woman, she was probably read more by men. Ehrmann's writings, though their reception is not clearly documented, seem to have been well disseminated and widely read by women, though the question, in turn, of whether Emilie von Berlepsch knew them is also unanswered. And there is no known evidence about whether either woman knew of Hippel's anonymous book about the improvement of women.

110. Sellner, "Appendix: Rauschenbusch-Clough," 219–21.
111. Berlepsch, *Caledonia,* 251–52.
112. Ibid. 252.
113. Pomerleau, "Emergence of Women's Autobiography," 36.
114. Berlepsch, *Caledonia,* 282.

CHAPTER 6: EXAMINING PASSION

1. Zantop, "Trivial Pursuits?" 15.
2. Schacht, *Future of Alienation,* 23–24.
3. SA81 181.
4. Blackwell, "Marriage by the Book," 138.
5. SA91 94–95.
6. Klopstock, *Wunderliche Dinger,* 12.
7. Ibid.
8. For a study of lesbian relationships in eighteenth-century Germany, Jenny von Voigts, who had an especially long list of foster daughters whom she had cared for, would appear to be a potentially promising subject—bearing in mind, of course, as Lillian Faderman has made clear for the nineteenth century, that behavior we today might label lesbianism was very differently understood then—Faderman, *Surpassing the Love of Men.*
9. SA81 74.
10. Schröder, *Hamburgische Schriftsteller,* 42.
11. Ibid. Since Schröder was writing his lexicon only eleven years after Albrecht's death, it is possible that he obtained this detail from someone who had known her.
12. Jones, "Surprising Fame," 83.
13. SA81 64–65.
14. SA91 54.
15. SA91 162.
16. SA81 22–23.
17. Cook, "Going Public," 40.
18. Kord, *Blick hinter die Kulissen*; Wurst, *Frauen und Drama im Achtzehnten Jahrhundert*; Hoff, *Dramen des Weiblichen.*
19. Kord, *Namen machen,* 67–68.
20. Bohm, "Authority and Authorship," 130.
21. Bohm, "Authority and Authorship," 130.
22. Roebling, "Sturm und Drang—weiblich," 70–71.
23. Maza, "The Rose-Girl," 401.
24. Prokop, *Illusion vom Grossen Paar,* 38.
25. Roebling designates her as "bürgerlich" ("Sturm und Drang—weiblich," 69), middle class as I am translating the term, but it seems to me that Albrecht draws on the prettified version of rural life familiar from the idyll—she includes

some idylls in the volume with the plays—to present Theresgen as an unusually privileged village girl who, since her stepfather works the land (with his own hands), must be considered a peasant.

26. Wurst, *Frauen und Drama im Achtzehnten Jahrhundert,* 72.
27. Prokop, *Illusion vom Grossen Paar,* 99.
28. Wurst, *Familiale Liebe,* 40.
29. SA-*T* 148.
30. SA-*T* 170.
31. Wurst's textual emendation; SA-*T* 163–64.
32. SA-*T* 165.
33. Roebling offers a detailed reading of how the count and Heinrich, functioning as two father figures, fail their daughter and are thereby morally disempowered in the play (Roebling, "Sturm und Drang—weiblich," 71–73).
34. Wurst, *Familiale Liebe,* 29.
35. Roebling, "Sturm und Drang—weiblich," 75; von Hoff, on the other hand, sees Theresgen as marked by death from the beginning of the play (*Dramen des Weiblichen,* 77).
36. SA-*T* 185.
37. Roebling, "Sturm und Drang—weiblich," 75.
38. SA-*T* 167.
39. Malcolmson, " 'What You Will,' " 32.
40. As far as is known, Sophie Albrecht's play was never performed, but Müller's was staged at a theater in Vienna. It is notable that when Austrian women became active as public writers in the eighteenth century, it was usually in connection with the theater (Dawson, "Frauen und Theater," 421).
41. Friederike Caroline Neuber (1697–1763), already notable as the director who introduced influential reforms into the practice of the German theater, wrote plays and dramatic prologues and epilogues. The actress Maria Antonia Teutscher (1752–84) wrote *Fanny, oder die glückliche Wiedervereinigung* "Fanny, or The Happy Reunion" idealizing passive femininity in the manner of the sentimental *Empfindsamkeit,* and saw herself rewarded with performances in Vienna. Another actress, Juliana Hain (1758–?), reworked in *Der Dichterling oder Solche Insekten giebts die Menge* "The Poetlet, or There Are Lots of Insects Like That" the stock eighteenth-century story of the immature and excessively bookish writer.
42. Wurst, "Elise Bürger."
43. See Dawson, "Catherine the Great: Playwright"; O'Malley, ed. and trans. *Two Comedies by Catherine the Great*; O'Malley, "Masks of the Empress"; and O'Malley, "Monarch and Mystic."
44. For a fuller account of these and other aristocratic female playwrights, see Dawson, "Frauen und Theater."
45. The status of these apparently unpublished plays requires further examination, especially because Susanne Kord, in the invaluable list of playwrights and their works that she attaches to her volume on German women dramatists, has found library locations for several of the works of these women. They are Sabine Elisabeth Oelgard von Basseritz ("Verzeichniß" 1790, 1:315), Karoline Baudissin (*Allgemeine deutsche Biographie*; see Kord *Blick hinter die Kulissen* 332), Karoline von Bentheim-Steinfurt (Goedeke 5:400), Anne Margarethe Hofmann (Sch 3:164, 167), Princess Ulrike of Mecklenburg-Schwerin, Countess Louise of Mecklenburg-Schwerin ("Verzeichniß" 1788, 1:138; see Kord, *Blick hinter die Kulissen,* 403 and 434), and the Princess of Thurn and Taxis (*Gotha Theaterkalendar* 173), as well as Elisa von der Recke and Charlotte von Stein, since their

plays, although written in the eighteenth century, were neither published nor performed until the nineteenth.

46. Dawson, "Reconstructing Women's Literary Relationships," 181, 211. In 1784, Sophie Albrecht was a rising young actress, and the aristocrat from the far north was making a trip through Germany, visiting as many important people as she could. Von der Recke evidently wrote to the young actress in the fall (Frels, *Deutsche Dichterhandschriften,* 233) and then, during a short stay in Erfurt, saw her at a concert which they were both attending (Becker, *Elise von der Reckes Reisen,* 84). The next spring, in April of 1785, von der Recke wrote to Albrecht again, a letter of introduction for a young painter (Albrecht, "Appendix: Albrecht's Correspondence," 211).

47. Albrecht also seems to have been passingly acquainted with Goethe (Hahn, ed., *Briefe an Goethe,* 1:381), but there is no evidence that this acquaintance was even nearly as important as the relationship with Schiller.

48. Schiller, *Werke; Nationalausgabe,* 23:137–38.
49. Ibid. 23:138.
50. Kord, *Namen machen,* 70–74.
51. These single women included Sophie Albrecht's sister (for volume one—if she subscribed again to volume two it was under a married name which is untraceable), friends such as Demoiselle Amalia Kopp in Erfurt (as with Madam, the borrowed French term signals her middle-class status) and Fräulein von Dachröden, and other readers like Fräulein von Dalberg, who was the sister of the governor of Erfurt and a convent member in Cologne. Basically, however, women's names were uncommon on the list, with a slight probability that when they appeared they were members of the aristocracy. Proper middle-class women, lacking a tradition as patrons of the arts but strongly affected, instead, by injunctions to remain private, seemed less likely to have their names on published lists. These considerations mean that it is impossible to determine how many of Albrecht's readers were men and how many women.

52. SA85 8–9.
53. The citation is from Betsy Draine's account of Linda S. Kauffman's *Discourses of Desire: Gender, Genre, and Epistolary Fictions* (Draine, "Refusing the Wisdom of Solomon," 160).
54. Becker, *Elise von der Reckes Reisen,* 84.
55. Walter, *Schrieb oft,* 29.
56. Schröder, *Lexikon der Hamburgischen Schriftsteller,* 43.
57. SA91 84.
58. SA85 101–102.
59. SA81 13–16.
60. Castle, *Female Thermometer,* 120–39.
61. Ibid. 123.
62. SA91 181–246.
63. SA85 211–12.
64. SA91 229.
65. Bovenschen, *Imaginierte Weiblichkeit,* 212–13.
66. MacArthur, "Devious Narratives: Refusal of Closure," 6.
67. Quoted in Kindermann, *Von der Aufklärung zur Romantik,* 5:633.
68. Albrecht, *Anthologie aus den Poesien,* 14.
69. If her poetry was inspired by moments of her own experience, then a loosening of the marriage must have begun even in Reval, when she was in her early twenties. She may have fallen in love there and someone, either the lover or her

husband, proved unfaithful. The fact that she published poetry on these topics in her home town and with the help of her husband raises the question whether her writing really does record events, and yet, the other fact that these poems, unlike most of the rest, have specific dates ("Im Februar 1778" or "Im Mai 1779") gives them a documentary quality. In 1780, a poem appears about loving "him" again.

70. Albrecht, *Anthologie aus den Poesien,* 14.
71. Jördens, *Lexikon deutscher Dichter und Prosaisten,* 550.
72. Schiller, *Werke; Nationalausgabe,* 23:137–38.
73. Geissler, ed., *Archiv weiblicher Hauptkenntnisse* 2:349.
74. Albrecht's new publishing and theater connections in Leipzig and Dresden opened a whole new region of potential readers to the poet, who until then had not had a single subscriber in either city—and none in Berlin or Prague, either. Now, however, she no longer had to rely on collecting subscribers, for Richter accepted her book without requiring that kind of prepayment. The resulting unidentifiability of her buyers makes tracing the further development of her readership impossible.
75. SA91 5–9.
76. Schiller reacted indifferently to the northward departure of his old friend; in 1797, he noted simply that she was gone and had been replaced by a Madame Hartwig (*Werke; Nationalausgabe,* 36,1:417). At about this time, one of Albrecht's Dresden admirers, Siegfried August Mahlmann (1771–1826), in a long letter reassured the actress that everyone was disillusioned with Madame Hartwig, although she had been very charming at first, and that he of course missed Albrecht's presence very much. Mahlmann also sent his greetings to her husband (undated letter).
77. Dawson, "Reconstructing Women's Literary Relationships," 180–81.
78. For Ehrmann's marital history see note 27 in chapter 5.
79. For details see Becker-Cantarino, *Der lange Weg,* 54–55.
80. It is alleged that Albrecht remarried—a man named von Hahn. And after his death she is supposed to have married her first husband again. While documentation on this is missing, it appears that the relation of the two Albrechts did not break off completely with their divorce. In 1801, they published a collection of stories together: *Erzählungen aus dem Dunkel der Vorzeit* "Tales from the Darkness of Long Ago."
81. *Teutscher Merkur* 1793: 176–77.
82. Grenz, *Mädchenliteratur,* 84.
83. Jördens, *Lexikon deutscher Dichter und Prosaisten,* 550. In 1978, Hadley noted that *Graumännchen* "had a certain fascination because of a light and easy style" and said that the author showed "restraint in presenting his mysterious events." In short, in praising the book Hadley assumed that S. Albrecht was male. Hadley, *Undiscovered Genre,* 106.
84. Karin Wurst mentions the role of incest in another woman's Gothic text, which might well make a good comparison with Albrecht's, Elise Bürger's narrative, "Dirza" ("Elise Bürger," 17).
85. SA-*ID* 118–19.
86. Gero von Wilpert, in his overview of the German ghost story from Middle Ages to the present, categorizes *Ida von Duba* as belonging to the Enlightenment, clearly a derogatory assignment in his system. According to his scheme, in Enlightenment ghost novels "everything mysterious, miraculous, and unreal in the plot is resolved in the end by a reasonable explanation, usually as mechanically staged visual tricks" (my translation, *Deutsche Gespensterschichte,* 124). Also,

the explanations are usually hinted at beforehand, sometimes in ways that invite the readers to apply their own detective skills to figure out how something works (*Deutsche Gespenstergeschichte,* 124–125). After mentioning three men writers of this type of ghost novel, Wilpert begins his comment on three women writers: "Astonishingly enough, the gentle sex too, working at home, took active part in the spread of ghosts." Eighteenth-century men, he seems to think, went to an office to write! Wilpert's total discussion of Albrecht is to characterize *Ida von Duba* as the "sentimental-moral story of an arrogant beauty" and to cite the full title of *Graumännchen*. In my view, the characterization that Wilpert proposes for ghost stories of German Romanticism actually better fits Albrecht's text. Countering the "de-poetization and secularization of life in the eighteenth century, the new view demands the re-poetization of life, the freeing of creative imagination from the limitations of reason, the transformation of knowledge back into the unconscious, and the production of a higher mythic condition"; he also speaks approvingly of the Romantics' effort to create "literature that addressed all classes" of readers (*Deutsche Gespenstergeschichte,* 184).

87. SA-*ID* iii.
88. Wurst, "Elise Bürger," 20.
89. My insertion; Albrecht, *Legenden,* iii–iv.
90. Castle, *Female Thermometer,* 8.
91. Neumann-Strele, "Sophie Albrecht, Lebensbeschreibung."
92. Albrecht letter to Schütte, [April 1816].
93. His name reappears in 1841 as one of the subscribers to the anthology of Sophie Albrecht's work that was published by Fr. Clemens in the effort to raise money for a gravestone for her.
94. Albrecht letter to Steinheim, n.d.
95. Dawson, "Appendix: Albrecht's Correspondence," 217.
96. The first preserved edition is dated 1839, the year before Albrecht's death. Because this is so late in her life and because the next edition, appearing in 1844, was already the third, it seems likely that Albrecht's first edition of the work was earlier. Altogether, the book went through at least six editions, all under the name of Sophie Albrecht, the sixth one printed in 1865.
97. Her emphasis; Albrecht, *Thüringisches Kochbuch,* iii.
98. Albrecht letter to unknown woman, 22 April 1839.
99. Albrecht, *Anthologie aus den Poesien,* 85–86.

CHAPTER 7: CONCLUSION: THE CONTESTING DISCOURSES OF THE NEEDLE AND THE QUILL

1. Schacht, *Future of Alienation,* 29.
2. SLR-*BM* 85–86.
3. Yet, it is also important that La Roche expresses her envy in a metaphor, which leaves out other important aspirants to rights. When she compares her knowledge with gold from Peru, and then disregards the Peruvians, she omits the people who not only supplied the labor to mine the gold, but also, who would, in the context of property rights, be considered the first owners of the gold. To La Roche, this other oppression and unfairness was not an issue.
4. [Schulz and Erbstein], *Almanach der Belletristen und Belletristinnen,* 5.
5. Schacht, *Future of Alienation,* 47, 48.

6. Quoted in Becker-Cantarino, "Gender Censorship," 83.
7. Becker-Cantarino, "Priesterin und Lichtbringerin."
8. Weigel, "Double focus," 65–67.
9. Lanser, "Writing Women into Romanticism," 173–74.
10. Haferkorn cites the figure 4300 for the total number of published writers (occasional to professional) in 1776 ("Der freie Schriftsteller," 625); my research indicates that not more than 2 percent would have been women. By 1800, he estimates that 2000 to 3000 writers were actually living from their publications; my research indicates that probably well less than 2 percent of that number were women.

Select Bibliography

The bibliography of works cited is divided into three main parts, with further subdivision of the first section.

I. Materials composed in the eighteenth century (even if published later)—or written in the eighteenth or nineteenth century by one of my five chosen writers.
    A. Sophie Albrecht
       1. Letters to and from Sophie Albrecht
       2. Writings published by Sophie Albrecht in her lifetime, in chronological order
    B. Friderika Baldinger
       1. Letters to and from Friderika Baldinger
       2. Published writings by Friderika Baldinger, in chronological order
       3. Cited review of Baldinger's *Lebensbeschreibung*
    C. Marianne Ehrmann
       1. Letters to and from Marianne Ehrmann
       2. Published writings by Marianne Ehrmann, in chronological order
    D. Philippine Engelhard nee Gatterer
       1. Letters to and from Philippine Engelhard-Gatterer
       2. Writings published by Philippine Engelhard-Gatterer in her lifetime, in chronological order
       3. Cited reviews of Engelhard-Gatterer
    E. Sophie La Roche
       1. Selected letters to and from Sophie La Roche
          a. Unpublished letters
          b. Published letters
       2. Writings published by Sophie La Roche in her lifetime, in chronological order
    F. Materials by other eighteenth-century women
    G. Further eighteenth-century materials written or, in the case of periodicals, edited by men

II. Nineteenth-century biobibliographies

III. Reference list of other works cited

This is by no means a comprehensive listing of all the materials I have relied on for my writing; it is most complete in identifying work I located by the five writers on whom I focus—Albrecht, Baldinger, Ehrmann, Engelhard-Gatterer, and, to a lesser extent, the prolific but also better documented La Roche—and in itemizing the nineteenth-century biobibliographies that include entries on one or more of the five. Writings by Albrecht and Ehrmann that I was unable to locate are omitted.

I. Materials composed in the eighteenth century (even if published later)—or written in the eighteenth or nineteenth century by one of my five chosen writers

I.A. Sophie Albrecht

I.A.1. Letters to and from Sophie Albrecht

Albrecht, Sophie. "Appendix: Sophie Albrecht's Correspondence with Identified Women [Elisa von der Recke, Sophie La Roche, Madam Herz, and Henriette von Montenglaut]." Ed. Ruth P. Dawson. In *In the Shadow of Olympus: German Women Writers around 1800*, ed. Katherine R. Goodman and Edith J. Waldstein. Albany: State Univ. of New York Press, 1992.
———. Letter to [Daniel Schütte]. [April 1816.] B: Albrecht. Deutsches Literaturarchiv, Marbach.
———. Letter to [unknown woman]. 22 April 1839. Ms. 5341. Freies deutsches Hochstift, Frankfurt am Main.
———. Letter to Friederike[?]. n.d. Ms. 13. Freies deutsches Hochstift, Frankfurt am Main.
Mahlmann, Siegfried August. Letter to Sophie Albrecht. n.d. Campe 3:226a. Staats- und Universitätsbibliothek, Hamburg.
Schiller, Friedrich. Letter to Sophie Albrecht. 17 April [1787]. Campe 4. Staats- und Universitätsbibliothek, Hamburg.
Steinheim, [Salomon Ludwig]. Letter to Sophie Albrecht. 29 January 1817. Campe 18. Staats- und Universitätsbibliothek, Hamburg.

I.A.2. Other works by Sophie Albrecht, in chronological order

Albrecht, Sophie. *Gedichte und Schauspiele.* Vol. 1. Erfurt: Albrecht und Compagnie, 1781. 2nd. ed: Dresden und Leipzig: Richter, 1791. [Reprint of one play, *Theresgen,* in *Frauen und Drama im Achtzehnten Jahrhundert,* ed. Karin A. Wurst. Cologne: Böhlau, 1991.]
Albrecht, Sophie, ed. *Aramena: eine syrische Geschichte, ganz für unsre Zeiten umgearbeitet,* by Anton Ulrich Duke of Braunschweig. Berlin: Rottmann, 1783–87.
Albrecht, Sophie. *Gedichte und prosaische Aufsätze.* Vol. 2. Erfurt: Albrecht und Compagnie, 1785. 2nd ed: Dresden und Leipzig: Richter, 1791.
———. *Gedichte und prosaische Aufsätze.* Vol. 3. Dresden: Richter, 1791.
[Albrecht, Johann Friedrich Ernst, and Sophie Albrecht?]. *Trümmer der Vergangenheit aus ihren Ruinen ans Licht gebracht.* Hamburg: B.G. Hoffmann, 1796. [Attribution in Preußische Bibliothek, section III below.]
Albrecht, Sophie. *Das höfliche Gespenst.* Altona: Bechtold, 1797.
———. *Legenden.* Vol. 1. Altona: Bechtold, 1797.
Albrecht, Johann Friedrich Ernst, [and Sophie Albrecht?]. *Erzählungen aus dem Dunkel der Vorzeit.* Hamburg: n.p., 1801. [Attribution in Preußische Bibliothek, section III below.]
Albrecht, Sophie. *Ida von Duba, das Mädchen im Walde: eine romantische Geschichte aus den grauenvollen Tagen der Vorwelt.* Altona: Bechtold, [1805?].
———. *Romantische Dichtungen aus der ältern christlichen Kirche.* Hamburg: Vollmer, [1808].
———. *Erfurter Kochbuch für die bürgerliche Küche.* Erfurt: Hilsenberg, 1839.

---. *Thüringisches Kochbuch für die bürgerliche Küche*. Erfurt: Hilsenberg, 1839.
---. *Anthologie aus den Poesien von Sophie Albrecht*. Ed. Fr[iedrich] Clemens [Gerke]. Altona: B. J. F. Hammerich, 1841.

I.B. Friderika Baldinger

I.B.1. Letters to and from Friderika Baldinger, not including those she wrote explicitly for publication

Baldinger, Frederika. Letters to Abraham Gotthelf Kästner. Cod. Ms. philos. 166:149. Staats- und Universitätsbibliothek, Göttingen.
---. Letters to Sophie La Roche. 31 January 1783, 16 May 1783, 23 November 1785. La Roche 56/I,4,16. Goethe- und Schiller-Archiv, Weimar.
Spangenberg, Dorothea [nee Wehrs]. Letters to Friderika Baldinger. 3 May 1782, 26 May 1782, and undated. Cod. Ms. philos. 166^b: 317–19, 321–24, and 325–28. Staats- und Universitätsbibliothek, Göttingen.

I.B.2. Other texts by Friderika Baldinger, in chronological order

Baldinger, Federika. "Ermahnungen einer Mutter an ihre Tochter am Confirmationstage." *Magazin für Frauenzimmer*. Strassburg 1782: 2: 825–.
---. Letters. *Magazin für Frauenzimmer*. Strassburg 1783, 1: 179–186, and 2: 99–103.
---. *Lebensbeschreibung von Friderika Baldinger von ihr selbst verfaßt*. Ed. Sophie von La Roche. Offenbach: Weiß u. Brede, 1791. Reprinted in *"Ich wünschte so gar gelehrt zu werden." Drei Autobiographien von Frauen des 18. Jahrhunderts*, ed. Magdalene Heuser, Ortrun Niethammer, Marion Roitzheim-Eisfeld, Petra Wulbusch. Göttingen: Wallstein Verlag, 1994.

I.B.3. Cited review of Baldinger's work

Anon. "Kleine Schriften" [Review of Friderika Baldinger's *Lebensbeschreibung*]. *Allgemeine Literatur-Zeitung*, 1792: 615.

I.C. Marianne Ehrmann

I.C.1. Letters to and from Marianne Ehrmann

Bürger, Gottfried August, and Marianne Ehrmann. *Briefe von Gottfried August Bürger an Marianne Ehrmann: Ein merkwürdiger Beitrag zur Geschichte der lezten Lebensjahre des Dichters*. Ed. Theophil Friedrich Ehrmann. Weimar: Industrie-Comptoir, 1802.

I.C.2. Published writings by Marianne Ehrmann, in chronological order

Ehrmann, Marianne. *Philosophie eines Weibs*. [Kempten]: N.p. 1784.
---. *Leichtsinn und gutes Herz oder die Folgen der Erziehung: Ein Original-Schauspiel in 5 Aufzügen*. Strassburg: Heitz, 1786. Reprinted in *Frauen und Drama im Achtzehnten Jahrhundert*, ed. Karin A. Wurst. Cologne: Böhlau, 1991.
---. *Amalie: Eine wahre Geschichte in Briefen*. 2 vols. N.p., 1788. Reprint, ed. Maya Widmer and Doris Stump, Bern: Haupt, 1995.
---. *Ninas Briefe an ihren Geliebten*. N.p.,1788.

———. *Ein Weib ein Wort.* [Reprint of *Kleine Fragmente für Denkerinnen.* N.p., 1789.] Ed. Maya Widmer and Doris Stump. Freiburg im Br.: Kore, 1994.
———. *Amaliens Erholungsstunden. Teutschlands Töchtern geweiht.* Vol. 1. Stuttgart: Im Verlag der Expedition des Beobachters, 1790; 2nd ed. Tübingen 1790. Vol. 2–3; Tübingen: Cotta, 1791–92.
———. *Die Einsiedlerinn aus den Alpen: Eine Monatsschrift zur Unterhaltung und Belehrung für Deutschlands und Helvetiens Töchter.* 2 vols. Zürich: Orell, Gessner, Füssli und Co., 1793–94.
———. *Erzählungen.* Heidelberg: F. L. Pfähler, 1795.
———. *Antonie von Warnstein: Eine Geschichte aus unserm Zeitalter.* 2 vols. Hamburg: Mutzenbecher, 1796–1798.

I.D. Philippine Engelhard nee Gatterer

I.D.1. Letters to and from Philippine Engelhard-Gatterer

Bürger, Gottfried August, and Philippine [Engelhard] Gatterer. *Ein Briefwechsel aus Göttingens empfindsamer Zeit.* Ed. Erich Ebstein. Leipzig: Dieterichsche Verlagsbuchhandlung, 1921.
Engelhard, Philippine. Letter to Abraham Gotthelf Kästner. 18 February 1788. StadtA Gö Autographensammlung Engelhard, Philippine. Stadtarchiv, Göttingen.
———. Letter to Friedrich Nicolai. 19 December 1803. Nachlaß Nicolai, Bl. 125–128. Staatsbibliothek Preußischer Kulturbesitz, Berlin.

I.D.2. Writings published by Philippine Engelhard-Gatterer in her lifetime, in chronological order

Engelhard, Philippine. *Gedichte von Philippine Gatterer.* 2 vols. Wien: Franz Haas, n.d.
[Engelhard], Philippine [nee] Gatterer. *Gedichte von Philippine Gatterer.* Göttingen: Dieterich, 1778.
———. "Engelhardin (Philippine) geb. Gatterer." *Grundlage zu einer Hessischen Gelehrten und Schriftsteller Geschichte.* 18 vols. Ed. Strieder, Friedrich Wilhelm. Göttingen: Barmaiersche Buchdruckerey, 1781–1819.
Engelhard geb. Gatterer, Philippine. *Gedichte von Philippine Engelhard geb. Gatterer.* Göttingen: Dieterich, 1782.
———. *Neujahrs-Geschenk für liebe Kinder.* Cassel: in Commission, 1787.
———. *Neue Gedichte von Philippine Engelhard geborne Gatterer.* Nürnberg: Georg Eichhorn, 1821.
Engelhard geb. Gatterer, Philippine, trans. *Lieder*, by Pierre-Jean de Beranger. Cassel: Bohné, 1830.

I.D.3. Reviews of Engelhard-Gatterer

Dz [unresolved cipher]. Review of *Neujahrs-Geschenk für liebe Kinder. Allgemeine deutsche Bibliothek* 80 (1787): 556.
Mr [unresolved cipher]. Review of *Gedichte von Philippine Gatterer. Allgemeine deutsche Bibliothek* 37 (1779): 476.
Pk [unresolved cipher]. Review of *Gedichte von Philippine Engelhard geb. Gatterer. Allgemeine deutsche Bibliothek* 54 (1783): 157–58.
Review of *Gedichte von Philippine Gatterer. Göttingsche Anzeigen von gelehrten Sachen* St. 140, 21. Nov. 1778. 1129–1130.

Review of *Gedichte von Philippine Engelhard geb. Gatterer*. *Göttingsche Anzeigen von gelehrten Sachen* St. 95, 8. Aug. 1782, 761–62.
Gatterer, see Engelhard-Gatterer.

I.E. Sophie La Roche

I.E.1. Selected Letters to and from Sophie La Roche

I.E.1.a. Unpublished letters
Anon. Letter to Sophie La Roche. [c. 1784]. La Roche I/5,6. Goethe- und Schiller-Archiv, Weimar.
Baldinger, see above I.B.1.
Gatterer, Helene. Letter to Sophie La Roche. 12 December 1784. La Roche I/1,17. Goethe- und Schiller-Archiv, Weimar.
Geßner, Judith nee Heidigger. Letter to Sophie La Roche. 20 February 1783. La Roche I/3,13. Goethe- und Schiller-Archiv, Weimar.
Grävemeier, [Molly] von. Letter to Sophie La Roche. 23 August 1784. La Roche I/4,20. Goethe- und Schiller-Archiv, Weimar.
Hagen, Christiane von. Letter to Sophie La Roche. 27 November 1783. La Roche I/4,19. Goethe- und Schiller-Archiv, Weimar.
Jerusalem, Friederike M. Letter to Sophie La Roche. 14 ? 1784. La Roche I/1,8. Goethe- und Schiller-Archiv, Weimar.
La Roche, Sophie. Letters to Susanne Bandemer. ? December 1794, 5 January 1795, 9 January 1795, 20 January 1795, 25 and 26 March 1795, 6 May 1795, 6 July 1795, 7 September 1795, 27 January 1797, 30 May 1797, 7 September 1797, 15 September 1797, 5 December 1799. Freies Deutsches Hochstift, Frankfurt am Main.
———. Letter to Susanne Bandemer. 10 December 1796. Wieland Museum, Biberach.
———. Letter to Emilie von Berlepsch. 11 May 1787. Sammlung Varnhagen. Biblioteka Jagiellonski, Cracow.
———. Letter to W.H. Dalberg. 12 June 1782. Cod. Germ. 4830, Ms. 59. Bayerische Staatsbibliothek, Munich.
———. Letter to Therese Huber. 13 March 1795. Sammlung Varnhagen. Biblioteka Jagiellonski, Cracow.
———. Letter to Jenny Voigts. 11 June 1784. Freies Deutsches Hochstift, Frankfurt am Main.
Recke, Elisa von der. Letter to Sophie La Roche. 30 March 1786. La Roche I/1,12. Goethe- und Schiller-Archiv, Weimar.
Stolberg-Stolberg, Katharina von. Letter to Sophie La Roche. 8 October 1783. La Roche I/3,8. Goethe- und Schiller-Archiv, Weimar.

I.E.1.b. Published letters
Hassencamp, R. "Aus dem Nachlaß der Sophie von La Roche." *Euphorion* 5 (1898): 475–502.
Jansen, Heinz. *Sophie von La Roche im Verkehr mit dem geistigen Münsterland*. Münster: Regensburg, 1931.
Boie, Heinrich Christian. "11 Briefe von Heinrich Christian Boie und Luise Mejer an Sophie LaRoche, 1779–1789." Ed. U. Schulz. *Wolfenbütteler Studien zur Aufklärung* 3 (1976), 67–97.
La Roche, Sophie. *Ich bin mehr Herz als Kopf: Sophie von La Roche, Ein Lebensbild in Briefen*. Ed. Michael Maurer. Munich: Beck, 1983.

———. *Lettres de Sophie de La Roche a C.-M. Wieland.* Ed. Victor Michel. Nancy: Berger-Levrault, 1938.
———. *Sophie Laroche: Ihre Briefe an die Gräfin Elise zu Solms-Laubach, 1787–1807.* Ed. Kurt Kampf. Offenbacher Geschichtsblätter 5. Offenbach: Offenbacher Geschichtsverein, 1965.

I.E.2 Writings published by Sophie La Roche in her lifetime, in chronological order

[La Roche, Sophie]. *Geschichte des Fräuleins von Sternheim.* 1771. Ed. Barbara Becker-Cantarino. Stuttgart: Reclam, 1983.
———. *The History of Lady Sophia Sternheim.* Trans. Christa Baguss Britt. Albany: State Univ. of New York Press, 1991.
[———]. *Rosaliens Briefe an ihre Freundinn Mariane von St**.* Altenburg: Richter, 1780–81.
———. "Eine Baad-Bekanntschaft." *Teutscher Merkur* 1781 I: 149–77.
———. "Mein Glüke, einer klagenden Freundinn gewidmet." *Magazin für Frauenzimmer* Feb. 1782: 92–101.
———. *Pomona für Teutschlands Töchter.* Speier 1783–1784.
———. *Briefe an Lina.* Speier: n.p., 1785.
———. *Neuere Moralische Erzaehlungen.* Altenburg: Richter, 1786.
———. *Journal einer Reise durch Frankreich.* Altenburg: Richter, 1787.
[———]. *Tagebuch einer Reise durch die Schweitz.* Altenburg: Richter, 1787.
———. *Briefe an Lina als Mädchen: Ein Buch für junge Frauenzimmer die ihr Herz und ihren Verstand bilden wollen.* 2nd ed. Leipzig: Gräff, 1788.
[———]. *Tagebuch einer Reise durch Holland und England.* Offenbach: Weiß u. Brede, 1788.
———. *Geschichte von Miß Lony, und der schöne Bund.* Gotha: Ettinger, 1789.
———. *Briefe über Mannheim.* Zürich: Orell, 1791.
———. *Erinnerungen aus meiner dritten Schweizerreise: Meinem verwundeten Herzen zur Linderung, vielleicht auch mancher trauernden Seele zum Trost geschrieben.* Offenbach: Weiß u. Brede, 1793.
———. *Briefe an Lina als Mutter.* Vol. 2–3. Leipzig: Gräff, 1795–97.
———. *Schönes Bild der Resignation.* 2 vols. Leipzig: Gräff, 1795.
———. *Erscheinungen am See Oneida.* 2 vols. Leipzig: Gräff, 1798.
———. *Mein Schreibetisch.* 2 vols. Leipzig: Gräff, 1799.
———. *Reise von Offenbach nach Weimar und Schönebeck im Jahr 1799.* Leipzig: Gräff, 1800.
———. *Schattenrisse abgeschiedener Stunden.* Added title page to *Reise von Offenbach* above.
———. *Liebe-Hütten.* 2 vols. Leipzig: Gräff, 1803–04.
———. *Herbsttage.* Leipzig: Gräff, 1805.
———. *Melusinens Sommer-Abende.* Halle: Societäts-Buch- und Kunsthandlung, 1806.

1.F. *Materials by other eighteenth-century women*

Bandemer, Susanne von. *Poetische und prosaische Versuche.* 2nd. ed. Berlin: Decker, 1802.
Becker, Sophie. *Vor hundert Jahren: Elise von der Reckes Reisen durch Deutschland, 1784–86.* Stuttgart: Spemann, 1884.
[Berlepsch, Emilie von]. *Caledonia.* 4 vols. Hamburg: B.G. Hoffmann, 1802–04.

———. *Einige Bemerkungen zur richtigen Beurtheilung der erzwungenen Schweitzer-Revolution und Mallet du Pans Geschichte derselben.* Leipzig: Dykische Buchhandlung, 1799.
———. "Einige zum Glück der Ehe nothwendige Eigenschaften und Grundsätze." *Teutscher Merkur*, 1791, 2.5:63–102; 2.6:113–34.
———. Letters to Herder. 24 November 1781, 28 December 1781?, 1 May 1783, 18 October [1787?]. Sammlung Varnhagen. Biblioteka Jagiellonski, Cracow.
———. *Sammlung kleiner Schriften und Poesien.* Vol. 1. Göttingen: Dieterich, 1787.
———. *Sommerstunden.* 1794. 2nd ed. Zürich: Orell, Füssli u. Comp., 1811.
Brun, Friederike, and Caroline von Humboldt. *Frauen zur Goethezeit: Ein Briefwechsel.* Ed. Ilse Foerst-Crato. Düsseldorf: n.p., 1975.
Einem, Charlotte von. *Aus dem Nachlaß Charlottens von Einem: Ungedruckte Briefe von Hölty, Voß, Boie, Overbeck u.a.; Jugenderinnerungen.* Ed. Julius Steinberger. Göttingen: Vereinigung Göttinger Bücherfreunde, 1923.
———. "Jugendgeschichte." In *"Ich wünschte so gar gelehrt zu werden": Drei Autobiographien von Frauen des 18. Jahrhunderts.* Ed. Magdalene Heuser, Ortrun Niethammer, Marion Roitzheim-Eisfeld and Petra Wulbusch. Göttingen: Wallstein, 1994.
———. Letters to Anton Matthias Sprickmann. 9 October 1776, 21 October 1776, 8 January 1777, 22 February 1777, 26 and 27 April 1777, 13 September 1777, 29 October 1777, 26 March 1778, 12 May 1778, 2 and 3 July 1778, 25 and 26 July 1778, 20 August 1778, 4 and 11 September 1778, 8 and 12 February 1779. Sprichmann Nachlaß 22/1–29. Universitätsbibliothek, Münster.
[Froriep, Amalie Henriette Sophie]. *Amalie von Nordheim, oder der Tod zur unrechten Zeit.* 2 vols. Gotha: Ettinger, 1783.
Glückel of Hameln. *The Memoirs of Glückel of Hameln.* Trans. Marvin Lowenthal. New York: Schocken, 1977.
[Hezel, Charlotte Henriette, ed.] *Wochenblatt für das schöne Geschlecht.* 1779. Reprint, ed. Hans Henning, Leipzig: Edition Leipzig, 1967.
Karsch, Anna Louisa. *Auserlesene Gedichte.* 1764. Stuttgart: Metzler, 1966.
———. *Herzgedanken. Das Leben der "deutschen Sappho" von ihr selbst erzählt.* Ed. Barbara Beuys. Frankfurt am Main: Societasverlag, 1981.
———. *Die Karschin, Friedrich des Großen Volksdichterin: Ein Leben in Briefen.* Ed. E. Hausmann. Frankfurt am Main: Societätsverlag, 1933.
———. *O, mir entwischt nicht, was die Menschen fühlen: Anna Louisa Karschin, Gedichte und Briefe, Stimmen von Zeitgenossen.* Ed. Gerhard Wolf. Berlin: Buchverlag Der Morgen, 1981.
Klencke, Karoline von. *Leben und Romantische Dichtungen der Tochter der Karschin.* Ed. Helmina [v. Chezy]. Frankfurt am Main: Wilmans, 1805.
Klopstock, Meta, nee Moller. *Briefwechsel mit Klopstock, ihren Verwandten und Freunden.* Ed. Hermann Tiemann. 3 vols. Hamburg: Maximilian-Gesellschaft, 1956.
———. *"Es sind wunderliche Dinger, meine Briefe": Meta Klopstocks Briefwechsel mit Friedrich Gottlieb Klopstock und mit ihren Freunden 1751–1758.* Ed. Franziska and Hermann Tiemann. Munich: Beck, 1980.
König, Eva, and Gotthold Ephraim Lessing. *Meine liebste Madam: Lessings Briefwechsel mit Eva König, 1770–1776.* Ed. Günter and Ursula Schenk. Munich: Beck, 1979.
Mereau, Sophie. *Das Blüthenalter der Empfindung.* 1794. Reprint, Herman Moens, Stuttgart: Akademischer Verlag, 1982.

———. *Lebe der Liebe und liebe das Leben: Der Briefwechsel von Clemens Brentano und Sophie Mereau*. Ed. Dagmar von Gersdorff. Frankfurt am Main: Insel, 1981.
Recke, Elisa von der. *Elisa von der Recke: Aufzeichnungen und Briefe aus ihren Jugendtagen*. Ed. Paul Rachel. Leipzig: Dieterich, 1902.
[———]. *Elisens Geistliche Gedichte, nebst einem Oratorium und einer Hymne von C.F. Neander*. Leipzig: Dyck, 1783.
[———]. *Elisens und Sophiens Gedichte*. Berlin: Vieweg, 1790.
———. *Familien-Scenen oder Entwickelungen auf dem Masquenballe: Schauspiel in vier Aufzügen*. Leipzig: Fleischer, 1827.
[———]. *Geistliche Lieder einer vornehmen kurländischen Dame mit Melodien von Hiller*. Leipzig: N.p., 1780.
———. *Mein Journal: Elisas neu aufgefundene Tagebücher aus den Jahren 1791 und 1793/95*. Ed. Johannes Werner. Leipzig: Koehler und Amelang, 1927.
———. *Nachricht von des berüchtigten Cagliostro Aufenthalte in Mitau 1779*. Berlin: Nicolai, 1787. Partial reprint, *Tagebücher und Selbstzeugnisse*. Ed. Christine Träger. Munich: Beck, 1984.
———. [Also see letter in 1.E. above.]
Schlegel, Caroline. *Caroline: Briefe aus der Frühromantik*. Ed. Erich Schmidt. 2 vols. Leipzig: Insel, 1913.
———. *Caroline und Dorothea Schlegel in Briefen*. Ed. Ernst Wieneke. Weimar: Kiepenheuer, 1914.
———. "*Lieber Freund, ich komme weit her schon an diesem frühen Morgen*": *Caroline Schlegel-Schelling in ihren Briefen*. Ed. Sigrid Damm. Darmstadt: Luchterhand, 1980.
Seidel, Charlotte Sophie Sidonie. *Hinterlassene Schriften*. Nürnberg: Bauer und Mann, 1793.
Spangenberg. See I.B.1. above.
Unger, Friederike Helene. *Julchen Grünthal: Eine Pensionsgeschichte*. Berlin: Johann Friedrich Unger, 1784.
[Wobeser, Wilhelmine Caroline von.] *Elisa oder das Weib wie es seyn sollte (allen deutschen Mädchen und Weibern gewidmet)*. Leipzig: Gräff, 1795.
Wollstonecraft, Mary. *Vindication of the Rights of Woman*. Ed. Miriam Kramnick. 1792. New York: Penguin, 1975.

1.G. Further eighteenth-century materials written or, in the case of periodicals, edited by men

Allgemeine Deutsche Bibliothek. 118 vols. Berlin: Nicolai, 1765–98.
Allgemeine Literatur-Zeitung. Jena: 1785–88, 1791-.
Baldinger, Ernst Gottfried. *Biographien jetztlebender Aerzte und Naturforscher in und außer Deutschland*. Jena: Hartung, 1768–72.
Boie, Heinrich Christian. "11 Briefe." See section I.E.1.b. above.
———. *Ich war wohl klug, daß ich Dich fand: Heinrich Christian Boies Briefwechsel mit Luise Mejer, 1777–85*. Munich: Beck, 1975.
Böttiger, Karl August. *Literarische Zustände und Zeitgenossen: In Schilderungen aus Karl August Böttiger's handschriftlichem Nachlasse*. Ed. K.W. Böttiger. 2 vols. 1838. Frankfurt am Main: Athenäum, 1972.
Flora, Teutschlands Töchtern geweiht: Eine Monatsschrift von Freunden und Freundinnen des schönen Geschlechts. Tübingen: Cotta, 1793–1803.
Forster, Georg. *Georg Forsters Werke: Sämtliche Schriften, Tagebücher, Briefe*. Berlin: Akademie Verlag, 1958-.

[Geisler, Adam Friedrich.] *Gallerie edler deutscher Frauenzimmer*. Vol. 1. Dessau: Buchhandlung der Gelehrten, 1784.
Geisler, Adam Friedrich, ed. *Archiv weiblicher Hauptkenntnisse für diejenigen jedes Standes, welche angenehme Freundinnen, liebenswürdige Gattinnen, gute Mütter, und wahre Hauswirthinnen seyn und werden wollen*. Vol. 2–3. Leipzig, 1788–89.
Gleim, Johann Wilhelm Ludwig. *Briefwechsel zwischen Gleim und Heinse*. Ed. Karl Schüddekopf. 2 vols. Weimar: Emil Felber, 1894–95.
Göttingsche Anzeigen von gelehrten Sachen. 1739–.
Hippel, Theodor Gottlieb von. *On Improving the Status of Women*. Ed. and trans. Timothy Sellner. Detroit: Wayne State, 1979.
———. *Über die bürgerliche Verbesserung der Weiber*. Vol. 6 of *Sämmtliche Werke*. Berlin: Reimer, 1828.
Hölty, Ludwig Christoph Heinrich. "Elegie eines Schäfers" and "Die Beschäftigungen der Menschen." In *Der Göttinger Hain*, ed. Alfred Kelletat. Stuttgart: Reclam, 1967.
Hutten, Johann Georg. Verzeichniss der Abonnenten auf *Pomona*. [Speyer]: n.p., 1787.
Iris. 1774/75–1776. 8 vols.
Jacobi, Johann Georg. *Sämmtliche Werke*. 8 vols. Zürich: Orell, Füssli u. Co., 1807–22.
———. *Ungedruckte Briefe von und an J.G. Jacobi*. Ed. Ernst Eduard Martin. Strassburg: K.J. Trübner, 1874.
Kant, Immanuel. "What is Enlightenment?" Trans. Peter Gay. In *The Enlightenment: A Comprehensive Anthology*, ed. Peter Gay. New York: Simon and Schuster, 1973.
Lichtenberg, Georg Christoph. *Briefwechsel*. Vol. 4. Ed. Ulrich Joost and Albrecht Schöne. Munich: Beck, 1992.
[Müller, Joh. Georg H.] *Schattenrisse edler teutscher Frauenzimmer oder unpartheyische Nachrichten von schönen und edlen Damen*. 2 vols. Halle: Hendel, 1784–85.
Nicolay, Ludwig Heinrich, and Friedrich Nicolai. *Die beiden Nicolai: der Briefwechsel zwischen Ludwig Heinrich Nicolay in St. Petersburg und Friedrich Nicolai in Berlin, 1776–1811*. Ed. Heinz Ischreyt. Lüneburg: Nordostdeutsches Kulturwerk, 1989.
Pütter, Johann Stephan. *Versuch einer academischen gelehrten Geschichte von der Georg Augustus Universität zu Göttingen*. 2 vols. Göttingen: Vandenhoeck-Ruprecht, 1765–88.
[Richter], Jean Paul. *Briefe, 1780–1793*. Ed. Eduard Berend. Vol. 3 of 3rd Division of *Sämtliche Werke: Historisch-kritische Ausgabe*. Berlin: Akademie, 1956.
Rousseau, Jean Jacques. *Emile or on education*. Trans. Allan Bloom. New York: Basic Books, 1979.
Schiller, Friedrich. *Schillers Werke. Nationalausgabe*. Ed. Julius Petersen et al. Weimar: Böhlau, 1943-.
[Schulz, Friedrich, and Karl Friedrich Wilhelm Erbstein.] *Almanach der Belletristen und Belletristinnen fürs Jahr 1782*. Uleitra, bey Peter Jobst Edlen v. Omai. [Berlin: Himburg, 1781].
Süssmilch, Peter, and Christoph Jacob Baumann. *Göttliche Ordnung in den Veränderungen des menschlichen Geschlechts, aus der Geburt, dem Tode und der Fortpflanzung deßelben erwiesen*. 4th ed. 3 vols. Berlin: Realschule, 1775–76.
Teutscher Merkur. 1773–1810. Microfilm. New Haven: Research Publications.

Theaterkalendar. Gotha, 1776-.
"Verzeichniß einiger jetztlebender deutscher Schriftstellerinnen und ihrer Schriften." *Journal von und für Deutschland.* 1788: 1.138–42, 2.109–110; 1789: 1.303, 2.109–110; 1790: 1.315–16, 378–82, 2.229–32, 554; 1791: 1.231–32, 2.978–76.
Voß, Johann Heinrich. *Briefe an Goeckingk, 1775–1786.* Ed. Gerhard Hay. Munich: Beck, 1976.
Zedler, Johann Heinrich. *Großes vollständiges Universallexikon aller Wissenschaften und Künste.* 64 vols. Halle: Zedler, 1732–50.

II. Nineteenth-century biobibliographies

Alberti, Eduard. *Lexikon der Schleswig-Holstein-Lauenburgischen und Eutinischen Schriftsteller von 1829 bis Mitte 1866.* 2 vols. Kiel: Akademische Buchhandlung, 1867–68.
Goedeke, Karl. *Grundriß der Geschichte der deutschen Literatur aus den Quellen.* 10 vols. Dresden: Ehlermann, 1884–1913.
Hamberger, Georg Christoph, and Johann Georg Meusel. *Das gelehrte Teutschland oder Lexikon der jetzt lebenden teutschen Schriftsteller.* 23 vols. 1797–1831. Reprint, Hildesheim: Olms, 1966.
Hanstein, Adalbert von. *Die Frauen in der Geschichte des Deutschen Geisteslebens des 18. und 19. Jahrhunderts.* 2 vols. Leipzig: Freund u. Wittig, 1899–1900.
Jördens, Karl Heinrich. *Lexikon deutscher Dichter und Prosaisten.* 6 vols. Leipzig: Weidmann, 1806–11.
Justi, Karl Wilhelm. *Fortsetzung von Strieders Hessischer Gelehrten und Schriftsteller-Geschichte und Nachträge.* Marburg: Garthe, 1831.
Lübker, Detlev Lorenz, and Hans Schröder. *Lexikon der Schleswig-Holstein-Lauenburgischen und Eutinischen Schriftsteller von 1796 bis 1828.* 2 vols. Altona: Busch, 1829–30.
Meusel, Johann Georg. *Lexikon der vom Jahr 1750–1800 verstorbenen teutschen Schriftsteller.* 15 vols. Leipzig: Fleischer, 1802–16.
Rassmann, Friedrich. *Pantheon deutscher jetzt lebender Dichter und in die Belletristik eingreifender Schriftsteller.* Helmstedt: Fleckeisensche Buchhandlung, 1823.
Recke, Johann Friedrich von, and Karl Eduard Napiersky. *Allgemeines Schriftsteller- und Gelehrten-Lexikon der Provinzen Livland, Esthland, und Kurland.* 6 vols. 1827–61. Berlin: Haude u. Spener, 1966.
Reden-Esbeck, Johann, ed. *Deutsches Bühnen-Lexikon.* Eichstätt: Stillkrauth, 1879.
Rotermund, Heinrich Wilhelm. *Das gelehrte Hannover.* Bremen: Schünemann, 1823.
Schindel, Carl Wilhelm Otto August von. *Die deutschen Schriftstellerinnen des neunzehnten Jahrhunderts.* 3 vols. Leipzig: Brockhaus, 1823–25.
Schröder, Hans. *Lexikon der Hamburgischen Schriftsteller bis zur Gegenwart.* 8 vols. Hamburg: Perthes-Besser, 1851–83.

III. Reference list of other works cited

Arnim, Bettina von, ed. *Die Günderode.* Frankfurt am Main: Insel, 1983.
Bartky, Sandra Lee. "Toward a Phenomenology of Feminist Consciousness." In *Feminism and Philosophy*, ed. Mary Vetterling-Braggin et al. Totowa, NJ: Littlefield, Adams, 1981.

Becker, Albert. *Schiller und die Pfalz*. Ludwigshafen a. Rh.: Waldkirch, 1907.
Becker-Cantarino, Barbara. Afterword to *Geschichte des Fräuleins von Sternheim*, by Sophie von La Roche. Stuttgart: Reclam, 1983.
———. Foreword to *Gedichte: Nach der Dichterin Tode herausgegeben von ihrer Tochter Caroline Luise von Klencke*, by Anna Louisa Karsch. 1972. Reprint, Karben, Germany: Verlag Petra Wald, 1996.
———. " 'Gender Censorship': On Literary Production in German Romanticism." *Women in German Yearbook: Feminist Studies in German Literature and Culture* 11 (1995): 81–97.
———. *Der lange Weg zur Mündigkeit: Frau und Literatur, 1500–1800*. Stuttgart: Metzler, 1987.
———. " 'Muse' und 'Kunstrichter': Sophie La Roche und Wieland." *Modern Language Notes* 99 (1984): 571–88.
———. "Priesterin und Lichtbringerin; Zur Ideologie des weiblichen Charakters in der Frühromantik." In *Die Frau als Heldin und Autorin: Neue kritische Ansätze zur deutschen Literatur*, ed. Wolgang Paulsen. Bern: Francke, 1979.
———. "(Sozial)Geschichte der Frau in Deutschland, 1500–1800: Ein Forschungsbericht." In *Die Frau von der Reformation zur Romantik: Die Situation der Frau vor dem Hintergrund der Literatur und Sozialgeschichte*, ed. Barbara Becker-Cantarino. Modern German Studies 7. Bonn: Bouvier, 1980.
———. "Zur Theorie der literarischen Freundschaft im 18. Jahrhundert am Beispiel der Sophie La Roche." In *Frauenfreundschaft - Männerfreundschaft: Literarische Diskurse im 18. Jahrhundert*, ed. Barbara Becker-Cantarino and Wolfram Mauser. Tübingen: Niemeyer, 1991.
Belsey, Catherine. Afterword to *The Matter of Difference: Materialist Feminist Criticism of Shakespeare*, by Valerie Wayne. Ithaca: Cornell, 1991.
Blackwell, Jeannine. "Marriage by the Book: Matrimony, Divorce, and Single Life in Therese Huber's Life and Works." In *In the Shadow of Olympus: German Women Writers around 1800*, ed. Katherine R. Goodman and Edith J. Waldstein. Albany: State Univ. of New York Press, 1992.
Blackwell, Jeannine, and Susanne Zantop. *Bitter Healing: German Women Writers from 1700 to 1830, an Anthology*. Lincoln: Univ. of Nebraska Press, 1990.
Bohm, Arnd. "Authority and Authorship in Luise Adelgunde Gottsched's *Das Testament*." *Lessing Yearbook* 18 (1986): 129–40.
Bovenschen, Silvia. *Die imaginierte Weiblichkeit: Exemplarische Untersuchungen zu kulturgeschichtlichen und literarischen Präsentationsformen des Weiblichen*. Frankfurt am Main: Suhrkamp, 1979.
———. "Is there a Feminine Aesthetic?" In *Feminist Aesthetics*, ed. Gisela Ecker. Boston: Beacon, 1985.
Brinker-Gabler, Gisela, ed. *Deutsche Dichterinnen vom 16. Jahrhundert bis zur Gegenwart: Gedichte und Lebensläufe*. Frankfurt am Main: Fischer, 1978.
———, ed. *Deutsche Literatur von Frauen*. 2 vols. Munich: Beck, 1988.
Brownstein, Rachel M. *Becoming a Heroine: Reading about Women in Novels*. New York: Penguin, 1984.
Brüggemann, Theodor, with Hans-Heino Ewers. *Handbuch zur Kinder- und Jugendliteratur von 1750 bis 1800*. Stuttgart: Metzler, 1982.
Burkhard, Marianne, ed. *Gestaltet und Gestaltend: Frauen in der Deutschen Literatur*. Amsterdamer Beiträge zur neueren Germanistik 10. Amsterdam: Rodopi, 1980.
Butler, Judith. *Gender Trouble*. New York: Routledge, 1990.
Castle, Terry. *The Female Thermometer: Eighteenth-Century Culture and the Invention of the Uncanny*. New York: Oxford Univ. Press, 1995.

Cocalis, Susan L. "Der Vormund will Vormund sein: Zur Problematik der weiblichen Unmündigkeit im 18. Jahrhundert." In *Gestaltet und Gestaltend: Frauen in der Deutschen Literatur*, ed. Marianne Burkhard. Amsterdamer Beiträge zur neueren Germanistik 10. Amsterdam: Rodopi, 1980.

———, ed. *The Defiant Muse: German Feminist Poems from the Middle Ages to the Present*. New York: Feminist Press, 1986.

Cook, Elizabeth Heckendorn. "Going Public: The Letter and the Contract in *Fanni Butler*." *Eighteenth-Century Studies* 24 (1990): 21–45.

Davies, Bronwyn. *Frogs and Snails and Feminist Tales: Preschool Children and Gender*. Sydney: Allen and Unwin, 1989.

Dawson, Ruth P. " 'And This Shield Is Called—Self-Reliance.' Emerging Feminist Consciousness in the Late Eighteenth Century." In *German Women in the Eighteenth and Nineteenth Centuries: A Social and Literary History*, ed. Ruth-Ellen B. Joeres and Mary Jo Maynes. Bloomington: Indiana Univ. Press, 1986.

———. "Catherine the Great: Playwright of the Anti-Occult." In *Thalia's Daughters: German Women Dramatists from the 18th Century to the Present*, ed. Susan Cocalis and Ferrel Rose in collaboration with Karin Obermeier. Tübingen: Francke/Narr, 1996.

———. "The Feminist Manifesto of Theodor Gottlieb von Hippel (1741–96)." In *Gestaltet und Gestaltend: Frauen in der Deutschen Literatur*, ed. Marianne Burkhard. Amsterdamer Beiträge zur neueren Germanistik 10. Amsterdam: Rodopi, 1980.

———. "Frauen und Theater: Vom Stegreifspiel zum bürgerlichen Rührstück." In *Deutsche Dichterinnen vom 16. Jahrhundert bis zur Gegenwart: Gedichte und Lebensläufe*, ed. Gisela Brinkler-Gabler. Frankfurt am Main: Fischer, 1987.

———. "Im Reifrock den Parnaß besteigen. Die Rezeption von Dichterinnen im 18. Jahrhundert (am Beispiel von Philippine Gatterer-Engelhard)." In *Frauensprache—Frauenliteratur? Für und Wider einer Psychoanalyse literarischer Werke*, ed. Inge Stephan and Carl Pietzcker. Vol. 6 of *Kontroversen, alte und neue: Akten des VII. Internationalen Germanisten-Kongresses, Göttingen 1985*, ed. Albrecht Schöne. Tübingen: Niemeyer, 1986.

———. "Reconstructing Women's Literary Relationships: Sophie Albrecht and Female Friendship." In *In the Shadow of Olympus: German Women Writers around 1800*, ed. Katherine R. Goodman and Edith J. Waldstein. Albany: State Univ. of New York Press, 1992.

———. Review of *Das Blüthenalter der Empfindung: Roman*, by Sophie Mereau and ed. by Herman Moens. *German Studies Review*, 6 (1983), 596–98.

———. "The Search for Women's Experience of Pregnancy and Birth: Eighteenth-Century Accounts." In *Anthropology and the German Enlightenment: Perspectives on Humanity*, ed. Katherine M. Faull. Bucknell Review 38. Lewisburg: Bucknell Univ. Press, 1995.

———. "Selbstzähmung und Misogynie: Frauen schreiben Verserzählungen im 18. Jahrhundert." In *Der Widerspenstigen Zähmung: Studien zur bezwungenen Weiblichkeit in der Literatur vom Mittelalter bis zur Gegenwart*, ed. Monika Jonas and Sylvia Wallinger. Innsbrucker Beiträge zur Kulturwissenschaft: Germanistische Reihe 31. Innsbruck: Univ. Press, 1986.

———. "Theodor Gottlieb von Hippel und seine Schrift 'Ueber die bürgerliche Verbesserung der Weiber.' " In *Akten des VI. Internationalen Germanisten-Kongresses*. Bern: Lang, 1980.

———. " 'Der Weihrauch, den uns die Männer streuen': Wieland and Women Writers in *Der Teutsche Merkur*." In *Christoph Martin Wieland, 1733–1813:*

North American Scholarly Contributions to the 250th Anniversary of his Birth, ed. Hans-Jörg Schelle. Tübingen: Niemeyer, 1984.

———. "Women Communicating: Eighteenth-Century German Journals Edited by Women." *Archives et Bibliothèques de Belgique* 54 (1983): 95–111.

Dedert, Hartmut. *Die Erzählung im Sturm und Drang: Studien zur Prosa des achtzehnten Jahrhunderts*. Stuttgart: Metzler, 1990.

Draine, Betsy. "Refusing the Wisdom of Solomon: Some Recent Feminist Literary Theory." *Signs* 15 (1989): 144–70.

Duden, Barbara. "Das schöne Eigentum. Zur Herausbildung des bürgerlichen Frauenbildes an der Wende vom 18. zum 19. Jahrhundert." *Kursbuch* 47 (1977): 125–40.

Dülmen, Richard van. *The Society of the Enlightenment: The Rise of the Middle Class and Enlightenment Culture in Germany*. New York: St. Martin's Press, 1992.

Eagleton, Terry. *Literary Theory: An Introduction*. Minneapolis: Univ. of Minnesota Press, 1983.

Ecker, Gisela, ed. *Feminist Aesthetics*. Boston: Beacon, 1985.

Ehrich-Haefeli, Verena. "Gestehungskosten tugendempfindsamer Freundschaft: Probleme der weiblichen Rolle im Briefwechsel Wieland-Sophie La Roche bis zum Erscheinen der *Sternheim* (1750–1771)." In *Frauenfreundschaft—Männerfreundschaft: Literarische Diskurse im 18. Jahrhundert*, ed. Barbara Becker-Cantarino and Wolfram Mauser. Tübingen: Niemeyer, 1991.

Eigler, Friederike, and Susanne Kord. *Feminist Encyclopedia of German Literature*. Westport, Conn.: Greenwood, 1997.

Eisenberg, Ludwig. *Großes biographisches Lexikon der deutschen Bühne im XIX Jahrhundert*. Leipzig: List, 1903.

Engelsing, Rolf. *Der Bürger als Leser: Lesergeschichte in Deutschland, 1500–1800*. Stuttgart: Metzler, 1974.

Faderman, Lillian. *Surpassing the Love of Men: Romantic Friendship and Love between Women from the Renaissance to the Present*. New York: Morrow, 1981.

Felman, Shoshona. "Women and Madness: The Critical Phallacy." In *The Feminist Reader: Essays in Gender and the Politics of Literary Criticism*, ed. Catherine Belsey and Jane Moore. Cambridge, Mass.: Blackwell, 1989.

Felski, Rita. *Beyond Feminist Aesthetics: Feminist Literature and Social Change*. Cambridge, Mass.: Harvard Univ. Press, 1989.

Ferguson, Kathy. *The Man Question: Visions of Subjectivity in Feminist Theory*. Berkeley: Univ. of California Press, 1993.

Figes, Eva. *Sex and Subterfuge: Women Novelists to 1850*. London: Macmillan, 1982.

Finke, Laurie A. *Feminist Theory, Women's Writing*. Ithaca: Cornell Univ. Press, 1992.

Flint, Christopher. "Speaking Objects: The Circulation of Stories in Eighteenth-Century Prose Fiction." *PMLA* 113 (1998): 212–26.

Folkenflik, Robert, ed. *The Culture of Autobiography*. Stanford: Stanford Univ. Press, 1993.

Frels, Wilhelm. *Deutsche Dichterhandschriften von 1400 bis 1900*. Leipzig: Hiersemann, 1934.

Friedrichs, Elisabeth. *Die deutschsprachigen Schriftstellerinnen des 18. und 19. Jahrhunderts: Ein Lexikon*. Repertorien zur Deutschen Literaturgeschichte 9. Stuttgart: Metzler, 1981.

Frühsorge, Gotthardt. "Die Begründung der 'väterlichen Gesellschaft' in der euro-

päischen Oeconomia Christiana: Zur Rolle des Vaters in der 'Hausväterliteratur' des 16. bis 18. Jahrhunderts in Deutschland." In *Das Vaterbild im Abendland I: Rom, Frühes Christentum, Mittelalter, Neuzeit, Gegenwart*, ed. Hubertus Tellenbach. Stuttgart: Kohlhammer, 1978.
Fuss, Diana. *Essentially Speaking*. New York: Routledge, 1989.
Gatens, Moira. *Feminism and Philosophy: Perspectives on Difference and Equality*. Bloomington: Indiana Univ. Press, 1991.
Geiger, Ruth-Esther, and Sigrid Weigel, eds. *Sind das noch Damen? Vom gelehrten Frauenzimmer-Journal zum feministischen Journalismus*. Munich: Frauenbuchverlag, 1981.
Gnüg, Hiltrud, and Renate Möhrmann, eds. *Frauen, Literatur, Geschichte: Schreibende Frauen vom Mittelalter bis zur Gegenwart*. Stuttgart: Metzler, 1985.
Goethe, Ottilie von. *Ottilie von Goethe: Goethes Schwiegertochter, ein Porträt*. Ed. Ulrich Janetzki. Frankfurt am Main: Ullstein, 1983.
Goodman, Dena. "Public Sphere and Private Life: Toward a Synthesis of Current Historiographical Approaches to the Old Regime." *History and Theory* 31 (1992): 1–21.
Goodman, Katherine. *Dis/closures: Women's Autobiography in Germany between 1790 and 1914*. New York University Ottendorfer series. New York: Lang, 1986.
Goodman, Katherine R., and Edith J. Waldstein. *In the Shadow of Olympus: German Women Writers around 1800*. Albany: State Univ. of New York Press, 1992.
Grant, Judith. *Fundamental Feminism: Contesting the Core Concepts of Feminist Theory*. New York: Routledge, 1993.
Greer, Germaine. *The Obstacle Race: The Fortunes of Women Painters and their Work*. New York: Farrar, 1979.
Grenz, Dagmar. *Mädchenliteratur: Von den moralisch-belehrenden Schriften im 18. Jahrhundert bis zur Herausbildung der Backfischliteratur im 19. Jahrhundert*. Germanistische Abhandlungen 52. Stuttgart: Metzler, 1981.
Grimm, Jacob. *Rezensionen und Aufsätze*. Vol. 4 of *Kleinere Schriften*. Berlin: Dümmler, 1869.
Grimm, Jacob, and Wilhelm Grimm. *Deutsches Wörterbuch*. 15 vols. Leipzig: S. Hirzel, 1854–1960.
Habermas, Jürgen. *Strukturwandel der Öffentlichkeit: Untersuchungen zu einer Kategorie der bürgerlichen Gesellschaft*. 1962. Darmstadt: Luchterhand, 1979.
Hadley, Michael. *The Undiscovered Genre: A Search for the German Gothic Novel*. Bern: Lang, 1978.
Haferkorn, Hansjürgen. "Der freie Schriftsteller. Eine literatur-soziologische Studie über seine Entstehung und Lage in Deutschland zwischen 1750 und 1800." *Archiv für Geschichte des Buchwesens* 5 (1963): 523–712.
Hahn, Karl-Heinz, ed. *Briefe an Goethe: Gesamtausgabe in Regestform*. Weimar: Böhlau, 1980-.
Hart, Gail. *Tragedy in Paradise: Family and Gender Politics in German Bourgeois Tragedy, 1750–1850*. Columbia, S.C.: Camden House, 1996.
Hausen, Karin. "Family and Role-Division: The Polarisation of Sexual Stereotypes in the Nineteenth Century—An Aspect of the Dissociation of Work and Family Life." In *The German Family: Essays on the Social History of the Family in Nineteenth- and Twentieth-Century Germany*, ed. Richard J. Evans and W.R. Lee. Totowa, N.J.: Barnes and Noble, 1981.
Hawkesworth, Mary. "Confounding Gender" *Signs* 22 (1997): 649–685.
Heidenreich, Bernd. *Sophie von La Roche—eine Werkbiographie*. Frankfurter Hochschulschrift zur Sprachtheorie und Literaturästhetik 5. Frankfurt am Main: Lang, 1986.

Herrmann, Ulrich. "Erziehung und Schulunterricht für Mädchen im 18. Jahrhundert." *Wolfenbütteler Studien zur Aufklärung* 3 (1976): 101–35.
Heuser, Magdalena. *"Ich wünschte so gar gelehrt zu werden." Drei Autobiographien von Frauen des 18. Jahrhunderts.* Ed. Magdalene Heuser, Ortrun Niethammer, Marion Roitzheim-Eisfeld and Petra Wulbusch. Göttingen: Wallstein, 1994.
———. "Zwischen Kochtopf und Verstandeserziehung, Briefe und Gelehrtenautobiographie: Dorothea Friderika Baldinger." In *Autobiographien von Frauen: Beiträge zu ihrer Geschichte*. Untersuchungen zur deutschen Literaturgeschichte 85. Tübingen: Niemeyer, 1996.
Hoff, Dagmar von. *Dramen des Weiblichen: Deutsche Dramatikerinnen um 1800*. Opladen: Westdeutscher Verlag, 1989.
Hohendahl, Peter Uwe. "Empfindsamkeit und gesellschaftliches Bewußtsein. Zur Soziologies des empfindsamen Romans am Beispiel von *La Vie de Marianne*, *Clarissa*, *Fräulein von Sternheim* und *Werther*." *Schiller-Jahrbuch* 16 (1972): 176–207.
Homans, Margaret. *Bearing the Word: Language and Female Experience in Nineteenth-Century Women's Writing*. Chicago: Univ. of Chicago Press, 1986.
Hull, Isabel V. *Sexuality, State, and Civil Society in Germany, 1700–1815*. Ithaca: Cornell Univ. Press, 1996.
Huyssen, Andreas. *Drama des Sturm und Drang: Kommentar zu einer Epoche*. Munich: Winkler, 1980.
Ingrao, Charles W. *The Hessian Mercenary State: Ideas, Institutions, and Reform under Frederick II, 1760–1785*. Cambridge: Cambridge Univ. Press, 1987.
Jelinek, Estelle C., ed. *Women's Autobiography: Essays in Criticism*. Bloomington: Indiana Univ. Press, 1980.
Joeres, Ruth-Ellen B. "'That girl is an entirely different character!' Yes, but is she a feminist? Observations on Sophie von la Roche's *Geschichte des Fräuleins von Sternheim*." In *German Women in the Eighteenth and Nineteenth Centuries: A Social and Literary History*, ed. Ruth-Ellen B. Joeres and Mary Jo Maynes. Bloomington: Indiana Univ. Press, 1986.
———. " 'We are adjacent to human society': German Women Writers, the Homosocial Experience, and a Challenge to the Public/Domestic Dichotomy." *Women in German Yearbook* 10 (1995): 39–57.
Joeres, Ruth-Ellen B., and Mary Jo Maynes, eds. *German Women in the Eighteenth and Nineteenth Centuries: A Social and Literary History*. Bloomington: Indiana Univ. Press, 1986.
Johnson, Claudia. *Equivocal Beings: Politics, Gender, and Sentimentality in the 1790s—Wollstonecraft, Radcliffe, Burney, Austen*. Chicago: Univ. of Chicago Press, 1995.
Jones, Ann Rosalind. "Surprising Fame: Renaissance Gender Ideologies and Women's Lyric." In *The Poetics of Gender*, ed. Nancy K. Miller. New York: Columbia Univ. Press, 1986.
Kaiser, Gerhard. *Aufklärung, Empfindsamkeit, Sturm und Drang*. Vol. 3 of *Geschichte der Deutschen Literatur,* Ed. Gerhard Kaiser. 3rd ed. Munich: Francke, 1979.
Kaplan, Carla. *The Erotics of Talk: Women's Writing and Feminist Paradigms*. New York: Oxford Univ. Press, 1996.
Kelly-Gadol, Joan. "Did Women Have a Renaissance?" In *Becoming Visible: Women in European History*, ed. Renate Bridenthal and Claudia Koonz. Boston: Houghton Mifflin, 1977.

Kiesel, Helmuth, and Paul Münch. *Gesellschaft und Literatur im 18. Jahrhundert: Voraussetzungen und Entstehung des literarischen Markts in Deutschland.* Munich: Beck, 1977.

Kiewning, Hans. *Fürstin Pauline zur Lippe, 1769–1820.* Detmold: Meyersche Hofbuchhandlung, 1930.

Kindermann, Heinz. *Von der Aufklärung zur Romantik.* Vols. 4–5 of *Theatergeschichte Europas,* 2d ed. Salzburg: Müller, 1972–1976.

Klüger, Ruth. "Zum Außenseitertum der deutschen Dichterinnen." In *Untersuchungen zum Roman von Frauen um 1800,* ed. Helga Gallas and Magdalene Heuser. Tübingen: Niemeyer, 1990.

Knodel, John. "Natural Fertility in Pre-industrial Germany." *Population Studies* 32 (1978): 481–510.

Kord, Susanne. *Ein Blick hinter die Kulissen: deutschsprachige Dramatikerinnen im 18. und 19. Jahrhundert.* Ergebnisse der Frauenforschung 27. Stuttgart: Metzler, 1992.

———. *Sich einen Namen machen: Anonymität und weibliche Autorschaft, 1700–1900.* Stuttgart: Metzler, 1996.

Kramnick, Jonathon Brody. "The Making of the English Canon." *PMLA* 112 (1997): 1087–1101.

Krull, Edith. *Das Wirken der Frau im frühen deutschen Zeitschriftenwesen.* Beiträge zur Erforschung der deutschen Zeitschrift 5. Charlottenburg: Rudolf Lorentz, 1939.

Lanser, Susan S. "Courting Death: *Roman, romantisme,* and *Mistress Henley*'s Narrative Practices." *Eighteenth Century Life* 13 (1989): 49–59.

———. "Review Essay: Writing Women into Romanticism." *Feminist Studies* 23 (1997): 167–90.

La Vopa, Anthony J. "Conceiving a Public: Ideas and Society in Eighteenth-Century Europe." *Journal of Modern History* 64 (1992): 79–116.

———. "Herder's *Publikum*: Language, Print, and Sociability in Eighteenth-Century Germany." *Eighteenth-Century Studies* 29 (1995): 5–24.

Loster-Schneider, Gudrun. *Sophie La Roche, Paradoxien weiblichen Schreibens im 18. Jahrhundert.* Mannheimer Beiträge zur Sprach- und Literaturwissenschaft 26. Tübingen: Gunter Narr, 1995.

MacArthur, Elizabeth J. "Devious Narratives: Refusal of Closure in Two Eighteenth-Century Epistolary Novels." *Eighteenth-Century Studies* 21 (1987): 1–20.

Madland, Helga. "Gender and the German Literary Canon: Marianne Ehrmann's Infanticide Fiction." *Monatshefte für Deutschen Unterricht* 84 (1992): 405–16.

———. "An Introduction to the Works and Life of Marianne Ehrmann (1755–95): Writer, Editor, Journalist." *Lessing Yearbook* 21 (1989): 171–96.

———. *Marianne Ehrmann: Reason and Emotion in Her Life and Works.* Women in German Literature 1. New York: Lang, 1998.

———. "Three Late Eighteenth-Century Women's Journals: Their Role in Shaping Women's Lives." *Women in German Yearbook 4: Feminist Studies and German Culture.* Ed. Marianne Burkhard and Jeanette Clausen. Lanham, Md.: Univ. Press of America, 1988. 167–86.

Malcolmson, Cristina. " 'What You Will': Social Mobility and Gender in *Twelfth Night.*" In *The Matter of Difference: Materialist Feminist Criticism of Shakespeare,* ed. Valerie Wayne. Ithaca: Cornell Univ. Press, 1991.

Maurer, Michael. "Das Gute und das Schöne: Sophie von La Roche (1730–1807) wiederentdecken?" *Euphorion* 79 (1985): 111–38.

Mauser, Wolfram, and Barbara Becker-Cantarino, eds. *Frauenfreundschaft—Männerfreundschaft: Literarische Diskurse im 18. Jahrhundert.* Tübingen: Niemeyer, 1991.
Maynes, Mary Jo. *Schooling for the People: Comparative Local Studies of Schooling History in France and Germany, 1750–1850.* New York: Holmes and Meier, 1985.
Maza, Sarah. "The Rose-Girl of Salency: Representations of Virtue in Prerevolutionary France." *Eighteenth-Century Studies* 22 (1989): 395–412.
Meinhardt, Günther. *Die Universität Göttingen: Ihre Entwicklung und Geschichte von 1734–1974.* Frankfurt am Main: Musterschmidt, 1977.
Meise, Helga. *Die Unschuld und die Schrift: Deutsche Frauenromane im 18. Jahrhundert.* Reihe Metro 14. Berlin: Verlag Guttandin und Hoppe, 1983.
Miller, Nancy K., ed. *The Poetics of Gender.* New York: Columbia Univ. Press, 1986.
Moers, Ellen. *Literary Women: The Great Writers.* New York: Anchor-Doubleday, 1977.
Möhrmann, Renate. *Die andere Frau: Emanzipationsansätze deutscher Schriftstellerinnen im Vorfeld der Achtundvierziger-Revolution.* Stuttgart: Metzler, 1977.
Möller, Helmut. *Die kleinbürgerliche Familie im 18. Jahrhundert: Verhalten und Gruppenkultur.* Schriften zur Volksforschung 3. Berlin: de Gruyter, 1969.
Mohanty, Chandra Talpade. "Under Western Eyes: Feminist Scholarship and Colonial Discourses." In *Third World Women and the Politics of Feminism*, ed. Chandra Talpade Mohanty, Ann Russo, and Lourdes Torres. Bloomington: Indiana Univ. Press, 1991.
Monter, E. William. "Women in Calvinist Geneva (1550–1800)." *Signs* 6 (1980): 189–209.
Nenon, Monika. *Autorschaft und Frauenbildung: Das Beispiel Sophie von La Roche.* Epistemata, Würzburger wissenschaftliche Schriften, Reihe Literaturwissenschaft 31. Würzburg: Königshausen u. Neumann, 1988.
———. "Sophie von La Roche: Schreiben für 'Teutschlands Töchter.' Überlegungen zur Funktion der Mutterrolle." In *Mutter und Mütterlichkeit: Wandel und Wirksamkeit, eine Phantasie in der deutschen Literatur*, ed. Wolfram Mauser and Irmgard Roebling. Würzburg: Königshausen u. Neumann, 1996.
Neumann-Strele. "Sophie Albrecht, Lebensbeschreibung." Handwritten copy from *Allgemeine Modezeitung*, Leipzig. 30 March 1885. 13: 81, in the Archive of the Freies deutsches Hochstift, Frankfurt am Main.
Nussbaum, Felicity A. *The Autobiographical Subject: Gender and Ideology in Eighteenth-Century England.* Baltimore: Johns Hopkins Univ. Press, 1989.
Offen, Karen. "Defining Feminism: A Comparative Historical Approach." *Signs* 14 (1988): 119–57.
O'Malley, Lurana Donnels. "Masks of the Empress: Catherine the Great's Polyphony of Personae and her Play *Oh, These Times!*" *Comparative Drama* 31 (1997): 65–85.
———. "The Monarch and the Mystic: Catherine the Great's Strategy of Audience Enlightenment in *The Siberian Shaman.*" *Slavic and East European Journal* 41 (1997): 224–42.
O'Malley, Lurana Donnels, ed. and trans. *Two Comedies by Catherine the Great, Empress of Russia: Oh, These Times!* and *The Siberian Shaman.* Russian Theatre Archive 15. Amsterdam: Harwood Academic Publishers, 1998.
Petschauer, Peter. *The Education of Women in Eighteenth-Century Germany: New Directions from the German Female Perspective.* Lewiston: Mellen, 1989.

———. "Improving Educational Opportunities for Girls in Eighteenth-Century Germany." *Eighteenth-Century Life* 3 (1976): 56–62.
Pomerleau, Cynthia S. "The Emergence of Women's Autobiography in England." In *Women's Autobiography: Essays in Criticism*, ed. Estelle C. Jelinek. Bloomington: Indiana Univ. Press, 1980.
Pott, Ute. *Briefgespräche: Über den Briefwechsel zwischen Anna Louisa Karsch und Johann Wilhelm Ludwig Gleim, mit einem Anhang bislang ungedruckter Briefe aus der Korrespondenz zwischen Gleim und Caroline Luise von Klencke*. Göttingen: Wallstein, 1998.
Preußische Staatsbibliothek. *Gesamtkatalog der Preußischen Bibliotheken*. 14 vols. Berlin: Preußische Bibliothek, 1931–39.
Prokop, Ulrike. "Cornelia Goethe, 1750–1777: Die Melancholie der Cornelia Goethe." In *Schwestern berühmter Männer: Zwölf biographische Portraits*, ed. Luise F. Pusch. Frankfurt am Main: Insel, 1985.
———. "Die Einsamkeit der Imagination. Geschlechterkonflikt und literarische Produktion um 1770." In *Deutsche Literatur von Frauen*, ed. Gisela Brinkler-Gabler. Vol. 1. Munich: Beck, 1987.
———. *Die Illusion vom grossen Paar*. 2 vols. Frankfurt am Main: Fischer, 1991.
Ramazanoglu, Caroline. *Feminism and the Contradictions of Oppression*. London: Routledge, 1989.
Roebling, Irmgard. "Sturm und Drang—weiblich; Eine Untersuchung zu Sophie Albrechts Schauspiel 'Theresgen.' " *Deutschunterricht* 48 (1996) 1:63–77.
Schacht, Richard. *The Future of Alienation*. Urbana: Univ. of Illinois Press, 1994.
Schieth, Lydia. *Die Entwicklung des deutsche Frauenromans im ausgehenden 18. Jahrhundert: Ein Beitrag zur Gattungsgeschichte*. Helicon: Beiträge zur deutschen Literatur 5. Frankfurt am Main: Lang, 1987.
Schlözer, Leopold von. *Dorothea von Schlözer: Ein deutsches Frauenleben um die Jahrhundertwende, 1770–1825*. Berlin: Deutsche Verlagsanstalt, 1925.
Schreinert, Kurt. *Benedikte Naubert: Ein Beitrag zur Entstehungsgeschichte des historischen Romans in Deutschland*. 1941. Reprint. Nendeln, Lichtenstein: Kraus, 1969.
Schulte-Sasse, Jochen. "Poetik und Ästhetik Lessings und seiner Zeitgenossen." In *Deutsche Aufklärung bis zur Französischen Revolution, 1680–1789*, ed. Rolf Grimminger. Hansers Sozialgeschichte der deutschen Literatur vom 16. Jahrhundert bis zur Gegenwart 3.1. Munich: Hanser, 1980.
Schumann, Sabine. "Das 'lesende Frauenzimmer': Frauenzeitschriften im 18. Jahrhundert." In *Die Frau von der Reformation zur Romantik: Die Situation der Frau vor dem Hintergrund der Literatur und Sozialgeschichte*, ed. Barbara Becker-Cantarino, Modern German Studies 7. Bonn: Bouvier, 1980.
Sellner, Timothy, ed. and trans. "Appendix: Rauschenbusch-Clough on Hippel and Wollstonecraft." In *On Improving the Status of Women*, by Theodor Gottlieb von Hippel. Detroit: Wayne State Univ. Press, 1979.
Simon, Philipp. "Schillers 'Berühmte Frau.' " *Euphorion* 17 (1910): 287–99.
Soliday, Gerald. "Some Recent Studies in German Family History." *Journal of Family History* 7 (1982): 425–434.
Spelman, Elizabeth. *Inessential Woman: Problems of Exclusion in Feminist Thought*. Boston: Beacon, 1988.
Spencer, Jane. *The Rise of the Woman Novelist: From Aphra Behn to Jane Austen*. Oxford: Blackwell, 1986.
Stenzel, Jürgen, ed. *Das Zeitalter der Aufklärung*. Deutsche Schriftsteller im Porträt 2. Munich: Beck, 1980.

Stephan, Inge. " 'So ist die Tugend ein Gespenst.' Frauenbild und Tugendbegriff im bürgerlichen Trauerspiel bei Lessing und Schiller." *Lessing Yearbook* 17 (1985): 1–20.
Stephan, Inge, and Sigrid Weigel. *Die verborgene Frau: Sechs Beiträge zu einer feministischen Literaturwissenschaft.* Literatur im historischen Prozeß, n.F. 6. Berlin: Argument, 1983.
Stummann-Bowert, Ruth. "Philippine Engelhard, geborene Gatterer (1756–1831)." In *"Des Kennenlernens werth": Bedeutende Frauen Göttingens,* ed. Traudel Weber-Reich. Göttingen: Wallstein, 1993.
Stump, Doris. "Eine Frau 'von Verstand, Witz, Gefühl, Fantasie und Feuer'. Zu Leben und Werk Marianne Ehrmanns." In *Amalie: Eine wahre Geschichte in Briefen,* by Marianne Ehrmann. 1788. Reprint, ed. Maya Widmer and Doris Stump, Bern: Haupt, 1995.
Todd, Janet. *Women's Friendship in Literature.* New York: Columbia Univ. Press, 1980.
Touaillon, Christine. *Der deutsche Frauenroman des 18. Jahrhunderts.* Wien: Braumüller, 1919.
Trouille, Mary Seidman. *Sexual Politics in the Enlightenment: Women Writers Read Rousseau.* Albany: State Univ. of New York Press, 1997.
Vansant, Jaqueline. "Liebe und Patriarchat in der Romantik: Sophie Mereaus Briefroman *Amanda und Eduard.*" In *Der Widerspenstigen Zähmung: Studien zur bezwungenen Weiblichkeit in der Literatur vom Mittelalter bis zur Gegenwart,* ed. Sylvia Wallinger and Monika Jonas. Innsbrucker Beiträge zur Kulturwissenschaft: Germanistische Reihe 31. Innsbruck: Univ. Press, 1986.
Vogt, Marianne. *Autobiographik bürgerlicher Frauen.* Würzburg: Königshausen u. Neumann, 1981.
Vulpius, Wolfgang. *Christiane: Lebenskunst und Menschlichkeit in Goethes Ehe.* Weimar: Kiepenheuer, 1953.
Wägenbauer, Birgit. *Die Pathologie der Liebe: Literarische Weiblichkeitsentwürfe um 1800.* Berlin: Erich Schmidt, 1996.
Walker, Alice. *In Search of Our Mothers' Gardens.* San Diego: Harcourt Brace Jovanovich, 1984.
Wallinger, Sylvia, and Monika Jonas, eds. *Der Widerspenstigen Zähmung: Studien zur bezwungenen Weiblichkeit in der Literatur vom Mittelalter bis zur Gegenwart.* Innsbrucker Beiträge zur Kulturwissenschaft: Germanistische Reihe 31. Innsbruck: Univ. Press, 1986.
Walter, Eva. *Schrieb oft, von Mägde Arbeit müde: Lebenszusammenhänge deutscher Schriftstellerinnen um 1800—Schritte zur bürgerlichen Weiblichkeit.* Ed. Annette Kuhn. Düsseldorf: Schwann, 1985.
Wartburg-Ambühl, Marie Louise von. *Alphabetisierung und Lektüre: Untersuchung am Beispiel einer ländlichen Region im 17. und 18. Jahrhundert.* Europäische Hochschulschriften, Reihe 1: Deutsche Sprache und Literatur 459. Bern: Lang, 1981.
Watt, Helga Schutte. "Woman's Progress: Sophie La Roche's Travelogues 1787–1788." *The Germanic Review* 64 (1994): 50–60.
Wayne, Valerie. Introduction to *The Matter of Difference: Materialist Feminist Criticism of Shakespeare.* Ed. Valerie Wayne. Ithaca: Cornell, 1991.
Weckel, Ulrike. *Zwischen Häuslichkeit und Öffentlichkeit: Die ersten deutschen Frauenzeitschriften im späten 18. Jahrhundert und ihr Publikum.* Studien und Texte zur Sozialgeschichte der Literatur 61. Tübingen: Niemeyer, 1998.
Weigel, Sigrid. "Double Focus: On the History of Women's Writing." In *Feminist Aesthetics,* ed. Gisela Ecker. Boston: Beacon, 1985.

Widmer, Maya. "Amalie - eine wahre Geschichte?" In *Amalie: Eine wahre Geschichte in Briefen,* by Marianne Ehrmann. 1788. Reprint, ed. Maya Widmer and Doris Stump, Bern: Haupt, 1995.

Wiedemann, Luise. *Erinnerungen von Luise Wiedemann geb. Michaelis, der Schwester Carolinens, nebst Lebensabrissen ihrer Geschwister und Briefen Schellings und anderer.* Ed. Julius Steinberger. Göttingen: Vereinigung Göttinger Bücherfreunde, 1929.

Wilke, Jürgen. *Literarische Zeitschriften des 18. Jahrhunderts (1688–1789); Teil II: Repertorium.* Sammlung Metzler 175. Stuttgart: Metzler, 1978.

Wilpert, Gero von. *Die deutsche Gespenstergeschichte: Motiv—Form—Entwicklung.* Stuttgart: Kröner, 1994.

Winkle, Sally A. *Woman as Bourgeois Ideal: A Study of Sophie von La Roche's* Geschichte des Fräuleins von Sternheim *and Goethe's* Werther. New York: Lang, 1988.

Winston, Elizabeth. "The Autobiographer and her Readers: From Apology to Affirmation." In *Women's Autobiography: Essays in Criticism,* ed. Estelle C. Jelinek. Bloomington: Indiana Univ. Press, 1980.

Wittmann, Reinhard. "Die frühen Buchhändlerzeitschriften als Spiegel des literarischen Lebens," *Archiv für Geschichte des Buchwesens* 13 (1973): 613–932.

Wolf, Christa. " 'Nun ja! Das nächste Leben geht aber heute an.' Ein Brief über die Bettine." In *Die Günderode,* by Bettina von Arnim. Frankfurt am Main: Insel, 1983.

Worley, Linda Kraus. "Sophie von La Roche's *Reisejournale*: Reflections of a Traveling Subject." In *The Enlightenment and Its Legacy: Studies in German Literature in Honor of Helga Slessarev,* ed. Sara Friedrichsmeyer. Bonn: Bouvoir, 1991.

Wurst, Karin A. "Elise Bürger (1769–1833) and the Gothic Imagination." *Women in German Yearbook* 13 (1997): 11–27.

———.*Familiale Liebe ist die 'Wahre Gewalt': Die Repräsentation der Familie in G. E. Lessings dramatischem Werk.* Amsterdamer Publikationen zur Sprache und Literatur 75. Amsterdam: Rodopi, 1988.

———, ed. *Frauen und Drama im achtzehnten Jahrhundert.* Cologne: Böhlau, 1991.

Wuthenow, Ralph-Rainer, ed. *Zwischen Absolutismus und Aufklärung.* Vol. 4 of *Deutsche Literatur: Eine Sozialgeschichte.* Ed. Horst Albert Glaser. Reinbek: Rowohlt, 1980.

Young, Iris Marion. "Gender as Seriality: Thinking about Women as a Social Collective." *Signs* 19 (1994): 713–38.

Zantop, Susanne. "Trivial Pursuits? An Introduction to German Women's Writing from the Middle Ages to 1830." In *Bitter Healing: German Women Writers from 1700 to 1830: An Anthology,* ed. Jeannine Blackwell and Susanne Zantop. Lincoln: Univ. of Nebraska Press, 1990.

Zionkowski, Linda. "Strategies of Containment: Stephen Duck, Ann Yearsley, and the Problems of Polite Culture." *Eighteenth-Century Life* 13 (1989): 91–108.

Index

acting and actresses, 237, 253–57, 265, 285, 313–16
admonitory tale. *See* moral or admonitory tale
aesthetics of literary texts, 35
Albrecht, Johann Friedrich Ernst, 295–96, 322, 331, 334, 341, 379–80n
Albrecht, Sophie, 25, 32, 33, 136, 191, 211, 279, 286–345, 348, 351–52; acting and theater, 254, 296, 299, 316–18, 330–31, 334, 341, 357n, 379n; aging 341–43; alienation, 287–89, 292, 297, 304, 324, 328, 333–34; birth and childhood, 295, 320; on death, 287–89, 305, 310–11, 322–28, 337–38, 343–44; divorce, 334–35, 380n; and *Empfindsamkeit* of alienation, 287–89, 311–12; father, 295, 322, 358n; husband (*see* Albrecht, Johann Friedrich Ernst); on love 288–301, 307, 345; on marriage, 288–90, 292, 297–98, 303–11, 312, 339, 345; marriages of, 295, 331, 334, 379–80n; mother, 295–96, 316; as professional writer, 26; publication record, 331–32; questionable motherhood, 322; readers and subscribers, 316, 318–19, 339–40, 343, 379n, 380n; on sexuality and passion, 32, 286, 291–92, 333, 345, 355n; on virtue, 286, 291–92, 296–97, 299, 307, 321, 332, 345. Works: cookbooks, 342–43, 345, 381n; "Fragmente" "Fragments," 327–28, 330; *Ida von Duba,* 335–40, 349, 380–81n; *Lauschen ist auch gut* "Listening is also good," 303; love poetry, 288–95, 312, 319, 332–34, 338, 344, 379–80n; moon poems, 294–96, 322, 332–34; patriotic poetry, 322–23; *Theresgen,* 231–32, 234, 302–14, 324, 333, 372n, 373n, 377–78n
Alembert, Jean le Rond d', 366n
alienation, 287, 319, 326, 346, 348–49; objective, 287–88, 319, 346–49; subjective, 287–89, 319, 328, 333, 347–49. *See also* Empfindsamkeit: of alienation
Allgemeine deutsche Bibliothek, 203, 206, 336
Anna Amalia, of Sachsen-Weimar, 131
anonymity, 26, 30, 83, 108, 140, 302, 350–51, 355n, 362n, 377n. *See also* self-naming
aristocracy, 14, 92, 232–33, 368n; as rival of educated middle class (*see also under* educated middle class), 18, 93–98; women of, 41, 45–47, 131, 313–14, 316, 378n, 379n
Arnim, Achim von, 216
Arnim, Bettina von (née Brentano), 151–53, 364n
audience. *See* readers and audience
Aufklärung. See Enlightenment
autobiography. *See* self-narrative

Baldinger, Ernst Gottfried, 66, 70, 86–87; affair with servant, 68–69, 360n, 361–62n
Baldinger, Friderika, 32, 37–91, 153, 158, 167, 183, 241, 277, 287; aunt, 48, 75; birth and childhood, 41, 295; and the body, 75, 90; brother, 41, 47, 50, 55–56, 60, 64–65, 70, 75, 117, 358n; childbirth, 70–71, 361n; class status, 45; daughters, 60–62, 74, 89 (*see also* Gehren, Amalie); death, 40; desire for autonomy, 68, 90; desire to write, 74–80; education and learning, 45–51, 55–56, 69–71, 75, 100, 281; and the Enlightenment, 32, 34,

403

42, 50, 68–69; 90–91, 152, 219–20, 340, 349 (*see also* Enlightenment, and Friderika Baldinger); father, 41–43, 47; husband (*see* Baldinger, Ernst Gottfried); insecurity as scholar and writer, 55–56, 72–73, 80–81, 86–87, 102; and Sophie La Roche, 30, 40, 81–88, 136, 147, 149, 154; marriage, 63–70, 87, 105, 360–62n; misogyny of, 37, 43–44, 63, 70, 73; mother, 41–42, 43, 47, 50, 58, 60, 62, 64–65, 70, 75, 116, 117; and patriarchy, 63–64, 72, 98–99; posthumous publication, 24, 361–62n; as private writer, 29, 38, 74, 354n; publication decision, 37, 74, 80–90, 93, 127, 170, 177, 222; readers (potential), 63, 86–87, 93; reading, 38, 45, 55, 357n; sexuality, 63, 67–68, 90; sister, 46, 47, 64, 75, 117; and Dorothea Spangenberg on Gatterer, 208–9, 371n; uncle, 45–46. Works: few publications by, 38, 76, 356n; *Lebensbeschreibung von Friderika Baldinger von ihr selbst verfaßt*, 30, 37, 40, 71–77, 80–81, 86–89, 273, 347; —, and its multiple prefaces, 40, 76, 86, 360n, 362n; letter writing of, 37–38, 50, 80, 82–85; other unpublished writings, 76

Bandemer, Susanne, 171, 335
Bartky, Sandra Lee, 229
Basseritz, Sabine Elisabeth Oelgard von, 378n
Baudissin, Karoline, 378n
Beaumont, Jeanne-Marie Leprince de, 49
beauty, 111, 172–73, 283–84, 307, 320–21, 325
Bechtolsheim, Julie von, 211
Becker, Sophie. *See* Schwartz, Sophie
Becker-Cantarino, Barbara, 358–59n, 368n, 370n, 380n
Bentheim-Steinfurt, Karoline von, 378n
Béranger, Pierre-Jean de, 216–17
Berlepsch, Emilie von, 32, 277, 282, 286; divorce of, 334, 374–75n; and Ehrmann and Hippel, 376–77n; on protofeminism, 221–22, 258–63, 274; on Wollstonecraft, 222, 283–84

Bernhardi, Elisabeth Eleonore, 131
Bernhardi, Sophie, 335
Bethmann, Elise, 319
Beulwitz, Caroline von. *See* Wolzogen, Caroline von
Bible and hymnals, as reading material 18, 45–46, 49, 57–59
biography, 76–77, 153. *See also* self-narrative
Bohl, Susanne, 77
Böhmer, Caroline. *See* Michaelis, Caroline
Boie, Heinrich Christian, 140, 177–78, 183, 188, 193, 216, 294, 360n
Boie, Luise. *See* Mejer, Luise
Bondeli, Julie, 64, 151, 368n
Bovenschen, Silvia, 107, 161–62, 329
Brachmann, Luise, 140
Brentano, Bettina. *See* Arnim, Bettina von
Brentano, Clemens, 140, 216
Brinker-Gabler, Gisela, 24, 356n
Britt, Christa Baguss, 106
Brun, Friederike, 272, 357n
Büchner, Georg, 375
Bürger, Elise (née Hahn), 313, 335, 375n, 380n
Bürger, Gottfried August, 176–77, 183–90, 207, 210, 216, 240, 313, 335, 370n, 375n
Burney, Fanny, 108, 251, 367n
Butler, Judith, 354n

Cagliostro, Alessandro, 367n
Carl August of Weimar, 341
"Caroline," (La Roche's purported reader-contributor), 135, 141, 142, 144–47, 367–68n
Castle, Terry, 326–27, 340
Catherine II, of Russia, 313
Catholicism, 250, 252, 295, 364n
Cervantes, Miguel de, 50
Charrière, Isabelle de, 257, 330
Chézy, Helmina von, 153, 335
Christianity, 44, 67, 194, 267, 341. *See also* Catholicism; Protestantism
class, 304–7, 349, 380n; impact on women writers, 28; and race and gender, 14; women's assignment to one, 18. *See also* aristocracy; educated middle class

Classicism. See *Klassik*
Claudius, Matthias, 216
Clemens, Friedrich. *See* Gerke, Friedrich Clemens
Cocalis, Susan, 24, 362n
conduct books for girls, 130–31, 329
convents, 245–46, 252, 254, 336, 379n
cookbooks, 23, 287, 342–43
corsets, 60–61
Cotta, Johann Friedrich, 264, 278, 347

Dachröden, Karoline von, 319–22
Dalberg, W. H., 365n
Dalberg, (sister of W.H. Dalberg), 379n
Damm, Christian Tobias, 196
Davies, Bronwyn, 20
Dawson, Ruth P., 369n, 378n
death: as literary theme, 196, 257, 267, 288–89, 323–28, 343–44 (*see also* Albrecht, Sophie: on death); in childbirth, 39, 51, 71, 83
Dedert, Hartmut, 233, 235
Diede, Charlotte, 335
divorce, 237, 250–52, 257, 259, 334–35, 374–75n. *See also under* Albrecht, Sophie; Ehrmann, Marianne
domesticity. *See* work: women's
Dörrien, Katharina Helena, 302
drama: as genre choice of women, 24–25, 28, 153, 286, 302–3, 313–16, 318, 328–29, 332, 346
dreaming. *See* sleep
Drebing, Lisette Charlotte, 360n, 361–62n
dressing and cross-dressing, 219, 252, 269
Duden, Barbara, 122
Dülmen, Richard van, 367n
Durkheim, Emile, 157

Eagleton, Terry, 35
Edgeworth, Maria, 108, 272
educated middle class, 13, 14, 17, 28, 38, 42; campaign for status, 17–18, 92–98, 199–200, 297
education: of men, 38 (*see also* university); of women and girls, 38, 46–47, 56, 90, 276, 344, 358n; —, in aristocracy, 41, 45, 46–47; —, capped, 17, 62, 114–15, 124, 281; —, concealment of, 54, 69, 99, 178; —, in educated middle class, 41, 45, 47; —, below educated middle class, 41, 45, 47, 57, 100; —, by family members, 18, 47, 57–61; —, inadequacy of, 100, 173–74, 176, 243, 350, 366n; —, and marriage 53, 62; men's criticism of —, 279; —, opposed by mothers, 57–60; —, by tutors and governesses, 47, 59. *See also* schools
Ehrich-Haefeli, Verena, 100, 102
Ehrmann, Marianne, 25, 31–33, 191, 214, 220, 221–85, 286–88, 340, 342, 344, 347, 351; as actress, 237; on alienation, 252, 264, 272, 333; birth and childhood, 236, 373n; and G.A. Bürger, 240, 375n; on divorce, 250–52; divorce, apparent, of 237, 334, 373n; and the *Empfindsamkeit* of alienation, 236, 241, 247, 258, 272, 275, 287–88; and the Enlightenment, 253, 269, 271–72; husband (*see* Ehrmann, Theophil Friedrich); as journalist, 263–81; on love, 249, 251, 254; marriages of, 236–37, 373n, 376n; parents, 236; as professional writer, 26; as protofeminist, 129, 228, 265, 274–78, 286–87, 376–77n; readers and subscribers, 375–77n; on reason and education, 276–77, 281; on sexuality, 223–24, 226–28, 242, 245–46, 251, 253, 255, 275; thinking woman notion 241, 245–48, 250, 252–53, 255–56, 258, 281, 285; uncle, 236; on virtue 249, 251; on women writing 277–78. Works: *Amalie* 231, 238–58, 263, 281, 286, 311–12, 320, 326, 335, 339, 372n, 374n; marriage in —, 246–52, 257, 259–60, 374n; *Amaliens Erholungsstunden* "Amalie's Recreational Hours" 240, 264–74, 373n; *Amaliens Feierstunden* "Amalie's Rest Hours," 240; *Antonie von Warnstein*, as *Amalie* renamed, 240, 336, 373n, 374n; dialog about the hairdo, 270–72, 330; "Das Ei" "The Egg" 268–69; *Die Einsiedlerinn aus den Alpen* "The Hermit Woman from the Alps," 240, 264, 272; *Graf Bilding* "Count Bilding," 238; handkerchief story, 222–28, 233, 237, 247,

253, 373n; *Kleine Fragmente* "Small Fragments," 238, 372n; *Leichtsinn und gutes Herz* "Frivolity and a Good Heart," 231, 234–35, 238, 306–7, 313–14, 372n, 373n; *Müssige Stunden* "Leisure Hours" 238–40; *Ninas Briefe* 232–33, 238–40, 372n; *Philosophie eines Weibes* "A Woman's Philosophy" 238, 248, 325; sketch of the sleepless night 265–68, 270
Ehrmann, Theophil Friedrich, 237, 240, 263–64, 273, 373n, 376n
Einem, Charlotte von, 128, 137, 294; and Friderika Baldinger, 46; childhood, 46; class placement, 46; and Philippine Engelhard-Gatterer, 167–68, 177, 182–84, 186; leaving autobiography unpublished, 89; reading, 49–50; values taught to, 58
Ekkard, Henrietta Elisabeth, 25, 66
emotion as validation of women's writing. See feeling woman
Empfindsamkeit "Sensibility", 25, 31, 33–34, 93, 103, 107, 161, 191, 266–67, 287, 290–91, 294, 307, 317–18, 329, 346, 369n, 373n; of alienation, 31, 32, 236, 241, 247, 258, 265, 272, 285, 287–89, 311–12, 346, 351 (*see also* alienation; Ehrmann, Marianne: *Empfindsamkeit* of alienation); of sympathy, 31, 154, 161–65, 174, 179, 222–23, 226, 266, 287, 346, 369n; religious, 31, 162, 267, 287; and readers 34, 162
enablement to write, strategies. *See* feeling woman; La Roche, Sophie: strategy; women writers
encyclopedia for women, 131
Engelhard, Caroline, 153, 213
Engelhard, Johann Philipp, 166, 213, 215
Engelhard-Gatterer, Philippine, 25, 31, 32, 136, 138, 153–220, 229, 241–42, 269, 277, 286–88, 300, 303–4, 325, 344–45, 347, 351, 360n; and G. A. Bürger, 183–90, 207, 240, 370n; childbearing and rearing, 213–14; childhood and education, 165–66, 216; death, 216; and Einem, Charlotte von, 177, 182–84; and *Empfindsamkeit,* 162, 174, 179, 266;

father (*see* Gatterer, Johann Christoph); justifying her writing, 168–75; on learning, 197–98; on marriage, 162–65, 198–202, 213; marriage of, 166, 213–16; Michaelis, Caroline, about, 155–58, 167, 171, 209; mother, 166, 181–82; readers and subscribers, 34, 81–82, 161, 173–75, 208–13, 371n; reviews of, 78–79, 199, 203–8; self-representations, 162–65, 168–76, 177, 179–81, 193; sisters, 165–66 (*see also* Gatterer, Helene); and taboo topics, 162–65, 208–9; on virtue, 161; writing for La Roche's *Pomona,* 215. Works: *Gedichte von Philippine Engelhard* "Poems by Philippine Engelhard," 193, 206, 208–9, 211–12; *Gedichte von Philippine Gatterer* "Poems by Philippine Gatterer," 191–205; *Neue Gedichte* "New Poems," 216; *Neujahrsgeschenk für liebe Kinder* "New Year's Gift for dear Children," 207–8, 212; poem on wedding night, 162–65, 209; poems on modesty, 158–59, 169, 171–72
England, 17, 125, 126, 142, 176, 183, 185, 227, 256, 282, 284, 348, 368n; novels in, 24, 108
Enlightenment, 33, 269, 271, 290, 326–27, 380–81n; and Friderika Baldinger, 30, 37–88 passim, 90–91, 346–47; and *Empfindsamkeit* 161, 236; and *Sturm und Drang* 230, 241; and universalizing language, 41, 349; and women, 25, 33–34, 38, 69, 73, 90–91, 103, 118, 129, 133, 151, 152, 219, 309, 340, 350
epic poetry, 24
essay, 23, 25, 125, 142, 153, 259–60, 264–68; as genre choice of women, 28, 329

Faderman, Lillian, 377n
fame for women, 86, 155, 171, 175, 197, 243, 264
fathers, 128, 246, 323, 358n; and girls' education, 47, 167; as mentors, 181–82; representation of, in La Roche, 112–13, 118; of women writers, 25. *See also under* Albrecht, So-

phie; Baldinger, Friderika; Engelhard-Gatterer, Philippine; La Roche, Sophie

feeling woman notion, 101–3, 117, 153, 162, 169, 183, 190–91, 245, 329, 345, 350

Felman, Shoshona, 354n

Felski, Rita, 20, 24, 355n

feminine culture. *See* women's traditional culture

feminine subjectivity in women's writing, 15, 146–54, 222, 240–42, 260–61, 290, 305, 328, 345. *See also* women writers

femininity: androcentric discourse of 38, 146; and being a woman, especially of the educated middle class, 15, 39, 81, 122, 248–51, 288, 319–22; scripted, 20–21, 100, 102, 153; (*see also* modesty, feminine; gender); *See also* gender; women writers

feminism in eighteenth century. *See* protofeminism

Ferguson, Kathy, 120–21

Fichte, Johann Gottlieb, 350

Fielding, Henry, 176, 256

Figes, Eva, 24, 108, 181–82

Finke, Laurie, 16, 355n

Flint, Christopher, 223, 225, 227

Flora, 264, 278

Forkel, Meta. *See* Wedekind, Meta

Forster, Georg, 73, 76, 358n, 371n

Forster, Therese. *See* Huber, Therese

France, 125–27, 142, 301, 304, 348, 365n, 368n

freedom, and women, 156, 174–75, 209, 217, 244, 274, 280, 296, 323–24, 350

French language and literature, 50, 58–59, 100, 151, 314, 363n; and German women writers, 368n

French Revolution, impact in Germany, 26, 229, 258–59, 267, 271–72, 276–77, 282–83, 322, 332, 335, 349, 352, 372n

Friedrich II, of Prussia, 313

Friedrich Wilhelm III, of Prussia, 132, 214

friendship model of interaction, 132–34, 143–44

Froriep, Amalie Henriette Sophie, 25

Frühsorge, Gotthardt, 362

Fuchs, Anna Rupertina, 24

Fuss, Diana, 254n

Gad, Esther, 356n

Gallitzin, Amalia von, 131

Gatens, Moira, 22

Gatterer, Helene, 138–39, 141, 358n

Gatterer, Johann Christoph, 165–67, 178–82, 211, 358n

Gatterer, Philippine. *See* Engelhard-Gatterer, Philippine

Gehren, Amalie (born 1768), 153, 361n

Gehren, Amalie (born 1799), 153

Geissler, Adam Friedrich, 332

Gellert, Christian Fürchtegott, 49, 57, 174, 193, 357n

gender, 13–36, 307, 317–18; attributions as historical constructs, 14; and class, 39, 93, 297; as crime and punishment system, 155–60, 168, 242, 352; and division of labor, 99, 290; historical change of, 99, 122, 245, 350; polarization, 14, 20, 152, 202–3, 245, 254–55, 258, 286, 301–2, 350. *See also* feminine subjectivity; femininity; self and identity; women writers

genius, 169–71, 188, 190, 232, 280, 348, 372n

genre: change of choice over time, 25, 318, 328–30; women's wide choice of, 15, 23, 24, 28. *See also specific genres*

George III, of England, 48, 165

Gerke, Friedrich Clemens, 343–44, 381n

Gersdorf, Wilhelmine von, 59–60

Gervinus, Georg Gottfried, 356n

Gessner, Judith née Heidigger, 130

Gessner, Solomon, 130

Giovane, Juliana. *See* Mudersbach

Gleim, Johann Wilhelm Ludwig, 193, 294, 369n

Göchhausen, Luise von, 64, 131

Goeckingk, L. F. G., 186, 190

Goeckingk, Nantchen, 67, 78–79, 186, 199,

Goethe, Catharina Elisabeth, 123, 366n, 370n
Goethe, Cornelia, 358n
Goethe, Johann Wolfgang, 33, 91, 122, 131, 211, 216, 235, 241, 294, 301, 358n, 379n; about Sophie La Roche, 152; *Werther* 49–50, 118, 305, 310–11
Goethe, Ottilie von. *See* Pogwisch, Ottilie von
Goldstein, Auguste von, 334
Goodman, Dena, 22
Goodman, Katherine, 19, 70, 362n
gossip, 160
Gothic in literature, 268, 287, 326, 335–40, 380n
Gotter, Luise, 167, 209, 371n. *See also* Michaelis, Caroline: to Gotter
Göttinger Hain literary group, 46, 132, 177, 185, 195, 360n
Göttingsche Gelehrte Anzeigen, 44, 203,
Gottsched, Johann Christoph, on women's education, 51, 199, 277
Gottsched, Luise Adelgunde Culmus, 24, 51, 53, 55, 66, 302–3, 314; *Spectator* translation 55, 69, 349, 358n
governessing, 253, 265, 281, 373–74n
Graffigny, Françoise de, 330
grammatical and metrical correctness, 182–83, 204–5
Grant, Judith, 155–57
Grävemeier, Molly von, 136–37
Greek language and literature, 51–52, 58, 100, 116, 173–74, 193, 358n
Greer, Germaine, 206
Gregorius, Johanne Elisabeth, 334
Grimm, Jacob, 32, 33, 216, 355–56n
Guillet, Pernette Du, 296
Günderrode, Karoline von, 351
Gutbier, Johann Christian. *See* Friderika Baldinger: father of *and also* brother of

Habermas, Jürgen, 132, 157, 183, 366n
Hadley, Michael, 380n
Haferkorn, Hansjürgen, 382n
Hagedorn, Friedrich von, 193
Hagen Christiane von, 137, 141

Hahn, von (Sophie Albrecht's alleged second husband), 380n
Hahn, Elise. *See* Bürger, Elise
Hain, Juliana, 378n
Hamburger Correspondent, 48
Hastings, Warren, 367n
Hausen, Karin, 16, 17, 222, 245, 254–55, 258, 278, 290
Hawkesworth, Mary, 354n
Heidenreich, Bernd, 107, 363n, 365n
Henrici, Charlotte Amalia, 51–52
Hensel (later Seyler), Friederike Sophie, 25, 334
Herder, Johann Gottfried, 162, 273, 277, 283, 374–75n
Herder, Karoline, 66
Heuser, Magdalena, 56, 68, 77, 87, 356n, 358n, 360n, 361n, 362n
Heyne, Christian Gottlob, 76
Heyne, Therese. *See* Huber, Therese
Hezel, Charlotte Henriette, 202
Hippel, Theodor Gottlieb von, 73–74, 258, 278, 282, 356n, 376–77n
Hoff, Dagmar von, 378n
Hofmann, Anne Margarethe, 378n
Hohendahl, Peter Uwe, 363n
Hölderlin, Friedrich, 132, 216, 273
Holland, 142
Hölty, Ludwig Christoph Heinrich, 195, 216
Homans, Margaret, 365n
household accounts, women writing, 14, 17, 18
housekeeping books and essays, 23, 276
Huber, Therese (née Heyne, then Forster), 73, 76, 167, 215, 355n, 356n
Hull, Isabel V., 103, 133, 135
Humboldt, Caroline von. *See* Dachröden, Karoline von
Humboldt, Wilhelm von, 319
Hungary, 256
Huyssen, Andreas, 230–34, 373n

identity. *See* self and identity
idyll, 25, 159, 193–94, 286, 304, 332
infanticide, 103
intention, lack of. *See* unintentionality topos
Irigaray, Luce, 354n

INDEX 409

Italian, 59, 100, 314, 363n
Italy, 253, 256

Jean Paul. *See* Richter, Jean Paul
Jerusalem, Friederike M., 64, 136–37
Jesus, 68
Jewish women, 29
Joeres, Ruth-Ellen B., 132–34, 366n
Johnson, Claudia, 253
Jones, Ann Rosalind, 296
journalism by and for women, 25, 28, 229–30, 263–81, 329. *See also* periodicals
justifications for writing or publishing. *See under* writing and publishing

Kalb, Charlotte von, 131
Kamienski, Karoline, 64, 211
Kant, Immanuel, 90–91,162
Kaplan, Carla, 143, 146–47
Karsch, Anna Luise, 24, 57, 66, 79, 128, 151, 153, 171, 206–07, 214–15, 279, 294, 335; and her daughter, 369n, 370n. *See also* Klencke, Karoline von
Kästner, Abraham Gotthelf, 60–62, 68, 72, 89, 153, 183, 211, 362n
Kelly-Gadol, Joan, 34
Kestner, Lotte, 211
Klassik (German Classicist movement), 28, 33, 122, 145–47
Kleist, Heinrich von, 216
Klencke, Karoline von, 79–80, 153, 335, 369n, 370n
Klettenberg, Susanna von, 64, 150
Klopstock, Friedrich Gottlieb, 49, 173, 193, 195, 205, 267, 280, 293, 357n, 359n
Klopstock, Meta (née Moller), 65, 66, 76, 81, 83–84, 89, 162, 267, 293, 359n
Klüger, Ruth, 369n
Knodel, John, 360n
Koch, Friederike, 57, 173–74, 196
König, Eva, 200, 293
Kopp, Amalia, 379n
Kord, Susanne, 24, 203, 205–6, 355n, 378–79n
Kortzfleisch, Sophie Eleonore, 231–34, 357n
Kramnick, Jonathon Brody, 183

Kranichfeld, Johann Wilhelm, 55–56, 70, 75, 84
Krockow, Luise von, 131
Krosigk, Ernestine, 356n
Krüdener, Juliane, 334
Krull, Edith, 230–31, 235, 273, 373n

La Fite, Marie Elisabeth de, 367n
La Roche, Georg, 108, 178, 364n
La Roche, Sophie, 31, 92–154, 158, 161, 176, 194, 214, 229, 241, 265, 271, 277, 286–87, 303, 319, 344–45, 347, 351–52, 373n, 380n; and age, 118; and Baldinger, Friderika, 30, 40, 81–88, 128, 147, 149, 154, 273, 361–62n; and the body, 149; brothers, 117–118; childbearing and rearing, 115, 178; criticizing men, 119–22, 153; daughters, 142, 153, 368n, 370n; death of, 152; easy and imitable style, 137, 141; and *Empfindsamkeit*, 93, 103, 107, 151, 154, 161–62, 266–67; and Enlightenment, 31, 93, 103, 129, 151–52, 219–20; father, 363n; genre choice and experiments, 108, 141, 143; girlhood and education, 100, 109, 128, 363n; honored in Froriep novel, 25; husband, (*see* Laroche, Georg); juxtaposition technique, 107–8, 124, 145–46, 152, 178–79; and literary group, 93, 132–47; on marriage, 102–16, 364n; mother, 59, 117–18, 363n, 364n; and needlework, 14, 17, 80; persona as older female relative, 118, 139, 144, 249; and professional writing, 26, 372n; readers and subscribers for, 81, 131–42, 237, 367n, 371n; on scholarliness and learning, 110–16, 123, 125–31, 198; self-representations in her writing, 127, 130, 141, 143, 147–52; on sexuality, 96, 97; sisters, 117–18; sons, 142; strategy of enablement, 32, 52, 98, 183, 191, 350 (*see also* feeling woman notion); supporting alternatives for women, 123, 141; and taboo topics, 103, 108–110. Works: *Briefe an Lina* "Letters to Lina," 130–31, 366n; *Briefe über Mannheim* "Letters about Mannheim," 116, 141–47,

364–65 n; *Geschichte des Fräuleins von Sternheim* "The History of Lady Sophia Sternheim," 24, 25, 92–98, 101–2, 104–10, 118, 120–21, 146–48, 169–70, 177–79, 232–33, 251, 256–57, 307, 329, 362–64 n, 370 n; education and scholarliness in —, 96, 98, 107, 364–65 n; virtue coalition in —, 93–98, 102; *Mein Schreibetisch* "My Writing Desk," 141–42, 147–52, 330, 368 n; *Melusinens Sommer-Abende* "Melusina's Summer Evenings," 152; *Pomona*, 53, 81, 84, 93, 109, 118–20, 123–30, 132–44, 211–12, 215, 264, 273, 276, 364 n, 365 n, 367 n (*see also* literary group; *Pomona* group); letters to and from readers of —, 127, 135–38; letters to Lina in —, 109, 123–26, 139, 142, 152–53, 365 n; *Rosaliens Briefe* "Rosalie's Letters," 110; "Der schöne Bund" "The Beautiful Band," 110–15; travel writings, 136, 142, 357 n, 367 n

La Vopa, Anthony J., 158–59
Landolt, Johann Heinrich, 115, 358 n
Lange, Charlotte. *See* Seidel, Charlotte
Lanser, Susan S., 351
Latin, 51–52, 58–59, 100, 116, 130, 191, 358 n, 364 n
Lavater, Johann Kasper, 365 n
leisure time, women's, 18, 79, 103, 197
Lengefeld, Charlotte. *See* Schiller, Charlotte
lesbian, 377 n
Lessing, Dorothea Salome, 358–59 n
Lessing, Gotthold Ephraim, 199–200, 231–32, 293, 303, 349, 358 n
letters: as genre, 25, 84, 137, 249, 251, 256; preservation of, 168
letter writing: by women, 21, 23, 80, 83–84, 101, 127, 138–40, 160, 167, 354–55 n. *See also under* Baldinger, Friderika: Works
Lewald, Fanny, 80
Lichtenberg, Georg Christoph, 71–72, 211, 213
Liebeskind, Margarete. *See* Wedekind, Margarete
literary confidantes, female, 160–61, 176–77, 182
literary group, 132–33, 138–41, 153–54, 367 n; goals, 135–36; and Sophie La Roche, 31, 123–25, 139–40, 371 n
literary history's treatment of women, 33, 355–56 n. *See also Empfindsamkeit*; Enlightenment; *Klassik*; *Sturm und Drang*; Romanticism
literary marketplace, 23, 160
literary public, women's participation in, 22, 157, 183. *See also* public sphere, bourgeois
literary salon, 133
Lohmann, Johanne, 334
Loster-Schneider, Gudrun, 147–48, 151, 368–69 n
Louise, of Mecklenburg-Schwerin, 378 n
Lucius, Christiane Karoline. *See* Schlegel, Christiane Karoline
Ludecus, Caroline, 140
Ludwig, Sophie, 54, 91
Lühe, Caroline von der, 87–88

MacArthur, Elizabeth, 330
Madland, Helga, 61, 231, 235, 269, 372–76 n
Mahlmann, Siegfried August, 380 n
Maria Antonia Walpurgis, of Saxony, 313–14
marriage, 61–71, 245, 286, 350; age at, 39, 66–67; and the "great pair," 122; intertwined with education and femininity, 53, 54, 62; as prostitution, 63–64; protofeminist analysis of, 258–63; represented in literature, 102–7, 111, 114, 162–65, 198–202, 285, 306, 310, 312, 374 n (*see also* Ehrmann, Marianne: *Amalie*); from women's perspective, 38–39, 62, 64, 65. *See also* divorce
McGrath, J. E., 133, 366 n
Meise, Helga, 355 n, 359 n
Mejer, Luise (later Boie), 67, 136–37, 294, 359–60 n
melancholy, 195, 233, 248, 252, 305, 324–26, 336
Mendelssohn, Moses, 206–7, 350
mentors and anti-mentors, male, 30, 160–61, 175–82, 184–90, 318, 347, 354 n

Mereau, Sophie (later Brentano), 66, 140–41, 335, 351, 355n, 374–75n
Mezger, Maria Dorothea, 375n
Michaelis, Caroline (later Böhmer, Schlegel, and Schelling), 66, 167, 203, 335, 351; to Gotter about Gatterer, 155–58, 171, 209, 335, 371n
Middle Ages, 269
military. *See* social advancement and status
misogyny, 243, 258–63, 279–80, 284–85, 375n. *See also* Baldinger, Friderika
Mnioch, Maria, 357n
modesty, feminine, 88–89, 156–61, 178, 196, 286
Mohanty, Chandra Talpade, 354n
Möhrmann, Renate, 261, 355n
Molière, 313
Moller, Meta. *See* Klopstock, Meta
Möller, Wendula Hedwig, 131
money. *See* writing for money
Montenglaut, Henriette von, 316, 335, 342–43
Monter, E. William, 360n
moral or admonitory tale, 125, 264, 269
More, Hannah, 185
mothers, 59, 128, 181–82, 246, 275–77, 323, 370n; representation of, in La Roche, 112–13, 116, 118. *See also under* Albrecht, Sophie; Baldinger, Friderika; education: of women and girls; Engelhard-Gatterer, Philippine; La Roche, Sophie
Mozart, Wolfgang Amadeus, 303
Mudersbach, Juliane, 136, 334
Müller, Elise, 312–14, 378n

narrators, in women's texts, 224–25
Naubert, Benedikte, 67, 273; her anonymity, 27
needle, 54, 80, 100, 352, 364n; as signal of gender, 13, 17
needlework. *See* work: women's
Nenon, Monika, 106–7, 110, 363n, 365n
Neuber, Caroline, 24, 314, 378n
Nicolai, Friedrich, 190, 203, 214, 367n, 375n
Nicolay, Ludwig Heinrich, 367n
nonwriter: definition of, 21, 354n

Novalis (Friedrich von Hardenberg), 216
novels: as women's genre choice, 23–25, 28, 318, 329, 346, 355n

object narrative, 223, 225
Offen, Karen, 274

patriarchy: in eighteenth-century Germany, 39, 61, 63–64, 69, 72–73, 89, 126, 153, 276, 278, 303, 309, 313, 320, 327
Pauli, Henriette, 64
Pauline, of Lippe-Detmold, 132
peasant women, 15, 29, 41, 45, 47
periodicals, for women, 18, 23, 214–15, 240, 268, 329. *See also* Ehrmann, Marianne: *Amaliens Erholungsstunden*, and *Einsiedlerinn aus den Alpen*; journalism; La Roche, Sophie: *Pomona*
Pernet, Hedwig Louise von, 302
Pfeffel, Gottlieb Konrad, 211, 273
Pichler, Caroline, 88, 357n
Pietism, 45, 76, 162
plays. *See* drama
Poe, Edgar Allan, 343
poetry: as genre choice of women, 23–25, 28, 125, 153, 259, 287, 328–29
Pogwisch, Ottilie von, 241
Pomona group, 132–44. *See also* La Roche, Sophie: readers; literary group
posthumous publication. *See* publication, posthumous
postscripts and margins, 82–85
Pott, Ute, 369n
private sphere: in homes, 22
private writers, 167, 321, 351–52, 354n, 354–55n; delimited, 21–23, 83 and genre choice, 23; made public, 177; women as and their influence, 24
Prokop, Ulrike, 122, 304, 364n, 366n, 370n
Protestantism, and girls' education, 41, 45, 250
protofeminism, 129, 228–30, 240–44, 286–87; defined, 221; and Emilie Berlepsch, 32, 221–22, 258–63, 274; and Marianne Ehrmann, 31–32,

228, 235, 252, 258, 265, 274–78, 376n
pseudomemoir, 222–25
pseudonymity, 26–27, 30, 208, 351, 355n, 371n; of Engelhard-Gatterer, 161, 178, 182, 215
public sphere: bourgeois, 21–23, 132–33, 156–57, 366n
public writers: delimited, 21–23, 89, 354n; and genre choices, 23; women as, 24, 34, 53, 202, 378n; —and their relationship to audience, 23, 351
publication, posthumous by women, 24, 83, 87–89

quill, 16–17, 54, 59, 80, 100, 352; as signal of gender, 13, 17, 364n

race, 14, 29, 273, 349
Radcliffe, Ann, 327
readers and audience: in literary groups, 133, 135–36, 138–41, 366n; of private letters, 23; women as, 38, 104, 136, 157–59; of women writers, 34, 86–87, 159–60, 318, 329, 368n, 376–77n. *See also under* Albrecht, Sophie; Baldinger, Friderika; Ehrmann, Marianne; Engelhard-Gatterer, Philippine; La Roche, Sophie; literary group
reading: extensive, 18, 58, 80; intensive, 18, 58
reading materials and books, access of women and girls to, 48–50, 58
reception, 160–61, 202–13, 347; formal, 31, 202–8 (*see also* reviews); informal, 31, 202, 208–10; nominal, 202, 210–12
Recke, Elisa von der, 132, 314, 316–17, 321, 334, 341, 378–79n
Reiske, Ernestine, 52
religion, 28, 71, 100, 335, 357n; and divorce, 250–52; in poetry, 173, 197 (see *Empfindsamkeit*, religious). *See also* Catholicism; Pietism; Protestantism
request device as excuse for writing, 56, 75–76, 82, 101, 127, 147
reviews, 23, 34, 160–61. *See also* Engelhard-Gatterer, Philippine: reviews; reception, formal

Riccoboni, Marie-Jeanne, 301
Richardson, Samuel, 49, 81, 176, 256
Richter, Carl Christian, 332, 380n
Richter, Jean Paul, 132, 212
Rococo, 193, 292
Roebling, Irmgard, 310, 372n, 373n, 377–78n
Romanticism, 32, 33, 167, 216, 265, 269, 284, 300, 327, 330, 335, 349–52, 380n
Rosa, Angelika, 374n
Rothberg, Friederike von, 136
Rousseau, Jean-Jacques, 22, 128, 146, 149, 151, 162, 199, 238, 248, 262, 283, 348–49; *Emil*, 99–101, 118; on the needle, 13
Rudolphi, Karoline, 64
Russia, 313, 341

Sagar, Maria Anna, 25, 355n
Schacht, Richard, 287, 333, 346, 349
Schieth, Lydia, 355n
Schiller, Charlotte von, 132
Schiller, Friedrich, 33, 132, 162, 216, 273, 278, 294, 368n, 376n; and Sophie Albrecht, 316–19, 330–31, 341, 379–80n; and Marianne Ehrmann, 255, 273; and *Sturm und Drang*, 231, 235, 255
Schindel, Carl Wilhelm Otto August von, 26–27, 33, 77, 79–80
Schlegel, Caroline (née Michaelis, also Böhmer and Schelling). *See* Michaelis, Caroline
Schlegel, Christiane Karoline (née Lucius), 67, 231–34, 357n
Schlegel, Dorothea, 335, 351
Schlegel, Friedrich, 345, 349–50
Schlieben, Wilhelmine, 64
Schlözer, August L., 53, 211, 356–57n
Schlözer, Dorothea, 53–54, 167, 274, 356–57n
scholarliness, 18, 19, 45, 51–55, 96, 98–99, 107, 114–16, 126–31, 364–65n; competing with women's traditional culture, 117; and opportunity, 44–45; requirements for, 51, 358n. *See also under* La Roche, Sophie
scholarly women and girls, 52–55, 57, 112–14, 130–31, 359n; separating themselves from other women, 43,

359–60 n. *See also* Ehrmann, Marianne: thinking woman; scholarliness
schools: and girls, 46, 47, 101, 104, 143, 280, 364 n, 370 n; Schulpforta, 41
Schröder, F. U. L., 341
Schröder, Hans, 377 n
Schubert, Johanne, 357 n
Schulte-Sasse, Jochen, 161
Schurman, Anna Maria van, 51, 114, 279
Schütte (Sophie Albrecht's friend), 342
Schütz, Henriette Hendel, 335
Schütze (Sophie Albrecht's friend), 343
Schwarz, Sibylle, 279
Schwarz, Sophie, 67, 321–22
Scotland, 256
scripts, life. *See* femininity: scripted; women writers: their positioning
secret writing, 171, 188
Seidel, Charlotte (née Lange), 67, 77–78, 162, 175, 267, 357 n
self and identity, for women, 15–17, 67, 118, 122, 134, 191, 241–42, 262. *See also* feminine subjectivity
self-censorship, 108, 175
self-deprecation and self-trivialization by women, 63, 77
self-naming, author's, 15, 26. *See also* anonymity; pseudonymity
self-narrative, 70, 76, 86, 88, 264, 330, 345–47, 374 n. *See also* Baldinger, Friderika: *Lebensbeschreibung*; Engelhard-Gatterer: self-representations; La Roche, Sophie, self-representations
Sellner, Timothy, 356 n
Sévigné, Marie de, 83, 127, 150
sexuality, 39, 96–97, 103–5, 165, 209, 291–94, 345, 355 n. *See also under* Albrecht, Sophie; Baldinger, Friderika; Ehrmann, Marianne; La Roche, Sophie
Seyler, Friederike Sophie. *See* Hensel, Friederike Sophie
Shakespeare, 313, 349
Singspiel, 303–4, 346
sleep in literary texts, 158–59, 268, 269, 304
social advancement and status of men and women, 38, 42, 44, 64

Solms-Wildenfels, Countess of, 67
Spangenberg, Dorothea, née Wehrs, 73, 167, 211, 371 n; to Baldinger about Engelhard-Gatterer, 208–9
Spectator. See under Gottsched, Adelgunde
Spencer, Jane, 176
Sprickmann, Anton Matthias, 184, 190, 294
Stadion, Count, 101, 178
Stael, Germaine de, 272
Stägemann, Elisabeth von, 334
Stein, Charlotte von, 314, 378–79 n
Steinheim, Solomon Ludwig, 342, 381 n
Stolberg, Luise, 359–60 n
Stolberg-Stolberg, Katharina, 64
strategy of enablement. *See* feeling woman; La Roche, Sophie: strategy of enablement; writing and publishing: justifications, validations
Stump, Doris, 372 n, 373 n
Sturm und Drang "Storm and Stress," 33, 34, 230–36, 238, 255, 287, 290, 373 n; and Ehrmann, Marianne, 32, 222, 241; and Enlightenment, 230, 236; influence on women writers, 25, 191, 303, 305, 372 n
subjectivity, feminine. *See* self and identity
subscription lists, 131, 139–40, 202, 318–19, 343, 371 n, 379 n; as alternative to court patronage, 23; collecting for, 81–82, 157. *See also* readers and subscribers *under* Albrecht, Sophie; Ehrmann, Marianne; Engelhard-Gatterer, Philippine; La Roche, Sophie
suicide, 231, 233, 288, 305, 310–12, 314, 323–24, 326–28
Sulzer, Johann Georg, 174, 196
Switzerland, 142, 272

Teutscher, Maria Antonia, 378 n
thinking woman. *See under* Ehrmann, Marianne
Thomson, James: "The Seasons," 119, 125–26, 140
Thon, Eleonore, 231–32, 234
Thurn und Taxis, Princess of, 378

Tieck, Ludwig, 349
Tiedeböhl (Sophie Albrecht's friend), 319
Touaillon, Christine, 230–31, 235, 363n
translators, women as, 368n
travel writing, 23, 28, 142–46, 153, 253, 256, 259, 329
Trouille, Mary Seidman, 91, 355n

Ulrike, Princess of Mecklenburg-Schwerin, 378n
Unger, Friederike Helene, 226
unintentionality topos, 83–84 ,159, 172, 178, 191, 225
university attendance, 38, 47, 50, 60, 98, 101, 104, 112, 132, 187, 280, 358n
Unzer, Karoline Dorothea Ackermann, 24, 335

validation of women as writers. *See under* writing and publishing by women
Varnhagen, Rahel von, 24, 274
verse tales, 23, 178, 193, 205, 329, 346
Verstand (intellect) in Friderika Baldinger's writing, 43–44, 48
violence, abuse, and sadism, 120–21, 248–49, 252, 257, 369n, 370n
Vogt, Marianne, 360n
Voigts, Jenny von, 136–37, 294, 377n
Volckmann, Anna Helena, 24
Voss, Johann Heinrich, 216
Vulpius, Christian August, 359n
Vulpius, Christiane (later Goethe), 359n

Wägenbauer, Birgit, 374n
Walker, Alice, 364n
Wallenrodt, Isabella von, 131
Walter, Eva, 21, 368n
war poetry, 215
Weckel, Ulrike, 367–68n
Wedekind, Margareta (later Forkel, then Liebeskind), 167, 334
Wehrs, Dorothea. *See* Spangenberg, Dorothea
Weigel, Sigrid, 355n
Weisse, Christian Felix, 50, 254, 314

Weissenthurn, Johanna Franul von, 314
Wesley, John, 367n
Wheatley, Phillis, 272–73
Widmer, Maya, 372n, 373n
Wieland, Christoph Martin, 31, 69, 114, 131, 193, 216, 259, 283, 335; and La Roche, 101–2, 147–48, 152, 169–70, 177, 363n, 367n, 368–69n
Wilhelmine, of Bayreuth, 313
Wilpert, Gero von, 380n
Winkle, Sally A., 107, 109
Winston, Elizabeth, 88
wish to be male or like a male, 45, 128, 217–20, 241, 320
Wobeser, Karoline von, 247, 374n
Wolf, Christa, 151–52
Wollstonecraft, Mary, 129, 172, 191, 222, 230, 236, 253, 277, 282–84
Wolzogen, Karoline von, 335, 368n
women writers, 15, 27; and femininity, 19–21, 32, 36, 89–90, 102, 153, 155–56, 160, 161, 170–72, 191, 204, 302; hurdles to, 36, 52, 74, 76, 81, 277; numbers and generations of, 15, 25, 102–3, 382n; and their readers, 158–60; trivialization of, 26, 355–56n. *See also* feminine subjectivity; private writers; public writers; writing and publishing
women's traditional culture, 116–17, 352, 364n
work: men's, 13, 18, 254–55; women's, 13, 254–55; —defined as nonwork, 16; —as housework and handwork, 54, 58–59, 77–80, 276; —as preventing writing, 77–80; —and simultaneous reading or writing, 58–59, 181. *See also* needle
Worley, Linda Kraus, 143, 145–46, 367n
writer, delimited, 21. *See also* private writers; public writers; women writers
writers, community of. *See* literary group
writing and publishing by women: for money, 214, 265, 281–82, 382n; justifications for, 30, 88, 101, 147, 168–75, 193; professionally, 26, 285, 382n; validation for, 15, 19, 36,